Jimmie Rodgers

The Life and Times of America's Blue Yodeler

Jimmie Rodgers

NOLAN PORTERFIELD

UNIVERSITY PRESS OF MISSISSIPPI   JACKSON

www.upress.state.ms.us

The University Press of Mississippi is a member of the Association
of American University Presses.

Originally published in 1979 by the Board of Trustees of the University of Illinois
First paperback edition 1992

Portions of this work have appeared as "Stranger through Your Town: The Backgrounds and
Early Life of Jimmie Rodgers," *John Edwards Memorial Foundation Quarterly*, 13:45 (Spring
1977), 4–16, and "Mr. Victor and Mr. Peer," *Journal of Country Music*, 7:3 (December 1978),
3–21.

Library of Congress Cataloging-in-Publication Data

Porterfield, Nolan.
  Jimmie Rodgers : the life and times of America's blue yodeler / Nolan Porterfield.
    p. cm.
  Includes bibliographical references, discography, and index.
  ISBN-13: 978-1-57806-982-8 (pbk. : alk. paper)
  ISBN-10: 1-57806-982-3 (pbk. : alk. paper)
    1. Rodgers, Jimmie, 1897–1933. 2. Country musicians—United States—Biography. I. Title.

ML420.R753P7 2007
782.421642092—dc22
[B]

                                                                           2006052934

British Library Cataloging-in-Publication Data available

To the memory of my father,
to Al,
and to
all who listen,
and understand

Contents

Preface ix

1   Looking for 1927 1

2   "Call Me James" 29
Spring, 1917–Autumn, 1923

3   Rain Down Sorrow 47
Autumn, 1923–January, 1927

4   Away Out on the Mountain 65
January–August, 1927

5   Mr. Victor and Mr. Peer 84

6   "All Right, George, I'll Just Sing One Myself" 104
August, 1927–February, 1928

7   "Mr. Victor's Got Lots of Money" 132
February–June, 1928

8   Hitting the Stars 143
June–August, 1928

9   "The Old Marster's Been Mighty Good to This Mississippi Boy" 156
August–December, 1928

10   The Show with a Million Friends 174
January–May, 1929

11   A Home Out in Texas 198
May–December, 1929

12   Swain's Follies 225
        December, 1929–Summer, 1930

13   A Sweetheart Not Far from Shawnee 242
        Summer, 1930

14   Fighting like a Lion 266
        August, 1930–February, 1931

15   Moonlight and Skies 284
        February–June, 1931

16   Going Down That Lonesome Trail 301
        June, 1931–June, 1932

17   "I Heard the Gang Singing 'Bury Me on the Lone Prairie'" 328
        July–September, 1932

18   Yodeling My Way Back Home 342
        Autumn, 1932–May, 1933

19   Endings, and Beginnings 359

Sources and Acknowledgments 366

The Recordings of Jimmie Rodgers 379

Appendix I: The Blue Yodels of Jimmie Rodgers 430

Appendix II: Jimmie Rodgers's Personal Appearances 432

Index 439

Preface to the New Edition

When *Jimmie Rodgers: The Life and Times of America's Blue Yodeler* was first published in 1979, little did I dream that it would still be in print for almost three decades. That circumstance is, most of all, a testament to Jimmie Rodgers's talent and genius, but I immodestly like to feel that, coming at a time when there was a lull in activity surrounding Rodgers, this book has played some part in keeping his memory alive and in documenting the extent of his influence on contemporary forms of American music.

The present edition is substantially the same as the original. Alert readers may note some dated references: CB radio, President Carter, double-knit suits. Many of my informants, written about in the present tense, have since passed on, and the list of places where Rodgers made personal appearances keeps expanding. Similarly, it's now documented that in his early railroading days he traveled further north (Cleveland) and west (Utah, California) than I was previously aware of. A few uncertainties in the discography have since been clarified or resolved. Most were quite minor; perhaps the most significant involves Rodgers's session on November 13, 1929, at which he recorded "Hobo Bill's Last Ride." The Victor logs show New Orleans as the place for that session, but the fact that only one title was recorded later led to speculation that it was done in Atlanta the following week. Now Rodgers's presence in New Orleans on November 13 has been confirmed. Otherwise, to the best of my knowledge nothing has come to light in the intervening twenty-eight years that materially changes or adds to the Jimmie Rodgers story.

Today, more than a century after his birth and over seventy years since he died, Rodgers's place in the annals of twentieth-century entertainment is taken for granted. For some time following his untimely death at thirty-five, he was little more than a dim specter haunting the margins of country and popular music, yet somehow his name and reputation survived. Reissues of a few of his 78s found a receptive audience in the late 1940s and early 1950s, prompting RCA Victor to release the first of several LPs that remained in the RCA catalog into the 1980s. In 1961, he was the first performer inducted into the Country Music Hall of Fame, proclaimed "The Father of Country Music" and "the man who started it all"—never mind that he had shunned the "hillbilly" image of his day and thought of himself as a pop star (which is not to say that he wouldn't happily embrace the notion that he had, indeed, sired something as bodacious as Country Music).

When the Songwriters Hall of Fame was established in 1970, Rodgers was among the first to be elected. As a major blues influence, he went into the Rock and Roll Hall of Fame with the inaugural class in 1986. Since 1992 every record he released has been available on CD, most notably in the Bear Family complete box set but also on many other labels.

Perhaps the major step in the re-emergence of Jimmie Rodgers as an important national figure was the Smithsonian Institution's reissue of thirty-six Rodgers sides in 1987, a Grammy nominee for both liner notes and best historical reissue. In 1995, Keith Carradine presented his one-man stage show, *My Time Ain't Long: The Jimmie Rodgers Story*, to standing-room-only audiences for three nights in Telluride, Colorado.

The process of canonization may have reached a pinnacle of sorts in September 1997, when the Rock and Roll Hall of Fame, the Country Music Hall of Fame, and Case Western Reserve University joined forces in Cleveland to present "Waiting for a Train: Jimmie Rodgers's America," a weekend conference of academics and performing artists. Noted scholars and music historians discussed such imposing topics as "Rodgers's Ongoing Legacy," "Rodgers and Race," and "Images of Rodgers's America." On the final evening a grand concert brought the event to a rousing full-tilt finale, with Ricky Skaggs, Guy Clark, Iris DeMent, Steve Earle, Levon Helm, John Prine, and a dozen others of equal fame and talent performing their favorite Jimmie Rodgers songs.

Simultaneously, Bob Dylan's Egyptian/Columbia label released *The Songs of Jimmie Rodgers: A Tribute*, featuring a wide spectrum of contemporary artists, from U2's Bono and Van Morrison to Steve Earle, Willie Nelson, and Dylan himself, demonstrating the scope and diversity of Rodgers's influence. The *Washington Post* proclaimed him "a signature figure in American popular music," a view echoed by *Newsweek*, the *St. Louis Post-Dispatch*, the *Daily Telegraph* in London, and other major publications here and abroad. Perhaps, though, the most telling proof of Rodgers's stature lies in the music: his tunes continue to be covered and his distinctive melodic ornaments and tags quoted among musicians whose great-grandparents boasted of hearing him "live."

One thing is certain: Jimmie Rodgers has not left the building.

Nolan Porterfield
2007

1

Looking for 1927

You know you're in the South when the waitress at breakfast says, "Toast or biscuits?" and brings grits, too, without asking. Regardless of what else you order, your plate arrives with a mound of grits in the middle of it. In the rural West Texas of my growing up, "grits" meant homemade hominy, with an acrid aftertaste of lye and ash, and I loathed them. But these grits, despite being Holiday Inn grits, are the real thing, with a puddle of butter floating in the middle and just the right amount of grain, white and steamy and gentle to the early-winter-morning palate. After the grits and scrambled eggs and country sausage and a fourth cup of coffee and all the news I can glean from yesterday's *Meridian Star,* the world looks a little better.

Outside, it is January in the Deep South, trying to be winter but not succeeding very well. The skies are low and grey, with a dampish mist in the distance and streets still glistening from last night's rain. Earlier, at dawn, I shivered coming over from my room to the restaurant, but that was not entirely because of the weather, and now a light jacket is ample against the clean, clear air. I like the weather. The world it encompasses stands out in strong relief, tangible and immediate, familiar even in its strangeness, gothic grey and filled with color just as I'd expected. As an omen, however, the weather is neutral. Things can go either way. And this is a day that began not without misgivings. The trip is a pilgrimage, of sorts, but I am not much for worshiping at shrines.

From my scuffled copy of the Holiday Inn Directory, I have tried to get my bearings: "Dwntn 3/4 mi; Key Field 3 mi; free trans.

Continental Trailways & Amtrack Terminals 1 mi; Merrehope Home
(antebellum) 3 mi; Mississippi Fish Hatchery 3 mi; Jimmy Rogers
Memorial Park 2 mi. . . ." I muse over the misspellings, remembering
how it irritated Jimmie Rodgers to see his name botched, and ask at
the desk for directions.

The youngish clerk, although he's lived there all his life, doesn't
know, and seems apologetic about it, yet a bit defensive, too, as if it
really isn't something worth knowing. The lady posting bills knows,
but seems equally defensive about that. A stout blonde with a beehive
hairdo out of the early Sixties, she gives directions in the flat tones of
a weary tour guide: "You jis take this road out yonder, clear on
downtown to where it jogs. Go a block past the jog, and that's Eighth
Street. Go down Eighth to Thirty-ninth Avenue, turn right at the light.
Takes you straight into the place. Can't miss it, sure enough."

I'm grateful for the clarity and grace of her instructions, but lack the
lady's confidence. It's that "jog" that worries me, and the city's
seeming contempt for street markers. Last night, arriving just at dark
in the rain, I missed a turn in the middle of freeway construction and
got lost. Of course, one does not really get lost in a city of 40,000, not
even an old country boy, but I circled the unmarked streets for half an
hour (largely as a result of that "jog," I now suspect) and wound up on
a one-way access road that took me five miles out of town in the wrong
direction before I got my bearings and found a place to turn around.
All to the strains of "Don't It Make My Brown Eyes Blue," emanating
from the local country music radio station.

This morning, ballasted with the Holiday Inn's No. 2 breakfast and
a street map, things go better. The jog successfully negotiated, I light
up a stale Roi-Tan that's been rolling around on the dash for two
months, and punch up the country music again. *"I hurt, all over-r-r-r
me . . . each, waking, mo-o-ment . . ."*

I believe it. If only he weren't so sincere. "The reason I like country
music is, it comes from the heart," says a legal secretary in
Tuscaloosa, Alabama, who has been to the Grand Ole Opry forty-three
times since 1954. "Country music is real *sincere.*"

"And it tells a story," says her mama. Mama, who is sixty-three,
sells real estate, does transcendental meditation, and is "Lady Hot
Lot" on the CB.

> *I tried, everythaaang . . . from new love, to whiskey . . .
> no other love can take the place   of yewwww*

and the whiskey, only helps me, until I'm so-ber-r-r-r
I'd like, to sleep, till I get, over-r-r-r   yewwwww[1]

My route has led me a long way, through the usual scatterings of commerce and cottage industry, past drive-ins, insurance agencies, and secondhand stores, into an area that is mostly residential. Up ahead I spot my destination, ease off the accelerator and lower the radio's volume, out of who knows what instinct—reverence, revulsion, fear or trembling. *I'd like to sleep, till I get, over-r-r-r yewww . . . but I know, I'd have, to sleep forever-r-r. . . .* Except for me, the park seems deserted, empty and grey and ugly, and as I ease the car through the entrance and across the first speed hump, a light mist begins to fall, blurring the windshield in front of me. The wipers make soft thumps in time with the low drone of the radio as I go on around the drive, looking for signs.

A lot of people, the secretary in Tuscaloosa and her mama to the contrary, don't like country music. Stan Kenton called it "a national disgrace" (a remark which one Nashville partisan promptly labeled "rigor mortis reflex babbling"). Jimmy Carter has given country music his seal of equivocation, allowing as how it keeps him in touch with his roots; and admission to the company of good ole boys and girls in some very select circles—the denim chic crowd, Media People, and hip academics—often depends on how many verses of old Hank Williams and Lefty Frizzell songs you can remember. Then there are the Real Folk in their double-knits and RV's tooling down the superslab listening to the eight-track, who bought almost half a billion dollars worth of country records and tapes last year and tune in faithfully to one or more of the nation's one-thousand-plus full-time country radio stations. But despite them all, the great bulk of the populace—and certainly its tastemakers—either ignore country music as best they can or regard it with ill-disguised contempt. Many actively loathe it.

Originally called "hillbilly" (never mind that the label, like "country," didn't quite fit), it was happenstance in its origins and undirected in its development, a sort of backward, ugly, show-biz stepchild that refused to go to school and learn from its betters but could not be kept locked up in the back room. There has been no other cultural phenomenon quite like it: devoid of discipline, lacking any guiding principle or serious concern save that of having fun and making money, country music grew from chance beginnings to fulsome maturity in less than fifty years, mostly as a diversion by and for the Great Unwashed, a bastion of all that is unsophisticated musically, uncultivated socially, and reprehensible politically. Curiously enough, some of its harshest critics are those who've grown up with it—that is, those who might logically feel it a part of their natural heritage.

Country music to most Americans means some big old raw dude in a sequined shirt fondling a gaudy guitar and whining about bad booze and busted hearts, simpleminded lyrics delivered with evangelistic fervor, televised in the thirty-minute syndicated slot between the Nightly News and the onset of prime time. Millions found its essence aptly symbolized by the grotesquely real image of Roy Acuff and Richard Nixon playing with Yo-Yos on the red-white-and-blue stage of the New Grand Ole Opry. At best, country music is equated with that which is otherwise shoddy in our land—the knobby-knuckled simple folk, truck-driver taverns, plastic flowers, laxative commercials, George Wallace, fast-food french fries, black-and-white porno, furniture from Sears, anklets-and-high-heels. In sum, Bad Taste.

There are exceptions. In that small scruffy city park in Meridian, Mississippi, where I drove one January morning in the rain, there stands an old Baldwin locomotive, a big eight-wheeler of the Consolidation type, circa 1904, garishly and badly trimmed in what might well be red barn paint and enclosed by a hurricane fence. Beside it is a monument to the men who drove such trains, and nearby is a second statue, inscribed to one trainman in particular, a thin, grinning young brakeman given to plunking on a guitar and making up songs with a peculiar vocal embellishment known as yodeling:

> His is the music of America;
> He sang the songs of the people he loved,
> Of a young nation growing strong.
> His was an America of glistening rails,
> Thundering boxcars and rainswept nights,
> Of lonesome prairies, great mountains,
> And a high blue sky.
> He sang of the bayous and the cotton fields,
> The wheated plains, of the little towns,

The cities and of the winding rivers of America.
We listened. We understood.

As poetry, the inscription isn't exactly a threat to Whitman, or T. S. Eliot, or even James Dickey.[2] But here, in this time and place, it's more than one expects, and a lot better than it has any right to be. In that fashion, it is an absolutely fitting memorial to Jimmie Rodgers, "The Singing Brakeman," known also as "America's Blue Yodeler" and yes, indeed, "The Father of Country Music."

The Father of Country Music. Jimmie would get a grin out of that one. The raucous wail of modern Nashville would baffle and bemuse Jimmie Rodgers as much as anyone else, although he would happily, if somewhat wryly, admit paternity and claim the credit. In his own casual, offhand manner, he was nothing if not upward mobile. Or perhaps it was just a unique expression of his Southern individualism, the "bald, immediate, unsupported assertion of the ego," as W. J. Cash described the type.[3]

Like the inscription on his monument, Jimmie Rodgers exceeded his limitations in strange and moving ways. For the first thirty years of his all-too-short life, he was more or less a failure at everything he tried, and in view of the fact that he was dying all the while of a terrible and debilitating disease, it is something of a miracle (or at least a happy accident) that he fathered anything, let alone an offspring as awesome and amorphous as "country music." He certainly wasn't much of a musician—couldn't read a note, keep time, play the "right" chords, or write lyrics that fit. All he could do was reach the hearts of millions of people around the world, and lift them up. They listened, and understood. It was still true in my early years, a generation after his death, and it is true today, more than half a century since Jimmie Rodgers first became, as the cliché has it, a legend in his own time.

In Rodgers's case, the phrase was literally true. Long before his premature death in 1933 at the age of thirty-five, he had become something of a folk hero, and the saga of the Blue Yodeler, often embellished by myth and romance, continued to flourish through time. It was a story with strong appeal to the public's sense of drama and destiny, marked as it was by the hero's humble origins, sudden success, fame and wealth, his early, tragic death—all the stuff from which we spin our popular gods and goddesses.

So dramatic in fact was Rodgers's real life that when I first began to trace it, I was sure that the telling of it would take the easy—perhaps

too easy—rags-to-riches pattern of so many show-biz biographies. For
openers, there was an almost unbelievable array of theatrical moments
which I might draw upon, re-create, novelize, or otherwise inflate for
full effect, after which all the others would swiftly fall into line: young
Jimmie winning an amateur talent contest at the age of twelve,
perhaps, and running off from home with a medicine show; or that
historic first recording session in Bristol, Tennessee: the frail young
railroader with show-business aspirations deserted by his own band,
the Jimmie Rodgers Entertainers, going back alone grimly determined
to face the big-city recording agent and winning the chance to make a
solo record that was destined to change history. Or, if one prefers *in
medias res,* the legendary scene a few months later, when Jimmie
Rodgers, his first record hardly released, goes up to New York in his
battered old Dodge with ten dollars in his pocket, checks into an
expensive hotel, calls up the busy recording executive, and allows as
how he just happens to be in town and, to be accommodating, will try
to find time to make some more records for Mr. Victor's Talking
Machine Company. Or perhaps a show-must-go-on story, one of the
dozens of times that Jimmie Rodgers got out of bed, downed a shot of
whiskey and chewed on a lemon to clear his throat and ease the chills,
and went out alone on a bare stage, propped his leg up on a chair,
flashed the audience a big grin, and began a song that would have them
on their feet by the time he got to the yodel. If one has a true taste for
bathos, there is finally (inevitably) the scene in Victor's Studio 1 on
Twenty-fourth Street in New York, May 24, 1933, where Jimmie
Rodgers lies on a cot in a rehearsal hall, marshaling his strength for
one more take before the microphone. Late in the afternoon he gets up
and records a piece of kitsch called "Years Ago," Tin Pan Alley's
notion in those days of what a "hillbilly" song ought to be, and
thirty-six hours later he is dead.

In between are hundreds of other set pieces, vignettes, moments of
glory and desperation, legends, cherished bits of fan lore. Some of
them, of course, turned out to be fabrications, either wholly or in
part. But that did not matter: others were more true than the telling
of them could ever be, and finally everything balanced out, for
the writing of a man's life is something more than, or other than,
the mere recording of it.

If the life of Jimmie Rodgers can be characterized by a single element, it would be impermanence. His early home life, continually subject to flux, was followed by a nomadic adolescence and the erratic rambles of an itinerant railroader; later, as a professional entertainer, he was forever on tour or simply going from here to there, living out the blithe conviction that while it may be "good times here, it's better down the road," as he put it. An outgoing, personable man with strong ties to his Southern homeland, he cultivated friends everywhere and found a home "anywhere I hang my hat." Yet in another, darker sense, he would always be, in the words of his own song, "a stranger passing through your town."[4] No one really knew him well; the old friends were always changing, being left behind. He would never quite find what he was looking for, if indeed he ever knew what it was. In the end, time and fate conspired against him, and it seemed enough that he knew that, bore it, and got his work done.

Rodgers's wanderlust may have been, to some degree, an inherited characteristic. Although little is known of his paternal ancestors, they were obviously of Irish origin (with whatever that may connote of restlessness, displacement, loneliness, and exile), caught up in the great flux of the eighteenth and nineteenth centuries, a time of increasing upheaval and migration around the world. In their pioneering study, *Jimmie the Kid,* authors Mike Paris and Chris Comber wrote only that the Rodgers family was "of Scots-Irish origin and may have descended from the trappers and hunters who had settled the Mississippi Valley in the early nineteenth century."[5] Even that was speculation. It is now known, however, that Jimmie Rodgers's grandfather, Zachary Rogers [*sic*], was born in Mississippi in 1841, probably in the east-central part of the state, and that he moved to the hill country of western Alabama sometime before the Civil War. Late in 1864 he enlisted (or was conscripted) into Capt. Rives's Supporting Force, 9th Alabama District, C.S.A.—and promptly deserted two weeks later.[6] It was an act not only appropriate to the character of Zack Rogers as handed down in family lore, but also a fairly wise and not entirely dishonorable one, considering that it represented an attitude shared by thousands of his fellow Confederates, more than 100,000 of whom had gone Over the Hill by 1864. Despite his apparent reluctance to make a formal stand against the Yankee hordes, Zack was nevertheless a true rebel and an unregenerate Southerner, a feisty, dyed-in-the-cotton son of Dixie, one of those "yeoman farmers" described in W. J. Cash's classic study as those who "might plow a little, hunt a little, fish a little, but mainly passed their time on their backsides in the shade of a tree, communing with their hounds and a jug of what, with a fine feeling for words, has been named 'bust-head.'"[7]

After the war Zack Rogers married Martha Woodberry, a Georgia native, and settled in Choctaw County, Alabama, where he raised mostly cotton, a little corn, and many children. The third of these, Aaron Woodberry, born in 1870, was a steely-eyed, strong-willed lad who decided he'd spell the family name with a "d" and left home in his early teens to work as a section hand with the Mobile & Ohio Railroad at Meridian, Mississippi, in the long-leaf pine region of the state. A fellow who takes a new spelling for his name has a sense for the power of the word, and is apt to be a man who knows who he is. From all accounts, Aaron Woodberry Rodgers suffered no crises of identity.

The Mobile & Ohio Railroad, later destined to play a formative part in the life of young Jimmie Rodgers, was one of the older and more prominent lines in that part of the South, originally chartered in 1848 to connect Mobile with the Ohio River near Cairo, Illinois.[8] Its fortunes, however, roughly paralleled those of the small Mississippi settlement built in the 1850's at the junction of the M&O and the Vicksburg & Montgomery line, whose promoters confused "meridian" with "junction" and fought a running battle for several years with local farmers who wanted to name the town "Sowashee" after a nearby creek. Both Meridian and the M&O flourished briefly before the Civil War, and both were practically destroyed by Sherman's troops in 1864. But twenty years later, when Aaron Rodgers went there to lay track and line roadbeds, Meridian was a thriving little town of 4,000, busy rising from its ashes and assuming some importance as a rail center. "The Mobile Road," as the M&O was popularly known, had survived the Panic of '73, prospered, and begun a broad program of expansion, building numerous branch lines and extending its northern terminus all the way to St. Louis. Simultaneously, tracks on its older, wide-gauge routes were being reset to conform to the new 4' 8½" gauge eventually adopted in 1886 as the national standard.

Times were still hard, but the worst of Reconstruction was over, and the growth of town and railroad reflected on a lesser scale the general postwar prosperity and spirit of enterprise that was sweeping other parts of the country. At the forefront was the rail industry itself, which nationwide had quadrupled its capital investment since 1865, more than doubled its dollar volume, and built some 70,000 route miles of new track during the 1880's alone. It was the onset of the golden age of railroading in America, a time when the very nature and spirit of the nation was being transformed by the mere fact that water heated into steam occupies 1,600 times its original space. From this simple but inescapable physical law came the great wailing, clanging locomotives and the twin rails of "high iron" that stretched away into nowhere but connected the whole country. From it too came the clattering telegraph, the water tanks and gingerbread stations, a new vocabulary ("cow-catcher," "dee-po," "caboose," "eight-wheeler"), and, inevitably, a new breed of men, whose lives were rivaled only (and briefly) by riverboat pilots and cowboys as models of fierce and epic proportions, of romance and individualism, true professionals. Many youngsters still yearn to fly, but what boy today really dreams of growing up to be an airline captain—or, for that matter, of engineering an Amtrak diesel?

The rapid growth of the M&O, coupled with Mississippi's heavy rains and shifting soils, meant plenty of work for those willing to man the section crews. Even though it was hard labor, done with pick and scoop and crowbar, with tie tongs and twelve-pound spike maul, for eager country boys like Aaron Rodgers it was easier on body and spirit than following a mule and moldboard plow up and down the Alabama clay hills. If the wages were not appreciably better, they were at least a lot more certain.

Aaron Rodgers was a willing and ambitious worker, a bit fast with his fists, perhaps, and possessed of an Irish temper; but generally a gregarious, likeable fellow who got along with the men on the section crew and made friends easily. He also had, in the vernacular of the time, a quick eye for the ladies, and his circle of acquaintances in Meridian soon included a number of local belles. Among them was sixteen-year-old Eliza Bozeman, whose father was a farmer and man of some means in the rural Pine Springs community a few miles northeast of Meridian.

The Bozemans, one may assume, were a rung or two up the social ladder from the red-clay bumblebee-cotton existence out of which Aaron Rodgers had come. At least their history is better chronicled, thanks largely to the efforts of the Reverend Joseph W. Bozeman, D.D., who in 1885 compiled and published an informative, if somewhat scattered and exuberant, account of the family. As a

Bozeman himself, the good Reverend was hardly an objective historian; further allowances must be made for his addiction to Victorian rhetoric and the vestiges of that peculiar, musty sort of ancestor worship more rampant in Savannah than in Shanghai. Nonetheless, the Bozemans as drawn from his account were a sturdy clan of farmers and craftsmen, a cut above the average, who went about their daily business of getting and spending, thriving and multiplying, not without a certain grace and sense of character.

Eliza Bozeman's ancestors were natives of Holland (the name was originally "Bosman" or "Boschman") who settled in Maryland along the eastern banks of Chesapeake Bay before the Revolution.[9] Later they migrated south into Virginia, the Carolinas, and Georgia, west to Alabama and Mississippi and beyond, following a pattern common to millions of the families, including in all likelihood that of Aaron Rodgers, which eventually populated the Old South. Eliza's great-grandfather, Meady Bozeman, settled in Georgia in the 1790's; her grandfather, also named Meady, married Lucy Carroll of Carrollton (described by the Reverend as "a woman of active, vigorous mind, great strength of character, and as fearless as a heroine") and moved into central Alabama, where he farmed and acquired a reputation as "a very fine mechanic" (i.e., carpenter). Said the Reverend Bozeman, "Houses that he built in Dallas County, Ala., fifty years ago, are still pointed out with pride as the work of Meady Bozeman. A large, fine-looking man, with blue eyes and ruddy face, full of life and jest, he was the delight of young people even in his advanced years."[10]

Eliza's father, Samuel Bozeman, was born in central Alabama in 1838. Two years later the family moved westward again, to Kemper County, Mississippi, some forty miles northwest of Meridian. Young Sam, only nineteen when his father died in 1857, went back to Lowndes County, Alabama, to work and farm with relatives. He was there when the Civil War erupted, and quickly enlisted (July 3, 1861) as a private in Company B, 14th Alabama Infantry. Captured at Gettysburg on the second day of Lee's bloody, doomed assault on the Union lines, he spent almost two years as a prisoner of war. Finally, in June, 1865, two months after Lee's surrender at Appomattox, he was administered the required Oath of Allegiance to the United States of America, given a battered Union Army Spencer carbine to replace the British Enfield he had surrendered, and released.[11]

Returning to Mississippi, Sam took up his father's trade as

carpenter and bridge-builder. He later bought land in Lauderdale County, near Pine Springs, and married a local woman, Mrs. Virginia Shine Robinson, who had been widowed by the war and left with two small daughters.[12] Through dint of luck and hard work, he prospered; by the 1880's his land holdings in the area were so large that the Bozeman place was known locally as "Sixteen Sections."

Eliza was the second of five children born to Sam and "Jennie" Bozeman, a frail, rather somber child whose seeming reticence and solemnity concealed a strong spirit and lively wit. Born in 1868, Eliza was two years older than Aaron Rodgers—almost seventeen when he began to court her in 1884. An exchange of letters in January of the following year suggests the growing intensity of their friendship, an easy familiarity beneath the outward forms of social decorum.[13] Aaron's note, cast in the elegant Spencerian script and formal diction of the time, is a model of etiquette and propriety, tending to belie his youth—he was barely fifteen—as well as his brief and spotty schooling. Addressing her as "Esteemed Friend," he asked for "the pleasure of carrying" (i.e., escorting) her to church services three weeks hence, "if there is any out there on that day."

Eliza's penmanship and spelling suffer by comparison, but her teasing reply, no less formally correct, tells a great deal about her lively character and the increasing familiarity of the relationship. She replied that she would "accept your company with pleasure" to preaching at Suqualena (a nearby community) and sent mock-threatening word to her half-sister Lena Griffin, who operated a millinery shop in Meridian: "Tell Lena if she don't send my old black vail home by you next time you come, I will snatch her ballheaded." Aaron had enclosed a picture of himself; she primly remarked that it was "very much esteemed," coolly signing herself, "Adieu, Your friend, Eliza Bozeman."

The elegant salutations and coy adieux soon fell by the way. By summer, "Miss Bozeman" had become "Eliza, My Dearest," and when he wrote in September, Aaron's note was brief and to the point: "You may look for me on the 13th inst. Truly yours, Aaron."

A month later, on October 18, they were married and moved into a modest but comfortable frame house on a small plot of land which Sam Bozeman had set aside for them a few hundred yards from his own home. They lived there only temporarily, however, for Aaron was soon promoted to foreman of the "extra gang," a section crew which operated on an erratic schedule at various locations, often being called away for days at a time to serve as troubleshooter or maintenance backup on some distant part of the division's lines. Whenever circumstances permitted, his new bride followed along, setting up household in a tent or boxcar on a siding in Lost Gap or Graham's Switch or Enterprise, surrounding hamlets that served as rail camps and division points. Soon even that irregular routine was further altered and interrupted by the arrival of two sons, Walter in August, 1886, and Talmage in January, 1890. During each confinement Eliza returned to her parents at Pine Springs, rejoining her wandering husband as soon as she and the babies were able to travel. Following the birth of Talmage, however, she suffered two successive miscarriages, and her health, never very robust, began to fail permanently. In all likelihood, she had contracted tuberculosis in the raw, shoddy rail camps where such diseases were endemic, and her case was aggravated by the general harshness of her nomadic life as a railroad section foreman's wife. The intervals at Pine Springs became increasingly frequent, and Aaron, in deference to her health, began to divide his time between railroading and attempts at farming the acreage he had acquired from his father-in-law. By the mid-1890's they had more or less taken up residence in the house Sam Bozeman had built for them as a wedding present, and it was there, on September 8, 1897, that Eliza Rodgers gave birth to her third and last child. Christened James Charles, he was a chubby, brown-eyed baby who quickly became the spoiled favorite of the family.

It was soon obvious that Eliza Rodgers's illness had grown chronic. In 1903 her health deteriorated rapidly, and she died, possibly in childbirth, sometime that year, when Jimmie was five or six. Although various branches of the Bozeman family were close by and offered to take Talmage and Jimmie (Walter, then seventeen, had already joined his father on the railroad), Aaron Rodgers, for reasons not fully known, declined and instead sent the boys to live for a time with his relatives at Scooba, Mississippi, and nearby Geiger, Alabama.

It would be the first of many moves for young Jimmie. Although he was never quite the poor orphan child later depicted in publicity and legend, he would not have a really permanent address again for more than twenty-five years, when, as a rising star in the entertainment world, he built his Texas "mansion"—and lived there barely eighteen months. So much moving about, coupled with the general instability of the family during his youth, has led to speculation about the possible psychological effects of such circumstances. Regardless of the conclusions one cares to draw, it seems clear that Jimmie preferred to stay on the move. It became the habit of a lifetime, and even as an adult, when the choices were his, he never settled down for long.

Jimmie's sojourn with his Rodgers relatives lasted hardly a year, for in October, 1904, his father married again and consolidated the family. The new Mrs. Rodgers was a Pine Springs widow named Ida Love Smith, whose son, Jake, from her first marriage, was three years younger than Jimmie.

Having once more assumed the responsibilities of a family, Aaron left the railroad in 1905 and made an all-out effort to support his wife and children by farming the land he still held at Pine Springs. He mortgaged eighty acres, along with "One Horse color Bay, about seven years old, also one Bay Mare—about eight years old" in exchange for "money, supplies & merchandise" as advances on that year's harvest.[14] Unhappily, the crop was short, and in the fall he was forced to sell the land to pay off the note. The following year, the family (now enlarged by the birth of a daughter, Lottie Mae) moved to Lowndes County, in the black prairie region of northeastern Mississippi, some eighty-five miles above Meridian; there Aaron made a short and ill-fated attempt at running an alfalfa farm. When that venture collapsed, he returned to work on the railroad, first at West Point, Mississippi, and shortly afterward back in Meridian, where he found a job as section foreman on the New Orleans & Northeastern Railroad. Again, their stay in Meridian was only temporary.

The family's economic condition was precarious, and in addition there was growing tension between Aaron Rodgers's sons and their new stepmother. Walter Rodgers, by this time twenty years old, had been pretty much on his own since joining the NO&NE the year before to become a conductor, but Tal and Jimmie were still at home and subject to parental guidance. However occasional and arbitrary that "guidance" may have been, it was nevertheless something they'd hardly been prepared for by the years of their mother's illness and the round of foster homes following her death. Now, during Aaron's frequent, lengthy trips away with the section crews, the two brothers chafed increasingly under the stern hand of Ida Rodgers. Strong willed and independent like their father, they apparently had never much liked their stepmother, and her strict rules and efforts at discipline, real or imagined, seemed more and more unbearable. Thus it came as some relief to all when Ida decided to take the baby, Lottie Mae, and join Aaron in his wanderings from one rail camp to another. The boys were sent to Pine Springs, where Jake was given over to the care of Ida's parents, the Loves; Tal and Jimmie went to live with their mother's maiden sister, Dora Bozeman, who upon the death of Sam and Jennie Bozeman a few years earlier had been left to preside over Sixteen Sections, the old Bozeman "home place."

To outward appearances, Aunt Dora was the archetypal old maid, one of those thin, sharp-faced spinsters who seemed to pass immediately from childhood to barren middle age, invariably mirrored in the collective family consciousness as a frumpy stick figure poking about in sunbonnet and gingham apron, tending gardens, raising chickens and someone else's children, ministering to generations of kin—martyred, in all the wrong senses, to a motion not her own. Beneath that appearance there was, happily, another, vastly different Dora Bozeman. True, she came to the role of Old Maid with all the likely credentials, right down to the inevitably tragic episode of a youthful lost love. But that only proved, if anything, that Dora took comfort in the old cliché about loving-and-losing being better than never loving at all. It signified, too, that she had at least had a youth, however painful, and had emerged from it whole—a warm, delightful lady, full of humor and patience, apparently free of the self-pity and narrowness that so often afflict those who find that life has delivered something less than promised. Keen intelligence was a Bozeman family trait, and Dora had her full share. She displayed a wide range of talents as a child, became an accomplished (if not especially inspired) pianist, and was, for a woman in that time and place, well educated. As befitted the daughter of a man of Sam Bozeman's position (in another country in another day, he might have been Squire Bozeman), she had "finished" at Cooper's Institute, a private academy for women at Daleville, Mississippi, and held diplomas certifying her to teach English and music. She did, in fact, teach music briefly, long before her nephews came to live with her. Her musical training was probably not the sort of thing that would have appealed to or much affected a young rapscallion like Jimmie Rodgers anyway. On the other hand, in view of the difficulty of establishing other immediate musical influences on Jimmie in these years, Dora's background in language, literature, and melody, her training in rhyme and rhythm, may well have been factors, however subliminal, in his development.

Tal was sixteen and Jimmie nine when they went to live with their Aunt Dora in late 1906, enrolling in school at Pine Springs for the winter term. Before his mother's death, Jimmie had attended a shanty school at Lost Gap, one of the rail points just west of Meridian where his father worked for a time. That initial brush with book learning ended abruptly when Eliza died, but after Aaron remarried, Jimmie had "started over" in the first grade at Pine Springs. The following year, when the family moved to the hay farm in Lowndes County, he and his stepbrother, Jake Smith, went to school briefly (and sporadically) at Artesia, several miles from the farm. They made the trip to school on the back of an ancient mule they called "'Sociation" (it belonged to the agricultural combine for which Aaron worked), over raw paths and primitive country roads that offered endless diversions and excuses to dawdle. As a consequence, they rarely got to school on time; more often than not, they never arrived at all. Sickness also contributed to Jimmie's absences that winter. He seemed to have inherited his mother's frail health and was increasingly susceptible to colds and respiratory infections.

Later that year he attended school in Meridian for a few months—or perhaps it is more correct to say that he was supposed to go to school there. Aaron had rejoined the railroad and was away from home frequently; Jimmie was at odds with his stepmother, and the "city" of Meridian presented infinite lures and fascinations to the would-be truant.

A busy, booming rail and trade center, turn-of-the-century Meridian was the largest city in the state (between 1900 and 1910 the population increased from 14,050 to 23,285). The diverse and sprightly Southern metropolis boasted multi-storied office buildings and hotels, an electric streetcar line, two telephone companies, brick streets, a professional baseball team, and, according to publicity, a "splendid" police force. In addition to lumber mills and cotton gins, a cannery, and a harness-and-saddle works, there were factories which produced steam boilers, eight-wheel lumber wagons, brooms, mattresses, and a variety of farm and household goods. Products were distributed from the complex of warehouses and shipping facilities of the seven rail lines which served the city and operated "shops" (roundhouse and repair stalls) there.

High above the hurly-burly of commerce and industry, the Finer Things in Life were cultivated by the Meridian Male College, the Meridian Female College (separate but, one assumes, equal), and the Moffit-McLaurin Institute for Girls. Mississippi Medical College was also located there, as were a normal school for Negroes and a conservatory of music which proclaimed itself "largest in the South!" Culture was further served by locally produced plays in the City Coliseum and by touring companies which appeared at the Opera House. Among professional entertainers Meridian had long had a reputation as a "show town," a good place to play. A Board of Trade publication of the time noted that "the fact that this city breaks the jump between the East and the South for expensive companies and leading stars touring the South may have some influence in the city's favor, but . . . we have here a large theatrical element . . . and [the city] is rated by managers as a theater town."[15]

The same publication also boasted that "Meridian is an ideal place for raising boys," for they are "not surrounded by temptations that beset them in other places." Indeed, Meridian must have been a fine place to be a boy, but hardly for the reasons the Board of Trade had in mind. Of course, the Greatest Temptation of All was liquor: "The city has for years operated under the prohibition laws," intoned the Board of Trade, "and the police force here makes the prohibition law prohibit [and] . . . for that reason the type of young man found here is much above the average in moral worth."[16] If young Jimmie Rodgers read that quaint bit of sententious puffery, he surely must have smiled. Only a few years later he would delight in telling the public that he'd left the railroad because of "trouble with Rule G" (forbidding the "use of intoxicants by employees"),[17] and when, on one of those infamous talking records with the Carter Family, he asks A.P. to "go get the ole boy [i.e., Rodgers] a little squirt," it is not so much an attempt to get a laugh as it is an entirely natural act, born of long familiarity with saloons and cups that cheer. Although he was never quite the heavy boozer that legend tried to make him, he consciously cultivated the image of the convivial drinking man. It was clearly something he'd acquired early, hanging around the railroad shops, the Negro joints along Fifth Street, the pool halls and tonsorial parlors where drinking men congregated.

Even if Meridian's prohibition laws did effectively prohibit, the spirited, feisty young Jimmie Rodgers was hardly at a loss for other temptations. In addition to the fine, delicious evils that emanated from the rail shops and pool rooms, there were countless alleys to roam, pranks to play, drugstores with Belgian marble soda counters and gaudy trinkets, and a succession of tatty carnivals, circuses, and medicine shows catering to the street crowds unable to afford the "expensive companies and leading stars" which played the Opera House. Among the acts and productions which appeared in Meridian in these years were "Polly of the Circus," Margaret Anglin in "The Awakening of Helena Ritchie," the Al G. Field Minstrels, and the Novelty Grahams, a song-dance-and-acrobatic team; under canvas were the Sun Brothers Shows (a carnival), the Ringling Brothers Circus, and W. I. Swain's Repertoire Company. "Captain" (eventually "Colonel") Swain would figure significantly in Rodgers's professional career years later. Young Jimmie, apparently starstruck from birth, was fascinated by any kind of show; he was particularly excited when the Gem and Elite theaters, both nominally vaudeville houses, began to show the newfangled moving pictures between acts. He and Jake ran with a gang of boys like themselves, an amorphous band of whelps who skipped school, rolled garbage cans through the alleys at night, sneaked into the "flickers," ran errands and did odd jobs for pocket money, peddled newspapers and jugs of molasses (and occasionally a jug or two of something harder), begged or chiseled what they couldn't earn, alternately loafed and hustled the time away. Jimmie's schooling during these few months in the fall of 1906 was mostly of the street variety, and while it may not have done much for his "moral worth," it became the foundation of both his art and his life, and served him well.

The nature of his existence was measurably altered when he went to live with his Aunt Dora a few months later. Nothing would permanently change his "rough and rowdy ways"—it was too late for that—but out at Pine Springs there were no alleys to roam or juke joints to frequent, and he was separated from daily contact with his closest cohort, Jake, who'd been sent to live with Ida's parents. In place of all that was a deepening relationship with Tal, then maturing into his late teens, a sober and reliable young man who had always been the most levelheaded of Aaron Rodgers's boys. In Aaron's absence, Tal became the nearest thing to a father for Jimmie at that crucial stage in his life, and the younger boy idolized him. Most of all, there was the calm and steadying influence of Dora Bozeman, who,

lenient and adoring as she may have been, nevertheless ran a
household: there were regular meals, chores to be done, a routine to be
followed. Other members of the Bozeman clan kept a sterner, if
ultimately less effective, eye on Jimmie.

In his adult years, largely for the benefit of reporters, Jimmie would
tell of the hardships of having to pick cotton as a boy and generally
emphasized the unpleasantness of his youth. It made good copy, and
there was more truth to it than to some of the other stories he told. On
the other hand, he was never the destitute orphaned waif, toiling away
at hard labor under the merciless hand of cruel elders, that some
accounts tended to portray. If his boyhood was sometimes harsh and
lonely, it was no more severe than that of his friends and playmates,
and the years that he spent with his Aunt Dora at Pine Springs were in
many ways idyllic. In those early years of the new century, the world
was still far away from rural Mississippi, yet life—its colors and
textures, thrills and pains—was intensely near: rich, pungent days of
earthsmells and horses, honeysuckle and pine and chicken manure,
hog-killings in the fall, windless wood smoke from distant cabins
curling through the chill November rains, winter's cold starlight and
the aching wails of trains in the night, flashing storms, the lush
summer land, heat-choked and brooding. It was a sniggering, rowdy
childhood of high jinks and swimming holes, peach-tree switches
and school picnics. Young Jimmie roamed the bottoms of Sixteen
Sections, swimming and fishing—he and Tal spent so much time
angling for catfish and perch in a little stream near Aunt Dora's farm
that it became known locally as "Rodgers Creek," and so appears on
county maps today. He chewed sugar cane and developed a lifelong
appetite for cornbread and milk; he foraged for chestnuts and scaly
barks, scrambled over the limestone hills with his Bozeman cousins,
dodged school, took to smoking, let his shirttail hang out, and avoided
Sunday School, much to the chagrin of his staunchly Methodist aunts
and uncles, who were already convinced that he would never amount
to anything. All but Aunt Dora. She kept the faith, and indulged
Jimmie, and the others went along. He was, after all, a Poor
Motherless Child (and "the runt of Uncle Aaron's litter," as his Cousin
Pearl Bozeman Harris said later, "so we took pity"), a rowdy and
unkempt waif who was difficult to discipline or keep in school, yet
somehow wise beyond his years, always into some devilment. But he
had a certain wistful Irish charm and a cocky grin, and they all loved

him in spite of his ruffian pranks and his stubborn disregard of bathtubs, schoolbooks, and Sunday manners.

Whatever formal learning Jimmie got—and it was a great deal, considering its brevity—was acquired largely during these few years at Pine Springs, from late 1906 until the early spring of 1911. For the first time (and the last, as it turned out), "James," as he was known to the family in those days, went to school more or less regularly. Sickness continued to take its toll, especially in the winter months, but with the community schoolhouse only a short distance from Aunt Dora's, it was almost impossible to play truant. Moreover, the schoolmistress, Miss Pearl Pope, was Aunt Dora's star boarder—which meant that, for Jimmie at least, the school day did not end when the last bell had rung. Miss Pope, like Aunt Dora, was a doughty but warm-hearted and sympathetic woman, and (like Dora also) she was to exert a lifelong influence upon Jimmie Rodgers. Although she was hardly a Miss Grundy, the mere fact that she lived at the Bozeman house and was in daily contact with "James" obviously meant that he got more exposure to book learning than he ordinarily would have. In any event, she took a close and lasting interest in the boy—perhaps all the more lasting because of her even closer interest in his older brother.

Meanwhile, Aaron Rodgers had more plans abrewing. In January, 1907, he wrote to Talmage on an NO&NE letterhead from Purvis, Mississippi, south of Hattiesburg, telling his son that he was on his way to Meridian and instructing Tal to meet him there at the Union Depot when he arrived on Train No. 8. "I want you to bring James and Jake to Mdn with you," he wrote. "I'd like for you to ask your Aunt Dora to make out her act. against me for Jas. Board & send by you so I can settle it." His letter further advised Tal that he had a job in mind for him ("dont arrange to work anywhere untill you see me").[18]

But apparently Tal, like his father, had a mind of his own. Things did not work out, and a month later Aaron wrote again, in a letter datelined "Meridian [Railroad] Shops, Feb. 8, 1907," claiming "the exclusive right and [on?] your services," and insisting that, although Tal could keep whatever money he earned, "you must leave your Aunt Dora." Simultaneously he wrote to Dora, "kindly and respectfully" asking that she "not retain my son any longer on your farm" because he was needed at home. Her reply, if she made one, is lost.

The "discussion" between Tal and his father went on for several months, but eventually Aaron realized that his son could not be swayed, and gave up. His last letter on the subject is interesting for its air of petulance coupled with his touching paternal concern for young Jimmie. Since writing to Dora, he said, he had reconsidered and was now willing to let Tal stay on the farm if that would make the boy and his meddlesome old aunt happy: "So go on and do as you like about it." He was adamant on one point, however. "Don't mistreat James," he declared, enclosing a dollar "to buy James some pants. It is all the bill I have." The letter ends with a postscript: "Kiss James for me."

The remark that "It is all the bill I have" may have been a comment on his financial condition, but more likely it meant simply that it was the only paper (and therefore mailable) currency on hand at the moment. Aaron Rodgers was never a prosperous man, but he worked steadily, paid his bills, had, from all accounts, good credit, and saw that his boys were taken care of, however random and haphazard that care might sometimes have been. Moreover, if a dollar seems a pittance today, one must remember that in that time it was almost enough to buy a boy's suit; a pair of top-quality overalls could have been had for half that amount.[19]

Whatever Tal's reasons for defying his father's orders to "come away from out there," he obviously had no sustained interest in farming. In January, 1908, he married Pearl Pope, and they soon moved to Meridian, where Tal had taken a job as a bill collector for the Dixie Credit Company. Early in 1911 Jimmie left Pine Springs also, ostensibly to live with Aaron and Ida in a house that Aaron had rented near the Meridian shops. But, as usual, Aaron was rarely home, and Jimmie fell into his old habit of making the rounds of relatives and acquaintances, dodging school, and learning the lessons of the street.

During this time one of his mother's younger brothers, Tom Bozeman, was an up-and-coming businessman in Meridian; among his several enterprises was the city's first "white enamel" barber-shop, a dazzling step ahead of the old-fashioned zinc-fixtured tonsorial parlors of the day. Located in the middle of a bustling triangle bounded by downtown, a complex of hotels and offices, and the railroads, Tom Bozeman's barbershop was a natural center of male social activity, a popular gathering-place for the city's elite—businessmen, politicians, baseball players, and travelers—as well as for policemen, railroaders, and other working men. It consequently became more or less a headquarters for thirteen-year-old Jimmie Rodgers. "Home" was often a daybed in the apartment of Tom

Bozeman—a bachelor at the time—above the barbershop. During business hours Jimmie hung around the shop, picking up bits of gossip and running errands for pocket change. He traded bawdy stories with traveling men, shot dice with the shine boys in a backroom, acquired from the pages of *Sporting Life* and the *Police Gazette* a quasi-literary taste for the sordid, sensational, and sentimental, and generally established himself as a tough but likeable street-wise kid who could hold his own with the best of them.

There is little in the life of Jimmie Rodgers to this point—the "formative years"—that would account for or foreshadow his eventual success as a musical entertainer, much less suggest that he would one day be a big-time personality, the idol of millions, a show business institution, and a dominant influence in the development of one of the greatest cultural phenomena in twentieth-century America, the "father" of the multi-million-dollar industry known as Country Music. In the early days of his professional career, he would tell a reporter that "My father and my two brothers and I all were musical," but there is little evidence of the nature or extent of their interests while he was growing up. His Grandad Zack had played a fiddle, which Tal Rodgers "messed with some" as a youth; but eventually Tal gave up the fiddle for the banjo, and after Jimmie began to make records, he and Tal would "woodshed" together when he was vacationing in Meridian between tours. Dora Bozeman had been trained in the "serious" music of her day—light opera and the more accessible classics—but there is scant basis for assuming that any of this background was more than passively absorbed by her young nephew James. Despite his aversion to church, he was no doubt familiar with its music, at least the old standard hymns which gravitate to almost every Southern consciousness; his preacher uncle, Samuel Bozeman, was also a fiddler, confining his repertoire entirely to religious music. Almost certainly Jimmie had also been exposed to secular country fiddling, the banjoing of medicine show minstrels, and occasional harmonizing among the patrons of Tom Bozeman's barbershop. Ultimately, however, the depth and degree of these possible influences can hardly be assessed from the meager, almost entirely circumstantial evidence available. The only direct clue to Jimmie Rodgers's musical beginnings rests in a single offhand remark he made to an interviewer years later: "I played the guitar at night after picking cotton when I was a kid." Whatever the sources of his inspiration or the origins of his talent, they had come early, down on the farm, long before he was drawn to the railroad gandy dancers and depot rounders chanting the blues.

Jimmie Rodgers apparently decided, very early and very definitely, that he wanted to be An Entertainer—one of those rare and select people who are called, almost as if by divine right or intervention, to rise in front of other, lesser humans and do things that dazzle, delight, and ennoble their poor benighted fellows. And with all the confidence and determination that later characterized the whole course of his struggle against impossible odds, he made up his mind and headed straight for the mark.

His first gawky venture into show business, a natural outgrowth of wisecracking and clowning for the barbershop crowd, was to organize a neighborhood "carnival." It's a game most children play at some time or another, but Jimmie approached it seriously. From Tal's wife (who was now "Sister Pearl") he filched several bedsheets, stitched together a "big top," and took the show on the road. Captured "several towns away," he produced enough money from the box office to pay for the sheets and glumly agreed to fold the tent and come home. A second time he outfitted a troupe and set off, sporting an expensive sidewall camping tent he'd charged to his father without the latter's knowledge; again he was tracked down and brought back.

Undaunted, he entered an amateur talent contest sponsored by Meridian's Elite Theater, promptly winning first prize for his vocal renditions of "Steamboat Bill" and "I Wonder Why Bill Bailey Don't Come Home" (which he had probably learned from popular cylinder recordings of the time). On the basis of that thin brush with fame, he wangled himself an appearance—unpaid, of course—with a medicine show then playing Meridian, and when the show left town a few days later, Jimmie Rodgers left with it. It was not quite the fulfillment of every boy's dream of running off to join the circus, but it was the best he could manage at the moment. This time he left with the knowledge, if not exactly the approval, of at least some members of the family. Tom Bozeman knew of the move, but made no real effort to stop him. Down the road a few days later, Jimmie wrote to his uncle, reporting the show's progress. The troupe was "making a little money and having a good time to," he said, and expected to reach Birmingham in a few days.

He may have gotten as far as Birmingham with the medicine show. However, it is more likely that he and the Good Doctor came to a parting of the ways soon after Cottondale, for, as Jimmie reported to his Aunt Dora, "I quit the show man because he wound [wouldn't] treat me Right." Undismayed at being a hundred miles from home and entirely on his own, the plucky thirteen-year-old soon found a job in West Blocton, a small hill town southwest of Birmingham. "Im working at Mr Tuggles," he wrote to Dora. The Tuggle brothers, T. C. and J. M., were tailors, "Specialists in Made-to-Order Garments," and proprietors of Tuggle's Yellow Front Photograph Gallery. The combination of needle and camera was a clever one, ingeniously appropriate to an age fascinated with the gadgets of fledgling technology and the inventions of "modern science." The Gallery not only did a brisk business in "the mug trade"—portraiture— but enabled the enterprising Tuggles to advertise a "measuring system" which was, to say the least, highly unusual: "We take a photograph of each customer which gives us the exact form and enables us to insure an absolute fit." Jimmie wrote to his aunt that "Mr [Tuggle] is paying me 50¢ a day and Bord, and I like my work." One can only speculate about his business efficiency, but socially he was, as always, a fast worker: "I have many frends here, and Sweet little girl to." In every town, in all his wanderings, there would invariably be a "Sweet little girl to" for Jimmie Rodgers.

Just how long he stayed in West Blocton is not known, but it is unlikely that he was there more than a few months. Dora wrote expressing her concern for his welfare and lack of schooling (to which he would reply, with as much reassurance as he could muster, that he would "try to go to School if I can next fall"). Nor was Aaron Rodgers oblivious to the potential hazards facing his youngest son. Sometime that summer he "retrieved" Jimmie from the Tuggles and brought him back to Meridian, probably with an eye to sending him back to school. However, Ida Rodgers died in October, and Aaron returned to the helter-skelter life of a section foreman on the M&O, taking Jimmie with him. By December they were with the extra gang in Macon, Mississippi, north of Meridian, where, as Jimmie wrote to Aunt Dora, "Papa is teaching me to line and surface track." Aaron had vague plans for putting his son in school at Starkville "after Xmas," but nothing came of them. Jimmie Rodgers's career as a railroad man had begun.

It has since become something of a commonplace that Jimmie Rodgers was first and foremost a railroader—a professional brakeman who happened into show business only because he was too ill to ride the "iron" any longer. With the passage of time, the railroad assumed a dominant place in the Rodgers mythos, becoming, as one enthusiastic writer put it, the very "symbol of his life."[20] It was almost as if he had cut his teeth on a rail spike, grown up counting cross ties, and (to quote another eminent scholar) "finally became a singer" only "as a desperate expedient," when sickness had forced him to give up the strenuous life of his chosen profession.[21] Obviously, Jimmie could hardly have grown up as the son of Aaron Rodgers without some passing familiarity with switch engines and water tanks and peddler freights and the special lingo of trainmen; from his earliest years he'd ridden handcars and rattling "crummies" and bantered with the brakemen and occasionally carried water for his father's section gang. Much later, as a full-time railroader—call boy, flagman, baggage master, brake-man—he no doubt came to "love" it as much as any man can love a thing that works him hard and pays him poorly, and he would always look back on those years on the high iron with great pride and more than a little romanticism.

However, all that has tended to obscure his much earlier and far more constant fascination with the world of entertainment, and his eager, if ill-fated, attempts to become a part of it. Show business was his true dream and calling; if hardly a Born Performer, he nevertheless sensed that he was born to perform, and would forever pursue the dream, no matter how brief and dark the reality of it might sometimes be. At fourteen his fledgling career as a performer had merely been brought to a momentary standstill; the rails provided the most immediate alternative, a paying job and a way of putting in time until the next opportunity presented itself. In future years he would, in fact, hold many other jobs—truck driver, day laborer, farmhand, mechanic, janitor, even dishwasher. His efforts to get back in front of an audience, while frequently postponed or shunted aside, were never abandoned.

Jimmie Rodgers was still a long way from being a polished performer, and undoubtedly he realized it. Years would pass before he found the exact blend of voice and instrument that so eloquently expressed his unique genius. Moreover, his stage aspirations, if openly admitted, would surely have earned him ridicule around the railyards. It was safer to bide his time, and learn what he could from the musically inclined amateurs, black and white, who manned the trains and worked the right-of-ways.

After all, James was only in his early teens, an awkward, growing boy beset with all the aches and uncertainties of adolescence. Some of the pains were actual physical ones, for although he had "fleshed out" and outgrown some of his childhood sicknesses, there were still frequent bouts with bad colds, pleurisy, and other chest ailments, even in the summertime. In August, 1912, he wrote to Dora from Artesia, Mississippi, where he and his father were working with the road crews of the Mobile & Ohio. He was confined to bed with chills and fever, "doctor here day and night," but had begun to improve. It was a hasty note. "I hope you are well. escuse Paper. answer soon."

As usual, they did not remain in one place very long. The following year Jimmie was in Oklona, up the M&O line, "running a [baggage] transfer car and making Pretty good money and having a good time." In November he wrote Dora that he planned to "come Down there Christmas if I can get off and spend (eat) xmas dinner with you all. Lottie May is at Mrs. Williams yet But he [Aaron] is going to take her away soon. Good luck to you all. Escuse paper and spelling."

School or no, his handwriting was improving, even if his orthography wasn't. He would forever take casual, often colorful, liberties with spelling, grammar, and punctuation; yet his letters of this period bear, in form and complexity, little resemblance to those of only a few years earlier. The voice that speaks through them is that of a very bright but sometimes troubled young man, increasingly conscious of himself and trying very hard to come to terms with that self. This is not to say that the letters are particularly "deep" or introspective, but even those invariable, touching little efforts to "escuse" himself for blunders of form or expression suggest an increasing attempt to identify a world beyond, and to measure himself against it. While it appears that Jimmie is mostly concerned with "making good money and having a good time"—a phrase that occurs again and again in his letters—what is really at stake is his dogged determination to escape the curse laid down against him by family and friends, the by-now-weary imprecation that Jimmie Rodgers is a lackadaisical kid who will never amount to anything. The strongest evidence of his new stance appears in a letter he wrote to Dora from Muldon, Mississippi, in May, 1914: "I am Making a Man out of myself now." To be sure, that statement is followed by the usual "And making Pretty good money"—the two notions forever conjoined but not necessarily coequal, even in his own set of values. There is now a Spencerian flourish to his signature (still "James"), bold if a bit erratic, mindful of the young Aaron, and written on the back of the letter, in his normal hand, is the inevitable "Escuse bad writing & spelling." *I am making a man of myself.* He is not yet seventeen and has, almost to the day, nineteen years to live.

It is one of the great clichés of country music, almost Keatsian in its romantic purity, that the artist must suffer. As Hank Williams later put it, "You've got to have smelt a lot of mule manure before you can sing like a hillbilly." Anyone who has heard Jimmie Rodgers sing "T.B. Blues" or "Lullaby Yodel" or "My Old Pal" will immediately recognize that Rodgers had lived what he sang, had suffered the pain and anguish, had gone through it in the most metaphysical sense, as Ishmael penetrated the whiteness of the whale and survived to translate it into a statement of common faith, some resonant, soothing litany, beyond mere words but instantly perceived, shared, understood. The distinctive note of Rodgers's personality was an unflagging exuberance, a jaunty optimism sometimes portrayed in almost pollyannaish proportions; but beneath that note there was the hard, cold reality, the certain knowledge that "my time ain't long." "I guess you got no business with the blues unless you can sing 'em," he said. That was his acknowledgment that the human condition is a hard day's work, and music helps to ease the burden. Although his own life would be a constant alternation of sunshine and shadow, it is remarkable that the darkness so rarely showed outside his music.

One of those rare moments surfaces in a letter he wrote to Dora from a railroad boardinghouse in New Orleans in June, 1916. After a brave—and all too familiar—start ("I have a good Job and making good money and doing fine"), the reality of his situation gradually emerges. He complains that he has not heard from his friend Sammy Williams: "Aunt Dora ask Sam whats the mater he can't write to me. I wrote him twice now and he has not ans one of my letters. Ask him if he got my card. . . ." Yet he is quick to make it plain that he doesn't really care (for after all, he is making a man of himself): "Tell him if he don't wont to write to me, he need not trouble him self." Take that, Sam Williams!

The problem, in fact, went much deeper than a casual slight from a boyhood chum. The whole world, it seemed, was against him: "I and [am] going to Elpaso Texas in a weak or 10 days I think. And if I can get the Job I am trying to get there I dont never indind [intend] to come to Miss. again all my People are down on me. Also my Brothers & father there." It was a rare note of self-pity, unrelieved by any of the dogged optimism that usually marked even his bleakest moods.

Years later he would sing of Texas as "the land of my boyhood dreams." Apparently none of them came true in 1916, for whatever the outcome of his projected trip to the Lone Star State, by early the next year he was back in Mississippi, working at various jobs and, as usual, courting a succession of "Sweet little girls," one of whom was to play a brief but significant role in his life.

NOTES

1. "I'd Like to Sleep 'til I Get Over You" (Roger Bowling). Copyright © 1974 ATV Music Corp. Used by permission. All rights reserved.

2. The inscription was composed by H. B. Teeter, at that time a Nashville newspaperman. Ernest Tubb to NP, Mar. 8, 1975.

3. W. J. Cash, *The Mind of the South* (New York: Alfred A. Knopf, 1941), p. 42.

4. "Anniversary Blue Yodel," words and music by Jimmie Rodgers and Elsie McWilliams. © 1929 by Peer International Corporation. Copyright renewed. Used by permission.

5. Mike Paris and Chris Comber, *Jimmie the Kid* (London: Eddison Press, 1977), p. 10.

6. *Roll 21, Capt. B. S. Rives' Supporting Force, Post of Selma, Alabama*, June 7, 1865, National Archives.

7. Cash, *Mind of the South*, p. 24.

8. For a concise history of the Mobile & Ohio Railroad and its evolution, see James Lemly, *The Gulf, Mobile and Ohio* (Homewood, Ill.: Richard D. Irwin, 1953), esp. pp. 308–14.

9. The place-name "Bozman" appears today on maps of Talbot County, Maryland.

10. Rev. Jos. W. Bozeman, D.D., *Sketches of the Bozeman Family* (Meridian, Miss.: Mercury Publishing, 1885), p. 105.

11. *Company Muster Rolls, Co. B, 14 Reg't Alabama Infantry*, and *Prisoner of War Registers, Fort Delaware, Delaware*, National Archives.

12. From her side of the family, Mrs. Robinson brought the blood of, among others, the Yankee admiral David Farragut, a distant cousin, and the New York actor and dramatist John L. Shine.

13. The "courting letters" of Aaron Rodgers and Eliza Bozeman, and Jimmie Rodgers's letters to his Aunt Dora Bozeman, are in the possession of Mrs. M. G. Harvey ("Virginia Shine") of Meridian, the daughter of Tom Bozeman and a cousin of Rodgers. I am grateful to Mrs. Harvey for access to the correspondence. Photocopies are in my files.

14. *Deed Records of Lauderdale County, Mississippi*, 51:504.

15. *Illustrated Handbook of Meridian, Mississippi* (Meridian: Board of Trade and Cotton Exchange, 1907), p. 14 *et passim*.

16. *Ibid.*

17. *Southern* [Railway] *News Bulletin*, Dec., 1928, p. 3.

18. The name is spelled variously "Talmage" and "Talmadge" in city directories of

the day, in newspaper accounts, and on public records. I have used Aaron's spelling throughout.

19. In a similar vein, there is the cherished story of little Jimmie begging milk from railroad restaurants to go with the cereal he'd "borrowed" around town. It was the kind of prank he came to be known for in his teens, but hardly something he had to do for nutrition. According to a lesser-known version, the incident took place on the farm, and it was sugar rather than milk that he was given, by a neighbor whose cows he sometimes tended. This account seems more credible, for Jimmie was rarely around the railyards as a child, and the Rodgers family, like most others in that time, regularly kept its own milk cows, whether on the farm or in town. (One of Aaron's letters to Tal mentions their "yearlings.")

20. Jerry Silverman, *Folk Blues: One Hundred and Ten American Folk Blues* (New York: Macmillan, 1958), p. 9.

21. John Greenway, quoted in Robert Shelton and Burt Goldblatt, *The Country Music Story* (Indianapolis: Bobbs-Merrill, 1966), p. 58; and in *Journal of American Folklore*, 70:277 (July, 1957), 232. See also Bill C. Malone, *Country Music, U.S.A.* (Austin: University of Texas Press, 1968), p. 84: "Although Rodgers had been fond of music since childhood, he made no serious efforts to build a professional career until tuberculosis forced his railroad retirement at the age of twenty-eight."

For this family portrait, Aaron and Eliza Rodgers posed in typical fashion with two of their children, sometimes identified as Tal (*faded figure at left*) and Jimmie, on Aaron's knee. The children's relative sizes, however, and their parents' youthful bearing indicate that the siblings are actually Walter and baby Tal, in a photo made about 1891.

In his mother's arms (*circle*), baby Jimmie appears with relatives in front of the Bozeman home at Pine Springs, about January, 1898. His brother Tal kneels in the center foreground, while brother Walter stands on the porch rail, holding Grandpa Bozeman's Civil War rifle. The two dandies sprawled at the left, looking as if they'd just ridden in with Butch Cassidy, are Jimmie's bachelor uncles, Meade and Walter Raleigh ("Rawl") Bozeman. Grandpa Sam and Grandma Jennie Bozeman are center, in front of the porch steps; others are various Bozeman uncles, aunts, and cousins. Aunt Dora is third from right, next to Eliza.

Jimmie about 1916, already a natty dresser and man-about-town.

Jimmie Rodgers's boyhood home at Pine Springs, only a short distance from the Bozeman residence. The building was destroyed by a storm in the 1960's.

Stella Kelly strikes a dramatic pose (*back row, center*) in this family portrait taken shortly before her marriage to Jimmie.

2 *Spring, 1917–Autumn, 1923*

"Call Me James"

"He was gentle and kind, he never spoke short to me," said Stella Kelly some sixty years later. "He was just as sweet as he could be, but he simply never had any money. Every week of our marriage I wrote to my father for money to pay the rent and other bills."[1]

Stella Kelly has not worried about paying the rent for a long time now. From her childhood on a hard-scrabble Mississippi cotton farm it has been a hard climb, with ample pain and anguish along the way—two early, failed marriages, the untimely death of a beloved daughter, sundry other tragedies and upheavals. But from the beginning Stella was ambitious and tough, and time has been good to her. She reminisces on the past amid the tasteful opulence of a rambling estate in a select residential area of one of the Southwest's larger cities. The living room, filled with art objects and a massive custom-made sofa, opens onto a grand balcony overlooking a tree-lined lake. Beyond is visible the complex of apartment towers, pools, and playgrounds designed and developed by Stella and her third husband, an eminent architect. Almost eighty, she is still a striking figure, an elegant, lovely woman whose form and bearing are that of someone easily twenty-five years her junior.

At eighteen she was an absolute heartbreaker, a swan-necked beauty with black hair, smoldering dark eyes, and skin as pure as Parian marble. But good looks were not all. Lowly born—like Jimmie Rodgers—of keen Irish stock, shaped by the musty, tumescent culture of the fin de siècle South, she grew up as a child of great will and a heady, compelling grace, delicate but animated, vivacious, sensible, and determined from an early age to escape her origins.

Stella's parents, George and Millie Catherine Kelly, were farm people in the central Mississippi community of Noxpater, near Louisville in Winston County. There Stella was born in 1898, the oldest of five children. By her early teens she'd acquired a poise and sophistication that belied her background, a manner combining Celtic vigor and Southern savoir faire. Such a blend has often resulted in the stereotyped Dixie Belle, all crinoline and mirrors-on-the-wall—or, in Stella's time, the erratic excesses of the Temple Drakes and Zelda Fitzgeralds, doomed flappers manqué. Vanity she had, but there was nothing light or frivolous about Stella Kelly, nothing self-indulgent. After graduation from high school in 1916, she somehow managed to enroll at Mississippi State University (then Mississippi A. & M.) at Starkville, something few girls of her means could afford. Her stay there was brief, and little is known about it, but the episode is significant for what it reveals of her desire and ambition. It was only the first of many arduous adventures she would undertake on the way to success.

Between semesters in the winter of 1916–17, Stella spent some time at home and then decided to go to Durant, some fifty miles away, to visit her cousin, May Conn, whose husband, Tom, was a fireman with the Illinois Central Railroad there. Today Durant is a sleepy hamlet of old houses, shady streets, and a few blocks of Edward Hopper storefronts, many of them empty. But around the time of World War I it was the center of a thriving farm community and an important service point on the Illinois Central's mainline, with the only heavy-repair rail shops and roundhouse between Memphis and Jackson, Mississippi.

One day in late January, 1917, Tom Conn brought a friend home for dinner, a lanky, likeable kid whom he introduced as J. C. Rodgers—or, as the young fellow said with a wink, "To close acquaintances, it's 'James.'" Very soon Stella was calling him James.

As Tom Conn explained to his wife and her cousin, James had been working "extra board" out of New Orleans and Jackson—that is, he had no regular train assignment and took whatever crew job he could get on extra trains or special runs. Hoping to find more permanent work in the shops at Durant, he'd come there, only to find no openings. Nevertheless, he stayed on, hanging around the depot and picking up odd jobs in the yards, working with maintenance crews, handling baggage, making occasional extra-board runs south to Jackson and north to Memphis. In really slack times he even "helped out" (which generally meant washing dishes) at a hash house near the station—something at which he'd had plenty of experience in his years of bumming around. It was a hand-to-mouth existence at best, but he was used to that—and at least it kept him within easy distance of the Conn home, where the pretty young visitor from Louisville had more or less settled in as a permanent resident, apparently giving up any notion of returning to school. That was fine with James, who came around regularly (usually dragging along an old banged-up banjo) for free meals and an evening of heartfelt, if clearly amateurish, serenading. The music did not impress Stella—years later, when she began to hear news of his records and professional appearances, she paid little attention because "I didn't think it would ever amount to anything. I didn't think he was very good." But if his music did not charm her, Jimmie Rodgers certainly did.

Theirs was, in true Rodgers fashion, something of a whirlwind courtship. For Jimmie it was not merely infatuation or a passing whim; he was, or believed himself to be, deeply in love and, typically, intended to waste no time. Just how much their relationship may also have been impelled by external pressures and events can only be guessed at—later there would be charges and countercharges, ugly rumors, and much speculation about the whole affair. But whatever the immediate circumstances and motives of those involved, other, larger forces were also at work. For some time it had been obvious, even in rural Mississippi, that the nation was going to war. At about the time when Jimmie and Stella met, Germany had resumed unrestricted submarine warfare, and President Wilson responded in March by arming American merchant ships. In that same month the government revealed German attempts to conspire with Mexico against the United States in the event of war, and, with U-boats taking an ever-increasing toll of American shipping in the Atlantic, public sentiment for entering the war reached new heights. In a speech in Rodgers's hometown that fall (a speech that Jimmie may well have heard), the egregious Governor Bilbo warned fellow Mississippians that the state was covered with German spies, baldly announcing that a dozen or more had been arrested while trying to steal blueprints of every sawmill in the state. Some Mississippians, like young Bill Faulkner,[2] a high school dropout in Oxford, not far away, were already trying to join the British or French services to Fight the Dirty Hun; others, including Sam Williams, Jimmie Rodgers's boyhood pal, would soon be donning U.S. Army khaki. It came as little surprise to anyone when, in early April, Woodrow Wilson went before the Congress and called for a war to make the world "safe for democracy." The House and Senate, reflecting the nation's dominant mood, instantly agreed, and Wilson's war resolution passed by overwhelming majorities. The date was April 6, 1917.

Three weeks later, on Tuesday, May 1, in nearby Lexington, Mississippi, a marriage license (misspelling the names of both bride and groom) was issued to "Mr. J. C. Rogers and Miss Stella Kelley." Their ages were given as "21 and 18 years respectively, being the statutory ages prescribed by law." In fact, Stella had celebrated her nineteenth birthday on March 19; Jimmie would not be twenty until September. They were married later that day, with only Tom and May Conn in attendance.

The newlyweds settled in a small apartment a few blocks from the Durant rail shops, where Jimmie had at last gotten what he hoped would be a steady job as an apprentice mechanic. In the first flushes of marital bliss, the young bride wrote a glowing, poignant letter to Dora Bozeman:

Dear "Aunt" Dora:
I know we've treated you badly, by not writing—but we've had so many to write to; that we can hardly get around. James speaks of Aunt Dora so often, & talks about you so much, that I feel as if I know you already.
    We're as happy as we can be—James is such a "dear." And I think this is the "cute" part: We're keeping house—
    Can't you come to see us Aunt Dora? We would be delighted to see you & have you with us at any time. I'm very anxious to meet James' father. We rec'd a letter from him today saying he had recently married again.
    James won't be in from work until 5:30 and it's so lonesome here while he's away.
    We expect to make Durant our home.
    I won't write any more. Please don't forget us. Here's hoping you'll like,

                                                            Your new neice
                                                            Mrs. James Rodgers

We expect to make Durant our home. One sees them, down through the years—James and Stella Rodgers, settling down, "making Durant their home," raising a family, keeping house (with a vengeance, beyond the time of its any longer being "cute"), growing older, fading away, good, strong, decent, anonymous American folk. Living happily every after.

So much for Great Expectations.

In less than two months, Durant was a thing of the past. In late June they moved to Louisville, Stella's hometown, and took up residence at the Parks Boarding House—or at least Stella did. The mechanic's job had not worked out, and Jimmie was on the road again as a boomer brakeman. His irregular hours—and paychecks—were taking their inevitable toll on the young marriage. "His work was not steady," Stella said later, with considerable understatement. She remembered also that "he drank quite a lot," but it is clear that that is merely a reflection; she objected not to his drinking, but to the money he spent or gave away: "He was kind, he was just as sweet as he could be, but he was the poorest businessman I ever saw." Easy come, easy go? "I don't know if it was easy come or not," said Stella, "but it was certainly easy go. Anybody on earth that would write him a card or call him for help of any kind, he would send them his last dime. Many times I have seen him fold the money up in an envelope and seal it . . . he had a funny way of planting his fist down on it to make it stick." She laughs gently, her voice soft and golden, honeyed now and then with the South, and the past: "envelope" is "EN-velup," the way my Texas grandmother used to say it.

The immediate problems were Jimmie's procrastination and seeming lack of ambition. "He would strum around on some instrument and fool away his time and money," Stella said, "and I wrote to my father [for money] every week of my life. Finally, my father said, 'Now honey, I tell you what, why don't you just mosey along home with us this time and when he gets straightened out he can come to get you.'" Although George Kelly enjoyed Jimmie's company and sometimes harmonized with him out on the front gallery, he had never looked with much favor upon his daughter's marriage to the impecunious railroad rowdy and erstwhile jack-of-any-trade; he stepped in with a strong hand, apparently undeterred even by the fact that Stella was by then two months pregnant. Later she would speak of the situation in only the vaguest terms, but her meaning is clear: "Jimmie tried to come, he tried any number of times to see me, but . . . all that was beyond my control. I thought it was most unfair, and I thought they [her parents] were trying to play God . . . but I've come to think it was the best thing they ever did."

With the marriage foundering, Jimmie drifted back to New Orleans. For a while he worked with an M&O section crew there, and later, with the war in full swing and the railroads under government control, he got on as a brakeman with the New Orleans & Northeastern (a subsidiary of the Southern Railway), working its regular passenger runs from New Orleans to Meridian. But Stella was still very much on his mind, and he tried several times to bring about a reconciliation. "He wanted to take me to New Orleans . . . but he never managed it," Stella said, suggesting that it was simply some vague act of fate each time which prevented them from getting together. Once she got as far as Meridian and the home of Tal and Pearl Rodgers before something interfered—lack of finances, or a change of mind, or some other passing whimsy. By the autumn of 1917 their separation was complete.

Sometime after Christmas, Stella's parents moved to Choctaw County, Oklahoma, near Hugo. For reasons known only to her, Stella, now in her eighth month of pregnancy, stayed behind. She went alone to Ackerman, Mississippi, a few miles north of Louisville, and took a room at the Heflin Hotel. There on February 16, assisted by Mrs. Heflin and a local physician, Dr. J. D. Weeks,[3] she gave birth to a daughter, whom she named Kathryn (her mother's middle name, given a "modern" spelling). Two weeks later Stella and the baby left for Oklahoma to join her parents. James was "a dear," but they had both been much too young and foolish. It would never have worked out. So long to Mississippi, to hard-scrabbling and railroad shanties, to a youthful fling at marriage with a wistful, shiftless, charming boy named James Rodgers. All that was behind her now, gone for good.

Conductor John Atwood met Jimmie Rodgers one day when the train he was working rolled into Laurel, Mississippi, at the south end of the Southern Railway's "hot foot run" from Meridian. Yard facilities were shared with the Southern's sister line, the New Orleans & Northeastern, and as Atwood walked down the house track to notify the extra gang to start switching cars, he saw a crowd of blacks kneeling in the shade of a boxcar on the sidetrack, rolling dice and keeping time with what struck Atwood as "a peculiar chanting rhythm" that came from under the car. "The chant was rolling off in that peculiar rhythm of the extra gang Negroes of the Southern Railway around the time of World War I," said Atwood. As he stopped to listen for a moment, he discovered that the music was coming "from a cheap guitar in the hands of a rather good looking lad in his teens." It was Jimmie, of course. When the game was broken up and the blacks sent back to work, he crawled out from under the car, climbed up on a pile of crossties, and began singing "Casey Jones," to Atwood's delight. "That sweet, mellow voice of Jimmie's impressed me then," he said, "as it has impressed millions since."[4]

Afterward, when Rodgers's railroad days were behind him and he was consciously cultivating a rakish public image, he would nurture the story that he and the NO&NE had parted company "because I kept havin' trouble with the ole 'Rule G.'" There is little doubt that by this time he was an accomplished tippler, but if his drinking had anything to do with his departure from the line, it is not reflected in the letter of recommendation written for him in January, 1925, by the trainmaster at Hattiesburg. "J. C. Rodgers has been employed by NO&NERR since January 9, 1918," wrote A. M. Tipton, "[and] on account ill health is going west and seaking such employment that he can get any favors shown him will be appreciated." Admittedly, it is not much of a recommendation, but Tipton was obviously fighting a recalcitrant typewriter—he gave his position as "Train Masiter"—as well as his own halting syntax and spelling.

The letter is noteworthy for several reasons. On the surface, it appears to account for a substantial span of time—almost seven years to the day—in Jimmie Rodgers's life. Moreover, it seems to document his longest term of regular employment to that time and, inasmuch as the NO&NE ran only between Meridian and New Orleans, to suggest a period of relative calm and stability. But in fact his association with the NO&NE was far from steady during these years, and his existence anything but routine.

For someone who rarely seemed to take life seriously, the breakup of his marriage had left Jimmie Rodgers more than a little shaken. In his own boyishly sentimental fashion, he had loved Stella deeply, and he did not give up hope of a reconciliation for a long time. But he was also a realist, well schooled in the hard ways of the world and only too aware of the limitations of wishful thinking. He may have mooned for a time, caught up in the melancholy of dull routine, the innate sadness of grimy switchyards and black trains moaning through the longleaf pines and shuttling down the delta in grey winter dawns. But summertime was coming, and at the end of the run lay New Orleans, the Paris of the Americas: warm Gulf breezes, bright lights, dark laughing ladies, and, most of all, music.

At the opposite end of his run was Meridian. Although Jimmie had never really lived there for any sustained period, it was home; he had relatives and many friends there, knew his way around, and found layovers there a respite from his hectic, rough-and-tumble life on the road. The thirty dollars a week he earned as brakeman and baggageman on Train No. 43 was no princely sum, even by the standards of the day. But when the work was steady, he could indulge in his favorite diversions: girlfriends, sporty clothes, phonograph records, and theater tickets, more or less in that order. More unusual was his affinity for perfumes, especially a scent known as Black Narcissus. Oblivious to those who might think the practice a bit strange, he habitually carried a small flask of it as a counter to the harsh odors of the railroads and, later, to relieve the smell of medicines and the sickroom. During these years—roughly 1918 through 1920—he shared an apartment on Fifth Street with his bachelor cousin Joe Bozeman, and even managed to make a down payment on a new Ford (which he could not pay for and eventually lost). Layovers in Meridian gave him a chance to stock up on Aunt Dora's home cooking, hang around the shops, go duding around town and renew old acquaintances—including one with a pretty sixteen-year-old preacher's daughter named Carrie Williamson.

Precisely when Jimmie and Carrie met is a matter of conjecture— there is some indication that he knew her as early as 1916—but the circumstances were later recorded in detail by Carrie. She was still in high school, "not thinking of young men, nor of marriage," she said, when Jimmie Rodgers appeared, almost literally sweeping her off her feet.

The Williamson home, a neat frame bungalow at 1609 Eleventh Avenue, had long been a popular neighborhood gathering-place for young people. The house not only accommodated Williamson children and their many friends, but also served as de facto social center for the newly organized First Methodist-Protestant Church, pastored by

the Reverend Mr. Williamson. Contrary to what one might expect
of a fundamentalist preacher's home in that narrow time and still
very conservative place, it was a warm and happy household—
"religious, but none of your stern, sour fanatics," as Carrie put it
later—with a worldly appreciation of literature and the arts. Like good
Methodists everywhere, the Williamsons were especially fond of
music; but unlike many, they knew secular tunes as well as hymns, and
if their tastes were rather predictably middle class—"light" classics
and the popular songs of the day—that was still more than could be
said for most people in their position. In light of the impoverished
social and educational background of both Reverend and Mrs.
Williamson, it was downright astonishing. To Carrie's parents must go
considerable credit for the generous sympathies and spirit of liberality
which they fostered.

The musical atmosphere of the Williamson household was an
immediate attraction to Jimmie Rodgers.[5] In Carrie's words, he "was
easily persuaded to go wherever there was music to be enjoyed—even
to a minister's house." Reckoning from her account, it was the summer
of 1919 when he first appeared there, in the company of another young
lady who was a close friend of the family. On their way to "a
professional concert" (more likely a dance or movie-and-vaudeville
bill), they stopped in unannounced to use the Williamsons' phone, and
caught Carrie in cold cream and kitchen gingham. "There was I, so
mortified I could have bawled," she later wrote, "and no escape. I'd
been taught to be polite to 'company'; make them welcome.
So—nothing to do except make my excuses as soon as possible—and
hurry to clean up a bit; fluff my hair and climb out of that house dress
into my pretty blue crepe. Then to rejoin the group now around the
piano. And steal embarrassed glances at the good-looking stranger.
Our 'company' stayed so long, enjoying this impromptu concert, that
they were somewhat late for the professional concert."[6]

Interested as he may have been in the Williamsons' piano, sheet
music, and songbooks (containing, said Carrie, "all the quaint,
old-fashioned songs he loved"), it was soon apparent that the real
object of Jimmie's attention was, as she put it, "my school-girl self."
Very soon he was showing up regularly, "barbered and shined," with
a box of candy and the inevitable banjo under his arm.

The seventh of the nine Williamson children—she was born August 8, 1902—Carrie occupied no special place among her sib-

lings. She was prettier than the other girls but less talented, quiet and reserved to the point of shyness but strongly independent. At sixteen, still in school, she was holding a full-time clerk's job in a department store downtown and paying room and board to her parents. The presence of Jimmie Rodgers immensely complicated her life, for it was a clear case of the attraction of opposites. He was just about everything she was not: high-spirited, gregarious, recklessly impulsive, and absolutely careless with whatever came his way, whether it was his money, his health, or his friends. Eventually he could come to respect at least one thing—his talent—but in those days it may have been simply his peculiar brand of independence, so different from Carrie's, which appealed to her; or perhaps it was nothing more than his cheerful optimism and his jaunty grin. Other members of the family, especially her older brothers, were well aware of Jimmie Rodgers's reputation around town. They did not take to the lanky brakeman so easily, and their opposition to the match grew as time passed and the romance intensified.

One further obstacle was that Jimmie was still legally married to Stella Kelly, although they had been separated for almost two years. That complication was resolved in November, 1919, when Jimmie filed for and was granted a divorce. The grounds were, in effect, desertion; according to the decree, Stella's whereabouts were unknown, and "complainant is entitled to the relief prayed for."[7]

The language was merely legalistic, of course: Jimmie Rodgers was never much inclined toward prayer in its strictest sense. There were dark spirits in him, but he seemed remarkably free from one element that haunted his Southern brethren: a sense of sin. Early in their courtship, Carrie promised him a kiss if he'd go to church. "He got the kiss, and kept his promise,"[8] she said, "by going to church at least once!" That pretty much indicated the order of his priorities: first the flesh, and then, if at all, the spirit. Later, struggling with hard times and the insidious disease that would kill him, he sometimes turned silent and withdrawn. His manner was taken for shyness by those who had not known him in these more carefree days, when he was full of pranks and quips and when life was a constant party. Carrie chided him for his hedonism, for spending his money recklessly and "parading the streets, serenading all the time" instead of resting up at the end of his railroad run. But even then Jimmie Rodgers was something of a fatalist, as anxious as any seventeenth-century poet to seize the day.

"Aw shucks, Carrie," he said, "what's money for, what's life for, if you can't enjoy 'em? I want to live—today. That old eight-wheeler might take a notion to leap the rails tomorrow." Exasperated, she would aim at the old wound from his childhood: "Everybody's saying you'll never amount to anything." To which he defiantly insisted, "I'll show 'em! I'll amount to something—someday." The most Carrie dared hope for was that he might eventually wear the coveted badge and uniform of a passenger conductor.[9] Jimmie himself was vague. Somehow "showing 'em" had to do with his playing and singing—but by now he'd seen the failure of his grandiose teenage schemes, had outgrown them, and cared to make no particular plans. There'd be plenty of time to plan later. For the present, it was a good life—far better than it had been (and in some ways better than it would be again, although he probably never thought of it that way). "Free, white, and twenty-one" was the popular expression; he turned twenty-two that fall of 1919 and was, finally, "making a man of myself," earning a man's pay and living the spirited life of a railroader and dandy-about-town. Yet in many ways he was still a boy at heart—and would forever be one. With 165 pounds on his 5'10" frame, he was robust, almost plump, brown-eyed and handsome in his boxback suit and polka-dot tie, with a katy straw set at a rakish angle over a shock of brown hair already beginning to thin. It was all too good to last.

The war years had been boom times for trainmen. When the rail industry was nationalized under the United States Railway Administration, jobs were plentiful and wages high. That situation began to change radically in early 1920, when the railroads were returned to private hands; corporate officials began to retrench in the face of declining freight shipments and the predicted postwar business slump. Jimmie Rodgers, with little seniority, lost his brakeman's job on scheduled runs of the NO&NE. It was a "temporary layoff," as opposed to an outright firing, but the net result was the same: he was back to the tough scuffle, empty pockets, roaming in search of work. Business was in a tailspin everywhere, beset by falling prices and labor disputes, and millions of returning soldiers had flooded the job market.[10]

For several months Jimmie hoboed around the country, visiting friends in Texas and working at whatever odd job came his way —section hand, roustabout, an occasional brakeman's run. He got as far as California before turning back, sometimes washing dishes in a roadside diner for the price of a meal, just as often doing without. Returning to the South, he found work for a time on the NO&NE's sister line, the Vicksburg, Shreveport & Pacific, running between Delta Point and Shreveport, Louisiana. One cold March morning, huddled in the "crummy" of a VS&P rattler freight, he scribbled a hasty note to his Aunt Dora, explaining that he'd "been going from place to place and havent had time to write." Times had been rough—"I have had to Pawn my watch to get money to eat on"— but now that he was working (at the usual "very good job"), he would send her the ten dollars she'd loaned him "soon as I can possibly get it." Apparently having settled that account to his satisfaction, he moved to a hurried finish—"This train is Runing so blooming fast I cant hardly write as it is." In closing he asked her to reply soon and, just incidentally, "if you can spare $5.00 please send it to me."

Matters did not improve. Soon he was out of work and laid up in Meridian with pneumonia. Nevertheless, within a month the impecunious railroader had proposed to Carrie Williamson, and she had accepted. On April 7, 1920, they were married, much to the dismay of her family and probably without her parents' approval or prior knowledge. If not exactly an elopement, the wedding was certainly a rushed affair. For Carrie, it meant leaving school in the midst of her senior year; at noon the day Jimmie proposed, she put aside her books and went to meet him downtown, where they bought the license and ring. After the ceremony, performed in the home of Jimmie's engineer friend, Jim Jackson, they caught the train to New Orleans for what Carrie later referred to as a "runaway" honeymoon. Exactly when her parents learned of the marriage is not known. It was probably not until the couple returned three days later, although there is some evidence that the Williamsons suspected what was taking place. (According to a prevailing rumor, one of Carrie's brothers met them at the station on their way out of town and demanded that Jimmie submit to a medical examination before leaving.)[11] In later years, Nate Williamson would take pride in announcing publicly, in his stately senatorial tones, that "Ah knew Jimmie Rodgahs long befoah he mahrried mah sistah," but in private he would not discuss the circumstances or divulge anything that he might have known about Jimmie prior to the marriage. In light of Jimmie's reputation, that reticence seems all too understandable.

Once presented with accomplished fact, however, the Williamsons determined to make the best of the situation. Jimmie Rodgers might be a rowdy and a shiftless no-account, but he was now a part of the family, and for Carrie's sake they accepted him, willingly if not enthusiastically, into the fold. It was a tightly knit group, bound not only by blood but also by geography—as many as four of the married Williamson children lived in the immediate neighborhood, forming a sort of family enclave around the block bordered on the east and west by Eleventh and Twelfth Avenues and on the south and north by Sixteenth and Seventeenth Streets.

It was here, with Carrie's parents or one of her brothers or sisters, that the newlyweds often found a home in the early years of their marriage. At other times, just as Eliza Rodgers had followed her wandering husband from job to job, Carrie went along when Jimmie, out of wanderlust or necessity, took a notion to see what was over the hill. "Throw your things together, kid," he would say. "We're leaving here for there." "There" was often a railroad boardinghouse or cheap apartment near the yards—"a one-room light housekeeping home," as Carrie generously put it. Soon, however—echoes of Eliza once again—she was back in Meridian, pregnant with their first child.

Laid off by the railroad throughout the latter part of 1920, Jimmie picked up odd jobs here and there, did day labor, and even drove a road construction truck over in Geiger, Alabama, where his father now lived in semi-retirement. But more often than not there was no work at all. Jimmie spent many days loafing around the rail shops and poolrooms, occasionally entertaining pals and hangers-on with his banjo or guitar. Always short of cash (although not nearly as desperate as they would soon be), Jimmie and Carrie were increasingly forced to rely on the hospitality of her family. They moved in with Carrie's sister and brother-in-law, Gladys and Mose Hunt, at 1617 Eleventh Avenue, next door to the senior Williamsons. "It didn't matter," said Mrs. Hunt later. "We were all poor and in the same boat. It was share-and-share-alike. Anyway, we were all young and carefree and happy. We had good times together."[12]

Even when Jimmie was working, their financial situation was precarious. "His pockets all had holes in them; any money that went into them went right out again," said Carrie,[13] echoing Stella's complaint. But Carrie, who lacked Stella's strong will and bounding ambition, preferred to stand by her man. Nagging him didn't do much good anyway, and as long as he gave her half of what he made, as he had vowed to do when they married, she was willing to help him enjoy spending his half. Still fascinated by show business—"any kind of show," said Carrie—Jimmie rarely missed a performance of any carnival, circus, or repertoire company touring the area, often taking the train to Jackson or some other nearby city to catch one of his favorites, the W. S. Walcott Original Rabbit Foot Minstrel Company or the Paul English Players, which, along with such popular units as the Blondin Shows, Crowley's Comedians, and the W. I. Swain Show, played regularly through the region in those days.

His other indulgence was phonograph records. According to Carrie, he bought them "by the ton."[14] Unfortunately, she listed none of the artists or titles which brought a gleam to the eye of the Father of Country Music. In addition to the standard fare of the day—old sentimental ballads, novelty instrumentals, and the New York stage hits—they surely included those new blues tunes that were sweeping the country and being advertised in the Meridian newspapers as early as 1921. But it was not merely for entertainment that Jimmie bought records. Almost completely self-taught as a musician and well aware that he was only a rank amateur, he nevertheless worked constantly to improve, playing the recordings over and over to learn whatever he could. In the process he inadvertently came upon the crucial elements that distinguish recorded performances from live ones, and developed into a discerning judge of what may be termed "recording presence," as opposed to merely correct execution. If the technicalities of musical annotation, timing, and proper pitch eluded him, he was drawn almost instinctively to the vitality a performer might transmit on record, the clarity of his pronunciation, the organic relationship between voice and instrument, and (most important of all) the nuances and authenticity of emotion that made a performance "live." Jimmie played the records again and again, listening for these qualities. One artist might be criticized for drowning out the vocal with his music, another for singing "too loud and whangy" and for slurring his words, still another for the bloodless monotony of his delivery—"no way tellin' if he's feeling bad about what he's singing, or good about it," Jimmie would say. He understood that, in person, an entertainer's appearance or gestures could compensate for these deficiencies and still win an audience; on record, the performance stood or fell solely and literally upon the quality of vibrations. It was no accident that Jimmie Rodgers's initial success came as a recording artist.

Although he eventually emerged as a true original, spontaneous, self-taught, and more or less immune to the finer points of musicianship, it would be unfair to suppose that Rodgers's attitude toward trained professionals was the sort of arrogant Know-Nothingism that often afflicts both the redneck amateur and the Nashville flash who boast that they play "strictly by ear." As Carrie pointed out, even playing by ear Jimmie obeyed no rules, but "he had no scorn for professional or other trained musicians . . . he never thought he was good; or that almost anybody else couldn't be better. He never thought there wasn't plenty of room for improvement in his own humble brand of music."[15]

In the early Twenties, however, Jimmie Rodgers was still a long way from perfecting even "his own humble brand of music." Conscious of his deficiencies, he nevertheless sought out opportunities to perform with other musicians, progressing from family sing-alongs around the Williamsons' piano to dance parties, picnics, and almost any social gathering that might provide him with an audience. In his rambles around the country he made friends with musicians and was widely accepted into that amorphous brotherhood of small-time entertainers, med show pitchmen, singing hobos, bandsmen, and part-time minstrels. In New Orleans, one of his acquaintances was a character named Goebel Reeves, a soldier of fortune and wandering troubadour who would later record as "The Texas Drifter" and other *noms de disque*. During one of Jimmie's layoffs from the railroad (if Reeves's windy account can be trusted), he and Reeves teamed up with a third musician named Lucien Parks to mount an impromptu road show, traveling around the country in an old Ford outfitted with a camper body, playing in bars and on street corners for gas money and expenses. According to Reeves, "I taught Jimmie how to yodel, and another mutual friend taught him to play the guitar."[16] That of course is a wild exaggeration, if not entirely imagined. It does seem likely, however, that Jimmie absorbed a great deal merely from touring with Reeves and Parks, and may well have begun his assimilation of the yodel, the blues, and his unorthodox guitar style during this period. In any event, the tour itself, like so many others he attempted, soon turned into a financial flop. Once more Jimmie was on his way back to Meridian.

On January 30, 1921, Carrie gave birth to a daughter whom they named Carrie Anita, after her mother and the actress Anita Stewart.

Having gotten back on the railroad that winter—temporarily, as it turned out—Jimmie was "up the line somewhere" when news of the baby's birth reached him. Although he desperately needed to put in his time on the job, the happy father paid a relief brakeman to take over the run and caught the first "varnish haul" back home. Over the years he might take a casual attitude toward his marriages, but he remained a devoted parent who lavished his love, his time, and what little money he had on his children. Later, when there was more money than time, he indulged them perhaps too lavishly.

The brakeman's job soon ended again. Jimmie took a cut to work as a flagman, but that job played out, too, and then he was back on the bum. He ranged far and wide, taking advantage of his railroad connections when he could, getting from "here to there" on his thumb when he couldn't, returning to Meridian when all else failed. He washed dishes in restaurants, pumped gas, drove a truck again, and may have even worked as a farmhand for a time in the fall of 1921.[17] It was a pattern that was to be repeated over and over throughout the early Twenties, a scrabbling, hand-to-mouth existence—"chicken one day and feathers the next," said Carrie—that grew increasingly desperate with each succeeding year. Railroad wages, on the decline since the war, had dropped to all-time lows by 1922. Jimmie was out of work most of that year, idled by frequent layoffs and by a national strike of the shop craft unions which shut down railroads all across the country in June. Practically the only source of information about Jimmie Rodgers's whereabouts and activities during this time is his wife, and her account is exceedingly brief and vague. Except to note the birth of their second daughter the following year, Carrie skimmed across the whole period in one telling sentence: "Happily confident, he would trail jobs here and there."[18] One thing is certain, however: Jimmie's old dream of entering show business had been renewed. Wherever he was, he had a banjo or guitar, and he was constantly practicing, emulating the sounds he heard on his favorite phonograph records, finding ways to improve on them, biding his time impatiently, waiting for another chance at the entertainer's profession. When it came, in the late fall of 1923, he was ready.

NOTES

1. Stella Kelly, interview, June 6, 1975. All interviews were conducted by the author, except where otherwise noted.

2. See Joseph Blotner, *Faulkner: A Biography* (New York: Random House, 1974), I:192. America's Blue Yodeler and its greatest modern novelist were almost exact contemporaries, born seventeen days and a scant 150 miles apart. Faulkner, who knew so well the native character and its rhythms, and who might have immortalized his fellow Mississippian in a line or two, chose instead to play Beethoven on the Victrola and moon over the literary ballads of Swinburne and Housman.

3. Deposition of J. D. Weeks, M.D., in the case of *Stella Harkins and Kathryn Rodgers* v. *Jimmie Rodgers*, Law 4502 (1932).

4. *Meridian Star*, May 24, 1975, p. 2A.

5. In a letter to Jim Evans, Elsie McWilliams wrote that her mother and father "sang for records on the old phonograph cylinder records" (*America's Blue Yodeler* [Journal of the Jimmie Rodgers Society], 1:4 [Fall, 1953], 2). Modern commentators, tending to forget that virtually all home cylinder machines were also capable of recording, have concluded that these were rare commercial recordings yet to be traced. Undoubtedly, whatever records the Williamsons may have made were done at home for their own enjoyment.

6. Carrie Rodgers, *My Husband, Jimmie Rodgers* (San Antonio: Southern Literary Institute, 1935), p. 17. Mrs. Rodgers's book is the source for all statements attributed to her and, where indicated, for the statements she attributes to Jimmie; hereafter it is cited as *MHJR*.

7. *Minutes of the Chancery Court of Lauderdale County, Mississippi*, 17:413.

8. *MHJR*, p. 20.

9. *Ibid.*, p. 19.

10. One of Jimmie Rodgers's friends was not among them. Sammy Williams had died in the Argonne Forest; in his memory Jimmie took the tune of "Where the River Shannon Flows," and the sentiments of several old traditional songs, and put together one of the two ballads that would eventually attract national attention and start him on the road to fame seven long, hard years later.

11. Confidential source.

12. Gladys Hunt, interview, Jan. 4, 1975, Meridian.

13. *MHJR*, p. 32.

14. *Ibid.*, p. 57.

15. *Ibid.*, p. 56.

16. Quoted in Shelton and Goldblatt, *Country Music Story*, p. 151; see also Malone, *Country Music, U.S.A.*, p. 150. The circumstances surrounding Rodgers's association with Reeves remain clouded by many unknown details. An extended account of Reeves's life and work, omitting the Rodgers episodes, is Fred Hoeptner's "Goebel Reeves, the Texas Drifter," *Old Time Music*, no. 18 (Autumn, 1975), 10–17; also Fred Hoeptner to NP, Apr. 25, 1977, and Dec. 15, 1978.

17. According to Paris and Comber (*Jimmie the Kid*, p. 24), he "tried his hand at farming." It seems highly unlikely that he ever "farmed on his own," as the colloquial phrase has it, or "put in a crop," in the sense of either owning equipment or sharecropping. More likely he merely did fieldwork for a few weeks at a daily or hourly wage. In response to my specific inquiry, Mrs. Hunt, who saw him regularly during this period, told me emphatically, "He was never a farmer to my knowledge" (interview, Mar. 8, 1975, Meridian). In this respect the accounts of Herb Quinn and others (see David Evans, "Black Musicians Remember Jimmie Rodgers," *Old Time Music*, no. 7 [Winter, 1972/3], 12–14) are unreliable and suggest little more than the kind of generic knowledge of Rodgers that accounts for so much of the folklore (in an immediate sense of the term) surrounding the man. Quinn's quaint analysis of

the origins of Rodgers's yodel is analogous to a tale which I have heard repeated in all seriousness by both blacks and whites: that Rodgers "invented" the yodel one day when he wenᴛ into a cafe, sat at the counter, leaned over to check the waitress's figure, and "yodeled," "I see your legs, lady-o-lay-de-heeee."

18. *MHJR*, p. 33.

3 *Autumn, 1923–January, 1927*

Rain Down Sorrow

In the years following World War I, show business at the grass-roots level was lively and diverse, an activity of the most august imagination. In addition to the familiar standbys—circuses, carnivals, Wild West shows, and minstrel troupes that roamed the land—there was a great proliferation of little theaters, tabloid companies, burlesque houses, medicine shows, magicians, freak acts, vaudeville bills, water circuses, aerial daredevils, and dozens more, most of them now long vanished, unknown or merely objects of nostalgic curiosity to recent generations of television addicts. Among the many forms that flourished and now languish forgotten was a glorious sort of folk theater–cum–private enterprise known as "tent rep"—companies of small-time actors organized under an owner-manager-director (and, often as not, co-performer), touring out-of-the-way hamlets and playing one-week stands under canvas. They presented a different play each night from their repertoire of tearjerkers, rustic romances, three-act farces, cornball melodramas, and other hoary chestnuts. Traveling a more or less regular route each season, year after year, tent rep companies such as Chase-Lister, Flora DeVoss, Harley Sadler's Own, Ted North Players, Justus-Romain, Swain's Dramatic Show, and Billroy's Comedians became standard fixtures in the territories they covered, "the living theater of the countryside," as one historian has called them.[1] Their actors and actresses were as well known and loved as any of Hollywood's idols, their plays as familiar and comforting as the Bible and the local social codes whose values, proscriptions, and prejudices they judiciously reaffirmed. Show owners were often more famous than their star performers—some, like Neil Schaffner, J. Doug Morgan, and Colonel W. I. Swain, established themselves as colorful, flamboyant characters; others, such as Paul English, Charlie Worthan, Les "Skeeter" Kell, Ted North, and Harley Sadler, were widely respected as both showmen and civic-minded businessmen.

One such impresario was the youthful proprietor of Billy Terrell's Comedians, which in the spring of 1923 was about to embark on its fourth season through the Mississippi Valley and into the South. At twenty-nine, Billy Terrell was already a veteran of fifteen years in show business, having literally run away from home as a boy to join a carnival, the Great Cosmopolitan Shows. Forming his own touring rep company after the war, Terrell had quickly prospered and was soon covering a territory that extended from southern Illinois to the Gulf and as far east as the Carolinas and Florida. For the 1923 season he had enlarged the cast and crew and added a number of the embellishments that every showman loved to boast: fresh scenery, a flashy bandwagon, "a beautiful line of paper" to advertise the "up-to-date bills" (as the plays were always known to show people), and most of all a new 2,000-capacity tent from Baker-Lockwood of Kansas City, the *ne plus ultra* of tentmakers.[2] In addition to Terrell, his wife, Bonnie, and his brother Brooks, the company that year was comprised of some twenty-five actors and musicians, several of whom "doubled in brass" to form a male quartet, a six-piece orchestra, and a ten-piece show band. Some also performed less illustrious chores in the cookhouse and on the canvas crew. It was not the biggest or best show on the road, but neither was it the shabbiest.

After touring the Upper Mississippi Valley during the summer, Terrell's Comedians played a week in Union City, Tennessee, then "made the jump" to northern Mississippi and began to work their way down the state toward the Gulf. They landed in Meridian in November. Despite heavy rains throughout the fall, business at the box office held up well, and Terrell decided to extend their Meridian run to two weeks.[3]

Toward the end of the first week, he was approached on the muddy lot by a smiling, jaunty young fellow decked out in what was obviously his best suit, a straw boater, and a bow tie. "Name's Jimmie Rodgers," the young man said, extending his hand. "I'm in show business myself. Thought maybe you could use a good act to liven things up around here."

Terrell knew a novice when he saw one. The less polite term for a towner who thought he could do better than the professionals was "apple-knocker." But something about the young fellow's genial manner appealed to Terrell. "That so?" he said. "Who've you been with?"

"Oh, had my own show for a while. Played around New Orleans with some fellas. Trouped all over, here and there."

Terrell smiled. "What sort of work you do?"

"Minstrel act, mostly. Play the banjo, guitar some. Do blues on the guitar, and blue yodeling."

"No, I mean what's your regular job?"

His story seen through, Jimmie scuffed the dirt. "Well, I railroad on the NO&NE, but we been laid off a few weeks, and I thought—"

"You live here in Meridian?"

"Sho enough."

"Son, don't never try to break in in your home town, where they know you. They'll razz you to death, even if you're good." But he was impressed with Jimmie Rodgers's brash confidence, and intrigued by something the young man had said. "Say, what's 'blue yodeling,' anyway? I don't think I've heard of that."

"Aw, it's a little something I been working on. Lemme try her out for you."

"Well, I'll tell you what. I'm busy as the devil right now getting ready for tonight's show, and I've got a dozen things on my mind. But if you'll come around next week, I'll take a listen."

In Terrell's hotel room a few days later, Jimmie struck off a few old vaudeville standards—"Hot Time in the Old Town," "The Daring Young Man on the Flying Trapeze," and his standby, "Bill Bailey"—all done to a banjo accompaniment distinguished mostly by its enthusiasm. Terrell was not particularly impressed until Rodgers began to noodle around on the guitar, lightly crooning bits and pieces of the blues he'd picked up from the gandy dancers, spike-drivers, porters, and roustabouts. The guitar work was no more polished than his banjo picking, but somehow he used the instrument effectively, almost as a natural extension of the lyrics and of the yodel, at once mournful and spritely, that punctuated each verse.

When he had finished, Terrell said, "Well, son, you've got something different, that's for sure. Tell you what. We're jumping to Hattiesburg this weekend, and if you want to go along, well, we'll give you a tryout down there." There was no talk of salary, not even a hint that he could stay with the show if he worked out, but Jimmie eagerly accepted the offer.

On Sunday afternoon, in a driving rain, he piled into Terrell's Oakland touring car with Billy, his brother Brooks, and Walter "Slim" Rozell, a musician in the show's band. The four headed for Hattiesburg, eighty miles away. Traveling over dirt roads (there were no paved highways in Mississippi at the time) they had to get out repeatedly and push the lumbering auto out of mudholes. Finally, having mired it up to the axles, they gave up and spent the night in the car, fitfully trying to sleep sitting up. The next morning a farmer and his mules pulled them several miles through the mud, and they got to Hattiesburg with barely enough time to clean away the muck and dress for the opening performance that evening.

Gathering the company hurriedly to issue his customary last-minute directions, Terrell announced incidentally that he'd brought along ("discovered" was the word he would later use, in line with hundreds of others who vied for the honor) a new member of the troupe, a "blue yodeler who is plenty good to my way of thinking."

"Yeah," quipped one of the players, "I'll bet his number will be plenty blue, all right." According to Terrell, "Jimmie and I had to listen to [a lot of other] wisecracks" from the veteran performers, whose half-serious jibes reveal a great deal about popular attitudes toward yodeling even in those days.

"What is a blue yodeler—a farmer?"

"Oh, I bet he's going to wear a Swiss outfit, with a green feather in the hat."

"I have it! Let's give him 'The Arkansas Traveler' for his entrance."

Clearly, blue yodelers were hicks, or cheap imitations, or both.

Terrell, who'd heard Jimmie and knew what he could do, finally lost his temper, as he recounted later, and told them off: "Listen, you bums, the first guy that makes a wisecrack during his act gets his two weeks' notice. Besides, he doesn't need the orchestra; he's a real musician, which is something this band could stand. You wisenheimers will please retreat to your music room when I start to introduce him."

Between acts of the feature bill ("Panther of the Sea," an adventure yarn) the olio curtain was dropped to allow the scenery change, and Jimmie went out to do his two numbers—one of the railroad "blues yodels" he'd auditioned for Terrell, followed by a parlor version of

"Frankie and Johnny," a juke song that had been around for years in one form or another but that was rarely performed in polite society. Terrell recalled what happened: "The big tent was packed that night and I gave him a real build-up. Out came Jimmie, with that big smile on his face. He walked to the center of the stage and started whipping that old guitar—then he pulled his train whistle and he had them in his hand." Making what was essentially his first professional appearance before a large paying audience, he was called back, according to Terrell, for three encores and received a standing ovation when he finally left the stage.

Terrell's recollections of the incident,[4] written long after Jimmie's death, were obviously colored by Rodgers's ultimate fame; it is always easy to spot the genius of an unknown in retrospect, once he has become a success. Yet there is little reason to doubt the essential accuracy of his story, for the substance of it would be replayed again and again during Jimmie Rodgers's career.

Despite Terrell's admonition to the other musicians to "retreat to the music room," most of them caught the act by peeping through the wings. Realizing their mistake, many came around after the show to shake Jimmie's hand and apologize for their earlier remarks. "From that time on," Terrell said, "Jimmie was a big favorite with the show as well as the audiences in the cities we played." (Those "cities" were mostly small towns between Hattiesburg and New Orleans.)

According to Terrell, Rodgers spent eight weeks with Billy Terrell's Comedians, eventually leaving because "he was homesick and said that old railroad was calling him back." In fact, Jimmie could not have spent more than a month with the show, and it is likely that he was summoned back to Meridian not by the NO&NE but by the death of his baby daughter, June Rebecca, three days before Christmas. His departure may also have been hastened by the fact that in those days the play was still the thing. Later in the decade, as tent rep tried to compete with radio and talkies, specialty acts and variety numbers acquired increasing prominence on the bill, providing Jimmie Rodgers with an important showcase for his talent. But at this point on a show like Terrell's they were still makeshift and haphazard, mere fillers to keep audiences placated before the show and between the acts of the dramatic offering. Generally such voids were filled, more or less as extra duty, by actors who could double—that is, those who could play some instrument, juggle, or do a novelty turn in addition to their regular acting chores. A solo act such as Jimmie's, however popular it may have been initially, was a dispensable part of the show, and Jimmie, who did not double and who offered a very limited repertoire, was soon hard pressed to earn his keep. He'd been touring with Terrell for little more than expenses anyway.

Summoned home by the baby's death, he rode a boxcar out of New Orleans and arrived back in Meridian without a cent to pay for the funeral. Carrie's family was hardly better off, but once again they came to the rescue, each one generously contributing what he could. The burial plot was provided by Mose and Gladys Hunt, who some years before had made down payments on several inexpensive lots outside the city, in a small suburb known as Bonita. There, scarcely nine and a half years later, the body of Jimmie Rodgers would be laid to rest, beside that of his infant daughter.

The baby's death marked the onset of a bleak time for Rodgers. For all the contrived pathos and melodrama of her account, Carrie probably spoke truly when she called it a "black hour [that] came near crushing [his] dauntless spirit forever." Together they shared the loss of their child, but it was Jimmie's private burden that his first attempt at professional show business, off to such a promising start, had dribbled away and finally come to nothing. Broke, out of work, and further than ever from his dream of "showing 'em," he suffered as patiently as he could, resuming the rounds of his old familiar hangouts, taking what comfort he could from the fellowship and the music that seemed to arise spontaneously around the cafes, poolrooms, and rail shops. Occasionally he would be invited to bring his banjo or guitar along to some club luncheon for carfare and a free meal, or to put together a small combo to play for a dance or other social function. But the money was hardly enough to pay expenses, let alone dent the pile of debts that was steadily accumulating. From time to time his name would go up on the extra board again, and he would be back on the high iron for a while as boomer brakeman.

Finally, leaving Carrie and little Anita behind in Meridian, he worked his way west that winter, through Texas and New Mexico to Arizona, Utah, and Colorado, going from callboard to callboard, riding any line that beckoned. After several months of this helter-skelter existence, he came home again, nursing a bad cold and hacking cough that had developed as he rode in the rain and snow atop boxcars which clattered through the mountains and across the windswept

winter plains. He shrugged off the illness and went back on the
NO&NE that summer, but even in the sunny Southland the ominous
cough hung on and grew worse. In September, Carrie noticed flecks of
blood in one of his handkerchiefs, and a short time later, while visiting
his father in Geiger, Alabama, Jimmie suffered a serious hemorrhage.

The local doctor announced a diagnosis, but it really wasn't
necessary. In that time and place, the symptoms of tuberculosis were
all too familiar. For decades the disease had been the leading cause of
death in the United States; between 1900 and 1925, T.B. claimed over
3.5 million Americans. During the year when it was diagnosed in
Jimmie Rodgers, some 90,000 people died of it, and at least twice that
many were afflicted .[5] Just as everyone recognized the symptoms, they
knew also that there was no certain cure, and little agreement about
how the disease should be treated. As with other fatal and mysterious
ailments, sufferers were confronted with a plethora of extravagant
theories, crackpot home remedies, and miracle cures. Luckily, the
Geiger physician was a prudent man. He may have been only a simple
country doctor, but his prescription was the rational distillation of
prevailing medical opinion on the subject: absolute bed rest and, if
possible, removal to higher terrain and a drier climate. The first was
eminently sensible and remains today a vital part of any long-range
program for recovery from tuberculosis, but it was unfortunately alien
to Jimmie Rodgers's nature; the second seemed quite out of the
question at the time, although it would eventually figure in some of the
more crucial moves in Rodgers's life. (Ironically, medical science
would later prove that altitude and atmosphere have no effect whatever
on the disease, beyond some superficial relief of its symptoms.)

Jimmie Rodgers reacted to the doctor's opinions in a manner that
scarcely changed over the years as his disease progressed toward its
inevitable consequence: he simply ignored the whole thing. Insisting
that "I'll be fine if you'll just get me back home [to Meridian]," he
dismissed the doctor and prevailed upon his family to let him out of
bed. As soon as he convinced Carrie that he was able to travel, she
brought him to her parents' house and tried to care for him there. But
soon even Jimmie realized that he was seriously ill. Although no
evidence has been uncovered to support the speculation that he may
have known he had tuberculosis several years earlier, the hemorrhage
itself indicates that the disease was at least moderately advanced by the
time it was diagnosed. In the days before X-ray examinations and

routine physicals became standard practice, that was not an uncommon occurrence. Tuberculosis is an insidious disease, characteristically displaying only slight, vague symptoms in its early stages and progressing at a highly varied rate, with long periods of inactivity and irregular eruptions that steadily increase in frequency and severity. In any event, while Rodgers and others around him may have suspected that he had T.B. earlier, he clearly did not face the issue until the hemorrhage made it unavoidable. Concerned at how long it was taking him to recover from what he continued to call "a bad cold," he at last reluctantly agreed to enter the tuberculosis ward of King's Daughters Hospital, a charity institution on the northern outskirts of Meridian.

After a few weeks of rest and proper diet, he began to feel better. Soon he was leaving the hospital without the doctor's permission to visit his family and his old hangouts around town, despite the fact that Carrie, often at great sacrifice, was visiting him regularly. "He was supposed to stay [in the hospital] for six months, but he just wouldn't stay put," said his sister-in-law, Gladys Hunt. "Jimmie was the restless type, you know. He stayed out there for a short while, then he'd get up and take a bus and come downtown [to her parents' home] and go back, you know, without the doctors' permission. They didn't like it, they told him he'd just have to stay put if they were going to help him at all. Finally, he was here for a while one time and when he went back they'd taken away the bedclothes, the sheets and all, and rolled up his mattress. They said, 'We just can't have this; you've either got to stay here all the time or leave, and we've put up with it all we can.' So that was that . . . and he never did go into a hospital again, until, you know, maybe there near the end."[6]

Through it all, Carrie worked at a variety of part-time jobs, in addition to caring for young Anita and making the long trip by streetcar and bus out to see Jimmie several times a week. As Christmas approached, she found a full-time, although temporary, job as a salesclerk in a downtown department store. Jimmie, out of the hospital now, jobless, and with time on his hands, again resumed his musical activities. Instead of playing the banjo or mandolin which he'd always preferred, he was turning increasingly to the guitar; according to Carrie, it somehow "seemed to suit his mood better" than the other instruments. Slim Rozell, whom he'd met while working with Billy Terrell, was back in town, and they teamed up with Jimmie's sister-in-law, Elsie McWilliams, to play for dances. A popular location for many of these events was Lauderdale Springs, a resort area northeast of Meridian, where an enclosed dance pavilion attracted crowds from miles around.

The Rodgers-Rozell-McWilliams trio made up in enthusiasm and versatility whatever they may have lacked in polish. The usual instrumentation was Rozell on fiddle, Rodgers on banjo or guitar, and Elsie McWilliams at the piano. Rozell, however, was a journeyman musician who played a variety of instruments in addition to the violin—from time to time he served as Terrell's "musical director" in charge of the orchestra and specialty bands—and he and Jimmie experimented with other combinations that involved a saxophone or trombone played by Rozell, with Rodgers alternating among the guitar, banjo, and mandolin. The idea, of course, was to sound as much as possible like the upbeat, jazzy, "modern" groups they were hearing on records. The tunes were those that Tin Pan Alley was popularizing across the country: "Doo Wacka Doo," "Who's Sorry Now?," "I'll See You in My Dreams," "How Come You Do Me Like You Do," "Jealous," and other hits of the day. Occasionally they might play a country waltz or an old sentimental favorite like "Daddy's Little Girl" or "Any Old Place I Can Hang My Hat Is Home Sweet Home to Me," but the Lauderdale Springs audiences were mostly young and modish, would-be sophisticates who scorned anything old-fashioned or rustic. Their parents might be attracted to the coarse, homely renderings of Fiddlin' John Carson and Henry Whitter, whose records were beginning to catch on in some parts of the country, but the boys in baggy pants and the girls with bobbed hair, even in rural Mississippi, were doing the Charleston and practicing fashionable cynicism set to the music of the blues rage that was sweeping the nation. The oldtime stuff was nasal, corny, and too narrowly regional to suit their tastes, although they had nothing against celebrating the South in song. There was a long tradition of such kitsch as "My Mammy," "Make My Cot Where the Cot-Cot-Cotton Grows," "Waiting for the Robert E. Lee," "Rock-a-Bye Your Baby to a Dixie Melody," and half a dozen musical tributes to the moon over every Southern state; but all that was nicely handled, thank you, by Northern composers and performers, and no half-baked locals need apply. At the same time, hardly anyone could escape the plaintive—if coolly commercial—strains of Vernon Dalhart's "Prisoner's Song"/"Wreck of the Old 97" (Victor 19427), which had gone on sale that fall and was rapidly becoming one of the recording industry's all-time successes. Later Rodgers would take from the emerging "hillbilly" trend whatever suited him or seemed natural, just as he did with other styles and repertoires. But in those early days most of the hillbilly records struck him as crude and largely unintelligible; he did not reject them so much as simply ignore them. Undoubtedly the primitive conditions under which many of them were recorded had something to do with his judgments. In any event, he paid little attention to the likes of Fiddlin' John, Whitter and Grayson, Blind George Reneau, and other hillbilly recording pioneers. Nor is it likely that he noticed a small item almost buried at the bottom of *Billboard*'s "Land O' Melody" page in January, 1925: "R. S. Peer, of the Okeh Record Company, left on Saturday last week, for Atlanta and New Orleans where he will supervise special recordings for the concern."

With characteristic enthusiasm, Rodgers envisioned a great future at Lauderdale Springs. He moved Elsie McWilliams's battered old grand piano out to the pavilion and talked about hiring additional musicians. But with the onset of winter weather, attendance dwindled, and the trio soon broke up. Rozell left for sunnier places, and Jimmie's attention turned to other matters so abruptly that Elsie's piano was never retrieved.

Refusing to admit the seriousness of his sickness—a stance he would maintain to the very end—Rodgers nevertheless realized that his days of railroading in the heavy, humid air of the South were numbered. With Trainmaster Tipton's letter of recommendation in his pocket, he formally ended his seven-year, on-again-off-again association with the New Orleans & Northeastern and, presumably, headed west, "seaking such employment as he [could] get." Once more he was traveling alone, for Carrie had gone to work again, this time as night clerk at the newsstand in Meridian's passenger depot.

It was at some point during this period, out in Oklahoma City, that a lean, hard-faced country boy named Raymond Hall struck up a conversation with an itinerant railroader in a speakeasy on the skid row section of Reno Avenue, down near the railyards.[7] The trainman was picking out runs on a scarred old guitar while the regular band took a break, and Hall, who also "chorded some," traded a song or two with him. Among the young Okie's compositions was a song called "Take Me Back Again," which he'd written while doing time in the state reformatory. The railroader liked it and asked for a copy of the lyrics. "I'd like to sing that to my old gal," he said. When they parted, an hour or so later, he wrote his name and address on a scrap of paper and gave it to Hall, saying, "Look me up if you ever write any more songs like that. Get in touch if you ever need anything." It was a casual gesture, part of the tradition of the road. Several years would pass before Hall, behind bars again on a life sentence for what he considered a rigged charge, would remember the railroader's words and what he'd written on the back of a greasy waybill: "J. C. Rodgers, % The Billboard, Cincinnatti, Ohio."

At the time, it had not seemed unusual to Hall that an extra-board brakeman would use "The Bible of Show Business" as a forwarding address.[8] "While we were talking," Hall recalled, "somebody in the speak there—one of his railroad buddies—called out, 'Say, Jim, sing us "Around the Water Tank." ' " When he finished, Hall complimented him, saying, "You got a good voice; why don't you do something with it?" "Well, I'm trying," the railroader said. "I do a little blackface now and then, work on the med shows or vaudeville wherever I can get it."

Without being precisely aware of it, Rodgers was in fact serving his apprenticeship. Now increasingly committed to becoming a professional performer, he took other jobs only when necessity demanded it and devoted most of his energy to improving his art and wandering wherever the chances of a show business connection, however shabby or tenuous, seemed most likely. In the process he was not only enlarging upon his already considerable knowledge of the ways of the world, but also making dozens of friends in all walks of life who would one day number among his staunchest fans. Some were relatively prominent citizens in the towns he passed through—police chiefs, judges, doctors, businessmen—but most were merely the working-class people for whom his music would eventually have its deepest and most abiding appeal. Among these were the many folk connected in some way or another with small-time show business—rep actors, musicians, med show "doctors," carnival workers, and even that legion of itinerant peddlers who called themselves "pitchmen," such colorful characters as Doc Zip Hibler, Mad Cody Fleming, Widow Rollins, Sergeant Poulos, Pens Patterson, the Canadian Kid, Sox Clark, Ask-Me Dodge, the Ragan Twins (Mary and Madaline), Paperman Dell, Sir Tom Rogers, Doc El Vino ("Lord Dietz"), Population Charlie, Professor Mayfield, and Joe "Fine Arts" Hanks, the punkmugger. Theirs was a loosely structured but very exclusive brotherhood into which the amiable, easy-going Jimmie Rodgers was readily accepted. Through these contacts he learned of various jobs with traveling shows, and no sooner did he get the news of one than he was aboard some freight train and headed toward it. Occasionally the information panned out, but more often than not he was left stranded in some out-of-the-way crossroads or given temporary work in the cookhouse or on the canvas crew to earn his way to the next stop. When he couldn't manage even that, he fell back on a gambit which he had, by this time, perfected into a minor art. Shined and shaved and dressed in his best—even on the road and down on his luck, he maintained appearances—he'd go into the nearest store where musical instruments were sold, pick out a moderately expensive guitar, and demonstrate his expertise with a song or two, charming the owner or clerk with show business stories and dropping impressive hints about his "current tour." Then he'd casually arrange to buy the instrument on credit. Next stop was a pawnshop, and after that the railroad tracks or highway out of town. Later, traveling through many of these same places after he'd become a star, he'd make a point of looking up the people he'd taken and repaying them, although he admitted that he missed a few because they were no longer in business or he'd forgotten their addresses. As the story got around, hundreds of hock shops all over the country suddenly began discovering and proudly displaying guitars that were "left here by ole Jimmie Rodgers."

Through the spring and early summer of 1925, he traveled with a scruffy little medicine show through Tennessee, Kentucky, southern Ohio, and Indiana, doing a "bally" in blackface to attract crowds and passing out Congo oil, liniments, and other home remedies peddled by the "Doc." In midsummer he left to join what Carrie described as "another street-show, a novelty attraction making larger towns." Within weeks, according to what Jimmie told her, he bought an interest in the new operation, then later took it over entirely and added "an Hawaiian show with a carnival"—only to lose the whole affair in a blowdown, the storms and high winds that were the scourge of every tent showman.

Between forays into show business Jimmie returned home at irregular intervals, picking up whatever work he could around the railyards. Somewhere along the way, passing into or out of Meridian, he became acquainted with a Southern Railroad engineer named Albert

Fullam, who later recalled their first meeting: "He was sitting on an express [baggage] truck, and a-strumming a guitar; he was dressed in a striped cap and striped jacket, which at that time was traditional railroad men's wear. He had a guitar, a bow tie, a thousand-mile shirt, and a package of Bull Durham." Like Ray Hall, Fullam sensed the common bonds between them, drawn by the open, easy Rodgers manner that would later magnetize theatergoers and record buyers. "It wasn't long before we was wising off at each other . . . and I asked him was he going south on the Queen ["Queen and Crescent"—the Southern Railway] and he said, yeah, he was laid off sick and was going back, dead-heading, and we wised off a lot at each other and had a pretty good time, and wound up in New Orleans, and worked together for some time."[9]

In the early fall of 1925, with the Florida land boom in full swing, Fullam decided to head for Miami, where the Florida East Coast Railroad was desperate for train crews. Jimmie, impetuous as always, said, "Well, I think I'll just mark off and go with you." After a few weeks of steady work on the Florida East Coast's Southern Division between Fort Pierce and Miami, Jimmie sent for Carrie and Anita. They settled into yet another of the cheap furnished apartments that became home whenever they left Meridian.

For a time, it seemed that Jimmie's tuberculosis had been arrested. He never talked about it, and Carrie found it easy to convince herself that he'd been "cured," her hopes buoyed by the sunny blue skies and warm ocean breezes of the Florida peninsula. But all too soon winter arrived there, too, and with it came the cold rains and pervasive dampness that revived the ominous rattle in Jimmie's chest and the strain in his already burdened lungs.

Later Carrie would write that "Jimmie worked steadily for the Florida East Coast Railroad for the better part of a year," but the company's records indicate that his employment there lasted barely five months, from September, 1925, until February, 1926.[10] It seems likely that he sent Carrie and Anita back to Meridian around the first of the year and then, after quitting the railroad, resumed his rambles during the spring and early summer, thus accounting for "the better part of a year" that he was away from Meridian. Rodgers's reasons for leaving Florida are not clear, but they probably resulted from several factors: his natural wanderlust, aggravated by a job that was leading nowhere and, far more immediately, by the feeling that he was further than ever from the world of entertainment. Furthermore, there was the gnawing realization (which he would never quite admit, even to himself) that he had not shaken his sickness.

This time he returned not to Meridian but to Geiger, Alabama, where he entered into still another curious and short-lived business arrangement—a roadside cafe operated in partnership with an old friend named W. C. Tyer. Tyer was also an amateur musician; apparently they thought the cafe would provide exposure for their musical talents, as well as for whatever culinary skill they possessed. But business was slow, and the arrangement did not last. By late summer Jimmie was in Meridian, his musical prospects dimmer than ever and the persistent pain in his lungs growing more and more intense. "I reckon we'd better head for Arizona," was the most he'd say, although both he and Carrie knew why. "Out West" had been his original destination when he left the NO&NE the previous year, and every doctor who had treated him and everyone he met who'd had any experience with "lungers" told him that the only hope was a high, dry climate. And lots of rest.

"I know a fella in Tucson—" he said. Possibly it was an acquaintance from an earlier trek to the West, in the days when he'd been a carefree boomer brakeman. For the first time in a long while they had a little money, carefully hoarded by Carrie from Jimmie's Florida paychecks. After a brief visit with the home folks in Meridian, they bought their first car—a secondhand Dodge—loaded it with everything they owned, and set out for Arizona. Jimmie's dreams of being an entertainer were again deferred. "If [his] thoughts turned longingly to the show-business at this time he didn't mention it to me," Carrie said. "His last experience [with his carnival the previous year] had been rather disastrous, financially. And our little family had, it seemed, to be torn apart for one reason or another, too often as things were."

If the climate in Arizona was what Jimmie needed, the work wasn't. As Carrie noted, "The Southern Pacific yards in Tucson are known to all experienced railroad men as being about the toughest spot—for a brakeman—in the United States." Her terminology was slightly off—technically, he was employed as a switchman rather than a brakeman, working only in the trainyard—but it was essentially the same backbreaking, dangerous job. Built on a steep grade, the Tucson yard required a veritable crew of switchmen when it came time to make or break up a train, two or three of them riding each cut of cars as it hurtled down the incline. Their job was to slow the speeding cars as they came together at the bottom, twisting the iron brake wheels by hand as far as they could, then tightening them down with a heavy wooden brake club inserted between the spokes for greater leverage.

Fifty years later, oldtime trainmen there remembered Jimmie as a likeable, happy-go-lucky sort, although there was general agreement that "as a switchman he wasn't too much."[11] Accidents were commonplace; a switchman might lose an arm or leg—or often his life—in an instant as the massive, rumbling freight cars crashed together, and tugging at stubborn brake wheels beneath the burning desert sun was no work for a frail man with bad lungs. Yet Jimmie stuck to it gamely, despite the nagging cough and the low-grade fever that would now smolder within him every day for the rest of his life.

On some days he simply couldn't muster the energy to face the work, when fever flared and the chills sent him back to bed. Each time his pay was docked, and soon there were weeks when he spent more days in bed than on the job. Their financial situation steadily deteriorated. The old Dodge was sold for money to live on, but that was soon gone, too.

Later Carrie emphasized the deterioration of her husband's health at this point, suggesting (without actually saying) that it was responsible for their leaving Tucson.[12] But Jimmie's musical aspirations may also have figured in the move. He might have set aside his professional plans, as she believed, but it was only natural that he turned to his music for relief from the hard work and dreaded sickness. Oldtimers on the Southern Pacific remember him singing duets with a switchman named Ferguson during their "bean periods" (mealtimes), and soon he was trying to augment his railroad pay by performing at various local functions. These began to interfere with his work on the SP's midnight shift, and when he was asked to play at a dance on the evening before Tucson's annual rodeo, the yard superintendent refused to let him off work. Jimmie kept the engagement anyway, and according to "old heads" around the yard, "this was the last any of the switchmen heard of him."[13]

Whatever the circumstances, Jimmie realized that things weren't working out in Tucson. Somehow he managed to obtain passes that got them to Texas. Stranded in San Antonio, they were down to thirty cents. Carrie's plan to get money for food by pawning her winter clothes went awry when they discovered that her suitcase had been sent to Galveston by mistake. The ever-resourceful Jimmie "made the rounds" and came back with a couple of dollars and new passes that would get them to Galveston, in search of the lost luggage and a job he had heard about.

They found neither, but did manage to collect insurance from the express company for what Carrie jokingly referred to as her "missing valuables." With that small sum Jimmie bought tickets to Meridian for Carrie and little Anita, and he persuaded his wife to take the baby and go on without him. The separation was brief; again the Williamsons came to the rescue and wired Jimmie that money for his fare.

A homebody by nature despite his rambling habits, Rodgers always seemed to flourish in Meridian. As Carrie put it, "A few weeks at home, rest, good meals, the joy of seeing again his beloved Dad and brothers, and of strolling around singing and playing with his pals, [did] wonders for the wandering brakeman"[14] But it was not all rest. Jimmie Rodgers may have been dilatory and erratic, but he was mindful of his responsibilities, and constantly nagged by the general notion around town that he would never amount to anything. Patient and helpful as they were, Carrie's family could hardly disguise their feeling that she had married a loser, and that wore on him also. As soon as he was feeling up to it, he looked for work again, took on any odd job, and kept a watchful eye on the extra board down at the dispatcher's office—although he was probably coming to realize that he would never be physically able to work the high iron again. For some time he kept up the pretense (when he left for Asheville, North Carolina, a month or so later, it was ostensibly to "see about a railroad job"), but in the meantime he did whatever he could to bring home a dollar. For a few weeks he even took over and operated (on a shoestring) a filling station at Fourth and Front Streets, until an enterprising customer gassed up and drove off without paying, taking with him the business's margin of operating capital.[15]

That fall of 1926, Jimmie Rodgers had passed his twenty-ninth birthday. "Passed" seems appropriate, for it is doubtful that he celebrated. He was at an age when most men of even modest ambition and a little luck can expect to have consolidated a few gains against life. Rodgers had the ambition but no luck, and precious little to show for his nearly three decades of hard-scrabbling: one failed marriage; another he could and did walk away from anytime; a dozen or so jobs, none of which he'd succeeded at; at least three attempts to run his own business, also failures; a couple of battered stringed instruments; numerous debts; and a disease that would eventually kill him, long before his time. A friend summed it up: "About all he had was the clothes on his back, a warped-neck guitar, and that cough in his lungs."[16] Perhaps he still had hope, too, but it was hardly the jaunty, open optimism of his youth. For too long now he'd been living proof of the old family axiom that he was the black sheep, a lazy, shiftless dreamer who would never realize any of his fanciful schemes. Try as he might to maintain his happy-go-lucky air and an outward show of confidence, it was with considerable apprehension that, in January, 1927, after reaching still another impasse, he prepared to leave Meridian once more.

NOTES

1. Jere C. Mickel, *Footlights on the Prairie* (St. Cloud, Minn.: North Star Press, 1974), p. 3.

2. *Billboard,* Feb. 3, 1923, p. 28.

3. *Ibid.,* Dec. 1, 1923, p. 28.

4. Published by Jim Evans in *America's Blue Yodeler,* 2:2 (Spring, 1954), 3.

5. U.S. Department of Commerce, *Statistical Abstract of the United States, 1925* (Washington: Government Printing Office, 1926), 48:72. Tuberculosis was probably the disease that killed Rodgers's mother, or at least hastened her death. It is unlikely, however, that Rodgers himself was born with it, as some stories have suggested; tuberculosis is rarely transmitted from mother to fetus, nor is it inherited. Yet the general physical characteristics which make one susceptible to it are genetic, and post-partum infection is common. In any event, it is possible that Rodgers first contracted T.B. as a child—the so-called primary infection that regresses only to erupt again, sometimes years later, in what is known as the reinfection stage.

6. Gladys Hunt, interview, Jan. 8, 1975, Meridian.

7. Raymond Hall, interview, Mar. 12, 1975, Texas State Penitentiary, Huntsville.

8. In those days *Billboard* offered a free letter-forwarding service to "all members of the profession." Each week's issue carried in its Letters Department a listing, sometimes extending over several pages, of the names of those for whom mail had been received. The addressee would then "call" for his mail by sending the newspaper a return envelope with his current address. "J. C. Rodgers" appeared on the list as early as Aug. 9, 1924, and is found there sporadically throughout the next several years, also in other forms: "Jim Rodgers," "Jas. Rogers," "Jimmy Rodgers," etc.

9. Fullam's story is heard on Hank Snow's album *The Jimmie Rodgers Story* (RCA LSP-4708). Although Fullam recalled the date of their first meeting as being 1927, other evidence rules that out, placing the episode within the chronology of 1925. Other minor errors in Fullam's account may be attributed to the passing of many years and to the circumstance that what he knew of Rodgers's earlier life he had learned from Jimmie, who was always known for his whimsical handling of facts.

10. Mrs. May Alexander, personnel administrator, Florida East Coast Railway, to NP, Apr. 14, 1975.

11. Pat Eggman, Tucson, to W. R. Meyers, United Transportation Union, May 2, 1978; Henry Young to NP, July 17, 1978.

12. *MHJR*, p. 46.

13. Pat Eggman to W. R. Meyers, May 2, 1978; Henry Young to NP, July 17, 1978.

14. *MHJR*, p. 52.

15. Gladys Hunt, interview, Mar. 8, 1975, Meridian.

16. Confidential source.

4 *January–August, 1927*

Away Out on the Mountain

Why Rodgers chose Asheville, North Carolina, as his destination that winter of 1927 remains something of a mystery. But there could hardly have been a more fitting or picturesque setting for what awaited him than that grand old mountain city of meandering streets and gothic mansions and brilliant blue skies steeped in American literary tradition, background for the great novels of Thomas Wolfe and a residence of William Sidney Porter (O. Henry). Still, the fair weather was some months away; a chill winter rain fell across the Land of the Sky as Jimmie climbed down from the train in the Asheville yard that grey January dawn and made his way up the tracks, carrying his guitar and a small, scuffed valise that held almost everything he owned.

Supposedly he'd come because he'd heard of a possible job with the Southern Railway there. In light of later events, however, there is little to indicate that he took the rumor seriously, or that it bothered him much when he learned, very quickly, that there was no job.

Asheville had other attractions. The center of a resort area high on a plateau surrounded by the Blue Ridge and Great Smoky Mountains, the city had long been popular with sufferers of lung diseases because of its light mountain air. In fact, Albert Fullam had earlier urged Jimmie to go there for his health; Fullam had relatives in the city, including an uncle, John Fullam, who was a conductor on the Asheville Division of the Southern. He assured Jimmie that his family would look out for him until he could get established. Although it is not documented, it also seems probable that Jimmie had already spent some time in Asheville during his travels, and that he was attracted to the city as a likely outlet for his musical aspirations. The region would prove to be immensely fertile ground for artists whose contributions to native American music would one day be writ large. From within a radius of a few dozen miles emerged such figures as the Carter Family, Skyland Scotty Wiseman, Dock Walsh, the Callahan brothers, the Mainers, Clarence Green, Clarence Ashley, Bascom Lamar Lunsford, the Dixons, Henry Whitter and Kelly Harrell, the Stonemans, Earl Scruggs, and many others. All this burgeoning activity surely did not go unnoticed by Rodgers, who may have already made his acquaintance with various local musicians.

Turned down by the railroad, he quickly fell back on other resources. John Fullam's son, Jack, a fireman with the Asheville Fire Department, found Jimmie a bed at the firehouse of Engine Company No. 2 and, true to Albert Fullam's word, loaned him money while he looked for work. Employment was not long in coming. Jimmie's guitar and genial personality made him popular around the firehouse, and he quickly made friends, moving easily in the world of firemen, cops, railroaders, and rounders from all walks of life. Through the Fullams he became acquainted with J. D. Bridgers, whose father owned a string of taxis; soon Jimmie was a part-time cabdriver, picking up a small but regular salary that enabled him to rent a room and move out of the firehouse. It also turned out that Asheville's new chief of detectives was Fred Jones, whom Jimmie had known some years earlier when Jones was a special agent for the Southern. Carrie would later write that Jones gave Rodgers a job as "city detective,"[1] but in fact the sinecure was considerably less than that. As one of the many hangers-on around police headquarters, Jimmie was employed from time to time merely as a sort of elevated errand boy, deputized (but not armed) to serve papers, chauffeur dignitaries, and perform other routine "go-fer" jobs.[2] These tasks combined rather naturally and easily with driving a taxi, and the extra money made it possible for Jimmie to send for Carrie and Anita. With the help of the Bridgerses, he finagled a place for them to live by offering his services as apartment house janitor in return for a rent-free cottage at the rear of the building. But all the while his real energies were directed toward the entertainment business, getting acquainted with local musicians and looking for ways to make money with his singing and playing. In later accounts he would invariably overlook the odd jobs, emphasizing instead his struggling career as a performer during those days in

Asheville. "I managed to make a living by entertaining, playing for dances and giving programs," he would tell reporters, "but it was hard sledding."[3] Difficult and unprofitable though it was, this course of events soon consumed most of his time. Claude Grant, who knew him as early as April, said, "He didn't have any other jobs [then]. He was always on the go, trying to book shows."[4]

Within a month or so of his arrival in Asheville, Rodgers was hanging out with a group of musicians that included Otis Kuykendall, and the Helton brothers, Ernest, Osey, Al, and Harry. Although the Heltons, like Kuykendall, earned their livings as painters, carpenters, or plasterers, they played regularly for dances and other social events in the area and had some slight claim to professional status. Ernest and Osey Helton had even "made records"—at least two sides each for the dime-store Broadway label in 1924, and one or two for Okeh the following year—and Ernest Helton would continue for several years to list his occupation as "musician." That was enough to impress Rodgers.

At about this same time his interest was also drawn to two events that had captured the whole town's fancy: the appearance of Will Rogers on February 15 at the City Auditorium, and the forthcoming debut of the city's first radio station. Will Rogers came, played to appreciative, standing-room-only audiences, and departed, but the excitement over local broadcasting continued to build. Although the initial impact of radio had been felt across the nation several years earlier, there seemed to be no letup in the public's fascination with voices out of the air, superhetrodyne circuits, enclosed speakers, "dx" reception, static suppressors, and call letters. Now that the novelty of tuning in faraway stations from the big cities had abated somewhat, it had become a matter of civic pride for towns the size of Asheville to promote stations of their own.

Since Asheville was in the center of a region that owed much of its economy to tourism, the city fathers were especially alert to the new medium's uses as a means of commercial promotion, made even more desirable by a rising boom in local real estate and land speculation during the mid-Twenties. The Asheville Chamber of Commerce, progressive and more active than most such heralds of civic boosterism, formed a special Radio Committee to promote the subject, and ultimately undertook to build and operate the station itself, at an initial cost of some $35,000.

By early 1927 equipment was being installed in three small rooms that had been built as a "penthouse apartment" atop the eight-story Flat Iron Building in downtown Asheville. A license had been obtained from the U.S. Department of Commerce assigning call letters WWNC ("Wonderful Western North Carolina"). A director for the station was hired, and the public found itself subjected to a barrage of publicity. While the studio was being outfitted and equipment tested, the initial broadcast was rescheduled several times, amid all sorts of speculation about programming and other matters that kept the public's interest piqued. An enthusiastic radio fan and writer for the *Asheville Times,* G. O. Shepherd, was appointed the newspaper's Radio Editor, signing himself "Station G.O.S.H." GOSH avidly reported each new development, counseling anxious owners of radio sets to be patient, and assuring them that the wait would be worthwhile: "Worry not a bit about the quality of [WWNC's] programs. Rest assured that this station is going to add materially to Asheville's reputation as a city from which there comes only the very best of all things."[5] Interviewing "Managing Director" J. Dale Stentz, he reported that while "a surprising amount of talent of the very highest order" was on hand, the station had no intention of "hogging the air" but would instead limit its broadcast time to a few hours a day and program only the best that was available. "'The voice of the skyland' is going to be at all times a voice of dignity," Shepherd wrote. "With J. Dale Stentz at the helm, there will be no cheap cavorting before the microphone." Stentz, former business manager of the Southern Methodist Assembly and a self-fancied baritone, stolidly announced that he would "insist on quality of voice and ability at instrument before allowing any performer to appear on a WWNC program." Moreover, added GOSH, "there'll be very little if any wisecracking from the announcing end of the equipment."[6]

Finally, on Monday, February 21, the station went on the air, broadcasting at 1180 kc. with "power sufficient to carry over the entire country." It was probably 500 watts; a few months later the power was increased to 1,000 watts, making it one of the four most powerful stations in North Carolina. At any rate, the initial broadcast was heard as far away as London, Ontario, and Waco, Texas (and by at least one mountain moonshiner who used his copper still as an antenna). The inaugural program went on the air at 7:00 P.M. with a "dinner concert" from the George Vanderbilt Hotel, followed by a male quartet comprised of "Messrs. Jones, Jones, Barnes, and Hartrick, with J. Foster Barnes, Baritone Soloist." Then came "popular piano numbers" by Arthur Wentge, and thirty minutes of "folk songs" by Bascom Lamar Lunsford, "The Minstrel of the Appalachians," accompanying himself on the guitar. There were, naturally, speeches by the mayor and other dignitaries, and the broadcast ended at midnight with music by the "WWNC Orchestra" and incidental solos by Mrs. Beth Roberts, soprano, Mr. George Hartrick, and Horace Seeley, tenor.

Rodgers would later claim that he "helped put WWNC on the air," but apparently the only performer who even remotely resembled a hillbilly that evening was Lunsford, a lawyer, teacher, and scholar of oldtime music. The *Asheville Citizen* termed Lunsford's appearance "a unique feature of the program . . . a truly Appalachian Mountain contribution, expected to bring much to the program as far as outsiders are concerned. It will probably be one of the features of the evening from the standpoint of distant listeners."[7]

The bulk of the station's regular programming was intended, as the opening broadcast suggests, to project an image of decorum and sophistication, "culture" and refinement. "Dinner music" by one or another hotel orchestra was programmed each evening; there was a weekly "Better Music Hour"; Bill Tilden, vacationing in the area, was brought on to discuss the social pleasures of tennis; and in March a "Beethoven Week" was dutifully observed. GOSH, tuning in other stations around the dial, admitted that he liked the "homily tunes" performed by Chubby Parker on Chicago's WLS. But the local rustics occasionally heard on WWNC caused him to comment, in what was obviously a pained effort at objectivity, "Mountain music—good, we suppose, for those who like it. Frankly, a little goes a long way with us, so we do not presume to criticize nor to praise."[8] Nevertheless, while the mountaineers and oldtime fiddlers offended Stentz's sensibilities as well, they proved popular with listeners and were heard with increasing frequency. Bascom Lamar Lunsford returned for several Sunday programs, and on March 17 "Helton's Old Time String Band" made its first appearance (followed, it is interesting to note, with "Baritone Solos by J. Dale Stentz"—as if, perhaps, to mollify his city listeners and soothe their anguish). The personnel of Helton's group were not listed, but Jimmie Rodgers may well have been among them—if not this time, then on one or more of the other occasions when they were called back in the following weeks. A reader of the

Asheville Times who signed himself "Uncle Wesley" wrote to the paper regularly, voicing his approval of almost everything broadcast on WWNC (it seems possible that he was an employee or other Interested Party). He especially liked Lunsford and the Helton band: "Bass Lunsford's mountain songs and the Heltons' music keep catchin' the fancy," Uncle Wesley wrote in one of his more exuberant moods. "If near to base fans don't appreciate 'han-me-downs,' [I've been listening to them] since I was knee-high to a duck an' ev'ry time Bass and the Heltons play my thots go back to a day when with mouth open and in juvenile restlessness a certain lad wished he could grow up to tickle a banjo and sing like old Eph Brown from the cabin up at Buzzard's Glory."[9]

The Heltons' predominantly oldtime repertoire did not have much appeal for Jimmie Rodgers, however. He arranged to form a duet with Otis Kuykendall and offer a program of their own, doing what the program log listed variously as "novelty selections" or "specialty numbers." Presumably these consisted mostly of snappy stage and pop tunes of the day, laced with what passed for light banter and clever repartee. If the evidence of later efforts—"Pullman Porters" and the talking records with the Carters—is any indication, this was probably pretty dismal stuff, but acceptable by the standards of that time. Rodgers may also have included rudimentary verses of what later became blue yodels. He and Kuykendall performed their first broadcast on Monday, April 18, in the 9:30 to 10:00 P.M. time period. GOSH, who made a point of reviewing practically everything aired over WWNC, somehow contrived to miss it, although he did note that "The program on Monday evening we understand has brought many favorable comments."[10] Rodgers and Kuykendall appeared again on April 28 and May 5, successive Thursdays (program logs and publicity suggest that Mondays and Thursdays were considered WWNC's "prime time"), and Uncle Wesley, who had a good word for everyone, offered his succinct appraisal: "Kuykendall and his partner are a treat."[11]

Meanwhile, on April 24-26, the 52nd District Rotary Clubs were holding their annual convention in Johnson City, Tennessee, some sixty miles from Asheville. Rodgers went there hoping to get on one of the many entertainment programs to be offered during the three-day meeting. Performers from all over the region were attracted to the event, among them a group from the Tennessee-Virginia border town

Carrie Williamson, about the time she met Jimmie (ca. 1919).

His trainman's bag packed for the next run, Jimmie says goodbye to Carrie and Anita in the Williamsons' front yard, Meridian, 1923.

Rodgers's "Hawaiian Show and Carnival" toured the Midwest and Ohio Valley in the spring and summer of 1925.

Businessman Jimmie Rodgers strikes up a tune with his partner, W. C. Tyer, in front of their cafe in Geiger, Alabama, summer, 1926. The children are Anita Rodgers (*left*) and Mickey Tyer.

Touring in the early 1920's, Rodgers and friends outfitted a Model T with camping facilities and played from town to town. Man at right may be Lucien Parks.

Jack Grant (*far right*) casts a suspicious eye on the leader of the Jimmie Rodgers Entertainers while Jack Pierce, Claude Grant, and Jimmie face the camera amiably in this rare snapshot taken at North Fork Resort, July, 1927.

An early professional pose. The imprint of a Washington, D.C., photographer's studio has suggested to some that the picture was made after Jimmie moved to the nation's capital in 1927, but it was probably only copied there, from a portrait taken about 1921.

Jimmie with Claude Grant, Asheville, 1927.

The Jimmie Rodgers Entertainers, "stars of stage and radio," in Asheville, May, 1927. Their bespectacled leader has handed his guitar to Jack Pierce in exchange for a banjo; seated in front are Jack and Claude Grant.

of Bristol, thirty miles north of Johnson City. The Tenneva Ramblers consisted of twenty-one-year-old Claude Grant, who did lead vocals and played the guitar; his brother, Jack, 24, on mandolin; and fiddler Jack Pierce, 19. At various times the act also included blackface comedian Smokey Davis, a cousin of the Grant brothers. All of them came from musical backgrounds and, despite their relative youth, were seasoned performers with substantial followings in their hometown and the surrounding area. Impressed with their music, Rodgers told them he was on the radio in Asheville, implying somewhat more prominence than he actually had, and suggested they join him there. "He told us to come on over and back him up and make a lot of money," Claude Grant recalled.[12] "Radio" had, for the Tenneva Ramblers, the same mystic attraction that it was exercising on other performers; across the nation artists were deserting vaudeville and other forms of entertainment en masse to go "on the air." As it happened, however, the Ramblers were booked up with dances and high school stage shows for the time being, and thus had to decline Rodgers's offer. He gave them a phone number where he could be reached and told them to call if they changed their minds.

Back in Asheville, Jimmie teamed up again with Otis Kuykendall for broadcasts over WWNC, but this was only a temporary, catch-as-catch-can arrangement which paid little, if anything. During these weeks there occurred some of the more momentous events for which the 1920's are remembered: Lindbergh flew to Paris, U.S. Marines landed in China, the flooding Mississippi caused widespread death and destruction, and the Hall-Mills murder case was in the headlines. But Jimmie Rodgers had little time for national affairs. He was busy with the more immediate concern of trying to get his struggling career as a performer off high-center and giving serious thought to certain changes in his repertoire, more anxious than ever to form what he was now beginning to refer to as his "hillbilly ork"—"musicians who can play my kind of stuff, and play it the way I want it played." Perhaps with the Tenneva Ramblers in mind, he told Carrie that "I'd like to find a couple of nice-looking single boys—not too highbrow . . . who'll be willing to work whatever date I can get—schoolhouse, barn dance, road house, beer-joint—anything. Be lucky if we make our expenses for a while. But here's what I figure. Folks everywhere are gettin' kind of tired of all this Black Bottom—Charleston—jazz music junk."[13]

In light of what he had been playing and the course of his later career, the logic which defined "my kind of stuff" seems curiously mixed and convoluted. On one hand, possibly as a result of his experience with the Heltons, he had begun to detect the latent appeal of "old-fashioned songs"—the sort of basic, pure folk material, "plantation melodies and old river ballads," he called them, that would soon account for his initial success across the nation. Just incidentally, that was exactly what Ralph Peer was listening for as he set out from New York that spring with the Victor Company's portable recording equipment. But of the titles Jimmie cited as examples—"Yearning" and "Forgotten"—one was a current hit straight out of Tin Pan Alley, and the other had been composed and popularized by a bass singer with the Bostonians Light Opera Company only twenty years before. Moreover, his disparagement of jazz is strangely at odds with some of his own best recordings of the very next year—"My Carolina Sunshine Girl" and "Waiting for a Train," for example, as well as such later hits as "Any Old Time," "Jimmie's Mean Mama Blues," "My Good Gal's Gone Blues," and especially "Blue Yodel No. 9," arrangements conceded by many jazz experts to be consistently solid, occasionally even brilliant. Their inclusion, along with five other sides of at least equal merit, in Brian Rust's initial compilation of *Jazz Records 1897-1931* suggests the quality of Rodgers's involvement with the jazz idiom and attests to the fact that his music, in those early days at least, transcended the narrow confines of what was then considered "hillbilly."

Rodgers's criticism of jazz, however, may have been largely directed at the current over-commercialization of the genre and at the mass craze for anything with a shrieking saxophone and a beat faster than three-quarter time. Nine out of ten popular songs had "Blues" in the title, or some connotation of Charleston, this overkill perhaps reaching a pinnacle of some sort in 1925 with "What-cha Call-em Blues" and "Charlestonette." (The latter offense was committed, it is worth noting, by a young man who would later write some of country music's most enduring hits and help found a Nashville dynasty. His name was Fred Rose.) By the late Twenties the resulting musical pollution, not unlike the backwash from Rock in the Sixties, was creating considerable disaffection even within the musical establishment, among composers, publishers, and recording companies. In 1926 *Billboard* had wishfully headlined that "Charleston

Rhythm Is on the Wane," and a similar verdict was announced by no less an eminence than Irving Berlin, who wrote to Sam Harris in almost the same words Jimmie Rodgers used: "The old fashioned ballads are becoming popular again. The public, I think, are tiring of jazz songs. . . ."[14]

But if Rodgers was unclear about what he meant by "my kind of stuff," any extended attempt to sort out the possibilities or to posit some consistent pattern of development only creates false dilemmas. As present-day country music aptly demonstrates, popular entertainment categories are inherently artificial. Although convenient and even necessary, they are ultimately of greater concern to the critics and commentators who stand outside them than they are to the composers and performers who shape and sustain them. True, a generation or so after Rodgers there would be an internal reaction against the use of "hillbilly" for what more identity-conscious artists decided ought to be "country and western," and recently teapot tempests have raged over the Nashville Sound versus Keepin' It Country. But in Rodgers's time such false and rigid distinctions did not exist—although, ironically, he involuntarily played a primary role in their evolution. In any event, throughout his career Jimmie Rodgers would display erratic and unpredictable (for which one may read "eclectic") tastes. The essential motive behind his style and repertoire, at any so-called stage of development, was the same one that has produced all truly popular entertainers: will it play in Peoria, or Pascagoula?

In late May, a month after they had met Jimmie Rodgers in Johnson City, the Tenneva Ramblers finished their current string of bookings at square dances and school auditoriums. They remembered the gangling, glib-talking ex-brakeman and called him from Bristol to see if his offer still held. Rodgers gave them his Asheville address and told them to come as soon as they could. None of the three owned a car but they talked a friend into taking them in his father's ancient Reo Speedwagon.

Seven flat tires and ten hours later they'd reached Elizabethton, scarcely twenty miles away. At a local cafe they literally sang for their supper and passed the hat for enough money to buy a used tire. (It soon gave out also.) By the time they topped the Blue Ridge Mountains, both back wheels were running on the rims. They parked the Speedwagon and waited for morning, when an old mountaineer in a Model T chugged along and picked them up. The remainder of the trip through the mountains was harrowing: the old gent drove along at open throttle and insisted on directing his passengers' attention to the scenery along the way, often taking both hands off the steering wheel to gesture at some point of interest hundreds of feet below the treacherous mountain road. "Like to scared that brother of mine to death," Claude Grant recalled, "though I expect that old man knew that road about as well as we knew our own bedroom."[15]

Finally they reached Biltmore, a suburb of Asheville, where they caught a streetcar into the city and inquired for the address Rodgers had given them, the place on Patton Avenue that Carrie described as "a little furnished cabin, a rear-cottage behind a big apartment house."[16] Although it was supposedly provided rent-free in exchange for Jimmie's services as janitor and furnace-tender, if he worked at anything other than trying to book appearances the Tenneva Ramblers had no knowledge of it.

Understandably, Carrie was less than enthusiastic about the three scruffy and disheveled country boys who appeared at her door that morning. "His wife didn't seem at all pleased to see us," Claude Grant said matter-of-factly. "She was a little stand-offish, not friendly, you know." Although later she glossed over the event, referring to the Grant brothers and Pierce simply—and anonymously—as "the three young musicians who . . . made up the humble hillbilly ork,"[17] at the time it seemed just another of Jimmie Rodgers's harebrained schemes, and one the family could scarcely afford. Neither she nor Jimmie had a full-time job, they were behind with bills all over town, and she could hardly face the grocer each week. As if his wife and child weren't enough responsibility, Jimmie had taken on the burden of three additional mouths to feed—never one to do things half way, he'd guaranteed the Tenneva Ramblers room and board while they were getting started. But if he lacked ready cash, there were other resources; Jimmie had friends—"knew people," as the saying went—and was always able to find someone he could call on. As Claude Grant explained it, "He took us to a place down on the square there, the Western Hotel; it was up over a store on the second floor, a place about like Jack Pierce's mother used to run [a boardinghouse in Bristol]. And he took us in there and . . . he knew the man, you know. There was room and board, so Jimmie told him we was over there to do some playing with him, and go ahead and put us up and he'd stand good for it."[18] Hungry and exhausted, the three musicians ate a big lunch and fell into bed.

Their trip from Bristol pretty much set the tone for the Tenneva Ramblers' association with Jimmie Rodgers. Rechristened "The Jimmie Rodgers Entertainers," they made their debut on WWNC on Monday night, May 30, at 9:30. For all of Jimmie's notions about "old plantation melodies" and "river ballads," their repertoire differed little from the sort of thing he had been doing since the Lauderdale Springs days and earlier—that is, a conglomeration of dance numbers, a few old theatrical standards like "Hot Time in the Old Town Tonight," and the popular tunes of the day, with an occasional traditional or "folk" song thrown in. Although as an all-string group they could not entirely escape the rural image, Rodgers was deliberately striving, as his name for the group indicates, to avoid the "oldtime" and "string band" connotations that other local groups flaunted. He was attempting to write and use more of his own material, and to the extent that the early raw versions of songs like "The Soldier's Sweetheart," "Sleep, Baby, Sleep," and "T for Texas" drew on "old-timey" sources, the Jimmie Rodgers Entertainers could qualify as what Carrie termed "a hillbilly string orchestra." But she seemed not to know, and Jimmie not to care, that the rustic purity of a given song was not necessarily guaranteed by its age or evolution. "Sleep, Baby, Sleep" is a case in point. The piece was certainly old enough, having appeared in its original form as far back as 1869; but it also had been, as Robert Coltman points out, something of a "towny-sounding" vaudeville hit, rather than the old mountain lullaby that Carrie thought it was.[19] The lyrics to "The Soldier's Sweetheart" had roots in a much more recent past, and its tune was derived from "Where the River Shannon Flows," written in 1905. "T for Texas" was merely another manifestation of the current blues mania, as commercial and up-to-date as any of the "Black Bottom, Charleston, jazz junk" that Jimmie railed against. So much for his theories about "old-fashioned" music.

Jimmie Rodgers's originality lay not in his material, but in the style that he was now busily perfecting and would eventually impose on whatever song he undertook, regardless of its source or genre. "I'm gonna make that old guitar of mine obey me yet," he told Carrie, "so it'll talk when I talk, and cry or laugh when I do."[20] Rehearsing the Entertainers, he insisted on "feeling," and on the authenticity of that feeling. "This kind of stuff oughtn't to be circus-ed," he told them, meaning that it shouldn't be performed with any sort of artificial extravagance. "It's gotta have pathos. Make folks feel it—like we do, but we gotta have the feelin' ourselves first. This is supposed to be pathetic."[21] If his choice of words was unfortunate, it was also accurate, and a clear indication that he understood precisely the nature of what he was undertaking.

A studio portrait of the Jimmie Rodgers Entertainers taken about this time shows them as anything but a "hillbilly band." Nattily dressed in business suits and beaming smiles, they might pass for a college quartet, with the balding, bespectacled Rodgers, looking much older than his twenty-nine years, as their kindly music prof. The instrumentation is curious: all hold banjos except Jack Pierce, who has Jimmie's 00-17 Martin guitar. Each was proficient on several instruments, however, and they presumably rearranged the instrumentation to suit the various numbers and styles they performed, as such groups commonly do. Their versatility is suggested by GOSH's review of their initial broadcast. Moved to qualified praise, he wrote: "Jimmy Rogers and his entertainers managed another period [of the evening], with a type of music quite a bit different than that presented just before [a recital by soloists from the Asheville high schools], but a kind that finds cordial reception from a large audience. Jimmy does things with a steel guitar and with divers other stringed instruments that are like magic in their harmony inducing proclivities."[22] Just who, if anyone, played the steel guitar is not known; in all likelihood, GOSH wasn't listening closely or simply did not know one guitar from another when he heard them over the air. But if he was something less than qualified as a music critic, his reference to "divers other stringed instruments" indicates the group's flexibility and their "harmony inducing proclivities."

A more discerning listener was *Asheville Times* columnist Wickes Wamboldt, who upon hearing "Sleep, Baby, Sleep" was so impressed by the "haunting, sympathetic, descriptive character" of Rodgers's voice that he called the station to ask who he was. Nobody, he was told. Just a bum—an out-of-work railroader who was "accommodating" the radio station as a volunteer. "Well, whoever that fellow is," Wamboldt told his wife, "he either is a winner or he is going to be. I could see him rocking the baby, crooning over it tenderly."[23]

But Jimmie Rodgers was not yet a winner. The Entertainers' stint on WWNC lasted only briefly, despite a steady flow of fan mail and smooth-talking Jimmie's ability to round up an occasional paying sponsor. The "hillbilly ork" did not appeal to J. Dale Stentz; their mixed repertoire and aspirations toward mass popularity took them out of the class of pure "folk artists" (like Bascom Lamar Lunsford and the Heltons!), yet they were still too raw to be really uptown, as befitted the dignified radio voice of Wonderful Western North Carolina. When Wamboldt heard they were being taken off the air, he called the station on behalf of the Jimmie Rodgers Entertainers, but to no avail. Their last program was broadcast on June 13.

As far as the Grant brothers and Jack Pierce were concerned, it was no great loss. "Jimmie told us that we was going to get paid [for the radio programs], you know," Claude Grant said. "I don't know how much; he never did tell us and he never did pay us anything. I guess he figured that his standing for the board bill would be enough. But he never did give us a penny from that radio station." Carrie, on the other hand, complained that even when the program had a sponsor, Jimmie's income was "so small that *by the time it was split among the entertainers* there was little left for our own family."[24]

To Jimmie, however, the program had been a matter of pride as much as money, and he was badly shaken by its failure. "They didn't give me a fair deal," he told Wickes Wamboldt in a broken voice. He'd gone on the air confident that he was on his way, and had been sure to let the folks back home in Meridian know about it: "Am playing over the radio, told you I'd amount to something someday." Now there was crow to be eaten, and it went down hard. "What scars us is not work, but failure," someone has written. One wonders how many scars Jimmie Rodgers could have borne had time and fate never tipped in his favor; perhaps eventually he would have withdrawn, grown cynical, maybe even given up. But in Asheville that early summer of 1927, as so many times before, he took still another lump, hitched up his pants, straightened his hat, and beamed the old familiar grin. "If I can't get 'em in town, we'll go to the woods," he said. "Anyway, I can bill the hillbilly ork now as popular radio artists. That's worth something."[25]

It had not been much of an asset in the past. He'd managed to book only one party date in Asheville while they were on WWNC, and an engagement at nearby Hendersonville was a total disaster. "I'll never forget the time Jimmie booked us at Hendersonville," Claude Grant recalled. "He made arrangements on the morning we were to play to get the school auditorium. He quickly got some handbills printed somehow and we spent most of the day around the drugstore in town playing and singing. But we went out there that night and only the janitor showed up." The usual problem, it seemed, was Jimmie's poor business sense—or at least his haphazard approach. "He could promote but he never bothered with the advance details," Grant said.[26]

Nevertheless, the hillbilly ork "took to the woods." Throughout his career, no matter how big his name became, Rodgers seemed to prefer touring the hinterlands, performing wherever he felt at home, with little regard for the size of the towns or the show-biz prejudices against "playing the sticks." "He loved the hillbillies, the same as he loved the common people everywhere," wrote Carrie, "and loved to be among them and with them." But it was necessity rather than love that put him on the road this time. Working out of Asheville, the Entertainers scoured the countryside for high school auditoriums and small theaters that might be booked. The summer heat, coupled with Jimmie's poor planning, conspired against them. Pickings were slim.

Traveling again to Johnson City, Tennessee, they heard news of a forthcoming Trade Exposition and Tri-State Fair, opening on June 27 and culminating in a big Fourth of July celebration, with parades, contests, and musical entertainment throughout the week. Rodgers went immediately to the promoter, a local strongman named A. B. Ritchie, who billed himself as Samson. Ritchie was quickly persuaded to put the Jimmie Rodgers Entertainers on the program, which already featured such attractions as a Hungarian dancer named Suzanne Chalupka, Professor Brown Pelgery and His Sixty-Foot Balloon, an old fiddlers' contest, a horde of Charleston dancers, a hog-calling contest, and four local couples who'd been persuaded to perform the exciting, death-defying feat of getting married in public during the week's events. Also scheduled were the Johnson brothers, Charles and Paul, local guitarists who could legitimately bill themselves as "Victor Recording Artists," having cut seven sides in Camden only a few weeks earlier. It seemed like a lucrative booking for the Jimmie Rodgers Entertainers, and Jimmie scurried back to Asheville to round up another musician or two—as the publicity indicates, he'd promised Ritchie "6—National Radio Artists—6."[27] Ernest Helton was persuaded to join them, and the sixth (if indeed there was a sixth) was probably Otis Kuykendall or Smokey Davis.

Among the other acts which appeared during the festivities, held at the local ball park, was a family group known as the Seven Tennessee Ramblers.[28] Organized by "Fiddlin' Bill" Sievers of Clinton, Tennessee, the group featured his daughter Willie on guitar and his son Mac on banjo. Fifty years later, from one brief encounter with Jimmie Rodgers, Mac Sievers remembered him distinctly: "Jimmie was a very friendly fellow and would be at the park before show time and sit in the shade and flump his guitar and play with us in some practice numbers. I've never met an easier-going feller . . . he was just *relaxed*. He could really yodel with the least effort I have ever seen. There was something about it that was just different. His act came on before ours and went over exceptionally well, but it was definitely different from the others. He'd sit and talk just like we're talking, but up there [on stage], there was something about him that'd just do them in. He had such a likeable disposition."[29] From Sievers's account, it appears that Jimmie did not play on stage, but simply sang and yodeled to Helton's accompaniment on guitar (in the same fashion that he would later record with Billy Burkes and Slim Bryant). Said Sievers: "This boy [Helton] played guitar for Jimmie and he would put some runs in there, like you hear in 'Right on Down through Birmingham,' seemed like they just took it so easy. They went over good, and . . . everybody commented on the easy way that [Rodgers] could yodel." Despite the popularity of their act, however, the Jimmie Rodgers Entertainers were doomed to another disappointment. On Saturday afternoon, July 2, as the exposition built toward its big Fourth of July climax on Monday, a heavy storm hit the city; hail and high winds destroyed part of the grandstand and forced suspension of all events for several days. Although Ritchie was later able to extend the affair through July 7, the momentum was gone, and many of the entertainers packed up and left. According to Sievers, most of them "barely got their expenses out of it."[30]

Back on the tough scuffle again, the Jimmie Rodgers Entertainers managed to pick up a one-night stand in Marion, forty miles east of Asheville. "We booked a theater there," Claude Grant recounted, "and went there and played a matinee and night show between pictures, and stayed overnight there." The next morning, as they were eating breakfast, the waitress told them of a possible job at the luxurious North Fork Mountain Resort about five miles from Marion. They drove out and Jimmie talked to the manager. "He was a pretty good talker," Grant said. "They squabbled around there and finally the man told us what he wanted, said that he had a lot of parties, big parties, come down from Asheville and want to dance, you know, and wanted to know if we could play dance music. Jimmie told him, yeah, we could do all right in that department, and so finally Jimmie made a deal with him to furnish us a cabin and, I think, ninety dollars a week is what he paid us."[31]

Leaving Rodgers's family back in Asheville, the four musicians moved into two cabins at the plush resort. There, in addition to room and board and the rather substantial salary (at least in comparison to the meager and uncertain dollars they'd been earning), they were given use of the extensive guest facilities: boats, riding stables, golf course, and tennis courts. To all appearances, Jimmie's health was fine—Grant had no inkling that he suffered from tuberculosis—and they spent much of their time riding and hiking. When they weren't otherwise occupied during the day, they rehearsed—about two hours a day, according to Grant. Each evening they provided music for diners from a wide veranda near the open dining room. "We'd just sit outside there," Grant said, "and play during the supper hour and when they'd get through, why, we'd play a little dance music and sing." Their offerings were essentially the same as those they'd played at WWNC: "Who's Sorry Now?," "St. Louis Blues," "Down the River of Golden Dreams," "Goodbye, Dixie, Goodbye," and other tunes which were considered smooth and sophisticated. In addition to providing dinner and occasional music, they also played for one or two dances each week. The Jimmie Rodgers Entertainers were immediately popular with the guests. "Naturally, some of them would come out [to the veranda]," Grant said, "and want to know where we was from and how long we was going to be there. We would play just about everything, square dancing music and other dance numbers. When we played for dinner it would be popular music, some country music also. We had a pretty good time."[32]

So good, in fact, that one wonders why they were willing to give it up. It was certainly the first steady job any of them had had for a long while, it was theirs for at least the remainder of the summer season, and they could hardly have wanted better working conditions. But Jimmie Rodgers had set his sights on bigger operations. He wanted to make recordings, for one thing, and had been following leads and writing letters to record companies for some time. The two giants, Victor Talking Machine and Brunswick-Balke-Collender, had politely turned him down, but he felt that he'd convince them of his talent if he could only audition in person. He had no doubt discussed his ambitions with Charles and Paul Johnson during the Johnson City fair, and they'd related their experiences with Victor; perhaps it was even from the Johnson brothers that he first heard of Ralph Peer and his vague plans for a field recording trip through the region.

Whatever the precise circumstances, Rodgers had already begun to look for some means of getting closer to New York, whence all blessings flowed. Baltimore came to mind—he had an uncle living there, a flamboyant, black-sheep member of the Bozeman clan, and Carrie's eldest sister, Annie, was nearby in Washington, D.C. He and Jack Grant were not getting along too well; in addition, Jimmie knew that the North Fork job would eventually end, perhaps sooner rather than later. A firm course of action had not quite crystalized when, almost literally out of the mountain sky, opportunity came.

Back in June when they first took to the road, the Jimmie Rodgers Entertainers had pooled their resources (mostly those of the Grant brothers and Jack Pierce) to buy an old Ford. It had barely gotten them to North Fork, and now Pierce decided that he and Rodgers would go back to Bristol to see if his father would help them get a newer one. In Claude Grant's words, "Jack's daddy was an awful good old man, and Jack talked him into buying him a car, an old '25 Dodge. Still, it was a good car, just two years old." Pierce's father was a barber and his mother ran a boardinghouse on the Virginia side of State Street in Bristol, a popular spot with railroadmen and local musicians. When Rodgers and Pierce went there to spend the night before returning to North Fork with their new car, they found the place unusually crowded with musicians. A man from the Victor Talking Machine Company was in town, they were told, auditioning acts in a vacant storage building right across the street. The next morning they went over to investigate and managed to introduce themselves to the Victor agent, Ralph Peer, explaining that they were members of a string band and were interested in recording. "Bring the whole bunch in," Peer told them, "and I'll listen to you. No promises. We'll see."[33]

They drove back to North Fork in a state of elation, only to find the Grant brothers somewhat less than enthusiastic about the idea. "Jack and I weren't sure we had anything to record that people wanted to hear," Claude Grant said. But Rodgers finally persuaded them, arguing that he was about to leave permanently for Washington, D.C., and that they might as well stop off in Bristol and take a shot at recording and maybe get in the big money. That, coupled with the fact that Claude and his brother were homesick and tired of wandering around in the mountains, convinced them to go. The Jimmie Rodgers Entertainers gave notice and left the next morning for Asheville to pick up Carrie and Anita.

Rodgers's instant mobility never ceased to amaze Claude Grant. "This little house they had [in Asheville] must have been furnished," he said, "because when we got back, he went in and told his wife we was coming to Bristol, and they put everything they had in suitcases. All they brought with 'em was clothes. Took about fifteen minutes, and we were on our way."[34]

To Carrie it had all the makings of another of Jimmie's wild and impulsive schemes, but her misgivings were silenced by his jaunty analysis of the significance of being recorded by a man named Peer for the Victor Company. "A victor is a winner, isn't he? And a peer is the top of the heap." It was an auspicious beginning. For once, he was right—in far more ways than he knew.

NOTES

1. *MHJR*, p. 61.

2. Interview with Bob Reese and Jesse James Bailey, Aug. 9, 1977, Asheville. Career law enforcement officers, now retired, both men worked closely with Fred Jones for many years and heard him speak often of Jimmie Rodgers. A longtime railroad officer, Mr. Bailey also served terms as sheriff of both Buncombe and neighboring Madison counties. Ninety years old when I talked with him, he was ramrod-straight and a keen talker, surely the most colorful and interesting informant interviewed. Mr. Bailey remembered Rodgers's early days in Asheville and attended his stage show there in 1929; his knowledge of oldtime music and his love for it are immense.

3. *Asheville Times*, Dec. 5, 1929, p. 8.

4. Claude Grant to NP, Oct. 11, 1975.

5. *Asheville Times*, Jan. 7, 1927, p. 3.

6. *Ibid.*

7. *Asheville Citizen*, Feb. 21, 1927, p. 1. For a fuller account of Lunsford, see Loyal Jones, "The Minstrel of the Appalachians: Bascom Lamar Lunsford at 91," *JEMF Quarterly* [John Edwards Memorial Foundation, UCLA], 9:29 (Spring, 1973), 2–8.

8. *Asheville Times*, Apr. 13, 1927, p. 9.

9. *Ibid.*, Mar. 20, 1927, p. 7B.

10. *Ibid.*, Apr. 24, 1927, p. 7B.

11. *Ibid.*, May 8, 1927, p. 6B.

12. *Bristol Virginia-Tennessean*, Aug. 2, 1972, p. 1B.

13. *MHJR*, p. 69.

14. *Billboard*, Apr. 3 and 24, 1926, both p. 21.

15. Claude Grant, interview by Glenn Sellers, June 1, 1975, Bristol.

16. *MHJR*, p. 63.

17. *Ibid.*, p. 89.

18. Claude Grant, interview by Glenn Sellers, June 1, 1975, Bristol.

19. Robert Coltman, "Roots of the Country Yodel: Notes toward a Life History," *JEMFQ*, 12:42 (Summer, 1976), 92.

20. *MHJR*, p. 20.

21. *Ibid.*, p. 74.

22. *Asheville Times*, May 31, 1927, p. 11.

23. *Ibid.*, Dec. 17, 1929, p. 4.

24. *MHJR*, p. 77. Emphasis added.

25. *Ibid.*, p. 82.

26. *Bristol Virginia-Tennessean*, Aug. 2, 1972, p. 1B.

27. *Johnson City Chronicle*, June 26, 1927, p. 12.

28. Not to be confused with the Tenneva Ramblers or with Dick Hartman's Tennessee Ramblers.

29. James "Mac" Sievers to NP, Dec. 12 and Dec. 27, 1976; interview by Charles Wolfe, 1974, Clinton, Tenn.

30. *Ibid.*

31. Claude Grant, interview by Glenn Sellers, June 1, 1975, Bristol. In the *Bristol Virginia-Tennessean* interview three years earlier, Grant said they were paid $180 a week. See also Dave Samuelson's liner notes to Puritan 3001, *The Tenneva Ramblers*. It now appears that the figure was $90 *per dance*. Normally, only one dance was held each week, but occasionally they played for two the same week and thus earned $180. Grant to Samuelson, Sept. 8, 1970.

32. Claude Grant to NP, Sept. 22 and Oct. 11, 1975.

33. Claude Grant, interview by Glenn Sellers, June 1, 1975, Bristol.

34. *Ibid.*

5

Mr. Victor and Mr. Peer

While there might be several senses in which Ralph Peer could be considered "the top of the heap," it was clear that the "Victor" in Victor Talking Machine meant winner. Jimmie Rodgers could hardly have known it, but that was the precise meaning which founder Eldridge R. Johnson had in mind when he named the fledgling company back in 1901.[1] A quarter-century later, the Victor Talking Machine Company was not only the undisputed champion of the phonograph industry, but also, in terms of return to investors, one of the most successful enterprises in the history of modern capitalism. By the end of the first year of operation, the $5,000 with which Johnson had founded the company had earned a net profit of $180,000, and twenty years later Victor had amassed assets of almost $40,000,000, with a cash surplus of over $9,000,000.[2] Between 1915 and 1925, every annual dividend had been at least 50 percent of the par value, and in 1922 a 600 percent stock dividend was declared, making millionaires of several dozen company executives and stockholders.[3]

Victor's financial success derived largely from its superiority in aesthetic as well as technical areas. Johnson, a Camden, New Jersey, machinist, had gotten into the business when he perfected a spring-driven motor for Emile Berliner's new flat-disc "gramophone" in 1896. Primarily interested in making and selling phonographs, Johnson cared little for the performing arts and even less for what is known in the modern recording industry as "artists and repertoire." Records were only something that had to be bothered with in order to give the phonograph its *raison d'être*.[4] But early in his business career,

Johnson recognized the prestige value of High Art in terms of sales and advertising. While Victor's initial success was largely due to his inventions and improvements on the phonograph—the spring motor and governor, the braking device, and especially the tapered, swivel-jointed tone arm which permitted the horn to be enclosed— Johnson shrewdly set about to compile a catalog of recordings second to none. He signed exclusive contracts with such eminences (and household words) as John Philip Sousa and Enrico Caruso, and then promoted his superior products with the most elaborate and expensive advertising campaigns the industry had yet seen. Nipper the Terrier listening to "His Master's Voice" quickly became one of the most recognized trademarks in the world, and, like the Victor record label itself, the dog endured as a familiar symbol cherished by generations of Americans. "Johnson was determined to turn his company into an American institution, to make the Victor pre-eminent among phonographs as the Steinway was pre-eminent among pianos," writes Roland Gelatt in his incisive history of the phonograph.[5] The heart of this master plan had been Victor's Red Seal series of grand opera and classical music recordings. "Caruso, the greatest tenor of modern times, makes records only for Victor," proclaimed an early advertisement. "Reading this," says Gelatt, "how could a prospective customer doubt the corollary, that the Victor was 'the greatest musical instrument in the world'?"[6] The organization grew by leaps and bounds into the 'Teens and through the war years; at the end of 1919 Victor's assets totaled $37,860,694, an increase of more than 700 percent since 1909. The home office in Camden had grown to a complex of buildings sprawled over acres of ground along the eastern bank of the Delaware River just across from Philadelphia, and the company also maintained extensive offices and studios in New York.

While priding itself in its classical catalog, Victor did not neglect the tastes of the masses. As Gelatt remarks, "then as now the bulk of record sales were confined to ephemeral, popular music."[7] One may well question Gelatt's sense of what lasts and what doesn't, but he admitted that the large sales of Victor's Red Seal Records were due as much to their "redolent snob appeal" as to whatever aesthetic satisfaction they provided. In any event, Victor's popular titles were not so widely promoted—for of course they didn't have to be. The company's operations in that area, especially from its beginnings until about 1920, have gone largely unexamined by cultural observers and social historians. However, the very first Victor catalog (1901) listed, in addition to selections by Sousa's Band, "Mr. Quinn, comic songs" and "Mrs. Chas. P. Lowe, xylophone solos"—items obviously directed at a mass audience hardly more sophisticated than those who bought the "coon songs," marches, and rube-comedy routines that were staples with Edison and lesser competitors. A year later Victor was recording "Uncle Josh" (Cal Stewart), perhaps the most popular monologist in recording history. The inimitable Sir Harry Lauder was added to the list in 1909, and Vernon and Irene Castle directed the recording of dance numbers for Victor in the years immediately preceding World War I.

The content of popular recordings varied little in the first decades of the commercial phonograph industry. Recordings made before 1902 are generally considered incunabula, and despite the many passing fads and fancies that followed, from minstrel ditties and marches to the talking monolog, ragtime, one-steps, and the raw beginnings of jazz, there was scarcely any change or innovation even through the Great War, and little of it is of more than passing interest today. In the 1920 Victor catalog—at the outset of a decade that would bring radically new forms and dimensions to popular entertainment—were listed only eighteen "Jazz Band Records," mostly by such slick commercializers as the Original Dixieland Jazz Band and Fuller's Jazz Band. Also for mass consumption were dozens of titles by popular actors and comedians like Al Jolson, Byron Harlan, Van and Schenck, Billy Murray, Ada Jones, and Elsie Janis; and a veritable horde of pop tunes by Joseph C. Smith's Orchestra, which performed, in effect, the duties of a "house band" for the Victor organization. Contrary to the notions of those who think Jimmie Rodgers invented the yodel, the 1920 catalog listed seventeen "Yodel Songs"—including a version of "Sleep, Baby, Sleep." A large group of titles were categorized as "Old-Time Ballads" (cross-indexed with "Stephen C. Foster"!), but "Folk Songs," as far as Victor was concerned, were those from foreign countries. "Hillbilly" of course had not yet been invented; the term's beginnings were at least five years away, when Ralph Peer, with the assistance of a group of musicians from Galax, Virginia, would name "the band that named the music." Vernon Dalhart, destined to record "the first million-selling hillbilly record" in 1924, was featured in the 1920 Victor catalog as a "light opera tenor," with such titles as "I'm Waiting for You, Liza Jane," and "Rock-a-Bye Your Baby with a Dixie Melody," watered-down, citified vestiges of the waning coon-song tradition.[8]

Success inevitably brought a certain hardening of the arteries, but Victor's dominance continued into the Twenties, despite the leveling-off of record sales and increasing signs of serious competition from radio—portents which the "Colossus in Camden" choose largely to ignore. Management had grown conservative and complacent; as Gelatt points out, the 1921 Victrola was practically identical with the original model of 1906. It was not until Johnson suffered a nervous breakdown in 1924 and annual sales dropped to $37,000,000 (compared to almost $55,000,000 for the newly organized Radio Corporation of America)[9] that the company shook off its torpor and pulled back into the running with the introduction of the electric recording process and the new Orthophonic Victrola. Within weeks Victor had orders totaling $20,000,000 for the new phonograph. By early 1926 sales of Victor records were twice those of its nearest competitor, Brunswick. Columbia, which had lost nearly a million dollars in 1925, was running a strong third.[10]

By the time Jimmie Rodgers made his first records for Victor, the man who'd named—and made—the company a winner was no longer at the helm. Eldridge Johnson apparently never much enjoyed his success; as early as 1901 he'd wanted to sell his stock and retire on the proceeds. Now in ill health and more tired than ever of the pressures of being a tycoon, he began to listen seriously to the multitude of business interests who regularly offered to buy his kingdom in Camden. Finally, in January, 1927—thirty years after Johnson had inadvertently gotten into the business by designing the practical spring-wound motor for Berliner—ownership of the Victor Talking Machine Company passed to two New York banking houses, Speyer & Co. and J. & W. Seligman & Co., for some $40,000,000. For his holdings Johnson received $22,229,960,[11] and retired, somewhat uneasily, to pursue his many hobbies, including deep-sea fishing and yachting around the world on various quasi-scientific expeditions. As time and fate would have it, Johnson had gotten out while the getting was good; but business continued to sail merrily along under the new owners. For the quarter ending June 30, 1927, only a few weeks before Rodgers went to Bristol, they reported a net profit of over $2,000,000.[12]

Throughout the Twenties, Victor's reputation was maintained by its strong record catalog, ballasted as always by the old reliable Red Seals and given new life by the growing popularity of jazz, in those days rising to the pinnacle of its development as an art form. Victor continued to pursue its policy of signing up the big-name bands, notably Paul Whiteman and Fred Waring, and to record the best-known popular singers and personalities of the day—Gene Austin, the Boswell sisters, Will Rogers, the Happiness Boys (Billy Jones and Ernie Hare), the Revelers, Jesse Crawford, Henry Burr, Frank Crumit, "The Silver-Masked Tenor" (Joseph White), Johnny Marvin, Vaughn DeLeath, and the team of Correll and Gosden, later famous as Amos 'n Andy. It should be noted, however, that Victor also took chances on hundreds of unknowns, many of whom—like Bernard Vessey, Fatty Martin's Orchestra, Arkansas Shorty, Dok Eisenburg and His Sinfonians, the Songcopaters, and Leroy J. Snyder II—remained largely and deservedly anonymous despite their brief flings as "exclusive Victor artists." The list extended, in what can only be seen as "public service" activity in Victor's continuing effort to present itself as a national institution, to the Princeton Seminary Male Chorus; Charles Kellog, "bird imitator and naturalist"; the Polish National Orchestra; speeches by Presidents Coolidge and Hoover and ex-President Arturo Allesandri of Chile; the Associated Glee Clubs of America ("1,200 Voices"); the Philadelphia Rapid Transit Band; the Minstrel Club of Asbury Park Kiwanis Club; the Hopi Indian Chanters; and yes, indeed, even the Mormon Tabernacle Choir.

The one thin spot in all this was the sort of entertainment just then coming to be known, disdainfully but profitably, as "hillbilly music." Somewhat ironically, Alma Gluck's "Carry Me Back to Old Virginny" (Victor 74420, 1915) had been the first Red Seal to sell a million copies,[13] and the Victor list had certainly included its share of rustics, real and imagined, through the years. But most of them—Murray Hill, Raymond Hitchcock, Charles Ross Taggart, Nat Wills, Burt Shepard, even Cal Stewart—were psuedo-rubes, rather than real hillbillies. The acts they created for stage or records were grounded in big-city notions of country people, rather than in the actual circumstances of rural life. Closer to the core, as early as 1922 Victor recorded two authentic, traditional fiddlers, Henry Gilliland of Altus, Oklahoma, and A. C. ("Eck") Robertson of Amarillo, Texas. However, the Gilliland-Robertson renditions of "Sally Gooden" and "Arkansaw Traveler" (Victor 18956) were not released until almost a year later. Even so, they were on the market several months before Okeh's initial recordings of Fiddlin' John Carson, now generally considered "the first" hillbilly records. But while the Gilliland-Robertson disc was well received by the public, Victor, whether from ignorance or mere inertia, failed to capitalize on its thin lead.[14] By 1924 the hillbilly field was almost entirely in the hands of three small companies—Okeh, Columbia, and Vocalion—so minor that previously they had hardly seemed worthy of Victor's notice. Now they were beginning to make waves with this upstart new variety of musical entertainment. Okeh had Carson, Henry Whitter, and a host of newly discovered lesser lights; Columbia, proclaiming that "the fiddle and guitar craze is sweeping northward," was pushing Gid Tanner and Riley Puckett with a national advertising campaign; and Vocalion (soon to merge with Victor's closest competitor, Brunswick) boasted Uncle Am Stuart, Uncle Dave Macon, and Blind George Reneau, all of whom would influence the emerging country music tradition. The best Victor could offer during this time was a hoked-up version of an old rural dance tune, "It Ain't Gonna Rain No Mo'" (Victor 19171), given hayseed lyrics and recorded with ukulele accompaniment by a Chicago radio performer named Wendell Hall. Among urban audiences the record passed for "hillbilly" and became a best-seller, but its only effect on the new form as a whole was to open Victor's eyes to the market value of something less sophisticated than, say, Paul Whiteman.

But the company remained cautious. Its attitude was best exemplified by the famous case of the 1924 Vernon Dalhart recording of "The Prisoner's Song"/"Wreck of the Old 97" (Victor record 19427), which did so much to legitimize the genre and convince recording directors that there was "gold in them thar hillbillies," however much they might oppose the music on aesthetic grounds. Dalhart had recorded "Wreck of the Old 97" for Edison discs and cylinders earlier that year, and when the release quickly showed signs of strength on the market, he tried to persuade Victor executives to let him record it for them. But it was only after months had passed, with Dalhart hounding them constantly and sales of the Edison version continuing to build, that Victor executives finally relented and reluctantly agreed to record the number. Their decision was no doubt prompted by the knowledge that still another competitor, Vocalion, was currently riding the crest with Blind George Reneau's version of the same tune.

Convinced by the unexpected success of "The Prisoner's Song" and "Wreck of the Old 97," Victor was now willing to promote Dalhart in further hillbilly efforts. But one star did not make a constellation—or much of a dent in the burgeoning market. Largely through luck, the company in 1925 discovered Carl T. Sprague, a Texan whose lode of traditional cowboy songs caught the public's attention and extended the boundaries of the emerging folk-music genre. However, while "Following the Cow Trail" and "When the Work's All Done This Fall" were comfortably, if unintentionally, close to a New York recording director's conception of commercial "hillbilly," they were still a long way from the Anglo-Scots-Appalachian manner of authentic folk musicians such as Carson, Whitter, Uncle Dave Macon, and Al Hopkins' Original Hill Billies. Not until mid-1926, after Victor had negotiated a rather unusual business arrangement with a former Okeh executive named Ralph Peer, did the company make serious progress toward filling the hillbilly gap in its catalog.

Late in life, Ralph Sylvester Peer would offhandedly summarize his career, with charming if somewhat calculated modesty, as "nothing more than the American success story."[15] If the pose was a bit disingenuous, the facts behind it were authentic enough. Almost from scratch, Peer had singlehandedly built an international business worth millions, earning for himself a niche as the man who "discovered" both the race and hillbilly recording industries. He also became a recognized authority on copyright law and amassed a personal fortune. Even in an area that was nominally his hobby—growing camellias—he had been accorded international fame and honor by professional horticulturists.

As an innovator and a brilliant businessman, Peer could accurately attribute his success to his own wit and energy, could honestly say that he was "self-made." But luck had also played a substantial role, as he often acknowledged.[16] In fact, he seemed to enjoy crediting the hand of fate, perhaps assuming that his talent for shaking it was also obvious to all. "It's the art of being where the lightning is going to strike," he said of his accomplishments. "And how in God's name you can detect that I don't know . . . but I've always been able to do it." Despite his success in the music business, Peer would look with mixed emotions on the circumstance that he owed his fortune and reputation to the likes of Jimmie Rodgers and the Carter Family. His camellias, it seemed, gave him far more personal satisfaction than hillbilly music.

Peer's entry into the recording business came early and in a natural course of events. At the turn of the century, his father, Abram Peer, sold sewing machines, phonographs, and Columbia records in Independence, Missouri, a Kansas City suburb, where the younger Peer was born on May 22, 1892. Although Edison had patented the phonograph as early as 1878, it was not until some twenty years later that the device began to acquire wide popularity as a source of home entertainment. By the time Ralph was ten or eleven and working on weekends in his father's store, the public's first real love-affair with the phonograph was reaching its height. The boy was as fascinated as everyone else by the sound of music and voices from the crackling wax discs and cylinders of that day. Thus attracted to the phonograph and record aspect of his father's business, young Peer quickly learned the release numbers of almost every title in the Columbia catalog; before he entered his teens he had assumed responsibility for ordering records and phonograph parts from the Columbia office in Kansas City. This led to part-time jobs with the company itself, and when Peer graduated from high school and married for the first time in 1910, he went to work full-time in the credit department of Columbia's Kansas City retail outlet. Soon he was promoted to credit manager and, in effect, ran the operation, although he had nothing to do with the actual recording processes. "At that time, recordings were very mysterious," he said. "They were made in some super-secret studio in New York, you see. It was really difficult to make these master recordings. So we never heard about recordings in Kansas City. That all came later. But I did learn the record business because I went right through the thing. I was the credit manager, retail manager, and I was traveling salesman. I wasn't old enough to be assistant manager, but that's what I was, in effect." In 1915 he transferred to the Columbia office in Chicago, where he "began to meet the top executives and really learn about the record business, how it was done." One experience that left a lasting impression was that of being assigned to look after W. C. Handy as he changed trains in Chicago on his way from Memphis to record in New York for the first time.[17]

After serving in the navy during World War I, Peer returned to the Columbia office in Kansas City. His former boss there, W. S. Fuhri, had gone to work in New York for the General Phonograph Corporation, makers of Okeh Records; and Fuhri soon hired young Peer away from Columbia to serve as assistant to Okeh's director of production, Fred Hagar. According to Peer, "That is where I invented the hillbilly and the nigger stuff." Strictly speaking, he was more or less right, but the language—racial and otherwise—bears adjustment. "Invented" suggests a quantity somewhat more known and a result more calculated than history will bear out. "Happened upon" is more nearly descriptive of what took place, and Peer was hardly alone at the miraculous event.

As the blues scholar Samuel Charters relates the story,[18] it was Fred Hagar, not Peer, who was responsible for the initial recordings by Mamie Smith in February, 1920. Those recordings of something new, called "the blues," sold in the thousands and started a fresh boom in the phonograph industry. Peer's contribution was simply to give the recordings a generic name—"Race," rather than the obviously more limiting "Negro"—and to promote them avidly. It is true that circumstances were ripe, and that Peer was quick to recognize and exploit the opportunity. The record business was sluggish everywhere, a result of the general downturn of the postwar economy. "Okeh was in a rather tough spot," as he pointed out. "They were competing with Victor [and] Columbia; and Edison was then important. They were selling maybe three or four million records a year, which was *nothing*. Something like this [Peer's innovation] was needed because it was really difficult in those days to compete." For his role in these events Peer would later be hailed as an "unsung folksong collector" and "a cultural documentarian of the first rank,"[19] but the man himself was somewhat more direct about his motives. Making records was a business, and profit, not posterity, was the incentive.

Peer's first brush with hillbilly music came in March, 1923, when a millhand named Henry Whitter from Fries, Virginia, walked into Okeh's New York office and announced that he was "the world's greatest harmonica player." Peer at first tried to get rid of him, but eventually agreed to give him an audition. "Finally I took him down to the recording studio and we ran off a half dozen of these things," Peer observed later, "and he *was* a great harmonica player, no doubt about that." At the time, however, Peer was apparently not so impressed. Despite his recollection that "we issued one or two recordings," Whitter's test pressings were in fact shelved and more or less forgotten until the sensational and quite unexpected success of Fiddlin' John Carson's first Okeh records a few months later.[20]

The events leading to the recording of "the first hillbilly record"— nominally "The Little Old Log Cabin in the Lane"/"Old Hen Cackled and the Rooster's Going to Crow" (Okeh 4890)—have been widely chronicled. According to the standard account, an Atlanta furniture dealer and Okeh record distributor named Polk Brockman was on a business trip to New York in June, 1923, when one evening he visited the Palace Theatre on Times Square and saw a newsreel of a Virginia fiddlers' contest. The film reminded Brockman of a fiddler well known in the Atlanta area, a feisty old codger who worked in the textile mills and painted houses for a living, performed in political campaigns, made moonshine, and played oldtime music over Atlanta's new radio station, WSB. Brockman made a note to himself—"Fiddlin' John Carson—local talent—let's record"—and promptly took his idea to Okeh executives. They hardly knew what to make of the scheme; until that time, commercial recordings had never been undertaken outside an established studio, with all the ponderous equipment and necessary baffling that recording supposedly required. However, Okeh's chief engineer, Charles Hibbard, had worked closely with Edison himself and had diverse experience in the field, much of it under experimental conditions. Hibbard convinced his superiors that recordings could be made almost anywhere, and he readily designed and put together the equipment that would be needed. Accordingly, Peer and Brockman arranged an expedition to Atlanta, sending Hibbard and his assistant, Peter Decker, to Georgia with the equipment while they stopped over in Chicago to attend an Okeh dealers' convention. A few days later Brockman arrived, rented an empty loft on Nassau Street, and began to round up Fiddlin' John and other local talent for Peer to audition.[21]

This generally accepted account of the historic event focuses on Carson—and, subsequently, on hillbilly music—as the prime motive behind the first field expedition by a commercial phonograph company. Peer, however, told a substantially different story. "We went down there to get Negro stuff," he said. "This fellow [Brockman] began scouting around but to my amazement he didn't know of any Negro talent . . . he went to the local Negro theater and he tried to find acts but nothing amounted to anything, so . . . I began to switch off, and I said, I better record a local dance band, I've got to do something about this. Finally there was this deal where he wanted me to record a singer from a local church. This fellow had quite a good reputation and occasionally worked on the radio. So we set a date with this fellow [but] his father was ill in some other town and he just couldn't make the date. So to take up that time, my distributor brought in Fiddlin' John Carson. He said Fiddlin' John had been on the radio station and he's got quite a following. He's really not a good singer, but let's see what he's got. So the beginning of the hillbilly [recording industry] was just this effort to take up some time. He would never have recommended Fiddlin' John except that we had a vacant date and the time would otherwise have been lost. So I can't claim that there was any genius connected with it—not on my part, not on his part."

The date was June 14, 1923. Whether by genius or mere chance, Brockman, Peer, and Fiddlin' John made history. In retrospect, it seems probable that Brockman had Carson in mind all along, but was only too aware of the response he would probably get from Peer, the Northern urbanite, if he confronted him directly with the rowdy old fiddler and his primitive music. Indeed, Peer's initial reaction was that the records were "horrible"; he finally agreed to press the five hundred copies that Brockman was willing to order for local resale, but he refused to give the release a label number or to place it in the Okeh catalog.[22] When Brockman (and Carson) sold the initial order in a few weeks and called for more, Peer's good sense—business, if not aesthetic—forced him to recognize a good thing when he saw it. He immediately brought Fiddlin' John Carson to New York for a lengthy recording session and signed him to an exclusive Okeh contract. As Robert Coltman has observed, "Peer was graceful enough, when time proved him wrong, to turn himself into one of old time country music's best friends."[23]

In the wake of Fiddlin' John's unexpected success, Peer recalled the earlier test pressings of Henry Whitter: "So I brought Whitter back to New York for more recordings, and I discovered that the dope could sing. So I began to make records where he would sing a chorus and play a chorus. All these things were so simple, but somebody had to learn them." It is not always easy to know whether Peer's tone was one of camaraderie or condescension, but his point is well taken. He was developing, from necessity and firsthand experience, techniques of arranging and recording that would become valuable assets to his later career and that would substantially influence the course of commercial country music.

Ultimately, it was not Fiddlin' John Carson or Henry Whitter, but the phenomenon of portable recording that would emerge as the most significant development to come from Okeh's 1923 sessions. Although the exact history of Peer's ensuing field trips for that company has yet to be charted, by early 1925 he had made at least two return trips to Atlanta and one to Dallas. In the process he discovered a number of important early artists, both black and white, whose contributions to the developing mainstream culture would otherwise have gone unrecorded. During 1924 and 1925 Peer consolidated Okeh's position in country music by recording such pioneers as Ernest V. "Pop" Stoneman, the Jenkins Family, and Kelly Harrell. The latter two would play roles in the early career of Jimmie Rodgers, for Harrell and the Reverend Andy Jenkins were composers as well as performers, and they became valuable sources for the song material on which Peer drew to augment Rodgers's meager repertoire. And of course it was during this time that Peer recorded a southern string-band from Galax, Virginia, and dubbed them "The Hill Billies," thus enshrining Al and Joe Hopkins, Tony Alderman, and John Rector as "The Band That Named the Music."

Late in 1925 Peer's association with Okeh ended. "I sort of got a big head," he said later. "I liked myself too much. I was making about $16,000 a year, a young man, you see, it was too much money, an enormous amount of money. That would be equivalent to $50,000 now [1959]. So I quit. I got into an argument with the president, who was a Jewish fellow named Heineman. I said, 'I'm tired of this anyway, so let's call it a day.' He thought I was bluffing because he couldn't imagine anybody quitting a job like that. Nevertheless, I just left and walked out."

With money in the bank, Peer was able to vacation for several months, confident that he could take his pick of jobs and resume his business career at will. There followed, however, a succession of failures and ill-timed ventures that left him, as he later admitted, "somewhat nervous and depressed." He spent a brief period as sales manager for a new sports car named Norma, "which didn't work out"; he then came up with a scheme to market apple pies nationwide, but could find no backers. Falling back on his years of experience in the phonograph business, he traveled down to Camden and approached the people at the Victor Talking Machine Company. "They found it very difficult to talk to me," he recalled later, "because of the enormous salary that I would expect. They said, 'Why, the treasurer of our company has been here for twenty-seven years and he only makes $7,500 a year. I found out later that he got a $28,000-a-year bonus. At any rate, they were trying to hire me for about $5,000 a year. Of course I had what they wanted—they couldn't get into the hillbilly business and I knew how to do it. I knew everything they needed, and I was sensible enough not to go to work for them just to go to work. But I couldn't make a deal. We didn't get anyplace."

Peer returned to New York, quite discouraged over the seeming impasse. That night he sat down and, drawing on what he'd learned from the Okeh field recording trips, outlined a plan of action. His idea was to have vast consequences, not merely for his own future, but for that of country music and the recording industry as a whole.

It had been realized, as far back as Fiddlin' John's recording of "The Little Old Log Cabin in the Lane," that while the song might have sold a million copies for Alma Gluck back in 1919, by the late Twenties the market for "familiar old standards" was very limited. The appeal varied from song to song, but Peer's early, pre-blues experience with Okeh had already shown him that (as he put it) the days of "standard vocalists making records of 'Home Sweet Home'" were long past. Of Carson's first disc Peer would say, "'The Old Hen Cackled' was all right, that wasn't very well known. But 'Little Log Cabin in the Lane' was too well known to everybody, it was an old minstrel song. But after that, when I worked with Fiddlin' John, I wouldn't let him record a thing like 'Silver Threads among the Gold' or anything that already had wide distribution. He had a repertoire of about three hundred songs that you've never heard of before, things he'd acquired in his circus days, from other performers. Of course, they were now all duly copyrighted and put over as new songs. That's where I first developed this idea that I didn't want any old material or standard songs."

In the midst of that casual comment, uttered almost as an afterthought, lies the momentous idea, the key term: "duly copyrighted and put over as new songs." That, Peer eventually realized, "is the basis for the whole business—the record business is founded on it today. It all comes from this point, that I never recorded an established selection, I always insisted on getting artists who could write their own music." When he was working with Carson, however, the full implications of copyright had not yet hit him. In Carson's case, Polk Brockman became the copyright owner; Peer, as he himself was quick to point out, was working for Okeh on a straight salary and had no financial interest in copyrights or royalties. "I didn't participate at all," he said, "except that I made a good showing for the company." Perhaps later it was reward enough to be able to say, as he often did, "I take credit for discovering all of it."

The realization that "essentially this was the business of copyrights" became the foundation of Peer's nascent plan. But even before he'd come to understand the singular value of copyrights apart from any other considerations, he had evolved a practice that was to form a necessary corollary: "Never buy a copyright." In the fiercely competitive world of popular music, supply has always exceeded both demand and quality. With hordes of hungry composers plugging their work, publishers in the early days of Tin Pan Alley were able to pick a likely tune from the thousands offered and, without paying any advance, sign the anxious tunesmith to a vaguely worded "contract" that was often little more than an option. If the publisher succeeded in getting exposure for the song (usually by offering it free to some established performer, adding other inducements when necessary), and if the tune showed signs of catching on, the publisher then attempted to convince the composer to sell the song outright, for as little as possible. As Peer explained it, "The publisher would send for the writer and he'd either take him out and give him a meal or get him drunk or something, but he would eventually end up by buying the copyright for, say, $100. He already knew it was going to be a success, you see, the cards were stacked against these writers, they didn't know what was going on."[24] From the beginning Peer disdained this practice, realizing that "you just can't do a continuing business with composers" on that basis. As commercial hillbilly music evolved, Peer recognized that the situation was especially crucial in that area. No single hillbilly number, regardless of its appeal, was likely to match a "pop" song in national sales; therefore the secret of financial success lay in "repeat business"—in cultivating performers who could write their own material or consistently produce it from traditional sources, either of which qualified for copyright. Peer saw that, although he might buy a song outright from a promising composer, other publishers would invariably rush in and, if necessary, raise the ante to lure the writer away. Moreover, if a particular tune happened to beat the odds and become a hit, the composer would likely expect a share of the riches regardless of what he'd been paid for the rights. Either way, there would be hard feelings between composer and publisher.

Consequently, Peer had begun to insist on a royalty contract. Its terms assigned the copyright to Okeh as the nominal "publisher" and stipulated that a royalty of $.005 per record was to be paid to the composer.[25] Whenever composer royalties had been paid by record companies in the past, the figure was standard; it amounted to 25 percent of the 2¢ per record set aside by the manufacturer as "mechanical" royalty and paid to whoever controlled the copyright. In some rare instances the recipient was the composer himself, but more commonly it was a music publishing firm. In the case of the early hillbilly discoveries at Okeh, there had been no "publisher" at all until Brockman set himself up in that role, taking over the copyrights of Carson and others he'd discovered, and consequently reaping a profit not only from sales of sheet music but also from the "mechanicals" paid by Okeh. More important, with the copyrights assigned to him Brockman controlled, and stood to gain from, all future use of the material, including copyright renewals. At about this time, Peer began to understand the value of merely holding title to ownership of a song. Given the twin necessities of finding new material and of having to pay royalties to each composer, he concluded that "this was essentially the business of recording [i.e., registering] new copyrights." The vital corollary was, of course, the axiom he'd learned previously: never buy a copyright, but merely secure an assignment of it in return for the promise of future royalties. Originally this arrangement had been formulated simply as a necessary method of dealing with amateur artists and composers, to assure a profitable and continuing source of material while ostensibly protecting the composer from exploitation by any third party. As a salaried employee of Okeh, Peer at that time had no financial stake in any of these practices.

Later, however, as he observed the intricacies of copyright provisions with Brockman's example before him, Peer realized the true significance of the seemingly minor feature that allowed a composer to assign his copyright to someone else: the *assignment* was practically as good as outright ownership. What with subsidiary rights and renewals, it might prove even more valuable over a period of time. In fact, if the assignee could somehow act also as "publisher"—an admittedly minor role where hillbilly music was concerned—he could actually collect *three times* as much on records alone as the composer (75 percent versus 25 percent of the mechanicals) with no cash investment at all. "This was my conception starting this hillbilly thing," Peer said later, "and it cost me thousands and thousands of dollars because I could have just as easily bought [the copyrights] for $25 each, or taken them for nothing, as far as that goes. But fortunately I wasn't quite that greedy, and therefore I built up the business." It was an astute stratagem, for in fact he didn't have to take the copyrights "for nothing." In return for future royalties (amount often unspecified), he got them anyway, in proper, legal transactions and with hardly any capital outlay.

"So by insisting on new material and leaning toward artists who could produce it for us, their own compositions, that created the so-called hillbilly business, and most of the nigger," Peer said. In the case of "so-called hillbilly," the concern for new songs which could be copyrighted was rather ironically complicated by the fact that the major attraction of early performers such as Carson and Whitter was their old-fashioned, nostalgic quality, appealing to their audiences' longings for days past and a simpler, vanished way of life. Peer, with his long experience in the recording industry and his acute business-man's sense of what would sell, was uniquely suited to resolve this seeming paradox. To these qualities were now added a new awareness of the value of original material and a determination to deal fairly with artists and composers. Hindsight allows us to see more clearly the effects of what he was surely too busy and too near to notice or care about. Pressured to produce material that was new (i.e., copyrightable) yet somehow authentic to their temperament and traditions, aspiring rural artists such as Jimmie Rodgers and the Carter Family fell back on two obvious sources: either they dredged up old, half-forgotten relics of the past, or they composed original songs that sounded like the old ones—music that connected with the past and extended the tradition. In the first process, valuable folk material was preserved, often improved upon; in the second, native genius was given a stimulus and a creative outlet that it would otherwise have lacked. The ultimate consequence was to significantly influence the evolution of a major segment of our native culture—its popular music—and to set basic patterns that shaped the future of country music as both industry and art form.

At the time, however, his eventual role in history was of little concern to Ralph Peer as he sat mulling over his experiences in the record business. He needed a job, and the world's greatest phonograph company had just turned him down, saying that it couldn't afford to pay him what he was worth. "I was rather discouraged, because there seemed to be an impenetrable wall," he recalled. "So I sat down and wrote a three-paragraph letter and said that I had considered the matter very carefully, and that essentially this was the business of recording new copyrights, and I would be willing to go to work for them for nothing, with the understanding that there would be no objections if I controlled these copyrights."

The reply from Camden came by return mail: Peer's offer was accepted. He was told to get in touch with Nat Shilkret, Victor's recording director in New York; "So I went in to see Nat, who was already a friend of mine, and he said, Well, I don't know what it is, what do you want to do? And I said, I have to get ahold of some hillbillies and bring them up to record them."

As Peer's statement indicates, recording in the field was not an initial part of the plan. In March, 1925, Shilkret himself had taken a portable unit to Houston and New Orleans, but the only "hillbilly" who showed up was Captain M. J. Bonner, "The Texas Fiddler," and the two sides he recorded then were the only ones he ever made. Victor had its reputation to protect, and the company was generally dissatisfied with the technical quality of recordings made on the portable equipment. During the middle Twenties Victor sessions were held in St. Louis, Chicago, Salt Lake City, and at various points on the West Coast, usually under conditions somewhat more stable than those which the Southern units would encounter, but they were nevertheless looked upon with little favor by the committee which directed recording operations.

Peer's first contribution to Victor's hillbilly list was apparently Kelly Harrell, whom he had, in effect, brought with him from Okeh.[26] Harrell recorded in Victor's New York studios in June, 1926; he was followed in September by another former Okeh artist, Ernest Stoneman. Later Peer had trouble remembering either of them, but he finally decided (incorrectly) that Stoneman was first. "'Ernest Stoneman and His Family,' I think we called them," he said, "one of those local groups with a fiddle in the background. Nothing terribly exciting, but of course as soon as we put the record out, Victor sold 60,000. Of course, I had figured this all out. Just a year from that time my royalty check was a quarter of a million dollars, that's for just three months." But other hillbillies were slow in coming in, and Peer earned his keep by arranging sessions for black musicians, including Bobby Leecan and Robert Cooksey, whom he'd become acquainted with while at Okeh.

As the hillbilly market continued to flourish and the demand for new artists grew, Peer convinced the Victor executives to mount an expedition to the South, into his old familiar stamping grounds. "Actually, they came to me for recommendations," he related, "and so I said I should make a trip into southern territory and find places where I could record and you'll have to supply me with a portable recording machine." Asked if this was an unorthodox procedure, he replied, "It was unknown. Only Okeh had ever done it. [Victor] would go out to record, for example, the San Francisco Symphony Orchestra during the World's Fair, but it wasn't a tremendous thing, and they were never satisfied with the general [recording] results. So I had to put over the thought that the hillbilly recording didn't need the same quality as Caruso. . . ."[27]

Peer's initial field excursion to Atlanta, Memphis, and New Orleans in February and March, 1927, was taken up largely with gospel singers and "race" artists, although it also resulted in the first recordings by the Georgia Yellow Hammers and the Carolina Tar Heels (Gwen Foster and Dock Walsh), groups that would enjoy sustained success and enter the pantheon of hillbilly pioneers. Still, there was the pervasive feeling in New York and Camden that the surface had hardly been scratched. Somewhere out there was another Fiddlin' John Carson, another Vernon Dalhart. Or even better, someone who combined the best qualities of both—Fiddlin' John's authenticity and Dalhart's commercial savvy. Someone who might even make hillbilly music a little more respectable while selling lots of records.

NOTES

1. E. R. Fenimore Johnson, *His Master's Voice Was Eldridge R. Johnson*, 2nd ed. (Privately printed, 1974), p. 56. See also Roland Gelatt, *The Fabulous Phonograph* (Philadelphia: J. B. Lippincott, 1955), p. 99.

2. Gelatt, *Fabulous Phonograph*, pp. 131, 209.

3. *Billboard*, Feb. 7, 1925, p. 22.

4. According to his "Son Fen," Johnson "would not permit a talking machine and records to be kept in the house" (*His Master's Voice*, p. 91). On one rare occasion, a Victor artist was entertained by the Johnsons: Mrs. Johnson's cultural aspirations led her to invite the company's reigning prima donna, Nellie Melba, to luncheon. Melba gave little Fen a wet smack, demanded protection from imaginary drafts, and in the midst of lunch told what she fancied was a clever story of ordering mousse in an outdoor restaurant, causing little children to run around screaming, "Madame Melba eats mice." The fastidious Johnsons were not amused. "That," said Son Fen, "was the first and last time that a Victor artist was ever invited to the Johnson home."

5. Gelatt, *Fabulous Phonograph*, p. 141.

6. *Ibid*.

7. *Ibid.*, p. 122. Today collectors think little of paying $10 for a random old 78 by Sophie Tucker, Fred Astaire, or Roy Acuff; the original recordings of Louis

Armstrong, Dilly and the Dill Pickles, Bob Wills, and Jimmie Rodgers regularly bring $50 and more. Conversely, most Carusos are hardly worth dusting off.

8. Beneath its entry for "Coon Songs and Specialties," Victor offered this explanation: "By 'coon songs' are meant up-to-date comic songs in negro dialect. The humor of many of these songs cannot be called refined, and for that reason we have distinguished them from old-fashioned darky humor, these songs being listed under 'Fisk Jubilee,' 'Negro Songs,' and 'Tuskegee.'" Of Dalhart, however, they said, "There is no burlesquing in Mr. Dalhart's singing of negro songs."

9. Gelatt, *Fabulous Phonograph*, p. 223.

10. *Billboard*, May 15, 1925, p. 22; Feb. 20, 1926, p. 21; May 29, 1926, p. 29.

11. This is the figure reported by Johnson's son in *His Master's Voice*, p. 119. According to Gelatt (*Fabulous Phonograph*, p. 246) and *Billboard* (Dec. 18, 1926, p. 22), Johnson received $28 million for his 245,000 shares.

12. *Billboard*, Aug. 27, 1927, p. 20.

13. Archie Green, "Hillbilly Music: Source and Symbol," *Journal of American Folklore*, 78:309 (July-Sept., 1965), 207.

14. Victor had also recorded the group that later became known as the Hill Billies, but their Victor sides were never released. (*Ibid.*, p. 213.)

15. Most of the statements which I have attributed to Ralph Peer were obtained from a series of interviews conducted by Lillian Borgeson in Hollywood between January and May, 1959. Because the individual interview sessions are undated and because no full transcript has been published or othewise circulated, there is little advantage in citing each statement separately. Many details of Peer's early life and all uncited statements by him are from the Borgeson interviews; any other sources are cited in these notes. Original tapes of the interviews are on file at the John Edwards Memorial Foundation, UCLA. Complete copies of the tapes and a full transcript are in my files.

16. Peer's deterministic world-view is also strongly reflected in his untitled account of his experiences with Rodgers: *Meridian Star*, May 26, 1953, p. 24.

17. In his autobiography Handy recounts at length his harrowing adventures between trains in Chicago during this trip, but (perhaps understandably) he does not mention any role Peer might have played in the musicians' hectic dash to catch the New York Central. Some years later it was Peer, along with Fred Hagar, who signed Handy and his band to record for Okeh. (See W. C. Handy, *Father of the Blues*, ed. Arna Bontemps [New York: Macmillan, 1941], pp. 171–73, 206.)

18. Samuel B. Charters, *The Country Blues* (New York: Rinehart, 1959), pp. 32–33.

19. See Green, "Hillbilly Music," pp. 206–7.

20. See Norm Cohen, "Henry Whitter: His Life and Music," *JEMFQ*, 11:38 (Summer, 1975), 58. As Cohen points out, the exact date and circumstances of Whitter's initial trip are yet to be confirmed. In the Borgeson interviews Peer implies that Whitter had written to Okeh earlier, and that the company ignored him. The consensus is that Whitter's test records, probably made in March, were never released but were simply redone when he returned to New York in December. Cohen (p. 61) reprints a bill of sale for "The Wreck of the Southern Old 97" made out to Fred Hagar, suggesting that Hagar, and not Peer, recorded Whitter. Green, "Hillbilly Music," p. 210, supports this view.

21. For a general account of these events, see Green, "Hillbilly Music," pp. 208–10, and Malone, *Country Music, U.S.A.*, pp. 40–42.

22. According to what Peer told Borgeson, a combination of Carson's performance

and the poor recording quality prompted his initial reaction. The figure of 500 records for the first pressing is Green's; Peer said that Brockman agreed to buy 1,000, which they manufactured and sent to him.

23. Robert Coltman, "Look Out! Here He Comes . . . ," *Old Time Music*, no. 9 (Summer, 1973), 17.

24. A notorious instance in country music was Darby and Tarlton's sale of "Columbus Stockade Blues" for $75. For what was then assumed to be clear title to "The Wreck of the Southern Old 97," Hagar paid Whitter $200, although of course that song later became the subject of one of the most protracted legal battles in copyright history. See Henry M. Belden and Arthur Palmer Hudson, eds., *The Frank C. Brown Collection of North Carolina Folklore* (Durham, N.C.: Duke University Press, 1952), II:512–16.

25. If the song appeared to have possibilities for sheet-music sales, an additional payment of 2¢ per sheet was stipulated. However, as Peer noted, hillbilly songs did not sell much in sheet-music form.

26. Earlier (in January, 1925) Harrell had recorded four sides for Victor independently of Peer, but it was not until he was taken up by Peer, then at Okeh, in August that his work began to catch on. His return to Victor the following year was clearly influenced by Peer. For a Harrell discography, see "Kelly Harrell & the Virginia Ramblers," *Old Time Music*, no. 2 (Autumn, 1971), 11.

27. Peer's remark suggests the general attitude of New York executives toward hillbilly music and musicians. (As for his statement about the San Francisco Symphony, Victor had recorded that group several times in the 1920's, but it is not at all clear what occasion Peer had in mind. No World's Fair or comparable exposition was held in San Francisco during the period.)

6 *August, 1927–February, 1928*

"All Right, George, I'll Just Sing One Myself"

During the spring of 1927, Peer began to plan another recording expedition into the South. In early June he traveled alone through the target area, selecting likely sites, arranging dates with some of his regulars, and searching out new talent. A phonograph dealer in the Tenneva Ramblers' hometown of Bristol gave him the address of a family named Carter in nearby Maces Springs, Virginia, who had been trying to arrange an audition with Brunswick; through an exchange of letters, they agreed to come to Bristol for a tryout with Peer the following month.[1] In other towns he contacted radio stations, music stores, and record dealers, eventually lining up recording dates in Bristol, Charlotte, and Savannah for July and August.

There had been cursory discussions with Victor about the budget for such undertakings. While working for Okeh, Peer's established practice had been to offer his hillbilly discoveries the standard royalty arrangement and to pay them a flat "performance" fee of $25 a side—"They were glad to get it," he said. So when Nat Shilkret asked him how much money he would need for a field trip, Peer told him, "Well, I don't think it's worthwhile unless I can do at least sixteen recordings. I'd have to give them about $400 for that, and it'd take four people and probably cost $300 for traveling expenses."

Shilkret was indignant. "You can't make any recordings for Victor at $25 apiece," he said. "That's just entirely too cheap. It might get out, and we couldn't stand that kind of publicity." Recalling the incident years later, Peer chuckled. "Victor, of course, was the company that had [Nellie] Melba and Caruso and they paid out enormous sums to dance orchestras and all sorts of people who couldn't sing. They were tops and they couldn't afford to be making selections for $25 each. So I said, Okay, then make it $50 apiece, so that set the minimum of $50 for a recording. I could have done it for half. But at an early age I had the sense to conform to whatever the company wanted. I never threw away money, but I did put a low point of $50 a selection, which was absolutely unnecessary. Most of them expected to record for nothing. On top of this $50, of course I gave them royalty on their selections. They thought it was manna from heaven."

Accompanied by his second wife, Anita Glander, who'd been his secretary, and two Victor engineers, Peer arrived in Bristol around the end of the third week in July and prepared to start the recording sessions the following Monday, July 25. "I can't tell you why I picked Bristol," he told an interviewer later. "It just seemed to be a likely spot." As usual, Peer's instincts were good; Bristol, like Asheville, was the center of a region fertile with musical activity, and out of Victor's sessions that summer came some of the finest and rarest examples of native American song. Peer's primary interest in oldtime music is borne out by the *Bristol Herald Courier*'s announcement of his arrival, in which it was noted that "In no section of the South have the pre-war melodies and old mountaineer songs been better preserved than in the mountains of East Tennessee and Southwest Virginia, experts declare, and it was primarily for this reason that the Victor Company chose Bristol as its operating base."[2] Conversely, the city was hardly the rustic village often depicted in liner notes and country music histories. With a population of some 25,000, it was a terminal point for the Norfolk & Western and the Southern railways and boasted two daily newspapers, three colleges, and a thriving tourist business.

For his operations Peer located a building at 408-10 State Street,[3] on the Tennessee side of the thoroughfare dividing the town; the site was just across the street from the boardinghouse operated by Jack Pierce's mother. The second floor, used from time to time as a warehouse by the Cox Hat Company, was empty except for some shelves of millinery materials, and it was there that the Victor engineers set up their equipment and a rented piano. A small story in the Sunday edition of the local newspaper observed that "several well-known native record makers will come to Bristol this week to record," and Peer began sessions the next day with his established star,

Ernest Stoneman. Their efforts that day resulted in some ten masters from the twenty-three takes performed by Stoneman and the various groups he'd brought with him. While Stoneman and his musicians rested on Tuesday, six sides were recorded by Ernest Phipps and His Holiness Quartet, a fine oldtime gospel group from Kentucky. Peer resumed with the Stoneman groups the next day, but, looking ahead, he became concerned that more new talent had not appeared to audition. A session had been set up later in the week for the Johnson brothers, whom he'd already recorded in Camden, and he sent to Princeton, West Virginia, some ninety miles north of Bristol, for Blind Alfred Reed, an amateur performer and composer whose railroad ballad, "The Wreck of the Virginian," had caught Peer's attention on his scouting trip through the area. The Carters were scheduled for the first session the following week, and Henry Whitter would eventually show up to record a couple of harmonica solos, but beyond that the appointment ledgers were blank, and prospects dim. "I then appealed to the editor of a local newspaper," Peer said, "explaining to him the great advantages to the community of my enterprise."[4] He also recounted how he'd gotten the editor's cooperation by giving him "inside information" about a proposed merger between Victor and RCA, enabling him to make "quite a bit of money out of it" on the stock market. However, considering that the merger was not even rumored in financial circles until the following year, the story must be discounted, or possibly credited to Peer's 1928 Bristol trip. In any event, the editor was invited to attend the Wednesday morning session, and his account of the event, printed on the front page of that afternoon's edition of the *Bristol News-Bulletin*, produced the desired results. Describing in detail "notables of this mountain country doing their best stunts for the microphone, turned into records, and spread at home and abroad," the story stressed Stoneman's growing fame and the fact that he had earned $3,600 in record royalties the previous year.[5] "After you read this," Peer said, "if you knew how to play C on the piano, you were going to become a millionaire. . . . This worked like dynamite and the very next day I was deluged with long distance calls from the surrounding region, [and] groups of singers who had not visited Bristol in their entire lifetime arriving by bus, horse and buggy, trains or on foot." He was exaggerating, certainly, but the resulting sessions produced a dozen or so new names, including such eventually important ones as B. F. Shelton, Alfred Karnes, and, of course, the Carter Family and Jimmie Rodgers.[6]

The Jimmie Rodgers Entertainers arrived in Bristol on the afternoon of August 3.[7] They went directly to Mrs. Pierce's boardinghouse, where they deposited Carrie and Anita; after tuning up their instruments, they went across the street to see Peer. The session that day had been one of the lighter ones, with only six numbers recorded by two groups, so Peer had time to audition the Entertainers on the spot. He was not much impressed by the dance tunes they'd been playing at North Fork, but Jimmie convinced him that they could come up with plenty of oldtime numbers, and Peer agreed to arrange a time for them to record the next day.

That night the musicians got together at the boardinghouse to rehearse. Jimmie had already announced his intention of leaving the group and heading north, so there arose the question of how they would be billed on the records they were about to make. Rodgers's role as nominal leader of the band had always been somewhat tenuous, but for several months the once-and-future Tenneva Ramblers had followed along, hoping that his promises of bigger and better things would work out. Looking back, they could see that he'd engineered precious few paying jobs—the North Fork engagement being a notable exception—and even worse was their general feeling that as a musician he really wasn't in their league. Now they were on home turf, and in no mood to have the spotlight hogged by a second-rate talent who talked a lot, produced little, and couldn't seem to stay put. No one was more aware of his shaky position than Rodgers himself, as evidenced by the fact that it was he who first raised the issue of billing. According to Claude Grant, "At some point [while they were rehearsing that evening] Jimmie brought up the question of how would we record; would it be 'Jimmie Rodgers and the Entertainers' or what?"[8]

The answer was a quick and firm no. Claude, an easy-going sort who apparently tried to act as mediator, suggested that they use "The Tenneva Ramblers" and credit the particular vocalist—himself or Jimmie—with the numbers that each sang. Jimmie countered with "Jimmie Rodgers and the Grant Brothers," which no one liked. One thing led to another, and tempers flared. Old wounds between Jack Grant and Jimmie were reopened, apparently stemming from Jimmie's casual approach to handling finances and paying bills the group had run up back in Asheville.[9]

Finally Jimmie told Claude, "I can't get along with Jack. I believe I'll just try to make a record by myself some way. Just sing with guitar." Claude, who was sympathetic to both sides, said that was all right with him. "I told him I didn't care one way or another, that we'd try to get some stuff together our own selves, you know, see if we could cut something. So Jimmie stormed out of the boardinghouse and went to Peer and asked if he could record alone, and Peer agreed. I remember after the argument, Jimmie said, 'All right, George, I'll just sing one myself.' He called everyone George. And he left."[10]

Ralph Peer saw the affair from a different perspective. As he later reconstructed events, it appeared to him that Jimmie had been merely "sort of a bus boy in a roadside stand [i.e., North Fork Resort]" and had fallen in with the band only as a means of getting transportation to Bristol. "I never heard that Jimmie performed at all in this restaurant," said Peer. "I think he was just a bus boy. But at any rate . . . he induced these boys to come down to try for a recording, so that he could come along himself. And of course, his only idea was to be just a member of the group, and I busted that up. But not to shut out Jimmie; in fact, the records would have been no good if Jimmie had sung with this group because he was singing nigger blues and they were doing old-time fiddle music. Oil and water . . . they don't mix."

Peer said that when the group first auditioned, he realized that Rodgers "was obviously trying to put something over on me. Of course I saw through this right away, but I didn't tell him that he was a fake. He came in with this string band, and they were going to be the recording artists and he was going to sing with them. But he was an individualist, he had his own style, so it wouldn't fit with a bunch of fiddles, you know, it was no good. And the selections—this string band, they just knew the dance music. So as I say, I didn't tell him he was a faker; I quickly figured out that he'd just used these fellows to bring him over, so in order that nobody's feelings would be hurt, I recorded the string band, gave them four [actually only three] selections . . . then I got Jimmie back alone and recorded him. . . ." Peer admitted that sympathy was partly his motive. "I did feel sorry for Jimmie on the first go-round. I saw what he was trying to put over, and I said to myself, I'll have to help this fellow all I can, but the only way to do it is to make two sets of recordings. This was all a new deal for Victor; they didn't have any oldtime fiddle music, so I knew if I recorded four selections by the band that it would be useful anyway. So I did that and I got rid of them quite early and I think I had Jimmie come back at night and record." Elsewhere Peer recounted that "I was elated when I heard him perform without the unsuitable accompaniment. It seemed to me that he had his own personal and peculiar style, and I thought his yodel alone might spell success. . . . I considered Rodgers to be one of my best bets."[11]

If this account is to be taken at face value, Peer himself was responsible for the separation of Jimmie Rodgers from the Tenneva Ramblers, motivated by a) his realization that they were mismatched, b) the fact that he felt sorry for Jimmie, and c) his perception of Rodgers's superior potential. These motives are logical and entirely credible in light of later developments—although one might wonder why, if Peer was so "elated"' with Jimmie's talent, he recorded only two sides, while the Tenneva Ramblers, allowed to perform "just so nobody's feelings would be hurt," got three. Unfortunately, Peer's version differs materially from Claude Grant's. Even more troubling, the time sequences related by Peer and by Grant are not borne out by the Victor files or master numbers.

However, if the two accounts are juxtaposed and allowances are made for certain errors of fact resulting from faulty memories, it seems clear that what actually took place was simply a chain of fortuitous coincidences. At the audition on August 3, Peer realized that the group was not a cohesive whole, but he made no attempt to resolve the problem, intending to deal with it somehow when they showed up to record. That night the group argued on its own and split up. Thus it may even have been with some relief that Peer greeted Jimmie the next day (Wednesday, August 4) when he appeared alone to seek an audition. This encounter presumably took place in the morning, and Rodgers became the first artist to record that day; according to Victor's files, the session began at 2:00 p.m. and lasted until 4:20. Jimmie Rodgers made his first record—and history—with little fanfare, but with considerable anxiety, frustration, and sweat. Getting two songs down properly on the wax masters required two-and-a-half hours and seven takes—more than any other artist, old or new, was permitted during the Bristol sessions.

These records were made under primitive conditions, even by the standards of only a few years afterward. Yet, as Peer was quick to point out thirty years later, the recording equipment was basically the same as that used for decades, until the advent of tape and sixteen-track mixing consoles: "Nothing that we know now [1959] that we didn't know then. It was all developed by Western Electric and they had this pretty much refined." The turntable itself was basically the same design as the one used earlier for acoustical recordings. It was driven by weights suspended from a tower rising some six feet off the floor ("just like a cuckoo clock," said Peer), a system which, with the addition of a mechanical governor, insured a constant rate of speed with far greater precision than either a spring or an electric motor, the latter being susceptible to line loss and other variations in current. As Peer pointed out, it was all practically handmade, with the tower constructed so that it could be folded up and transported in the trunk of a car. "The electrical equipment was just a separate panel board," he said, "very much like that used today. We were able to simulate room tone or take it out, we could do all that because we had condensers on the equipment." In Bristol this was fortunate, for the "studio" itself was simply a huge bare stockroom, furnished with nothing more than a microphone on a stand, a light-and-buzzer combination by which the engineer signaled the performer to begin, and many cubic feet of "room-tone." Said Claude Grant, "The acoustics was bound to have been bad. "I don't see how they got the fidelity."[12]

Sound quality was one of Peer's lesser worries as he undertook to plan a recording session for the excited young Mississippian with the winning grin and dark radiance in his eyes. Peer's business was based on finding songs that could be copyrighted, and Jimmie Rodgers had a decidedly limited repertoire. "We ran into a snag almost immediately," Peer wrote later, "because in order to earn a living in Asheville, he was singing mostly songs originated by the New York publishers—the current hits."[13] Later it became obvious that that was Jimmie's natural inclination; he would always consider himself a "popular entertainer," and his forte, when he eventually found it, lay in his ability to blend the traditional and the modern. At the moment, however, he was ready to do whatever was necessary to seize the opportunity before him, just as throughout his career he would bend to any commercial breeze— and, as often as not, turn it into a gale. Peer explained what he needed to "get over" on records—some of this hillbilly stuff that was catching on like wildfire, but it had to be more or less "new" so they could get composer royalties. Jimmie recalled the old ballad, sung to the tune of "Where the River Shannon Flows," that he'd worked over some years back in memory of his boyhood chum, Sammy Williams, a casualty of the Great War. The mournful tone and lush sentimentality of "The Soldier's Sweetheart" were properly archaic, yet the mention of "this awful German war" (liltingly pronounced by Jimmie as "wawh") and the song's tacitly pacifist message identified it as the product of its own time, the Twenties milieu that had had its fill of No Man's Land and letters written by commanding officers to report the deaths of loved ones. There was a certain folk-poetry quality in it, too, in phrases like "golden finger ring." Never mind that it was a maiden's song sung by a male; things hadn't gotten so sophisticated that anyone would notice. Like most of the other songs that would be credited to Rodgers, "The Soldier's Sweetheart" was not so much composed as simply compiled. But there could be no mistaking the power and genuine emotion in his rendition of it.

Peer was sufficiently impressed with the song, and Jimmie, fired by the fever in his veins as well as by his perennial optimism, wildly promised that, given a few days, he could have dozens more songs ready. But of course they didn't have that much time—Peer was scheduled to move on to Charlotte—so for a pairing they settled on the yodeling lullaby, "Sleep, Baby, Sleep," that Jimmie had made popular on WWNC, although Peer was none too happy that the song was in public domain and, he felt, uncopyrightable.[14] It has been thought that Rodgers's version was only a pale imitation of Riley Puckett's 1924 recording (Columbia 220-D), but in fact the two performances have little in common except the title and a similar tune. Jimmie was obviously familiar with Puckett's recording, but his lyrics are derived from other sources and modified to highlight his fluid, melodic yodel. Puckett's raw, often hollow falsetto suffers by comparison, and his rendition lacks the driving clarity of Rodgers's, although these flaws may be attributed in part to the acoustical process by which the earlier record was made.

Carrie complained that "Sleep, Baby, Sleep" was a "thousand-years-old lullaby," one of those "quaint old-timey things" that would only bore the public.[15] Eventually, when there was speculation as to why he had not picked a sure winner like "T for Texas" for his first record, she would offer Jimmie's reasoning: he feared that the catchy lyrics of a "blue yodel" might detract attention from the quality of his voice and guitar, and he wanted Victor's "deciding board" to judge him solely on his performing ability. "If they do happen to like me—my voice and my playin'—and these pretty old-fashioned numbers," he said, "why then they'll have sense enough to know I can put over all those old hill-billy things, sentimental or rowdy."[16] Much wisdom in that—but one cannot be sure whether it was foresight on

Jimmie's part, or an explanation supplied by Carrie long after the fact. It seems more likely that "T for Texas" had not been perfected at that stage—even Carrie has Jimmie saying, "I've got 'em [the blue yodels] all right, but I haven't got 'em all worked out good yet."[17] Moreover, Peer, who observed with some disdain that Rodgers had been "singing nigger blues" previously, would probably not have let him use such material at that time even if it had been in shape. Peer was still on a determined quest for "hillbilly music" (or whatever would pass for it back in New York) and was willing to invent it on the spot if necessary. He had not yet realized the potential of his future star, nor had he detected the real nature of Rodgers's talent and the true originality that would take him in directions Peer never dreamed of at the time. For all his Southern origins and shanty Irish upbringing, Rodgers was very much a product of the American mainstream, with his eye firmly fixed on the main chance. But curiously enough, he was also, long before the term was coined, a hipster: self-contained in his strength and weaknesses, shrewd and cool and keenly alert to the pains and ecstasies of the shared human experience. If "hip" did not exist in his time, then mercifully neither did "hillbilly," "country," "pop," "soul," or "folk." If they had, Jimmie Rodgers's polestar would have been, simply and absolutely, "popular," in the broadest possible sense. He wanted to do it all, and if that meant dressing up in overalls or a cowboy suit and wailing folksy ditties for a while, he'd do it.

And so it was that on a sultry August afternoon he stood before the microphone on the bare floor of a deserted hat warehouse and performed the awkward rustic songs that Mr. Victor and Mr. Peer apparently wanted to hear. But it was not the incongruities of the situation that concerned him, or even the flush of tubercular fever, for by now that was a familiar part of every day's exertions. Uppermost in his mind was the realization that this was the chance he'd wanted so long and worked for so hard, and now it had come almost too soon and in a way that he was scarcely prepared to handle. Still uncertain of his skill with the guitar and accustomed to performing the established material of other composers, with other musicians, Jimmie Rodgers was suddenly alone, with nothing but his gumption and his Martin and two songs he'd cobbled together. Little wonder that he recorded four takes of "The Soldier's Sweetheart" and three of "Sleep, Baby, Sleep" before he got them right.[18] In each case, it was the last take which was issued; the earlier ones, if they are ever uncovered, might well reveal a progression, in the space of a few hours, from a nervous amateur to one who was reasonably, or at least acceptably, polished, and secure in the knowledge that his critics and detractors were wrong. When the chips were down he could "show 'em." Lacking the early takes, however, posterity can only speculate on the errors and frustrations Rodgers had to overcome. "The fact that he did only two selections indicates that we had a little trouble with the recording quality," Peer said later, with considerable tact and understatement. "We probably had to do them over two or three times each, or he may not have had anything [else] ready."

Later, Carrie would relate the colorful account of how Jimmie had gestured to her from the studio window across the street, how she'd grabbed up little Anita (and coincidentally bumped into sister-in-law Lottie Mae, just off the train from Geiger), how all three had rushed over just in time to hear Jimmie record, how Carrie had pleaded desperately with Peer to let her "darling dear" record just one more side—"Give him a chance to show how he can yodel the blues"![19] It's a grand story, now ingrained in the public consciousness and surely central to any Hollywood treatment.

According to Peer, however, it never happened. "That's highly imaginary," he said. "Carrie was no place around." Queried specifically, he insisted that he did not meet her until months later: "I don't know when she first came into my life, but it was not then [at Bristol] or for many months after." He was, in fact, under the impression that she was still in Meridian. "If Carrie and the child were over in a hotel [in Bristol] I knew nothing about it, and later when he came up to Camden, I met him at the railroad station and no Carrie, so if Carrie was on the trip, I can't substantiate it. It really doesn't make much difference. She never had a thing to do artistically with any of Rodgers's work, either the records or his personal appearances, so far as I know."[20]

With a hundred dollars from Peer for his two test sides and a short-term option agreement in his pocket, Jimmie checked himself and Carrie into Bristol's best hotel, as confident of his future as if he'd just signed to play the Palace. Radiating enthusiasm, Rodgers seemed blissfully unaware that all over the country dozens of other young men with equally high hopes were making test records and would never enter a studio again. That night, as planned, Jimmie and Carrie put young Anita and her Aunt Lottie Mae on the train for Alabama, where

Anita would stay with her grandparents until her parents could get established "somewhere near Camden."

Returning to their hotel from the station, they encountered a salesman Jimmie had known in Asheville. The man mentioned that he'd enjoyed hearing the Entertainers on the radio, and asked how things were going. Jimmie blithely announced, "Well, I'm under contract to the Victor phonograph company. Just made a recording here today; and I'm going to be broadcasting again soon. Washington, D.C., I guess." That was a bit much even for Carrie, proud and supportive though she was. What's more, as she said later, "Jimmie never changed expression when I pinched his arm." The years of struggle had made her a realist, and she knew her husband's easy, dreamy ways only too well. As he lingered in the lobby to look through the evening papers, she mused to herself: "I bet he's hunting to see if the Associated Press wires are carrying the news yet—the news that Jimmie Rodgers has just made his first record for the Victor Company."[21]

They left Bristol the next day for Washington in the Dodge that Jack Pierce's father had bought for the Jimmie Rodgers Entertainers. "I still don't know how he wound up with that car," Claude Grant said, implying that Jimmie was up to old tricks, "but he sure left the next day with it."[22] In fact, Jimmie bought the car with money wired from Washington by Carrie's sister Annie, who was working in the office of the Superintendent of Documents at the Government Printing Office. Like the rest of the Williamsons, Annie was generous to a fault, especially where Jimmie and Carrie were concerned. She not only wired them the money, her entire savings, but also insisted that they come to Washington and stay with her while Jimmie waited for word from Victor. As she recounted the circumstances years later, "I had just that very day put three hundred dollars in my savings account, money I had saved bit by bit, and it was all I had. Then came Carrie's wire, asking for just that amount, saying how desperate they were. Well, I worried and worried over it all day long, until finally my supervisor saw that I was very upset and took me aside. We talked it over, and she agreed that I ought to send the money. Well, it was 'family,' you know—Carrie was my sister, and I knew she'd see that the money was paid back somehow." She laughed softly. "But what I didn't know was how long it might take!" Just how long it took is not recorded, but Annie Nelson proudly acknowledged that she was eventually "paid back many times over."[23]

The immediate prospects certainly weren't very good. In Washington, the exhilaration of having "phonographed for Mr. Victor" soon faded. In the lull that followed, even Jimmie's spirits began to sag. Making the rounds of booking agents and radio stations, he got caught in a rainstorm and came home with chills and a fever that put him in bed for days. Over his objections, Carrie went to work as a tearoom waitress. She had hardly any choice, for other than the secondhand Dodge they owned little more than the clothes on their backs, and winter—a harsh Northern winter—was on its way. And as she pointed out to her husband, he needed a decent wardrobe not only for the sake of his health but also to impress booking agents. Jimmie, who'd always dressed in style and taken pride in his appearance, had to agree.

Within weeks of his arrival in the nation's capital, he had business cards and letterhead printed up, proclaiming him "National Radio Artist—Victor Record Artist." The former claim was backed up, of course, by nothing more than his very brief stint on one small station in North Carolina, while the latter derived from a single as-yet-unreleased recording. He managed to pick up a few random engagements, playing cheap luncheon dates and filling in between movies in small suburban theaters, but as Carrie put it, "sophisticated Washington refused to be bothered with him." His bad cold hung on, ofter accompanied by severe pleurisy pains, a common problem with advancing tuberculosis. But for Jimmie the show, whenever he could get one, had to go on. On more than one occasion he got out of bed and went out to perform for a precious few dollars, running a high fever and with a plaster taped to his ribs to blunt the pain and keep him from breathing too deeply.

His spirits rose with the approaching date for the release of his first record. Victor sent him several advance copies late in September. A few days later he wrote "Dear little Aunt Dora" to tell her about it, ever so casually, dropping fanciful hints of a grand promotional tour that did not, of course, ever materialize. He gave her the title and catalog number of his forthcoming record, and told her to visit the Williamsons in Meridian "and get them to Play it for you, Cause you cant Buy it till Oct 7th however I got hold of 2 or 3 and sent 1 to them."

A darker side of the letter concerns his acknowledgment of several debts, which he always insisted on spelling "depts": "Aunt Dora I guess you heard about the way I left some of my Depts there when I left but I couldn't help my self at that time but I think I can Pay all my Depts by Febuary if not sooner."

All said and done, he was still a Southern country boy, a long way from home and suffering the indignities of Yankee weather and Yankee table fare. "Wish you would send me or have some body send me," the letter ends wistfully, "5 Gals of Pure old Country Ribon cane lasses C.O.D. Your nephew, Jimmie Rodgers."

Although "Sleep, Baby, Sleep" was given the "A" side of the record and would eventually emerge in the public's estimation as the stronger of the two initial cuts, his letter bears out what is suggested by the order of recording and other evidence—that to Rodgers himself, "the name of my record is *the Soldier's Sweet Heart*" (his emphasis), with "Sleep, Baby, Sleep" merely "the other side." While the latter had been successful enough back in Asheville, and despite Jimmie's improvements on the old standard, it was nevertheless a cover version of someone else's popular record.

On October 6, 1927, the first major talking picture opened in New York. Any connection between this movie and jazz was "purely coincidental," said one scholar later,[24] but *The Jazz Singer,* for all its schmaltz and superficiality, ushered in an era of vast technological and cultural change that would radically affect the lives of people around the world. Its consequences were many, but the one which would ultimately have the greatest impact on Jimmie Rodgers's career was the fact that, as one historian succinctly put it, the film "sounded the death knell of live show business."[25]

The very next day, with considerably less fanfare, Rodgers's first record went on sale in music stores across the country. During subsequent weeks Jimmie haunted the stores and made repeated calls to Victor's Washington distributor to check on sales. Told that it was moving faster than most first releases by an unknown artist (especially considering that, typically, it had been given little advance promotion), he confidently waited for Victor to call him, convinced that he was the center of the universe and oblivious to the slow pace at which the business world, and especially the world of recording, moved in those days. To the impatient and ever-impetuous Jimmie Rodgers, who did not have forever and knew it, each day became a year. As the weeks passed and no call came, he grew increasingly fretful, afraid

Peer had tried and failed to locate him, or (even worse) had forgotten him. He began to worry that using "old-timey stuff" on the first record had been an error; maybe he should have insisted on "T for Texas" even if it hadn't been polished the way he wanted it. Maybe he should have shown them his strong suit—the bluesy, catchy yodel songs—right off.

Finally, around the middle of November, tired of being in limbo, he reached a decision: if he'd not heard from Peer by the end of the month, he would go to New York and confront him in person. In the meantime, mindful of Carrie's concern for their small daughter back in Geiger, he sent for Anita without his wife's knowledge and arranged a surprise reunion on Thanksgiving Day. A few days later, marshaling their combined cash resources (which totaled, according to Carrie, "ten whole dollars"), he headed for New York in the clattering grey Dodge.

Later Peer insisted that he had written to Rodgers but received no reply, and that he finally located him by phone. It is quite possible that he did (or at least intended to), although the available evidence indicates that it was Jimmie who initiated the phone call. In New York, Rodgers went not to Victor or Peer, but straightaway checked into the expensive Hotel Manger at Seventh Avenue and Fiftieth Street, casually showing the desk clerk a copy of his record and telling him to bill his charges to the Victor Talking Machine Company. As he explained to Carrie later, "I just naturally like the best, and I believe in taking it." His reading of the value which Victor placed on prestige was somewhat keener than Peer's had been when he suggested to Shilkret that they pay the "hillbillies" only twenty-five dollars a side. "I figured they were a powerful firm and wealthy, and I was one of their artists," said Jimmie. "Course, they'd want me to do 'em proud—and I did."[26] It was an act entirely characteristic of Jimmie Rodgers—audacious and irresistible as he was, full of charm, sure of his own ability, a confidence man in more happy ways than one. But just beneath this brash and cheery exterior were several dark and more complex entities. For all his presumption and bravado, he was still a nervous country boy scarred by years of hard traveling, a proud, brooding soul with a burning ambition. Possessed of a raw and surging talent, he also had a certain awesome sense of that talent's brief intensity. He was dying, and he knew it.

From his room at the Manger, Jimmie placed a call to Peer. In the same offhand manner that was becoming his professional style, he mentioned that he happened to be in town and allowed as how he might spare some time to make another record or two. To his credit, Peer seems always to have taken Jimmie with a certain amount of humorous detachment, and not a little sympathy. Of course, he had seen the sales reports, and he clearly had business on his mind that November afternoon when he heard Jimmie's jaunty Mississippi drawl at the other end of the wire. But surely Carrie wrote with rare perception— and telling honesty to both parties—when she commented that "underneath that painfully casual drawl, he must have sensed [Jimmie's] repressed eagerness, wistful longing—even fear."[27]

Prompted by a mixture of commerce and compassion, Peer agreed to arrange a second recording session. "We'll have to take a run over to the factory, in Camden," he told Jimmie, and called Victor to schedule the event for the following week. It proved to be a decision of paramount importance, for out of that session would come the one big record that catapulted Jimmie Rodgers into national prominence and established him as "America's Blue Yodeler." The successes of that early, eventful session led to a sequence of recordings which altered and shaped the patterns of emerging hillbilly music, materially contributing to the legitimization of the genre in the canon of American culture.

His confidence substantially bolstered, Jimmie took the train down to Philadelphia, where Peer met him and drove him to the swank Walt Whitman Hotel in Camden. In a rehearsal hall that evening they got together to plan the next day's session, and Peer quickly discovered problems. "When we went over his new selections," he wrote later, "I found them mostly incomplete or not properly timed. We worked hard far into the night getting enough material in shape. . . ."[28] Despite Jimmie's earlier assurances that, given time, he could have "dozens of songs" ready, the limited, if not downright impoverished, condition of his repertoire was now obvious. He had written to Carrie's sister, Elsie McWilliams, in Meridian, asking her to help him with some "original ballads for future recording" ("I know you can do it as you write up stuff for your church programs"), but she'd not yet had time to respond.[29] Finding suitable songs presented difficulties for Rodgers throughout his professional career, and he often found himself scrambling to produce "original" material to fill the demand. Although sóme 83 percent of the Blue Yodeler's recordings carry his name as composer or co-composer, he actually wrote very little of the material, and was always dependent on a variety of random sources—his sister-in-law, amateur composers, Tin Pan Alley hacks —for suitable songs.

The meagerness of Rodgers's own resources is borne out by the fact that three of the four songs recorded at the second session were written by others. Jimmie's sole contribution was included not because Peer was impressed with it, but only because it was needed to fill the fourth side. "Actually, we did not have enough material," Peer said, "and I decided to use [one] of his blues songs to 'fill in.'"[30] The song, of course, was "T for Texas" (which Peer released as "Blue Yodel"), and it became, significantly, the big hit of the session. But even the Blue Yodels were garnered from communal sources; exactly how much of "T for Texas" originated with Jimmie Rodgers is open to question. At the time of recording, "Mother Was a Lady" was intended to be offered for copyright as a Rodgers composition, under the title "If Brother Jack Were Here." Just who came up with the song is not certain, but Jimmie had probably learned it years before and convinced Peer (and perhaps even himself) that he'd written it, or at least "fixed it up" from traditional and therefore copyrightable sources. When the record was released eight months later, it turned out to be an old show tune still under license to Joseph Stern and Edward B. Marks, who demanded royalties and threatened to sue. Peer learned a lesson from this experience, and thereafter he kept a closer eye on the "original material" proposed by his star. "Jimmie would bring in some famous old minstrel song and just do it word-for-word, and of course I'd stop that immediately. I'd say, 'You didn't compose that.'" Although later Peer claimed that "we never had one of them challenged, successfully or otherwise," he obviously chose to forget "Mother Was a Lady."

Peer had hoped to begin recording at the first of the week, but it was now obvious that Jimmie needed more time to rehearse and prepare the new songs that his presumptive manager and publisher had to provide on the spot. If Rodgers lacked a repertoire, he was at least a fast learner; it helped, too, that the material Peer provided could hardly have been better suited for him. Whether by pure luck or by virtue of professional instinct—probably a combination of both—Peer settled on "Away Out on the Mountain" and "Ben Dewberry's Final Run," both of which came from composer-performers he had known during his days at Okeh. "Away Out on the Mountain," by Kelly Harrell, might well have been a lyrical account of Rodgers's own odyssey into the Land of the Sky, with its rugged lofty slopes; "Ben Dewberry" was a railroad tragedy song, a sort of "Casey Jones" out of "Wreck of the Old 97," by the Reverend Andy Jenkins, Atlanta's blind preacher and balladeer. It was familiar ground to Jimmie Rodgers, and Peer was surprised and delighted to find that in less than a day Rodgers had made the song his own, quickly polishing and assimilating the material into his natural idiom. The recording session was rescheduled for Wednesday afternoon, November 30, in Victor's famous Studio 1, in the former Trinity Baptist Church at 114 North Fifth Street in Camden. There, as is frequently pointed out, such luminaries as Stokowski, Toscanini, John McCormack, and Sir Harry Lauder were also recorded.[31] On the morning of his second appearance before the Victor microphone, Rodgers was preceded in the studio by Fred Waring and His Pennsylvanians, recording that current sophisticated rage, "I Scream, You Scream, We All Scream for Ice Cream." But of course Waring's Pennsylvanians wore tuxedos, even in the studio.

The four sides which resulted from Jimmie's session are quintessential Rodgers, standards which remain deep in the consciousness of three generations of fans. Together, "Ben Dewberry's Final Run," "Mother Was a Lady," "T for Texas," and "Away Out on the Mountain" constitute a capsule representation of Rodgers's entire career in both manner and material—a railroad song, a sentimental ballad, a blue yodel, and a rambling man's whimsical paean to the haven of his dreams. All four were delivered with the verve and clarity that were uniquely his, distinct from all other performers past and future. It was ground Jimmie Rodgers would cover again and again, sometimes differently, occasionally better, but never more authentically.

Lyrically, "Ben Dewberry's Final Run" is typical of dozens of accounts of railroad wrecks set to music, almost formulaic in its design and strategy, and reminiscent of Newton and Seibert's "Casey Jones" (1909) in many words and phrases—"put your head out the window, watch the drivers roll," "we may reach 'Frisco [Atlanta], but we'll all be dead," and especially the verse:

> Casey Jones said just before he died:
> "There's two more roads that I'd like to ride."
> Fireman said, "What could that be?"
> "The Southern Pacific and the Santa Fe."[32]

Jimmie had ridden them both, but preferred the names of two lines more deeply rooted and immediate in his own experience. Lacking Andy Jenkins's original lyrics, one cannot cite Rodgers's contributions with any certainty; had they been substantial, he would probably have shared in the copyright credit, as commonly happened later on. But obviously the "old Northeastern" replaced the Southern Pacific because the NO&NE was Jimmie's favorite, and the rhyming "Santa Fe" in the original was emended to "A&V" (Alabama & Vicksburg), a minor branch line which only those who'd labored on it, as he had, would be inclined to preserve in song.[33]

Rodgers's recording of the song provided the first evidence of his developing skill with the guitar, in strong contrast to the plain, merely adequate accompaniments on the Bristol sides. He'd clearly been spending time in the woodshed, learning to "make that old guitar obey." Of course, he was never an accomplished, orthodox musician; technically unconventional, largely self-taught, he simply over-powered the instrument and brought it under control as an organic extension, like the yodel, of his singing voice. On "Ben Dewberry" his exuberant guitar work supplants the yodel entirely as lyric embellishment, marked by the driving runs that were to become his trademark—the flamboyant progressions, the heavy, mellow bass beats, an overall sense of dominance and control. To be sure, confidence is the earmark of these Camden performances. His poise is further attested to by the length of the session and number of takes: where he'd required seven takes and almost two-and-a-half hours to record two sides in Bristol, four were recorded at Camden in about the same time. None required more than the two takes which were routinely made in those days to provide a protection copy. In one instance—oddly enough, "Mother Was a Lady"—the first take was considered good enough for release.[34]

Although he recorded several of them over the years, Rodgers's "mother" songs were never particularly distinguished. "Mother Was a Lady" is no exception. He probably did not know it well—"jovial" is pronounced "jo-full," "approaching" comes out "frotching," and there is other evidence of haste. While his rendition is suitably straightforward (any excess would have been a disaster), the song itself, despite a certain moldy charm, is mawkish and unrealistic, typical of the late Victorian period in which it first appeared and probably sentimental even by the standards of 1896. But Rodgers never flinched in the face of sentimentality, and often he succeeded in making it work for him. In 1934 one of the song's composers, Edward B. Marks, spoke realistically when he said, "I believe that our popular music, after some 25 years of comparative wishy-washiness, is going to come back to the vitality of the '90's. Perhaps the ballads of those days, 'After the Ball,' 'My Gal Sal,' 'Take Back Your Gold,' 'A Bird in a Gilded Cage,' 'In the Baggage Car Ahead,' or the two that I perpetrated myself, 'Mother Was A Lady' and 'The Little Lost Child,' may seem absurd and stilted today. But dozens of good scholars have come forth and have said that those same tearjerkers are so typical of what Sig Spaeth calls the anti-macassar period they will be the folk songs of tomorrow."[35] In any event, Rodgers's revival of the maudlin old stage tune, paired with E. T. Cozzens's fine composition, "Treasures Untold," from the following session, found a substantial audience among the millions whose emotional lives still depended upon induced dramatics.

If "Away Out on the Mountain" had been written with Jimmie Rodgers in mind, as is sometimes suggested, the song could hardly have been better suited to his purposes, or more appropriate as an expression of his own outlook, at once whimsical and serious, comic and profound. All too often he'd "packed his grip for a farewell trip" and kissed Susie Jane goodbye; if the land of his dreams was populated by zany animals in a variety sufficient to give Noah pause, it nevertheless embodied the hobo's vision of a place where one could "feast on the meat, and the honey so sweet."[36] The rain and the hail might still come bouncing, but there was a grizzly-bear coat to wrap oneself in, and a love to find, there in the Land of the Sky. Shades of his own past—of Wonderful Western North Carolina and all kinds of north winds and vile snakes and squirrels, so many you can't count 'em. Never mind that the eagle roosted on rocks of something he called "the spontain," or that "love" had to rhyme with "turtle dove"; in Jimmie Rodgers's clear, heady declaration, it was as original as the beavers paddling on walking canes and as natural as love itself. The song was clever and catchy the way a distinctly new tune should be, and yet so authentically "oldtimey" that only a few years after its release an eminent folklorist "collected" it in the wilds of northern North Carolina and proclaimed that, while "I have found no trace of this song elsewhere . . . it bears its own evidence of being a folk song." It might even be, he speculated, "a relic of the days of Davey Crockett"![37]

One cannot know just how popular "Away Out on the Mountain" might have been by itself, but coupled with "Blue Yodel" it sold hundreds of thousands in the original release and brought Kelly Harrell a check for almost $1,000 as composer's royalties for the first three month's sales.[38] The song's initial impact was such that it was "covered" by no less than Nathaniel Shilkret and the Victor Orchestra, among several others, in what surely must have been a jarring juxtaposition of form and content. The song left its imprint on an even more widely known lyric in a similar vein, Harry "Mac" McClintock's "Big Rock Candy Mountain[s]," recorded the following year.

The undisputed hit of the session, and the prototype for a dozen distinctive songs to follow, was of course the song Jimmie called "T for Texas." Issued as "Blue Yodel," it was an amalgamation of old blues stanzas which, in the best traditions of the genre, he had welded together and refurbished into a reasonably consistent narrative of betrayed love and projected revenge. The manner in which the song was received by both the recording company and the public is somewhat curious, however, and suggests a relevant commentary on the continuing debate over "black blues" versus "white blues." While no one could seriously suggest that Jimmie Rodgers was another Blind Lemon Jefferson or Robert Johnson or even Furry Lewis, his performance of "Blue Yodel," insofar as it is a direct, serious, and authentic rendering of the material, is scarcely distinguishable from that heard on dozens of black blues recordings of the time. Indeed, some of the early reviewers were apparently confused about the color of Rodgers's skin. It is true that his guitar is less exotic and his enunciation clearer than that of the fieldhands and gandy dancers he emulates, but the same raw pain is there, the same sense of loss and defeat, the same stoic note of endurance. Above all, "Blue Yodel" manifests the subtle tension that is the core of the blues: at once comic and tragic, burdened and free, soul-prisoned and at the same time purged by the very act of pronouncing one's bondage.[39]

Rodgers's white audiences, however, seem to have heard only the jokes. "Blue Yodel," for all its success, was perceived as a parody, or at best a "novelty song." In pre-release blurbs to its dealers Victor hawked the record as "Popular Song for Comedian with Guitar" and, incredibly, praised the artist for his "grotesque style." In a similarly muddled vein, one reviewer, none too sure of the singer's pigmentation, referred to "his engaging, melodious, and bloodthirsty 'Blue Yodel'"—for of course everyone knows how violent those blacks are, what with their owlhead pistols and switchblades and pearl-handled razoos. The reviewer was Edward Abbe Niles, who, to state the case fairly, was one of the best friends of American folk and popular music of the day, and one of the very few to write intelligently and sympathetically about jazz, blues, and other fledgling forms of recorded entertainment.[40] Niles had broad interests and a generous heart, but the cultural chasm separating his life as a Wall Street lawyer from the raucous country blues and hillbilly wails was often simply too great to bridge. By the time of "Blue Yodel No. 3," he had Rodgers properly categorized ("White Man Gone Black"), but his ill-disguised tone of condescension suggested that he'd merely realized that these were all just good old blackface jokes—and if they weren't particularly funny, well, that was part of the White Man's Burden. Rodgers's "singing and guitaring," he wrote, "are as easy and lazy as ever, but [he] needs a gag-writer, for he is running short of verses." When Professor W. C. Handy, in his boiled shirt and frock-tail coat, wrote, "I hate to see that evenin' sun go down," it was a blues line; but when Jimmie Rodgers sang it, it apparently wasn't. Perhaps the passage of time and the falling away of many class and racial distinctions have allowed us easier insight into the complexities of the situation, yet the suspicion remains that what is musically white or black resides all too often in the ear of the listener. The debate over just what constitutes "blues" will continue, but we could do worse than settle for the simple, ancient definition that Jimmie Rodgers took to heart, and sang about in "Jimmie's Texas Blues": "the blues ain't nothing but a good man feeling bad."

If Ralph Peer's account is to be taken at face value, "Blue Yodel" proved to be the sleeper of Rodgers's second session, recorded more or less as an afterthought to "fill in" because they did not have enough material. Without actually claiming the credit, Peer also managed to imply that he was responsible for naming the piece: "When we recorded the first blues, I had to supply a title, and the name 'blue yodel' came out."[41] The phrasing is vague enough to allow one to think that perhaps Jimmie had some hand in it also. He would not become "America's Blue Yodeler" for some months yet, until, according to Carrie, the billing was suggested by a Washington radio announcer. Billy Terrell indicated that Jimmie was using the term as early as 1923, although it appears that he thought of it then rather casually, as something not particularly unique, but merely descriptive of what he was doing: singing the blues and yodeling between verses. In time, his blue yodels would become, as Bill Malone has deftly put it, "Rodgers' unique contribution to American folksong."[42]

The yodel itself has been the subject of extended interest among fans and scholars alike. Many of the former remain convinced that Rodgers "invented" it, while the latter sort in frustration through complex social flux and unwritten history in search of its true origins. While falsetto vocal embellishments were common in popular music long before Rodgers was born, it is difficult to know which of several likely sources contributed to his assimilation of the device. The possibilities include, at the very least, the classic Alpine warble, the black field hollers and rhythmic shouts of gandy dancers on the railroads, and a yodeling tradition on the popular stage passing back through vaudeville to the roots of minstrelsy as early as 1840, with re-connections at that point in Afro-American culture. A lateral line of influence may have been the American cowboy, who in his romantic manifestations was supposed to be a native yodeler, although the "cattle calls" of Western movies and recordings may in fact owe as much to Jimmie Rodgers as to the yippy-ki-ays of the old cow trails. In all likelihood, it was one or more of its professional forms that attracted Rodgers to the yodel, rather than any immediate experience with it in his native environment (as, for example through the work songs of black railroad laborers). The relationship between Rodgers's yodel and either field hollers or cowboy crooning is tenuous at best. Evidence of cause and effect, influence and reinforcement, is simply lacking.

What really matters about Rodgers's yodel is that, regardless of where he got it, he made it totally and uniquely his own. In the process of assimilation he created an entertainment and artistic phenomenon that captured the public's fancy to a degree rarely equaled in modern show business. Robert Coltman's assessment is worth quoting at length:

> Once Rodgers had recorded his first Blue Yodels, everything changed. His suave, rueful vernacular songs made him the first real people's popular singer, stylistically ten years ahead of his time, breaking the long dominance of golden voice and stage manner. All this was not to be digested at once, and imitators often sounded inane; indeed, the typical Rodgers hit was fragmentary, insubstantial, held together by his wry, remarkable personality and the signature of his yodel. Hearing it, one

catches one's breath as his voice slips mischievously over the break.
Doubtless he was well aware of the yodel's value to his career; virtually
all his songs had it worked in somewhere, and he wore each yodel like
an old shirt, supremely at ease. In his throat it shed its Swiss starch and
its black inversion, the voice blurring upward as easily as water over a
mossy stone, making other popular singers of the time sound as if they
were standing at attention wearing tight-fitting tuxedos. Rodgers'
yodeling is perhaps the simplest type of all, scorned by many yodel
devotees. But what he did with it was magnetic, inimitable, and not at
all easy.[43]

Eventually Rodgers and the yodel would become synonymous to
millions of Americans. In the early stages of his professional career,
however, it was still something less than an indispensable part of his
performances. He did not yodel on the very first song he recorded,
"The Soldier's Sweetheart," and apparently was as surprised as anyone
else that "Sleep, Baby, Sleep," with its lullaby yodel, proved to be the
more popular side of the record. Within eighteen months of its release,
he would claim that "Sleep, Baby, Sleep" had sold more than two
million copies; by that time he'd obviously come to appreciate the
yodel's appeal. But of the first six sides he recorded, the yodel is heard
on only three. With the immediate success of "Blue Yodel" that winter
of 1928, Rodgers became, indelibly, "America's Blue Yodeler." From
then until his death, virtually every record featured the yodel or some
form of falsetto.[44]

Ironically, Rodgers so popularized the yodel that within a decade it
was as dead as Dalhart's disaster songs, killed off by the wretched
excesses of a horde of imitators whom the Blue Yodeler had set to
wailing and warbling from every phonograph and radio. For a time in
the Thirties no country singer could hope to succeed without the yodel;
a dozen years later it was on the scrap heap along with ragtime, bird
imitators, and musical saws, an object of derision among audiences
and performers alike. Eddy Arnold recalled the old gent who drawled,
with a sneer, "Thet demned Jeemie Rodgahs, he taught *everah* country
boy to yodel," pronouncing the final word in a manner that suggested
its proximity to white trash, head lice, and the itch.[45] Today Rodgers's
yodel is the most formidable barrier separating him from unsympa-
thetic modern audiences, but anyone willing to approach his work
on equal terms will soon learn to distinguish between stage yodelers
in Alpine hats and the authentic voice, pure and simple, that speaks
to all human experience.

Jimmie's hopes of returning to Meridian for Christmas did not materialize. The strain and excitement of the second recording session left him weakened and physically vulnerable to the harsh Northern winter. Shortly after returning to Washington, he took a cold which lingered for weeks and brought renewed aggravation to his tubercular lungs. He was always at the mercy of any slight respiratory disorder, and the pleurisy which invariably accompanied a cold made the pain of breathing almost unbearable at times. Alcohol brought a certain temporary relief, but Rodgers, to the extent that he could be considered a drinking man, looked upon liquor as a pleasant garnish to good times, not as medicine. If he took notice of his illness at all, it was to joke that at least it entitled him to "prescription whiskey" and spared him the miseries of Prohibition rotgut that afflicted everyone else. Over the years his consumption would increase steadily, giving rise to stories of alcoholism and debauchery, but in fact he drank only in a failing effort to numb the physical pain and did not enjoy his dependence upon liquor.

Although he was sick throughout December and the Rodgerses were living mostly on Carrie's wages as a waitress, Christmas that year was a happier occasion for the family than it had been in a long while. They were still sharing Sister Annie's small house at 1151 Third Street N.E., in a strange city far from most of their family and friends. But they were together, and things were looking up. Jimmie seemed on the verge of achieving his lifelong ambition to become a professional entertainer, and since the previous Christmas his accomplishments had been only slightly less than spectacular. Within the past six months he had appeared on radio, headed his own band briefly, and made numerous paid appearances. None of these jobs had been exactly big time, but he had certainly gained a wealth of experience. Most important, he had, in little Anita's words, "phonographed for Mr. Victor," not once but twice, and his first record was selling briskly. His optimism finally seemed justified, although there were still the same old money shortages and illnesses to contend with. Carrie as well as Jimmie suffered from the Northern winter, and medical bills drained off any excess that might have remained after food and rent bills were paid.

In January, the arrival of Jimmie's first royalty check further dampened their spirits. While he had envisioned hundreds, if not thousands, of dollars pouring in, three months' sales of "Sleep, Baby, Sleep"/"The Soldier's Sweetheart" brought him a mere twenty-seven dollars "and some odd cents." While there is no way to substantiate Carrie's statement that it later proved to be "the largest royalty statement ever sent out to a beginning solo artist on the Victor lists" (which seems unlikely), it nevertheless represented a sale of about 6,000 records—considerably better than anyone expected of a virtually unheard-of hillbilly singer.[46] But this was little consolation to Jimmie, who'd staked everything on the expectation that his first record would catapult him to immediate wealth and fame. That first royalty check was, in Carrie's words, "a bitter blow to his professional pride." Coming on top of a siege of colds and pleurisy, it put him to bed, "a weary, unhappy figure."[47] He wrote to his Aunt Dora that both he and Carrie had been sick. "Im always down with Cold since I have been up in this country. I make lots of money here but I cant seem to get ahead to save my life." Doctors and drugstores, he said, "get just about all I make here of late."

As usual, he was longing for the sunny South and "some of them good ole turnip Greens" that Dora was raising in her garden. Despite homesickness and depression, a note of the old optimism crept in. Although it was only February, Jimmie was looking ahead. "The good ole summer time is Coming now," he wrote, "and I think my luck will change."

NOTES

1. According to the standard account, the Carters were attracted to Bristol by an advertisement or story in the local newspaper. The strongest evidence is Sara Carter Bayes's letter to John Edwards (Dec. 27, 1955): "So there was an ad come out in the Bristol, Va.-Tenn., paper for all talent to come to Bristol to try out on records. So we three decided to go. . . ." See also Charles Wolfe, "Ralph Peer at Work: The Victor 1927 Bristol Sessions," *Old Time Music*, no. 5 (Summer, 1972). In the Borgeson interviews, however, Peer was quite clear and precise in recounting how he'd learned of the Carters on an earlier trip and made arrangements by mail for them to audition. Although he is not always the most reliable source in such matters, other circumstances tend to bear him out here.

2. *Bristol Herald Courier,* July 24, 1927, p. 3.

3. The address is most often shown as 408 State Street. However, an apparently authoritative article in *Billboard,* Oct. 29, 1966 ("Parking Lot Site Was Scene of Glory," p. 62), gives the number as 410. In all probability, the building encompassed both street numbers.

4. Peer in *Meridian Star,* May 26, 1953, p. 24.

5. See Wolfe, "Ralph Peer at Work," p. 12.

6. See *Meridian Star,* May 26, 1953, p. 24. The extent to which Peer's cleverly engineered newspaper publicity was directly responsible for the discovery of Jimmie Rodgers is a matter yet to be resolved. In his account for the *Star* twenty-six years

later, Peer wrote, "Jimmie Rodgers telephoned from Asheville. . . . He had read the newspaper article and was quite sure that his group would be satisfactory. I told him to come on a certain day and promised a try-out." Yet in the Borgeson interviews—among other contradictory accounts—he implied that he had first heard from Rodgers by mail at the time of his initial scouting trip through the area in June. Close scrutiny of the circumstances tends to substantiate Claude Grant's version, given in the fourth chapter—that Rodgers learned about Peer from the out-of-town musicians who'd gathered at the boardinghouse of Jack Pierce's mother, just across the street from where Peer was recording. There is also reason to believe that Rodgers had gotten some inkling of the upcoming Bristol sessions from the Johnson brothers at Johnson City earlier in the month; but it seems obvious that if he had known the exact date—either from the Johnsons or from reading the first story (July 24)—he would have been on hand when the sessions began, rather than showing up in the middle of the last week. In any case, he and the Entertainers were some ninety miles away, at North Fork, when both newspaper accounts appeared. The group was playing regularly each day and, at the time of the second story (July 27), was presumably in demand for the upcoming weekend dances. Subsequent events suggest the following sequence: Rodgers and Jack Pierce, unaware of any recording activity in Bristol, went there on Monday, Aug. 1 (when the weekend was over and business light at the resort). They got Pierce's father to help them buy a car, and then went to Mrs. Pierce's boardinghouse to spend the night before returning to North Fork. There, from various visiting musicians (who may have shown the news clippings to bear out their stories), they learned of Peer's presence in town. They talked to him the next morning—Aug. 2—and then returned to North Fork that day, gave notice, and played their last engagement that night. The next day they returned by way of Asheville to pick up Carrie and Anita, arriving in Bristol again that afternoon, Wednesday, Aug. 3. It is quite possible that sometime during this period Rodgers did indeed telephone Peer—locally from Mrs. Pierce's on Tuesday, or later by long distance from North Fork or Asheville—to confirm that the group was on its way. In addition to producing the record sessions, Peer was busy with dozens of other details; he could hardly have been expected to remember the pattern of events in exact detail.

    7. In the interview by Glenn Sellers, Claude Grant recalled the date as being Aug. 1, but he was also under the impression that they recorded on Aug.2. In general, his account supports the conclusion that the entourage reached Bristol the day before recording, i.e., on Aug. 3.

    8. *Bristol Virginia-Tennessean*, Aug. 2, 1972, p. 1B.

    9. Later, Claude Grant was pointedly vague about the exact nature of the differences between his brother and Rodgers: "I never will say what, but Jimmie tried to pull a fast deal on him one time and Jack never forgot it" *(ibid.)*. Whatever the circumstances, Jack Grant stands chronicled as one of the few who were immune to Jimmie's charm.

    10. *Bristol Virginia-Tennessean*, Aug. 2, 1972, p. 1B.

    11. *Meridian Star*, May 26, 1953, p. 24.

    12. Claude Grant, interview by Glenn Sellers, June 1, 1975, Bristol.

    13. *Meridian Star*, May 26, 1953, p. 24.

    14. "Sleep, Baby, Sleep" dates back to a stage version composed in 1869 by S. A. Emery. See Robert Coltman, "Roots of the Country Yodel . . . ," *JEMFQ*, 12:42 (Summer, 1976), 91–92. By 1908 it had been issued anonymously as a "yodle song" on the Oxford label (sold by Sears, Roebuck), and about 1918 Ward Barton and Frank Campbell recorded a "new version" for Victor. In 1953, the year when he finally copyrighted it, Ralph Peer recalled the title as "Rock All Your Babies to Sleep"

(*Meridian Star*, May 26, 1953, p. 24). It was an understandable error, but only one of many that indicate his hasty and often less than accurate accounts of events long past.

15. *MHJR*, pp. 108, 109.

16. *Ibid.*, p. 126.

17. *Ibid.*

18. There may actually have been many more fluffed attempts; the number of "takes" shown in the log were only those carried to completion for possible use.

19. *MHJR*, pp. 105–10.

20. Efforts to clarify the conflicting accounts with members of the family and those close to Carrie have met with silence. Elsie McWilliams would say only, "If that's what Carrie wrote, that's the way it was."

21. *MHJR*, p. 122.

22. *Bristol Virginia-Tennessean*, Aug. 2, 1972, p. 1B.

23. Annie Nelson, interview. May 18, 1976, Ft. Worth.

24. Marshall Stearns, *The Story of Jazz* (New York: Oxford University Press, 1956), p. 179.

25. Robert C. Toll, *On with the Show* (New York: Oxford University Press, 1976), p. 354.

26. *MHJR*, p. 148.

27. *Ibid.*, p. 147.

28. *Meridian Star*, May 26, 1953, p. 24.

29. See *America's Blue Yodeler*, 1:14 (Fall, 1953), 2.

30. *Meridian Star*, May 26, 1953, p. 24.

31. One of Rodgers's idols, Gene Austin, had also recorded there—although the song that was to make him famous the following year, "My Blue Heaven," was recorded in New York, and not, as Carrie writes (*MHJR*, pp. 151–52), in Camden. Victor had purchased the old church for recording purposes because of its unique acoustics. See Gelatt, *Fabulous Phonograph*, p. 215.

32. Norm Cohen, in *Long Steel Rail: The Railroad in American Folksong* (Urbana: University of Illinois Press, 1981), concludes that "Ben Dewberry's Final Run" actually represents an older family of texts and tunes than does the popular vaudeville version of "Casey Jones."

33. A badly garbled text of the recorded lyrics, showing "father" for "fireman," "troublous switch" for "trestle and switch," "while she starts to roll" for "watch the drivers roll," and other errors, was published by Peer International in *The Legendary Jimmie Rodgers: Memorial Folio, Vol. II*, 1967.

34. If there was a substantial difference (as there surely must have been) between the acoustics of Trinity Church and those of the warehouse in Bristol, the Victor engineers certainly compensated for it. Except for a slightly better balance between instrument and voice on the Camden recordings, the quality is almost indistinguishable from that of the sides made by field equipment.

35. *Billboard*, Dec. 29, 1934, p. 37.

36. "Away Out on the Mountain," words and music by Kelly Harrell. © 1928 by Peer International Corporation. Copyright renewed. Used by permission.

37. Belden and Hudson, eds., *Frank C. Brown Collection*, III:371.

38. "Kelly Harrell and the Virginia Ramblers," *Old Time Music*, no. 2 (Autumn, 1971), 8. Ostensibly, Harrell's composer royalty was $.005 per record (25% of the 2¢ per record "mechanicals" royalty). At this rate, his initial check represents a sale of 197,000 records for the first quarter.

39. A recent point of view holds that blues songs were all fun and entertainment,

innocent of personal tragedy or serious intent. Jeff Todd Titon quotes Nick Perls of Yazoo Records: "The whole sadness thing about country blues is white publicity bullshit." (See *Early Downhome Blues* [Urbana: University of Illinois Press, 1977], pp. 58–59.) Are we to believe, after all, that blacks really are just a bunch of happy folk who have rhythm? I think not. Even Handy speaks of "the well of sorrow from which Negro music is drawn. . . . It's strange how the blues creep over you" (*Father of the Blues*, p. 149). There's no denying the genuine and intentional humor of many blues lyrics, but it seems to me more nearly accurate to say that some blues are humorous, some serious, and the best a little of both. Today this same serio-comic tone—call it the ironic voice, if you will—defines what is best in modern Nashville heartsongs. Compare the embarrassingly over-earnest moanings of Buck Owens or Bill Anderson with the performances of Willie Nelson and Waylon Jennings, who know it's better if you can grin a little along with your broken heart.

40. For representative samples of Niles's work and relevant comments cited here relating to Rodgers, see *The Bookman*, 67:5 (July, 1928), 565–67; 68:1 (Sept., 1928), 75–77; 68:3 (Nov., 1928), 327–29; 68:4 (Dec., 1928), 457–59.

41. *Meridian Star*, May 26, 1953, p. 24. Asked about the term "Blue Yodel" by Borgeson, Peer said, "That was my invention. I invented that." Yet he knew so little about the series that he insisted that "T for Texas" was not "Blue Yodel No. 1" ("I don't think so—I couldn't tell you what the first one was") and authoritatively stated that "I think I went back and marked them all 'Blue Yodel'—'Blue Yodel No. 1, 2, 3, 4, 5,' so forth *up to 16* . . ." (emphasis added). There were, of course, only thirteen Blue Yodels, including "Jimmie Rodgers' Last Blue Yodel," unnumbered.

42. Malone, *Country Music, U.S.A.*, p. 95. See also Bruce Cook, *Listen to the Blues* (New York: Charles Scribner's Sons, 1973), p. 164.

43. Robert Coltman, "Roots of the Country Yodel," pp. 92–93.

44. The single exception, after Rodgers's second recording session, is "My Blue-Eyed Jane." On at least a dozen others what is heard is not, strictly speaking, the yodel, but a falsetto employed within a hum, moan, or key phrase. Even so, the sound is distinctly his own, the signature that made Rodgers the most unique yet widely imitated entertainer of his time.

45. *The History of Country Music*, radio transcription, 1973. Copy in my files.

46. This figure is based on a royalty of $.0045 per record, the rate reported by both Claude Grant and the Carter Family for their initial recordings. (Claude Grant, interview by Glenn Sellers, June 1, 1975, Bristol; John Atkins, "The Carter Family," *Stars of Country Music*, ed. Bill C. Malone and Judith McCulloh [Urbana: University of Illinois Press, 1975], p. 102.) It is not clear whether this represented the performance royalty, the composer royalty, or both, but there is no reason to believe that Rodgers was to be paid differently. When "Blue Yodel" became a hit that spring, a new yearly contract was negotiated and the percentage was raised substantially, probably to about 1¢ per record. The rate continued to increase each year until the Depression. Minuscule as their first royalties may have seemed to the performers, it was only through Ralph Peer's generosity (and shrewd business sense) that they got any royalties at all. Most early country artists were simply paid a flat fee, or promised royalties which they never received.

47. *MHJR*, p. 154.

7 *February–June, 1928*

"Mr. Victor's Got Lots of Money"

Once more Jimmie Rodgers's blind optimism, voiced with little to justify it except his faith in himself, triumphed over the odds. Before 1928 ran its course, he would broadcast his own weekly radio show from the nation's capital, headline a major vaudeville tour through the South, and make a triumphant return to his hometown. Soon his record royalties alone were earning him $2,000 a month, and he was on his way to fame and stardom.

Rodgers's fortunes had begun to change almost at the very time he wrote to his aunt, complaining that "I can't get ahead to save my life." Although his second record was not scheduled for release until April, Peer and the Victor reviewing committee, impressed by the continuing steady sales of the first one, took another look at "Blue Yodel." Despite earlier reservations about it, the number had developed as the strongest side of Rodgers's second session. Now the executives decided to pair it with "Away Out on the Mountain" and put the record into limited distribution early in February. The initial response confirmed the wisdom of that move, and Peer immediately called Jimmie to arrange a third session, to be held in Camden on February 14 and 15.

Peer's position in the industry at that time was unique. Although an independent businessman, he was, in effect, pioneering in the role of what came to be called, in the Thirties and Forties, an "A&R man," a position more commonly known in the record business today simply as "producer"—the person involved in locating talent and material and pairing the two appropriately, overseeing arrangements, and often directing the actual recording operations from the control booth or studio floor. It was a role that would have vital impact upon the evolving music-and-recording business, and to Peer must go major credit for creating and defining its function. As was the case with his "discovery" of race and hillbilly music, it came about with little deliberation or regard for the historical consequences; but it was clearly the force of Peer's personality and his peculiar combination of talents that made it work.

Like many successful businessmen, Peer was both conservative and innovative. On one hand, he relied on cautious planning and coldly efficient, proven management practices; on the other, he understood the need to take risks and disliked doing things a certain way simply because they had always been done that way. Where the artistic side of the business was concerned, he was ready to experiment, to explore all the possibilities of the music and performer at hand, to avoid settling into some safe routine that the public might soon tire of. With the entertainment world undergoing rapid and dynamic changes, the time was ripe for such a temperament, although eventually it created certain ironies and dilemmas that manifested themselves in the career of Jimmie Rodgers.

One irony lay in the very nature of commercial hillbilly recording and marketing. For all the efforts of those who would try to characterize Peer as the Francis James Child of American Folksong, it was not his interest in native culture but his willingness to take business risks that had first led him to hillbilly music. Paradoxically, the same quality that made it profitable for Peer—its quaint, native (and therefore copyrightable) origins—also accounted for its consequent popularity with modern generations who'd never heard it, or who remembered it only with nostalgic longing. Much of hillbilly music's success came about because it struck people as something "new" and "original"; continuing the paradox, the more successful the music became, the more Peer's capacity for innovation was set at odds with his businessman's instincts never to tamper with a winner. The presence of Jimmie Rodgers helped bring these conflicts into focus, although the dilemma was something Peer came to realize only gradually. He faced it in various fashions, and with varying results, over the years.

In a business where sticking with any successful formula, however vapid and moldy, has become a way of life, Peer's continuing demand for something fresh was a radical, sometimes even dangerous departure. Like any method that seeks to be creative and original, it was not always successful. But it worked more often than not, and despite occasional aesthetic flubs it created, without particular design or intent, the vital atmosphere in which Jimmie Rodgers's latent, unique talents might develop and flourish. At first neither Peer nor Rodgers knew what Jimmie was capable of; Rodgers had some ideas of his own, but they were as yet unformed. Peer stood ready to deal with them in whatever shape they might emerge, but meanwhile he went ahead with his own perceptions of his new protégé's situation.

One such perception stemmed from the fact that Rodgers's first six sides had been recorded solo. Peer felt it was time for Jimmie to try recording with accompaniment, for the sake of variety if nothing else, and he urged him to locate suitable musicians for the third session. In view of the "mismatch" he had detected between Rodgers and the Tenneva Ramblers and his initial feeling that Rodgers performed best alone, it is interesting to note how soon after Bristol this decision was reached. Also puzzling is the fact that Peer was about to leave on another field trip and knew he would not be present at the session to approve Jimmie's accompaniment or to oversee the recordings. One inevitably concludes that Rodgers was not really being "handled" in any strict sense, and that Peer's instructions about accompaniment may simply have been in the form of some vague suggestion for future consideration. In any event, Jimmie took him literally and began to spread the word among his few scattered contacts around Washington that he was looking for instrumentalists.

Through the grapevine, the news reached a draftsman and part-time musician named Ellsworth Cozzens. An acquaintance of Cozzens had met Rodgers in a local music store and, learning of his interest in locating musicians, arranged to introduce him to Cozzens and another guitarist, Julian Ninde.[1]

Ninde, originally from Colonial Beach, Virginia, was the son of a country doctor. While working as a clerk in the State Department during World War I, he had acquired an interest in string music from a co-worker who had constructed a three-stringed "guitar." This led to a brief series of mandolin lessons, but Ninde was uncomfortable with the wrist motion required by a flat pick. Finding himself also more inclined to memorize tunes than to read from music, he gave up formal lessons and turned to the standard guitar, playing by ear and using a

Ralph Peer at the prime of his career.

It's the same song, with different labels. The original issue (*above*) was withdrawn after a few weeks, when Marks and Stern threatened to sue for copyright infringement. Copies of "If Brother Jack Were Here" are now rare.

Jimmie inscribed this professional pose to accompanist J. R. Ninde following their February, 1928, recording session.

Rodgers's early accompanists, Ellsworth Cozzens (*seated center*) and Julian R. Ninde (*seated right*), with other members of the Blue and Gray Troubadours in Washington, D.C., 1924. Others in the group are Harry Angell (*seated left*) and Buck Moore, Charlie Smith, Lou Gramlich, and "Doc" Stats (*all standing*).

Coat and tie set aside, Jimmie relaxes with his new Weymann guitar.

Elsie McWilliams, shown in a recent photograph, reminiscing about the songs she helped Rodgers write. The piano, strewn with Rodgers song folios and other mementos, replaced the one Jimmie left at Lauderdale Springs in 1925.

thumb pick. He had then met Cozzens, a versatile stringed instrumentalist who was equally adept on steel or standard guitar, mandolin, and banjo. A victim of polio in his childhood, Cozzens walked with a limp and carried a cane. Despite his handicap he led an active and quite normal life; during the War he served in the Marine Corps with a four-man recruiting unit which played at fire halls and other local spots to attract recruits. To Cozzens's amusement, people assumed that his limp was the result of a war wound, and he became the glamorous center of attention wherever they played.

When Cozzens met Ninde he was working as a draftsman and estimator for his father's construction business and playing steel guitar in the evenings at a Georgetown hotel. Ninde, meanwhile, had left the State Department and gone to work for a Georgetown sand and gravel company. The two men became fast friends, sharing mutual interests in hunting and fishing as well as in music. During the early Twenties they joined an informal Georgetown group which called themselves the Blue and Gray Troubadours, playing together on evenings and weekends mostly for fun, occasionally booking dances and other local events for pay. The Blue and Gray Troubadours apparently had few professional aspirations; of the group, only Cozzens and Ninde ever recorded, and their recorded performances are limited to the six sides on which they accompanied Rodgers.

During their first practice session, Jimmie learned that Cozzens had composed several songs of his own, and since he was short of material as usual, he expressed an interest. Jimmie himself had been working diligently on several blues-and-yodeling songs (strictly speaking, they were not yet Blue Yodels), and had also received a batch of material from his sister-in-law, Elsie McWilliams. From these varied sources the three musicians culled eight or ten of what they considered to be the best numbers. After only two or three practice sessions Jimmie pronounced the group ready, loaded them into the old Dodge touring car, and took off for Camden. They lodged, in true Rodgers style, at the swank Walt Whitman Hotel—at Victor's expense, of course.

It is difficult to explain Ralph Peer's absence from this very important third session. There Rodgers would more than double his previous output, recording for the first time with accompaniment and backed by what was, essentially, a pick-up band. Peer was by now aware of Jimmie's sales potential (if not entirely convinced of his artistic merits), and the very fact that the accompaniment was Peer's idea indicates that he was anxious to guide his new discovery and provide him, at some expense, with suitable support. Certainly he had not forgotten Jimmie's misguided attempts to record with the Tenneva Ramblers, nor was he unmindful of the shortcomings of Rodgers's repertoire. Yet somehow he was content to let Jimmie not only pick the group, but also prepare whatever material was at hand and select the numbers to be recorded. The only explanation seems to be that Peer's field trip to Memphis and Atlanta had already been arranged, and there was no way for him to change his schedule. Moreover, he surely left knowing that, regardless of the results of the session, he would exercise final judgment over whatever was to be released. Perhaps he had already sensed that the roots of Rodgers's artistry were deep in some luminous essence of his fevered frame, transcending matters of mere musicology; or perhaps he simply felt that a weak song now and then, or an occasional fluff or error in timing, didn't really matter much. Jimmie was, after all, only a "hillbilly singer," however much he might think himself in the mainstream of show business. Had he been an up-and-coming operatic tenor, or even one of the new radio crooners, he would undoubtedly have been given more attention. As it happened, he was left in the care of Peer's wife.

Anita Glander Peer was also her husband's secretary; consequently, she had considerable knowledge of recording operations. She knew little about this new so-called hillbilly music, however, and had little interest in it. She was even less prepared to cope with the likes of Jimmie Rodgers, an upstart, unpredictable Southerner who alternately charmed and teased her, smelled of perfume, camphor, and drugstore booze, and in general took a seemingly casual approach to what she considered to be the serious business of making records.

The initial session was scheduled for 6:00 p.m. on February 14, but it was delayed for almost an hour while Jimmie looked for a fruit stand where he could buy some lemons, which he had taken to sucking on, along with a sip of bourbon, to clear the phlegm from his throat before each performance. Finally maneuvered by Mrs. Peer to the studio, Rodgers, Cozzens, and Ninde—later dubbed "The Three Southerners" on the record labels—were introduced to the recording engineer and told that they had only a few minutes in which to tune their instruments and warm up. "Shoot, son," Jimmie said, "we're ready to go. This train been building steam all mawnin'."

Their hasty rehearsals had pointed up the same problems Rodgers encountered whenever he tried to perform with other musicians. An individualist to the core, and much more concerned with the general "feel" of the thing than with strict matters of timing and pitch, he was apt to launch into an unrehearsed guitar run or add extra measures at the end of a line, to the total frustration of whoever was trying to follow him. Like most of his later accompanists, Cozzens and Ninde were taken with his outgoing personality, his exuberance, and his optimism, and they happily suffered along. "The foul-ups didn't bother Jimmie," Ninde said later, bemused by the recollection. "He simply wasn't aware of them, and went cheerily on his way to the end of the song."

They had picked one of Cozzens's compositions, "Dear Old Sunny South by the Sea," to start the session. With Jimmie merely strumming along on the uke behind Cozzens's emphatic steel and mandolin leads and Ninde's strong second on guitar, it went well—so well, in fact, that the first take was later chosen for release. But as the evening wore on, Jimmie tired and began to have increasing difficulties with timing. Before each master take, which was recorded directly onto the wax disc, numerous tests were made in order to determine volume, tone, and microphone placement. Eventually Jimmie's more blatant errors were showing up not only on the wax tests, but in the middle of a master as well, requiring the take to be scrubbed and started over. Years later Ninde's most vivid memory of the evening was of Anita Peer standing at the studio window, clenching her fists and wincing each time they "messed up" and had to begin again.[2]

Ruffled by neither Mrs. Peer's nerves nor his musicians' discomfort, Rodgers plowed on through the evening's schedule—"Treasures Untold" (another Cozzens song, destined to become a standard in the Rodgers canon), "The Brakeman's Blues," and "The Sailor's Plea"—despite repeated fluffs and lost beats. After several masters had been ruined in mid-record, the annoyed engineer came out of the control booth and sternly reminded them that the discs cost fifty dollars apiece. To this Jimmie replied with a grin, "That's all right, son. Just turn 'em over—Mr. Victor's got lots of money!"[3]

The next morning they were back in the studio to record four more sides, all written (or compiled) by Rodgers. The first, "In the Jailhouse Now," would become, in Carrie's words, "a surprise hit everywhere—even though it had been done for years."[4] In those days Rodgers was still a long way from being the Father of Country Music, as the original sheet music for "Jailhouse" clearly indicated. Bidding for a popular audience, the cover labeled the tune a "fox trot" and depicted a very uptown sheik and flapper behind bars. It was, as Archie Green has written, "obviously non-rural in design and appeal . . . directed at an urban audience more accustomed to 'red hot' fox trots than to barn dances."[5] "Jailhouse" became one of the earliest "crossovers"; cover recordings were made by several commercial orchestras and jazz bands, including Boyd Senter and His Senterpedes (on whose version are heard both Jimmy and Tommy Dorsey). "The tune is out of meter and we had a little trouble getting it ironed out to my satisfaction," said Senter, adding, "but it sold as well as most of my records,"[6] which in those days were immensely popular. *Variety,* reviewing Senter's cover of "Jailhouse," praised it as "sizzling blues."[7]

The three other sides which Rodgers recorded that morning— "My Lovin' Gal Lucille," "Memphis Yodel," and "Evenin' Sun Yodel"— were all clearly in the mode of "Blue Yodel," obvious attempts to capitalize on the earlier song's popularity. "My Lovin' Gal, Lucille" and "Evenin' Sun Yodel" would in fact be released as "Blue Yodel—No. II" and "Blue Yodel No. 3," respectively, starting a chain of sequels that would not be completed until "The Women Make a Fool out of Me" was recorded at Rodgers's final session in May, 1933. Renamed "Jimmie Rodgers' Last Blue Yodel," it was released in December, seven months after his death. (The title was not only appropriate as a grim, and marketable, reminder that the Blue Yodeler was gone, but it also avoided the macabre necessity of assigning the next number—thirteen—required by the sequence.)

Although Ninde was present at the morning session on February 15, he did not play on any side recorded that day; Rodgers probably felt they'd satisfied Peer's request for accompaniment, and he was more at ease with his own guitar for the remaining numbers. Cozzens accompanied Jimmie on two sides, playing a somewhat subdued banjo on "Jailhouse" and steel guitar on "Lucille." Although the steel takes only one break, it provides a subtle reinforcement throughout, and distinguishes "Blue Yodel—No. II" from "T for Texas" sufficiently to counter the occasional complaint that "all the Blue Yodels sound alike." Throughout, the series would reflect widely varying arrangements, accompaniments, and approaches.

When they'd finished in the studio, the trio visited some friends of Ninde's in the area; later that evening they entertained informally at a country club outside Camden, appearing as "Victor Recording Artists." On the way back to Washington after the performance, Jimmie, who'd had his full share of lemons and bourbon, went to sleep in the back seat. The old Dodge had no heater, and the chill winter air brought on a coughing spasm so severe that Cozzens and Ninde were afraid he might die before they could get help. But Jimmie convinced them it was nothing unusual, and finally, with the help of more whiskey, he brought the coughing under control and went back to sleep.

According to Ninde, he and Cozzens were each paid twenty-five dollars and their expenses for the trip to Camden, and Cozzens was to share in the composer royalties for "Dear Old Sunny South by the Sea" and "Treasures Untold." Later stories allege that Cozzens sold one or both songs outright for a nominal fee and subsequently came to feel that he'd been taken advantage of. Such tales are contradicted by both Ninde and Dorothy Devers, a longtime friend of Cozzens, who insisted that he continued to receive royalties for several years and always looked with pride and satisfaction on his brief collaboration with Rodgers.[8] In later years Cozzens apparently became something of a recluse, which may partially explain rumors of his disaffection. In a 1959 interview Peer noted that "Treasures Untold" was "a pretty big seller, and time went along and this fellow Cozzens just simply disappeared. We've never been able to locate that fellow. I think there's quite a bit of money due him if we could possibly find him."

Rodgers's association with Cozzens and Ninde appears to have been as amiable as it was short lived. On one or two occasions Cozzens took Jimmie to activities of the Blue and Gray Troubadours; but there was simply no place in the group for the Singing Brakeman, whose musicianship was at best erratic and whose finest performances were solo. It mattered little to him anyway, for the general release of "Blue Yodel"/"Away Out on the Mountain" in April brought national recognition and placed him in the front ranks of the entertainment world. That month his second royalty check arrived from Victor; it amounted to more than $400 and reflected the sale of some 100,000 records, mostly of "Soldier's Sweetheart"/"Sleep, Baby, Sleep." Today, with extensive advertising campaigns, disc jockey promotion, and network television exposure, 100,000 records would be a creditable sales figure for the first six months of any artist's career. In that primitive era it was nothing short of phenomenal.

Back in December, billed as "The Singing Brakeman," Jimmie had begun a series of weekly broadcasts over Washington's WTFF, radio station of the Fellowship Forum. WTFF was a low-power, minor league operation, on the air for only three evening hours four days a week, but it provided Jimmie with local exposure and useful experience. More important, it helped him live down the debacle back in Asheville, when he'd written home to Meridian that he was a radio star, only to find himself out in the cold within days. Now, with more than a little confidence he could write Dora Bozeman that he was "the Monday nite feature on Radio Station W.T.F.F." and send back heady word of his success to the Meridian papers. One account, with strict fidelity to the American Dream, was actually headlined "Ex-Local Boy Making Good." Said the story,

> Jimmie Rodgers, formerly of this city where he helped the NO&NE run passenger trains to New Orleans and back, is making quite a hit in the radio broadcasting field, having his program broadcast from practically every large station. Jimmie is quite an expert on every kind of a stringed instrument, [and] has written several songs and made several records for the Victor Company, the sales of his records topping the list, and yet Jimmie doesn't know one note from the other, playing all his music by ear. . . . It is predicted by the Victor Co. that he will be the yodeling headliner of the country within a very short time.[9]

If some of the details were a bit vague, the exaggerations were innocent enough. That would show 'em, all right; Jimmie Rodgers was indeed, at long last, Making Good.

For the WTFF broadcasts, in addition to plugging his own records and trying out new material, he dipped into his shaggy repertoire of old vaudeville standards, unearthing such chestnuts as "Jeanie," "The Daring Young Man on the Flying Trapeze," and "There's Going to Be a Hot Time in the Old Town Tonight." Also heard were a liberal sprinkling of current hits, including Gene Austin's "My Blue Heaven," then at the crest of its popularity. Austin's 1925 recording of "Yearning" had been one of Jimmie's favorites, and now, as a fellow Victor artist, Rodgers followed the crooning tenor's career with even greater interest.

Despite recurring bouts of illness, Jimmie continued to work local dates around Washington throughout the spring, appearing at luncheons, in neighborhood theaters, before fraternal organizations—

anywhere a paying crowd might gather. With the general release of "Blue Yodel" in April, he began advertising himself as "America's Blue Yodeler." Although he had used the term in a casual fashion earlier, it probably became his major professional billing at the suggestion of a WTFF announcer, Ray McCreath, who had ambitious plans to become his manager and book a nationwide tour.[10]

Meanwhile, the popularity of his records continued to grow. Carrie's brother, Nate Williamson, drove up from Meridian that spring for a visit, and Jimmie took him on a tour of the city. Years later, Williamson recounted the experience in his stately Southern drawl: "That, you see, was before I really knew he was destined to be a famous man. Jimmie invited me to get in the car with him and take a ride in downtown Washington, and as we drove through the streets rather slowly, in every block his voice would come from a music house, sometimes from more than one music house in the same block. I'd never heard anything that way and . . . of course, I learned that's why he wanted me to take the ride with him, just to let me hear how the whole city was listening to Jimmie Rodgers." A few weeks later, back in Mississippi, Williamson and his wife left for a drive to the Gulf Coast. "As we rode along, at the break of day and before the rising of the sun," he recalled, "my attention was directed to almost every farmhouse—it was his voice and his yodeling, such as I'd heard in Washington. It came from almost every house. I knew then he was destined to be great."[11]

The same notion was beginning to occur in Camden. By the middle of May, with four Jimmie Rodgers records on the market, Victor executives discerned that their vagabond yodeler from Mississippi was about to set a new sales record for the quarter, and they issued a call for—as Carrie put it—"more—more—more!" Accordingly, Peer arranged to hold a session in New York during the last week in May. "We want to do eight or ten numbers this time," he told Rodgers, and the ever-enthusiastic Jimmie eagerly assured him that he was ready.

But of course he wasn't. The spirit was more than willing, but the repertoire was weak. He had on hand three or four songs which Elsie McWilliams had sent from Meridian, hastily scribbled off and annotated, in response to an earlier call for material; however, since Jimmie couldn't read the music, he had been able to "work out" only one of them, "The Sailor's Plea." Now he needed more songs, and he needed Sister Elsie to teach them to him.

Elsie McWilliams hesitated. Her own family always came first; with three small children and a husband to look after, she was in no particular mood to go traipsing off to Washington. Moreover, she wasn't at all sure she'd be able to come up with the kind of material Jimmie wanted and needed. But, after thinking it over, she agreed. Helping Jimmie Rodgers out of tough spots had become something of a habit in her family.

NOTES

1. Julian R. Ninde, Sr., interview by Armand Beard, May, 1975, Annandale, Va.; Beard to NP, Oct. 6, 1975.

2. *Ibid.* Peer himself apparently took a more relaxed view of the random hazards so common in the earlier days of recording. Charters recounts an incident which occurred during a Memphis field trip the previous year: a session of Will Shade's Memphis Jug Band was interrupted by Charlie Williamson, who walked into the studio and plopped his stiff derby down on the piano in the midst of a take. "There was a hollow bang when he put it down and Son [Shade] was sure the test was ruined. He looked at the control-room window and Peer was standing there laughing at the whole scene. Victor issued 'Stingy Woman Blues' anyway, with the incidental noises by Charlie Williamson." Charters, *Country Blues*, p. 76.

3. Ninde, interview by Beard, May, 1975, Annandale, Va.

4. According to Bill Randle, a version of "Jailhouse" was being sung on the radio as early as 1922 by Ernest Rogers, former *Atlanta Journal* reporter, stage star, and pop recording artist. See Randle, "History of Radio Broadcasting and Its Social and Economic Effect on the Entertainment Industry" (Ph.D. dissertation, Western Reserve University, 1966), p. 420. See also *MHJR*, p. 186.

5. Archie Green, "Commercial Music Graphics: Nine," *JEMFQ*, 5:14 (Summer, 1969), 60.

6. Boyd Senter to NP, Apr. 7, 1975.

7. *Variety*, July 24, 1929. The number was also covered by such diverse talents as the Memphis Jug Band (recording as "The Memphis Sheiks," Nov. 21, 1930) and Gene Kardos's Orchestra (Apr. 7, 1932).

8. Ninde, interview by Beard, May, 1975, Annandale, Va.

9. *Meridian Star*, undated clipping in the papers of Mrs. M. G. Harvey.

10. *MHJR*, p. 158. The exact origins of the phrase cannot be pinpointed, but Rodgers probably used it casually in some form prior to moving to Washington. While Carrie gives McCreath credit for promoting it, she also implies (p. 92) that she had thought of using it as early as Asheville. Billy Terrell's account indicates that Rodgers was calling himself a "blue yodeler" as far back as 1923.

11. Interview, Jan. 8, 1975, Meridian.

8 *June–August, 1928*

Hitting the Stars

Over the phone, Elsie McWilliams's voice is bright and immediately cordial, although she has no idea who I am, or may be. "Why, of course," she says, "you just come on out here and we'll talk. Be glad to see you."

I have visions of some poor old lady—she must be close to eighty—very lonely, a shut-in perhaps, desperate for company, anxious to reminisce and relive the past. But something in her voice tells me it isn't that way at all. When I ask what would be the best time for me to come, she says, "Why, just any time at all. Any time you can catch me here. I have lots of errands to run, things to look after all over town, and there's always folks in and out around here, but you just come on anyway. We're always glad to see the Jimmie Rodgers fans. You just come any time."

The house is a colorless bungalow on a terrace above the street, in a neighborhood that is not so much run-down as simply taken for granted. Fifty years ago, in Jimmie Rodgers's time, it was a new and thriving addition; now the sidewalks are cracked and the hedges go unclipped and the small, single-family dwellings are beginning to show their age. I identify my destination by the neat sign above the door of the screened-in porch: "E. R. McWilliams." The initials, of course, are those of Mr. McWilliams—Edwin Richard, or "Uncle Dick," as he is known around town. For more than forty years he carried a badge and gun for the City of Meridian; he loved to dance, charm the ladies, and tell funny stories. A tough, gentle man, once he was described as the sort who'd invite you into his house and say, "If you spit on the floor at home, why, spit on it here." He was one of Jimmie's favorites, and whenever Rodgers was in the area Dick McWilliams traveled around with him as "bodyguard," drinking companion, and fellow prankster. Now, as I will shortly learn, he lies in the front bedroom, crippled and mute, slowly dying.

I knock several times. Although I am expected, it is clear that no one is anxiously awaiting me. I hear a radio playing; eventually, after another of my raps, the volume is lowered and finally the door is opened. She is thinner than I imagined, but I recognize Mrs. McWilliams from photographs dating back twenty years. For an instant she peers at me without expression, a wary housewife prepared to cut off the spiel for potato slicer, encyclopedias, insurance. But when I introduce myself, the smile is there immediately, and the warmness in her eyes. She comes out to open the door of the porch, talking a steady stream. She's been sitting with her husband, he's sick, you know, but he loves the radio and likes to have someone sit with him, this place is just a mess but come on in anyway. This afternoon she has to pick up some things at the store and run errands, but we'll have a nice long chat, let me light the heater in this front room and we'll sit there. But first come across the hall and meet Mr. McWilliams.

Afterward, in the crowded, comfortable parlor—the very room itself is overstuffed—we talk about Jimmie Rodgers and Elsie McWilliams. She has told the stories over and over through the years, for I have read or heard them all before, practically word for word, but her voice and her manner are as fresh as if the year were 1928.

"Nothing would do but that I go to Washington," she says, recalling that spring. "I had already written three or four songs and sent them up there, but he didn't take anything but 'The Sailor's Plea.' He said, 'I don't have no musicians up here that can do 'em right. I want to hear you play 'em and sing 'em, so I'll know what I like, and how they're supposed to be done.'

"So nothing would do but I come up there. When he called that time, he said, 'They tell me I've got to have four songs ready for recording in New York at a certain date.' Says, 'Sis, get me four songs and come up here and sing 'em to me. I'll pay your expenses and all.' Well, at the time, my children were all well, and school was out, and everything. So I said I would."[1]

In the meantime, Ray McCreath had persuaded Jimmie to take him on as "personal manager" to arrange show dates and publicity. Although their association would prove to be short lived, McCreath had resigned his job at WTFF and was devoting full time to promoting "America's Blue Yodeler." His grandiose plans included network radio performances and an extensive personal-appearance tour across the nation.

When she left Meridian in mid-May, Elsie McWilliams expected to be away from home for only a week or so. After spending several days in Washington "woodshedding" the new numbers with Jimmie, they left for New York, accompanied by McCreath, who planned to do advance work along the way. In Manhattan, however, they learned that Ralph Peer had been called to Chicago by the illness of his mother. He left instructions for Jimmie to have Carrie and Anita join them in the city and vacation at Victor's expense until he could return in a few days. It was the family's initial taste of luxury, their first tangible evidence that the hard times were finally over, and they made the most of it. Carrie, troubled by the terse wire that summoned her, had hurriedly left her waitress's job and rushed up on the train, expecting to find Jimmie suffering a relapse, possibly near the point of death. Instead, he met her with a sly grin and a new blue Buick, in place of the battered Dodge that had been in the family since Bristol. They toured the city, took in Coney Island, ate in the best restaurants, and generally reaped the pleasures of the nation's greatest metropolis at the pinnacle of its glory, in the days before the Big Apple withered under bureaucracy, tax burden, and urban blight. "We just settled in at the Manger Hotel," said Elsie McWilliams, "and had a good time, doing the very best things you could imagine, and enjoying life."[2] Finally, after a week, Peer wired and told them to go back to Washington; his mother had died and he would be unable to return as planned. The session was rescheduled for the middle of June in Camden, and Jimmie and Elsie were instructed to have four additional songs ready by then. Elsie resigned herself to a long stay up North.

Back in Washington, she recalled how Jimmie had talked of his family and early life as they drove along on the trip to New York. Moved by his close attachment to his father, she composed "Daddy and Home" from things he'd said about "the best friend I ever had," the man who "tried to bring me up right." Similarly, Jimmie's recollections of his railroad boardinghouse days in the Crescent City inspired "My Little Old Home Down in New Orleans" (although, as in the case of other numbers she helped with, Elsie did not receive credit for it). Other songs had random origins. "Mississippi Moon" was Elsie's attempt to match the effort of a friend who had written a similar ditty entitled "Alabama Moon."[3] Her fascination with the name of another girlhood friend, Haydee, resulted in "My Little Lady." ("I'd never heard that name before; it just stuck with me," she said, "so I decided to make a song around it.") "Lullaby Yodel" was "just another cradle song; his first one ["Sleep, Baby, Sleep"] had been so popular, and I wanted something similar to it." To her surprise, Jimmie's heartfelt rendition of "Lullaby Yodel" convinced many of his listeners that it was autobiographical. "They would say, 'Oh, it's too bad—his wife left him and took the baby,'" she remarked later, laughing. "I said, 'Law, I was just writing a song.'"[4] But the incident illustrates what lay at the heart of the Rodgers phenomenon, the unique quality that was to shape the nature of his place in entertainment history, his image both public and private. Taking raw material from varied and often unlikely sources, he synthesized it, made it completely his own, and delivered it with such utter conviction that time and again his audiences transferred what he sang not only to his own life but to theirs as well. To many, Jimmie Rodgers made "sincerity," "honesty," and "heart" the compelling forces of country music.

In contrast to the origins of "Mississippi Moon" and "My Little Lady," inspiration for the other remaining songs—"My Old Pal" and "I'm Lonely and Blue"—was more generic and less immediate, derived as they were from the great stock of professionally composed sentimental ballads and love songs in vogue since the 1890's and before. Asked about influences upon her, Elsie McWilliams is typically vague: "Oh, I've always had music around the house— records playing or the radio on. But I don't know that I paid attention to any of it before Jimmie got me interested in it."[5]

Line by line, note by note, day and night, Jimmie and Elsie—"the music-factory," as Carrie called them—hammered out songs. It was hard work and serious business, for despite the casual, sometimes cavalier approach that Rodgers affected for public consumption, he was a perfectionist, and his instincts were those of a professional in the strictest sense of the word. As Carrie has written, "when working out any composition of his own, words and music, he refused to be content until it 'sounded just right.' If a phrase, a measure, seemed to lack free emotional swing, he worried it to rags; and then, figuratively, sewed the rags up again until it 'fit his ears.'" As she pointed out,[6] he had no rules but his own—formal musicology would have "crushed the spontaneity, the whimsical charm that was the really vital part of that singing Irish heart of his." Yet in adhering to the standards and demands of his own "natural music," he was an exacting craftsman, a true maker in the precise and unconventional manner of an instinctive poet. "He blandly ignored the matter of rhyming unless it 'just happened,'" wrote Carrie. "He would even change the pronunciation of a word if necessary for more pleasing rhythm. He scorned alike context, subject sequence and all the tenses; sometimes even the genders! And plurals and singulars got themselves gaily tangled up continuously. No matter. Did it sound right? That was all that mattered to Jimmie Rodgers, minstrel. He wanted to be sure that voice and strings expressed his moods perfectly; told the stories he had to tell, whether carefree and rowdy or heart-throbbingly tender." If Carrie's prose occasionally warmed to a blush, her perceptions on this point were accurate.

With the addition of "Never No Mo' Blues" (Elsie's one attempt to try her hand at Rodgers's yodeling blues form), they had, on the eve of their departure for Camden, the required eight songs. Carrie prepared an elaborate dinner to celebrate, and Jimmie, feeling his oats, whirled her around the table, brandishing his guitar at the same time. "With you and my old guitar," he called out, "I'm gonna hit the stars," punctuating the outburst with a yodel. Carrie brushed him away with a laugh, calling the rest of the family (they were still living with Annie and Alex Nelson) to the table. But the musical wheels kept turning in Elsie's head, and while the others ate she turned back to the piano to work out the song that soon developed as "You and My Old Guitar." They went to Camden the next day with nine songs instead of eight, Elsie having suffered a cold dinner in solitude as the price for her compulsive inspiration.[7]

It seems unlikely that Jimmie and Elsie gave much thought to the overall nature of their joint efforts, or that they were conscious of any new departure evolving out of it. As far as they were concerned, they were merely mining a familiar lode, often (as with "Lullaby Yodel," "Never No Mo' Blues," and others) deliberately attempting to duplicate what had already proved successful. Yet there is a distinct tone to the Rodgers-McWilliams material which sets it apart from what preceded it and, to some degree, from what was to follow.

"Domesticated" seems a reasonable term to describe it, for in contrast to the earlier jailhouse ditties, railroad tragedies, hobo songs, and blue yodels, the numbers written or co-authored by his sister-in-law and recorded at Jimmie's fourth session all show a marked involvement with syrupy love songs and sentimental serenades to home and hearth. The real difference, however, lies less in subject matter than in execution.

"Never No Mo' Blues" is a case in point. Although she probably contributed to several blue yodels, Elsie would never allow her name to go on them, for she considered the idiom rather crude and impolite. "I helped him straighten them out," she said, laughing, "but I didn't want my name on them. I've always been mighty straight-laced. Sometimes he'd say something in there that I didn't think I wanted my name to."[8] "Never No Mo' Blues" was the sole exception, because it was mostly her creation. Significantly, in contrast to Jimmie's raw and sometimes faintly bawdy blues, with their maverick stanzas and driving exuberance, "Never No Mo' Blues" emerged as little more than an innocuous farewell to faded love, organically unified and carefully polished. That, perhaps, is the distinguishing note of the Rodgers-McWilliams material: it was, in several senses of the word, "composed," betraying the smooth and steady but all-too-removed hand of the songwriter. In this respect is resembles uptown efforts to write folksongs, as opposed to the more natural and authentic sources of Rodgers's earlier material. Modeled as many of them are on New Yorkish notions of what rural music should be, such titles as "Mississippi Moon," "My Old Pal," "You and My Old Guitar," and "I'm Lonely and Blue" are barely run-of-the-mill even by Tin Pan Alley standards, although still superior in their own way to much of the hokum that professional hacks would later palm off on Rodgers and Peer.

As a songwriter, Elsie McWilliams had her limitations; her lyrics are derivitive, commonplace, and occasionally downright banal on the page, only slightly removed from "moon-June-spoon-tune" clichés. At the same time, hers was a fertile and lively imagination, coupled with wide-ranging interests and a natural affinity for narrative that gave her songs a force and cohesion often lacking in Rodgers's own work. If she was not a writer of great songs, she surely produced material that compares favorably with better-known professional efforts of the day—"Jeanine" from *Lilac Time* (1928), for example, and the cowboy kitsch "written in Manhattan by men from Indiana," as John Updike put it, obviously thinking of writers like Hoagy Carmichael and Cole ("Don't Fence Me In") Porter.[9] Even Fats Waller was capable of a line such as "your heart has changed its mind," which would surely draw knowing smirks if sung by any country artist.

Ultimately, Elsie McWilliams's greatest virtue as Rodgers's collaborator arose from her unique position as a member of the family: she knew where Jimmie's native instincts lay, understood his strengths and weaknesses, and possessed the insight and the ability to direct her talents to reinforce his. As a result even her most mediocre efforts—"I'm Lonely and Blue," for example—become, through his handling, substantial achievements. Judged solely on the basis of their lyrics (the words as sung, rather than on the page), several of the recordings from the fourth session—"My Old Pal," "My Little Old Home Down in New Orleans," "Daddy and Home," "Lullaby Yodel," and "Never No Mo' Blues"—are as good as any Rodgers ever did. At least one, "My Little Lady," has become a classic. All were immediately popular with his audiences and sold well.[10]

The Rodgers-McWilliams collaboration was ultimately short lived—he recorded only one of her songs after 1929—but her contributions played an early and vital role in shaping the direction of his career. "A few other artists have recorded some of my numbers since Jimmie's passing," she wrote in 1953, "but no one has ever seemed to understand the spirit behind the songs and make them reach the hearts of the people like he did."[11]

In May, 1928, Jimmie Rodgers's fourth record—"Blue Yodel—No. II"/"Brakeman's Blues"—was released, and by midsummer his royalties were averaging over $1,000 a month. For Jimmie, who'd confidently predicted success all along, it was only the beginning, but Carrie still found it difficult to believe that their hard times were over. Although he'd finally convinced her to quit her job at the tearoom, she worried that she might have to go back anytime. What Mr. Victor had given he could likewise take away, and Jimmie, careless as ever with a dollar, was spending money as fast as it came in, buying cars, clothes, and any gimcrack that caught his eye. Carrie took small comfort in the fact that he was as generous with everyone else as with himself, and she carefully hoarded that half of his income which had always been hers, against the inevitable day when it would all be over.

As Jimmie Rodgers prospered, so did those around him. Victor's net profit for the second quarter (April-June, 1928) grew to $1,270,686, on sales of almost $10,000,000—a net gain of $226,436 over the corresponding three months of the previous year. Profits for the first six months of the year amounted to almost $3,000,000, up more than $1,000,000 from the first half of 1927.[12] Just how much Rodgers contributed to that success is a matter of speculation, but his role must have been substantial, in view of the fact that Ralph Peer's copyright royalties for the second quarter alone soared to almost $250,000. Peer's earnings were in fact so phenomenal and sudden that, to mollify Victor and avoid drastic taxes, he quickly found it necessary to form several wholly owned corporations to disperse the profits. "As I collected these copyrights," he explained later, "I'd divide them [among the corporations] on the recording sheets, which was just a device, not to cover up exactly, but at least not make it too obvious that I was taking out large sums of money." From this procedure was spawned, among others, Southern Music Publishing Company, Inc., which eventually was to become the flagship of the Peer organization. By the end of the year Southern Music alone was so profitable that executives in Camden were pressuring Peer to sell it to Victor, which they viewed as the "parent company" and thus entitled to both profits and a managerial voice.[13] Victor itself closed out the year with a net income of $7,269,523—only slightly below its peak in the mid-Twenties, before radio and the talkies had become serious competition.

In assessing the probable impact of Jimmie Rodgers upon the fortunes of those who'd undertaken to promote him, one must acknowledge that Victor's operations were wide and diverse, and hardly subject to wild fluctuations because of the presence of any newcomer, however auspicious his debut. After all, classical music was still what mattered in Camden. Victor's Red Seals were the firmament, and Caruso, although long dead, the only True Star.[14] Far beneath, on the popular scene, Whiteman and Waring and Gene Austin continued to rule, and below them were a dozen or more studio standbys, old hands like Vernon Dalhart, Frank Luther, and Johnny Marvin, who were not about to be dislodged by some yodeling yahoo out of the boondocks, no matter how well his records sold. Similarly, Rodgers was only one of many artists in Ralph Peer's stable, and there is not much evidence to suggest that at this stage Peer thought of him as anything more than a somewhat fortuitous discovery, one who probably wouldn't last long once the initial novelty had worn off. ("The professional life of a recording artist is never more than three years," he'd told Jimmie at the second session.) It seems hardly a coincidence, however, that Victor could report its best sales in several quarters at the very time of Jimmie Rodgers's debut, or that Ralph Peer, after only three Rodgers royalty statements, would suddenly find himself with more money than he knew what to do with. Rodgers was proportionately a greater asset to Peer than to Victor, but both would soon find him a major source of income in the uncertain times ahead. Unfortunately, their financial relationships in later years cannot be charted with any accuracy; after 1928 Victor was absorbed by RCA and no longer issued separate profit-and-loss figures, while Peer's affairs were steadily submerged in the machinations of an international conglomerate.

With his professional star ascendant, Rodgers was now beginning to count among his social acquaintances a number of prominent show business personalities. In New York in May he'd met one of his longtime idols, Gene Austin, and discovered that they had a great deal in common. Although Austin was younger and had come to fame much sooner, they were both Southerners, and both had had show business in their blood from an early age. Born in Texas and reared in Louisiana, Austin had led a life every bit as tumultuous and eventful as Jimmie's. At fifteen he ran away from home to join a circus; he later rode with Pershing's expedition into Mexico, and served as an army bugler in France during World War I. Before he was old enough to vote, he'd gone to college, formed his own dance band, and embarked on a career in show business. By the mid-1920's he was an established vaudeville performer, a popular recording artist, and the composer of such standards as "How Come You Do Me Like You Do" and "When My Sugar Walks Down the Street." He had even taken a brief (and largely anonymous) fling into hillbilly music a few years earlier, accompanying Blind George Reneau and Uncle Am Stuart on several sides. Over the years he'd become something of a fixture around the recording studios, turning out sentimental ditties like "A Boy's Best Friend Is His Mother" and covers of popular hits such as "Yearning," which had caught Jimmie's attention. "My Blue Heaven," which he'd recorded for Victor the previous September shortly after Rodgers's debut in Bristol, had finally catapulted him into the big time, and he was currently at the height of his popularity.[15]

Jimmie's acquaintance with Austin was renewed in June, when the latter came to Camden not long after Jimmie's fourth session to complete a series of recordings he'd begun there earlier with a popular whistler named Bob MacGimsey, from Louisiana. The following month Austin and his wife brought down from New York their new $25,000 yacht, fittingly christened *Blue Heaven*. Sailing it up the Potomac to Washington, the Austins hosted a Fourth of July picnic for Jimmie and Carrie aboard ship.

As two of the top recording artists in the country, Rodgers and Austin had reason to celebrate. "In the Jailhouse Now," released in April, was climbing to third on Victor's Ten Best Sellers, ahead of records by Whiteman, Waring's Pennsylvanians, Frank Crumit, Johnny Marvin, and even Austin's current hit, "Ramona," which, with an advance sale of 400,000, had already earned the artist $50,000 in fees and royalties.[16] Over plates of Carrie's fried chicken their conversation soon turned to business. Jimmie's health had improved with the arrival of warm weather, and he was anxious to capitalize on the growing success of his records with many personal appearances. Peer had talked of a nationwide vaudeville tour, but nothing had come of it. Meanwhile, Rodgers was playing the random one-nighters that Ray McCreath managed to come up with, happy to be working at all. When Austin heard about it, he shook his head. "No use wasting your time with shotgun and neighborhood houses," he told Jimmie. "You can fill a major theater just as easy." That was all the encouragement the eager and always enthusiastic Rodgers needed.

At the time, however, theatrical conditions in Washington were mixed, reflecting trends across the country. Talkies were on their way, but the national craze for sound had not yet hit. Although big-time vaudeville, pressed from all sides and dying of its own inertia, had only a few years to live, the five major Washington theaters open that summer—the Fox, Loew's Palace and Columbia, and Stanley-Crandall's Earle and Metropolitan—continued to book what were known as "vaudefilm" bills. These consisted of first-run pictures, still mostly silents, alternating with live entertainment. Strictly speaking, it was not vaudeville in the traditional sense, but three or four acts which, although they received individual billing and performed separately, were advertised as a "revue" under some general theme, along the lines of the unit acts known as "movie presentations."

For some months the New York–based Keith-Albee-Orpheum organization, one of the nation's oldest and largest theatrical concerns, had been negotiating with the Stanley-Crandall interests to take over S-C's principal Washington theater, the Earle, at Thirteenth and E Streets, and to reinstitute a policy of straight vaudeville. Near the end of July the talks fell through, and K-A-O resolved to reopen its own Keith Theater in the capital. While discussions with Stanley-Crandall were underway, the Earle had been booking its acts from week to week, resisting any long-range commitments pending the outcome of the proposed merger.[17] Under these somewhat unusual circumstances, with Gene Austin's backing and help from Peer with the New York booking offices, Rodgers was able to secure a week's engagement at the Earle, opening Saturday, August 4.

One measure of Jimmie Rodgers's booming popularity that summer is the fact that in this, his first big-time personal appearance, he was given headline billing above a group of seasoned vaudeville performers. The program—"a refreshing summertime revue" called "Moonlight and Roses"—included Charlie Althoff, a popular oldtime musician and rube comic known as "The Yankee Fiddler"; the Lovey Girls, a teenage sister act; dancer Frank Seifert; and the Kardo Brothers, "The Boys of 1,000 Songs." Master of ceremonies was Joe Bonbrest, a favorite with Washington audiences.[18] It was "four-a-day," with half-hour performances between showings of the feature film, "Home James," starring Laura La Plante.

Two days before he opened, Jimmie went down to rehearse with the house orchestra. Undisturbed by all the hubbub and fancy paraphernalia of a "deluxe house," so calm in fact that his quiet, unassuming manner was taken for shyness, he good-naturedly suffered the hazing of the stage crew, who'd singled him out as a novice. Offered mock-important advice and assailed with endless questions about props and lighting, he won them over by insisting, with a grin, that all he needed was "a box to prop my foot on, and a coal oil lamp."

On opening night, dressed in his brakeman's outfit, the blue jumper and striped cap, his railroad watch and prized heavy gold Albert watch-chain, he went onstage to the orchestra's lively rendition of "Frankie and Johnny," which he'd begun to use occasionally as a theme song. He put one foot up on a wirebacked drugstore chair which the prop master had provided, cradled his new Weymann guitar on his knee, gave the audience a big grin, and promptly captivated them with "Blue Yodel," "Brakeman's Blues," and "Ben Dewberry." They called him back for an encore and wanted more—as the *Washington Post*'s reviewer reported, "Jimmie Rodgers, 'The Singing Brakeman,' would have come back some five times if a certain Saturday audience had had their way about it."[19] But the show had to stay on schedule. Still, Jimmie took his hurried bows with the high elation that comes only to a performer who knows he's knocked 'em dead. There would be other appreciative audiences throughout the week, and more opportunities for lengthy encores once the show had loosened up.

Despite Jimmie Rodgers's personal success, however, the box-office business for the week was only mediocre, Washington sweltered in the heat and humidity of high summer, and attendance was down at theaters all over town. *Variety* attributed the falloff to a number of factors: in addition to the weather, there was a notable lack of strong features in town, and the Earle had only recently enjoyed a successful vaudefilm run that had been held over until its regular audience began to dwindle, reducing "carry-over" for the new bill.[20]

To Jimmie, however, his week at the Earle was nothing short of a triumph. Aside from a substantial salary, he'd gotten star billing and what amounted to rave notices from the newspapers, and the exposure would soon lead to an even bigger and more protracted engagement. There was, finally, a certain happy symmetry in the timing of his national debut. As Carrie was quick to note, it had come one year to the day after he'd crossed State Street in Bristol to record for Ralph Peer.

NOTES

1. Interview, Jan. 4, 1975, Meridian.

2. *Ibid.*

3. Obviously not the same "Alabama Moon" as that copyrighted by George Hamilton Green in 1920.

4. Interview, Jan. 7, 1975, Meridian. In a similar vein, when asked about the origins of "The Sailor's Plea" (her husband served in the army during World War I), she said, "I was just writing a song. I'd never known any sailors."

5. *Ibid.*

6. *MHJR,* p. 58.

7. Interview, Jan. 9, 1975, Meridian. See also the *Chicago Sun-Times,* Jan. 1, 1976, p. 74.

8. Interview, Jan. 4, 1975, Meridian.

9. John Updike, *Rabbit Redux* (New York: Alfred A. Knopf, 1971), p. 124.

10. Exact sales figures are missing, of course, but the best evidence available from several informed sources suggests that sales of Rodgers's first twenty or so releases—down to the beginning of the Depression—fluctuated between 250,000 and

500,000 copies. Original issues bearing the Rodgers-McWilliams sides are among those most commonly seen today, further attesting to their popularity.

11. *America's Blue Yodeler*, 1:4 (Fall, 1953), 3.

12. *Variety*, Aug. 8, 1928, p. 49.

13. Charters (*Country Blues*, p. 62) asserts that "In January, 1928, [Peer] and Victor set up the Southern Music Publishing Company to handle the copyrights for much of the company's music. The capital came half from Peer and half from Victor." In the Borgeson interviews, however, Peer gave a detailed account of the history of Southern Music and insisted that "I used $1,000 to start Southern Music, and that's it."

14. For the first time in their history, however, Victor's Red Seal records were in a decline. See *Variety*, Oct. 10, 1928, p. 53.

15. For a brief account of Austin's career, see Roger D. Kinkle, *The Complete Encyclopedia of Popular Music and Jazz, 1900–1950* (New Rochelle, N.Y.: Arlington House, 1974), II:524–25.

16. *Variety*, June 27, 1928, p. 57.

17. *Washington Post*, Aug. 4, 1928, p. 16. See also *Variety*, June 6, 1928, p. 31, and Aug. 8, 1928, p. 32.

18. Carrie wrote (*MHJR*, p. 180) that "Jack Pepper was master of ceremonies for the Earle." However, as publicity and reviews clearly establish, Pepper (of the team of Salt and Pepper, and later married to Ginger Rogers) had already ended a lengthy run there, plagued by recurring illness. It is possible that he was still around during Rodgers's rehearsals, but Bonbrest handled all m.c. duties during the engagement. See *Washington Post*, Aug. 5, 1928, p. 2A, and Aug. 6, 1928, p. 14.

19. *Washington Post*, Aug. 6, 1928, p. 14.

20. *Variety*, Aug. 15, 1928, p. 9.

9 *August–December, 1928*

"The Old Marster's Been Mighty Good to This Mississippi Boy"

Jimmie Rodgers's engagement at the Earle was heady stuff, but his week of "four a day" in the nation's capital left him physically and emotionally drained. An option with Stanley-Crandall provided for an extended tour of the chain's neighborhood theaters around Washington, but Jimmie was in no condition for the hectic pace and continued strain. After a few appearances he gave up the tour for a much-needed rest.

In the year since Bristol he had had precious little time to relax, enjoy the rewards of success, and take stock of what was happening to him professionally. The money rolling in from record royalties was a clear enough indication that he'd arrived; now bundles of fan mail arrived every day, and scrapbooks began to bulge with press notices. More flattery came in what was proverbially its sincerest form—other artists began to cover his hit records, adding to both his composer royalties and his stature in the entertainment world.[1] In September his own recording of "Blue Yodel"/"Away Out on the Mountain" was released in England to favorable reviews and surprisingly strong sales, marking the beginnings of an international following that would grow in scope and intensity through the years. By that time the Rodgers-McWilliams records, with their distinctly different flavor, were further expanding Rodgers's appeal in the United States.

Following their marriage, Alex and Annie Nelson had purchased a home on Abbey Place, N.E., in Washington, with the intention of turning over the Third Street house to Jimmie and Carrie. But with summer now passing and despite all his professional options, Rodgers was certain of only one thing: he wanted to avoid the rigors of another Northern winter. He was also getting itchy feet; rarely had he stayed in one place for as long a period as they'd spent in Washington. Accordingly, he and Ray McCreath began to make elaborate plans for a tour of one-nighters across the country. Jimmie sat for a new professional photograph by Apeda in New York; the famous pose of him in street clothes, polka-dot tie, and straw boater, cradling his 00-18 Martin was incorporated into handbills and newspaper advertising mats heralding the colossal "Coast-To-Coast Tour of America's 'Blue Yodeler' IN PERSON!" Offering "A Program Of The Greatest Variety and Filled With Entertainment and Surprise," Rodgers was to perform with "His Company of Entertainers," although it was clear from the beginning that he had no intention of carrying along any additional acts. Instead, he planned to book local talent, trusting to luck that they'd be professional enough to suit his needs.

Initially, the best McCreath could come up with was a meager string of dates in small independent theaters through the Carolinas, Georgia, and into Florida. But such a tour would mean doing what Jimmie liked best—playing and singing to small-town audiences at their downhome, everyday simplest—and it would at least pay the expenses and provide a reason for getting back to his beloved Southland. He was all set to start out when Ralph Peer called with important news.

Although a personal management contract was a customary part of his initial agreement with each new artist, Peer never showed much interest in the day-to-day routine of overseeing the progress of their careers outside the recording studio. In the early days Rodgers had tried various small-time agencies or would-be managers; in addition to McCreath, he'd been booked by the Henry F. Seal Agency in Washington and by Paul Dempsey of the Herbert Hooey office in New York, and there later followed a virtual parade of figures who were nominally, but only briefly, his "agent" or "manager." Rodgers never hesitated to act on his own when the chance presented itself, and gradually he more or less took over the business of booking his own tours and personal appearances. Peer was generally contented with this arrangement, stepping in only—as in the case of the Earle booking—when he felt the situation was important enough to require his attention and clout. Of course, he remained ready to exploit any major opportunity to promote his new star, who, as he realized that summer of 1928; was growing increasingly restless and dissatisfied in Washington.

Peer therefore set to work with the New York vaudeville agent Jack Adams and, after several weeks of negotiations, managed to book Rodgers into a lucrative spot on the Loew Circuit's "Southern Time" for the coming fall tour. In light of Jimmie's relative obscurity, the chaotic atmosphere then prevailing in Loew's New York booking offices, and the shaky condition of vaudeville in general, this was a major coup. Among the larger vaude "wheels" touring out of New York, Loew's Southern Time was one of the best known and most prestigious, a widely touted road show which played several Midwestern and Northern cities (including Boston, Toronto, and Montreal) as well as Loew's first-class theaters in the South's major cities. To be sure, it was no longer vaudeville in the old, pure sense; in recent years each weekly unit had been functioning largely as a presentation bill for a featured movie, and the decline of live entertainment nationally had caused the tour to be cut to ten cities from sixteen the year before. Nevertheless, as far as Jimmie Rodgers was concerned, Loew's was the Big Time. At a reputed salary of $500 a week,[2] he was delighted to join the bill, scheduled to open in Norfolk, Virginia, on November 5. Peer, who was about to leave New York on an extended field recording trip, also arranged to meet Jimmie in Atlanta later that fall for the latter's fifth Victor session. America's Blue Yodeler was suddenly facing a very busy schedule, and despite the vagaries of his health and Carrie's nagging doubts, that was exactly the way he wanted it.

For good measure, Peer had also made a deal with the Publix chain; Jimmie was to appear in several of their theaters down the Eastern Seaboard, fleshing out the thin itinerary that Ray McCreath had put together. McCreath, one-upped by Peer and foreseeing little demand for his services, went back to the radio business, another name on the lengthening list of "managers" who would come and go in the course of Jimmie Rodgers's career.

The Rodgers family left Washington in mid-September. Planning a long-awaited visit (for which read "triumphant return") to Meridian before opening on the Loew Circuit, Jimmie sent his wife and daughter on to Mississippi by train so that young Anita could start school there. With a hired driver at the wheel of the new blue Buick, he set out to play the "indie" dates and Publix houses that McCreath and Peer had booked, together with other appearances that he arranged himself along the way. In Miami, there was a brief reunion with Gene Austin, and a one-nighter at the Olympia Theater, where on the following Sunday Jimmie entertained, by request, the huge Interdenominational Men's Bible Class. Apologizing that he knew no "church songs," he gave them instead "In the Jailhouse Now" and "Frankie and Johnny," and received a standing ovation. Then it was time to head back up toward Meridian, by way of Atlanta, to meet Ralph Peer and his recording equipment.

Peer's excursion that fall to Memphis, Nashville, Atlanta, and Bristol was to be one of his longest and most productive. In thirty-five sessions in Memphis throughout September, he recorded some of the greatest bluesmen of all time, including Furry Lewis, Ishman Bracey and Charlie McCoy, Cannon's Jug Stompers, Will Shade's Memphis Jug Band, and the legendary Jim Jackson. A week was spent in Nashville recording a number of early Grand Ole Opry performers whose fame on radio at the time outstripped their popularity on records; ironically, barely half the sides recorded there were ever released by Victor, and Nashville was in effect "written off" by the recording industry.[3] In Atlanta, Peer recorded Rodgers, Henry Whitter, Blind Willie McTell, the Georgia Yellow Hammers, the Carolina Tar Heels, and others. The Bristol sessions resulted in new sides by several old hands, including Alfred G. Karnes, Ernest Phipps, the Stonemans, the Stamps Quartet, and a new group called the Smyth County Ramblers; this last was distinguished, if for nothing else, by the fact that it included Jack Pierce, late of the Tenneva Ramblers, and Malcolm Warley, who had taught Claude Grant to play the guitar.

Rodgers arrived in Atlanta almost a week before he was scheduled to record. He checked into the Robert Fulton Hotel and went off on his habitual tour of clubs, dance halls, and "speaks," visiting wherever musicians and entertainers might congregate, making friends and looking over the local talent. On his rounds he ran across a small jazz combo whose sound he liked, and he persuaded them to let him sit in with them and try a few of the numbers he had in mind for his upcoming session. Pleased with the results, Jimmie took a phone number where he could reach them when the time came.

As usual, Peer was receptive to the idea of backing Rodgers with other musicians, and he readily approved the group when he heard them. It was a happy decision, for the records which Jimmie made with Dean Bryan, C. L. Hutchison, John Westbrook, James Rikard, and George MacMillan are among his very best. One can only lament that his association with these musicians was so brief, and that it resulted in only four sides. But those four sides reveal Rodgers at the top of his form, and at least one of them—"Waiting for a Train"—has found an enduring place in the musical consciousness of several generations. Country music purists and culturally naive "fans" of contemporary styles sometimes deride the jazz element in these recordings as dated or corny, but in fact it is skillfully executed and totally authentic, a sound true to its own day and in turn a testament to the agelessness of Rodgers's artistry. To the time-wise, to musicians, and to those who listen for the total performance, this duality is immediate and authentic, a source of brilliance. Admittedly, the flavor that emanates from these recordings is peculiarly era-bound, the musty yellow-gold aura of the late Twenties (a quality so lovingly caught and nurtured by Merle Haggard in his own versions of the tunes). Yet they speak as directly to the modern sensibility as the latest multi-tracked, over-dubbed chart-climber out of Nashville.

The band's power and cohesion is most apparent when they jam between choruses, notably during the break led by Hutchison's cornet on "My Carolina Sunshine Girl" and behind Rikard's clarinet solo on "Waiting for a Train." The brass and reed share a brief but equally wailing outburst on "California Blues" (Blue Yodel No. 4), prompting Rodgers to sound off: "Man, man, let's go to town!" But even more vital is the way this obscure pickup band works throughout to reinforce Rodgers's vocals, shoring him up at every strategic point, floating in strong and solid yet with just the proper restraint. The steel guitar, played left-handed by John Westbrook, deserves special attention, as those lavish but delicate licks behind the first verse and chorus of "My Carolina Sunshine Girl" clearly demonstrate. There's more of the same throughout "California Blues," where the entire band functions, together and variously, in a call-and-response to Rodgers's lyrics and yodel. The mood is clearly infectious, and Jimmie caught it, responding with the uniquely vigorous, free-swinging performances that would engage the sympathies and emotions of millions as few others of his time ever did.

The group had good material to work with. In particular, "My Carolina Sunshine Girl," a substantial success for Rodgers, seems to deserve a better fate than later years have accorded it. Actually inspired somewhere in the Carolinas on his way to Atlanta, the song is perhaps his best composition outside the Blue Yodels (which were, after all, mostly pieced together from fragments which had long resided in the collective blues consciousness). Despite its obvious debts to the hoary Tin Pan Alley laments over the wretched heartlessness of some Southern belle, Rodgers's contribution to the venerable tradition exhibits a certain fresh and compelling quality. Its structure, at least, is unusual; unlike the published sheet music, which indicates a standard thirty-two-bar chorus, Rodgers in his recorded version repeats only the last sixteen bars. He ends the doleful complaint with a slight turn that deftly transforms the mood of his suffering, as he concludes that although "the sweetest angel in this world" has left him thoroughly miserable, he really ought to laugh at her "little old photograph" instead of weeping over her. It took the likes of Jimmie Rodgers to make such a song serious and wistfully humorous at the same time; no one else would do as well until Hank Williams came along twenty years later.

The jazz backing for "California Blues" added still another dimension to the evolving Blue Yodels and demonstrated once again how versatile the form could be in Rodgers's hands. With "Blue Yodel No. 3" just released and doing well in the stores, it was at this point that Peer decided to continue the series indefinitely under its generic title. He began to stockpile likely blues numbers for later issue in the sequence, generally listing them on the recording logs simply as "Blue Yodel #—," in addition to whatever title Rodgers might originally have given them. "California Blues" thus became "Blue Yodel No. 4" and was tabbed for release in February, 1929, as soon as the current backlog of Rodgers-McWilliams numbers had reached the market.[4] It was an immediate hit and became one of the most popular of all the Blue Yodels, so pervasive that it eventually passed into rural tradition and was collected as an "anonymous folksong" by an ambitious but benighted academic, too pure to be tainted by listening to hillbilly music on the radio or records. The professor described it as "a blues song that I have not found recorded elsewhere [that is, anywhere other than his "folk" source], though the feeling it expresses is common in Negro song."[5] He was correct enough in his assumptions about the "feeling," but "California Blues" was not the only Jimmie Rodgers composition to be ignored by the intelligentsia until cleansed and sanctified in the respectable stream of "folksong."

Like the other Blue Yodels, "California Blues" owes its strategy and many of its lines to traditional blues sources, but Jimmie's brassy throwaway in the last stanza ("I can't understand how come you treat me like you do-doodle-do/Now if you don't want me, mama, it's a cinch I don't want you")[6] appears to be a wry nod in the direction of Gene Austin, whose "How Come You Do Me Like You Do?" had been a big hit a few years earlier. Rodgers rarely showed professional jealousy, but Austin remained a minor thorn in his side for several years, until the crooning tenor's popularity waned in the early Thirties.

No doubt the success of "Blue Yodel No. 4" may be partially attributed to its pairing with "Waiting for a Train," one of Jimmie's all-time biggest hits. The original pairing sold some 365,000 copies,[7] second only to "T for Texas"/"Away Out on the Mountain," which ultimately peaked out at close to 1,000,000 records. Later, almost everyone connected with him tried to claim a hand in the composition of "Waiting for a Train," although (as Norm Cohen, D. K. Wilgus, and others have pointed out) the lyrics can be traced back to a stage recitation from the mid-1800's, and there is evidence that Jimmie was singing his own version as early as 1925.[8] Through the years numerous variants and cognates had evolved under such titles as "Danville Girl," "Wild and Reckless Hobo" (or simply "The Reckless Hobo"), and, perhaps the best known of all, "Ten Thousand Miles from Home."[9] In one manifestation the song was rendered in three-quarter time, a version which the legendary Texas fiddler Prince Albert Hunt committed to record as "Waltz of the Roses" (Ok 45375) in 1929. The widespread popularity of versions other than Rodgers's is attested to by the fact that many country musicians today still disagree over the proper time signature, thus accounting for what Dave Evans has described as "probably the low point of my music-listening career": Mississippi bluesmen Skip James and John Hurt trying to perform a duet of "Waiting for a Train" with one playing waltz time and the other 4/4.[10]

Ralph Peer's account of how the song evolved in Rodgers's hands is enlightening for what it reveals of Peer's attitudes about using traditional material and his role in shaping what Rodgers recorded. Despite their earlier run-in with Edward B. Marks over "Mother Was a Lady," Peer apparently trusted his protégé and later insisted that "he could record anything" he wanted to. As for "Waiting for a Train," which Peer admitted is "really an old minstrel song": "Somebody sent him a garbled version, and Jimmie said, 'Well, I know that song.' So he picked up his guitar and he starts to do this thing. Well, Jimmie only knew, I think, two chords on the guitar and couldn't fit the words. So anyway, he had to sing it, and he *didn't* know it—he could only think of about two-thirds of it. Then I found that he couldn't use the old tune because he couldn't play in that key, so he had to change the tune around. It turned out to be a wonderful song—better than the original, actually."[11]

Elsie McWilliams later claimed that she "put music" to the lyrics. Whatever the circumstances of its composition, "Waiting for a Train" was eminently copyrightable. As Peer put it, "It was in the public domain anyway, but the way he changed it, it was obviously a great song. So I didn't hesitate to put his name on it." (Prince Albert Hunt, for one, held a contrary view of the song's authorship; but he was probably wrong, and didn't live long enough to do anything about it, anyway.[12])

Peer was right about one thing: "Waiting for a Train" is a great song. Although Professor Arthur Palmer Hudson dismissed it as "one of many nondescript hobo songs,"[13] its lyrics, whatever their source, are as close to poetry as anything Rodgers ever recorded. Backed by the tightly controlled but appropriately wailing bluesy accompaniment, he delivers the lines with an authenticity born of his own experience, the burnished memory of those many times, not long past, when he'd been stranded alone and far from home, wet and hungry and hustling his way back to Dixie. "Waiting for a Train" also gave Jimmie an opportunity to introduce on records the train whistle so popular with his live audiences. Like his yodel, the whistle was a vocal flourish which could sound the gamut of moods and emotions. On "Waiting for a Train" it is high and lonesome and fading, for all its brevity almost another instrument in the group.

As with the other records he cut during this session, the whole of "Waiting for a Train" emerged greater than the sum of its parts, Jimmie Rodgers and his tatty little pickup band pushing each other further than any of them realized they were going. Together they were good enough to salvage even the weakest of their four songs, the almost embarrassingly bad "I'm Lonely and Blue," which Jimmie had tried and failed to bring off solo at his previous session. With the band's strong, steady rhythm behind him and Westbrook's steel weaving through the lyrics, he gave up the weak falsetto punctuation he'd previously affected, apparently in a misguided effort to strengthen his solo performance and the thin lyrics. Now he met the song head on and turned a thoroughly mediocre ditty into one of the staple love ballads of the day.

In 1928 it was a hard day's trip from Atlanta to Geiger, Alabama, where Aaron Rodgers was living in retirement. But Jimmie hired another driver to take the wheel of his Buick and arrived rested and full of pep, excited by his first visit home in almost two years. Despite the upheavals of his childhood, or perhaps because of them, he'd always been close to his father—"Daddy and Home" had a deeper meaning for him than any of the similar songs he sang. The two of them were alike in many ways, gregarious, happy-go-lucky, full of gentle pranks, Irish sentimentality, and Southern gab. Aaron of course took great pride in his youngest son's rising career, and showed him off grandly among his cronies in the small village of Geiger and relatives in nearby Scooba, Mississippi. For Jimmie it was time to stock up on Southern home cooking, renew old friendships, and sit around making music with the local boys who brought their instruments and gathered wherever he happened to be.

A few days later he was in Meridian, where he could fully savor the sweet smell of his success. Less than two years earlier he'd drifted out of town on the bum, leaving behind a string of bad debts and a reputation not much better. To his harshest critics—and there were quite a few of them—he had been a sickly, no-good yokel who couldn't or wouldn't work to support his family, an idle drifter who had some crazy notion of picking a guitar and singing on records and being in show business. Now he was back, driving a new Buick and wearing sporty clothes, flashing a big diamond ring and showering money and gifts all over town. They heard his voice coming over the radio and on records in every music store, and they read about him in all the papers. "MERIDIANITE WINS FAME AS SINGER, VISITS HOME" was the *Meridian Star*'s headline version of local-boy-makes-good,[14] and although the story didn't quite make the front page (out of spite, some felt), Jimmie bought dozens of papers and spread copies around wherever he went. He was certainly entitled to a bit of self-promotion. In view of how far he'd come and against what odds, he might have been forgiven even an occasional swagger. But while he might boast a bit, arrogance and conceit were never a part of Jimmie Rodgers's style. Considering how the town had treated him, he handled himself with admirable restraint, if not downright humility. "Besides," said one

Good Ole Boy, "if it's true, it ain't braggin'." By that standard, Jimmie Rodgers wasn't bragging—much.

He no doubt took a certain proper satisfaction in proving how wrong people had been about him. Among other things, he was still living down that false start in Asheville. Now there were many ways to settle old accounts, and one of them was in the most literal fashion: he went around town paying all of his old bills, often insisting that interest be added to those that were long delinquent. "When he was down, Jimmie just assumed that the world owed him a living," said an old friend, "and when he was up, he thought it was just as natural for him to pay it back."[15]

First came family. The Williamson, Hunt, and McWilliams households were soon heaped with gifts, as were those of Jimmie's brothers, Walter and Talmage. There were presents for adults as well as an endless stream of toys for nieces and nephews. Where some impulsive purchase alone would not suffice, as in the case of his father and Aunt Dora, a substantial check was tucked in with the bric-a-brac, perfumes, sweaters, and Coney Island souvenirs.

Fans and friends gathered everywhere he went, and he tried to be as free with his time as with his money. He was especially anxious to see old friends on the railroad, but there were simply not enough hours in his busy schedule. "Please say for me that I regret not being able to get around to all my old railroad buddies," he told the *Star*. "My time is so limited that I can't possibly see them all. It's good to be home again and I wish I could stay longer, but I start a tour over the Loew Circuit on Nov. 3rd and must leave for Atlanta Sunday" (October 28).[16]

Atlanta was only a stopover; the tour actually opened at Loew's State in Norfolk on November 5. But Jimmie could hardly be blamed for wanting to squeeze in a few extra days to relax and prepare for the tour. Much as he looked forward to it, boyishly anxious for the footlights and applause of the Big Time, he knew also that Loew's four-a-day would be an exhausting grind.

As the undisputed headliner, he got the prominent position in newspaper promotions and on theater marquees. He was still performing in brakeman's garb and proudly emphasizing his railroad days to interviewers and audiences, yet his billing was invariably "America's Blue Yodeler"; newspaper pictures and theater displays showed him in street clothes, sometimes even in formal dress replete with tuxedo jacket and shiny bowler. Almost never was "The Singing

Brakeman" used in his advertising or publicity (although it reappeared later, amended in one notable campaign to "The *Yodeling* Brakeman"). Perhaps he wanted it that way, or maybe it was simply characteristic of the times. At any rate, this hazy public image was to persist throughout his career, suggesting that Rodgers was never quite sure what his professional stance should be—or that, despite his usual careful attention to detail, he simply wasn't much concerned about his image from one time to the next. He was always reaching for the widest possible audience, and so he may have instinctively avoided any single identity that might limit his appeal. Another explanation is that, in a time before the packaging of stars became both an art and an obsession, the diverse, free-wheeling nature of show business allowed him to appear in whatever guise he might choose. Certainly it made little difference to his audiences, although today one wonders what he might have gained (or sacrificed) with the benefit of modern promotional techniques.

The Loew's bill which Rodgers headlined was a strong, balanced unit. Opened by the inevitable dog act—in this case, Al Gordon's Comedy Canines, one of the best—it included the Three Ryans ("Frolics of the North and South"), comedians Faber and McIntyre, and Frank and Milt Britton's Brown Derby Orchestra, a classy show band specializing in novelty routines similiar to those later popular- ized by Spike Jones and His City Slickers. Rodgers, as the headlined single, appeared in the coveted feature spot, "next-to-close." A Norfolk newspaper was sufficiently impressed to detail just what a sensation he was:

> Jimmie Rodgers, one of the latest recording finds, made his formal debut at Loew's State Monday and won the distinction of being the first recording artist who has ever received a personal stage triumph on a vaudeville bill here. Rodgers appears on the stage costumed as a railroad brakeman, with his guitar, which has won him fame and much cash, tucked under his arm. He sings five songs in a soft Southern voice and yodels parts of them. His Mississippi dialect, which is genuine, charms the audience. Before his third song, a request number, the capacity matinee audience joined in an ovation for the singer whose real ability as an entertainer was undisputed before he had completed his second song. Rodgers' Loew Circuit debut was the most auspicious from every standpoint. He made probably the biggest hit ever put over by a record artist on a vaudeville bill.[17]

The judgment was confirmed by another local paper, whose reviewer called Loew's bill "top-notch, the best this humble critic has seen there." Singling out Rodgers for special praise, the writer noted his widespread fame on records and concluded, "To see him in person and hear him sing is a real treat."[18]

The day after Rodgers opened in Norfolk was federal election day. Loew's added a special Tuesday late show that ran until 12:30 a.m., during which returns from the presidential contest were read from the stage. Like many other Americans, especially Democrats and Southerners, Rodgers viewed the national political scene with somewhat bemused disinterest. Although by instinct and temperament he was always on the side of the underdog, during the mid-Twenties he'd been too busy looking after himself and his family to argue much with "Coolidge Prosperity"; now that he was getting a share of it, he could hardly dispute the popular notion that the Republicans had at least been good for business. Much as he liked Al Smith's stand on Prohibition, Hoover's promise of "two chickens in every pot and a car in every garage" had a happy ring to it—especially for those who, like Jimmie Rodgers, had suffered chicken one day and feathers the next.

The election results indicated that most of the country felt the same way. Hoover carried forty of the forty-eight states, including six in the Democrats' previously "Solid South" (but not Jimmie's native Mississippi). In the electoral college Hoover took 444 votes to Smith's 87. The country revved itself up for four more years of pleasure and profits, and Jimmie Rodgers turned confidently back to his flourishing career. It was a good time to be riding high.

After a week in Atlanta, where Rodgers again garnered rave reviews ("Honors Captured at Loew's Capitol by 'Blues' Singer"),[19] the unit moved to Memphis. There Jimmie received one of his warmest receptions. He was close enough to home to be considered a local boy, and he provided colorful copy for the newspapers. "Yes, sir, buddy, the good old Marster up yonder has been mighty good to this long-legged Mississippi boy," he told one of the many reporters who interviewed him incessantly. "It's a darn sight easier yodeling and plunking my banjo forty-five minutes a day than it was putting in sixteen hours for the railroad. But doggonit, I used to have fun."[20] There was a fervent effort to keep the fun going. Old friends and even passing acquaintances drove up from Mississippi to join the party that went on almost constantly in his dressing room, and Jimmie welcomed them all. "Tell more to come," he announced to the papers, adding, "All you railroad boys want to remember there won't be any observance of Rule G [prohibiting intoxicants] when you come to see me." Said Jimmie, with a wink, "That danged rule always caused me a lot of trouble."[21] On one occasion the festivities spilled over to the composing room of the *Press-Scimitar*, where Jimmie, togged out in his brakeman's outfit, went to look up an old printer friend from Meridian—and, just incidentally, got his picture taken for the evening editions.[22]

Oddly enough, the Birthplace of the Blues had acquired a reputation as a poor vaudeville town. But Memphians turned out in large numbers for Rodgers's performances, and local reviewers recorded their enthusiasm in no uncertain terms:

> Jimmie Rodgers, with some new and some old "blues," breezed into Memphis yesterday for a week's stay at Loew's State Theater, and when Jimmie had finished his first appearance last night there wasn't a cold hand in the house.
>
> Rodgers and his mandolin stopped the show. This boy from the railroad yards, so he says, and his highly censored songs from the same place, won the audience and held it, despite the strong competition from the other acts on the bill.[23]

Memphis had found a favorite, and Jimmie reciprocated by writing a song dedicated to the city, "Memphis Day," which he introduced during a special broadcast over WMC.[24]

The last week in November was free, and Rodgers took advantage of the time off to stop over again in Meridian and to pick up his car and visit with his brother Tal, now a detective with the Meridian police force. Tal got out his mandolin, and the two spent much of their time together on the back porch, having what Jimmie later referred to as "a regular jamboree."

By the time he opened in New Orleans on December 3, some substantial changes were taking place in Rodgers's act. For reasons that he was never very explicit about, he had begun to discard the railroad garb and "The Singing Brakeman" stage tag, instead donning street clothes and placing renewed emphasis on his billing as "America's Blue Yodeler." Songs with broader "pop" appeal—"Blue Yodel," "In the Jailhouse Now," and "Frankie and Johnny"—were

Sunday amusement-page spread in the New Orleans *Times-Picayune*, December 2, 1928, shows the early popularity of "Jimmy" Rodgers, whose 1928 tour on Loew's Southern Time Circuit was given similar attention in major newspapers along the route.

Record sleeves publicizing popular and hillbilly artists were a rarity in 1928. Along with Rodgers (*upper right*), this jacket featured Bud Billings (Frank Luther), the Stamps Quartet, the Carter Family, the Georgia Yellow Hammers, Jilson Setters, Tal Henry and His North Carolinians, and Walter Kolomoku's Honoluluans.

Jimmie and his father remained close through the years, and Jimmie took great delight in introducing Aaron to audiences whenever the two traveled together.

Jimmy Meets a Pal

Jimmie's habit of finding old friends wherever he went is illustrated by this clipping from the *Memphis Press-Scimitar*, November 23, 1928.

The straw boater and figured bow tie were Jimmie's personal trademarks. Smiling and seemingly healthy, he posed for this professional portrait sometime in 1929.

When better cars are built I will buy one
Yours
Yodeling
Jimmie Rodgers

Breaking into the big time, Jimmie bought his first new car, this gleaming 1928 Buick sedan, and exuberantly endorsed it with his own version of the manufacturer's slogan.

replacing the railroad songs in the act, and of course in the Crescent City he sang "My Little Old Home Down in New Orleans," to the wild approval of the crowd. Up to this point he'd alternated among the banjo, mandolin, and guitar in personal appearances, but now audiences wanted to hear the sound they knew from his records, and he began to use the guitar almost exclusively. He still did a railroad song now and then and regaled listeners with stories of his days as a trainman, but "The Singing Brakeman" seemed too much a novelty, associated with the plethora of "singing waiters," "singing messenger boys," and "singing secretaries" (there was even a "singing grave-digger") who were flocking to show business in those days. The tag implied an amateur, some moderately talented workingman who'd merely left the job for a while to warble a few notes. However vague and inconsistent Rodgers's image of himself might have been, he certainly saw himself in more professional terms than that.

Jimmie's popularity in New Orleans is attested to by a huge picture spread in the Sunday *Times-Picayune* that featured him prominently, attired in business suit and fedora and cradling his new Weymann guitar. His photo was surrounded by professional poses of Dolores Del Rio, Jean Hersholt, Charles "Buddy" Rogers, and other famous names whose films or acts were playing in town that week.[25] An interview in the *New Orleans States* was accompanied by a photo of Jimmie in his bow tie and black bowler.[26] Headlines read "Jimmie Rodgers Tops Loew's Bill in Blue Yodeling" and "$1500 a Week Salary for Orleans Brakeman." During the week he was a guest at Tulane University's Side Liner Club Banquet at the Jung Hotel, where he sang several songs and received a standing ovation. As in other cities, his dressing room at the State, on the corner of Canal and Rampart, was packed with well-wishers and old friends, among them the many railroad men, in high positions and low, whom he'd known in his days as a boomer brakie. He hosted what amounted to a floating open house, with the crowd dividing its time between the theater and his suite at the Jung. In the city where only a few years earlier he had walked the streets hungry and out of work, he was very nearly the toast of the town. Proclaimed the *Times-Picayune*, "America's famous singer and yodeler of 'blues' songs, Jimmie Rodgers, recording artist, headlines an all-star vaude-ville program at Loew's State theater this week, and those familiar with his singing hail his appearance as one of the notable events of the current season."[27] In another story the paper observed that his music "derived from mountaineer, Negro, and railroad lyrics," and noted, with rare perception for that time, that "he and his composers are gradually building up an imperishable folk-literature in song in America." Rodgers, the story concluded, was "one of the few yodelers at all worth listening to."[28]

A reporter for the *States* caught him one morning in the Jung's coffee shop having breakfast with the posh hotel's manager, Steve Barco, and G. H. Lehleitner, the Victor representative for the area.[29] As they talked, the strains of "The Soldier's Sweetheart" came from a nearby radio, and the reporter commented on Jimmie's deep drawl. Rodgers replied with the old cliché about taking the boy out of the country but not the country out of the boy, and proceeded to explain "how I happen to be making fifteen hundred simoleans per week and sitting here in the Jung while two years I walked on Canal Street with holes in my shoes and my stomach empty." The ensuing tale was typical of the curious mixture of fact and fiction that was to give rise to so many legends, especially the one about his "overnight success." Recounting his railroad days, he admitted (truthfully enough) that "I was kind of a black sheep and couldn't stick long to a job," touched on his mother's early death "when I was four" (not quite accurate), and told how "the Victor recording manager, R. S. Peer, in New York, heard me over the air and next morning I found a telegram waiting" (created out of whole cloth). The first record, he said, was "one of the best national sellers," and his second—that is, the second to be released, "Blue Yodel"/"Away Out on the Mountain"—"put me ahead of Paul Whiteman and Gene Austin for sales." Neither claim can be substantiated; the latter, although doubtful, at least shows whom he considered the competition and indicates the direction in which he was aiming. The Victor man, Lehleitner, despite his obvious interest in plugging his product, observed merely that the eight Rodgers records then in distribution "rank among the nation's best sellers." More important, he told the reporter, "Rodgers has universal appeal," and the sales figures from such far-off places as England, Africa, India, Australia, and Japan would soon bear him out.

One can only speculate about Rodgers's reasons for propagating the notion that he was "discovered" by Victor while broadcasting on WWNC. Beyond the fact that the tale has certain dramatic, B-film flair, it may simply have been a quick and convenient way to account for his recording debut. In any event, he'd begun to plant the story as early as Norfolk, and it appeared in the December, 1928, issue of the

Southern (Railway) *News Bulletin*, obviously at Jimmie's instigation.
Here he embellished the account a bit by asserting, as he'd hinted
earlier, that he'd been forced out of railroading and into show business only because of "trouble with Rule G." In relating the "interesting story" of "How Jimmie Rodgers came into prominence as an
entertainer," the *News Bulletin* coyly observed, "It seems in his railroading days, between 1918 and 1924, he had quite a bit of trouble
with 'Rule G' (all railroad men know what Rule G is) and he had to
part company with the NO&NE." This was hardly the sort of thing that
a house organ would publish without the subject's approval. Rodgers's
hand in the story is evident further along: "Jimmie says 'Rule G' does
not bother him any more now and he thinks in a few years he will be
able to go back to his old job as brakeman on the NO&NE." There is
no mention of the real reasons for leaving—his health and his
long-standing desire to become a professional entertainer—and that
feeble line about going "back to his old job as brakeman" seems little
more than a tactful gesture for the benefit of Jimmie's acquaintances in
the rail industry. The story ends, however, on an authentic note:
"[Jimmie] extends a cordial invitation to his railroad friends, especially
Southern Railway fellows, who might see his vaudeville act to come
back-stage and give him the latest sand-house gossip and talk shop
with him."[30] It was an invitation he would repeat in many interviews,
and he meant it. His true calling—entertainment—came first, but
while the Singing Brakeman might give way to America's Blue
Yodeler on the stage, in private life he was, as he told the *States*
reporter, simply "a railroad man."

Following New Orleans there was a week at Loew's Houston, where
the tour ended for Jimmie Rodgers. The unit headed north without
him; his spot in *Variety*'s listing for the opening date in Evansville,
Indiana, on December 17 is replaced with the simple notation, "One
[act] to fill." It has been speculated that Rodgers's contract originally
called for appearances in only the five Southern cities on the circuit,
but Peer is on record at the time as saying that he was "booked for
twelve weeks," i.e., the full tour.[31] Turmoil in Loew's booking offices
and the rumored cancellation of the road show may have had
something to do with his departure, but geography and weather seem
to be the most likely factors. Jimmie simply decided that he wanted no
more Northern winters—"up with the ice and snow"—and elected
instead to remain on the balmy Gulf Coast.

In any event, he was not out of work for long. Less than a week after closing in Houston, he did a "guest appearance" with the Paul English Players, a prominent tent repertoire company, and then signed for a limited engagement with the show's coming road season scheduled to open in Mobile. Although a tent show might seem a comedown from the Loew Circuit, "rag opry" had been one of Jimmie's true loves since the time he toured with Billy Terrell. He was also well acquainted with the English show, having attended its performances back in the days when he was a young trainman and would-be performer. Moreover, English offered him what was for tent rep a record high salary, and the show's scheduled opening date after New Year's would allow him to spend the holidays in Meridian, catching up on some much-needed rest. It had been a sensational year, but the strain was beginning to show.

NOTES

1. The first cover was probably Frankie Marvin's "Blue Yodel"/"Away Out on the Mountain" (Br 3979), released during the summer of 1928. Riley Puckett had recorded "Blue Yodel" (Col 15261) in April, but it was not on sale until later that fall.

2. Peer mentions this same figure somewhat vaguely in the Borgeson interviews. In 1928 he was reported as saying that Rodgers was "making over half a thousand a week" for the tour (*Bristol Herald-Courier*, Oct. 28, 1928, p. 1). Interviewed while playing in New Orleans that December, Rodgers himself claimed he was being paid "fifteen hundred simoleans per week" (*New Orleans States*, Dec. 4, 1928, p. 7). Half that amount would seem to be a liberal estimate.

3. For a full account of the Nashville sessions, see Charles Wolfe, *The Grand Ole Opry: The Early Years, 1925–1935* (London: Old Time Music, 1975).

4. The sequence in which the Blue Yodels were recorded and released coincided until early 1931, when the tune that had been recorded as "Blue Yodel No. 8" was rejected and replaced by "Muleskinner Blues," which until that time was listed as "Blue Yodel No. 9" both in Victor's files and on Rodgers's lyric sheet. This accounts for the error in Brian Rust, *The Victor Master Book, Volume 2 (1925–36)* (Hatch End, Middlesex: By the Author, 1969), p. 320, which mistakenly lists master BVE 56617 as "Blue Yodel No. 8." At this juncture the normal sequence of recording and release was resumed. When Victor first began to mine the Rodgers lode after his death, BVE 56617 was dug out and released as "Blue Yodel Number Eleven" (with the number spelled out). Ironically, and perhaps erroneously, it was actually released three days *after* "Blue Yodel No. 12." See Appendix I.

5. Belden and Hudson, eds., *Frank C. Brown Collection*, III:563.

6. "Blue Yodel No. 4," words and music by Jimmie Rodgers. © 1929 by Peer International Corporation. Copyright renewed. Used by permission.

7. See Norm Cohen's introduction to Johnny Bond, *The Recordings of Jimmie Rodgers: An Annotated Discography*, JEMF Special Series no. 11 (Los Angeles: John Edwards Memorial Foundation, 1978), p. vi.

8. See Norm Cohen, "Railroad Folksongs on Record—A Survey," *New York Folklore Quarterly*, 26 (June, 1970), 103 (JEMF Reprint no. 15); D. K. Wilgus, *Anglo-American Folksong Scholarship since 1898* (New Brunswick, N.J.: Rutgers

University Press, 1959), p. 276; interview with Raymond Hall, Mar. 12, 1975, Texas State Penitentiary, Huntsville.

9. Folksong scholar G. Malcolm Laws, Jr., originally (1950) cited "Ten Thousand Miles from Home" (H2) as an "anonymous folksong," but in his revised edition of *Native American Balladry* (1964) he felt obliged to note that "John Greenway . . . *says* that this piece was composed by Jimmie Rodgers, *a popular singer* from 1927–1933, whose phonograph records sold in the millions" (emphasis added).

10. David Evans, "Black Musicians Remember Jimmie Rodgers," *Old Time Music*, no. 7 (Winter 1972/3), 14.

11. Despite his claim that he helped Jimmie "dish it up," in the Borgeson interviews when Peer tried to sing "Waiting for a Train," he began with the wrong word and wrong line ("Starts out with that line, 'A-waiting . . .'" he announced confidently), quickly faltered, and gave it up.

12. Ken Harrison to NP, Apr. 11, 1975.

13. Belden and Hudson, eds., *Frank C. Brown Collection*, III:428.

14. *Meridian Star*, Oct. 24, 1928, p. 8.

15. Confidential source.

16. *Meridian Star*, Oct. 24, 1928, p. 8.

17. Unidentified clipping in the papers of Mrs. M. G. Harvey.

18. *Norfolk Virginian-Pilot and the Norfolk Landmark*, Nov. 6, 1928, p. 9.

19. *Atlanta Constitution*, Nov. 13, 1928, p. 19.

20. *Memphis Press-Scimitar*, Nov. 22, 1928, p. 8.

21. *Ibid.*

22. *Ibid.*, Nov. 23, 1928, p. 2.

23. Memphis *Commercial Appeal*, Nov. 20, 1928, p. 8.

24. "New Memphis Song Is Being Written by Jimmie Rodgers," *ibid.*, Nov. 23, 1928, p. 3. What became of "Memphis Day" has never been learned, but it apparently did not survive long after its initial performance, or ever find a place (as the newswriter suggested it would) alongside "Beale Street Blues," "Memphis Blues," or even Jimmie's own "Memphis Yodel," which had just been released that month.

25. New Orleans *Times-Picayune*, Dec. 2, 1928, sec. 4, p. 1.

26. *New Orleans States*, Dec. 4, 1928, p. 7.

27. New Orleans *Times-Picayune*, Dec. 2, 1928, sec. 4, p. 1.

28. *Ibid.*, Dec. 3, 1928, p. 21.

29. *New Orleans States*, Dec. 4, 1928, p. 7.

30. *Southern* [Railway] *News Bulletin*, Dec., 1928, p. 3.

31. *Bristol Herald-Courier*, Oct. 28, 1928, p. 1.

10 *January–May, 1929*

The Show with a Million Friends

We sat in the living room of Bill Bruner's neat, modest brick home on the west side of Meridian. The previous year Bruner had suffered a serious stroke that left his speech impaired and part of his right side paralyzed. During long months in the hospital and a nursing home, he'd made a slow but substantial recovery, almost by sheer force of will; now he was home, able with the help of a part-time nurse's aide to care for himself through the day while his wife worked in a downtown department store. He was glad to be home, happy to see visitors for short periods of time and to talk about the old days when he was making records for Okeh in New Orleans and New York, touring with tent shows and playing over the radio, billed variously as "The Yodeling Messenger Boy," "The Singing Salesman," and "The Yodeling Ball Player." All too soon there would be lean years as an oil company clerk and then a carpet salesman for Sears, Roebuck, but Bill Bruner was not one to be bitter or maudlin over the unfortunate brevity of his career as a professional entertainer. He had wanted it to go on, of course; but instead of bemoaning the course of fate, he preferred to remember the plush times on the way up—expense-paid trips to the recording studios, stories about him in the trade magazines, the fancy Pullman compartment in which he toured with a big show through the Southwest. The story he cherishes most concerns a guitar—or, to be accurate, two guitars. One is an expensive L5 Gibson that he shows off proudly to visitors. The other was a small Spanish guitar that he gave away more than twenty-five years ago. But that's getting ahead of the story.

The winter of 1929 was damp and chilly across the state of Mississippi. In Meridian, the overcast skies on Groundhog Day foretold a mixed blessing for those who followed Nature's signs. Winter might soon be over, but in the meantime there seemed little prospect for immediate relief from the interminable rain and cold.

That week a convoy of trucks and fancy touring cars, all painted gleaming white, rolled into town through the grey drizzle; the vehicles contained the traveling tent show of the Paul English Players. As the crew began setting up canvas on a lot near downtown, bright posters and a flurry of publicity captured the townspeople's attention, lifting the gloom of the long weeks of bad weather. "Comedy!—Action!—Thrills!" "Extra Added Concert Attraction!" "Big Canvas Theatre—Well Heated!" Any show in town caused excitement, but this one was something really special, for the "Extra Added Concert Attraction" was a native son, and the entire week was to be, as the *Meridian Star*'s headline proclaimed, "Homecoming for Jimmie Rodgers."[1] The town had been hearing about its famous Blue Yodeler ("a local boy making good," one music store actually advertised). Now here he was, making his first professional appearance in his hometown. The legend of the ex-railroader and the magnetism of his music were already exerting their powerful, almost hypnotic, hold on the American public's imagination. The excitement was all the greater in the place where hundreds had (and everyone now claimed to have) known him when he was just plain James C. Rodgers, a rookie brakeman on the NO&NE.

At the time Bill Bruner was a seventeen-year-old messenger boy for Western Union. He'd caught the Jimmie Rodgers fever in a big way, and spent all his spare time strumming a guitar and learning every new Rodgers song as soon as it appeared on record, consciously emulating the style of his idol. Bruner's regular hangout was a cafe near Fifth Street and Thirty-first Avenue; between delivering messages and parcels around town, he loafed there with the regular crowd of coffee-drinkers and picked out Blue Yodels on his cheap guitar. The Paul English tent happened to be just across the street, and during the week of the company's run young Bill spent more and more time at the cafe. Several members of the English troupe, including the show's comic, Happy Gowland, came around regularly, but Bruner had seen Jimmie Rodgers only during the show's nightly performances, each of which the boy had faithfully attended despite the strain on his meager finances. Regular admission cost 50¢, plus 20¢ for a reserved seat and an additional 25¢ for the Extra Added Concert Attraction—in a day when the standard rep show admission was the famous "10-20-30" (10¢ for reserved seats, 20¢ for children, and 30¢ for adults).

On Friday, with a week's pay in his pocket, Bruner decided to treat his girlfriend to the show. The scheduled play had a racy title— "Companionate Marriage"—but nothing else that would bring even the faintest blush to a maiden aunt, and Bill especially wanted to impress his girl by taking her to hear Jimmie Rodgers in person. Given a chance to compare the two, she'd readily see that her beau sounded just like the great Blue Yodeler himself.

They were waiting expectantly for the curtain to rise when Paul English, the impresario himself, stepped out from the wings and raised his arms for silence. A handsome, dapper man, dressed in a tuxedo for his lead in the evening's drawing-room comedy, English was an impressive figure before the crowd of farm families, clerks, and shopgirls. As quiet fell across the audience, English announced that although there had been a slight delay, the show was about to begin. In the meantime, he wondered if there was a fellow named Bill Bruner in the crowd. Heads turned in Bill's direction, and a low murmur rose. Spurred on by his girl's admiring gaze and the applause from friends around him, the surprised youngster managed to stand up shakily and identify himself. English promptly motioned him backstage. There the showman took his arm solicitously. "Some of my company tell me you sing and play like Jimmie Rodgers. Is that right?"

"Well, I try awful hard."

"Do you have your guitar?"

"No, it's at home."

"Can you get it? We'll send you in a cab. Jimmie is too sick to go on, and we want you to take his place. Will you do it?"

Bill hesitated. "Don't you want to hear me first?"

"Happy Gowland has heard you. The comedian over there. He was in the restaurant today while you were playing. He says you sound just like Jimmie, and I'll take his word."

Still in a daze, Bruner found a cab, went across town for his guitar, and returned as English was about to introduce the concert attraction.

"Many of you have been hearing Jimmie Rodgers here this week," he told the audience, "and you've also seen him around town, where he's been making personal appearances at the music stores. Unfortunately, being out so much in this damp weather, he's caught a bad cold—." The crowd saw what was coming, and began to groan its disapproval. "However, we have with us another Meridian boy who is also a fine entertainer. He sings and plays in Jimmie's style, and we think he deserves a chance to show you what he can do." Learning that Rodgers's replacement was "another Meridian boy" helped to mollify the crowd, and English silenced the last dissenters by offering a full refund at the box office to anyone who still wanted his money back after hearing "Bill Bruner, the Yodeling Messenger Boy."

Bruner did four or five numbers, ending as Jimmie characteristically did with a rollicking version of "Frankie and Johnny." The enthusiastic audience brought him back for six encores. A lengthy story in *Billboard* called it "a typical Horatio Alger incident in which the youthful hero steps in at the critical moment and saves the day." According to the trade journal's report, "The crowd went wild over the boy's efforts, and his imitation of Jimmie was so good that one could shut one's eyes and imagine one of Jimmie's records being played. The young artiste was a huge success, and when he returned to the dressing room, Manager English found him not in the least affected by his success. Altho he had gone over so big he was not the least bit excited about it and as far as we can find it was not necessary to refund any money at the office."[2]

Young Bruner took great pride in the fact that no one asked for a refund; at the time that seemed as important as his ability to do an "almost perfect imitation" of Jimmie Rodgers. But his biggest thrill came the next evening, when English invited him back to the show as a guest and took him to Jimmie's dressing room in a small tent near the main canvas. Although many stars would have resented being upstaged by an unknown, Rodgers greeted the boy warmly, complimented him on his performance, and thanked him for helping out. "Jimmie gave me ten dollars," Bruner recounted, "and I was tickled to death. Of course I thought that was it, and I started to go." But Jimmie stopped him, went over to an instrument case, took out a guitar, and handed it to the boy. Recalling the incident years later, Bruner's gentle Southern voice wavered slightly. "He said, 'Bill, this is a guitar I made some of my first records on, and I want you to have it.' Well, I just filled up—I didn't know what to say. Finally, I managed to thank him."[3]

For more than twenty years the guitar was Bruner's prized possession, but finally, caught up in the excitement of the first gala

Jimmie Rodgers Memorial Day in 1953, he presented it in a public ceremony to Hank Snow's son, Jimmie Rodgers Snow, "because I felt like that was what Jimmie would have wanted me to do." He will not say he's sorry to have parted with it, but, reflecting on the younger Snow's subsequent withdrawal from show business and the guitar's disappearance from public view, he clearly laments the loss. In its place is the handsome big Gibson, valued at more than $400, which a Meridian businessman presented to Bill as a gift when he heard of Bruner's selfless act in giving up the instrument he cherished so much. "Now," says Bruner, with a soft, wistful smile, "this is my Jimmie Rodgers guitar." Since the stroke, he hasn't been able to play the Gibson, but he cradles it gently on his lap, making chords with his good left hand while a visitor strums for him. They both like the sound.

Although cover records of Rodgers's hits had appeared earlier, Bill Bruner was among the first to pay tribute to the Blue Yodeler's style by trying to imitate it note for note. On the evidence of the eight sides he made for Okeh in December, 1929, and February, 1930, he was neither the best nor the worst of dozens who yodeled dutifully and picked out a few Rodgers-like guitar runs in vain attempts to capitalize on Jimmie's following. An accomplished guitarist even in his youth, Bruner played in the Rodgers fashion of strong, simple chords and bass run embellishment, and his yodel was an almost exact replica. Practically identical also were his phrasing and pronunciation, as might be expected from their common cultural and geographical background. The major difference that distinguished Bruner was the heavier timbre of his voice—on those early records, possibly because of the rudimentary equipment, it carries more substance and maturity than one expects of a seventeen year old. Transcriptions made in a radio studio in the late 1940's reveal a smooth, easy tenor of the Gene Austin–Rudy Vallee radio crooner style (singing such numbers as "Buttons and Bows," "San Fernando Valley," "I Wonder Who's Kissing Her Now," and "Smiles"). Except for a couple of sides, notably "Singing the Blues with My Old Guitar" and his own rather clever version of "He's in the Jailhouse Now" (both on Ok 45438), Bruner's commercially recorded material was quite thin, little more than pale imitations of the softer and more sentimental love ballads that even Rodgers was hard pressed to save. Bruner's titles in this vein include his own compositions, "My Pal of Yesterday" and

"That's Why I'm All Alone" (Ok 45400), "Just a Little Dream" and "A Gal like You" (Ok 45463), as well as two tunes which Elsie McWilliams wrote for him, "My Old Home Town Girl" and "School Day Dreams" (Ok 45497).

Bruner's first record sold well enough for Okeh to call him to New York for six more sides, but by that time the country was headed into the Depression, and down with it went Bill Bruner's recording career. Although one account later suggested that "he had little ambition to be a professional performer . . . and soon retired from music,"[4] Bruner insists otherwise. "I never really retired," he says. "Once you're in it, you don't retire from show business." For several years he kept plugging, trying for another break, even standing in again on other occasions for the ailing Jimmie Rodgers. But gradually it became clear that his career was going nowhere. The Depression was not the only cause, as Bruner himself is the first to point out; ironically, it was the very nature of his initial success—the reflected glory of someone else's achievement—that led to his early decline. "Where I made my mistake, I tried to be an imitator," he says, a little wistfully. "I should have gotten away from that and struck out on my own. No matter how good an imitator gets, he's nobody but an imitator."[5] There could be only one Jimmie Rodgers, as dozens of other aspiring Blue Yodelers would eventually learn.

While Bill Bruner stood in for him on that chilly night in 1929, Jimmie Rodgers was being put to bed in his suite at the Lamar Hotel, wracked by severe pleurisy pains and 103-degree fever. He had in fact been seriously ill for many days, and his Meridian physician, Dr. Inman Cooper, had repeatedly warned him to go to bed and stay there. Rodgers had, of course, ignored those orders, but finally he'd collapsed in his dressing room that night, only minutes before curtain time. Dr. Cooper was called, took one look, and immediately insisted that the headliner be put to bed. Jimmie argued as vigorously as he could, maintaining that a shot or two of bourbon and a lemon to clear his throat would see him through; but he was clearly in bad shape, and at last he allowed himself to be carried to the doctor's car and driven back to the hotel.

Given the medical technology of the time and the already advanced state of Rodgers's disease, there was not much Dr. Cooper could do for him except get him off his feet and try to make him as comfortable as possible. The fever and excessive strain on his lungs caused Jimmie's pulse rate to accelerate wildly, and the pain from the pleural infection was so severe that he could breathe only in short, shallow gasps. It was all he could do to hold back the coughing spasms that sent pleurisy pains stabbing through his chest. Over the years he'd gone through most of the conventional painkillers then available, and Dr. Cooper had finally resorted to administering small but increasing doses of morphine to slow his pulse and put him at ease. By early 1929 the dosage had reached a quarter-grain. Given the nature of the drug, even that would soon have to be increased.[6]

Jimmie's collapse had been imminent for some time. He'd suffered a flare-up at Christmas and had been warned then by Dr. Cooper that he needed absolute bed rest. Instead, three days after New Year's, in a move widely heralded in show business circles, he'd rejoined Paul English for the season's opening in Mobile. His initial appearance with the show before Christmas had been a great success; according to *Billboard*, "the appearance of Jimmie Rodgers on the program had the effect of doubling the company's business," despite the fact that Mobile was "a bad show town."[7] English decided that a name headliner was what he needed to revive the public's interest in live entertainment and compete with the current craze for talkies, which had had his business in a slump for several months. It was a novel idea for tent repertoire, and *Billboard* gave the story prominent play on its front page: "Paul English Tent Show Pays Act $600 a Week / Jimmie Rodgers, Popular Recording Artiste, Works Only as Concert Feature, 20 Minutes Nightly—Great Possibilities Seen in Idea." According to the story:

> Playing a vaudeville headliner at $600 a week with a tent show is the bold stroke of Paul English. . . . The high-priced performer is Jimmie Rodgers, popular Victor recording artiste, known as America's blue yodeler. He was signed by English for five weeks at $600 weekly as an experiment. . . .
>
> Rodgers works only as a concert feature, about 15 to 20 minutes a night, and Manager English reports that he has doubled the show's concert business. The concert admission prices have been increased from 20 to 25 cents, and recently in Jackson, Miss., the show's concert receipts ran in excess of $1,000. Tieups are arranged with the Victor dealers in all the towns played, thus cutting the show's advertising expense to almost half.

The use of name attractions by tent shows is a new departure in the canvas show field and is being watched with eager eyes by other tent-show operators. It is English's intention to use a name act regularly if the present venture proves successful. Great possibilities for increasing tent-show attendance are seen in the idea, which is expected to go big in towns where good vaudeville is not to be had in any other way.

The idea has advantages for the vaudevillian, too, Rodgers says. . . .[8]

As the story suggests, Paul English was one of the more astute and progressive entrepreneurs in his field. Still in his thirties, he'd spent most of his adult life in show business, and had fronted his own company since 1920. A native of Bristol, Tennessee, coincidentally the very town where Rodgers's professional career had really gotten its start, English was an alumnus of Colonel W. I. Swain's flamboyant operation, where he'd learned to act, pitch baseball on the show's amateur team, and chart a somewhat steadier course than the irascible, erratic old Colonel. By the mid-1920's the Paul English Players—"The Show with a Million Friends"—had become a popular favorite throughout the South. The Depression would eventually deal English a tragic fate, but his contributions to the brief but culturally vital history of tent repertoire were significant. For a few short years in the late Twenties and early Thirties he had few equals as a purveyor of popular entertainment, and he justly deserved his reputation for having "the best and cleanest show in the business."

By 1929, although the national economy was still booming, even the best tent shows were finding it difficult to compete against radio and talking pictures. For English, signing Rodgers at a big salary was something of an act of desperation, for he'd been forced to cut back radically on other parts of the show. As *Billboard* reported,

Paul English has "lowered his sights" somewhat since last year, and has framed his present show along more practical lines, in accordance with current conditions. He boasts a strong company which is meeting with success all along the line, and his expenses are $800 less than last season [even, apparently, with Rodgers aboard]. English has disposed with the orchestra platform and the large band and orchestra. A six-piece novelty orchestra now is furnishing the music. Manager English states that the past season has taught him a lesson, and altho he does not intend to sacrifice his ideals entirely, he plans to emulate the example of his friend, Col. W. I. Swain, and stick a bit closer to the earth.[9]

The wisdom of his choice of models remained to be seen. Swain would go under, too, but it is doubtful that anything could have saved tent rep. It was simply an idea whose time had passed.

Meanwhile, the Paul English Players were busy getting the 1929 season underway. Among the acts, in addition to Rodgers and comedian Happy Gowland, were the novelty band, billed as "Happy Cook's Kentucky Buddies"; Eva Thomas, "a radio blues singer"; and a would-be recording artist named Buddy Baker. (Baker eventually made several sides for Victor, only two of which were released; in the English show he also doubled as an actor.) The featured plays were advertised as "all new" and included such bills as "The Elder Brother," "Some Baby," Why Wives Worry," "Keep to the Right," "Companionate Marriage," and a modern version of that old stage chestnut, "Ten Nights in a Bar Room."

The show opened its road tour in Gulfport, Mississippi, during the second week in January. Despite bad weather, a cramped lot, and stiff competition from dog races, the talkies, and George B. Wintz's popular musical show *Rio Rita*, which was playing day-and-date, the English box office turned away more than a hundred people and grossed several hundred dollars on the opening concert feature alone. Although the inclement weather continued, the company reported "good business" throughout the week. Rodgers and other members of the cast were invited to do a thirty-minute broadcast over the local radio station, WGCM.

The company's debut in Jackson the following week was plagued by more rain, but the show broke its previous attendance record in the state capital: grossing over $1,000 on opening night, later in the week it took in that much on the concert alone. Heavy downpours throughout the next week, in Vicksburg, dampened everyone's spirits and cut box office receipts to merely "fair." Jimmie had come down with a bad cold in Jackson and couldn't seem to shake it; he was also beginning to suffer from the steady grind that had hardly slackened since he left Washington the previous summer. As usual, he seemed totally oblivious to his health and never called attention to it, although several members of the troupe saw that he was in trouble and sometimes barely able to go on. Near the end of the Vicksburg stand he seemed to recover a bit. He accepted an invitation, along with other cast members, to visit the country estate of F. S. Walcott, owner of the famous Rabbit Foot Minstrels, an act Jimmie had often admired in his own days as a wandering and luckless troubadour.

Despite near exhaustion and the precarious state of his tuberculosis, Rodgers showed no intention of letting up. Victor had released all but five of the sides he'd recorded, and the company was clamoring for more to replace the dwindling supply. Peer wired him with plans for another recording session, to begin February 21 in New York, and Rodgers was already arranging to leave English a week early in order to make the trip. From Vicksburg he wrote to his rowdy uncle, "Rawl" Bozeman, in New York, enclosing his schedule for the coming weeks with the notation, "am leaving for N.Y.C. Feb. 18th to make more Records. Stoping at the Roosevelt Hotel there."

After Vicksburg the company jumped to Meridian. There, in addition to his regular performances, Jimmie took on the extra strain of personal appearances and autograph sessions each afternoon at the hometown music stores. Subjected to persistent rain and cold every day, his condition quickly worsened. Still he shrugged off all attempts to get him to rest or take care of himself, toughing it through the nightly shows with shots of whiskey. His audiences saw only his jaunty, happy-go-lucky side as he toted out his wire-backed drugstore chair and his favorite Martin guitar, propped up his foot, broke into a grin, and literally yodeled their blues away. But backstage the crew noticed Rodgers sitting in the chair more often than not, yodeling less and less, breathing hard, cutting his performances shorter and shorter. He left the chair onstage when the curtain went down and came off soaked in cold sweat, still grinning but working hard for control over the fever in his veins and the rasping ache in his lungs.

Somehow he lasted for four days, determined not to let the homefolks down. He was used to the fever, but by Friday the congestion and pleurisy were so bad that any breath deeper than a faint whiff caused unbearable chest pains. That afternoon he got through the autograph party at F. A. Hulett & Son Furniture Co., went down to the lot for the evening show, reached his dressing room, and simply ran out of breath. Blacking out, he groped for a chair and fell over it.

To the cast of characters in this heightening drama were now added Dr. Cooper, Bill Bruner, and Horatio Alger. Dr. Cooper looked on the collapse as something of a mixed blessing. At least it would keep

Rodgers in bed for a while, something the doctor been trying to accomplish ever since he began to treat him. He also took advantage of the situation to arrange for a chest x-ray, not a common practice in that time and place, so that he might determine more exactly the extent of Jimmie's disease. The results showed "active pulmonary tuberculosis in both lungs, with cavities in both apices [that is, in the top of both lungs], and severe pleurisy at the base of the right lung." The patient was, Cooper concluded, "in severe trouble." He estimated that unless Rodgers took better care of himself, he would live only another year or two.[10]

The prognosis had little effect on Jimmie. To the doctor's dismay, he was up the very next day, insisting that he felt fine and showing every intention of going on stage that night, arguing that The Show Must Go On. But that was little more than allegiance to a catch phrase, and hardly characteristic of a hardened realist like Jimmie Rodgers. To be sure, his sense of professionalism often kept him up and going when other men would have dropped. But the real motives behind what others saw as a cavalier disregard for his health were deeper and more fundamental, rooted in what may fairly be termed a stoic's tragic sense of life, unspoken but clearly acted upon. Early in the course of his disease, Rodgers had accepted its conditions and the certainty of his death; but he was equally certain that he would not meet it cringing or crawling, nor did he want to live out his dying in the sickroom atmosphere of sanitoriums, tepid nostrums, hot water bottles, and false cheer. It was as if he sensed that death would come anytime he let it, anytime he gave in to it, but by simply ignoring the spectre he could hold it off long enough to get his work done. Poor and luckless, he had chosen to act as if he owned the world; now, dying, he chose to live.

The attitude was, in some respects, symptomatic of the disease itself, a pattern of behavior that Rodgers shared with other sufferers of tuberculosis. When empire-builder Cecil Rhodes learned that he was dying of it, he shrugged off the advice of his doctors and redoubled his workload. Chekhov, who also died of the disease, was himself a trained physician; he steadfastly refused to diagnose his own condition for what he knew it was, pretending it to be only a minor indisposition. Similar reactions were reported in case after case. Because of the progression-regression-progression pattern of the disease, the patient may be ill one day and seem much improved the next, although his condition is always in a general downward spiral. In any event, it was clear that Rodgers would do whatever he wanted, and that no one could change his mind if he decided to ignore the whole thing. Dr. Cooper managed to exact Jimmie's promise that he'd rest as much as he could over the weekend, but Saturday night found him back in the tent to close the hometown stand, and on Monday he drove to Hattiesburg, south of Meridian, to join the show for its next opening. A week later he was on his way to New York.

Ralph Peer probably was not aware of the current state of Rodgers's health when he called him north to record again, and he certainly knew nothing of Jimmie's recent collapse. What is debatable is whether events would have been altered much if he had known. That is not to suggest that Peer was ever deliberately careless with Rodgers's health, but only that he was often simply too busy and too far removed from the situation to act in the best interests of Rodgers's well-being. Moreover, Jimmie invariably insisted that he was feeling fine and ready to go, and to the extent that Peer relied on his entertainer's own assessment, his responses to the matter were often affected as much by business considerations as by therapeutic ones. It has often been assumed that, following the Blue Yodeler's emergence as a hot property in mid-1928, Peer attempted to schedule his field recording trips around Rodgers in order to conserve the singer's energy and lessen the strain of long trips north to Camden and New York.[11] Peer himself may have helped foster that notion, although it does not square well with the circumstances of the last several sessions, which required Rodgers to travel great distances at the very time when he was least able to do so. Jimmie's health undoubtedly figured in Peer's plans, but even he did not hesitate to point out that "the principal idea [for recording Rodgers in various cities] was to provide [him] with variegated accompaniment so that he would have as many back-grounds as possible."[12] Peer obviously developed a genuine liking for his protégé, a circumstance which, given the differences in their backgrounds, temperaments, and outlooks, was more than a little remarkable. At the same time, however, his personal attitudes toward the relationship were invariably bound up in the day-to-day business of merchandising phonograph records and securing copyrights. Even when he cautioned Jimmie to take care of himself, the advice was couched in business terms—"Watch your health carefully, as it is worth more than ten thousand per"[13]—implying that, if asked "How much more?," he could have come up with a figure.

Rodgers, although an increasingly valuable asset, was still only one horse in a busy stable. At this point he was somewhat incidental to Peer's grand design (never quite achieved) of breaking into what was then the popular music field. "I was always trying to get away from the hillbilly," Peer said, "and into the legitimate music publishing field. . . . What I was doing was to take the profits out of the hillbilly and race business and spend that money trying to get established as a pop publisher."[14] Toward this end, near the close of 1928 Peer had agreed to transfer control of the lucrative Southern Music Publishing Company to Victor, in an arrangement whereby he was to retain control of the copyrights, with the stipulation that Victor assign to Southern Music all material "of popular nature that might be recorded" by the company, regardless of source.[15] Peer's flirtations with what he thought of as popular music help one to understand many of the curious turns and twists in Jimmie Rodgers's recording career and explain the more extreme combinations of musicians that were put together with him in the studio. All this, of course, could not have happened had Rodgers himself not been a willing and able accomplice.

Peer had encouraged "variegated accompaniments" all along, but only occasionally had he had much to do with selecting the musicians or actively participating in the necessary arrangements, rehearsals, or repertoire whenever Jimmie recorded with accompaniment. However, by the time of the February, 1929, sessions Peer had detected Jimmie's own aspirations for attracting a broad and diverse audience beyond the limitations of "oldtime" or "hillbilly," so he stepped in with plans for producing half a dozen sides that he felt would work to their mutual advantage. Peer planned to capitalize on Jimmie's eclectic style and popular appeal, backing him with what Rodgers would later refer to as an "uptown ork." As Peer recalled, "I brought Jimmie to New York the first time he ever recorded with a professional orchestra. I induced Victor to get an 18-man combination [Peer characteristically thought big: there were actually only six musicians], so it cost a lot of money to get these arrangements made and Victor was stewing about it, but I forced it through." He was quick to admit, however, that "the records weren't too good, because Jimmie wasn't at ease." As Peer put it, Jimmie liked to take "liberties," meaning that he played the music the way he felt it and ignored the conventions of notation, for of course he couldn't "read" anyway. With the orchestra, said Peer, "he couldn't take any liberties, so he wasn't comfortable. . . . he was really at ease

[only] when he was playing his own guitar. So I considered it was an experiment that didn't work out."

As far as Peer was concerned, the fault was largely Jimmie's, because "the orchestra was perfect." The consensus of others, however, is that it was terrible—so incredibly corny that "Desert Blues," for example, derives a certain notoriety and compelling charm from the very fact of its atrociousness. But bad as it is, "Desert Blues" is far from the worst song Rodgers ever recorded. The lyrics are catchy, at least, and Jimmie delivers them with particular verve. His wry, gleeful tone suggests that he had at least taken the measure of the band and decided he could make it fit the material.

The same accompaniment, somewhat restrained, provided backing for "Any Old Time," probably Jimmie's personal favorite of all the songs he recorded. Held off until the first chorus by Rodgers's strong solo guitar, the band then joined in to thump and whack along with him to the end, in a performance that, to be generous, can be called suitable. At bottom, it is merely archaic—dated, in the worst sense—and perhaps much of that is due to the instrumentation, notably the inclusion of a tuba. The song itself deserved Rodgers's affection. "Any Old Time" has held up well over the years, finding receptive audiences and loving treatment in the hands of later artists. Maria Muldaur's 1974 rendition, liltingly modern and at the same time thoroughly faithful to the original, attests to the song's timeless appeal.

Whatever may be the ultimate judgment of these two numbers, Peer's first attempt at a "variegated accompaniment" was far from the instincts that had led him to Bristol two years before, and it provided clear evidence that his vaunted role as a "folksong collector" and "cultural documentarian of the first rank" was largely incidental. To his credit, he quickly saw the folly of continuing that particular experiment, although other, more successful efforts would follow. The orchestra was dismissed, and Rodgers returned to the ease of his own guitar and the comfort of taking whatever "liberties" he pleased.

Back in the studio two days later, Jimmie recorded a fifth Blue Yodel, introduced by one of those engaging, breakaway guitar runs that were to become his trademark. First awkwardly listed on the recording logs as "Ain't No Blackheaded Woman Can Make a Fool out of Me," the song took that title from the catch line of a vagrant stanza in the black tradition; it eventually became ensconced in another of those scholarly folksong collections, identified as "clearly a Negro blues song."[16] That same day Rodgers recorded two more numbers, a conventional love lament entitled "I'm Sorry We Met," and "High Powered Mama," which ranks among the best of his hard-driving, lowdown blues tunes.

These sessions, together with numbers already on hand, provided Victor with only enough Rodgers material for the company's next four or five monthly releases. The recording committee wanted more, but Jimmie had used up everything he had ready. There were obligatory rumblings of discontent from the committee, but, assured by both Rodgers and Peer that by midsummer they'd have material for another session, the company readily renewed Jimmie's contract. Meanwhile, Peer had his eye on other promising show business developments. With the recording sessions now out of the way, he and Jimmie turned their full attention to more immediate matters.

In the film industry, a vogue had long existed for so-called short subjects—ten- or fifteen-minute travelogs, comedies, newsreels, and, with the coming of sound, musical acts. Almost an extinct form today, the "short" had evolved to large degree out of vaudeville. As live variety entertainment in the theaters declined, short subjects grew in popularity as a replacement for the vaude bill in smaller cities. The talkie boom was creating an unprecedented demand for film of all kinds, and many production units were concentrating exclusively on shorts, operating their studios and labs around the clock. The craze for sound (All Talking! All Singing!) made the major phonograph companies logical sources for talent, as well as for studio facilities. When Warner Brothers introduced its Vitaphone system back in 1927, the film company had approached Victor with plans to sign the latter's recording stars for talking shorts; nothing tangible came of the discussion, and the contracts eventually expired. In early 1929, Columbia, then struggling to establish itself as a major independent, announced big plans for a tieup with Victor in which it would produce an extensive series of shorts, using Victor talent and sound facilities. "Under the setup Columbia will have at its disposal the modern, fully-equipped studio of Victor at Camden, N.J.," reported *Billboard*, "and will be in a position to draw for talent from the wide field in which Victor is represented, from opera stars down to vaudevillians."[17]

As one of Victor's top artists and a proven success in vaudeville, Rodgers was a natural choice for such a project. Peer lost no time in seeing that he was signed and arrangements for production initiated, with actual filming scheduled for later in the year at Victor's Camden studios. As Rodgers's publisher, Peer would of course receive the standard "mechanical" royalties from the film, and in terms of exploitation it was a rare opportunity for Jimmie to gain national exposure in the hottest medium of all.

Peer also turned his attention again to national vaudeville, where renewed activity promised another substantial booking for his yodeling protégé. Many optimistic observers felt that the decline in live entertainment had bottomed out. After all, it could hardly get worse, they said—and kept saying, until the Depression arrived less than a year later. The trade magazines, whistling past the graveyard as usual, were proclaiming "a new era": "VAUDE. COMING BACK ALL OVER COUNTRY!" "Financial Survey of Amusement Industry Predicts Bright Outlook for the Long Term!"[18]

Amid the happy but premature cries of resurrection, the Radio Corporation of America, Victor's parent company, took controlling interest of the Keith-Albee-Orpheum Circuit, one of the country's oldest and largest vaudeville chains. Actually a conglomerate of several regional "wheels," K-A-O owned and booked the Mother Church of Vaudeville, New York's Palace Theater; the firm traced its origins back to pioneer showmen Benjamin Franklin Keith and Edward F. Albee, and to the once-grand Orpheum Circuit which had dominated the West at the turn of the century.[19] Reconstituted as R-K-O (Radio-Keith-Orpheum), in early 1929 the organization set out to breathe new life in vaudeville by restoring the confidence of performers and audiences alike, cleaning up its theaters, putting an end to shoddy practices in the booking offices, attracting new acts, and framing the durable older ones in fresh combinations.[20] Along with the sailing of the *Titanic*, Wilson's Fourteen Points, and near-beer, it was one of the Great Exercises in Futility, noble and courageous but ultimately wrongheaded, doomed by greater and more complex events than any of its astute and well-meaning executives could have foreseen or coped with.

But meanwhile the upbeat mood was infectious, and Peer felt that conditions were ripe for booking another headline tour for his rising star. The new alignment of a major vaudeville circuit within the RCA corporate structure no doubt improved his chances, or at least opened a few doors, although the two subsidiaries, R-K-O and Victor, were operated independently of each other. Peer and Jimmie met with Charles J. Freeman, booking agent for R-K-O's Interstate Time, to work out the details of a summer tour of Interstate's houses in the South and Southwest, at a reported salary of $1,000 a week.[21]

Facing several weeks "at liberty" until the R-K-O opening, Jimmie hauled out the ad mats and handbills for the "Coast-to-Coast Tour" he'd begun in Washington the previous fall. Booking engagements wherever he might find them, he headed west, barnstorming his way toward Texas and then to Oklahoma, where the R-K-O tour was to open in May.

A few blocks off Nashville's Music Row, and several light years away, I found the office of Showay Productions, quartered in the cramped, cluttered front room of an old brick bungalow. A walk painted in rainbow colors led to the door, and out in the yard was a strange shrub covered with the tattered remnants of fake dollar bills. Houses up and down the street had signs out front proclaiming the occupancy of recording studios, music publishers, agents, and sundry related cottage industries, the swarming little fish that feed on the bony fringes of Nashville's largest enterprise.

President of Showay Productions, Inc., is Bennie Hess. He is also its producer, chief engineer, head of promotion, and star recording artist. The other executive position is held by Dorothy Collins, who is general manger and president of the Bennie Hess Fan Club. She is also Mrs. Bennie Hess. Until recently, Bennie shared artistic honors with his son Troy, who began making records at the age of three and was billed for years by his father as "The World's Youngest Recording Star." The frizzy shrub in front, it turns out, was a bit of on-site publicity for one of Troy's early records called "The Money Tree," for which they had high hopes. Bennie spent a lot of time and cash promoting Little Troy Hess. If he accomplished little else, he at least managed to get the tyke photographed with practically every big star in town, and has the pictures to prove it. One of the first things a visitor to Showay Productions gets to do is turn through Troy Hess's scrapbooks, all eight of them, and admire Little Troy in his white hat and cowboy suit, getting kissed by Dolly Parton or outmugged by Buck Owens. Some people around Nashville thought Bennie was exploiting the youngster, but when *Country Music* said so in print, Bennie promptly sued the magazine for several million dollars. He eventually dropped the suit. Now that Troy is moving into his surly teens, he has considerable competition for his title, although no one really seems to care much about who is the World's Youngest Recording Star.

Bennie, among his other accomplishments, might lay claim to being one of the world's oldest. In his early sixties, he isn't as old as Ernest Tubb or Roy Acuff, but then he isn't as well known, either. Bennie Hess would probably check in about ninety-seventh on a list of One Hundred Famous Unknown Recording Artists. Back in the mid-Forties he made a side or two for Decca and Mercury, and since then he's released dozens on small-time labels, mostly his own. But Bennie never stops trying. He has, as he says, six irons in every fire and the world is burning up. High on his current list of projects is a deal that will restore singing cowboy movies to their former glory, starring Bennie Hess as the Fighting Western Balladeer.

On the other side of the ledger, there isn't a mean bone in Bennie Hess's body, and for all his grand schemes and constant self-promotion, he is totally without guile. When the conversation turns to Jimmie Rodgers, his eyes grow moist with genuine emotion, and his voice breaks now and then. He stops answering the phone and gets downright rude to the dough-faced country boys who come up on the porch lugging guitars and hustling their wares, wanting to know if he's listened to their demo yet and whether Mr. So-and-So has talked to him in their behalf. Bennie sets the chain latch and through the barely opened door gives them his version of don't-call-me: "Yeah, yeah. Well, I talk to you about that next week sometime. I'm real busy now."

What he's busy doing is telling me all sorts of wondrous things about Jimmie Rodgers. Bennie Hess, you see, knew Jimmie Rodgers. Sometimes it seems that half the conscious population between 1927 and 1933 knew Jimmie Rodgers. The problem is that nearly all of them are frustratingly vague about dates and particulars. Bennie is no exception. When he was just a small boy, it seems, Bennie traveled around with Jimmie Rodgers, and he has Jimmie's first guitar and the master of every record he made, "plus twelve that were never released," songs that Bennie wrote for Rodgers's last recording session. He performs several Jimmie Rodgers numbers for me, and tells how people fainted when he sang them at the Rodgers Memorial Celebration in Meridian, thinking it was Jimmie come back. Then he is off on another tangent about his dear old dad and Carrie Rodgers on her deathbed and his own checkered career in show business. "See, my dad knew him back in Mississippi when Jimmie was just a little boy. Then he got him a job on the railroad, and Jimmie practically lived with my folks there, off and on. Far back as I can remember he'd be there." The version I usually hear begins, breathlessly, "Why, my old mother *raised* Jimmie Rodgers." Jimmie's foster parents, "cousins," boyhood pals, and illegitimate children would populate a small city.

As Bennie's stories veer from subject to subject, I begin to search for some hard place to get my bearings, a date or name that might bring the information into focus. He's telling me about Carrie giving him Jimmie's guitar and all the record masters, and then he's off on the time Jimmie began playing theaters and how Bennie's folks trusted Jimmie and let him take Bennie along on his tours. What year was this, I ask? Bennie makes a stab but gives up, pleading, "I was just such a little bitty feller back then, see, and that's been a long time ago." From the birthdate he's given me, I doodle a little math in my head and calculate that he was thirteen in 1927 when Rodgers began recording, nineteen when the Blue Yodeler died. Bennie attended the funeral; he remembers everything about it except the date, the weather, where the services were held, and the names of the people he met there.

Yet some of the casual details that he hits on are simply too minute, exact, and awesome to be made out of whole cloth. I begin to wonder if perhaps he isn't talking about Jimmie's earlier years, before Bristol. Probing that avenue only sends him off on the time, back in the Twenties, when his dad and some other railroaders chipped in to raise $465 to buy Jimmie his first new guitar, the Martin D-35 which Bennie now shows off as "Jimmie Rodgers's first guitar, and the first Martin ever made." C. F. Martin began making instruments in 1833; by 1940 the most expensive guitar in the company's catalog was the F-9 Grand Auditorium, priced at $250. That year, more than a decade after Rodgers first recorded, a new 00-18 model similar to the one he used at Bristol cost $40.

I despair of ever getting enough solid facts to document, and decide instead to hone in on those twelve unreleased masters and the songs he supposedly wrote for Rodgers. When Bennie fails to produce anything, I will be able to write it all off as another Rodgers myth, one more wondrous but grandly inflated figment of the imagination. About those masters—are they actually the original metal parts from Victor? How are they marked? Again the vague responses, the studied evasions. Is "Prohibition Has Done Me Wrong" among them? Well, now, I had that one, but I was going home in the wagon one day and—. Can I see the others? Well, I tell you what, they're stored away, place is a big mess, see, somebody broke in here and tried to steal my secret invention for 3-D recording, did I tell you about that—?

With a sort of malicious detachment, I keep herding him back to the subject, refusing to let it pass, pushing to see just how far he will go and how at the last minute he will try to save face and send me away thinking he has what he doesn't have, and has done what he hasn't done, although both of us will know better, and each will know that the other knows. So I am mildly surprised when, after we have been over it several times and the words are no longer working, he finally ambles away into the back room and returns with a cardboard box. By this time the number has shrunk from twelve to two, and when he takes them from the box I see that they are not Victor masters from the Thirties, but plain, unlabeled studio acetates of a much later vintage. Bennie shows them off with a flourish, talking a mile a minute, but as far as I'm concerned we're back to square one. For all I know these are home recordings of the World's Youngest Recording Star, although I try not to put it so bluntly. If I could only hear them, just a groove or two maybe, in the interests of Pure Scholarship—. Well, I dunno, see, I really don't have anything to play 'em on, record player just quit working, and the quality's not very good, you probably can't tell what's on 'em.

Still I refuse to give up. In response to the steady pressure, he's gone through the motions of trying to hook up a dilapidated old turntable and tone arm. The whole thing is so obviously wrecked that I know it will never make a sound, much less track a record; but eventually he manages to wedge a stick under the arm at the proper angle, and the needle responds when he flicks it with his thumb. This is certainly going beyond the call of duty. Now I am really anxious to hear his story when it turns out to be the wrong record or too garbled to understand or, as I begin to suspect, a recording of Bennie or someone else doing a close imitation.

I should have trusted my instincts. At the time what I heard—all too eager for it—was the voice of Jimmie Rodgers, singing something called "Tennessee Mama Blues."

> There's bears in the mountains, fish in the deep blue sea
> There's bears in the mountains, fish in the deep blue sea
> And there's a lot of pretty women in the hills of Tennessee.[22]

The yodel was missing, and an electric steel guitar had been over-dubbed, but the voice, I thought then, was unmistakable. Bennie let it play through before putting on the other one. We listened to "I Love You Yet," a simple love song typical of dozens that Rodgers did. Still, its modern flavor should have been a clue; it had none of the musty Depression flavor that I'm so accustomed to hearing on Rodger's records, but instead sounded eerily close to the bubbles-in-my-beer jukebox ballads of Ernest Tubb a decade later, and the movie smoothies that Gene Autry did in the early Forties.

I was never able to pinpoint the true source of these recordings or the circumstances surrounding their origin, but at the time I rushed to the conclusion that they were raw tests, home recordings which Rodgers made on a lathe he was known to have had at the Kerrville residence. I should have listened to all the people who had warned me about good old Bennie and his penchant for self-promotion. His story about people fainting because he sounded so much like Rodgers should have alerted me; still, I had just heard him, live, doing Rodgers's songs, and I was certain it wasn't *him* on the records. Several years were to pass before I learned my mistake, through a process too long and boring to relate, and only after Bennie himself had issued the two cuts as "The Last Songs of Jimmie Rodgers" ("The Singing *Breakman*"!). Never try to outhustle a hustler.

Perhaps the happiest result of the whole affair was that it sent me back to Bennie's other stories about Jimmie Rodgers.[23] As in the case of the records, I was never able to get a consistent chronology from him or dig out many hard facts, but afterward enough of it fell into place to convince me that the broad outlines had some basis in actuality. Bennie's father, Festo "Cap" Hess, had probably been a neighbor of Aaron Rodgers, either at Pine Springs or in one of the other small communities in the area where Aaron worked on the M&O when Jimmie was growing up. Cap Hess took up railroading himself, and around the time of World War I he helped young Jimmie find work around the yards in New Orleans. Shortly afterward Hess moved to central Texas, north of Austin, to work for the Santa Fe; Jimmie followed along, boarding with the Hesses and picking up whatever railroad work he could find, with Cap Hess's help. This was intermittently during the period from about 1918 to 1923; Bennie recalled Jimmie being gone frequently during 1920 while courting Carrie, although he misremembered many of the details and the circumstances of their subsequent marriage. Jimmie came by to visit only sporadically in later years, but in the spring of 1929 (Bennie thought the year was 1928, but it clearly could not have been) he was back as a recording star and rising entertainer, booking personal appearances around the state on what he advertised as a "Coast-to-Coast Tour." This was the period that Bennie remembered best, when Jimmie took the fifteen-year-old youngster around with him as he played the small towns near Chriesman, the tiny hamlet where the Hesses made their home. Booking a theater in a likely town, Jimmie would fill his car with pretty local girls and drive around the city square, yodeling out the window to advertise that evening's show: "Hey, hey. This is Jimmie Rodgers, folks, and I'll be singing and playing for you at the theater tonight. Tell 'em 'bout me." On one occasion, Hess remembers, "two of the prettiest women I ever saw came up to him and offered to take him for a ride around town, you know, show him the sights and all that. 'Oh, no, thank you,' Jimmie says, 'I'd love to, but I've got my son here with me'—that's me he's talking about, see—says, 'I'd just love to go with you, but I can't go off and leave my son.' He's using me, see, to keep out of trouble." Bennie tells of a time when Rodgers arrived in some town to find only a single, crudely lettered sign advertising his upcoming appearance. "Man, he really got mad about that sign. He was squatted down there, looking at it, and some fellow came up and asked him for a match, and maybe I ought not to tell this, but Jimmie hit that guy and knocked him clear out in the street. Then we went right back to the depot to catch the next train out. Somebody there asked him if he wasn't going to play there that night, and Jimmie said, 'Hell, there ain't enough money in this town for me to sing here.'"

After a performance in Temple, Texas, Rodgers took Bennie back to their hotel to put him to bed and caused a near calamity when he opened the window and sat in it, playing his guitar and singing. "Liked to scared me to death, I was just a little feller; see, and that was back when the only cars around were Model T's and Baby Overlands, and as Jimmie started singing, people was jumping out of their cars to listen, some was even forgetting to pull the handbrakes, and they were running into each other out there. I never heard so many wrecks in my life, I mean I was *scared*, and there was a knock on the door and three po-lice—I just knew they was gonna arrest him and take him off and I'd be there all alone. But all they done was, they just said, 'Mr. Rodgers, would you please hold it down some, we got a mess on our hands out there.' So he moved away from the window, but he kept right on picking and singing. He was some Jimmie, I'll tell you that."

Bennie last saw him in the spring of 1933, when Jimmie stopped by the Hess home in Chriesman to rest on his way to San Antonio after a performance near Houston. It was then, says Hess, that he gave Rodgers the two songs we'd heard on the acetates; Jimmie pinned the lyrics on the back of a rocking chair and sang them while Bennie picked out the tunes. Hess also claims, probably with some justification, that earlier he'd given Jimmie verses to "Train Whistle Blues" and "I'm Lonesome Too," and that he supplied "most of the words to what is now known as 'Jimmie Rodgers' Last Blue Yodel.' At that time it was supposed to be another numbered Blue Yodel. Jimmie added 'The women make a fool out of me' to the end of each verse." Asked why he was not credited with the authorship of these songs, he says, "I was too timid to even show them to Jimmie, but my dad told me to. We didn't know what publishing or copyrights were in those days. When I saw him the last time, he said, 'Son, I'll see that you keep the rights to these songs' ["Tennessee Mama Blues" and "I Love You Yet"], but of course they weren't released." He cannot explain why they were not issued or even entered in the recording logs, except to hint vaguely at some sort of conspiracy against him. "But I didn't care about that," he says. "I was proud to give them to Jimmie. I loved him so much and it gave me a great thrill just to know he would record my songs." My conversations with Bennie Hess raised more questions than they answered, but there is no mystery about Bennie's sincerity or the emotion in his voice when he talks about Jimmie Rodgers.

NOTES

   1. *Meridian Star*, Feb. 1, 1929, p. 17.
   2. *Billboard*, Apr. 6, 1929, p. 30. Other details of this episode were obtained in interviews with Bill Bruner, Jan. 6, 1975, and May 29, 1976, Meridian.

3. Interview, Jan. 6, 1975, Meridian. According to Bruner, the guitar was a Martin, probably an 00-18 (but clearly not the same instrument Jimmie used at Bristol). See, however, Prynce E. Wheeler and Walter W. Fuchs, "Wo Sind Jimmie Rodgers' Gitarren Geblieben?," *Hillbilly*, no. 38 (June, 1971), 5, which identifies it as a Mexican guitar of unknown manufacture. Inquiries to Hank Snow have gone unanswered.

4. Paris and Comber, *Jimmie the Kid*, p. 81.

5. Interview, May 29, 1976, Meridian.

6. Deposition of I. W. Cooper, M.D., in the case of *Stella Harkins and Kathryn Rodgers* v. *Jimmie Rodgers*, Law 4502 (1932). An eighth of a grain is considered standard dosage.

7. *Billboard*, Dec. 29, 1928, p. 30.

8. *Ibid.*, Feb. 16, 1929, pp. 3, 30.

9. *Ibid.*, p. 30.

10. Deposition of I. W. Cooper, M.D., in *Harkins and Rodgers* v. *Rodgers*.

11. See *MHJR*, p. 186.

12. *Meridian Star*, May 26, 1953, p. 24.

13. *MHJR*, p. 227.

14. Asked by Borgeson to name some hillbilly artists for whom he was responsible, other than Rodgers and the Carters, Peer said, "Oh, I've tried so hard to forget them. . . ."

15. Peer's original offer had included copyright assignments on "all of the material that I have collected or will collect in the future," but for various reasons Victor hedged. When they finally came around, he altered that provision so that he retained full control of everything copyrighted through 1928. The question of who held the copyrights became a moot one anyway when he bought Southern back from Victor in 1932, and for all his machinations he acquired very little popular material. "I never got anything," he said, "because the stuff I wanted would have to come through the A&R Department in New York, and . . . they'd say, why, he's not even really a publishing company, it'd be dangerous to give him one of these things. So they just stalled off on me. . . ." He agreed, however, that "they were right about it. I just wasn't organized to take advantage of this. [Southern] was just a name, you see. Just a name, you might say, to prevent the treasurer from finding so much money going to one man."

16. Belden and Hudson, eds, *Frank C. Brown Collection*, III:564.

17. *Billboard*, Feb. 9, 1929, p. 22. See also *Variety*, July 11, 1928; Oct. 3, 1928, p. 7; Jan. 23, 1929, p. 21; and Mar. 20, 1929, p. 73.

18. See, e.g., *Billboard*, Feb. 9, 1929, p. 10; Jan. 19, 1929, p. 3; Mar. 30, 1929, p. 10; July 27, 1929, p. 10.

19. Toll, *On with the Show*, pp. 269–73.

20. *Variety*, Feb. 6, 1929, p. 65, and Mar. 27, 1929, p. 35; *Billboard*, Feb. 23, 1929, p. 12. See also numerous other stories in the vaudeville sections of these "trades" throughout the period.

21. *Kerrville Mountain Sun*, Apr. 25, 1929, p. 1.

22. "Tennessee Mama Blues," words and music by Bennie Hess. © 1973 by Showay Productions. Used by permission.

23. Interviews, Mar. 11 and 12 and June 3, 1976, Nashville; Bennie Hess to NP, Mar. 20, Apr. 28, and June 14, 1976; also "Memoirs [Memories] of Jimmie Rodgers," by Bennie Hess, unpublished monograph, n.d.; copy in my possession.

11 *May–December, 1929*

A Home Out in Texas

Growing up around O'Donnell, Texas, twenty years after Jimmie Rodgers died, I heard many stories about the time he supposedly played there. He got drunk and threw beer bottles off the balcony of the local hotel, they said, and at least half a dozen happy homes disintegrated in his wake. Much as I wanted to believe that he'd been there, in that same dusty, dull little West Texas hamlet where I spent so much time whiling away the weary, fevered hours of adolescence, I'd heard enough stories about Jimmie Rodgers even then to know better than to accept them at face value. Anyway, nothing ever happened in O'Donnell, Texas. Why would America's Famous Blue Yodeler show up in such a small, out-of-the-way tanktown?

The High Plains region is dotted with dozens of crumbling little burgs just like O'Donnell, half-deserted villages with little future and even less past. Most of them hardly existed before World War I; they flourished briefly in the Twenties with an influx of settlers from the farmed-out, boll weeviled bottoms of East Texas and beyond, and then gradually rotted away, victims of future shock, fast living, and freeways, of cultural homogenization and changing economic patterns that doomed the quarter-section cotton farm and replaced it with "agribusiness" conglomerates. Today O'Donnell is a veritable ghost town; one strains to realize that, at its peak in the late Twenties, the place was a bustling community of several thousand souls, seriously contending for prominence among its neighboring rivals, Tahoka and Lamesa. Looking back, however, it is easy to see that the town never really had a chance, situated as it was between two county seats, skirted by the main highway, only forty-odd miles from the emerging metropolis of Lubbock, and at the mercy of a single-crop economy. Why, indeed, would Jimmie Rodgers play O'Donnell, Texas?

Yet when I got around to checking, years after I heard the stories, I found out that he did perform there. Only three towns in the area could boast a personal appearance by America's Blue Yodeler in the spring of 1929, and O'Donnell was one of them.

I still don't know exactly why, and perhaps it doesn't really matter. There is some reason to believe that Rodgers was familiar with O'Donnell from previous rambles through the region; perhaps he even had old friends there. Substantial evidence that he made some new ones at least partially bears out the rumors I'd heard. Finally, the location may simply have seemed promising and convenient, roughly halfway between the two larger towns he played in the same area. O'Donnell in 1929 was still years away from the deteriorating relic I knew as a boy, and Jimmie Rodgers was known to have played in even smaller, more remote places.

A week before he was to perform there, the *O'Donnell Index* gave the event a banner 72-point headline across the front page: "JIMMIE RODGERS APPEARS HERE APRIL 6TH."[1] Although Jimmie himself obviously planned the itinerary and took an active part in promoting the tour, actual arrangements were made through Victor's Dallas distributor, the T. E. Swann Music Company, whose West Texas representative, Burt Ford, handled the details and acted as advance man.

Rodgers arrived on Friday, April 5, from Big Spring, where he had appeared the previous week. That evening he was guest of honor at a party hosted by the local theater-owner and his wife, and attended by the town's more socially prominent young couples. It was this event which gave rise to later rumors of dalliance and divorce. Although the stories can't (and probably shouldn't) be documented in detail, they are numerous enough and agree substantially enough to indicate that they have some basis in fact. "Various games were enjoyed by those present for a time, until the honor guest was finally persuaded to favor the crowd with some of his most popular numbers," said a later social note in the *Index*.[2] What the paper didn't report was the exact nature of the games that were played, or the realignment of partners; when Jimmie Rodgers left town following his performance the next evening, his host's wife left also, and although she returned some days later, her marriage soon ended in divorce. Townsfolk attributed a rash of marital discord to the Blue Yodeler's sojourn in O'Donnell. Adjusted for the normal exaggeration in matters relating to Jimmie Rodgers, the actual figures seem to be two divorces and three separations. Judged by the groupie standards of a later day, it didn't amount to much—but O'Donnell was clearly not as dull as I'd been willing to believe.

Jimmie Rodgers's romantic exploits are legendary, second only to the fabrications about his drinking and serving time in prison. "He'd just take any woman wherever he found her," said Ralph Peer, whose close working relationship with Rodgers would seem to qualify him to speak on the subject. But Peer would also have it believed that Jimmie's rampant libido was attributable to his illness. "A tubercular person has three times the sexual activity as normal," he blandly asserted, although of course the exact opposite is more nearly true. It would be exceedingly naive to believe that Rodgers was the saintly, true-loving husband that his family and zealous fans have understandably tried to depict; on the other hand, neither was he the wayward profligate that Peer and rumors tended to describe. The real wonder is that Rodgers had any energy at all for amorous activity.

Equally inexplicable is the source of his undeniable sex appeal. Gaunt, balding, and big-eared, he did not gyrate like Elvis or croon seductively in the fashion of Crosby or Sinatra. Perhaps it was his roguish grin and cool air of command; he sang with the voice of experience, and the songs said, "I've been there before, and I know what I can do." When he told them he could get more women than a passenger train could haul, or do more switchin' than their mainline had ever done, they believed him. Surely the most exotic evidence of his visceral magnetism is a female puberty rite reported among the Kipsigi tribe of East Africa, to whom Rodgers is something of a minor deity. Introduced to the phonograph only recently, the Kipsigis were inordinately attracted to Rodgers's records and soon elevated him to the position of a demigod, addressed in the native tongue as "Chemirocha." Rodgers, imagined as a sort of centaur, half-man and half-antelope, is the spirit to whom young Kipsigi maidens appeal as they sing their song, *Chemirocha*, and seductively invite him to dance with them.[3] Somewhere, chuckling to himself, Jimmie Rodgers is piping a short, gleeful yodel over that one.

A week after his appearance in O'Donnell, Rodgers played a two-day engagement at the Palace Theater in Lubbock, performing twice a day to capacity audiences despite day-and-date competition from the Christie Brothers Circus. Noting his unusual popularity, a local reviewer commented, "Rodgers plays his own accompaniments, on a guitar, and plays as entertainingly as he sings. His act sticks to the type of blues songs that have made him famous and that seem to please the most people. Such whimsical numbers as 'In the Jailhouse Now,' 'Way Out on the Mountain,' 'Brakeman's Blues,' and 'Waiting for a Train,' are offered. . . ." Other stories referred to him as "the Victor record yodeling phenom" and observed that "in fourteen months [he] rose from a jobless railroad brakeman to a headlining vaudeville performer with an income that runs anywhere from $1,800 a week into dizzy figures"—as though $1,800 a week wasn't dizzy enough![4]

The trip through Texas, despite all the hoopla about a "Coast-to-Coast Tour," had really been planned only as an interim venture, a sort of working vacation that would give him additional exposure and keep the money rolling in as he moved closer to his Oklahoma opening with R-K-O. After the Lubbock engagement he returned to Madisonville, north of Houston, where Carrie had been visiting relatives. Together they traveled to the resort town of Kerrville in the famed Texas Hill Country for a brief rest before setting out for Oklahoma.

Kerrville, as Carrie had learned, was widely known as a center for the treatment of pulmonary diseases. Several private sanitoriums were located there, as well as a large Veterans Hospital (popularly referred to as "Legion," having been established originally by the American Legion) devoted exclusively to the care of patients suffering lung disorders. Although neither talked about it, Jimmie's recent collapse while touring with Paul English was very much on their minds. After years of roaming, there was also a growing need to find somewhere to settle down, now that Anita was growing up and Jimmie needed a stable base of operation. The only places where they'd ever stayed put for any length of time were Meridian and Washington. Jimmie made no bones about his distaste for the nation's capital, with its humid summers and bitterly cold winters, and the muggy Mississippi climate was equally hard on him. They'd both liked Asheville, but it rained a lot there, too, and the winters could be harsh. The ideal location, according to the accepted medical doctrine of the day, would have dry air and mild weather the year around, and would be high above sea level, where the lighter atmosphere supposedly made breathing easier for lung patients. Arizona and California were too far away, but Texas might have possibilities, and Kerrville was one.

With the town crowded by tourists and the families of patients at the various sanitoriums, housing accommodations were scarce. Jimmie and Carrie managed to lease a private residence on Earl Garrett Street, near downtown Kerrville. The local folk received them warmly, showed them the town, and in general made a big fuss over the famous personality in their midst. Jimmie was introduced to the area's more prominent citizens, including L. A. Schreiner, son of the town's founder, and was given a special tour of Schreiner's private game reserve. As early as the previous summer, when Gene Austin was showing off his *Blue Heaven* yacht, Jimmie had talked of building a big home, ostensibly in Meridian, and naming it "Blue Yodeler's Paradise."[5] Now, moved by the local hospitality and a fondness for Texas that dated back to his years as a wandering teenager, he decided that Kerrville was the place to settle down. Only a week later the *Kerrville Mountain Sun* announced his decision in bold front-page headlines: "Famous Singer to Make Home in Kerrville / Jimmie Rodgers, Victor Recording Artist, Will Build Here." According to the news account, "Henceforth, Kerrville will be home to Jimmie Rodgers, famous Victor recording artist and known to thousands of radio fans throughout the world as the 'Blue Yodeler' . . . Rodgers plans to build a home in Westland Hills, to cost approximately $20,000. He considers Kerrville the ideal place for rest and recreation after his strenuous tours over the country, and the people here are among the most hospitable he has ever met in his extensive travels, he says."

Rodgers's "sudden rise to fame," said the *Mountain Sun*, "reads like a page from Horatio Alger's books." In a day when editors were still working the rags-to-riches angle for all it was worth, Bill Bruner clearly had no corner on the market. The lengthy story went on to repeat many of the fables Jimmie had perpetuated, including the account of how his singing over WWNC had "brought a Victor representative to Asheville, and Rodgers became a sensation practically overnight." The age at which he was orphaned dropped from the standard four years to two (it was actually six), and sales of "Sleep, Baby, Sleep" were reported to be 2,000,000 copies. "Today his annual income derived from royalties on Victor phonograph records approximates $100,000 . . . [and] his contract for the [upcoming] vaudeville tour calls for $1,000 a week."[6]

Although he would be out of town most of the summer fulfilling his pact with R-K-O, Rodgers continued to be a hot topic in Kerrville.

Stories of the tour's successes were dutifully reported in the local papers, along with accounts of Jimmie's new cars. (Within three months that year he bought two Fords, both equipped with every imaginable gadget.) Townsfolk also kept a close watch as construction began on Blue Yodeler's Paradise. Walter Rodgers left his conductor's job with the Southern Railway and came out to Kerrville to accompany his brother on the tour as "business manager" (another professional arrangement that lasted only briefly), and Jimmie, squeezing all he could out of his celebrity status, arranged an appearance at the local movie house on the Sunday prior to his departure. Local Victor dealers joined in to promote the show, and he played two performances to packed houses.

The following Tuesday, May 7, he left Kerrville for Miami, Oklahoma, to open the R-K-O Interstate tour. Rodgers headlined a bill that included the Seven Nelsons ("Europe's Latest Acrobatic Sensation"), comedians Morton and Stout, and the Shaw-Carroll Dance Revue. It was essentially an "intact unit"—R-K-O's term for a roadshow made up of independent acts but booked together for a given number of weeks. After a split-week opening at Miami's Coleman Theater on May 16,[7] the schedule called for a week in each of ten major cities: Tulsa, Oklahoma City, Fort Worth, Dallas, San Antonio, Houston, New Orleans, Little Rock, Birmingham, and Atlanta, closing on July 26. For Rodgers it was a grueling grind in which any one city became a replica of all the others. Doing four shows a day, seven days a week, left little time for rest during the run, and "making the jump" between cities every Friday often meant traveling all night. Still, in every city he squeezed in one or two radio broadcasts and made several appearances at music stores to sign autographs and records, or simply to shake hands and chat with the hundreds of fans who turned out.

On the Loew Circuit a year earlier, he'd been billed as "America's Blue Yodeler" while appearing onstage in brakeman's garb. As if that were not illogical enough, the procedure was now curiously reversed. Although now he was back to "The Singing Brakeman" or even more frequently "The *Yodeling* Brakeman" in advertising and publicity, he performed in street clothes, often topped off with a wide-brimmed Western hat. A Dallas critic scolded him for giving up the railroad image: "Picture Mr. Rodgers and his harmony in some dim-lighted caboose and you can imagine the hit he must have been in his railroad days. We'd advise him to arrange a setting like that for his act. Nothing is charged for this counsel."[8] Otherwise, the reviews were practically unanimous in their praise. In Houston, where the show broke all attendance records and hundreds were turned away, the *Post-Dispatch* observed that Rodgers's name "is applauded before he appears." Said the *Atlanta Constitution*: "Jimmie Rodgers seems to get better every time he appears on a local stage." Even the Dallas critic singled him out as the hit of the "unusually qualitative vaudeville bill" and praised him for his unique style and clear voice. "He is in high favor throughout," admitted the reviewer, "and even his long-drawn-out stories appear to please." Writing for the *Dallas News*, John Rosenfield called the bill "the best program from start to finish that this chronicler has seen in five and twenty years." The only sour note came, oddly enough, in Birmingham, where the *Post*'s critic complained that the stage program was "spotty" and "mediocre"— noting, however, that Rodgers was roundly applauded by the audience.[9]

But while they were enthusiastic, the reviews were fewer and briefer than before, carried farther back in the papers and often buried under bigger, more immediate show business news. Since Rodgers's Loew tour the previous year, a drastic change had taken place in popular entertainment, all as the result of a singular phenomenon: the mushrooming vogue for talking pictures. Quite simply, talkies were taking over, creating shock waves throughout the industry and sending live entertainment running for cover. With many a whimper and a bang, vaudeville slipped into its final decline. Everywhere theater ads and newspaper publicity reflected the radical new trend, in phrases now memorable only for their quaintness. "100% Talking—100% Entertainment," proclaimed the movie ads. "Hear Douglas McLean Talk for the First Time." "Mary Pickford in the ALL SPOKEN Show 'Coquette.'" "A talking drama of wild passion—also talking comedy and Pathe News." Paramount's famous mountain logotype was draped with an "All Talking" banner across its snowy slope; the trademarks and publicity of other studios were similarly defaced in deference to the mania for sound. R-K-O, true to its word, bravely continued to give its vaude bills strong promotion, but there was simply no way their stage shows could compete with the hullabaloo over talkies.

In Tulsa, R-K-O's Orpheum Theater had just been wired for sound, and Jimmie Rodgers shared top billing with the "Gala Opening of Our

Vitaphone and Movietone Talking Pictures Presenting Warner Bros. Latest Talking Picture." (It was *No Defense,* with Monte Blue and May McAvoy—"vivid and enthralling drama of a bridge that collapsed and a love that endured!") He also had to compete with the *Tulsa World*'s "Miss Tulsa" beauty contest in the same theater. By and large, however, Rodgers's audience remained loyal despite the many other bids for their attention. His radio broadcast at the end of the week, starring on the weekly Rialto-Orpheum Radio Show over KVOO, brought the usual deluge of mail, telegrams, and telephone requests.[10]

Rodgers's R-K-O unit was booked for the grand opening of Interstate's new multi-million-dollar Majestic Theater in San Antonio on June 14. The vaudeville bill was enlarged to eight acts for this gala event, and an all-out promotional campaign spotlighted Rodgers, the undisputed headliner and a local boy to boot. (Kerrville was only sixty miles away.) First-nighters included Texas Governor and Mrs. Dan Moody, the Mexican consul in San Antonio with a delegation of officials, and other distinguished guests. A capacity audience, most of them in formal dress, crowded the lavish new theater, advertised as second only to New York's Paramount in size and elegance, to witness a boggling array of entertainment that included the expanded vaude bill and William Fox's latest talking-film extravaganza, *Movietone Follies.* ("All talking—All singing—All dancing—The first film follies for the talking screen!") Jimmie did four numbers—"Blue Yodel No. 4," "Daddy and Home," "Treasures Untold," and "In the Jailhouse Now"—and was called back for several encores. He got prominent headline treatment in the papers ("Famous Victor Artist Tops Vaudeville, Movietone Follies on the Screen"), but despite the crowd's enthusiasm for him, the reviews were limited to sundry misstatements and the casual observation that "He is doing a most entertaining act of singing, yodeling, and musical numbers."[11] A critic for the *San Antonio Light* complained that the length of the opening night bill "somewhat marred" the occasion: "The film's similarity to a musical comedy stage show, made up of song and dance acts mostly with little thoughtful plot, made the show seem like one continuous vaudeville act."[12] It was clearly not the wisest programming ever devised.

In New Orleans this time there were no private guest appearances or lengthy interviews with the press, but reviewers duly noted Jimmie's impact on his audiences. A writer for the *Times-Picayune*, suffering grammatical lapses but accurately catching the essence of Rodgers's appeal, wrote that "Jimmie Rodgers, Victor recording artist who has the headline spot, plays a guitar as if he'd grown up with one on his lap and gags when he isn't singing blue songs [meaning, one assumes, that he told jokes between blues—not "blue"— songs]. You might call him a 'gentleman actor'—he has a slightly different line than others of his profession."[13] The *New Orleans States* reported that "he had to take several bows and give many encores. He has a pleasing and crooning voice which went over well with the audience."[14]

The tour ended in Atlanta on July 26. Headed back toward Texas, Jimmie stopped off in Meridian to meet Carrie and rest up for a couple of weeks, but (as usual) he was busy most of the time, working with "Sister Elsie" on new material. Peer had arranged to hold his next recording session at the Jefferson Hotel in Dallas beginning on August 8.

Arriving in Dallas with his wife and sister-in-law, Jimmie registered at the Jefferson and took off on his habitual round of theaters, union halls, and night spots. Along the way he heard about a musician named Joe Kaipo, a Hawaiian guitar player (in both senses of the adjective: a native of Honolulu, Kaipo specialized in the so-called steel or "Hawaiian" guitar in vogue at the time). Learning that Kaipo was working at a swank west Dallas speakeasy known as the El Tivoli Club, Rodgers went to catch his act. But Kaipo and the other musicians had been given Saturday night off, so Jimmie left a note for him, asking Kaipo to call the hotel to discuss working on the upcoming recording session.

Except for his brief and rather random association with Jimmie Rodgers, little is known of Joe Kaipo. Even the circumstances which brought them together were, as the foregoing indicates, mostly a matter of chance, as was frequently the case with Rodgers and the musicians who accompanied him. Apparently Kaipo had a reputation of sorts among musicians in the area; he'd gotten the El Tivoli job largely as a result of his passing acquaintance with two Fort Worth youngsters, Billy and Weldon Burkes, whom he'd met only a short time before Rodgers contacted him. Ironically, the Burkes brothers, especially Billy Burkes, were to play a far more prominent role than Kaipo in Rodgers's developing career.[15]

Although he was only seventeen at the time, Billy Burkes was a show business veteran who had appeared professionally as early as 1922, when he was ten. Taught to sing by his musically inclined parents, Burkes's initiation into show business had come about in 1921, when the famous C. A. Wortham carnival played his hometown, Wichita, Kansas. Billy and his brother Weldon, a year and a half older, went down to the lot without any money, hoping to sing and pick up enough change among the sideshow crowd to pay for admission to the main tent. Wortham himself, one of the legends in the business, heard them performing. The next day he offered the boys' father $1,000 plus expenses for them and their mother, for a ten-week summer tour. Unhappily, all the boys got out of the offer was a headline in the paper—"Wichita Boy Singers Thrill Carnival Crowds; Offered $1,000 to Go with Wortham."[16] The elder Burkes declined the offer, and the boys glumly returned to school. The following year, however, they entered an amateur contest sponsored by Brunk's Comedians, another traveling rep show, and were so popular with the crowds that they began to appear whenever the show played in Wichita and neighboring towns. Eventually they were hired to tour with a Brunk's unit under the management of Texan Harley Sadler, who later, as the owner of his own company, became one of the Southwest's best-known and most beloved showmen.

During this time the Burkes brothers were essentially vocalists. When the family moved to Fort Worth about 1924, however, they became acquainted with a traveling salesman named Fred Stewart, who taught them both to play the ukulele. Lacking an instrument of their own, they improvised with an old gourd mandola, stripped down to four strings and tuned like a uke. They were also adept at making their own instruments, creating a one-string "guitar" out of a cigar box and broom handle that Billy thumb-picked like a steel, using a perfume bottle as a slide. For Christmas that year they both received Martin ukuleles and began to spend their free time playing for street crowds and neighborhood parties. One of their more lucrative enterprises was to ride the Dobbs Safety Coach bus runs between Fort Worth and Arlington, playing for tips; sometimes they made as much as eighty dollars on a weekend—"more money than we knew what to do with," according to Billy Burkes. Their repertoire consisted of "popular music of the day" and old standbys such as "Silver Threads among the Gold." School held less and less attraction for the talented brothers, and soon they were devoting all their time to performing. By 1927 they were playing regularly in local vaudeville houses, and that same year they toured statewide on the Publix circuit, ending with an engagement at the "million-dollar" Aztec Theater in San Antonio. Between shows Billy went over to catch the bill at the old Majestic, where Nick Lucas was headlining. Captivated by Lucas's light, intricate guitar work, he made up his mind on the spot to give up the uke and learn to play guitar. Back in Fort Worth, he bought a mail-order guitar for fifty dollars and struggled along with it before falling heir to a friend's old Gibson. With that instrument and a near-perfect ear, he soon mastered the technique, developing a style in conscious imitation of his idol, Nick Lucas.

In the ensuing years the Burkes brothers found plenty of work. By the summer of 1929 they had landed a job "strolling floors" at the exclusive El Tivoli—roaming among the tables and playing requests during the regular band's intermissions. Shortly they were joined by Kaipo, and the trio was an immediate success.[17] Working strictly for tips, they were soon making several hundred dollars every night. When the waiters complained that their own tips were suffering as a result, the group was asked to take Saturday nights off to allow the waiters a fair share. Thus they were absent when Rodgers showed up to hear Kaipo.

Handed Rodgers's note when he came to work the next day, Kaipo called Jimmie at his hotel and arranged for an audition the following morning. Perhaps apprehensive about meeting a star of such stature, Kaipo prevailed upon Billy Burkes to go along with him, "to break the ice." Burkes was reluctant at first, not because he shared Kaipo's awe, but, on the contrary, because he was decidedly unimpressed by Jimmie Rodgers. He had, in fact, gone with a friend to one of Jimmie's R-K-O appearances in Fort Worth back in June—and left during the performance. "I just didn't care too much for Jimmie's music—that type of music," he recalled later. "I hadn't been around any of it." But Kaipo finally persuaded him to go along for the interview, and (somewhat to Burkes's surprise) Rodgers hired them both on the spot. He then put them to work woodshedding the material he planned to record.

"That was the hardest day's work of my life," Burkes said. "His sister-in-law would hand Jimmie some lyrics, he'd search around for a tune to it, and I'd try to follow him on the guitar, try to find the right chords." When Burkes felt he had the tune under control, he'd take

Kaipo off in a corner and try to teach it to him—"Joe's ear for music wasn't too fast"—so he could work out a lead on the steel. Ceiling fans provided the only relief from the sweltering summer heat; by the end of the day the musicians were all weary. Jimmie seemed to suffer no more than the others, however, and scheduled another rehearsal for the following morning.

By mutual agreement, Weldon Burkes came along the next day, and the addition of his ukulele seemed to make things go better. "Just that little ukulele made a difference in the combination," Billy recalled. "I'll tell you, there's a lot of music to be had out of a little uke."

Ralph Peer liked what he heard from the group, and they went into a makeshift studio in the Jefferson Hotel's banquet hall on Thursday, August 8. The first side they recorded, "Everybody Does It in Hawaii," provided an appropriate debut for the group, oriented as it was to pop styles and the Hawaiian fad of the day. With Rodgers singing two verses and a repeat of the lengthy chorus, the band had little room for individual virtuosity; but the accompaniment is solid and vigorous, carried along by Billy Burkes's strong seconding on the standard guitar. The song itself, trivial but ingratiating, was one of Rodgers's more blatant appeals to a pop audience. A last-minute entry in the schedule, it had been composed only the night before it was recorded. Earlier, Kaipo had talked expansively about the splendors of Hawaii (claiming, among other things, that his father was mayor of Honolulu), and Peer joked that he'd have to arrange a session there. "Yeah," said Jimmie, "I'd like to have me one of them hula-hula girls." That night, unable to sleep because of the heat, Elsie got up and scribbled off a few verses based on phrases from the conversation that had stuck in her mind. When she sang it for the musicians at breakfast the next morning, they took to it immediately, and Peer decided to record it while they were so enthusiastic.[18] The song's double entendre, appropriate to Rodgers's image and risqué enough to be catchy, was nevertheless pretty mild stuff to audiences accustomed to the likes of "How Come You Do Me Like You Do?" (1924), "Makin' Whoopee," and "Do What You Did Last Night" (both 1928). But when the record was released, *Variety*, on one of the rare occasions when it deigned to notice Jimmie Rodgers, huffed that "dealers should use discrimination and not sell this into polite families or for juvenile consumption." The complaint, apparently, was that "It's never made clear what everybody does in Hawaii. That leaves the sensitive listeners in a state of unrelieved embarrassment."[19] Curious as that statement seems, it merely reflected the typical coy stance of *Variety*, which delighted in printing spicy divorce stories, national scandal, and deliberately scurrilous gossip—all cynically cast in a tone of weary indignation. Perhaps the only faint shock that arises today from "Everybody Does It in Hawaii" is that the lyrics came from Elsie McWilliams, who would not allow her name on any of the Blue Yodels because "I've always been mighty straitlaced."

The second song, "Tuck Away My Lonesome Blues," was likewise a spur-of-the-moment production. Peer heard Kaipo playing the music, which he had composed long before, and suggested that they would record it if he could come up with suitable lyrics. Kaipo complained that it had taken him a year just to work out the tune, whereupon Peer said, "Give it to Elsie." She listened to the music once, jotted off some lyrics in shorthand, then transcribed them "without revising a single word."[20] Peer gave his okay, and the tune was scheduled for the afternoon session. The result was one of Rodgers's better recordings, but one that for unknown reasons is often neglected in discussions of his work.

For "Tuck Away My Lonesome Blues," the group was joined by whistler Bob MacGimsey, who had appeared frequently on radio and records with Gene Austin and others. A prominent lawyer and cotton planter in his native Lake Providence, Louisiana, MacGimsey was known as "the only man in the world who can whistle three tones at once" (the so-called harmony whistling heard on the Rodgers record). He took seriously his title as National Champion Whistler. To a university professor who theorized that "whistling is an unmistakable sign of the moron," MacGimsey replied, "I'm not sure what degree of nit-wit that makes me . . . but if you're asking me, it's hardly fair to say that whistling has any more to do with a man's mentality than his playing the bass viol. And, if so, what about the yodelers and the Swiss bell ringers? The surest sign of a moron is how he thinks and not whether he whistles, plays the fiddle or indulges mumbly-peg."[21] MacGimsey's performance on "Tuck Away My Lonesome Blues" provided a pleasant, if now dated, interlude; his presence was clearly another concession to the popular taste of the time, but one that would leave no lasting effect on the substance of Rodgers's work.

As the sessions progressed, Kaipo's performances on the steel guitar grew more confident, contributing materially to the strength of two of

Jimmie's best numbers, "Train Whistle Biues" and "Jimmie's Texas Blues." Once again Rodgers drew on the communal stock of old blues verses, and once again, like all the good bluesmen, he transformed them into his own personal statement of hard luck and faded love, of stoic endurance and the release, bordering on rapture, that comes from sharing the experience. "Yes," he sang, "I know how it feels when you're feeling so doggone blue." In "Texas Blues" one finds even that hoariest but best of lines—"The blues ain't nothin' but a good man feeling bad." The lyrics are new all over again when he sings them, talking along between verses, shouting "Hey, sweet mama!" and imploring "Have mercy, Lord," yodeling on down the line after the band has faded.[22]

For some time Rodgers had planned to record "Frankie and Johnny," an old stage number that he had known most of his life and had used frequently in personal appearances. Peer was not very enthusiastic about it, for he knew there was little chance to claim composer royalties on the song. While "Frankie and Johnny" was certainly as "traditional" as other songs that Jimmie had put his name on, it was much better known and had, in fact, already been recorded several times during the early Twenties by such artists as Al Bernard (Brunswick 2107), Fate Marable (Okeh 40113), and even Carl Sandburg, who termed it a "classical gutter song." Only two years earlier it had been a minor hit for Frank Crumit (who, according to Vance Randolph, once claimed "complete authorship" of the song). But Jimmie kept working with it, changing a word here and there, and Peer finally decided that they might be able to copyright it as an "arrangement."[23]

Over the weekend Rodgers resumed his prowls around town, accompanied by young Billy Burkes. In a dancehall in the black section of east Dallas they ran across a jazz band that Jimmie liked, and he persuaded the group to come down to the Jefferson on Monday to record "Frankie and Johnny" with him. According to Burkes, "the band sounded real good with Jimmie," but, for reasons unknown, Peer rejected the take and instead issued a solo version which Rodgers had done two days before.

The Dallas session ended with several attempts to record "Home Call," which Elsie McWilliams said she "wrote up several different ways." Although Rodgers later recorded a satisfactory solo version, no takes of "Home Call" from this session were released until the early

1960's, when what was perhaps the most bizarre version of all—with Jimmie and Kaipo accompanied by a musical saw—appeared on the LP album entitled *Jimmie the Kid.*

The Burkes brothers and Kaipo returned to their job at the El Tivoli, and Jimmie headed for Kerrville. But, as usual, Rodgers had big plans for the future, and he told the musicians that he would be in touch with them again as soon as the details were worked out. Peer was talking about another vaudeville tour and was already making arrangements to return to Dallas in the fall for another recording session.

In his absence from Kerrville that summer, Rodgers had appointed three prominent businessmen, J. L. Pampell (the local Victor dealer), E. A. Prescott, and W. A. Fawcett, to handle his affairs and to look after the construction of his new home. The San Antonio architectural firm of Morris and Noonan was commissioned to draw up the plans; the contract was let in June, and building began in late July. According to the Kerrville *Mountain Sun* the cost had risen from $20,000 to $25,000—considerably less than the figure publicized today, but still an imposing sum, at a time when the average three-bedroom brick residence in Kerrville was being built for less than $5,000.[24] But even while Blue Yodeler's Paradise was going up, Jimmie's star was somewhat eclipsed by a Houston oil man, who erected a $150,000 "summer home" on his ranch property near the city. There were numerous other mansions of similar magnitude in the vicinity.

In early September, Rodgers wrote to the Burkes brothers, to whom he had clearly taken a liking: "Well things are fixing to break now. I have just heard from New York and I am to open about the middle of October. But between now and then I am to record again and also make a short talking picture." He outlined the arrangements under which the musicians would work for him; they were each to be paid sixty dollars a week, plus a bonus of fifteen dollars a week at the end of the run (or as Jimmie alternately phrased it, "you will receive seventy-five dollars each per week but fifteen dollars each week will be held out until your contract expires.") They were instructed to get in touch with Joe Kaipo and offer him the same terms. Jimmie's plan was to bring the three of them to Kerrville for rehearsals, "for which I will pay your transportation, eating and sleeping expenses." He suggested also the possibility that they would play several barnstorm dates in the meantime, receiving a commission that would equal or exceed their regular salary.

One Day Only

COAST-TO-COAST TOUR

OF AMERICA'S FAMOUS "BLUE YODELER"

JIMMIE RODGERS

IN PERSON!

Famous
Victor Star
and

HIS COMPANY OF ENTERTAINERS

IN A PROGRAM OF THE
GREATEST VARIETY AND FILLED
WITH ENTERTAINMENT AND SURPRISE

Not a city, town or village in America but knows "Jimmie Rodgers" and his "Blue Yodel," his happy, care-free songs, and his guitar. Only a few cities can hear him as his tour is limited on account of his recording engagements with the Victor Talking Machine Company.

LYNN THEATRE

O'DONNELL, TEXAS, Saturday, April 6th, 1929

Tickets on Sale at Corner Drug Store, O'Donnell, Texas; Cannon Variety Store, Lamesa; Thompson Drug Store, Tahoka.

1st show from 6:30 to 9:00 p. m.   2nd show from 9:00 to 11:30

The notorious "Coast-to-Coast Tour" never quite made it from sea to shining sea, but Jimmie revived the idea from time to time, using this ad layout as the focus of his publicity. The "company of entertainers" was almost invariably composed of locals recruited on the spot, but in places like O'Donnell, no one seemed to mind.

The cowboy image and the lore of the West fascinated Rodgers, but there is no evidence that he performed in the elaborate, if reasonably authentic, **getup** shown in this rare photo, made **about** the time he moved to Texas in 1929.

Still shot from *The Singing Brakeman,* Rodgers's movie for Columbia Victor Gems, fall, 1929.

"Jimmie Rodgers's Guitar Hounds" was Jimmie's joking reference to this group of musicians who accompanied him on some of his best-known records. *From left:* Billy Burkes, Weldon Burkes, Joe Kaipo, Rodgers. Photo taken in Houston during their Texas tour in the autumn of 1929 and inscribed to Charlie Burkes, eldest of the three brothers.

Getting in touch with Kaipo proved to be the most difficult part of the arrangement. A likeable but pugnacious sort, he seemed to have an affinity for Texas jails. Shortly after the recording sessions were over, he'd gotten into an argument with a cab driver, started a fight, and wound up in the Dallas pokey. That ended the El Tivoli job, and the Burkes brothers had gone back to free-lancing. Although Kaipo had disappeared after his release in Dallas, he was traced to Wichita Falls, where the Burkes boys found him in the local calaboose once more. Finally, with the help of their father and after much difficulty, they succeeded in getting him bailed out, just in time to answer Rodgers's summons to Kerrville.

Jimmie met the three at the San Antonio railroad station, drove them out to Kerrville, and put them up at a hotel. Once they were settled, he took them down to a local haberdashery and bought each one a complete new wardrobe. "When we walk down the street," he told them, "and people say, 'There's Jimmie Rodgers' boys,' I want you to look like a million dollars even if you haven't got a dime."[25] They spent a few days rehearsing and working up an act, then set out on the road in one of Jimmie's new Fords to "barnstorm a few dates," as he put it. Oil activity around the West Texas towns of Sonora and Ozona had swelled the population with drilling crews and pipeline workers, and Jimmie decided that area would be a good place to start. He sent one of his Kerrville buddies, R. T. "Jerry" Gerard, a fellow T.B. sufferer, ahead to contact local theaters and to publicize the Blue Yodeler's coming. But Gerard failed to make the arrangements on time, so the entertainers drove up to San Angelo, where they succeeded in booking a two-day stand at the Municipal Auditorium.

Joe Hanks, a nomadic portrait photographer known to pitchmen and carny workers around the country as "Fine Arts," was working San Angelo at the time. He sent a "pipe" to *Billboard*:

> I have framed [teamed up with] Professor James A. Black, better known as "That Man Black—He Makes the Camera Click." Guess I will have to re-route, as California is his only ambition for the winter. Our old friend, Jimmie Rodgers, is here for a two-day stand with his guitar and many yodels. Guess I'll go over and say "Hello." Business seems good. I see lots of good cigars smoked by more or less mediocre pedestrians, which is a pretty good sign. . . .[26]

Hanks's casual "Guess I'll go over and say 'Hello'" was the response of thousands. Everywhere Jimmie Rodgers went, he encountered old friends from his roustabout days, railroaders and pitchmen and knights of the road, and always he was ready with a handshake, a "loan," and a swig or two of his prescription bourbon.

Contrary to Fine Arts's cheery prediction, business was only fair in San Angelo. Rodgers and his troupe returned to Kerrville to bide their time while Jimmie took stock of the situation and looked for other likely locations. After a week or so they took off again, headed this time for the Gulf Coast, where Jimmie had booked appearances in Beaumont and Port Arthur.

Meanwhile, Ralph Peer was on his way back from Memphis to Dallas to set up another recording session. He detoured through Port Arthur to meet Rodgers and discuss some bad news concerning one of their current projects. Back in August, Jimmie had announced— around Kerrville, at least—a whopping sixty-eight-week tour at $3,000 a week on R-K-O's big-time circuit, extending from New York to San Francisco.[27] It mattered little that the actual figures were ultimately a great deal less, or that the arrangement was only tentative, because now the whole affair was about to be cancelled. While Wall Street's bull market continued its headlong charge to dizzying heights, show business in general and vaudeville in particular had fallen into turmoil, beset by rumor and uncertainty. Amid the furor caused by talking pictures and generally unsettled entertainment conditions throughout the country, R-K-O temporarily suspended all new vaudeville bookings, leaving its famous fifth-floor booking office in the Paramount Building practically deserted.[28] Rodgers took the news with characteristic good humor, despite his obvious disappointment. He found some consolation in the fact that details had been completed with Columbia for the short film he was to make. As further balm, Peer arranged for him to record again in Dallas in mid-October.

After the last show in Port Arthur, Joe Kaipo and Weldon Burkes decided to celebrate with a night on the town—an outing which culminated in a friendly, inebriated brawl in their hotel room. Although Rodgers paid for the damage and convinced the manager not to file a charge, Peer took a dim view of such goings-on.

Despite the altercation, Jimmie took the Burkes brothers and Kaipo with him to Dallas for his next recording session. In retrospect, it is difficult to understand why he did so, for he recorded four of the six numbers solo, and used the full group (rather ineffectually at that) only on "Whisper Your Mother's Name." With one or two exceptions, the recordings from that session are among Rodgers's least inspired. For the first time, perhaps in deference to his adopted state, he performed a couple of Western-oriented numbers. Although they were to have substantial impact on the emerging "singing-cowboy" image in movies and on record, neither "Yodeling Cowboy" nor "The Land of My Boyhood Dreams" offers anything out of the ordinary. The latter may suggest some clue to his mood, as he placed in himself in the role of an old wrangler, growing feeble and heartsick, whose "days are nearly done." Rodgers himself would probably have brushed aside any such psychological speculation, and rightly so; the dangers of digging deep meanings out of commercial song lyrics are many. Still, the evidence is there, on record: the thin, listless guitar work, the voice that sounds as if it is merely going through the paces, the occasional slurs ("hastedly" for "hastily," for example), and above all the weak and insipid material. "I've Ranged, I've Roamed, and I've Travelled" was so poor that it was held for release until long after Rodgers's death, when Victor was scraping out the last bit of treacle—and pocket change—from the Blue Yodeler's barrel.[29]

The happy exceptions to this criticism are "My Rough and Rowdy Ways," one of the more fortunate results of the Rodgers-McWilliams collaboration, and "Blue Yodel No. 6," which, although barely up to the standard of others in the series, succeeds on the strength of the form and Rodgers's obvious affection for it. His recording of "My Rough and Rowdy Ways" has, in addition to the backing of Joe Kaipo's steel guitar, the further advantage of its material. The song is autobiographical, in the best sense of the term; close to the core of Rodgers's life and personality, it was material he felt comfortable with, unlike the sentimental paeans to Mother, pop love ballads, and hokey campfire songs he felt called on to record during this time.

Precisely one week after the Dallas session the nation's financial establishment staged its most dramatic and tragic show of the age, concisely chronicled in *Variety*'s famous headline: "WALL ST. LAYS AN EGG."[30] But the real effects of the stock market collapse would not be felt for some time, and Jimmie Rodgers, who paid little attention to national affairs anyway, had more important matters on his mind. The most immediate problem, as always, was that of finding suitable song material to keep up with the growing demand. Soon after Bristol he had taken to stashing away any scrap that might prove useful—bits of lyrics from oral tradition, poems, greeting card verses, slogans;

anything with the germ of an idea that might be developed into a song. Still, he was constantly pressed to come up with the finished products.

An unexpected source of material appeared in a West Texas farm boy named Waldo O'Neal. Like many others in that era, O'Neal had been born into a rich heritage of rural music. As a small boy he'd watched the silent westerns of William S. Hart and Hoot Gibson, and later had fallen sway to the string bands and yodeling crooners that emanated from primitive radio speakers and scratchy phonograph records. Like many others also, his idol was Jimmie Rodgers.

O'Neal had begun scribbling down poems and song lyrics while still in his teens. "I ordered a cheap guitar from Montgomery Ward," he remembered years later, "and sang my songs to family and friends, usually fitting them to some familiar cowboy tune."[31] In 1928 he composed a mournful dirge about a dying tramp, in the vein of hundreds of similar hobo songs.[32] His sister was much impressed by the song, which he called "Hobo Bill's Last Ride," and she suggested that he send it to Jimmie Rodgers. "I laughed and said, 'Do you think he would sing any song I wrote?'" O'Neal recalls. At her urging, however, he mailed a copy of the lyric to Jimmie in care of the Victor Talking Machine Company, adding that he sang it to the tune of "Waiting for a Train" and hoped that might be helpful. Interestingly enough, O'Neal was completely unaware that Rodgers had ever worked on the railroad—another indication that, even by 1929, the "Singing Brakeman" image had never quite established itself, or had already been superseded by "America's Blue Yodeler."

Months passed, and O'Neal had almost forgotten about mailing the song away when one day his father returned from town with a big smile on his face. In his hand was a letter from Rodgers, containing a check and a contract for use of "Hobo Bill's Last Ride."[33] Naturally, O'Neal was elated. He later supplied several additional songs, four of which were eventually recorded by the Blue Yodeler.

Just when and where "Hobo Bill's Last Ride" was recorded is something of a mystery. In fact, Rodgers's precise whereabouts between the October recording session in Dallas and the November sessions in Atlanta remain to be documented. During that time he went to Camden to film his talking short, *The Singing Brakeman;*[34] and according to Victor's files "Hobo Bill's Last Ride" was recorded in New Orleans on November 13. If those files are correct, however, he recorded only that one side in New Orleans—an extremely curious circumstance which many observers have remarked upon. On the other hand, there is the story, credited to his brother Tal, that Jimmie cut a dozen or more sides in the Crescent City at that time.[35] This assertion is given credence by a gap in Victor's sequence of master numbers following "Hobo Bill's Last Ride," suggesting that the missing numbers were assigned to test pressings or private recordings by Rodgers that never found their way into the production files. The number of missing matrixes, however, does not match the figure given by Tal Rodgers. Elsie McWilliams speaks of being with Rodgers at a recording session in New Orleans, but she is not sure of the date and offers other details that conflict with the files. (She says, for example, that she wrote "Mississippi River Blues" in New Orleans and that Rodgers recorded it there,[36] although rather conclusive evidence shows that the song was recorded in Atlanta later. She also mentions that "Never No Mo' Blues" was recorded in New Orleans, but it had been done in Camden a year and half earlier and had in fact been in release for more than a year.)

The strongest evidence of error in the Victor files for the New Orleans session comes from William T. "Billy" Burkes. A genial, modest gentleman who through the years quietly cherished his association with Rodgers, Burkes had the distinction of accompanying Jimmie on more records (seventeen) and working with him longer than any other musician. Experts and enthusiasts have long agreed that the guitar heard on "Hobo Bill's Last Ride" is not Rodgers's; although years had elapsed since it was made, Burkes listened to the recording and had no doubts that it was he who played the accompaniment, offering convincing evidence to bear out his statement. "I played Jimmie's Weymann guitar on this particular tune," he pointed out, "and you can notice the difference in tone, in the way it recorded. My, that was a beautiful instrument." Burkes was equally certain that the number was not recorded in New Orleans, and that he never recorded there with Rodgers. "The files must be fouled up someplace," he said. "For Jimmie to come to New Orleans just to cut one side—that just doesn't sound like the way they operated." Burkes's conclusion: "To my recollection, 'Hobo Bill' was made in Atlanta."[37] Aural evidence supports this view; as with the succeeding Atlanta recordings, the tone is brighter, the mood more mellow, and Rodgers's voice has regained the clarity and enthusiasm so lacking in Dallas.

Whatever the circumstances of its origins on record, and despite the inherent sentimentality of the form, "Hobo Bill's Last Ride" is in several ways an improvement over the Dallas sides which preceded it, thanks in no small part to Elsie McWilliams's reworking of the song. It seems to belong quite properly to the repertoire—mixed, but on the whole successful—which Rodgers recorded in Atlanta, in a series of sessions lasting from November 25 through 28.

A week earlier, back in Fort Worth, Billy Burkes had received a phone call from Rodgers, who was stopping at the Baker Hotel in Dallas. Would Burkes be interested in working with him on another recording date, and possibly some concerts after that? As for Weldon Burkes and Joe Kaipo, it was no secret that Jimmie had not been entirely pleased with them during the barnstorming tour. Moreover, he implied, there was Peer's heavy hand to contend with. "Ralph wasn't too happy about that little fracas in Port Arthur," he told Burkes. Both Peer and Rodgers liked Billy's work, however, and felt that he had proved himself both on the road and in the recording studio. "I'll pay you $25 a day when we make records, or put you on a straight salary at $75 a week, whichever you want," Jimmie told him.[38] "I'm not trying to break up your act, but the job's there if you want it."

Burkes had little trouble making up his mind. Although the worst shock waves from Wall Street were yet to hit North Texas, business conditions had been shaky for some time. Since the El Tivoli engagement, the trio had limped along from one pick-up job to another, contending with erratic bookings, spotty salaries, and Kaipo's penchant for picking fights and landing in jail. Burkes accepted Rodgers's offer, opting for the weekly salary.

A few days later he took the interurban over to Dallas and went up to Rodgers's room to discuss travel arrangements and other details of the projected tour. Jimmie decided to go to a nearby luggage and music store to shop for a briefcase, and he asked Burkes to go along. After picking out the briefcase, they both drifted toward the back of the store, where the stock of Martin guitars was displayed. "They'd just brought out their first 'f-hole' model," Burkes recalled. "Jimmie strummed around on it, then handed it to me. We looked at some others. I personally liked a round-hole model they had better, and when Jim asked me which was best, I said that one, even though it was about thirty dollars cheaper. The round-hole really sounded nice, and it cut real well on records." Rodgers bought the guitar, and they took a cab back to the hotel. When they'd finished their plans for the Atlanta trip, Burkes started to leave. "Wait a minute," Jimmie said, holding up the guitar. "Aren't you gonna take this along and show your folks what I gave you?" Recalling the incident years later, Burkes paused, looking away. For him the story needed no comment.[39]

Rodgers and Burkes traveled to Atlanta in their own private Pullman drawing room. With an eye toward booking personal appearances once the recording sessions were over, Rodgers also brought along Jerry Gerard, his Kerrville buddy. Although Gerard had fouled up the earlier tour in Texas, Jimmie sympathized with him because of his tuberculosis and gave him work largely out of charity. It was only one of many such instances of the Blue Yodeler's casual philanthropy.

Despite the gloomy weather that greeted them in Atlanta, Jimmie was in high spirits. They checked into suites at the Henry Grady Hotel and went over the next day to a recording studio which Peer had set up in the meeting hall of the Atlanta Woman's Club building on Peachtree Street. There Rodgers first met his fellow "hillbilly pioneers," the Carter Family, who were just finishing a series of sessions that would produce some of their all-time classics: "The Cyclone of Rye Cove," "No Telephone in Heaven," "A Distant Land to Roam," and "Jimmie Brown the Newsboy."

Peer had lined up a substantial array of talent for Victor's Atlanta sessions, including the Stamps Quartet, the Georgia Yellow Hammers, and Blind Willie McTell. Noting that these were ample to keep the studio busy, Rodgers opted for brief after-dinner sessions throughout the week, a schedule which allowed him to rest and enjoy himself during the day. "We could have cut all those sides in two days," Billy Burkes said, "but Jim didn't want to rush anything, or push anybody too hard. We had all the time in the world. It was really grand." Burkes felt that Rodgers had other motives, too—that he generously spread the work out over several days so Burkes would get a full week's salary. "No two ways about it," he said. "Jim was the grandest guy I ever worked for. He was just great to me."[40]

The six sides recorded in Dallas the preceding month had all been done in one day. Working at a slower, more deliberate pace in Atlanta, Rodgers put down only eight numbers (nine if "Hobo Bill" is included) over a period of four days, and the change paid off. Much of the material was scarcely better than what he had struggled with in Dallas, but, rested and relaxed, buoyed no doubt by the change of scenery and happy to be back in the Deep South, Rodgers was able to take on such mediocrities as "That's Why I'm Blue" and "Why Did You Give Me Your Love" and, with strong backing from Burkes, produce records of substantial merit. From these sessions came two of his very best blues, "Mississippi River Blues" and "Anniversary Blue Yodel (Blue Yodel No. 7)," the latter highlighted by Burkes's rippling Nick Lucas runs. "Nobody Knows but Me" and even "That's Why I'm Blue" also reached wide popularity with his fans. "Nobody Knows but Me" is plagued by the silly, perhaps deliberate, evasiveness of its lyric— apparently no one but the singer does know why he's so mournful about being in jail while at the same time boasting that he'll leave "worth my weight in gold." But there, as elsewhere, Billy Burkes's delicate guitar work and Rodgers's jaunty delivery rescue what would otherwise be a dreary experience. Merle Haggard's rousing reprise (Capitol SWBB-223) demonstrates just how good the song could be. "That's Why I'm Blue" is another of those Rodgers-McWilliams anomalies, a successful recording that had every reason to fail. On paper the lyric is trite; Rodgers was tired and kept rushing the tempo, and Burkes, by his own admission, was unnerved by Jimmie's habit of inserting a different yodel each time they rehearsed it.[41] But perhaps these are things only a purist would note. At any rate, Rodgers's public loved the rendition.

Yet it must be admitted that the session produced some clinkers. From the standpoint of the song itself, "She Was Happy Till She Met You" is my own nominee (perhaps finishing in a dead heat with "I've Ranged, I've Roamed, and I've Travelled") for the worst thing Jimmie Rodgers ever recorded. Apparently "She Was Happy" was difficult even for Rodgers to digest; Billy Burkes remembered that it caused them "a rough time" and required "many takes."[42] For reasons only they would know—composer royalties being the most obvious— Rodgers and Elsie McWilliams were willing, maybe even anxious, to take credit for its composition. However, the song was actually one of those fin de siècle horrors from the great age of melodrama and morbidity, written by Charles Graham and Monroe Rosenfeld and copyrighted in 1899. By 1932, when Rodgers's recording was released, the real authors were either dead or too embarrassed to raise any protest.[43] "A Drunkard's Child" is only slightly better, perhaps because its pure and unabashed sentimentality is even more deliberately achieved, coming as it did from the Reverend Andy Jenkins, Peer's old hand at tears and flapdoodle.

The recording that emerged after Rodgers's death as "Blue Yodel Number Eleven" deserves comment, for at this juncture the regular sequence of recording and numbering the Blue Yodels was interrupted. In Atlanta the song was entered on the Victor log as "Blue Yodel No. 8," but when a review of the test pressing back in Camden revealed that the performance was inferior, the record was placed on hold. The numerous takes required to get it on wax and the fact that it was the only side attempted that day attest to the circumstances behind the recording's poor quality. Rodgers was not feeling up to par, and the repeated takes only tired him more and led to numerous timing errors. The lapses are minor enough to bother only a trained musician, but neither Rodgers nor Burkes was satisfied with the results. Whether Rodgers would have agreed to the number's eventual release can only be speculated upon. In any event, it was the first of his records to be rushed into distribution following his death.

The last side recorded in Atlanta was "Why Did You Give Me Your Love," another lyric supplied by Elsie McWilliams. Although he received no credit (nor did he expect any), Billy Burkes was largely responsible for the music; he commented later that "I put too many chords in it for Jimmie's type of music."[44] Perhaps because of the relatively complex structure, recording the song also caused considerable difficulty. Although the result is agreeable enough by the standards for pop love tunes of that day, "Why Did You Give Me Your Love" was also among those cuts that went unreleased until after Jimmie's death. The recording of it marked the virtual end of the Rodger-McWilliams collaboration. Although "Miss Elsie" had no doubt contributed to other scraps that Jimmie would later add to and polish, the only composition of hers that he subsequently recorded was the fine religious number, "The Wonderful City," in June, 1931.

From Atlanta, Rodgers and Burkes traveled to Chattanooga. There they met an old acquaintance of Jimmie's, the fiddler Clayton McMichen, who had recorded with Gid Tanner's Skillet Lickers and, as "Bob Nichols," had cut several sides for Columbia. McMichen was promoting fiddle contests and other stage shows in the Chattanooga area, and Jimmie discussed with him the possibility of a local concert appearance. Negotiations were begun to book Chattanooga's Memorial Auditorium, but December 13 was the first available date. Rodgers, restless as always and unwilling to linger while the arrangements were made final, decided to visit Asheville, some two hundred miles away, where he had old friends and many memories. If things worked out, he might book a few shows there in the meantime.

Accompanied by Burkes and McMichen, Rodgers arrived in the Land of the Sky during the first week in December. Three years before, when he'd first drifted into Asheville sick and on the bum, the town had greeted him with about as much enthusiasm as it showed for the winter wind gusting down across the mountains. His reception this time was a great deal different.

NOTES

1. *O'Donnell Index,* Mar. 29, 1929, p. 1.
2. *Ibid.,* Apr. 12, 1929, p. 1.
3. Paul Oliver, "Jimmy Rodgers," *Recorded Folk Music,* 2 [:2] (Mar.-Apr., 1959), 10.
4. *Lubbock Morning Avalanche,* Apr. 12, 1929, p. 12; *Lubbock Sunday Avalanche-Journal,* Apr. 7, 1929, p. 6.
5. *Memphis Commercial Appeal,* Nov. 23, 1928, p. 13.
6. *Kerrville Mountain Sun,* Apr. 25, 1929, p. 1.
7. Although the Coleman billed its stage acts as "Senior Orpheum Vaudeville— Only Orpheum Circuit Vaudeville between Kansas City and Tulsa," the theater was actually a "pop-time" house, booking two bills a week. The "last half," normally Wednesday-Thursday-Friday, was booked to units just beginning their road tour, as a sort of warm-up. Rodgers's unit, however, played there only two days (Thursday and Friday) before moving on to Tulsa.
8. *Dallas Times-Herald,* June 10, 1929, p. 8.
9. For these reviews, see (in order): *Houston Post-Dispatch,* June 24, 1929, p. 5; *Atlanta Constitution,* July 23, 1929, p. 24; *Dallas Morning News,* June 10, 1929, p. 4, and June 11, 1929, p. 12; *Birmingham Post,* July 16, 1929, p. 17.
10. See *Tulsa World,* May 18–24, 1929, *passim.*
11. *San Antonio Express,* June 16, 1929, sec. D, p. 17.
12. *San Antonio Light,* June 15, 1929, p. 14.
13. New Orleans *Times-Picayune,* July 1, 1929, p. 18.
14. *New Orleans States,* July 1, 1929, p. 7.
15. The ensuing account of William T. "Billy" Burkes's life and association with Rodgers was compiled from the following sources: Billy Burkes, interview by Jim Griffith, Mar. 11, 1976, Tucson; Jim Griffith to NP, Mar. 26, 1976; interviews by NP, Mar. 29, 1976, Jan. 23, June 5, and July 10, 1977; Billy Burkes to NP, Apr. 14, May 24, July 21, and Oct. 27, 1976; Jan. 12 and Oct. 8, 1977. The spelling of Billy Burkes's name has been the source of some confusion. During the time he toured with Rodgers, it was assumed by the family to be "Burke," although Jimmie, with characteristic disdain for orthography, also spelled it "Burks" and "Burkes" in correspondence and on his lyric sheets. Years later, having occasion to obtain a copy of his birth certificate, Billy learned that the legal form was actually "Burkes," and he has used that spelling since.

16. Unidentified clipping in the papers of Billy Burkes.

17. Burkes did not remember just when or how they met Kaipo, but he thought his father knew him and brought him to their home one day.

18. Elsie McWilliams, interview, Jan. 7, 1975, Meridian.

19. *Variety*, Jan. 8, 1930, p. 121.

20. Elsie McWilliams, interview, Jan. 7, 1975, Meridian.

21. *Memphis Commercial Appeal*, Oct. 18, 1931, sec. IV, p. 2.

22. "Jimmie's Texas Blues," words and music by Jimmie Rodgers. © 1930 by Peer International Corporation. Copyright renewed. Used by permission.

23. In *The Legendary Jimmie Rodgers: Memorial Folio I* (1967), "arranged by" is replaced with "words and music by." For a concise account of the possible origins and checkered history of "Frankie and Johnny," see Vance Randolph, *Ozark Folksongs* (Columbia, Mo.: State Historical Society of Missouri, 1948), II:125–36. Among several "folk" versions, Randolph prints one (pp. 135–36) that is almost identical with Rodgers's. As late as 1944, "Frankie and Johnny" was still having problems with the censor. A version copyrighted by Jerry Livingston and Mack David was the subject of a terse memo from the Breen Office (MPPA) to Louis B. Mayer of MGM. Producer Arthur Freed proposed to use the number in his forthcoming film, *Ziegfeld Follies*, but the censors found it "unacceptable from the standpoint of the Production Code, on account of its flavor of prostitution and excessive sex suggestiveness." The song was deleted. See Hugh Fordin, *The World of Entertainment: Hollywood's Greatest Musicals* (New York: Doubleday, 1975), pp. 121–22.

24. *Kerrville Mountain Sun*, June 27, Aug. 1, and Aug. 22, 1929, all p. 1. See also *Kerrville Times*, July 25, 1929, p. 1.

25. Billy Burkes, interview by Jim Griffith, Mar. 11, 1976, Tucson.

26. *Billboard*, Oct. 19, 1929, p. 80. See also *San Angelo Evening Standard*, Oct. 2, 1929, p. 2.

27. *Kerrville Times*, Aug. 22, 1929, p. 1.

28. *Variety*, Oct. 16, 1929, p. 38.

29. The difficulties during this session are further indicated by the fact that three and sometimes four takes were required. "The Land of My Boyhood Dreams" was recorded in ¾ and 4/4 time, and, on one of the rejected takes, in *both* time signatures within the space of a few bars. (See Bond, *Recordings of Jimmie Rodgers*, p. 14.) Billy Burkes corroborates that Rodgers was tired and "kept hurrying the tempo," especially on "Whisper Your Mother's Name" (Burkes to NP, Oct. 27, 1976).

30. *Variety*, Oct. 30, 1929, p. 1.

31. Waldo O'Neal to NP, Feb. 6, 1976.

32. Compare, e.g., Laws H3, "The Dying Hobo."

33. As a later letter reveals (Jimmie Rodgers to Waldo O'Neal, Apr. 22, 1930), the amount was probably $25 and the "contract" a bill of sale.

34. *Kerrville Times*, Nov. 21, 1929, p. 1.

35. See Alton Delmore, *Truth Is Stranger than Publicity*, ed. Charles K. Wolfe (Nashville: Country Music Foundation Press, 1978), pp. 99–100. As Wolfe points out, the story does not agree with other known details of Rodgers's recording history, but provides a rather strong indication that at least one session was held in New Orleans. A careful search of New Orleans newspapers and other public records for the period in question failed to produce any evidence of Rodgers's presence there.

36. Interview, Jan. 7, 1975, Meridian.

37. Billy Burkes to NP, Oct. 26, 1976, and interview, Jan. 23, 1977, Tucson.

38. These figures are roughly comparable to studio scale for recording musicians at that time: one session (not to exceed three hours), $20; two sessions, same day (not

to exceed five hours), $30; overtime, $2 per fifteen minutes or fraction thereof. See *Variety*, July 24, 1929, p. 70.

39. Interview, Mar. 29, 1976, Tucson.

40. Interviews, Mar. 29, 1976, and June 5, 1977, Tucson; Burkes to NP, Jan. 12, 1977.

41. Burkes, interview by Jim Griffith, Mar. 11, 1976, Tucson; Burkes to NP, Oct. 27, 1976.

42. Burkes to NP, Jan. 12, 1977.

43. Randolph prints, without comment, a variant (309E) of "The Drunkard's Lone Child" that is practically identical to the song Rodgers recorded. See *Ozark Folksongs*, II:401–2.

44. Burkes to NP, Jan. 12, 1977.

12 *December, 1929–Summer, 1930*

Swain's Follies

"Jimmie Rodgers Left City Broke; Returns as King of 'Blue Yodel.'"
So proclaimed a front-page headline in Asheville that week, and
Jimmie Rodgers loved every minute of it. As in Meridian, he had old
scores to settle, and there was no better way to do it than by making the
rounds, leaving in his wake a shower of greenbacks and happily
soaking up the adulation of those who'd kicked him when he was
down, laughed at his ambitions, or merely ignored him. For the benefit
of WWNC, which had unceremoniously given him the gate and
written him off as "just another bum," he generously repeated the
now-aging yarn about Victor officals hearing his broadcasts. When a
reporter asked whether he planned to appear on the local station again,
Jimmie grinned his publicity-picture grin and said, "Sure I will. I'll tell
the world if there's anything I can ever do to help old WWNC, they'll
find me coming across."[1] It was a gentle turn of the screw. Although
Jimmie's tongue was no doubt angled toward his cheek, he genuinely
meant what he said, and went out of his way to arrange several
broadcasts that week.

Asheville's City Auditorium was booked for Thursday and Friday
nights (December 6 and 7), and local Victor dealers ran a saturation
advertising campaign which again proclaimed the "Coast-to-Coast
Tour" of America's Blue Yodeler and, in half-inch type, the sale of
"Over 12,000,000 Victor Records by this Artist." General admission
tickets were 50¢ and 75¢, orchestra and reserved seats $1.00, stiff
prices at the time. By early Wednesday, the 1,200-seat auditorium was
completely sold out for both evenings.

Rodgers and his entourage lived it up at the elegant Battery Park

Hotel overlooking the city, entertaining Jimmie's old friends and enjoying life in general. "Traveling with Jim was just wonderful," Billy Burkes said. "He was the greatest guy in the world. When you were with him, you never paid for a meal, and it didn't matter how many there were in the party. He picked up the tab."[2] Rodgers told a reporter for the *Asheville Citizen* that "my main idea in coming back here was to see all my old friends who stuck by me when I was a down-and-outer." He issued his standard public invitation for "all my old friends to come up and see me," and when they came he made sure they enjoyed the best of everything.[3]

For his Asheville appearances Rodgers added to the act a fourth musician, Otis Elder, and Lee Holden, a blackface comedian billed as "Texas Tom." The standing-room-only crowd heard him perform the numbers that had made him famous—"In the Jailhouse Now," "Waiting for a Train," "Blue Yodel," "Away Out on the Mountain" (a local favorite, for obvious reasons), closing with "My Carolina Sunshine Girl," which brought down the house.

On Saturday, Rodgers, Burkes, and McMichen drove down to Spartanburg, South Carolina, to play a one-night stand at the Rex Theater. It was another of Jimmie's impetuous moves, conceived on the spur of the moment, but even though there was little time for advance promotion they again played to a capacity audience.[4]

Their greatest success came the following week back in Chattanooga, where for two consecutive nights they packed the Memorial Auditorium with hundreds of cheering fans. The *Chattanooga Times* theater editor made no effort to disguise his disdain for such goings-on. "Artistically, the Jimmie Rodgers entertainment at the auditorium last night left much to be desired," he sniffed, echoing the general attitude toward "hillbilly music" among those who wore white collars, or aspired to. But he could hardly ignore the crowd's reaction, and had to admit that "judging from the appreciation of the audience of more than 1,400, it was a huge success." He elaborated: "Rodgers can certainly yodel and his every effort was greeted with storms of applause from the audience. He was recalled time after time while persons from the arena called for their favorites with which they have become familiar through phonograph records." On both nights long lines formed at the theater, and during the box office's first hour of operation on Friday, ticket receipts exceeded $500. The crowd was even larger on Saturday night. It clearly galled the reviewer to report that "more people were

Asheville Citizen, *December 5, 1929*

Asheville's warm greeting to Rodgers when he returned in 1929 was in sharp contrast to the troubled times he'd known there earlier.

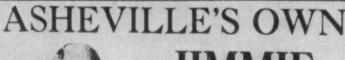

ASHEVILLE'S OWN
JIMMIE RODGERS

Appearing in Person

Thursday and
Friday Nights

Auditorium

OVER

12,000,000
VICTOR RECORDS

BY THIS ARTIST

Drop in our store and hear the records
and you will enjoy the concert better

We Will Gladly Play Them For You

Dunham's Music House
The Home of High Grade Pianos

Asheville Citizen, *December 5, 1929*

This ad's bold claim shows Jimmie's penchant for extravagant publicity. In less than a week, the sales figure had leaped from seven million, announced as Rodgers passed through Chattanooga, Tennessee.

Chattanooga Times ad, December 13, 1929, publicized Rodgers's standing-room-only performances in that city.

Clayton McMichen and Rodgers in Tupelo, Mississippi, December, 1929, near the end of a tour that began in Asheville, N.C.

Billy Burkes with Jimmie, Tupelo, Mississippi, December, 1929.

entertained by the yodeler and his assistants than witnessed any performance of grand opera presented in the auditorium last week."[5]

For the Chattanooga shows, the act had been substantially expanded once more. Hugh Cross, a fine guitarist and vocalist who recorded with both McMichen and Riley Puckett, was added to the band, as were a couple of other local musicians, William Krug, a clarinetist, and Earl Van Arsdale, who played string bass. Others on the bill were Howard Campbell, a magician, and the blackface comic "Texas Tom" Holden, who rejoined the show from Asheville.

Rodgers's repertoire remained much the same as in Asheville, although "Blue Yodel" ("T for Texas, T for Tennessee") obviously got more attention than "My Carolina Sunshine Girl." McMichen and Burkes were given a big hand for their version of "The Cacklin' Hen," presumably a variant of Fiddlin' John Carson's "Old Hen Cackled and the Rooster's Going to Crow." A surprise crowd-pleaser was a jazzy arrangement of "Weary River" done by Burkes and the two pick-up musicians, Van Arsdale and Krug. Rodgers heard them "noodling around" with it in the dressing room before the show and told them to include it in the program. "We really hadn't worked on it much," Burkes recalled later, "but it sure brought down the house." Rodgers closed the show with "Frankie and Johnny," and when the whole group was called back for an encore, they performed a rousing rendition of "St. Louis Blues."[6]

The following week Rodgers, accompanied by Burkes, McMichen, and Holden, played a couple of one-night stands in the Tupelo-Pontotoc area, not far from Meridian. After that the group disbanded. Christmas was coming, and Jimmie was anxious to get back to Kerrville, to his family and their new home. In 1929 he had toured almost constantly, made a movie, and recorded twenty-seven sides for Victor. It would never be quite the same again.

My father was a simple and exceedingly gentle man, clever with his hands but unschooled and lacking the academician's obsession with facts and precise dates. A Texas farm boy, he had left home and worked at a dozen jobs and traveled over most of the western United States by the time he achieved his majority. The year that he was twenty-one was the same year that the history books tell us the Great Depression began. When my father talked about the Depression, however, his mind was usually on something that happened along about 1931 or maybe 1933. Sometimes it was later, and once, I remember, it was even 1927. He was hazy about beginnings and endings. For my father and thousands like him—mostly farmers and laborers and small businessmen—there had always been a Depression. Hard times, like Tolstoy's happy families, tend to be all alike.

To those of us who only read about it, the Wall Street Crash of Tuesday, October 29, 1929, conjures up images of a sudden and dramatic catastrophe. On one side of the time line in our minds, people are whooping it up, tossing tinsel, dancing the Charleston, riding in big cars, and counting their stock market profits; on the other they are jumping out of windows, selling apples, and standing in breadlines. In the rural South and Southwest, which was to be the center of Jimmie Rodgers's activity for the remaining three-and-a-half years of his life, people like my father took little notice of Wall Street. They went on about their business, such as it was, struggling for a dollar, falling in and out of love, marrying, settling down, moving on—more often than not to the tune of "T for Texas" or "In the Jailhouse Now," or whatever new song they heard over the radio or off a record that somebody had scraped up enough money to buy.[7]

Most people in show business—the rank and file, certainly—shared that attitude and economic situation. There was always money, if not room, at the top, but only a few ever realized the wealth and security of the big time. Great masses of show people rightly considered themselves professionals but earned their livelihood as performers or entrepreneurs in the lower reaches; their acts made up the mainstay of show business—pop-time vaudeville, circuses, carnivals, tent repertoire, showboats, amusement parks and fairs, burlesque, stock companies. For these hardy folk, real life had little connection with what went on in Washington or New York or even Hollywood.

Throughout the Twenties, while the rest of the nation's economy had been steadily ascending the roller coaster with no summit in sight, show business had been riding the peaks and troughs. The advent of talking pictures, although a boon to the industry in general, had also created great upheaval and displacement. Silent stars and technicians suddenly found themselves out of fashion, exhibitors went broke trying to cope with the flood of cheap pictures and new equipment, and producers tore their hair over the public's fickle attachment to whatever was Hollywood's latest rage. In the rush to capitalize on any patentable talkie gimmick, hordes of small corporations sprang up overnight and vanished almost as quickly, taking with them an excess of now-forgotten sound devices: Dramaphone, Qualitone, Vitovox, Vocafilm, Biophone, Vitaphone, Photophone, Bristolphone, and dozens of others that *Variety* called "syncromaniacs." Radio was entertainment's glamor baby, but there, too, competition among performers was stiff, and the chances of success far from certain. Big-time vaudeville was on its last legs, the popularity of phonograph records had peaked in mid-decade, and survival out on the road continued to depend on the manager's skill at booking routes and putting together bills that would draw, subject always to the vagaries of local economic conditions, the weather, the county sheriff, alcoholic bill-posters, and a thousand other intangibles. One town would be a bloomer, another a "red one," and often it was only by the seat of his pants that a carny boss or tent show manager could know in advance which was which.

These conditions had long prevailed at the grass roots level. At best, they'd been none too good, and time would elapse before anyone would notice that they were getting worse permanently; it would be even longer before the cause would be traced back to that Black Tuesday in October. In the heart of the country, away from the show business centers of New York, Chicago, and Hollywood, the whole year of 1929, even before the Crash, had been one of the leanest on record. Those involved in live entertainment—vaudeville, carnivals, stock, tent rep, and the like—blamed radio and talkies, and to a large extent their complaint was well founded. But other factors were involved as well. For one thing, traveling shows, especially carnivals, had acquired a notorious reputation as gyps, and while most operators were essentially honest, there were enough shady characters among them to taint the rest. More serious was the growing rigidity and depletion of the entertainment form itself. Like any other businessmen, showmen of the period were reluctant to tamper with success, and they were still trying to draw crowds with the same sorts of things that had brought audiences flocking twenty years before, during a simpler, more naive era. It was a perverse sort of economic Darwinism, with an ironic and ultimately fatal twist: the acts that were surviving were by definition the most prosperous, but their very success had made them complacent, dull, and stylized, lacking in imagination and poorly suited to meet the dazzling new competition from movie screens and loudspeakers. In the end, they were victims not merely of new technology in the entertainment industry but of radical and permanent change in the social and economic character of the nation. In retrospect, it seems unlikely that any innovation could have withstood the onslaught. As the Thirties began, however, it was not only a slowly growing awareness of the general business depression but also a lurking suspicion that what they offered was thin and outdated that spread fear and trembling among the ranks of show folk in tent rep and other live attractions.

One downhome impresario who kept his finger on the public pulse—or fancied that he did—was the volatile, flamboyant character known as Colonel Swain. A showman of the old school, W. I. Swain— "Old Double Eye" to his less fervent admirers—was sort of a cross between P. T. Barnum, William Randolph Hearst, and a snake-oil salesman, at once charming and outrageous, a self-made and widely self-proclaimed Rugged Individual. Swain put together unusual, sometimes daring shows, quarreled with theatrical unions, fought one-man battles with state legislatures, insulted everyone's intelligence (including his own), and liked to boast, contrary to the experience of many who worked for him, that "I never stalled a payday." In his habitual black suit ("of the mid-McKinley period," said one observer), with his shock of snowy hair and his immaculate linen set off by a flowing white bowtie "knotted carelessly enough not to conceal a diamond collar button," the Colonel cut an impressive figure. For more than forty years he was a dominant presence in the tent theater business across a dozen or more states, ranging through the Mid-South, South, and Southwest.[8]

Introduced to show business at an early age, Swain in the course of his six decades of professional life tried his hand at almost every kind of live entertainment that could be put on a stage or under a tent. While still in his teens he'd toured with circuses—Nathan, Jukes & Calvin, Pogie O'Brien, and even Barnum & Bailey—during the heyday of the Big Top before the turn of the century. In 1891, turning to somewhat loftier pursuits, he formed Swain's Comic Opera Company and set out on a tour of Midwestern theaters, playing Gilbert and Sullivan and other light opera of the day. Then, as now, Art paid poorly; the road show was a dismal failure, even after Swain hired a comedian to burlesque his own productions. "I considered light opera the most wonderful entertainment and, according to my thoughts, the public would certainly go wild [for it]," he wrote later. "That was the last time I considered what I wanted in the way of amusement, but [instead] consulted and studied what the public wanted." From high culture he turned to what he openly and even proudly referred to as "hokum"—slapstick comedy, novelty music, flash acts, melodrama, and lots of razzle-dazzle. What the public wanted, he decided, was anything that "appeals to our various emotions, heart pangs, laughter, love or hate." But most of all "it must be imbued with a spirit of the present, close to nature and sex."[9]

When his Comic Opera Company folded, Swain hired a blackface comedian, a sketch team, and an organist, rounded up several yards of canvas sidewalling, and hied himself to the backwoods—Poplar Bluff, Missouri, to be exact. With his hokum bill, essentially what was known in those days as "variety" or "vode-vee," he opened to capacity crowds. From that time on, Giving the Public What It Wanted was Swain's stock in trade. In the next few years he owned or managed dramatic and vaudeville shows that played both in theaters and under canvas throughout Illinois, Iowa, Kansas, and Missouri. The shady practices of house managers in those days soon turned him against theaters, and in 1904 he took his first tent show into the South. Thereafter he operated exclusively under canvas, a confirmed believer in the magic of the Big Top. The crowds which flocked to see Swain's Dramatic Company in those days undoubtedly included young Jimmie Rodgers, whose hometown was a regular stand on Swain's route.

The feisty showman prospered in the boom years during and immediately after World War I. He acquired a 3,000-acre ranch near Dwight, Kansas, and elaborate winter quarters in the heart of New Orleans, where he bought an office building and huge lot at Gravier and Telemachus for storing the equipment of his several units when not on tour. In those days it was still "Captain Swain"—he did not promote himself to Colonel until about 1925, although the title became more or less official a few years later when it was honorarily bestowed upon him by the bumptious Governor Bilbo of Mississippi.

For the benefit of show business colleagues and competitors, Swain took great delight in publicizing his comings and goings, as well as his grievances with trade unions, lawmakers in various states who tried to impose regulations on itinerant businessmen and entertainers, and anyone who threatened what he considered to be the American Way of Life—the right to make a buck, by hook or by crook. At one point, besieged by the Forces of Evil (this time in the form of Actors'

Equity), he took large ads in the trade papers to insist that his actions were "justified by persecutions" and pouted defiantly that "we are simply trying to retain our status as citizens of the United States."[10] During the intervals when things were calm, he published his vacation itinerary (but never his show routes, the better to keep competition guessing): "Statler Hotel, St. Louis, January 23, 24; Muehlback, Kansas City, 25, 26; then Swain Ranch, Dwight, Kansas, two weeks. Glad to meet show people. Especially want Basso-profundo, Toe Dancer, and Clarinetist." His promos were invariably laced with personal notes and folksy bits of dietary advice that would warm the heart of any contemporary natural-food faddist: "Be my guest at ranch, 5 a.m. breakfast. Eat pure pork sausage with a knife, catch warm cream from the separator; all free of benzoate of soda and formaldehyde."[11] His worries about bodily pollution apparently did not extend to tobacco, however; he had a special taste for Cuban stogies with "the most utterly magnificent cigar band" one observer had ever seen. He burned a dozen a day, and eventually died of lung cancer.

For all his reactionary attitudes and devotion to hokum, Swain was something of a progressive when it came to framing a show. "Variety" was one of his catchwords—"you must have the 'menu' of your show consist of a variety so that something on the 'card' will please all," he advised. "New" was another treasured shibboleth. "It is also necessary to be alive to the requirements of this rapid age. This is an epoch of evolution. What was seemly and fitting in the past years would not fill the wants in an amusement way today."[12] As a result, Swain's pit bands played jazz "regardless of my personal dislike for it," and he showed remarkable candor in discussing the attractions of what he called "the presence of feminine beauty and the eccentricities of present freakish fashion"—that is, Sex. It was a subject that most other tent rep managers, mindful of their small-town puritanical audiences, either avoided or clouded in mists of pious platitudes. "Clean family entertainment" was the common boast, although practically every show, no matter how pure it pretended to be, pandered to fleshly urges with risqué titles, double-entendre punchlines, and smirking comedians. Said Swain pointedly, "I have tried to divert the attention of my audiences from the legs of the women [in the show] to their extreme gowns and costumes, but I am ready to acknowledge 70 per cent are in favor of the legs."[13]

With the general decline of live entertainment in the late Twenties,

Swain had begun to experiment with different attractions, varying dramatic offerings with increasing doses of vaudeville, sideshows, and novelty acts. He had opened his 1928 season with an attempt to restore some of the lost vigor and ballyhoo to tent rep by playing upon its kinship with the gaudier, more extravagant atmosphere of the circus. In place of the usual orchestra and theater setting, he offered a brassy marching band, sawdust on the floor, pennants flying from the tent poles, balloons all over the place, and an extended bill of concert attractions in addition to the staple dramatic fare. This effort was only moderately successful, but the continued economic slump in the winter of 1929-30 convinced the Colonel that ever more drastic measures were necessary if the coming summer tour was to succeed.[14]

The first hint that something was brewing reached the profession in early January, 1930, through a small and innocuous item in Bill Sachs's *Billboard* column:

> Col. W. I. Swain, one of the most successful and experienced tent show managers in the game today, is one of those who has something up his sleeve for the coming season. Just what it is we are unable to say, for the Colonel, now in training on pork sausage and pancakes at his ranch in Dwight, Kan., has steadfastly refused to divulge his secret "until the proper time comes. . . ."[15]

It is unlikely that anyone held his breath while Colonel Swain waited for the "proper time," but with business in a tailspin and daily rumors of shows closing or failing to open on schedule, considerable attention was given to any promotion that might bring new life to the box office. A further hint of what Swain had in mind came in early March: a professional "call" was announced in the trade journals, notifying "all people engaged" to report in New Orleans for rehearsals of a show to be known as "Swain's Hollywood Follies."[16]

Swain's plan, although not unheard of, was nevertheless a rather radical innovation for a touring tent rep company, requiring substantial overhaul of the usual operation. The repertoire bills were discarded entirely and replaced with a lavish musical comedy production involving a larger cast and more complicated staging. Although individual acts were to be featured—notably a tabloid musical entitled "Hawaiian Whoopee"—the bill was designed to play as a single unit, the same show every night through an entire season of one-night stands, in contrast to the one- and two-week runs normally played by a rep company. This was perhaps the most unusual and demanding part of the new scheme; the mere logistics required extensive preparation, careful planning of routes and transportation, and larger crews to handle teardown and setup.

The show also required, in Swain's estimation, one additional fillip—a star of considerable stature, some name attraction whose very presence could capture public attention and help insure box office success. It had to be someone who'd already attracted a following; yet Swain had no intention of paying the salary that a really big Broadway or Hollywood personality would demand, even if one could be persuaded to tour in a tent, which in itself was highly unlikely.

The Colonel did not have to look far for an answer to his problem. He remembered the splash that his protégé, Paul English, had made the year before when he'd hired the lanky, yodeling record artist known as "The Singing Brakeman," and he was well aware of the growing popular appeal of "America's Blue Yodeler." From almost every standpoint, save perhaps that of health, Jimmie Rodgers was an obvious choice—a proven crowd-pleaser, an established attraction who despite his celebrity status actually preferred to barnstorm in the boondocks. Although his name was rapidly becoming a household word in the very area where Swain intended to tour, Rodgers's limited exposure outside the South and West meant that he was still something less than a national star, and therefore could not command as large a salary as many of his peers—Gene Austin, for example—even though his records often outsold theirs.

For Rodgers, who had been playing random, catch-as-catch-can theater dates and high school auditoriums in those early months of 1930, the most compelling argument for touring with Swain was that the tour would allow him to stay active and earn some steady money while doing the very thing he most enjoyed—entertaining small, essentially rural audiences. There was also the notion, at least given lip service, that traveling with Swain and playing only one show each evening would be easier on him than attempting another round of the "four-a-day" in distant cities. But surely Rodgers did not undertake an arduous four-month tour of one-night stands with any serious belief that it would not strain his already precarious condition.

Indeed, even before the tour could get underway, he suffered another collapse while attempting to play a three-day movie house engagement in Carthage, Mississippi, near Meridian. Realizing he was too sick to sustain his one-man show, he'd been forced to hire a local band, the Freeny-Cannon Trio, to alternate with him on stage and allow him to rest as much as possible. Facing sellout crowds on home territory, Rodgers struggled through two nights of the engagement, performing solo as long as he could and then bringing out the band to take over. Finally he began to hemorrhage on Saturday morning, and although the bleeding was stopped, the doctor insisted that he cancel the final show and stay in bed.[17] Less than two weeks later, despite this severe setback, Jimmie Rodgers was on his feet and ready for the opening of Swain's Hollywood Follies.

Colonel Swain unveiled the full details of his new scheme on March 8, when the Swain-Rodgers association was announced to the profession in a *Billboard* advertisement:

W. I. SWAIN SHOW COMPANY, Inc.

PRESENTING

◢JIMMY RODGERS◣

THE PREMIER VICTOR RECORD PRODUCING STAR, WITH

SWAIN'S HOLLYWOOD FOLLIES and WAIKIKI HAWAIIANS

In Musical Comedy. One-night-stand Tent Show. WANT four Union Billposters, two must drive car; $40.00 per week and transportation after joining; $5.00 bonus if stay season.

TO FAIR SECRETARIES, CANADA, NORTHWEST AND SOUTHWEST UNITED STATES, INCLUDING TEXAS—On account of Mr. Rodgers being as strong, if not the strongest, drawing card to any show, we can contract with you for one day or a week, during your Fair, and we consider we will draw a greater number of paid admissions than any other attraction you have ever played. Write or wire Swain Building, New Orleans, La.

As the fine print indicates, Swain was prepared for a truly international tour, or at least one that would reach a major portion of the United States. Such bookings never materialized, however. The route of "Swain's Hollywood Follies of 1930" was eventually limited to five states, although the troupe played some seventy show dates in that territory and covered more than 3,000 miles. Borger, Texas, was the closest most of the performers ever got to Hollywood.

In newspaper accounts and other publicity, much was made of the show's size: according to the most frequently cited figure, it carried a roster of sixty-one. Swain's original call had been for "A 36-People Musical Comedy," and that number was far closer to fact. The cast was comprised of about twenty performers, plus the regular stage band of seven musicians. There was also the "executive staff" (mostly members of the Swain family), tent crew, cooks, and dining-car attendants. The complete entourage did not number over forty, counting all the Swains, in-laws, and hangers-on. But of course the portly Colonel had a reputation for being poor at figures: when it came to reporting box office receipts or the scope of his operation, he was known to err somewhat on the side of excess, whereas at other times, when it suited circumstances, he displayed a flagrant poormouth. If he had a company of twenty, it was said, he'd advertise them as fifty—and make sure that only ten or fifteen could be found when the train conductor came around to count fares.

All things considered, Swain's Hollywood Follies still properly boasted a substantially larger complement than the average tent rep company, which normally carried only a dozen or so people. In addition to Rodgers, the featured performers included blues singer Eva Thomas (who'd also toured with English when Jimmie was on that show), comedian Jimmy Vann, who specialized in Irish dialect and characters, and Alfred and Lucille Freita, who had put together an act known as Freita's Hawaiians—which Swain changed to the Waikiki Hawaiians—in "Hawaiian Whoopee."

Following three weeks of rehearsals in New Orleans, the show opened in Independence, Louisiana, on March 29. "Huge crowd greets players at opening," reported *Billboard;* "first-night gross nearly $1,000." Again, allowances must be made for Colonel Swain's mathematics, but evidence indicates that, in its early stages at least, the company was indeed a success. At any rate, as *Billboard* noted, "The outstanding hit of the show . . . is Jimmie Rodgers, Victor recording artist."[18]

Traveling aboard three specially designed railroad cars, the troupe moved up through central Louisiana and played three dates in southern Arkansas before jumping across to Texas. On April 9, Swain's Hollywood Follies played to a sellout crowd in Jefferson, hometown of Vernon Dalhart. After two weeks of one-night stands in the area, the company moved into North Texas. Crowds flocking to Paris for the April 23 show jammed city streets, and traffic around the square came to a standstill that afternoon as Rodgers appeared on the courthouse lawn to advertise the show with an impromptu concert.[19] Two days later he packed them in in Gainesville, the birthplace of another professional rival, Gene Austin.

Texas businessman Townsend Miller was growing up in Gainesville during this time; he vividly remembered Jimmie Rodgers's impact on the town. "For weeks [his appearance] was almost the only topic of conversation," Miller has written. "The visit of a President wouldn't have created more excitement. . . . I was one of the luckier kids in town. That afternoon after school and after the tent was erected, I went to the site. A bunch of us youngsters were 'hired' to set up the folding chairs. When we finished, a flashily-dressed Damon Runyon-type character called us down to the foot of the stage. Standing above us, he tossed a double handful of pennies into the air for all of us to scramble after as our pay. Even more important, we each got a free pass to the show. And that's how I got to see and hear the legendary Jimmie Rodgers perform. I can still see him, sitting under that big tent on a portable stage, this time wearing the cocked straw hat, singing and yodeling his songs of the common people."

Miller accurately gauged Rodgers's unique appeal. "It would be almost impossible to exaggerate the popularity of Jimmie Rodgers during the late '20s and early '30s when he was alive and recording," he pointed out. "It was akin to the frenzy the big bands generated during the swing era of the late '30s and early '40s. It equaled the devotion and oftimes frantic adoration of the fans of Frank Sinatra and Elvis Presley. However, there was a difference in Rodgers' popularity. It was more subtle and deeper . . . [it] spread across all age brackets."[20]

All along the Swain route there were friends and acquaintances among the crowds, and Jimmie went out of his way to greet them and spend time reminiscing about the old days when they were hoboing around or railroading together. In Nocona he ran into an old pal named Claude Townsend, an oilfield worker and amateur musician whom Jimmie had known in his barnstorming days. Townsend invited him home, and Jimmie spent the afternoon on the family's big front porch, strumming his guitar and making a lasting impression on Townsend's six-year-old daughter, Dorothy. Recalling his visit years later, Dorothy Townsend (now Mrs. Guy Long of Alvin, Texas) said, "I was really too young to know who he was, but I knew just from the way everyone else carried on that he must be Somebody. He certainly didn't act like a star—he was just as friendly as the folks next door—but he was really dressed up, all in black, with a vest and tie and white shirt—and it wasn't even Sunday! That made an impression on me." As the child hovered just out of reach, listening to her father and the awesome stranger as they talked and played their guitars, Rodgers playfully scooped her up in his arms and sat her on his knee. "He was lighting a cigarette," she said, "and he had a beautiful monogrammed lighter. I'd never seen a cigarette lighter before. He spent the longest time showing me how it worked and letting me play with it. Then he told me it was mine to keep. I still have it, after all these years. I've always remembered him as such a warm, gentle person." Later in the afternoon, Jimmie walked out to his car and produced a silver flask—"the first one of *those* I'd seen, too," said Mrs. Long, laughing. "He asked my father, who didn't drink, if it was all right for him to have one, and my father sent my mother for ice and water. He drank it just that way, straight from the flask, with ice-water chaser, through the rest of the afternoon."

Ads and news releases invariably contained a note to the effect that "Mr. Rodgers says he is very anxious to meet all his friends and especially the kiddies." It was genuine. "Jimmie Rodgers must have been to all children what he was to me," Mrs. Long said. "I didn't know what the word 'hero' meant in those days, but I can remember always feeling so important because he held me on his lap and gave me the cigarette lighter, which I've treasured all these years."[21]

Dorothy Townsend's experience was typical of those which occurred over and over, wherever Rodgers went. This sort of behavior made him a genuine hero to people who desperately needed and deserved one. They rewarded him by paying a day's wage for one of his records, by traveling miles to see him in person, by naming their children after him, and by carrying on the memory of America's Blue Yodeler long, long after he was dead and out of fashion.

Over the rails of the Texas & Pacific, the Missouri, Kansas & Texas, and the Colorado & Southern railroads, Swain's Hollywood Follies passed along the northern rim of the Lone Star State, reaching Clarendon, in the Texas Panhandle, in early May. There Jimmie made an earnest effort to locate Waldo O'Neal, the originator of "Hobo Bill's Last Ride," who lived nearby. O'Neal had sent him lyrics for several new tunes, including "Pistol Packing Papa" and "Mean Mama Blues," which Rodgers hoped to record at his next session. There was also a song O'Neal called "I'm a One Man's Mama Now," a line or two of which later turned up in "Jimmie the Kid."

Rodgers had written to O'Neal from Clarksville, Texas, back in April. His letter reveals a great deal about the process through which he (and Peer) acquired new material. As Ray Hall would do later, O'Neal had indicated that he preferred having a royalty arrangement, rather than selling his songs outright. Rodgers urged caution: "I don't know if you are wise or not regarding this royalty business, but it is a good racket and very hard to get into." For the material O'Neal had submitted, Jimmie offered "Our regular stipulated amount," with the further inducement that he would "put your name on the records with mine, also sheet music, as half composer of the number," adding, "Mr. O'Neal, please bear in mind that I am not trying to get your song for the trifle sum of $25.00 or $50.00, but that is our limit on song lyrics or poems."[22] This agrees precisely with Peer's account years afterward. Despite the vaunted assertion that "I never bought a copyright" but instead always insisted on paying composer royalties, Peer clearly had no qualms if the artists themselves bought material, which of course he could then copyright. In fact, he seems to have encouraged the practice. "People would send Jimmie songs," Peer admitted, "usually just lyrics, and if he liked them he had instructions from me, he would buy these lyrics and pay them twenty-five dollars, fifty dollars, something like that, and have them sign a full bill of sale. Buy them outright." Even Andy Jenkins, an established composer in his own right, had to share billing and royalties, whether Rodgers added anything to his material or not. Explaining how Rodgers came to use Jenkins's songs, Peer said, "Jenkins would send me the material and I'd go over to Jimmie and if Jimmie liked it, why, we'd take it. I think we usually cut-in Rodgers." The "cut-in," as songwriter Sammy Cahn explains in his autobiography, *I Should Care*, "was anyone who could get your song recorded, published, or played, which meant his name appeared on the song."[23] It was a common practice in the music business, and most of the amateurs who supplied Rodgers with material were eventually convinced to settle for the meager one-time fee and the glory, real or imagined, of having their work recorded by America's Blue Yodeler.

Rodgers had no luck in locating his collaborator in Clarendon, although he did encounter O'Neal's parents on the street before the show and chatted with them at length. When it turned out that O'Neal was working in Amarillo, Jimmie suggested that the next day his father bring the young man to Panhandle, where the Follies would be playing. In Clarendon that night, Jimmie gave "Hobo Bill's Last Ride" a prominent place in his act, announcing to the audience that one of his biggest hits had been written by a hometown boy. Unfortunately, O'Neal never got to meet his idol; when he drove to Panhandle the following afternoon, a Swain offical told him that Jimmie had been called to nearby Borger "on business" and would not return until late that evening. Pressed for time, and thinking he would have other opportunities, O'Neal left. "Later, Jimmie wrote and invited me to come visit him at Kerrville," O'Neal recalled wistfully. "Somehow I never got around to it. I was such a great admirer of him. As the old cliché has it, 'in my eyes he could do no wrong.' " A few days after Rodgers's death, O'Neal received a letter from Peer, informing him that the fifty dollars Jimmie had paid him in advance for "One Man's Mama" was being deducted from the earnings on his other songs.[24]

NOTES

1. *Asheville Citizen*, Dec. 3, 1929, p. 9.
2. Billy Burkes, interview by Jim Griffith, Mar. 11, 1976, Tucson; by NP, Mar. 29, 1976.
3. *Asheville Citizen*, Dec. 3, 1929, p. 9. Throughout his stay in Asheville, Jimmie repeated for reporters all the standard myths, such as that he was "discovered" as a result of the WWNC broadcasts and that his record sales totaled twelve million copies; perhaps the most extravagant story was one concerning Carrie, "the little country girl I married." Boasting that he'd bought her a new Packard for Christmas (which he had), he added, "She and the baby, Anita, eight years old, are going into the talkies with me next year. We are going to make a picture called 'The Singing Brakeman' for the Columbia Picture Company" (*Asheville Times*, Dec. 5, 1929, p. 8). The statement is especially curious in light of the fact that he had already made a short subject with that title, and did not mention it. For other stories relating to the Asheville trip, see *Asheville Times*, Dec. 3, 1929, p. 10B, Dec. 4, 1929, p. 10A, and Dec. 17, 1929, p. 4.
4. Billy Burkes to NP, Oct. 27, 1976. Local newspapers carried large advertisements but no stories or reviews. See the Spartanburg, S.C., *Journal and Carolina Spartan*, Dec. 5, 1929, p. 7, and Dec. 6, 1929, pp. 5 and 6.
5. *Chattanooga Times*, Dec. 14, 1929, p. 10. See also *Chattanooga News*, Dec. 10, 1929; and *Chattanooga Times*, Dec. 3, 1929, which cites Rodgers's record sales at seven million copies. (In Asheville the very next day the figure had climbed to twelve million.)
6. Billy Burkes, interview by Jim Griffith, Mar. 11, 1976, Tucson; by NP, Mar. 29, 1976.
7. "The immense crisis of capitalism that began in New York October 23, 1929, did not at first affect Texas. The real pinch only began in 1931. . . . The mass of Texans were still poor in 1928; they were more adapted to relative poverty than the American groups now hit the hardest. . . . In fact, a striking phenomenon of this era was that more Texans remembered the disastrous drouth and dust storms of the 1930's than the Depression itself . . ." (T. R. Fehrenbach, *Lone Star: A History of Texas and the Texans* [New York: Macmillan, 1968], p. 650).
8. *Billboard*, Dec. 13, 1924, pp. 16, 27; Jan. 3, 1925, p. 4; "Col. W. I. Swain's

Python Story" (from the New Orleans *Times-Picayune*, n.d.) reprinted in *Billboard*, Oct. 12, 1929, p. 31. I am also indebted to Al Lindberg, who supplied many additional details concerning Swain and the world of tent repertoire in general.

9. *Billboard*, Dec. 13, 1924, p. 16.

10. *Ibid.*, Jan. 3, 1925, p. 4.

11. *Ibid.*, Jan. 23, 1926, p. 4.

12. *Ibid.*, Dec. 13, 1924, p. 16.

13. *Ibid.*

14. *Ibid.*, Apr. 28, 1928, p. 26; Aug. 31, 1929, p. 28; Jan. 18, 1930, p. 30.

15. *Ibid.*, Jan. 18, 1930, p. 30.

16. *Ibid.*, Mar. 1, 1930, p. 31.

17. For an expanded account of this episode, see Tony Russell, "The Freeny Story," *Old Time Music*, no. 8 (Spring, 1973), 15–19.

18. *Billboard*, Apr. 5, 1930, p. 30.

19. *Paris* (Tex.) *Morning News*, Apr. 23, 1930, p. 2; Tony Thomas to NP, May 9, 1975; interview, May 17, 1975, Hugo, Okla.

20. *Country Music*, 1:9 (May, 1973), 32.

21. Telephone interview, Feb. 12, 1977.

22. Jimmie Rodgers to Waldo O'Neal, Apr. 22, 1930; O'Neal to NP, Jan. 8, 1976.

23. Sammy Cahn, *I Should Care* (New York: Arbor House, 1974), p. 35. "The big scam around the music business," writes Cahn, "was and is that the greatest of all cut-ins was Mr. Al Jolson, who has his name on practically every hit he ever sang (or perhaps he'd never have sung). The second greatest must be Mr. Irving Mills, the famed music publisher, whose name appears up alongside Duke Ellington's on many of Ellington's hits. Another prominent cut-in was supposed to be Mr. Billy Rose. I am not sure if Billy Rose really deserved that rumor but I *do* know that Mr. Rose once, when hiring me to do one of his Aquacade shows, told me, 'I can't wait to hear what we're going to write.'"

24. O'Neal to NP, Dec. 2, 1975; Jan. 8 and May 12, 1976.

13 *Summer, 1930*

A Sweetheart Not Far from Shawnee

Throughout much of the Southwest, the summer of 1930 was the driest on record. Under the blazing, cloudless sky, scraggly cotton wilted and turned brown on the stalk; lakes and creeks shrank to puddles, their banks gridded with cracks. The land baked to a hard yellow mass, and where it had no cover to hold it, the topsoil shifted and stirred and gusted along in the hot wind, sometimes rising in howling, gritty swarms of dust that covered the sky and shut out the sun. It was as if the economic torment settling over the nation had here been redoubled by the very elements of Nature, inflicting compound misery on the people of the region.

Swain's Hollywood Follies, mounted amid high hopes and grandiose pronouncements, struggled gamely into the teeth of the twin furies of drouth and depression. From the Texas Panhandle the troupe turned northeast, angling across the narrow neck of Oklahoma toward the Kansas border. Moving by rail through the central part of the Jayhawker State, the show played to dwindling audiences as the summer wore on. Even in Swain's home territory between Topeka and Abilene the locals stayed away in droves; the Colonel muttered imprecations against "these damn farmers that come to town with two bucks and a celluloid collar, and go home without changing either of 'em." True to the trouper's traditions, both Swain and Rodgers continued to ballyhoo the show as long as they could, sending out glowing reports to generate public enthusiasm while trying to calm their own worst fears. As late as mid-May *Billboard* headlined "Swain's 'Idea' Clicking Big," applauding the Colonel for "offering something entirely different in the way of tent-show entertainment." Rodgers was quoted as saying, "We are doing capacity business, giving 'em three hours of red-hot entertainment. What I mean by red-hot entertainment is that there is not 10 seconds between acts and numbers during the three hours' program. This looks like a good bet to me, and just a little tip to other vaudeville actors in this old U.S.A.—get something for yourself out in the wide open spaces and let the theaters alone."[1] Rodgers may have stood behind the statement, but it shows more than a little of the Swain touch, especially in the gratuitous dig at theaters, one of the Colonel's longtime phobias. Apparently both Swain and Rodgers were increasingly concerned that the tent operation was contributing to their poor drawing power, so much that they felt compelled to alter their advertising to explain why a big-name attraction was playing in a "rag opry." The explanation took the form of "a personal letter from Jimmie Rodgers,"[2] clearly the product of Old Double Eye Swain and his bill-poster prose. Datelined "Hollywood, Cal., Season 1930" and addressed to "My Dear Public," the "letter" said:

I am delighted that I am to meet you in person and sing and play for you. Won't this be grand! And especially I never expected such dreams would be a reality. All this has been made possible by the greatest showman of the age, Col. W.I. Swain [after all, the Colonel's ego was in trouble, along with his pocketbook]. The salary he is paying me establishes me as the highest salaried Victor Record star.

Now my dear friends, I will appear in person with Swain's HOLLYWOOD FOLLIES each night, and by the way the Hollywood Follies have a great big company of good looking young men and pretty girls, comedians and singers and vocal quartette and novelty entertainers—and the finest advanced style wardrobe. In fact Col. Swain is bringing a big Hollywood production to you, and I also wish to state the show excels any Broadway show. I assure you I am glad to be the star on such a grand show.

Unless I explain, you may wonder why myself and such a wonderful show presented by so wonderful entertainers are appearing in a tent. Because theaters are not available, being entirely controlled by picture interests, thus road shows cannot get theater bookings. However, Col. Swain's present plan of presenting this big city show in a tent makes it possible for you, my friends, to hear and see me and meet me, also to enjoy the big show, of which I bear the distinction of being star.

I will sing and play my songs that you request, until, well perhaps you will tire of me. I hope you are wearing out all my records playing them. I want to shake hands with you. I also want to meet the kiddies.

                                        Sincerely,

                                        JIMMIE RODGERS
                                        (America's Blue Yodeler)

Swain cut prices (to $1.00 per couple and 30¢ for children, from a top of $1.00 per adult and 50¢ child's admission), and business began to pick up a bit after the show swung back down into Oklahoma. In the meantime, however, a new problem arose—or more accurately, what had become an all-too-common problem recurred. Rodgers's health took another turn for the worse, and once again he was too sick to perform.

Roy Hogan, Swain's business manager, had been with Paul English the year before when young Bill Bruner had stood in for the ailing yodeler in Meridian. Now Hogan was able to contact Bruner with an offer to come out and perform the same chore for Swain. Bruner joined in mid-May and remained with the show until it closed in July, long after Rodgers had departed. Swain often sent the youngster out to perform without announcing Rodgers's absence, and Bruner's imitation of the Blue Yodeler was so good that audiences often left thinking they'd seen Rodgers himself.[3]

Shortly after Bruner's arrival, the show took a week off to reorganize, rest up, and make the jump to Ada, in southeastern Oklahoma. On the way Swain and Rodgers took a side trip to visit another renowned showman, Major Gordon W. Lillie, the famous "Pawnee Bill," who'd toured with Buffalo Bill's Wild West Show and later established his own unit, with headquarters and western museum near Pawnee, northwest of Tulsa. The following day Jimmie sent his Aunt Dora a postcard from Pawnee Bill's Trading Post. On one side was a picture of the post's interior, on the other a cryptic message: "Had dinner here yesterday." What he didn't report was that the main course had been roast of buffalo, which Jimmie found a little too exotic for his old-fashioned, Southern-fried tastes. A kid at heart, however, he had a grand time going over Major Lillie's collection of guns and western Americana. As his guests were leaving, Lillie remembered the "buffalo hide" Jimmie had sung about in "Away Out on the Mountain," and the Major presented him with one, expertly fashioned into a fine rug. According to Carrie, it was made from the hide of the same buffalo they'd had for dinner.[4] In any event, Jimmie cherished the outside far more than what it had contained. A genuine friendship had been struck, and Rodgers later visited Major Lillie on several occasions.

On May 22, 1930, the *Hughes County Tribune* in Holdenville, Oklahoma, ran an advertisement over the signature of the J. W. Sturges & Sons Piano Company, announcing that on the following Saturday, May 31, Jimmie Rodgers was coming to town. "You Have Heard Him on the Victor in Such Song Hits as—" said the headline; listed below were the titles of eight of Rodgers's current releases.[5] As was the case wherever he went, word of the Blue Yodeler's imminent appearance soon became a topic of conversation everywhere.

In Wewoka, some ten miles away, a pretty, dark-haired divorcée found the news particularly intriguing. She was Stella Harkins, née Kelly, formerly Rodgers, and she had traveled a long and adventurous path in the dozen or so years since she parted from the gangling young Mississippi railroader with the perennial hole in his pocket.

After coming to Oklahoma from Mississippi, Stella had continued the struggle, against substantial odds, to rise above her origins and to establish some measure of independence for herself and her baby daughter. She acquired a teaching certificate, attending classes while her mother kept the baby, and was employed by a country school in rural McCurtain County. In the far southeastern part of the state, this region had long been known for its rugged, often violent way of life.

In 1922 Stella married Richard Harkins, son of a rather prominent family in the small town of Fort Towson, east of Hugo.[6] Less than three years later Harkins and Stella's brother, Hugh Kelly, were involved in the shooting death of a man named Elmer Coker, and Harkins was convicted of manslaughter. Despite persistent rumors that Harkins killed Coker "because of Stella,"[7] neither contemporary newspaper accounts nor court records provide much insight into the cause of the incident. Harkins pleaded self-defense and argued that the dead man "used vile, opprobrious, insulting and provoking language at and toward the defendant, or about the defendant's wife."[8] The jury found him guilty, however, and he was sentenced to fifteen years in the Oklahoma State Penitentiary, of which he served less than three years before being paroled.

While Harkins was in prison, Stella made up her mind to divorce him. Moving to Hughes County, east of Shawnee, she found a job in the rural community of Benedict, teaching seventh- and eighth-grade English. A former pupil, Ellen Fraser (later Kiker), remembered her as "a kind and likeable teacher, though it seemed her mind was on something else and not altogether on teaching." Her daughter, Kathryn, about ten by that time, was "a sweet and beautiful little girl," according to Mrs. Kiker, who added, "We kids thought it was great, her being the daughter of yodeling Jimmie Rodgers and being in school with us."[9]

Popular wherever she went, especially with the menfolk who courted her avidly, Stella fixed her intentions on being something more than a country schoolteacher. In the late Twenties, through a friendship with an official in neighboring Seminole County, she acquired a job at the courthouse and moved to Wewoka, the county seat. In short order she became the county clerk's invaluable assistant, and, according to those who knew her, "ran" the office.

As time neared for the appearance of Swain's Follies in Holdenville, Stella found herself with conflicting emotions. For two or three years word had been filtering down of her former husband's rising success in the entertainment world, but Stella had received the news about Jimmie Rodgers with only passing interest and rather wry amusement. After all, she'd long ago dismissed his show business aspirations as foolish nonsense, and she had little use for any of the moaning, nasal hillbilly clowns whose silly records and radio broadcasts seemed to fill the air in those days. They sounded too much like the music she'd grown up with, evocations of the life she'd struggled so hard to escape. Anyone with the slightest notion of Culture knew such performers and songs were a blight on the nation's sensibilities. Opera and the classics were still a bit heady for rural Oklahoma, but there were all these nice new radio crooners and handsome dance orchestras with tuxedos and slicked-down hair; if one wanted to hear our "native rhythms," Paul Whiteman was the very thing. For all the attention he was getting, Jimmie Rodgers was only another hick from down in Mississippi, a country boy who'd rather pick a guitar than work for a living. Besides, he *yodeled*, and toured with a traveling tent show. Still, her daughter bore his name, and Stella couldn't deny that he was something of a celebrity. She knew she'd have to see him, if only to satisfy her curiosity. And—only incidentally, of course—to give him a big surprise.

Stella I wish you
and yours all the
Happiness on earth.
Sincerely
Jimmie Rodgers
6-1-30

Jimmie Rodgers
America's Blue Yodeler
Exclusive Victor Artist

One of two pictures given to Stella during their "reunion" in 1930.

Kathryn Rodgers,
about 1934, four
years before her death.

A rare copy of the famous "thumbs up" publicity pose, inscribed to the daughter of his marriage to Stella Kelly: "To My Sweet little Daughter, Kathryn Rodgers. Sweet Heart I love you. from your Dady Sincerely Jimmie Rodgers 5/31/30."

In the hoariest of melodramas, a poor lost waif approaches the dapper stranger, tugging at his pants leg and whimpering "Daddy, daddy," in a piteous voice. "Get away, kid," growls the hero-heavy, visions of paternity suits dancing in his head, before learning that the erstwhile orphan with the golden ringlets is indeed his own long-lost child. From all accounts, that was the scene, with minor modifications, that took place following Rodgers's performance in Holdenville. Astonished as Rodgers must have been to see his former wife backstage, he recognized Stella at once and greeted her warmly. Momentarily, recovering from the shock of it all, he was beaming proudly and showing a genuine delight at being the father of a child whose existence he apparently had never even heard of until that moment.[10] On the spot, he autographed one of his famous "Thumbs Up" publicity pictures for her, inscribing it "To My Sweet little Daughter, Kathryn Rodgers. Sweet Heart I love you. from your Dady Sincerely Jimmie Rodgers 5/31/30." In light of later events, others would have reason to look upon that act as precipitant, or at least naive; but there is no evidence to show that Rodgers felt so, or that he ever changed his attitude toward the daughter he was to know so briefly. For him, it was enough that she bore his name, as well as a remarkable resemblance ("a spitting image," in the words of one acquaintance). Always adaptable to whatever life brought him, Jimmie took to instant fatherhood as he did to everything else—openly, generously, and with as much enthusiasm as he could muster.

The next day was Sunday, an open date for the Swain show. Although he was running a temperature and feeling the effects of his exhausting schedule, Jimmie drove to Stella's apartment in Wewoka with a carload of presents for Kathryn—"everything he could find to buy for her," said a friend. Included were a bicycle, roller skates, camera, clothes, and a bulldog puppy which they named Aby (the acronym of "America's Blue Yodeler").[11] That same day he inscribed two pictures for his former wife, one rather bland and formal, apparently intended for public display: "Stella I wish you and yours all the Happiness on earth Sincerely Jimmie Rodgers." The other, signed simply "Jimmie," contained a more personal message, showing perhaps where his real interests lay. It read, "Stella, please be good to Kathryn and I know you will." What he did not know was the length to which Stella might go to follow his advice, or that her efforts in Kathryn's behalf would eventually embroil him in some of the more troublesome and unpleasant episodes of his last years. At the moment, it seemed enough that their surprise reunion had gone so well and was now behind him. He had pressing professional matters to attend to.

At this eventful point the Swain-Rodgers partnership, already under strain, came apart completely. For some weeks Jimmie had been plagued with poor health, and meeting Stella again, coupled with the elation of discovering his new daughter, did not help matters. For his part, Swain grumbled that Jimmie kept shortening his performances and frequently couldn't appear at all—which was true, although Bill Bruner was there to fill in and keep the show running fairly smoothly. Swain also blamed Jimmie for the poor business they'd encountered, claiming that Rodgers was "more or less a stranger" in Kansas and Oklahoma.[12] That charge had little validity, especially in the Sooner State, where even today Jimmie Rodgers fans are legion. Moreover, Swain should have been able to draw audiences in Kansas, his own home territory. Obviously he couldn't, business and weather conditions being what they were.

Later Swain threatened to sue Rodgers, implying that a contract had been broken. But Jimmie's letter to Waldo O'Neal back in April makes it clear that even then Rodgers was planning a recording session for May or June, and his plans were hardly kept from the Colonel. Swain fueled the dissension by negotiating a replacement for Jimmie without his star's knowledge, eventually signing Ben Turpin, the old comedian of silent films. Turpin, now long past his prime, had joined the troupe in late May; Jimmie generously stayed with the show as headliner while Turpin got his act together and Swain prepared new billing and publicity. By the time he encountered Stella, however, he was in need of rest, worn down by the rigors of more than two months of one-night stands and constantly ravaged by fever and coughing.

The regular Follies show, with Rodgers headlining, had been advertised for an appearance in Wewoka on Tuesday, June 3. But during the preceding weekend Swain posted paper and took large ads for the Wewoka date, announcing Turpin's "First Personal Tour"— and using the same "My Dear Public" letter for Turpin, with only slight changes, that he had run over Rodgers's signature, again plugging Colonel Swain as "the greatest showman of the age" and explaining why "myself and such a wonderful show" were appearing in a tent.[13] By the time Swain and Turpin played in Wewoka, Jimmie was in Memphis, checking into the Peabody Hotel. He wrote to his father in Geiger, telling him he was "awful tired and worn out" and would soon be on his way to Meridian for a few days' rest.[14]

A week or so in his hometown put him back on his feet, and arrangements were completed with Ralph Peer to begin a new series of recordings on the West Coast later in June. While Swain's Hollywood Follies and their washed-up movie star struggled on through the boondocks and backwaters of Arkansas and Louisiana, Jimmie Rodgers headed toward Southern California and the nation's film capital aboard the Southern Pacific's luxury Sunset Limited, as if to prove just who really deserved the "Hollywood" billing.

By early July, it was clear to everyone that Colonel Swain's hot idea had been more folly than Follies, and the big ballyhoo in the trade publications ended with a thud. "Reverts to Old Policy," headlined *Billboard.* "Col. W. I. Swain cuts personnel after unsuccessful tour with 'Follies.'"[15] Turpin had proved to be a dismal failure, and Swain retired to New Orleans to fire people, lick his wounds, and ponder his next move. By early fall he was back on the road again with a combined dramatic-and-musical-comedy show ("Two Show Units Working as One Combination"). With only half the old cast trying to do twice as much, it met with scattered success and closed before the end of the year.[16] The wily old Colonel would continue to mount some sort of tent enterprise each year throughout the Depression, but his shows grew progressively smaller, thinner, and more ragged. Never again would there be anything as spangled and ambitious as "Swain's Hollywood Follies of 1930." By 1935, the once-grand and peripatetic old showman had run aground in the tiny hamlet of High Island, Texas, operating a "shooting gallery" movie house and trying to unload the remnants of his last tent rig. A year or so later he died, broke and feeble, on the last few acres that remained of his ranch at Dwight, Kansas.[17]

Despite the darkening Depression, demand for Jimmie Rodgers records remained firm. Oklahoma fiddler Tony Thomas recalls long lines of country folk forming in front of the music store in Hugo whenever news of the Blue Yodeler's latest release was posted; all were prepared to spend a day's pay (and for some it was more than that) for a single, fragile 78 rpm record containing only two songs by their hero. "Today, a day's wage is twenty dollars and more," Thomas says pointedly. "Would anybody pay that much for a new release by some rock star—any rock star?"[18] A popular story has it that the standard order in general stores became "a sack of flour, a slab of bacon, and the latest Jimmie Rodgers record." Although Rodgers's appeal is generally considered to have centered in the South and Southwest, his popularity on records extended across the nation, even into urban and more sophisticated areas not otherwise identified with the early days of country music. Talking with an elderly gentleman who'd fronted dance orchestras and owned a record shop in a Midwestern city during the Thirties, I tried to feel him out about Rodgers and similar performers of the time, but quickly learned that he had no use for "hillbillies." Whenever the topic came up, he quickly turned it aside, and because he had so many other interesting things to talk about, I gradually gave up. After several conversations, however, I happened to ask whether he had perhaps stocked a few Rodgers records in his store from time to time. "Stocked a few? I stocked 'em all," he said, barely able to hide his disgust. "Sold thousands of 'em. Kept me in business all through the Thirties."[19]

Since the onset of Rodgers's initial success, Victor had been issuing about eight Rodgers records each year, averaging one release every six weeks. Even at that modest rate the company found it increasingly difficult to build a stockpile from which satisfactory releases could be drawn. The number of sessions[20] grew annually, from two in 1927 to three in 1928 and five in 1929, the peak year. These sessions produced, in terms of assigned matrix numbers, six sides in 1927, twenty-one in 1928, and twenty-seven in 1929. Of these, at least half a dozen had been deemed unsatisfactory; although they were eventually released after Jimmie's death, they were clearly not up to the standard that Victor, Peer, and Rodgers would have preferred to maintain. Instead, all concerned had to cope as best they could with the vagaries of Rodgers's health and the ever-present difficulty of finding suitable material. By the summer of 1930 the Victor vaults contained masters for only three or four more Rodgers releases; busy with the Swain tour and other personal appearances, Jimmie had not been to a studio since November. In the interval, however, he'd put together a substantial amount of material, and he informed Peer that he was ready "to make plenty of records." As it turned out, the series of sessions in Hollywood in June and July was the most protracted of his career, and the only time in 1930 that he was to record. From these sessions came fourteen sides—almost a year's supply, at the normal rate of issue—of which half a dozen or so have become Rodgers "classics."

The Hollywood sessions were planned as another working holiday, an opportunity for Jimmie to rest, soak up some California sunshine, and tour the film capital while at the same time replenishing Victor's storage vaults. The trip was also another dream come true for Jimmie Rodgers, for although he did not go to Hollywood for the entertainer's usual reasons—to make movies—it afforded him a chance to see and meet his screen idols and to travel in the upper reaches of the profession. Unfortunately, he was too ill to enjoy his stay fully, but few around him realized just how sick he was. As usual, he went to considerable lengths to conceal his discomfort and refused to be catered to on account of his health.

Jimmie and Carrie arrived in Hollywood around the middle of June and settled into the Barker Hotel on Miramar. Rodgers had not really recovered from the last flare-up that had taken him out of the Swain tour (although in any event "recovery," in his case, was a highly relative term). Nevertheless, he went to work right away, putting his material in shape and rehearsing with the various backup groups that Peer had lined up for him.

Victor had only recently completed its new quarter-million-dollar West Coast plant on Santa Monica Boulevard, covering most of the block bordered by Orange Drive, Romaine Street, and Sycamore Avenue. Constructed primarily to accommodate the company's expanding involvement in sound-on-film synchronization, the new building was also designed with rehearsal rooms and studios for disc recording, to augment the R-K-O facilities in nearby Culver City on which Victor had previously relied for its West Coast operations.[21]

Having managed a few days' rest between rehearsals and sight-seeing, Jimmie began to feel better and grew daily more anxious to get on with the recording schedule. His initial day in the studio—Monday, June 30—was a long and ambitious one, with morning and afternoon sessions of several hours. Accompanying him were two groups that were to epitomize the best that came out of his work in Hollywood— Lani McIntire's Harmony Hawaiians, and a jazz-oriented combo under the nominal direction of pianist Bob Sawyer, a local studio musician.[22] The day's work produced "My Blue-Eyed Jane," backed by the Sawyer contingent, and, with McIntire's Hawaiians, "Moonlight and Skies" and "Why Should I Be Lonely?"

"My Blue-Eyed Jane," which had originated with a niece of Elsie McWilliams's husband (but which was probably reworked by Elsie herself), transcends the mediocrity of its love/turtledove lyrics as a result of Rodgers's lilting delivery and the driving, buoyant energy of the jazz accompaniment. One of the least "country" of all Rodgers's songs, "My Blue-Eyed Jane" has nevertheless found a place over the years in the repertoire of many country artists—Hank Snow's version is especially fine—and it rightly deserves to be ranked among Rodgers's most memorable recordings. "Moonlight and Skies" was to become one of his most popular sides in many parts of the country, especially in Oklahoma. On the other hand, "Why Should I Be Lonely?" belongs to a small group of similarly bland pop love songs from the Hollywood sessions—"Take Me Back Again," "I'm Lonesome Too," and "For the Sake of Days Gone By"—which are distinguished by little more than the excellent but all-too-subdued accompaniments of McIntire's string group. The concept of the "flip side"—pairing a weak song with an obviously stronger one and thereby stretching the material—was just then beginning to develop, and, as Peer pointed out, Jimmie "only did these other [i.e., "soupy sentimental"] songs to balance the catalog."

The origins of "Moonlight and Skies" and the convolutions surrounding it are many and complex. It is possible that Rodgers first heard it back in the early Twenties on that occasion when he was passing time in a speakeasy down on Reno Avenue in Oklahoma City and struck up a conversation with another rambling man—Ray Hall—who also "picked a little" and wrote songs in his spare time. It may have been "Moonlight and Skies," or an early version of it, that attracted Jimmie's notice and resulted in his telling Hall to "write me in care of *Billboard* if you get any more songs like that." By 1928 Hall, who'd been in trouble with the law most of his life, found himself behind bars once again, convicted of manslaughter in Wichita Falls, Texas (probably without adequate or proper defense). Shortly afterward he was involved in a prison break at a state workfarm near Sugarland, during which a guard was killed. The details are sketchy and confused, but, according to Hall's account, he was mistakenly given another convict's identity and found himself serving not one but two life sentences. Feeling he'd been railroaded, he began to look around for help and remembered the lanky brakeman who'd told him to "get in touch if there's ever anything I can do." Because he'd been held in solitary confinement for long periods, Hall did not know that the itinerant trainman was now on his way to fame as America's Blue Yodeler, but he sent off a letter to Rodgers, addressed to *Billboard*, hoping for any kind of support he could get from the outside.[23]

Jimmie never forgot a name or face, and he remembered not only Hall but the songs they'd sung for each other in the Reno Avenue dive. When he received Hall's letter in mid-1929, he'd been busy with recording dates, the R-K-O tour, and a hundred other matters; but he had wired Hall immediately, promising to help in any way he could and asking Hall, in the meantime, to send him whatever song material he might come up with. Hall responded with a version of "Moonlight and Skies." At that stage, according to Hall, it was "a sort of cowboy song," done to the tune of "Little Mo-Hee" or "The Lass o' Mohee." ("It was one I had loved to hear my own dear mother sing in the Indian Territory days.") Jimmie replied that he wanted a "convict song, like the one Dalhart did."[24] Hall, staring out over the red brick towers of Huntsville's central unit—known, appropriately enough, simply as "Walls"—no doubt found himself singularly qualified to fill that request.

The second version, essentially the one recorded, reached Jimmie shortly and was added to the growing stack of material in his files, to be pulled out and put into final shape the following summer in Hollywood. Acting independently, Hall sent a copy to the U.S. Copyright Office; his copyright was registered on October 28, 1929.[25] It was only the beginning of a long and complicated, if often dormant, legal struggle that has not yet been resolved.

While "Moonlight and Skies" is marred by a few ragged lines ("A robbery we planned / So decided to start"), its popularity is easy to account for. Although hardly intentional, the Hall-Rodgers collaboration melded a lyric with strong autobiographical identity to both composer and performer. The narrator's story of his pal Blackie, the attempted robbery, Blackie's death ("with a shot through his heart"), and his own ensuing capture all closely parallel the account of what happened to Hall in Wichita Falls. And the song had its private appeal as well to Rodgers, who really did have "a sweetheart . . . back in old Oklahoma, not far from Shawnee"[26]—his newly discovered daughter. Like the child in the song, she may well have beseeched her father not to leave her (at least in his own imagination). Only a few months after the December release of "Moonlight and Skies," Rodgers told a reporter that it had been "by far the best selling record I ever made for Victor"[27]—a statement which, despite the song's considerable success, can only be explained as wishful thinking, testament to his affection for the number.

On the second day Jimmie worked alone in the studio to record two takes of "Pistol Packin' Papa," an entertaining bit of bawdy rendered with innocent good cheer. The approach was an entirely natural one, characteristic of the impish Jimmie Rodgers, with his small-boy charm and sly grownup grin. As he told Carrie, "If they like you when you're nice, they'll forgive you when you're naughty."[28] While his ribaldry was certainly mild by later standards, this attitude undoubtedly had its impact on the increasing freedom and openness which country artists now enjoy in dealing with subjects that were, in the past, only euphemistically hinted at or entirely forbidden.

After "Pistol Packin' Papa," Rodgers was unable to sustain the pace that he had set for himself the first day; he soon settled into an easier routine of afternoon sessions in which he would record only one or two numbers. Even at that rate he was taxing himself, and occasionally he had to miss a day or two from the studio in order to rest up. Still, over a period of almost three weeks he gamely kept coming back, determined to complete what he'd undertaken.

On July 5, accompanied only by McIntire on standard guitar, he recorded his interesting variation on "St. James Infirmary," renamed "Those Gambler's Blues," one of several older titles traditionally attached to the song. Both "St. James Infirmary" and "Those Gambler's Blues" had been the subject of much litigation; only a month earlier a New York Appellate Court had ruled that neither was in public domain but in fact had been copyrighted by Mills Music Company. Although the court admitted that " 'Gamblers Blues' is an old gutter song of the Southern slums," others were enjoined from using either title or any similar tune.[29] Just why Peer allowed Rodgers to record it is unknown—apparently he was simply unaware of the legal complications—but Southern Music proceeded straightaway to register it as an "arrangement," and the issue was fortunately never raised by the legal copyright-holders. As in the case of other songs, later Peer-Southern folios credited "words and music by Jimmie Rodgers."

Sometime early in his recording career, possibly as a result of the difficulties of working with various accompanists, Rodgers had begun to rely more and more on what may be referred to as "lyric sheets." They are not, strictly speaking, lead sheets, for few of them contain any musical notation. However, they served the same purpose, providing a sort of script to be used in the studio, indicating the key for a given song, chord changes (in some instances), pauses, breaks, yodels, and even the supposedly spontaneous spoken phrases which frequently punctuate the blues numbers. Lyric sheets for some forty-five Rodgers titles are extant, several in multiple versions. Taken collectively, they offer interesting insights into the processes and procedures by which he composed, published, and recorded his material. Often they include vital information concerning his accompaniment, the number of takes, the time of the session, and other incidental details. Each contains the lyrics of one song, usually in typescript and often with variant or rejected lyrics. Rodgers's revisions and notations appear in his own hand. Many are written on the back of letterheads from hotels in the cities where he traveled and recorded, suggesting clues to his whereabouts and to the sequences in which certain songs were composed.

Valuable as these sheets are, they are far from complete and provide only slight basis for conventional textual or bibliographical analysis. In rare instances it is possible to see a given song in several stages of composition, but generally one is rewarded with only a minor change here, a word inserted or deleted there, an altered title, a few chord changes, and some discographical information. Several sheets bear no notations at all and obviously represent the last stage of the process, or perhaps are even "clean copies" typed up for Rodgers's files. Most tantalizing of all are the omissions: the earliest sheet is for "That's Why I'm Blue," recorded in Atlanta in November, 1929. Although the file is more complete near the end, missing are sheets for some of the most interesting and problematic numbers, such as "Mississippi River Blues," "The One Rose," and, especially, "Hobo Bill's Last Ride." These disappointments are to some degree offset by the preservation of the lyrics for "Prohibition Has Done Me Wrong," the only master never issued (and now apparently lost), and the sheet for "Blue Yodel No. 9," recorded at the famous and much-debated session with Louis Armstrong.

The lyric sheet of "Those Gambler's Blues" shows the extent to which Rodgers had "St. James Infirmary" in mind. An early, aborted version on the back of the sheet begins, "Went down to St. Joe's

infirmary. . . ." As finally recorded, "Those Gambler's Blues" is a
rather inventive reworking of the old standard; although probably too
close an imitation to stand up under legal scrutiny had it been
challenged, the song nevertheless demonstrates Rodgers's ability to
embellish a traditional narrative and make it his own, condensing and
rearranging stanzas, adding details from his own experience, and
generally smoothing out the lyrics to make it fit the delivery he felt was
most natural. The opening line, for example, was first written, "It was
down in Old Billy's barroom"; troubled by the awkward alliteration,
Jimmie changed the proprietor's name to "Big Kid," which not only
sings better but also conjures up the image of a character far more
appropriate to the tough, sinister world of that dive "on the corner
beyond the square." The lyric sheet further indicates Jimmie's simple,
straightforward approach to musical notation. In rehearsing the song
he apparently decided—as the recording bears out—that he wanted to
end the first stanza on a low note and the second slightly higher,
alternating in that fashion throughout. Accordingly, on the page he
propped up before him in the studio, he simply wrote "Down" at the
end of the first verse, "Up" at the end of the second, "Down" again on
the third, and so on to the end, with the added reminder between the
fourth and fifth stanzas to "hum, yodel."

Jimmie hoped to record several numbers with McIntire's Hawaiians
the same day that he did "Those Gambler's Blues." He and McIntire
went into the studio that morning, and the rest of the group was called
for an 11:30 a.m. session. But by noon Jimmie was exhausted and
suffering a high fever, so the band was dismissed.[30] The intervening
Sunday allowed him to rest up, and all the musicians returned on
Monday afternoon for a session which lasted more than three hours. In
that time, however, they were able to record only two numbers, "I'm
Lonesome Too" and "The One Rose." The latter, a simple but
haunting composition by McIntire, has the unfortunate distinction of
being among the last Rodgers sides to be issued, after the song had
been made popular by Larry Clinton, Bing Crosby, and a host of others
in the late 1930's. Peer later admitted that he was to blame; he simply
forgot that the agreement with McIntire called for the record to be
released within a year after it was recorded. When Victor, unaware of
the stipulation, failed to issue it on time, McIntire took the tune to
another publisher, who succeeded in having it recorded by a number of
big-name artists. Consequently, the one side that might have been
Jimmie Rodgers's best claim to pop fame suffered the ignominy of

being issued as a "cover." The incident is merely typical of the helter-skelter way that his career was managed.

The next day, still running a high fever, he attempted to record "For the Sake of Days Gone By," but gave it up after two unsatisfactory takes. A note on Victor's recording logs for the session indicates: "Rodgers' voice husky. Could not make any more."[31] But the very next afternoon he and McIntire's group returned to do two more takes of the song; with the added embellishment of Bob Sawyer's light-fingered piano work, they succeeded so well that their first master that day was selected for release.

A day later, on July 10, Rodgers recorded one of his finest jazz sides, "Jimmie's Mean Mama Blues," a lilting, energetic number sparked by Sawyer's studio band. Sawyer himself devised the music for Waldo O'Neal's lyrics, which (like so many of Jimmie's own compositions) are at once original and derivative. The line "I'm going to leave this town just to wear [*sic*] you off my mind" appears in W. C. Handy's "Shoeboot's Serenade" of 1915 and was probably no more original even with Handy than were other vagrant lines such as "I woke up this morning with the blues all around my bed" and "The blues ain't nothing but a fatal heart disease," which both he and Rodgers drew upon.[32] But Jimmie's treatment of "Mean Mama Blues" catalyzes the familiar words and music, merging them into a unique, organic whole: all his life he would "crave the peace of miles," and he knew how to sing, with his own particular twist, "I've been from several places, and I'm going to be from here."[33] The ultimate strength of "Jimmie's Mean Mama Blues" lies in its total performance, in the infectious energy with which it is delivered, further distinguished by an arrangement that is clearly a product of the Jazz Age and yet years ahead of its time as country music. This progressive quality is best illustrated by the rousing first break, which the band approaches at full tilt and then drops out completely, leaving Jimmie to carry vibrantly through the bridge with only his guitar and effusive yodel. The band blows right back in for the second verse and then wails an instrumental chorus of its own; the third break is again done solo, by Sawyer, and they all join in for a slam-bang finish behind Jimmie's yodel. It is an inspired piece of work, reminiscent of Rodgers's 1928 Atlanta recordings, and all carefully worked out. The lyric sheet carries the notation, in his hand, for each break—"Guitar & Yodel," "Band," "Piano," and "Band up, yodel."

Two more sessions finished the week. "The Mystery of Number

Five," something of a throwback to Jimmie's earlier, pseudo-folksongs, with its "little maiden with a teardrop in her eye" and the formulaic warning to "you railroad men," was recorded on July 11, along with "Muleskinner Blues" (issued as "Blue Yodel No. 8").[34] The following day he did "In the Jailhouse No. 2," a number which, according to Carrie, he dashed off in a few minutes at the hotel in response to Peer's request for a sequel to his big hit of two years before. Despite the fact that he was still suffering the effects of his latest relapse—a Hollywood doctor's name and phone number are written on the back of "The Mystery of Number Five"—these sides reveal Jimmie at the top of his form and mark one of the rare instances this late in his career when he recorded solo, accompanying himself on guitar. The brash, exuberant "Blue Yodel No. 8" is especially fine, featuring yet another variant on the form, in which the base line is not repeated. Heard also is one of Jimmie's more protracted and—for him—complicated guitar runs, the sort of sharp, solid fret work and booming bass notes that, although rarely performed on his records, became identified as his trademark and were widely copied. The lyrics of "Muleskinner Blues" are themselves superb, and the song has attracted a number of country singers over the years. Unfortunately, it is rarely performed as Rodgers originally did it. For reasons unknown, Peer's published version bears no resemblance to the song Jimmie recorded.

Whether deliberately or by mere happenstance, the pièce de résistance of the Hollywood sessions was saved until last. After three days of rest and recuperation, Jimmie arrived at the studio to record a blues number he'd entitled "Standin' on the Corner" and found that his accompanist for the session was a rising young trumpeter named Louis Armstrong. As Armstrong's biographers, Max Jones and John Chilton, remark, "How this improbable partnership came into being remains one of jazz's unsolvable riddles."[35] I suppose we are entitled to say that it is also one of country music's unfathomable mysteries, but Jones and Chilton's emphasis upon jazz is only one more indication of Jimmie Rodgers's diversity and his distance, in his own time, from what has traditionally been derided as "hillbilly music."

In light of Ralph Peer's modest boast years later that "I invented Louis Armstrong" back in the days at Okeh, one may assume that Rodgers's very brief association with the great Satchmo was merely a natural result of Peer's acquaintance with both performers. Armstrong had only recently moved to the West Coast and was anxious to get whatever work he could find. An old hand at studio jobbing, he undoubtedly made the rounds and encountered Peer (who knew him, but had hardly "invented" him). Although Armstrong as a musician was of course superior to Rodgers, their work together was not as "improbable" as Jones and Chilton seem to feel. Jimmie was, after all, a bluesman, despite the pallid pigmentation of his skin, and had been making jazz-oriented recordings since early in his career. For his part, Armstrong, upon recording a country-western LP in 1970, observed that it was "no change for me, daddy, I was doing that same kind of work forty years ago."[36] The divisions, more imagined than real, existed largely in the minds of naive fans and feckless scholar-critics more intent on writing about music than on listening to it. No one understood the universality of music, and especially of jazz, better than Louis Armstrong. "I always say a note's a note in any language if you hit it on the nose," he remarked.[37]

Which is not to assert that Jimmie Rodgers always did. Commenting on "Blue Yodel No. 9," the Rodgers-Armstrong side which grew out of "Standin' on the Corner," Jones and Chilton correctly assess the performance: "Restrained authority marks Louis' solo; in the backings he sounds apprehensive whilst contending with the problem of following the singer's markedly individual concept of bar lines"[38]—a kind way of saying, as many of Jimmie's accompanists did in less polite terms, that the Blue Yodeler couldn't keep time. Despite the vague sense of uneasiness that one detects in both performances, "Blue Yodel No. 9" is a signal achievement, one that fans of both musicians can justifiably cherish. If to some extent Armstrong carries the side, he carries it sympathetically, immersed in a mode of expression natural to singer and musician alike: the anguished, defiant, and ultimately triumphant language of the true blues. As for the lyric itself, a number of listeners have commented on its similarity to "Frankie and Johnny," at least in the general stance and setting. Whether this constitutes a strength or weakness is debatable; a more serious distraction seems to be the abruptness with which the narrative ends, unresolved. Rodgers's lyric sheet reveals, however, that the original version contained three additional stanzas, two of which extend the "Frankie and Johnny" parallel and deal with the actual shooting, and a final, appropriate verse about the graveyard, that lonesome place where they "lay you flat on your back and through [*sic*] the dirt down in your face"[39] (a traditional stanza later incorporated into "T.B. Blues"). Apparently the full complement of verses, with Armstrong's trumpet breaks, simply consumed too much time, and the last three were cut. The resulting truncated version, then, can be attributed not to a faulty sense of narrative, but to the exigencies of 78 rpm recording.[40]

For a number of years, until Armstrong's presence on "Blue Yodel No. 9" was definitely established by Jones and Chilton, the recording provided grist for the mills of discographers, and the argument over the identity of the piano player, who perhaps deserves more credit than yet accorded, has continued to simmer. John Edwards guessed, incorrectly, that it was Earl Hines, and, like the equally mistaken idea that Boyd Senter and Mickey Bloom were part of Bob Sawyer's studio band, his speculation has caused problems for later chroniclers willing to take it all too literally. Conversely, Brian Rust, in his first edition of *Jazz Records, 1897-1931*, credited the piano to Lil Hardin Armstrong, but jazz aficionados familiar with the work of Satchmo's second wife have been unable to confirm her presence on the basis of aural evidence. Jones and Chilton assert categorically that the pianist is "definitely not Earl Hines or Lil Armstrong,"[41] providing substantial detail to show that Lil and Louis were separated at the time and not working together. Consequently, it seems somewhat anticlimactic to offer the evidence of Rodgers's lyric sheet—but there it is, written at the bottom of "Standin' on the Corner," in the same hand that made revisions, indicated breaks, and preserved the names of his accompanists:

> Recorded in Hollywood 7-16-30
> Louis Armstrong Trumpet, Lillian on Piano

Perhaps the unfortunate omission of a last name allows the discussion to go on.

A somewhat greater mystery, although one of far less consequence, surrounds a curious recording session in which Rodgers participated the following day, his last studio date in Hollywood. Together with an ex-vaudevillian named I. N. Bronsen, he recorded a blackface sketch, without music, called "The Pullman Porters," on the order of the dialogue recordings popularized by the Two Black Crows. As Hiram and Hezekiah, a sort of poor man's Amos 'n Andy, Bronsen and Rodgers struggle through a flat, tasteless script in which the Clever Darkie (Rodgers) shortchanges the Dumb Nigger (Bronsen) in a money swap, reads him a telegram announcing the birth of a son—the supposed joke is that his wife knows nothing about it—and performs miscellaneous other nonsense. Rodgers, an accomplished blackface actor from his medicine show days, has the right voice and proper inflection, but he is never able to find the pace or to cope with the atrocious material. Bronsen, something less than mediocre throughout, alternates between awkward pauses, hog-on-ice ad libs, and reading one, word, at, a, time from a script that doesn't quite make sense. Just how this strange affair came about is anyone's guess, but the general consensus is that it was done merely as a test and was never seriously considered for release. This assumption is supported by the fact that it was given a four-digit master number, out of sequence with all other West Coast recordings of the same time, and tucked away in a remote corner of Victor's files. Rodgers fans can be grateful. "The Pullman Porters" is of little value except as a curiosity.[42]

Hollywood had not been all work and no play for Rodgers that summer. To the extent that his health permitted, he socialized, made a round of movie-colony parties, and lunched on several occasions with film executives and other celebrities. The talking short which he had made for Columbia the previous year was then in national distribution, and there may have been some notion in the back of both his and Peer's minds of pursuing further film offers when they went to California. It soon became obvious, however, that his health, the deepening Depression, and a number of other factors would not allow such plans to materialize.

Although Carrie would refer to *The Singing Brakeman* as "the best selling short of its time,"[43] there is little to support that claim; nor does the movie itself convey much of the personal magnetism that captivated audiences who saw Rodgers perform in person. This may be attributed not only to the film's brevity and low budget, but also to the relatively primitive filming techniques in those very early days of talking pictures. Within only a year or so, important advances would be made in lighting, set design, and camera placement. Rodgers was filmed during that brief transition period from silents to talkies, when movies suffered many of the shortcomings of both forms with few of the virtues of either. Immobilized in its soundproof casing, or "sweat box," the camera was static, and the movement of actors had to

take place near the microphone, which was often hidden on a wall of
the set or in some piece of furniture. Within the confines of time and
space imposed on him, Rodgers can do little more than walk out, set
his eyes against the harsh lights, sing his three songs—"Waiting for a
Train," "Daddy and Home," and "Blue Yodel"—and make an exit.
Compared to the amateur-theater delivery of the Elderly Lady and the
Waitress with whom he chats briefly, Jimmie's performance is smooth
and natural enough; yet there is little of the spontaneity and breezy
charm reported by those who saw him perform in person. Every word
or gesture is obviously planned and carefully rehearsed. Graphically,
the movie exaggerates his worst features: the long, thin face, the jug
ears and hooked nose, the tilted upper lip that gave the impression that
he was catching whiffs of some faintly disagreeable odor as he sang.
The slow filmstock of the day produced a pallid, almost ghostly skin
tone against the dark background of the set, an effect only heightened
by eye and lip makeup and a sidewall haircut that might well have been
administered by some barber-school dropout. Jimmie Rodgers was not
the most handsome candidate for film stardom; but then neither were
the likes of James Cagney and Edward G. Robinson, or even Bing
Crosby, to whom Rodgers bore a passing resemblance. As most of
Jimmie's professional stills reveal, he was normally a far more
photogenic figure than depicted in *The Singing Brakeman*.[44]

Despite all this, the film is of singular cultural and historical value,
preserving the Father of Country Music in action as he sings interesting
variants of three of his most popular songs. At the very least, it offers
visual refutation of Ralph Peer's blithe assertion that "Jimmie only
knew two chords on the guitar."[45] A few of them may have been
entirely of his own invention as he worked up and down the frets, but
he was at home wherever the tune might take him. "Jimmie Rodgers
would probably laugh at the idea that he was a great guitar player,"
said C. F. Martin III, who knew him and who made some of his
favorite instruments, including the one he plays in the film, "but he had
the good taste and the right touch that make guitar accompaniments
effective."[46] That's the appropriate note, and one which *The Singing
Brakeman*, our only pictorial evidence, aptly bears out: the instrument,
although secondary to the vocal performance, is a vital and fitting part
of it, a natural extension of the bardic power that was the basis of
Jimmie Rodgers's art. "It is the heart," said Quintilian, "which renders
men eloquent."

NOTES

1. *Billboard*, May 10, 1930, p. 30.

2. *Henryetta* (Okla.) *Daily Free Lance*, May 30, 1930, p. 2.

3. Bill Bruner, interview, May 29, 1976, Meridian.

4. *MHJR*, p. 234.

5. They were "Whisper Your Mother's Name," "A Drunkard's Child," "The Yodeling Cowboy," "Blue Yodel No. 6," "Tuck Away My Lonesome Blues," "My Rough and Rowdy Ways," "Frankie and Jimmie" (an interesting slip), and "Everybody Does It in Hawaii."

6. According to a brief filed by her lawyers in the child support case, Stella sued for divorce from Rodgers after moving to Oklahoma, but no record of the decree has been found.

7. Confidential sources.

8. *State of Oklahoma* v. *Richard Harkins and Hugh Kelly, District Court of Choctaw County, Oklahoma*, Case #1482. See also unidentified newspaper clipping, "Harkins Trial Is Started in District Court," in court file.

9. Ellen Fraser Kiker to NP, July 14, 1975.

10. A source close to the Bozeman family relates that Jimmie's Aunt Dora had received a birth announcement at the time of the baby's arrival, but no evidence has been uncovered to indicate Jimmie's knowledge of the child prior to the appearance in Holdenville.

11. Stella Kelly, interview, June 6, 1975.

12. *Billboard*, July 19, 1930, p. 30.

13. *Wewoka* (Okla.) *Times*, May 27, 1930, p. 3; *Holdenville* (Okla.) *Daily News*, June 1, 1930, p. 5; *Wewoka Daily Times-Democrat*, June 2, 1930, p. 5.

14. Jimmie Rodgers to Aaron Rodgers, June 3, 1930; letter in Jimmie Rodgers Memorial Museum, Meridian.

15. *Billboard*, July 19, 1930, p. 30.

16. *Ibid.*, Sept. 16, 1930, p. 31; Jan. 31, 1931, p. 26. The route of Swain's Follies, which in earlier weeks had been faithfully reported to *Billboard*'s Route Department, disappeared after the issue of June 28, 1930.

17. *Ibid.*, Apr. 20, 1935, p. 23; Mickel, *Footlights on the Prairie*, p. 107.

18. Tony Thomas to NP, May 9, 1975; interview, May 17, 1976, Hugo, Okla.

19. Confidential source.

20. As used here, the term "session" covers those periods, often involving several appearances in the studio over many days, when Rodgers had traveled to one city or another for the specific purpose of recording. See note 3 in "The Recordings of Jimmie Rodgers."

21. *Variety*, July 11, 1928; Oct. 3, 1928, p. 7; Mar. 20, 1929, p. 73.

22. The musicians who made up these groups have not been identified. Sawyer's group was presumably comprised of union musicians and may have changed from session to session. It has been speculated that McIntire's steel guitarist was Sam Koki (Bond, *Recordings of Jimmie Rodgers*, pp. 22, 28; Dirk P. Vogel to NP, Mar. 25, 1978). Vogel (to NP, Mar. 4, 1978) also suggests that it may have been Bob True. McIntire, born December 15, 1904, in Honolulu, came to the mainland in the mid-Twenties, joining Sol Hoopii's Novelty Trio on the West Coast. The group recorded on various obscure labels, including Sunset and Hollywood, before signing with Columbia in October, 1926. From time to time McIntire headed his own contingent, and he later scored and appeared in a number of early Hollywood musicals, including *Waikiki Wedding, Honolulu*, and *South of Pago Pago*. In the late

1930's his orchestra backed Bing Crosby on numerous recordings. From 1947 until McIntire's death in 1951, the group was in residence at the Hawaiian Room of New York's Lexington Hotel (Dirk P. Vogel to NP, Mar. 4 and 25, 1978).

23. Raymond Hall, interview, Mar. 12, 1975, Texas State Penitentiary, Huntsville; see also Tom Miller, "Prisoner 60339 Sings the Blues," *Country Music,* Feb., 1975, pp. 25–27.

24. Hall, interview, Mar. 12, 1975; to NP, Apr. 6, 1975. The revised version, substantially that recorded by Rodgers, was collected by Vance Randolph and included in *Ozark Folksongs,* II:162; he cites two "folk" sources, a newspaper, and "a phonograph record, Montgomery Ward, 1938."

25. United States Register of Copyrights, E unpub. 12715; Copyright Office to NP, July 21, 1975.

26. "Moonlight and Skies," words and music by Jimmie Rodgers. © 1931 by Peer International Corporation. Copyright renewed. Used by permission.

27. *Lufkin* (Tex.) *Daily News,* May 31, 1932, p. 6.

28. *MHJR,* p. 185.

29. *Variety,* May 14, 1930, p. 73; see also *Billboard,* Mar. 28, 1931, p. 40; Bond, *Recordings of Jimmie Rodgers,* p. 25 (note by Norm Cohen).

30. Victor files. See Randle, "Jimmie Rodgers: An Annotated Discography," (unpublished manuscript, in files of JEMF), p. 15n.

31. *Ibid.,* p. 16n.

32. Citing these and other such floating stanzas, Paul Oliver writes, "These words come from no special blues, but from a hundred, or a thousand. See *Aspects of the Blues Tradition* (New York: Oak Publications, 1970), pp. 18, 90.

33. "Jimmie's Mean Mama Blues," words and music by Waldo O'Neal, Bob Sawyer, and Jimmie Rodgers. © 1931 by Peer International Corporation. Copyright renewed. Used by permission.

34. "The Mystery of Number Five," words and music by Jimmie Rodgers. © 1931 by Peer International Corporation. Copyright renewed. Used by permission. (Copyright information supplied by the music publisher occasionally varies from that shown in Victor's files.) "Muleskinner Blues" was recorded as "Blue Yodel No. 9," but changed to "Blue Yodel No. 8" when the previously designated No. 8 was withheld and later issued as "Blue Yodel Number Eleven."

35. Max Jones and John Chilton, *Louis: The Louis Armstrong Story* (Boston: Little, Brown, 1971), p. 236.

36. *Ibid.*

37. *Ibid.,* p. 214.

38. *Ibid.,* p. 236.

39. "T.B. Blues," words and music by Jimmie Rodgers. © 1931 by Peer International Corporation. Copyright renewed. Used by permission.

40. These are the two omitted stanzas:

>She says there aint no use
>To holler scream and cry
>I'm gonna kill you Daddy
>You know the reason why
>
>That fourty four
>Cracks so loud
>It sounds like a bulldog
>Up in the clouds

41. Jones and Chilton, *Louis,* p. 236.

42. "The Pullman Porters" has lately surfaced on a bootleg LP, Endangered Species ES-13.

Another minor curiosity of Rodgers's trip to California arises from a brief item in the *Kerrville Mountain Sun* of Oct. 23, 1930, headlined "Song Hit Written by Kerrville Man." The story concerns a song entitled "Smiling Silvery Moon," composed by Rocco Muscotto of Kerrville and published by J. S. Unger. According to the story, the song was "introduced in Hollywood, Cal. from the manuscript, by Jimmie Rodgers." See also *Billboard*, Sept. 6, 1930, p. 26. Efforts to discover the circumstances of this "introduction" have been unsuccessful, but the song was obviously not recorded because Peer did not hold the copyright. In any event, it tends to contradict Peer's assertion that Rodgers "never sang a song publicly that he hadn't recorded."

43. *MHJR*, p. 232.

44. Paris and Comber comment (*Jimmie the Kid*, p. 88) on the incongruity of "a blue-denimed brakeman in a tumble-down lunchroom playing a $1,500 guitar. . . ." Perhaps even more out of place were his silk hose and shiny "low quarter" dress shoes, in place of trainman's brogans. The value of the guitar is another cherished Rodgers myth; C. F. Martin III, whose craftsmen made the instrument, has pointed out that "when new the retail price of the guitar with case was about $300.00," noting however that at the time it was "about the highest priced guitar made" (C. F. Martin III to Leo Leriche, Aug. 5, 1959; copy in my files). Added Martin, "The only basis for such valuation [$1,500] would be the sentimental value attached to an irreplaceable instrument." When Ernest Tubb sent the guitar to the Martin factory for repairs in the mid-Fifties, he valued the shipment at $1,000.

45. Earlier, however, in his *Meridian Star* article (May 26, 1953, p. 24), Peer wrote: "As a guitarist, he was an individualist, that is, he had his own way of selecting his chords and was what can best be described as a 'natural' guitar player. I remember that another artist during the year 1931 spent a great deal of time learning one of Jimmie's 'wrong' chords. Whatever [Jimmie] used always sounded right, but upon examination it was quite often not the chord which ordinarily would have been used. This provided individuality for all records in which his guitar playing predominated amongst the accompaniment, but quite often it was a problem to find musicians and other artists able to fall into the spirit of his recording style."

46. C. F. Martin III to Leo Leriche, Aug. 5, 1959.

14 *August, 1930–February, 1931*

Fighting like a Lion

Mention a song called "T.B. Blues" today, and most people give you a brief look of disbelief, followed by sniggers and curious shakes of the head. Boy, what those oldtime hillbillies couldn't think of! The notion of a prominent entertainer singing about the disease that was killing him—especially a disease so old fashioned, ludicrous, and disgusting as tuberculosis—strikes them as a rather literal (and pathetic) sick joke, on the macabre order of, say, Nat King Cole huskily warbling some merry ditty about lung cancer.

Only a generation or two ago, tuberculosis was a very real and ordinary occurrence. At the turn of the century up to 90 percent of the American adult population had been afflicted with it at some time, and as late as 1950 it was still the leading cause of death among Americans between the ages of 15 and 34.[1] So prevalent was tuberculosis in the nineteenth century that it was not only domesticated into everyday life—euphemized as "consumption" or "phthisis"—but also idealized into something of an aesthetic *force majeure*, giving rise to the tradition of fainting ladies and pale, fastidious poets. To many it was "the disease of genius": Keats, Shelley, Elizabeth Barrett Browning, the Brontë sisters, Chopin, Balzac, Paganini, Emerson, Gauguin, Dostoevsky, Thoreau, and Stephen Crane all had it, as did dozens of other prominent figures. But so did a hundred thousand lesser mortals who contracted it as a result of living in filthy slums or rural hovels and toiling long hours in bad weather, deprived of proper food and health care—conditions rarely conducive to producing works of genius or creativity. Tuberculosis penetrated to all levels of society. In the

1920's and '30's, if you didn't have it, you knew someone who did. My father's eldest sister died of it, and two of his brothers suffered it but survived, thanks to medical advances during World War II. T.B. sanitoriums dotted the country, and every community had an invalid "lunger" or two, lurking along the streets or nestled away in a back bedroom. I remember, from childhood, a tall, gaunt man named Theodore John Henry Gass, whom everyone called Thee, with a soft *th*, slurred behind the teeth. Thee Gass was distantly related, by marriage, to my mother's side of the family, and with his wife and two scrawny children lived in a tiny three-room shack (the ceilings in two of the rooms were so low that Thee couldn't stand up straight in them, and everyone laughed about that) across the road from my grandfather's farm, where Thee rented a quarter-section of hardscrabble cotton land. For years Thee had had T.B. and was, among us children, an item of minor curiosity. Although he worked in the field and seemed otherwise normal (if a bit dense and stolid), at family gatherings the dishes he ate from were set aside separately to be boiled, and we were warned, privately, not to touch him or get too close. As his disease progressed, I was not allowed to enter the shack they lived in, or, finally, even to cross the road to play with his kids whenever I visited my grandparents. At last, all through the hot Texas summer of 1944, Thee Gass lay dying in that gloomy, airless shack, in the one room in which, if he could have stood up, he might have raised his head without touching the ceiling. In high August the neighboring farmers came to plow and lay-by his crop, and the womenfolk gathered at noon in my grandparents' yard to spread dinner beneath the huge, leafy Chinese elms. Saying grace, the country preacher got down hard and quoted from Romans 6: "What shall we say then? Shall we continue in sin, that grace may abound? God forbid. How shall we, that are dead to sin, live any longer therein? . . . For the wages of sin is death, but the gift of God is eternal life. . . ." He spoke of those times "when it rains down sorrow," and everyone knew that that allusion was not to the Bible but to Jimmie Rodgers; and from the sequel[2] to "T.B Blues," the preacher concluded his offering with what were for him its most comforting (if innocuous) lines—" 'Just say in your mind your troubles you've forgot, good old contentment is going to help you a lot'; in the name of Jesus Christ we pray." The soft Methodist "amens" murmured across the flat, shimmering fields. A month or so later they buried Thee Gass, and on the way home from the funeral I remember my mother, who sometimes worked as a nurse for the doctor in town, talking about a new drug called streptomycin that would cure tuberculosis.[3]

Up to that time, treatment of T.B. had amounted to little more than "rest," and that was something which Jimmie Rodgers seemed constitutionally incapable of. Constantly plagued with flare-ups in California, he'd gone back to Kerrville with the notion of remaining there indefinitely, completely inactive, until he'd accomplished another of his seemingly miraculous "recoveries." A few weeks after his return in late July he assured Peer that "I have been getting lots of Rest since I got home," even though his letter teems with news of fraternal doings (he was active in both Elks and Masons), a trip to Galveston "to see the Bathing Beauties," and all sorts of professional matters, including arrangements for having his songs scored, advances against royalties, and the possiblilty that Colonel Swain "is going to Sue Me for fifty grand." ("I ain't a Dam bit afraid of that," said Jimmie confidently.) There is also a note of appreciation for a case of his favorite whiskey which Peer had arranged to have brought in at El Paso and waiting for Jimmie on his way home from Hollywood.[4]

In August, Jimmie and a group of his Kerrville buddies traveled to Breckenridge, near Fort Worth, to attend a political rally and hear ex-Governor James E. Ferguson speak in behalf of his wife's candidacy for the state's highest office.[5] The Fergusons constituted a long and colorful, if not always glorious, tradition in Texas politics. A vague neo-populist with a minor talent for demagoguery, Pa Ferguson was nevertheless an astute politician who had accomplished considerable reform during his initial term of office back before the Great War. Also something of an opportunist, he made many enemies and created widespread controversy. In 1917, as a result of a heated battle with the University of Texas and charges that he'd accepted payoffs from the brewing industry, he was impeached and prohibited from ever again holding state office. Undeterred, he entered his wife as a candidate in the 1924 election, and Ma Ferguson rose to sudden notoriety as the state's first woman governor. Pa of course continued to run the office, but both Fergusons gained great popularity among the rank and file, who saw them as champions of the "little man" and who, in the words of one historian, "equated commonality with real democracy and professed to see social value in being 'common as an old shoe.'"[6] Defeated in their race for a third term in 1926, the Fergusons decided to try again four years later, and Jimmie Rodgers became one of their more ardent supporters.

Sometimes accused of lacking a political stance in that crucial period of national upheaval, Rodgers was in fact a thoroughgoing democrat, in the broadest sense of the term. If his social consciousness lacked sophistication, it was all the more intense and unequivocal, a product of instinct and heritage, and rooted in his simple dictum that "The underest dog is just as good as I am—and I'm just as good as the toppest dog." He said it with pride and with modesty, and he lived by it devoutly. Like most people, he had little time or use for abstract theories of government or high-level political maneuvering, and (like many other voters) he may have sometimes confused style with substance, as in the case of the Fergusons. At the same time, it is easy to understand why Jimmie, along with thousands of other Texans, was attracted to the wily, ebullient Pa Ferguson and his plain but jovial wife, who'd become a mother figure for many in the state. The Fergusons were for the common man, they insisted, and if they actually did little for him legislatively, they at least put on a good show, took his mind off his troubles, and allowed him the satisfaction of feeling that one of their own was running things. It is also worth noting that Ma Ferguson originally entered politics as an anti-Klan candidate—largely a political maneuver that was never acted upon (because the overt threat of the Klan had melted away), but one which surely delineates the position of the Ferguson camp on a crucial issue. Another plank in the Ferguson platform may have had special appeal to Rodgers: their previous administrations were famous—and, strangely enough, widely popular—for the broad use of executive clemency for convicted felons. Jimmie may have seen in this some hope for his friend Ray Hall, in whose case he had taken a genuine interest. In any event, he followed the campaign avidly. "Well I'm hoping Ma Furgerson gets Elected Goviner of the State of Texas," he wrote to Peer. "Looks pretty good for her here."[7] His prediction did not hold: Ma was beaten by Ross Sterling, a Houston oil man and contractor, although she would return two years later to eke out one more victory. By that time Jimmie Rodgers was scarcely in any condition to concern himself about politics.

Although Rodgers tried to give everyone the impression that he'd gone back to Kerrville to rest until his health improved, life there was hardly less hectic than performing on the road. In the year since Blue

Yodeler's Paradise was completed, Jimmie had been there barely half the time, and even now, despite the accelerating progress of his disease, he was never home for very long. There were hunting trips with his Kerrville cronies and frequent excursions to the Mexican border towns with Houston businessman Earl Moore, who later served as another of Jimmie's business managers, and with Will Horwitz, a flamboyant Texas entrepreneur and theater-owner. Horwitz's business interests included the Mexican radio station XED in Reynosa; he enlisted Jimmie's services to inaugurate the station's first broadcast, and they frequently returned, in high spirits, to contribute to XED's programming—which was normally chaotic anyway—with a bit of impromptu yodeling and singing.[8]

Rodgers's daughter Anita remembered one of her father's excursions to Medina Lake, south of Kerrville, with his good friend Sunny Blevins. Blevins was a tall, genial San Antonian with a career in law enforcement, serving at that time as Bexar County's chief probation officer. "Daddy and Sunny had been up there at the lake, fishing and 'hoorawing,'" said Anita. "Which means of course they were having a few drinks, too." On the way home Jimmie's yellow Ford roadster jumped a ditch, wrenching Jimmie's back and loosening several of Blevins's teeth. "Somehow they managed to get home," Anita said, "and you should have heard all the carrying on. Daddy was on the couch, yelling 'Oh, my back, my back,' and Mr. Blevins was in the kitchen spitting blood in the sink, and still they were joking and cutting up like two fools. When Mama saw Mr. Blevins spitting in the sink, she got mad and bawled him out, said, 'Why Sunny, I know you're in pain, but how dare you spit in my sink!' She shooed him out of the kitchen, still bleeding, but that didn't seem to put a dent in the way they were carrying on. Finally the doctor came and they got Daddy upstairs, with a few snorts along the way of course, and made him as comfortable as they could. And I'll be darned if the doctor didn't come back in an hour or so, with a sort of sheepish grin on his face. He said, 'You know, I was having so much fun over here, and I know Jimmie's gonna be all right, so I thought I'd just drop back, maybe have another drink and talk some more.' And those fools sat up half the night, Daddy and Sunny both in pain but laughing and joking all the time."[9]

One of Jimmie's closest companions during this time was a Kerrville neighbor, real estate dealer John Furman, whose son Dick occasionally traveled with them on jaunts around the country. The younger Furman later recalled their adventures with wry amusement. "They weren't hard drinkers," he said genially, "just steady. They'd take a social drink. And all the other drinks were social drinks. They just kept on having a social drink, and another social drink, and one after that, all day."[10] Jimmie had a boyish yen for all cars, but he especially loved Model-A Fords, which he bought and traded constantly. His favorite was a 1930 touring car that he called "Thirsty, the Christmas Tree" because it was the one he used whenever he was headed for some serious drinking, and because it was loaded with every gadget and accessory he could find, including special pockets built into each of the front doors, to hold his .32 owlhead pistol and a fifth of whiskey. All along the border were Mexican towns famous for their red-light districts—known as "Boys' Towns"—and it was Thirsty that carried Jimmie and John Furman to their favorite haunts in Piedras Negras and Villa (now Cuidad) Acuna, the latter of which boasted the grandest Boys' Town of all, the mecca of male Texans for hundreds of miles around.

Most of Carrie's efforts during this time were directed, as one Kerrville resident said, toward "trying to keep Jimmie under control and getting him to take care of himself," but her concern seemed only to make matters worse. Jimmie took a permanent suite at the Gunter Hotel in San Antonio, and whenever things at home got too complicated he would load up his pals and drive down to the Alamo City for a week or more of fun and games. This of course only contributed to the already tense situation at home. When Billy Burkes first knew Jimmie in 1929, "he and Carrie weren't living too close, even then."[11] Burkes's view was supported by others. "Jimmie loved that little ole daughter of his," Dick Furman said. "He was a fool about her, but I don't believe he was near as crazy about his wife as the publicity tried to make it."[12] Ralph Peer felt that Carrie nagged her husband too much. "She and Jimmie didn't actually get along awfully well, not for any sustained period," he said. "He was always traveling, getting away. You see, he needed somebody who had confidence in him, and a man and his wife, that's a different thing. A wife, normally, will become a little supercritical of this man who she sees day and night." Rodgers undoubtedly felt a strong obligation to his wife for all the years of hardship she'd suffered alongside him;[13] and he had no reason to divorce her, for he came and went as freely as if there were no marriage. Yet it was not his style to quarrel with her, either, and whenever he felt crowded he simply left and waited for the domestic seas to calm. For her part, Carrie's devotion to her husband was genuine enough. But, more important, as Mrs. Jimmie Rodgers she enjoyed a life of ease and prominence that exceeded anything she'd dreamed of, and she had no intention of giving up the marriage, troubled as it sometimes was. Despite Jimmie's occasional wayward- ness, there were compensations.

"If either of us saw something we longed to possess, we bought it—without a second thought," Carrie wrote.[14] The money rolled in—$100,000 a year from record royalties alone, according to the publicity blurbs. But it rolled out again just as quickly. Medical bills continued to mount, and the expense of maintaining Blue Yodeler's Paradise, along with several hotel suites at the same time, was a considerable strain. As always, Jimmie remained generous to a fault with everyone, constantly giving money away or loaning it without security (which amounted to the same thing) to anyone who needed it—or who could make it appear so. He was forever investing in some highly touted but ultimately doomed business scheme. Usually these affairs were related to show business in some way; he put money into a short-lived guitar-making enterprise, and into several tent shows that failed. One of his more curious ventures involved the purchase of an Orange Julius franchise for Kerrville. This, it turned out, was largely a sinecure for another of his ne'er-do-well friends; it, too, lasted only a short while. He was perennially appealing to Peer for advances against royalties—"I have asked Gilmore [Peer's assistant, Bob Gilmore] to let a grand come through on the 15th," he'd written after returning from Hollywood. (Peer readily admitted, however, that "I never lost anything on Jimmie Rodgers." That, for him, was a rare case of Putting It Mildly.) At least, said Carrie wistfully, "it may be said of us that we kept cash in circulation—much of it—in Texas all through the Great Depression."[15] Free spending was fairly endemic in their social circle, among the landed gentry, health spa proprietors, real estate promoters, and doctors who comprised the core of Kerrville's population, and the effects of the nation's economic catastrophe were a long time in reaching the wealthy little resort town. As the first full year of the Depression drew to a close, the Kerrville *Mountain Sun* asserted that "Talk of Hard Times Is a Myth," reporting local Christmas sales up substantially over 1929.[16]

Somehow, despite the social whirl, Jimmie's health improved

Lani McIntire, in a rare photo of Sol Hoopii's Novelty Trio in the mid-Twenties. *From left:* Glenwood Leslie, Sol Hoopii, McIntire.

"Blue Yodel No. 9," with uncredited backing by Louis and Lillian Armstrong, was widely promoted in newspaper ads, as Victor sought to spur lagging Depression sales.

Bizarre but appropriate, this 1973 drug advertisement drew on "T.B. Blues" to promote a new antibiotic forty years after Rodgers's death.

"I've been fighting like a lion; looks like I'm going to lose. I'm fighting like a lion; looks like I'm going to lose. 'Cause there ain't nobody ever whipped the TB blues."

TB Blues: Words & Music by Jimmie Rodgers

A major advance in the treatment of one of the world's most frustrating diseases.

The hopelessness of the fight against pulmonary tuberculosis was plaintively recorded by the "Father of Country Music," Jimmie Rodgers, in 1931—two years before he lapsed into a coma and died.

Today's victims have new hope—an antibiotic from Dow, Rifadin®(rifampin).

In initial treatment, regimens* containing rifampin and a companion drug may reduce the need for lengthy hospitalization, thus permitting the patient an early return to his community and productivity.

Rifadin has also shown significant results in many patients unresponsive to previous therapy.

Regimens containing Rifadin are usually well tolerated, which should encourage outpatients to stay with your prescribed, completely oral regimen. However, side effects and adverse reactions as described on the next page, can occur.

*NOTE: Rifampin must always be used in combination with one or more antituberculosis drugs.

300 mg. capsules

Rifadin®
rifampin

DOW PHARMACEUTICALS
 The Dow Chemical Company
Indianapolis, Indiana

See next page for full prescribing information.

This 1930 Ford Phaeton was only one of the many cars that he owned, but Rodgers preferred it for short tours and weekend jaunts around Texas. The inscription is to John Furman, his close friend in Kerrville: "I hope dad Burn yo hide you make 10 million in 1930, how's Dat.?"

Rodgers and Peer with their families on the patio of Blue Yodeler's Paradise, fall, 1930. *From left:* Rodgers, Mrs. Peer, Anita Rodgers, Peer, Mrs. Rodgers.

ORANGE JULIUS
== FOR ==
KERRVILLE
Served for the First Time
THURSDAY, SEPTEMBER 3rd, AT 7 A. M.
n the Schreiner Building Next to the Guadalupe Ca

GET ACQUAINTED WITH THIS WONDER DRINK

You'll Be Surprised How Good and Different Orange Juice Can Be.   See It Made On the New . . . .

SUNKIST EXTRACTOR

emember That the Julius Drinks are Made from Fresh Fruit. Juli rinks to be served are: Orange, Lemon, Lime, Grape Fruit and Oth

DON'T FORGET THE VARIETY

JIMMIE RODGERS
America's Blue Yodler
Franchise Holder

J. E. EDEN
Manager

Orange Julius franchise was another of Jimmie's short-lived business ventures.

The team of Rodgers and Rogers pauses for a photo in front of Blue Yodeler's Paradise during their whirlwind tour of Texas in January, 1931.

again—or possibly he simply convinced himself and those around him that it had, reacting to the restlessness and high nervous energy that is symptomatic of tuberculosis. In any event, he began making plans to go back to work. Ralph Peer and his wife had stopped by for a brief visit on their way back to New York from the West Coast that fall, and Peer had suggested bringing portable recording equipment to San Antonio for a session early in the coming year. Accordingly, Jimmie began working again on new material.

In October the Blue Yodeler was in the Big Thicket area of East Texas, "booking a few barnstorming dates before Christmas." From Houston he notified *Billboard* that while in Lufkin he'd run across his old friend, minstrel Lasses White, and sent his regards to all "the minstrel gang." "Just bought myself a new seven-passenger car," he added, "and I have all my recording for Victor finished until next February. Business conditions seem to be better in East Texas than any place I have seen recently."[17] After that, he was off to Meridian for Christmas. His doctor there told him sternly that he had less than a year to live if he didn't take care of himself. Jimmie piped a yodel, winked, and took a swig of prescription whiskey. He'd been listening to Dr. Cooper's warnings for a long time now.

"Sure am glad to know that Will Rogers is one of my fan's," Jimmie had written to Ralph Peer. "I wanted to meet him B4 I left Calif but you know how things were when I left I was in a hurry to get home." Everyone, including America's Blue Yodeler, was a fan of Will Rogers. Back in 1927, when Jimmie was still struggling for his first break, he'd probably been in the audience for the cowboy-humorist's performance in Asheville.

Disappointed at not getting to meet his idol in Hollywood, Jimmie took particular notice when he learned some six months later that the famous humorist would be touring the Southwest; he had offered to make a series of personal appearances to help the Red Cross raise money for the victims of drouth and Depression. For some time Rodgers had also been disturbed over reports of growing unemployment and the plight of farm families in drouth-stricken areas, and he was contemplating a similar benefit tour of his own. "Jimmie was always sorry for the fellow who was worse off than he was," said Peer, finding that somewhat difficult to understand. "It was hard to find those people, but he would find them."

Hearing of Will Rogers's projected tour, Jimmie felt that their efforts might be combined, and despite his awe of Rogers's stature in the entertainment world he sent a wire offering his services.[18] The Ambassador of Wit promptly accepted, and plans were made to open the tour with a gala show in San Antonio on Monday, January 26.

There was to be a brief preliminary appearance in Austin, a *pro forma* ceremony in the state's capital to pay proper respects, garner publicity, and draw the Legislature's attention to needed relief measures. Rogers, accompanied by his eighteen-year-old son, Will, Jr., arrived there on January 25, announcing that he was "just down here to do something about unemployment among the ex-Governors of Texas."[19] Joined by Jimmie, who grinned from ear to ear in boyish delight, the humorist joked about the imagined vaudeville team of Rogers and Rodgers, "the world's only yodeling rope-throwers." A warm friendship was established on the spot.

The event made a lasting impression on young Will Rogers, Jr., whose admiration for America's Blue Yodeler revealed the curious cultural prejudices of the time as well as a keen perception of Rodgers's true appeal. "I had all of his records, playing them on an old crank Victrola," he said later. "I and my friends were 'sophisticates' . . . and we considered most hillbilly [music] cornball. But not Jimmie. To appreciate him was a mark of intelligence. So when he joined my father on his drouth relief tour, I thought it a perfect mating. . . . Dad, of course, was a great admirer of his."[20]

The next day they flew to San Antonio, where they were met at the airport by a delegation of prominent citizens headed by Jimmie's good friend, Mayor C.M. Chambers. As Will Rogers stepped out of the plane, Hizzoner extended his hand in greeting. "Welcome, Mr. Rogers. I am the Mayor of San Antonio." "Well, sir," said the irrepressible Rogers, "I'm glad to meet you anyway."[21]

Everywhere they went, huge crowds gathered. There was a grand reception that afternoon in the Crystal Ballroom of the Gunter Hotel, attended by local dignitaries, society figures, big brass from Fort Sam Houston and Kelly Field, officers of the Old Trail Drivers Association—"just about everybody who counted," rhapsodized Carrie. Everybody except the folks for whom the benefit was being staged. Although Jimmie understood the necessity of catering to high society—these were, after all, the people who were sponsoring the tour—he was not exactly pleased with the exclusiveness of the gathering, nor was he particularly quick to respond to suggestions about his part in the performance coming up that evening, despite his high regard for the person making them. "Jimmie was very positive of what selections he wanted to sing," said Peer, "and he listened to what Will Rogers wanted him to do and he tried to conform to that and he did conform to it, but he picked his own selections to do and he didn't need anybody to advise him as to what was good for him." The affair that evening went smoothly, however, and the capacity crowd in San Antonio's Memorial Auditorium contributed almost $9,000 to aid the needy. Throughout the tour, performers paid their own expenses and received no salaries; gross proceeds were turned over to the Red Cross. On several occasions, when he felt the take hadn't been large enough, Will Rogers even contributed substantial sums from his own pocket.

Included on the San Antonio program were Eduardo Martinez and his band; Joseph Rubiola and Mrs. Saphia-Bosch, performing what was termed "native dancing"; Chester Byers of Fort Worth, world championship trick roper; and, of course, Jimmie Rodgers, "hill-billy blues singer of recording fame and radio fame" (one of the first instances in which the "hillbilly" appellation was hung on him, evidence of its growing use to categorize a particular style of performance).[22] Also scheduled to appear were the Revelers, Victor's popular male quartet and stars of a network radio show for Palmolive soap. The group, composed of Lewis James, James Melton, Elliott Shaw, and Wilfred Glenn, was delayed in New York and did not join the tour until it reached Dallas later in the week.

The star of the show, of course, was clearly Will Rogers. Everyone else, including Jimmie (whom the humorist introduced as "my distant son"), took decidedly second billing. But no one seemed to mind; despite his celebrity status, the slow-talking, low-key Oklahoman was hardly one to provoke professional jealousy, and the other performers laughed along with the audience at his witty gibes directed at human follies and the inflated egos of those in high places. Poking fun at Governor Ross Sterling and the twenty-two bathrooms on his Sugarland Estate, Rogers said, "Your Governor goes home every Saturday night for a bath. That is a good thing. I've seen your Governor's mansion in Austin. It must have been designed by a specialist, probably Chick Sale's grandfather." The controversial Wickersham report on Prohibition had resulted, as near as he could make out, in eleven men agreeing on one thing collectively and on

eleven different things individually. The only solution to Prohibition
was a device to register voters' breaths: "The ballot and the breath
must correspond before they can be counted." As Carrie Rodgers
reported, "A good time was had by all."

The rigid cultural division of the day is worth noting. While Will
Rogers captivated his audiences with honest, homespun humor and
Jimmie Rodgers was yodeling their blues away with "T for Texas" and
"In the Jailhouse Now," San Antonians in high society were attending
a recital of "traditional negro melodies," which had, curiously enough,
been "composed" by a local *artiste*. Said a social note in the
newspaper, "The traditional negro melodies composed by Alice
Mayfield were sung by Beethoven Maennerchor and directed by Albert
Schaeffer. The composer was at the piano. The melodies included,
'Galilee' and 'Honey in de Comb.' "[23] (One can believe "Honey in de
Comb"—but *Beethoven Maennerchor*?! Where, indeed, are the snow
jobs of yesterday?)

Following the huge success of the San Antonio benefit, the Red
Cross entourage was scheduled to leave the next morning by plane for
Abilene. However, steady rains and muddy runways forced cancellation of the take-off. The irony of a benefit tour for drouth victims
getting bogged down in mud gave everyone a laugh, but they had a
schedule to maintain, and time was running out.

Jimmie Rodgers came to the rescue, commandeering his wife's new
Packard for Will Rogers, Rogers's son, himself, and a driver. With the
rest of the troupe jammed into a second car provided by Earl Moore,
they headed west, leaving Carrie stranded in San Antonio and, for a
time, wondering who'd stolen her car. The Abilene show, originally
planned for that afternoon, was rescheduled for the following day; but
there was still an evening performance to be given in San Angelo,
more than two hundred miles away. Kerrville was along the route, and
Jimmie insisted they stop by Blue Yodeler's Paradise for a hasty lunch.
The stop was something of a shock for the Rodgers housekeeper,
Anna; but long accustomed to her employer's irregular habits and
impulsive gestures, she was equal to the task of whipping up a meal for
two carloads of celebrities. While they waited, Jimmie arranged for a
round of picture-taking, and insisted on showing off his famous visitor
to the town. A crowd gathered as they parked the chauffeur-driven
Packard by the picturesque Guadalupe River that runs through the
business area. Will Rogers stuck his head out and said, "So this is

Kerrville," as though he'd traversed land and sea in search of it. "He was the same old Will of the screen and stage," reported a representative of the *Mountain Sun*. "A shock of hair protruded beneath his hat, and during his brief visit he never missed a stroke in his gum chewing." The reporter was disappointed, however, that although the famous cowboy-philosopher chatted amiably with the townsfolk who gathered, he "never gave away any comedy stuff." Concluded the writer, a little petulantly, "he doubtless left that for the cash customers in San Angelo."[24]

With lunch out of the way, the group resumed the trip, arriving in San Angelo only minutes before the show was to begin in the Municipal Auditorium, where Jimmie had appeared on his shotgun tour in the fall of 1929. The show went off without a hitch before another capacity audience. Jimmie and Will, at least, were seasoned performers and accustomed to last-minute arrivals and hasty openings; box office receipts totaled $6,353, reportedly the largest in the city's history.[25] The next morning the entertainers drove on to Abilene to play the show that had been postponed. There improved weather conditions made it possible for Rogers's famous aviator friend, Frank Hawkes, to join them. Jimmie sent his driver back home with Carrie's car, and the entertainers flew to Breckenridge for an appearance that afternoon. By evening they were in Dallas to present an enlarged, three-hour extravaganza, the sixth benefit performance in three days. It turned out to be the biggest disappointment of the tour: fewer than 2,000 people showed up in the 5,000-seat auditorium, a surprise to everyone, since Will Rogers's last two appearances in the city had packed the house and his movies played to record box office receipts. Blame was laid to conflicting bookings, poor publicity, and the failure of the newspapers to support the enterprise. Noting that San Antonio had contributed more than twice the meager $3,856 collected in Dallas, and that even the small cities had frequently topped that amount, the show's star was openly displeased. "Rogers Grumbles at Size of House, but Gives Show," reported the *Dallas Morning News*. "The comedian swallowed his disappointment and gave a good-humored, zestful show," said the reviewer, perhaps trying to make amends. But some of Rogers's barbs were noticeably sharper than usual, as when he poked fun at the Trinity River navigation problems, a perennial object of civic concern. "I can't understand why you people spend so much money on that mangy little river," Rogers said, with unspoken inference to the niggardly amounts they spent on charity. "Why don't you get some buckets and move it out of here?" The Blue Yodeler's contribution to the evening was noted only briefly, with a maximum of misinformation: "Jimmy Rodgers, celebrated banjoist and crooner, now retired to his farm[!] at Kerrville, joined the Will Rogers party to assist in the entertainment."[26]

Rodgers left the tour temporarily in Dallas, having learned that Peer was on his way to San Antonio with the portable recording equipment. He went directly to the Alamo City and checked into his suite at the Gunter for a day's rest before digging into preparations for the recording session. But, as usual, there were many interruptions, with phone calls, visits with friends and fellow musicians, and business decisions to be made. The circumstances surrounding this session are not clear, but apparently Peer had planned his trip primarily around Rodgers, hoping to find enough other local talent to make the excursion worthwhile. He did not have much luck, and when he discovered that even his star was poorly prepared, having just come off the road and suffering from his usual scarcity of material, Peer decided to cut his stay to only two days.

Jimmie was able to line up several local musicians to accompany him on short notice, mostly struggling young semi-professionals whom he had gotten to know during his rambles around San Antonio. Charles Kama, a fine steel guitarist, and M. T. Salazar, who played standard guitar, had recorded for Victor earlier, although their first sides were never released. The string bass player, Mike Cordova, worked occasional dates with Kama and Salazar in local nightspots. For one side the group was enlarged to include Jimmie's friend Shelly Lee Alley and his brother Alvin, violinists who'd appeared on Dallas's WFAA as early as 1923 and worked with several pop-oriented bands at other Texas radio stations.[27] Despite the hurried and somewhat hectic conditions under which they were recorded, the three sides which Rodgers cut with these musicians are among his best and most representative.

The first, sung to the accompaniment of only Jimmie's and Kama's guitars, was the enduring "T.B. Blues." As both an artistic achievement and a statement of his own mortality, "T.B. Blues" Blues" is perhaps the ultimate manifestation of Rodgers's curiously dual attitude toward the disease that was killing him. For obvious reasons of taste and "image," the nature of his poor health was never named in news stories or publicity; but Jimmie himself made no effort to conceal it from those with whom he associated, nor was it any secret to most of his audiences, who, when he was occasionally caught by a coughing spell onstage, were known to applaud sympathetically and shout, "Spit 'er up, Jimmie, and sing some more."[28] Yet he rarely spoke to anyone about his health and appears to have simply ignored the whole matter as much as possible. This seeming ambivalence may help to explain why "T.B. Blues" is at once intensely authentic and yet calmly impersonal, as if the ominous disease and certain death are someone else's afflictions. How otherwise could he sing, so eloquently, so stoically, "I've been fighting like a lion, looks like I'm going to lose—'cause there ain't nobody ever whipped the T.B. blues"?[29] In one sense, the distance with which he performs suggests that he approached the song much in the manner of any other that he sang for commercial gain—it no more meant that he really had T.B. than, say, "Moonlight and Skies" meant that he'd been in prison, or "Lullaby Yodel" attested to marital trouble. But from beginning to end, from the singer's refusal to let his "good gal" make a fool of him by telling him he doesn't have T.B., to the final acknowledgment that "that old graveyard is a lonesome place" where "they put you on your back, throw that mud down in your face," "T.B. Blues" is both an artistic achievement and the most eloquent evidence of Jimmie Rodgers's tragic vision. It was a vision borne of his own courage and will, of his great zest for life and his own coming to terms with the transience of it, a vision substantial enough to elevate him to the ranks of those poets and painters and artisans whose work illuminates and eases all our human lives.

When Jimmie Rodgers sang "T.B. Blues," his audiences knew that he meant it—and that was one of the things, amid all the hillbilly hokum of the day, that distinguished him from the likes of Vernon Dalhart and Carson Robison. It is what country music fans mean today when they bestow their highest accolade on an artist by calling him "sincere." Corny, perhaps; but in a world where, as Joan Didion has suggested, the greatest evil lies in taking nothing seriously, a little sincerity goes a long way.

Of course, singing about tuberculosis was neither original nor exclusive with Rodgers. Several recordings entitled "T.B. Blues" preceded his version, and others continued to appear in the following years, as long as the disease remained a familiar presence. Whether tuberculosis was more socially acceptable in the Twenties and Thirties than now is debatable, but singing about it was nothing new in Rodgers's time. Blues stanzas mentioning the disease had been commonplace for years, and Jimmie was probably familiar with Willie Jackson's 1928 version (Columbia 14284). Early in 1929 he had written to Ray Hall in the Texas State Penitentiary, asking for "your version of 'T.B. Blues,'" together with any old random blues verses Hall could remember. As it happened, the prison farm where Hall was then located had originally been set up as a camp for tubercular prisoners, and it retained among its inhabitants much of the lore and atmosphere of the disease. Hall sent him what he had, and "Jimmie changed words here and there and some of the phrases—that's the way he worked."[30] One of Rodgers's more inspired alterations involved picking up the graveyard verse, originally part of "Blue Yodel No. 9," and fitting it in as the last stanza. He also decided to replace his usual yodel between verses with the falsetto refrain, "I've got the T.B. blues," subtly altering and reinforcing the blues form, producing a composition that, if not original, is nevertheless unusual, a tight, cohesive whole distilled from some of the best blues lines floating around in the collective consciousness.

The entire contingent of back-up musicians was assembled to record "Travellin' Blues," a song which was destined to be a Rodgers standard, revived over the years with considerable success by other artists such as Lefty Frizzell and Merle Haggard. Although Jimmie shared composer credit for "Travellin' Blues," it was largely the work of Shelly Lee Alley, whose performance on the recording contributed to Rodgers's ubiquitous influence upon the emerging patterns of country music. Until the time of his association with Rodgers, Alley's background and instincts had directed him primarily toward pop music. "Travellin' Blues" brought together, in however rudimentary a fashion, the strains of several musical traditions, notably jazz-blues and those elements of popular music most directly derived from older, "folk" roots. The combination was nothing new for Rodgers, but the particular instrumentation of the string band, highlighted by the Alley brothers' violins—the sound was not yet quite that of fiddles—caught the attention of younger musicians such as Bob Wills, the fledgling genius who was to make western swing an indelible part of American musical culture. Once more, without much plan or conscious intention, Jimmie Rodgers was breaking new ground.

The session was concluded with "Jimmie the Kid," a pleasant bit of fanciful, if harmless, self-promotion. Originally the idea of Jack Neville, one of Rodgers's San Antonio buddies, "Jimmie the Kid" is the least distinguished of the three sides recorded that day, but it has gained moderate popularity for its supposed autobiographical elements. Someday it may be documented that Jimmie did indeed ride all those roads he sings about, but as "parts of the life of Jimmie Rodgers," the song is about as reliable as all the other myth and puffery written about him. Once past enumerating the colorful railroad names, the lyrics fall into simple-minded non sequiturs and predictable rhymes; the six verses and alternating yodels take up so much time that the record's saving grace, Charles Kama's clean, progressive steel guitar, is squeezed into only one brief, eight-bar break.

On Monday, February 2, Jimmie rejoined the Will Rogers benefit tour in Oklahoma City. In the next two weeks Rogers and his entourage appeared in some thirty-seven cities and towns in Oklahoma and Arkansas; all told, they played fifty towns in eighteen days and raised more than $225,000 for the Red Cross. At the outset Rogers had made a rough itinerary of the trip, but it was often altered at the last minute by weather conditions and the need to fit in three, and sometimes four, performances a day. Existing newspaper accounts and publicity releases often conflict regarding dates and personnel. "It was a slam-bang affair, with some connections made, and some missed," said Will Rogers, Jr., long afterward. "I doubt if it could ever be reconstructed perfectly."[31]

Although Jimmie Rodgers's name appeared prominently in advance publicity for most of the show dates, the last clear evidence that he was still with the tour came from Ardmore, Oklahoma. On February 4, the *Ardmoreite* reported that during the show on the previous day, Will Rogers had again introduced Jimmie as "my distant son," after which "Rodgers sang several numbers and was well-received." Will, Jr., remembered that Jimmie "was on that tour for only a few dates . . . he was too ill for the hard work of daily touring (and it was a very hard tour: flying, driving, talking, arranging, in and out of small hotels)." It was a loss that both father and son regretted. Said Will, Jr., "On several other occasions, Dad made appearances in the Southwest, and whenever I asked about Jimmie Rodgers, I was told he was too sick. Dad, of course, was a great admirer of his. He recognized the team they would have made."[32]

Jimmie may have stayed with the tour as far as Hot Springs,

Arkansas, another resort town he was known to visit for rest and relaxation. But now he had more immediate problems than his health to worry about. Stella had reappeared again.

NOTES

1. U.S. Department of Commerce, *Statistical Summary of the United States, 1950* (Washington: Government Printing Office, 1951). See also Saul Solomon, M.D., *Tuberculosis* (New York: Coward-McCann, 1952), pp. 37–49 ["Statistics"].

2. "Whipping That Old T.B.," words and music by Jimmie Rodgers. © 1933 by Peer International Corporation. Copyright renewed. Used by permission.

3. There is, of course, no "cure"; modern drugs, in fortuitous cases, merely arrest the growth of the disease. The lowered incidence and mortality rates today are largely due to generally improved health conditions which prevent the initial spread of tuberculosis, and to the use of chemotherapy.

4. Jimmie Rodgers to Ralph Peer, Aug. 10, 1930, in the files of the Country Music Foundation, Nashville. As the letter indicates, Rodgers joined the Elks shortly after returning from Hollywood. His membership in the Masons dated from Aug. 9, 1920, when he was initiated into the John L. Spinks Lodge No. 507 in Meridian. On Dec. 31, 1930, he was passed to Fellowcraft, and he was raised to Master Mason as of Jan. 5, 1931. His membership was moved Aug. 3, 1931, to Blue Bonnet Lodge No. 1219 in San Antonio, where he received the Scottish Rite degrees May 11–14, 1931, and affiliated with Alzafar Temple (T. K. Griffis, Grand Secretary, Grand Lodge of Mississippi, to H. O. Grauel, May 26, 1975; Roy E. Dunsmore, General Secretary, Scottish Rite of Texas, Valley of San Antonio, to H. O. Grauel, Aug. 26, 1977). For a concise account of Rodgers's involvement in Freemasonry, see *New Age*, 86:9 (Sept., 1978), 21–23.

5. *Kerrville Times*, Aug. 21, 1930, p. 1.

6. Fehrenbach, *Lone Star*, p. 646.

7. Jimmie Rodgers to Ralph Peer, Aug. 10, 1930; copy in my files.

8. Horwitz, whom *Billboard* called "one of the most aggressive Texas showmen," was, like Colonel Swain, a fierce competitor and staunch foe of unions. He pioneered in offering cut-rate talkies at his Iris Theater in Houston, and was once sued for pelting striking musicians with rotten eggs. See *Billboard*, Nov. 24, 1928, p. 24, and Mar. 2, 1929, p. 3. In 1932 Horwitz and XED ran afoul of federal lottery regulations (*Variety*, Apr. 19, 1932, p. 41).

9. Interview, May 23, 1973, San Antonio.

10. Interview, May 21, 1976, Kerrville.

11. Interview, Jan. 23, 1977, Tuscon.

12. Interview, May 21, 1976, Kerrville.

13. See, e.g., *Asheville Times*, Dec. 5, 1929, p. 8: "The best fun of having made good and having plenty of money pouring into the coffers is in being able to give 'the little country girl' he married all the fine things she wants, [Rodgers] said. 'When I worked on the railroad she got up at daylight to make my hot coffee and fry my eggs before I started on the day's work, and she did it without complaint. Now I can give her all kinds of things, and I do too.'"

14. *MHJR*, p. 228.

15. *Ibid.*

16. *Kerrville Mountain Sun*, Dec. 18, 1930, p. 1.

17. *Billboard*, Nov. 8, 1930, p. 38.

18. *MHJR*, p. 240.

19. *Austin Statesman*, Jan. 26, 1931, p. 1.

20. Will Rogers, Jr., to NP, Oct. 17, 1977.

21. *San Antonio Light*, Jan. 26, 1931, p. 2A.

22. *San Antonio Express*, Jan. 26, 1931, p. 18, and Jan. 27, 1931, p. 3.

23. *Ibid.*, Jan. 27, 1931, p. 24.

24. *Kerrville Mountain Sun*, Jan. 29, 1931, p. 1; see also *Kerrville Times* for that date.

25. *San Angelo* (Tex.) *Evening Standard*, Jan. 28, 1931, p. 1.

26. *Dallas Morning News*, Jan. 29, 1931, p. 10.

27. For a brief account of the Alley brothers' career and discography, see *JEMFQ*, 9:29 (Spring, 1973), 33–34. Note, however several errors: Joe Kaipo was not present at this session, nor are the Alley brothers heard on "Jimmie the Kid."

28. Anita Rodgers Court, interview, May 23, 1973, San Antonio.

29. "T.B. Blues," words and music by Jimmie Rodgers. © 1931 by Peer International Corporation. Copyright renewed. Used by permission.

These lyrics appeared in a 1973 medical journal advertisement (reproduced in this book). See John P. Morgan, "Famous Persons Who Have Had Tuberculosis: Jimmie Rodgers and Dow Pharmaceuticals," *JEMFQ*, 15:54 (Summer, 1979).

30. Raymond Hall, interview, Mar. 12, 1975, Texas State Penitentiary, Huntsville.

31. Will Rogers, Jr., to NP, Oct. 17, 1977.

32. *Ibid.*

15 *February–June, 1931*

Moonlight and Skies

On February 3, 1931, a suit for civil action was filed in the District Court of Comanche County, Oklahoma, naming as defendant "Jimmy Rogers." The plaintiffs were "Stella Harkins, in her individual capacity and Katherine Rogers, by Stella Harkins, her mother and next friend." Their petition alleged that Kathryn's father, despite his wealth and prominence, had failed to make any provision for the support of the daughter of his first marriage. Pointing out that at the time of his divorce from the child's mother he was "without property," the petition observed that since that time he had "come into possession of large sums of money and valuable properties, and is known as a recording artist, making records for the Victor people, and appearing in theatres as a public singer for pay, and draws large sums of money each month as royalties upon the records he makes. . . ." Consequently, the plaintiffs asked that Rodgers be ordered to pay child support of $250 a month for five years (when Kathryn would be eighteen), "or a sum equal to $15,000." Additionally, he was to pay her mother $5,000 "to reimburse Stella Harkins for her work and labor and support of his child during the last twelve (12) years."[1] In 1931, the average family income was $125 a month. Twelve million Americans were unemployed.

Soon after the surprise reunion with her former husband the previous summer, Stella had begun to reflect upon the magnitude of his success. She decided that it was only right and proper that he contribute to his newly discovered daughter's welfare; furthermore, she calculated that she herself had something coming—back pay, in effect, for being a kind and loving mother all these years. In due course she had made suggestions to this effect, but when the random sums Jimmie sent from time to time fell short of her expectations, her requests became demands. Carrie, of course, had been appalled by the situation from the beginning. Half-suspecting some sort of subtle pressure that might eventually tie up the whole estate, she set herself firmly against paying anything. Jimmie, true to his nature, increasingly withdrew from the whole affair. One angry, nagging woman was more than he cared to cope with; two were an absolute calamity. He had all he could handle anyway, merely trying to keep on his feet and manage the day-to-day details of his career. But now Stella's threats of legal action had suddenly become a stark reality, and he could no longer ignore the situation.

Years later Stella would claim that the whole idea of a lawsuit had originated with Jimmie himself—that he had told her he wanted to contribute to Kathryn's support, but explained that, because Carrie was adamantly opposed, the only way he could do so was through a legal judgment.[2] Even if that circuitous reasoning made sense, it is not borne out by court records.

Jimmie's public acknowledgment of Kathryn as his daughter the previous summer presented a serious obstacle to his attorneys. He (or they) decided he ought to have second thoughts about it, and should raise what they hoped would be substantive questions about the child's paternity. His battery of lawyers, headed by Carrie's brother, Meridian attorney Nate Williamson, began an extensive investigation into the background of Stella Kelly Rodgers Harkins. In their formal response to Stella's suits the attorneys presented the court with a detailed account of her past, comprised of what were claimed to be "facts unknown to the defendant at [the time of their marriage] and . . . not known to him until the year 1930." The paramount fact, according to the document, was that when Jimmie and Stella first met, she was already pregnant by another man (named in the brief); she had in effect deceived Rodgers into marrying her "for the purpose of covering her shame." The real father, it seems, was already married and therefore unable as well as unwilling to make an honest woman of her. Furthermore, in the language of the response, "this defendant at the time of said marriage was an inexperienced youth and was a minor of tender years, and was without the advantages of education, travel or worldly experience, working at odd jobs at the time in restaurants."[3] Could this "inexperienced youth of tender years" be the same fellow who'd run off to join a medicine show when he was only thirteen, lived on his own for years, and railroaded across half the nation when most boys his age were still in high school? At the time of his marriage to Stella, Jimmie was in fact a scant six months away from his twenty-first birthday; he may have been a little hazy in the head, but he was hardly inexperienced or unworldly.

The lawyers also made a rather flagrant effort to guard Rodgers's financial flanks by suddenly denying all the carefully nurtured publicity about thousand-dollar-a-week salaries and million-selling records. They flatly rejected Stella's claims that he was earning "large sums of money," pointing out with some validity that "his income depends upon his ability to carry on his public engagements, and upon the number of records sold, all of which is of an uncertain and fluctuating nature." More to the point, they drew attention to the advanced stage of his illness: "His vitality has been undermined and his nervous system and general health are so impaired and decreased that he is scarcely able to carry on and do the work mentioned in the line of his profession."[4] Such statements were all true enough; but later, when his attorneys tried to use Jimmie's health as an excuse for his failure to appear in court, they would have a devil of a time squaring that with the fact that he was off somewhere recording or making a stage appearance. Ultimately, the core of their defense was that Jimmie had accepted Kathryn as his daughter through ignorance and had innocently believed what Stella had told him about the child at their reunion in Holdenville.[5] It was merely the beginning of a long, messy legal affair that would drag on for many months, bringing little credit to either side and only contributing to the misery of Jimmie Rodgers's last years.

Life still had its bright spots. In late February, Jimmie traveled to Austin, accompanied by several of Kerrville's prominent citizens, to be sworn in as an honorary Texas Ranger by the state's adjutant general, William Sterling. To Jimmie it was a signal honor, for he loved the lore and tradition of the Old West and relished the accoutrements of honorary membership in one of the world's most famous law enforcement agencies—a gold badge and permit for his pistol, a siren for his car—with none of the rigors or responsibilities of being a real Ranger. Like his membership in the Masons and the Elks, being a Ranger appealed to that part of Jimmie Rodgers that found fulfillment in fraternity and the camaraderie of good fellows. In a time before "law and order" had become a euphemism for bureaucratic shenanigans and the preservation of the status quo, it was an honor in which he might justifiably take pride. Not incidentally, it also put him on equal footing with his new friend and recent co-star, Will Rogers, who had also been inducted into "that old Ranger band." The news earned Jimmie a squib in *Billboard*, and it received front-page attention in the Kerrville papers. The *Mountain Sun* proudly announced that " 'The Yodeling Texas Ranger' is Jimmie Rodgers' new title," adding, however, that "yodeling will continue to be Rodgers' chief business. His job of being a Texas Ranger is merely incidental."[6]

The following month Jimmie returned to Austin to appear as the featured attraction at the Texas Rotary Club's statewide convention. His Texas Ranger "boss," General Sterling, was chairman of the committee which issued the invitation, and Jimmie took delight in pretending that it was "an order from my superior officer." The Rotarians responded to his performance with characteristic enthusiasm, and Jimmie in turn showed his appreciation by presenting Sterling with one of his special Weymann guitars.[7]

Whenever there was a lull, Rodgers would cast about for some way to make things happen. Usually this meant undertaking an impromptu barnstorming session around the state. On rare occasions a drinking buddy or two went along, but often he was accompanied only by Cliff Bass, a young auto mechanic from Florida whom Jimmie hired to take care of his cars and chauffeur him around. Booking methods varied from place to place. Sometimes local friends made the arrangements, and occasionally Rodgers wrote or called ahead to theater managers or other likely contacts. But more often than not he simply drove into town, arranged to rent the local movie theater or high school, took his guitar over to the town square to draw a free crowd, and then gave a paid performance that same night, almost always to a standing-room-only audience. Folks everywhere knew about Jimmie Rodgers, and although some of them were reluctant at first to believe that he was really there in person, playing their own town, they soon learned that he was as much at home in Sweetwater or O'Donnell as in front of a

Victor microphone or on the stage of some fancy big-city theater. Vernon Dalhart and Gene Austin might make a lot of records, but they didn't come out into the boondocks to rub shoulders and tell bawdy jokes and laugh with the plain folks who bought them. The effects of the Blue Yodeler's tours had been apparent for some time. Just when the first baby was named after Jimmie Rodgers isn't known, but there would be many to follow; and everyone had a personal story to tell about him—what Jimmie had said the time he played Wetumpka or Conroe, how he'd given his guitar to a blind newsboy in McAlester, the way he sang his way out of jail after killing his girlfriend, the time he invented the yodel, ran off with the mayor's wife, threw beer bottles off the hotel balcony, shot up the city square, or paid off the mortgage for a destitute widow. Most of the stories were pure fabrication, a few had some basis in fact, but all were derived from the simple, eloquent circumstance that Jimmie Rodgers was a genuine hero to those who needed one most—the plain, ordinary people across the land.

By mid-March he was back in Meridian, "fooling around in his home town," according to *Billboard*, and "planning to go into the tent-show business with a partner for the coming season."[8] The projected partner was none other than his old associate, Paul English, who'd lost his rep show to bad business and was now managing Radio Station WCOC in Meridian. On March 19 Rodgers loaned English more than a thousand dollars—a substantial sum in those days—and two weeks later *Billboard* reported that English was about to open a tab show (i.e., a condensed musical production) in Bogalusa, Louisiana. Whether Rodgers appeared in connection with the show is unknown; in any event, the company folded within a couple of months. English, the once astute and prosperous showman, went on to a series of similarly ill-fated schemes, another victim of the Depression. In July he wangled a job promoting Miss Louisiana, and he later managed a string of shotgun theaters in Mississippi for a short time. In September he opened a night club near Baton Rouge, but it went broke in four months. When last heard from several years afterward, English was operating a "studio of dancing, singing, and dramatics" at Shreveport. The money he borrowed from Rodgers was never repaid; at the time of Jimmie's death, it was written off as "uncollectable."[9]

By May, Rodgers had returned to the Kerrville–San Antonio area, where he rested and prepared for an upcoming recording session in Louisville, Kentucky. Although pressed as usual for new material, he'd had a chance to put together a few pieces that he thought Peer would like, including two from his convict composer, Ray Hall.

However, a problem had arisen in connection with Hall. Victor was preparing to release "Moonlight and Skies," recorded the previous summer in Hollywood, and Jimmie had sent Hall the usual fifty-dollar fee and contract (which was, in effect, a bill of sale). Although Hall had accepted that arrangement for "T.B. Blues," which was already in the stores, on "Moonlight and Skies" he reneged, sent the money back, and asked for a royalty contract. Apparently he considered "T.B. Blues" to be substantially Jimmie's work—he had merely supplied a batch of maverick stanzas from which Rodgers could pick and choose. But "Moonlight and Skies" was another matter entirely. Hall looked on it as his personal creation; not only had he gone to the considerable trouble of having his original version copyrighted, but the revision which Rodgers recorded was Hall's as well, done while the composer was serving time in solitary and written to Jimmie's specification. Perhaps Hall raised the issue also because he saw it as a possible means of calling attention to what he considered his wrongful imprisonment, and a way of getting outside help with his legal troubles.

In any event, Jimmie decided to visit Hall in order to resolve the matter. As an honorary Texas Ranger and an immensely popular celebrity in the state, he had little trouble arranging access to Huntsville (although Hall later hinted that the warden tried to prevent the visit). Rodgers had with him an advance copy of "Moonlight and Skies"; he and Hall listened to it on Hall's portable Victrola in the visitor's area of the prison "bull ring" and talked over the matter of copyrights, royalties, and composer credits. Just what agreement they reached is unknown, but the record was released four months later, with the two men sharing authorship on the label. Rodgers's visit to Hall, however, was not prompted solely by business matters; as Peer remarked, "He was really sorry for [Hall], he tried to help him. He went out of his way to help this fellow." Peer obviously found the whole thing hard to believe, but Hall remained forever convinced that he would have gotten out of jail long before if Jimmie had lived. "Too bad for me Jimmie Rodgers died," he said.[10]

Almost from the beginning Rodgers's recording sessions had been rather helter-skelter affairs, with little deliberate plan or consistency in the selection of material. But for sheer variety nothing rivals the conglomeration assembled during the 1931 Louisville sessions. During a single week that June he ran the gamut from risqué yodeling blues to a gospel song, and in between were pop ditties, a cowboy number, two dialogue skits with the Carter Family, a pseudo-folk tearjerker from Tin Pan Alley, a comic railroad ballad, and a piece of funky jug-band jazz.

For a clue to some connecting thread, some intentional pattern or professional motive at this reasonably advanced stage of Rodgers's career, one looks in vain at the order in which these sides were released. Evidence suggests that the primary reason for the Louisville sessions was to pair the Stars of Country Music—Peer implied as much, and certainly "Jimmie Rodgers Visits the Carter Family" was among the first of the Louisville sides to go on sale, heralded by what was a very considerable advertising campaign in those dark Depression days. Yet none of the other sides that Rodgers made with the Carters in Louisville was released until long after his death. "Looking for a New Mama," one of the more undistinguished yodeling blues numbers, was issued in September, but the much superior "Gambling Polka Dot Blues" did not appear until the following February. The most musically interesting side recorded in Louisville, "My Good Gal's Gone Blues," was not released until 1935. Almost half of the Louisville masters were still in Victor's vaults, unprocessed, when Rodgers died.

Too many random factors impinged upon the selection and marketing procedures for one to use the release dates to draw any firm conclusions about the nature of the Louisville sessions, but the order of release does suggest that Peer and Victor were as confused as anyone else by the hodgepodge which Rodgers had recorded. In this thoroughly mixed bag nothing much stands out, and some of what was attempted had every reason to turn sour. The surprise, perhaps, is that all of it is as good as it is. In one respect, the broad diversity of the Louisville material may be seen as further evidence of Rodgers's continuing search for a professional identity, testament to his willingness—and ability—to explore a range of styles and musical modes. More likely it was merely the random result of his poor health, harried private life, and the ever-present necessity of coming up with new material, regardless of source or quality.

Jimmie's visit to Ray Hall at the Texas State Penitentiary had taken place on June 5, a Friday.[11] Victor's field unit was scheduled to begin recording in Louisville, more than a thousand miles away, on the following Tuesday. Traveling in his new Chrysler touring car, Rodgers arrived in town with barely a day to spare and fewer than half a dozen selections ready to record. Some of these were only semi-finished, and all needed further polishing. But he had at hand his trusty old briefcase full of lyric scraps and ideas, and he set to work in his usual hectic but somehow productive fashion. The effort took more stamina and concentration than one would think possible, considering the state of Rodgers's health and the long trip, in those days before interstate highways and air conditioning; but from these scattered beginnings he would somehow, in the week that followed, produce enough material for eleven sides. With a little help from his friends.

Pairing Jimmie with the Carters was Peer's idea, one that had taken shape while he was recording the Carter Family two weeks earlier in Charlotte, North Carolina. Peer had always shown an inclination for the slightly bizarre in arranging Rodgers's sessions, although at the time bringing together two of Victor's hottest properties was a logical venture, not nearly so inappropriate as one senses today when listening to the results of their collaboration. After all, Rodgers and the Carters were currently the most successful acts in hillbilly music—and "hillbilly" it is, for despite the emphasis on Jimmie's western image in these sessions and his established appeal as a pop entertainer, one must acknowledge that the hillbilly label was beginning to attach itself to him with increasing frequency, a circumstance which being linked with the Carters certainly did nothing to alter.

Yet while Rodgers and the Carters appealed to similar audiences and shared common rural origins, there were significant differences between them, differences that would become fully apparent only with the passing of time. Putting A. P., Sara, and Maybelle together with Jimmie Rodgers was not exactly an attempt to mix oil with water (axle grease and STP might be a more fitting metaphor) but, as the results indicate, the risks were considerable. It is to everyone's credit that their joint efforts were brought off with reasonable success, in some places even with positive verve.

Victor's Louisville sessions that summer were, aside from those of Rodgers and the Carters, largely devoted to black musicians and selections aimed at the so-called Race market—low-down blues, jug bands, and the gospel music of "sanctified singers." The sessions, which were held in a makeshift studio set up in a vacant storeroom on Main near Sixth Street, began on June 9, while Rodgers and the Carters were still in the midst of their hasty preparations for recording together. The following day they were ready with two numbers, "Why There's a Tear in My Eye" and "The Wonderful City."

The first, a suitably benign lament composed in the mold of thousands of mountain ballads about falsely accused lovers, was apparently intended as A. P. Carter's contribution to the session, for he did not play or sing on any of the sides. Carter was even more adept than Rodgers at appropriating song material out of the tributaries, commercial as well as traditional, which filtered down toward the mainstream. He may well have felt that he'd really written "Why There's a Tear in My Eye" from bits and scraps he'd heard in the Virginia mountains, but in fact the song was merely an uptown replication of the old sentimental ballad form, composed and copyrighted only three years earlier by Carson Robison under the title "An Old Man's Story."[12] As a composer, Robison, a jack-of-all-musical-trades in New York, was nevertheless a proficient imitator of the oldtime style. Accompanied by Maybelle, Jimmie and Sara render "Why There's a Tear in My Eye" in a properly plaintive fashion. Their combined talents are equally appropriate to Elsie McWilliams's fine gospel number, "The Wonderful City," which Jimmie had apparently been carrying around in his briefcase for some time. Despite its considerable merits as a devotional, the song was something he could never have quite brought off by himself. The Carters, with their long-standing involvement in "inspirational music," provided the ideal accompaniment.

The next morning, shifting from the sacred to the engagingly profane, Jimmie recorded what is probably his most blatantly bawdy number, "Let Me Be Your Side Track." Originally untitled, it may have been performed with some notion of including it in the Blue Yodel sequence—there was only one other, "Blue Yodel No. 9," in Victor's vaults at the moment—but the earthy lyrics clearly gave it a character of its own. The stanza which ultimately provided the title phrase is another of those communal blues verses one encounters throughout Rodgers's work, a cousin to dozens of similar statements derived from the same formula: "Let me be your ——— till your ——— comes; I can do more ——— than your ——— ever done." Jimmie delivers it with special relish and a particularly audacious yodel. Although rumors have suggested that he sometimes found it necessary to censor certain lyrics or at least to restrain Jimmie's supposed penchant for making explicit references to sex, liquor, and drugs, Peer was well aware that such subjects were not only an ingrained and vital part of the blues tradition but, even more important, one of the reasons for their commerical success. Rodgers actually used them more sparingly than many of his contemporaries, both black and white. Furthermore, as numbers like "Everybody Does It in Hawaii" and "What's It?" attest, he could deliver the most boldly suggestive line with disarming innocence. That pleasantly roguish quality of calling up all sorts of gamey pleasures without giving offense to anyone's maiden aunt was Rodgers's stock in trade, inherent in his manner, voice, and material. It seems unlikely that Peer would have risked tampering with it. In any event, there is little evidence to indicate that anyone had reservations about "Let Me Be Your Side Track"; it was among the first sides from the Louisville sessions to be issued, barely six months later. The only regret which collectors express over this title is that neither of the two takes on which Rodgers is accompanied by the fine St. Louis bluesman, Clifford Gibson, was ever issued. One of those takes—a wonderful contrast to what was issued—finally surfaced in 1990.

Later in the day Jimmie was again joined by the three Carters in the first of several attempts to record the music-and-dialogue skits which Peer apparently had intended as the focal point of their collaboration. As one may readily imagine from the finished results, matters did not proceed smoothly. Despite their considerable musical talents and continuing success as recording artists, the Carters had remained a stolid and professionally unsophisticated group, with little inclination or ability for developing the sort of stage presence that had always been one of Jimmie Rodgers's major assets.

Although Sara Carter later recalled that Peer had the speaking parts ready in a finished script at the beginning of the session, Rodgers's files reveal working copies, typed on the back of letterheads from the Tyler Hotel in Louisville, where he was staying. These session sheets, which contain numerous changes in Rodgers's hand, suggest that the skits were put together hastily, perhaps overnight, by Jimmie and Peer, and were to a large extent worked out and polished in the studio. This haste may account for some of the problems which ensued. In any event, three takes of each skit were attempted, unsuccessfully, that afternoon. The Carters, especially A.P., repeatedly had trouble delivering their lines; according to stories that filtered out, tension rose as Rodgers grew tired and impatient from the long hours and many fluffs.

The following day they all settled down and managed to get through both scripts more or less successfully in a single take. The two sides which resulted are surely the most curious items in their recording careers, yet no fan of either Rodgers or the Carters would be without "Jimmie Rodgers Visits the Carter Family" or "The Carter Family and Jimmie Rodgers in Texas." Lame and ill conceived as they are, the sides are at least historically significant. Listeners willing to muster a bit of simple charity toward them are repaid with engaging performances that are guilelessly revealing and charismatic in their very artlessness.

In the first skit, frail rustic jokes about revenuers and coon dogs provide an excuse for Sara and Maybelle to render a few pleasant strains of "My Clinch Mountain Home" and "Little Darling Pal of Mine." Jimmie's easy, offhand manner is in strong contrast to the stiffness of the Carters, who are obviously clutching their scripts and straining at every word. An attempt is made to play up Jimmie's Western image ("You're the first cowboy we've seen in a long time"). Amid other aimless chitchat, Rodgers is suitably impressed by the imaginary Virginia scenery (a plug for "My Clinch Mountain Home") and accepts the offer of "a little squirt" of mountain dew, punctuating his enthusiasm with the famous yodel and laugh. At one point, even A. P. sounds almost relaxed and natural, delivering the supposed punchline to a joke, the point of which has apparently been lost with the passage of time. They all join in the finale, a rousing chorus of minstrelsy's moldiest fig, "A Hot Time in the Old Town Tonight."

"The Carter Family and Jimmie Rodgers in Texas" is more of the same, this time with the roles of host and guests reversed. Again, the Western setting is emphasized with a verse of "Yodeling Cowboy," sung by Jimmie for openers. The jokes—mostly concerned with Texas and Jimmie's love for his adopted state—aren't much fresher, but they at least make sense. Jimmie's fine statement about the blues—"I guess you've got no business with the blues unless you can sing 'em" (apparently extemporized, for it does not appear in the script)—leads naturally and effectively to his and Sara's virtuoso performance of "T for Texas." On the whole, "The Carter Family and Jimmie Rodgers

Rodgers inscribed this publicity photo to the Carter Family during their recording sessions together in Louisville in the summer of 1931.

"Jimmie Rodgers visits the Carter Family," Louisville, June, 1931. *From left:* Rodgers, Maybelle Carter, A. P. Carter, Sara Carter.

JIMMIE RODGERS
visits the
CARTER
family

Hear them sing together on one record

JIMMIE RODGERS and the CARTER FAMILY
RECORD NO. 23574

A great event . . . and a great record!

Hear them today!
An RCA Victor Product

Latest Victor Hits

The music you want   when you want it

Memphis Commercial Appeal, *October 23, 1931*

Meeting of the stars received a flurry of unusual publicity in 1931. Even in the flush 1920's, neither Rodgers nor the Carters had been so lavishly promoted.

in Texas" is superior; why it was held for release until 1937 while its counterpart appeared within four months of the session remains a mystery.

With the Meeting of the Stars out of the way, the Carters departed. Jimmie settled in for another four days, working with a wide spectrum of accompaniments that resulted in some of his more interesting recordings. No single side from these sessions is particularly distinguished, yet all of them reveal Rodgers in solid form, consistently producing work of far greater merit than might be expected of any performer in his condition.

At the Dallas sessions in October, 1929, three of the six titles he recorded had been cowboy songs, his initial foray into the genre. As the sketches with the Carter Family suggest, the romantic connotations of Texas were on his mind again; now, after an interval of almost two years since "Yodeling Cowboy," "Land of My Boyhood Dreams," and "I've Ranged, I've Roamed, and I've Travelled," he returned to the subject in song once more. "When the Cactus Is in Bloom" is one of his more successful efforts at composition, and his recording of that song, with the fine backing of Cliff Carlisle on steel guitar and Wilber Ball on standard, was the sort of thing that would have a pervasive impact on the singing-cowboy school of cinema then on the verge of erupting in Hollywood. To be sure, it is ersatz Western—a little more stylized, more "written" than older, more authentic songs of the range. But as a prototype, and a good one, "When the Cactus Is in Bloom" compares favorably with almost any of the sagebrush serenades later cranked out by celluloid wranglers gathered around the old campfire on Sound Stage 2B.

Carlisle and Ball were just breaking into show business at the time, performing as "The Lullaby Larkers" over Louisville's WLAP and WHAS and picking up whatever other entertainment work they could find in the area.[13] Jimmie apparently heard their radio broadcast and asked Peer to get in touch with them through their agent, Ward Keith. Carlisle remembered the arduous conditions in the studio—"hot as blazes"—and the poor state of Jimmie's health. "He coughed and spat up a lot," he said, "and seemed rather tired and weak a lot of the time. We'd go down and cut a couple of masters, might have to cut and re-cut if the grooves ran together, especially in hot weather. Then we'd take Jimmie back to his hotel and Carrie would put him in bed for an hour or so, then we'd repeat the action." But Carlisle, like many others, was most impressed with Rodgers's courage and high spirits in the face of his adversity. "Even though he was a sick individual," Carlisle said, "he knew how to laugh and joke some. He was a great guy; you would have loved him like a brother. We did."[14]

Carlisle and Ball returned the following Monday to accompany Jimmie on "Looking for a New Mama," a rather conventional yodeling blues, but one which is of some interest because of their presence and because it features Rodgers playing the ukulele. Carlisle and Ball had been hired for only two sides, but when they finished that afternoon Jimmie said, "Everybody meet here at 8:00 p.m. We're going to Cunningham's for supper." Cunningham's was one of the city's more popular dining spots, famous for its frog legs. "Everybody loved frog legs," said Carlisle. "We all had a great time."

That same day Jimmie had recorded Raymond Hall's "Gambling Polka Dot Blues," later popular with many other artists and probably best known in the Bob Wills–Tommy Duncan version. Hall, like Elsie McWilliams, was something of a simplistic rhymester, given to stylized phrases and stereotyped situations, but occasionally he reached for the unusual and caught it. "Gambling polka dot" possessed unique connotations of dice and domino spots, the designs of a deck of cards, and other imagery associated with gambling—even including, perhaps, the shirt and tie patterns favored by "sports" like Jimmie Rodgers. Moreover, Hall was capable of carrying through with a lyric, fitting together terse, trenchant lines into a unified whole, as demonstrated also by "Southern Cannonball," his other composition which Rodgers recorded in Louisville. Unlike most trains commemorated in country song, the poor old Southern Cannonball is a piece of junk, whose defects not only play havoc with the singer's love life but eventually drive him away from railroading altogether. Perhaps unintentionally, the hackneyed language ("I once loved a maiden, she was fair and tall";[15] the notion of a railroader spending his honeymoon in "the magic islands") only serves to heighten the comic tone. The last verse of "Southern Cannonball" is a model of compression, delivering two reversals and the ultimate insult: despite everything the railroader can do, "the train refused to run," and he has to be married in an old boxcar. The extent to which Rodgers was involved in forming these lyrics into a tight narrative cannot be determined, for his worksheets are missing. However, even the yodeling blues that he recorded in Louisville are marked by consistent thematic structure, in contrast to the diffuse, random verses that characterized earlier such numbers.

Piano accompaniment for "Gambling Polka Dot Blues" and a number recorded the following day, "What's It?," was provided by Ruth Ann Moore, staff pianist at WLAP. Her easy, stride-influenced style bears some resemblance to that of Elsie McWilliams, which someone once described as "church-house rag"—secular but restrained. Miss Moore's work is pleasant enough, but probably more appropriate to "What's It?," a clever ditty in the vaudeville vein which was composed by Jimmie's San Antonio pal Jack Neville, possibly under the influence of a popular Ben Bernie tune of that year, "Who's Your Little Who-zis?" Neville originally called it "My Dog Faced Gal," a title with obviously limited appeal. The substitute which Rodgers supplied, on the other hand, is almost too cryptic. A pop-oriented tune coming in the middle of Rodgers's career, at a time when his hillbilly image was gathering force, "What's It?" remains a minor effort, of interest largely as a novelty.

Most appealing of all the sides Rodgers made in Louisville was "My Good Gal's Gone Blues," recorded at the final session with a group of black musicians generally credited as the Louisville Jug Band. Properly speaking, they were Clifford Hayes's Dixieland Jug Blowers, but the two groups were so closely identified and their personnel so interchangeable that it seems to matter little that Rodgers's discographers, following Victor's files, have confused them.

Earl McDonald's Original Louisville Jug Band was something of a local institution, with origins dating back to the early years of the century. As early as 1913, when Clifford Hayes joined the group as fiddle player, it was already a familiar fixture at Churchill Downs during Derby Week. Wealthy horsemen and Derby patrons hired the group for private parties in Louisville's posh hotels, and the performers' popularity with the sporting crowd led to engagements in New York just prior to and during World War I, at about the time when various white musicians were importing "dixieland" up the Mississippi River, commercializing it, and turning it into a national fad. The emerging phenomenon of jazz quickly caught Clifford Hayes's attention; as jug-band historian Fred Cox has observed, it became his aspiration "to achieve musical success far beyond his role of a country fiddler in a jug band."[16] In contrast to the popular and conscientious McDonald, however, Hayes was a devious sort and often at odds with his fellow musicians. His reckless private life and habit of pocketing more than his share of the band's proceeds soon led to trouble, and about 1919 he left to form his own group, the Dixieland Jug Blowers.

Throughout the Twenties a tenuous but profitable alliance existed between the two organizations, with McDonald dominating the local scene and Hayes booking a steady stream of out-of-town engagements and recording dates.[17] Hayes was a successful promoter, but he was far less adept at getting and keeping good musicians to play the dates he booked, probably because of his reputation for dishonesty and a bad temper. Consequently, he was frequently forced to turn to his former employer for personnel. McDonald respected Hayes's talents as a musician and was apparently willing to help out, even to the extent of offering his own services on the jug.

Clearly this sort of arrangement on the part of Hayes brought the group to Victor's makeshift studio. On his lyric sheet of "My Good Gal's Gone Blues," Rodgers noted simply "Accomp. Clifford Hayes and Band 5 colored." Just how he and the group came to be paired is unknown, but Fred Cox speculates that the arrangement was quite impromptu; Rodgers probably overheard the band while they were rehearsing, was intrigued by what he heard, and asked them to do a number with him. It also seems possible that Jimmie was familiar with McDonald's jug band—essentially the same personnel—as a result of hearing their widely popular weekly program on WHAS in Louisville.[18]

Rodgers's lyric sheet for "My Good Gal's Gone Blues" offers considerable insight into the process through which the song evolved. Scribbled on one side of the page, in a hand other than Jimmie's, are raw bits and scraps of blues verses and random phrases. None of them is very good, but enough are thematically related to the finished song to show that they were the raw material from which Rodgers worked. The opposite side of the sheet demonstrates how he put the elements together, selecting a phrase here, trimming one there, and distilling them into a cohesive blues statement that moves, in three simple verses, from the formulaic lament for a lost love to the optimistic anticipation of "some high grade loving" from a "new mama."[19] He obviously recorded from this very page, for the sheet also contains his "impromptu" remarks between verses and other instructions, such as "Whole Band take Chourse" or "Whole Band. Talk some." After the first verse he wrote, "Play it, Boy, Play it," exactly as it is spoken on the first two takes; however, on the released Take 3, he says "Blow it, boy, blow it."

The fact that Rodgers reduced the lyrics to only three blues stanzas suggests that the selection was intended as a showpiece for the band, and they came through in fine style. The somewhat unusual instrumentation, not entirely representative of the true jug bands that worked the streets, is nevertheless singularly appropriate to the amalgamation of musical forms and traditions which had found a focus in the talents of Jimmie Rodgers: Clifford Hayes's bluesy country fiddle, the clean, single-string pick of Cal Smith on guitar (much of their work together reminds one of Django Reinhardt and Stephane Grappelly), and the jazzy, moaning clarinet of George Allen, a brilliant if sometimes erratic musician.

Immediately after they recorded "My Good Gal's Gone Blues" with Rodgers, these same musicians returned to the microphone to accompany black vocalist Ben Ferguson on a number entitled "Please Don't Holler, Mama" (Vi 23297). A comparison of the two recordings suggests some rather startling implications for those who wish to debate the interesting, if ultimately pointless, question of Jimmie Rodgers and "white blues" versus "black blues." Although the lyrics differ, "My Good Gal's Gone Blues" and "Please Don't Holler, Mama" are, musically speaking, practically identical, note for note and break for break—as identical as one might reasonably expect of jazz musicians who, for whatever reasons, were attempting to repeat a given performance without a score. Regardless of the conclusions one cares to draw, it must at least be said that if nothing else proves Jimmie Rodgers's natural affinity for the authentic blues idiom, "My Good Gal's Gone Blues" clearly does. One can only puzzle over the fact that Peer (or his successor at Victor, Eli Oberstein) chose not to release the number until two years after the Blue Yodeler's death.

NOTES

1. *Stella Harkins and Kathryn Rodgers* v. *Jimmie Rodgers*, Law 4502 (1932).
2. Interview, June 6, 1975.
3. Amended answer to petition, *Harkins and Rodgers* v. *Rodgers*.
4. *Ibid.*
5. *Ibid.*
6. *Billboard*, Mar. 14, 1931; *Kerrville Mountain Sun*, Feb. 26, 1931, p. 1; see also *Kerrville Times*, Mar. 5, 1931, p. 1.
7. Malone, *Country Music, U.S.A.*, p. 90. According to various accounts, the guitar was a one-of-a-kind prototype, supposedly worth $1,500. See Wheeler and Fuchs, "Wo Sind Jimmie Rodgers' Gitarren Geblieben?," which asserts that it was the only such instrument made by Weymann before the company suspended its manufacture of guitars. In fact, the Jimmie Rodgers Special was a standard production model, priced at $90 ("complete with plush lined case") and marketed by Weymann

for several years before the company went out of business in the mid-Thirties.

8. *Billboard,* Mar. 28, 1931, p. 45.

9. *Will Book, Lauderdale County, Mississippi,* 6:471. For English's activities during this period, see *Billboard,* Mar. 14, 1931, p. 25; Apr. 4, 1931, p. 24; July 18, 1931, p. 21; Sept. 12, 1931, p. 20; Jan. 16, 1932, p. 24; Dec. 31, 1932, p. 44; Apr. 29, 1933, p. 54; and July 15, 1933, p. 20.

10. Interview, Mar. 12, 1975, Texas State Penitentiary, Huntsville; Hall to NP, June 3, July 27, Aug. 3, 1975, and Jan. 23, 1976. At the time of my initial interview with Hall at Huntsville, the warden told me that "the only way he'll ever leave here is feet first." However, on Jan. 20, 1976, Hall was paroled, some forty-eight years after his first conviction in Wichita Falls. On Mar. 31, 1977, he was granted a full pardon and restoration of his civil rights. Hall, who died in 1982 in Memphis, Tennessee, continued to insist through the years that he did not sell "Moonlight and Skies" outright, but was given a royalty contract, which he later lost, and has never received a cent for the song. A search of records in the U.S. Copyright Office reveals Hall's original registration of the title in 1929, but a 1931 entry for the same title, registered to Southern Music, shows only "words and melody of Jimmie Rodgers." Both Hall and Rodgers are listed in a 1940 assignment through which Southern transferred the song to Peer International; otherwise Hall's name does not appear on any of the numerous assignments and renewal registrations, and it was dropped from many later reissues of the recording.

11. Hall has asserted that the year was 1930, but prison logs and other evidence do not support this.

12. See notes accompanying *The Carter Family on Border Radio* (JEMF 101), pp. 26–27.

13. Cliff Carlisle to NP, Mar. 9 and Apr. 18, 1978; Wilber Ball to NP, May 15, 1978.

14. Carlisle to NP, Mar. 9 and Apr. 18, 1978. The state of Rodgers's health is confirmed both by Ball and by Sara Carter (interview by Henry Young, May 29, 1971).

15. "Southern Cannonball," words and music by Jimmie Rodgers and Raymond Hall. © 1933 by Peer International Corporation. Copyright renewed. Used by permission.

16. Liner notes to *Clifford Hayes and the Dixieland Jug Blowers* (Yazoo 1054); also Fred Cox to NP, Mar. 7, 27, and Oct. 28, 1977.

17. Essentially the same personnel comprised the groups known as the Dixieland Jug Blowers and (minus jug) Clifford Hayes's Louisville Stompers, which began recording for Victor as early as 1926 and returned regularly until the Depression ruined the record business.

18. Fred Cox to NP, Mar. 7, 1977. It seems likely also that Peer was acquainted with Hayes as a result of producing earlier sessions with Will Shade, who knew Hayes. (See Charters, *Country Blues,* p. 76.)

19. "My Good Gal's Gone Blues," words and music by Jimmie Rodgers. © 1935 by Peer International Corporation. Copyright renewed. Used by permission.

16 *June, 1931–June, 1932*

Going Down That Lonesome Trail

Sickness ruled the last years of Jimmie Rodgers's life. By 1930 —much earlier than generally recognized—his daily routine as well as larger professional matters were dominated by his disease, regardless of how much he might try to ignore it or pretend that all was normal. A sort of silent conspiracy evolved between him and those around him: trips were undertaken, tours scheduled, and even the day's activities planned to accommodate his need for rest and the always imminent possibility of collapse. He dreaded the atmosphere of the sickroom, but a bag of medications traveled everywhere with him, and getting pain-killing drugs on the road often consumed time and precious energy. The dishes he ate from had to be boiled—one reason that he increasingly preferred the newfangled "tourist courts" to his usual hotels—and precautions taken against infecting little Anita. Whether he got out of bed in the morning often depended on how severe the nightsweats had been. Most vexing of all were the coughing spells and their vile, bloody sputum. There had been hardly a day since 1924 when he'd been entirely free of the fever or the raw, billowing pain in his lungs, and by the time he went to Louisville in June, 1931, he was almost constantly wracked by pain and labored breath.

Even at Bristol, four years before, he'd been sicker than anyone realized. On at least half a dozen occasions since, he'd collapsed or simply had to give up and go to bed, wheezing and railing and cussing all the way. Once or twice the chills and spasms had been so bad that Carrie and those attending him fully expected him to die. Yet every attack seemed only to make him more determined to ignore the whole business; time after time he would shake off the effects of a particularly severe seizure, climb out of bed, put on his shoes, and go back to work.

From Louisville he went to Meridian to rest and try to recover some of the energy that recording sessions always drained away. There he could loaf and, with his old buddies, gab about what he called the railroader's favorite subjects—"whiskey, women, and back pay." After a week or so he decided to return to Texas by way of Oklahoma to visit his old friend Pawnee Bill and celebrate the Fourth of July. He sent off one of his notes to *Billboard* with news of his activities, motivated as much by the simple boyish thrill of seeing his name in print as by the desire for professional publicity. He mentioned that he would be accompanied on the trip to Oklahoma by his "trusty guitar and, maybe, Mrs. Rodgers."[1] Whether intentional or not, that seemingly innocent little "maybe" was a sign of the steadily increasing distance between them. Back in June he'd mentioned to Ray Hall, almost a complete stranger, that he and his wife were practically separated. "He told me," said Hall, "'That old gal don't know what it's all about.' I didn't want to get into it; it wasn't none of my business. But it was pretty clear they weren't getting along."[2]

By late summer they were back in Kerrville, but Jimmie stayed only long enough to join up with the first touring rep show he could find and take to the road again. It was, of all things, Colonel Swain's Original Show Company.[3] Whatever had passed between the two men the previous summer was forgotten, at least temporarily, while Jimmie and the Colonel scrabbled together for any loose cash out in the Texas hinterlands that fall.

Their association lasted only a few weeks, through the cotton harvest season. In mid-November Jimmie returned to Kerrville, announcing, as he had several times before, a forthcoming vaudeville tour on one of the major circuits. Again nothing came of it. *Billboard*'s story of the proposed tour carried the observation that "Jimmie's health, which has been out of kimbo for some time, has greatly improved in the last several weeks."[4] That seems to have been wishful thinking on Jimmie's part. According to Peer, "his health conked out, and the deal [with R-K-O] was never consummated. It was in Northern cities and we decided that if he went through those snow storms, he'd just die, so we had to call it off." By that late date, however, vaudeville was in a state of ruin anyway, a circumstance which probably contributed as much to the cancellation of the tour as did Jimmie's health.

Rodgers was certainly not well, but if his condition made a Northern tour inadvisable, it did little to slow the hectic pace of his other activities. On November 4 he'd been well enough to attend Will Rogers's fifty-second birthday party in San Antonio, and shortly afterward he traveled to Meridian and back to attend to matters relating to Stella's lawsuit. Throughout the fall and early winter there were repeated business trips to San Antonio. By Christmas he was onstage again, performing with Leslie "Skeeter" Kell's rep show in Houston, and making big plans for a spring tour.

Will Rogers's birthday party had been a special thrill. Jimmie was one of only half a dozen special friends invited to a private dinner in Rogers's suite at the Gunter Hotel. "I don't know what they ate," said Carrie, "—chili, I suppose,—but Will Rogers sent me his splendid birthday cake."[5] Jimmie took particular pride in a *San Antonio Express* account of the event which referred to him as the "famous singer of cowboy songs and yodeler, no relation to Will, but for long a close friend."[6] They'd met only twice and had known each other for less than a year, but both were men to whom friendship, once established, had a special meaning. The newspaper had not exaggerated.

Jimmie's reunion with Will Rogers was one of the few bright spots of the period. As 1931 drew to a close, there were all sorts of nagging problems. In addition to the upheavals caused by Stella's lawsuit, a growing quandary had arisen over what to do with Blue Yodeler's Paradise, which had proved expensive to maintain and too far removed from the centers of Jimmie's operations. His medical expenses continued to mount, at the very time when his income had begun to suffer from the worsening Depression. His records were still selling, unlike those of many other artists, but in steadily declining numbers. A run-of-the-mill Rodgers release that would have sold 500,000 copies two years earlier was now lucky to reach 30,000 paying customers. By the end of the year the figure would drop to half that.

Always there was the one concern that overshadowed all others: the steadily deteriorating state of Rodgers's health. He'd long ago accepted that his condition was terminal; what bothered him most was the troubling question of how long he'd be able to stay on his feet and keep working. Despite all the grand pronouncements about record royalties and high-salaried personal appearances, money had for some

time been a matter of growing stress in the Rodgers household. It is
doubtful that they had ever been completely solvent, but during the
first heady days when Jimmie was riding high—from the spring of
1928 until early 1930—the cash flow had carried them along from
royalty statement to royalty statement, from one occasional road tour
to the next, ample enough for them to quickly assume the Grand Style.
In the beginning there'd been ready money for a down payment on
the Kerrville "mansion" and the seemingly endless stream of big cars,
guitars, jewelry, fine clothes and furniture, any gimcrack that caught
their fancy, not to mention the cost of Jimmie's constant travels—
always first class, of course—and other professional expenses. After
all, in those whirlwind days before the Crash, the whole country
had been buying and spending as if there were no tomorrow. For
Jimmie Rodgers, of course, that rationalization was all too literally
appropriate, and at rock-bottom the sure knowledge that he might be
dead any day was reason enough for scattering cash across the land.
But now while the effects of the Depression were beginning to be
felt, household expenses continued to mount, inflated by the ever-
increasing costs of Jimmie's medical care. In Carrie's words, "All the
money Jimmie Rodgers could possibly bring in would, it seemed,
never be enough."[7] Yet, somewhat paradoxically in view of his
spendthrift nature and lifelong disregard for money matters, Jimmie
was quick to express concern over the situation, to suggest cutbacks,
and to redouble his efforts to play every available tour or personal
appearance to keep the money coming in. To some degree his behavior
reflected his genuine concern for what might happen to his family,
especially young Anita, once he was gone. Beyond that, given the sad
state of his health and all the other torments that plagued him, this
driving determination to remain active during these last years can be
explained only as the expression of his great courage and his
indomitable will to stay on his feet.

There had been no dramatic decline in his condition that fall; rather,
he merely experienced a steady downward spiral as his disease
progressed into its final stages. The effects were starkly visible.
Whatever weight Rodgers had ever carried was gone; shadows lined
his face and eyes, and his skin had assumed the soft milky hue
of someone already dead. So ravaged was he by this time that
photographs were rarely taken. Like the disease itself, other consequences were insidious, gradual but cumulative. The morphine doses

were steadily increasing, along with his consumption of alcohol and any other painkiller that might blunt the searing ache that now accompanied every breath. On one of their trips to San Antonio, Rodgers and John Furman took along young Dick Furman, who was struck by Jimmie's condition as they left Kerrville. "He was in a lot of pain; he didn't say anything but you could tell," Furman said. "He looked depressed, and he *was* depressed. But along the way, he took something, and he perked up right away and started singing."[8] Constant activity was another way of dealing with the disease. But some saw Jimmie's behavior merely as a desperate, chaotic flight from oblivion. One Kerrville resident who knew Rodgers during his last days there spoke of him, not unkindly, as "a spindle-assed ragged rat, running from hole to hole."[9] That statement was as apt, perhaps, as it was harsh.

Among the new Rodgers records in the stores that fall and winter were some of the last fruits of the previous summer's Hollywood sessions, including "Blue Yodel No. 9" and "Moonlight and Skies." The first of the Louisville sides were appearing also—"Looking for a New Mama" in September and "Jimmie Rodgers Visits the Carter Family" in October. "What's It?" was released the first week in December, and later that same month Victor issued "Let Me Be Your Side Track," backed with a studio gimmick which, as a simple curiosity, is perhaps of greater interest today than when it first appeared. This was "Rodgers' Puzzle Record," containing, on one side, segments of three previously issued songs—"Blue Yodel," "Train Whistle Blues," and "Everybody Does It in Hawaii"—which had been remastered to run in alternating grooves, spiraling parallel to each other across the record. The supposed "puzzle" was that, with three different lead-in grooves on the rim, the listener could not determine in advance which song would play when the needle was set down. Similar contrivances were being widely marketed by other phonograph companies in an effort to boost lagging Depression sales. The puzzle-record device itself had been around for years, however, apparently dating back to the days when life (in the parlor, at least) was simpler—and duller. Victor had a particular fondness for the gimmick; as early as 1915 the company's catalog had carried an item entitled "The Conundrum (What Will I Play Next?)," which was described as "Four short selections, vocal and instrumental, any one of which the needle may decide to play." In the early 1930's a series of similar records was released by Harmony and its several dime-store subsidiary labels such as Velvet Tone, Clarion, and Odeon, possibly including Benny Goodman and Tommy Dorsey among the studio musicians who recorded them.[10] Many of these same sides were also issued by Okeh from leased masters. Puzzle records were also popular abroad; Rodgers's contribution to the genre was released in England, India, and Australia. Today the original Victor issue is extremely rare and sought after by collectors.

By the time "Rodgers' Puzzle Record" appeared in late December, Jimmie had taken steps to resolve one of his more pressing problems. Blue Yodeler's Paradise was put up for sale, and the family began preparing to move to San Antonio, where he bought a comfortable duplex bungalow in the suburb of Alamo Heights. Leaving Carrie to attend to details of the move, Jimmie headed for Houston to join the tent rep company of Skeeter Kell and His Gang as the "Added Feature" for Christmas week.

Leslie Kell, like Paul English and Colonel Swain, was a familiar name in the tent theater business and, like them also, a veteran showman who would not survive the Depression. As a Toby character and knock-about comedian, he'd worked with many shows over the years; he had headed his own operation since the early Twenties, when the company was known as Skeeter Kell's Comedians and toured the area around Kell's hometown of Springfield, Missouri. For a time the show played only Missouri and bordering states, but Kell gradually evolved a regular route that covered the South and South-west, centered at Hemphill, Texas, where by 1928 he'd established permanent winter headquarters. In those palmy days the company had played as many as 178 consecutive weeks, touring across six or seven states; but, as the Depression closed in, Kell's route steadily shrank until the bulk of his engagements were within a few hundred miles of Hemphill. In June, 1931, for the first time in his career, he had been forced to close the season early, sadly observing that business was "hopeless." Less than a week later fire destroyed the company's permanent quarters and much of its equipment.[11]

In any other business, such a disaster would have been the final blow—but tent showmen were a markedly resilient lot, proudly surviving fires, blowdowns, and assorted other disasters time after time with borrowed tents, makeshift scenery, and loyal performers willing to stick it out, in the best show-must-go-on tradition. Skeeter Kell and His Gang opened the fall season on time, and within a few months the show was completely re-equipped. A huge new tent seating 1,500 boasted a modern ventilating system, gas heaters for the winter tour, and an elaborate display of colored lights and pennants. On the roster were some sixteen performers, a ten-piece orchestra, and a tent crew of seven. It was an impressive outfit for those troubled times, and with it Kell was able to work his way out of the tanktowns and secure a lucrative spot in Houston, at McKinney and Crawford Streets near the city's established theatrical district. "The Kell show is one of the finest tent shows to play Houston since 1922," said *Billboard* when the company opened there in late November. Business was so good the first week that Kell announced a special benefit performance for the weekend and donated the proceeds to Houston's relief fund for the unemployed. The cast and crew settled in for an indefinite run.[12]

In earlier years Kell had run a rather conventional operation, offering the staple dramatic fare of all tent rep companies; he emphasized hayseed comedies and Toby shows which featured the impresario himself in the familiar role of the country bumpkin. Special material or vaudeville had been used only sparingly, before the show or as filler between acts of whatever play comprised the main bill. Recently, however, the structure of the show had begun to change, in response to pressures from radio, talkies, and the depressed condition of business in general. Over the years Kell had developed the "Skeeter" character—a variant of the stock Toby role—to the point that it had taken on an identity of its own, apart from the standard dramatic situations of hackneyed old plays. Kell had proved adept at tailoring his own material and using the character to give the entire show a new and distinctly different flavor. Tinkering with the old scripts and adapting them to suit the purposes of one's own show was a common practice among rep managers—the less scrupulous obtained the bulk of their season's bills simply by scrambling titles and interchanging a few key scenes from copyrighted plays—but Kell's alterations went further than most, sometimes producing material so different from its sources that it might properly be termed original. As an opening bill, for example, Kell had developed what today would pass as a "sit-com." "Skeeter Kell's Gang" featured Kell; his wife, Amber Wymore; their small son, Leslie, Jr.; and other members of the troupe playing themselves in supposedly real-life situations. Many of the lines came from stock sources, but the characters were "real" and the plots often derived from their own experiences, as filtered through Kell's imagination. Further, while the average rep show carefully confined itself to plays that were notoriously simpleminded and moralistic, Kell found that for the somewhat sophisticated Houston audiences he could turn to material that was, if not exactly controversial, at least topical. One of his more popular productions in this vein was an updated version of the old chestnut, "Ten Nights in a Bar Room," retitled "The 18th Amendment" and changed into a comedy that poked fun at the foibles of Prohibition—something no rep show would have dared attempt out in the Baptist-belt boondocks.

Straight vaudeville, too, was playing an ever-increasing part in Kell's efforts to lure audiences. In addition to a full complement of jugglers, jokesters, and novelty turns between acts of the plays, he was also experimenting with a tabloid musical revue featuring fan dancer Holly Desmond. Houston crowds loved the revue, and as they continued to jam the tent, Kell had begun to search for other "Added Feature Attractions" to keep the momentum going.

Jimmie Rodgers was a natural choice. Although his foothold on national fame had never quite been secured, he was then at the height of his popularity in Texas, largely as a result of his many grass-roots travels around the state. Texans, more than any of his other audiences, felt they knew him; he was one of their own.

Kell took additional advertising in the Houston newspapers to announce the Blue Yodeler's appearance, and the crowds continued to turn out in large numbers all during Christmas week.[13] Following the December 24 performance, a huge tree, "the talk of the Houston show world," was set up and decorated in the center of the stage, and Christmas was celebrated under the big top by the cast and crew and a select group of visitors. Among the latter were Carrie Rodgers and young Anita, who'd driven down with friends from San Antonio for the occasion. Gifts were distributed, refreshments served, and speeches made; according to one account, the party went on "until the wee small hours."[14]

Party or no, and Christmas or no, the next day was Friday—show day as usual. Jimmie Rodgers and "The 18th Amendment" packed them in; according to *Billboard*, "the big Kell tent was overflowing." Business was so good, in fact, that success caused some extra excitement they could have done without. Houston police sent word of a tipoff that the box office was to be held up on Saturday night. Kell placed extra guards on duty, and, said *Billboard*, "a battery of sawed-off shotguns and other weapons of warfare were placed around the proposed point of attack."[15] Only Jimmie Rodgers seemed to enjoy all the commotion, making a show of hauling out his .32 revolver and shining up his fancy diamond-studded Texas Ranger badge. When the bad guys failed to appear, he jokingly claimed credit: "Even these Houston robbers is smart enough not to tangle with a Ranger— 'specially one that yodels."

Business continued to hold, and Kell announced an extension of the Houston run "at least thru the month of January and possibly February." Although he'd been engaged initially for only one week, Jimmie stayed on, alternating with other headline attractions. These included Texas Ann's Wild West act and John Mansell's "Hollywood Revue," a mini-musical with the added gimmick of a recording machine which made free records of members of the audience talking or singing.[16]

It soon became obvious that Jimmie was staying with the show for reasons other than merely playing out the run. In mid-January he and Kell announced ambitious plans to form a partnership and launch an entirely new company in the spring; they would tour from Texas to the Northwest and up into British Columbia, eastward through Canada to New York, and back to Texas for the winter stock season. According to *Billboard*, "the proposed new show would move on two cars, making one- to six-night stands, using plays with a railroad or circus atmosphere. Jimmie Rodgers would continue as the headliner, with L. Desmond's New York Roof Garden Revue serving as the musical comedy feature." Further plans called for daily women's matinees and an elaborately uniformed street band for parades and town concerts. Ample financing, said the new partners, had been assured.[17]

The ambitious venture had hardly been announced when signs of trouble appeared. Despite Kell's intention of remaining in Houston "at least through January," the show pulled up stakes on January 23 and prepared to move to San Antonio. Publicity reports at the time insisted that the company had closed "in a blaze of glory and to a well-filled tent," but it seems clear that all was not well. En route to San Antonio, Kell booked a week's engagement in nearby Luling; he announced that the show was intact, pointing out specifically that "Jimmie Rodgers,

Victor recording ace who appeared with the Kell Company in Houston and [Luling], will go with the show to San Antonio."[18] But when Skeeter Kell and His Gang opened in the Alamo City on February 1, Rodgers was on his way to Dallas for a week-long recording session. Reports from Kell's short-lived San Antonio run made no further mention of the Blue Yodeler.[19]

Shorn of his star attraction, buffeted by bad weather and heavy competition from Harley Sadler's popular tent show, Kell was forced to close after a few weeks and disband the company.[20] Despite tentative plans to reopen again at the Houston location "in the near future," the grandiose Kell-Rodgers partnership, like so many of Jimmie's schemes, was heard of no more. In all likelihood it was a victim purely of economic conditions, rather than of any falling-out between the proposed partners. Their initial claim of sufficient "financial ability to launch the new venture" appears to have been made with fingers crossed, as encouragement to would-be investors whose support never materialized.

Rodgers had other irons in the fire. In mid-January, again at the invitation of General W. W. Sterling, he'd been back to entertain the Austin Rotarians and sat at the table of honor with the state's new governor, Ross Sterling. It was pretty tall cotton for a country boy from Mississippi, and although Jimmie was suitably impressed, he had the presence of mind to bring up Ray Hall's case in a subsequent conversation with General Sterling, the state's chief legal officer. Sterling assured Rodgers that he would look into the matter. "From the way he talked," Jimmie wrote in a touching letter to Hall, "he was in your favor[,] said he would see The Governor and if nothing else he would try and make it easy for you so you could put in your time on writing Songs and Poetry and doing things that would help you & all man kind."[21] There were not many unschooled rounders of Jimmie Rodgers's background who equated "writing Songs and Poetry" with helping mankind.

During this time arrangements were completed with Radio Station KMAC in San Antonio for a regular weekly program.[22] Scheduled for Tuesdays at 4:00 p.m., the broadcasts were primarily devoted to the playing of Jimmie's records, but there was also the understanding that, whenever he was in town and his health permitted, the studio would be turned over to him for a live broadcast. Jimmie considered it an ideal arrangement, for although the money involved was only minimal, it provided a regular outlet and valuable publicity at a time when he needed whatever help he could get to maintain his popularity.

Rodgers's involvement with radio broadcasting has received scant attention through the years. It may never be accurately chronicled, given the sporadic nature of his radio work, which was broadcast for the most part over secondary stations in the days when logs were filed haphazardly and air checks were rare. Nonetheless, radio was a vital adjunct to his other professional activities. Seen from a historical standpoint, the advantages were also mutual: while radio provided Rodgers with valuable exposure, his use of it in those formative years of regional and local broadcasting helped influence the directions rural programming would take in the decades to follow.

Although Asheville's WWNC had not (as he liked to tell it) actually given Rodgers his start, radio had figured prominently in his career almost from the beginning. In Washington he had lost little time in getting on WTFF, and while it was one of the capital's smaller, weaker stations, a connection with it allowed Jimmie to bill himself as a "National Radio Artist" and provided a springboard to his first major vaudeville bookings. Touring the Loew circuit in 1928, he'd wangled a broadcast or two in almost every city along the way, plugging his stage appearances and garnering special attention in the papers, especially in Atlanta and Memphis, where he was heard on WSB and WMC respectively. Playing with Paul English in early 1929, Rodgers had continued the practice in smaller towns where there were stations, showing up at all sorts of primitive studios and offering impromptu— and usually unpaid—performances on the air. Radio appearances became a regular adjunct to his R-K-O tour that summer, for the booking chain and its theaters sponsored regularly scheduled weekly programs in most major cities to publicize their current vaudeville bills, and headline performers were expected to broadcast as part of their routine chores. Some stage stars, feeling that local radio was beneath them, considered this task to be only an imposition and performed grudgingly, if at all. But Jimmie relished the opportunity, and he was heard delivering his familiar yodels and rowdy jokes over such stations as KVOO, Tulsa; KOMA, Oklahoma City; WBAP, Fort Worth; WFAA, Dallas (where the program was termed "a recital" by "the latest record and radio sensation"); KPRC, Houston; WBRC, Birmingham; and KLRA, Little Rock. In Fort Worth he sang "In the

Jailhouse Now" and got stacks of fan mail; his initial broadcast in Houston netted seventy-five phone calls and ten telegrams while he was on the air, as a result of which he was called back later in the week to play as many requests as possible.[23]

Even by the time KMAC instituted its regular Jimmie Rodgers show, ten years after such stations as Atlanta's WSB had pioneered in programming oldtime music, rural radio was still in its infancy, only just beginning to find a place in the native culture. Its coming of age was now being hastened, of course, by the decline and disappearance of other entertainment forms, notably vaudeville and windup phonographs. Charting the impact of radio on country music in those years of crucial change and development between 1930 and 1934, Bob Coltman has accurately noted how "the brash young medium of radio became America's single most popular form of entertainment, with its intimacy, its dreamglow, its knack of getting inside the head."[24] And much of what was filtering into the heads of country folk across the land came from Jimmie Rodgers. Largely because of radio in general and Rodgers in particular, there were striking differences between the country music of 1929 and that of 1935, for, as Coltman stresses, "Jimmie Rodgers had been singing '30s—or '40s, or '50s—country music since 1927." That Rodgers was clearly ahead of his time is further borne out by Bill Randle's extensive analysis of the content of his songs. While Randle tends to slight the influence of black music and traditional folk sources in order to emphasize what he correctly sees as Rodgers's stronger affinities with the popular music of his day, he accurately observes that "Rodgers' songs are far more 'modern' than 'old time' and represent a new synthesis of country and hillbilly music rather than the older, 'sentimental' styles that preceded 1920."[25] More to the point is Coltman's analysis of the fusion of many disparate elements which made Rodgers's records and radio broadcasts the vanguard of the "new sound":

> He had pioneered in blues in country singing, had introduced Hawaiian, jazz and pop combos as backup bands and made the first unabashed use of contemporary popular style. Though by some accounts he never quite conquered his shyness on stage, he was at his best in a [radio] studio. He sensed intuitively how to communicate in this new, remote, and to some artists rather alien fashion, and his warm, ingratiating personality would have made him a radio mainstay had he lived.[26]

In the early Thirties, before Nashville emerged as the sole mecca of hillbilly music, as the popularity of the phonograph died away and field recording trips were becoming a thing of the past, country boys who had show business aspirations put on their silk shirts and butterfly boots, packed up their Sears, Roebuck guitars, and headed for the nearest radio station to show everyone they could do it just like Jimmie Rodgers.

By 1932 there could be no doubt that the record business, which had been Rodgers's professional mainstay, was in dire trouble. Gross income during the previous year had dropped almost 90 percent, and there would be further drastic losses in the coming months. Total sales in the United States for 1932 would reach a scant 6,000,000 records, barely 6 percent of the number sold only five years before.[27]

With business in a tailspin, Victor, like the other companies, had reduced its recording activities and fallen back on the substantial backlog housed in its vaults. Hillbilly records were still selling better than others, curiously enough, and one of the reasons for their continued sales was even more curious. In the days before radio stations were required to log and pay royalties on copyrighted "mechanicals," records had become a quick and inexpensive way of filling air time. But the tastes of most stations tended toward light classics and current pop hits, whose publishers and artists complained that the stations not only used their material without paying for it, but also ruined record sales by playing choice items over and over until the public tired of them. Hillbilly records, viewed with disdain by most programmers, were not given much air time; consequently, the small but loyal audiences for hillbilly music had to buy the records if they were to enjoy their favorite songs regularly.[28]

Jimmie Rodgers's fans were even more faithful than most, and a steady (if much diminished) market continued to absorb Victor's monthly Rodgers releases. According to Peer, "For at least three or four years, any Jimmie Rodgers record would be expected to sell a million eventually. That's like five million today [1959]. It's incredible." By early 1932 the figure had plummeted to around 15,000 copies per release—pathetic in comparison to even the weakest earlier issues, which consistently sold in the hundreds of thousands. Still, Rodgers's sales were double and sometimes triple those of his nearest competitors in the hillbilly field, and there was always hope that the next release would hit big and signal a return to the former days of glory. That prospect, coupled with his steady track record, made Victor willing, if not overly anxious, to maintain a backlog of "issue-able" Rodgers material. By this time that backlog had shrunk to two or three sides. Although the salad days of the field recording expeditions were essentially over, Victor executives decided to send a crew out one more time to record the company's premier hillbilly star.[29]

The sessions were scheduled to begin in Dallas on February 2. Peer, hoping to avoid a repeat of the previous year's rather unproductive journey to San Antonio, had urged Rodgers to prepare as much material as he could. Special effort was also made to round up local talent that would further insure the success of the trip. In addition to Rodgers, those recorded in the ensuing two weeks would include Jimmie Davis, later "Louisiana's Singing Governor," and a quartet known as the Fort Worth Doughboys, which contained in at least two of its members—Milton Brown and Bob Wills—the genesis of what would come to be known as Western swing.[30]

As the Depression worsened, Peer's vaunted field expeditions were beginning to lose favor with Victor executives, and his involvement in the tangled corporate structure of Southern Music made his relationship with the company even more precarious. As Peer put it, "Next thing I knew they had hired another fellow who technically was my boss. In other words, he was the man in charge of the hillbilly and race business. If I wanted to put on a recording expedition or something, why, I had to do it jointly with him. So I didn't like this at all, but I fell into it." The "fellow" was Eli Oberstein, a former bookkeeper for Okeh Records, and the friction between them was all the greater because Oberstein owed his job at Victor initially to Peer himself. "I knew him [at Okeh]; he was a live wire," Peer said. "He's a Jew and he'd had all the tenacity, had impressed me as a good man. That's what I needed to produce a sort of sales department for what I had picked up [through the transfer of Southern Music to Victor]." Under the terms of the sale of Southern Music to Victor in 1928, Peer still held control of all copyrights, and Victor had agreed to channel into Southern all the popular material they recorded. But the company's A&R men regularly discovered ways of circumventing the provision. Even when an occasional pop item managed to wind up in the Southern catalog, Peer found Victor decidedly unenthusiastic about promoting it. He'd gotten Oberstein installed in the Victor sales department with the idea of having someone on the payroll there to look after his interests. Unfortunately, Oberstein had "a mind of his own," as Peer put it, and quickly saw where opportunity lay. "He got an obsession," Peer said, "he wanted to take [the field recording and copyright business] from me—he saw how I was operating and he wanted to take this over from me." According to Peer, Oberstein eventually began a campaign to squeeze him out; but before that could happen, external events made it desirable for RCA to sell Southern Music back to Peer, who took advantage of the situation and began to back away on his own, leaving the field to Oberstein. Peer maintained a loose relationship with Victor for many years, but he was never again the fair-haired boy he once had been. This turmoil was only beginning in early 1932 as Peer planned the Dallas session, but, with Oberstein covertly looking over his shoulder, the pressure was on, and it may well have influenced the character of these sessions and the selection of Rodgers's material.

For the eight sides he recorded in Dallas that February, Rodgers turned back to old, familiar territory—prisoner's songs, bindle-stiff ballads, and the laments of moonstruck lovers, in such numbers as "Roll Along, Kentucky Moon," "Hobo's Meditation," "My Time Ain't Long," "Ninety-nine Year Blues," "Mississippi Moon," and "Down the Old Road to Home." Compared to the random, at times almost experimental repertoire of the Louisville sessions the previous summer, they were all rather conventional and undemanding, pleasant enough but not particularly exciting. The few exceptions include "Blue Yodel No. 10," "Home Call," and, perhaps, "Ninety-nine Year Blues"; but even those were built on safe ground, rather than extending Rodgers's talent in any significant direction. The meagerness of his own resources and his continued dependence upon "co-composers" is pointed up by the fact that seven of the eight sides originated wholly or partly with someone else—a rather ironic circumstance for a performer who'd established himself (with Peer, at least) as the composer of his own material. On the other hand, the single best performance of the Dallas sessions was Jimmie's solo rendition of the one song he could take credit for himself—"Blue Yodel No. 10"—demonstrating once more the unique, individualistic quality of his genius. (Although, again, with regard to the authorship of the song, one cannot be sure how much of it originated with him and how much came through the communal "blues line.")

If distinguished by little else, the 1932 Dallas sessions are noteworthy for the musicians who were rounded up, on short notice as usual, to accompany Rodgers. Among those who provided back-up on the first day's recordings was a young guitarist named Bill Boyd, who would soon contribute materially to the development of Western swing with the formation of his own group, the Cowboy Ramblers, and later star as a singing cowboy in a brief series of Hollywood shoot-'em-ups. Boyd is heard on both "Roll Along, Kentucky Moon" and "Hobo's Meditation," hitting licks that sound a great deal like those of Jimmie Rodgers—altogether natural, considering that Boyd was one of the Blue Yodeler's most ardent fans and had learned to play by listening to Jimmie's records. Only twenty-one at the time, he'd already established himself on Dallas radio stations WRR and WFAA, and it was through officials of the latter station that he was contacted and asked to join the Rodgers session. That brief appearance with his idol was an experience Boyd never forgot, although for years it was largely unknown to anyone else; his identity, along with those of the other musicians on those sides, was not revealed. Asked by an acquaintance long afterward why he'd never discussed it, Boyd said that when he first told his friends that he'd worked with Jimmie Rodgers, no one believed him. Rather than be accused of boasting falsely, he'd simply remained silent. His presence, however, is confirmed by Rodgers's lyric sheets, which also list the other musicians: Dick Bunyard, steel; Red Young, "mandoline"; and Fred Koone, string bass. The three were, like Boyd, radio staff musicians on either WRR or WFAA. Bunyard and Koone also gave music lessons locally, and all of them played in various pick-up bands in the area.[31] Bunyard would later record with Jimmie's cousin, Jesse Rodgers.

Playing with Kell in Houston, Rodgers had again encountered his old favorites, the Burkes brothers, and had brought them along with him to Dallas for sessions later in the week. They were joined by Fred Koone, the only one of the first group to be held over. The experience was not particularly pleasant; Jimmie was feeling bad, and the raw condition of the material only contributed to their problems. "My Time Ain't Long," which had come in rough form from Waldo O'Neal, proved especially troublesome. Said Billy Burkes later, "We worked fifteen hours on that one day, and never cut it. Next morning when we came back, the first time we cut it, they sent it to the master. If it hadn't been for Fred Koone, I don't think we would have cut it then, because Fred sat down with Jimmie and just made note-like diagrams on a piece of paper for the yodel, so he could tell whether to go up or come down on it. That's the only way we got it recorded, because he was changing the yodels on us so much. That was the hardest tune I ever cut with him."[32] And, one might add, it was largely wasted effort, despite the title's tragic and all too appropriate connotations. The lyric is a disappointment; rather than the hero's stoic confrontation of his pending doom, in the fashion of "T.B. Blues," the song is a condemned convict's farewell to his dear old Mom—stilted, mawkish, and moralistic. Not certain whether he should yodel high or low, Jimmie seems to have opted for a safe, subdued middle. With eight overblown verses to squeeze in, he had little time for anything more. The band clearly felt the same pressure: Billy Burkes makes the most of the steel guitar, but generally the musicians—Burkes, his brothers Weldon (standard guitar) and Charlie (uke), and Fred Koone on bass—are reduced to little more than thumping along dutifully behind the vocal.

They fared better with "Mississippi Moon" and "Ninety-nine Year Blues." The latter, another of Ray Hall's sardonic commentaries on life behind bars, is rendered in a fittingly serio-comic fashion, down-and-out blues sung with a tip o' the wink and punctuated by Jimmie's running commentary: "Hey, buddy," "Good mawnin', Judge," "Lawd, I wish I wuz dead." As with "My Good Gal's Gone Blues" and most other instances where he talked between verses, the patter was carefully worked out in advance and written down, attesting to Jimmie's professionalism. At the same time, working from a script cost him nothing in spontaneity or originality, for at the microphone he never hesitated to alter or amend the lines according to the way that particular performance "felt." Clearly, the feeling of "Ninety-nine Year Blues" was somewhat more complex than that of the average song, attempting as it did to impose a wry and humorous tone on the deadly serious subject of life imprisonment. Hall had caught the essence in one verse: "All these old bootleggers come here and do their time, and leave me here grinding on the same old ninety-nine."[33] Musically, Jimmie and the band achieved the proper blend of light and heavy with the roving, delicate flat pick of Billy Burkes on standard guitar across Koone's solid bass anchor and the steady seconding by Rodgers and Weldon Burkes.

Billy Burkes took up the steel again for "Mississippi Moon," a remake of an Elsie McWilliams tune that Jimmie had first attempted back in 1928. He'd given it up after two takes and repeated errors in timing, but now, with Koone and the Burkes brothers for reinforcement, he decided to try again. Five takes were necessary—an excessive number, even for Rodgers—but they eventually produced a satisfactory tribute to the moon above Jimmie's native state, adding one more entry to the ranks of such lunar ditties as "Alabama Moon," "Dixie Moon," "Roll Along, Kentucky Moon," and, as Jimmie must have noted with a twinge, Gene Austin's popular "Carolina Moon."

Fred Koone stayed on one more day to second Jimmie on the plaintive and memorable "Down the Old Road to Home," another of those Rodgers sides which succeeds in spite of itself. Simple, unembellished, always bordering on sentimentality but never quite crossing into saccharin, it is the sort of archetypal Rodgers ballad that filtered into the lives and hearts of many Americans on the move, a long way from home, "with a troubled mind and a heart full of pain."[34] Millions were suffering those conditions when the song was released in the fall of 1932, but its deep appeal to the basic human condition has gone undiminished through passing years and changing times.

On Saturday, Jimmie returned to the studio alone to record another Blue Yodel. At the time it had no number; in fact, it was even considered for release under the title "Ground Hog Rootin' in My Backyard," the loss of which surely no one mourns. Eventually it became "Blue Yodel No. 10," and together with the other title recorded that day—a remake of "Home Call"—it demonstrated once again that Jimmie Rodgers was at his best when performing solo, unencumbered by musicians fretting about whether he should yodel high or low and bothering him with such trivial things as timing. There was nothing wrong with Jimmie Rodgers's sense of timing, except perhaps that it was entirely his own, private and esoteric, but absolutely right for whatever he wanted to do. And what he did on "Blue Yodel No. 10" was to revive the old Rodgers magic—the bold, fluid guitar work that had always been a vital extension of his singing; the jaunty stance of the suffering but indomitable bluesman; the simple, instinctive yodel that so many tried to imitate but never achieved because, like the guitar, it was an organic part of the whole.

Jimmie's yodel was not a gimmick or contrivance "tacked on," but his pure essence, a distillation of all his pain and delight, of everything he had to say and everything that was unspeakable. In "Blue Yodel No. 10" it all came together in a blues lyric that, in the best traditions of the genre, manages to be sad and funny and suggestive all at the same time. The soul-weary lover finds "there's been a ground hog rootin' round my yard at night" and ponders what it is about his pretty mama that gives him the blues: "It ain't your drop-stitch stockings, it ain't your blue buckle shoes." The essence of the blues situation—and very nearly pure folk poetry as well—is a verse like "Got me a pretty mama, got me a bulldog too; my pretty mama don't love me, but my bulldog do." Finally, there is the proud disclaimer, as the bluesman admits that he "ain't no sheek [*sic*] man" anyway, and he salvages what he can in the stoic assertion that "it's my regular grinding gets me by in this world."[35]

From singing about his regular grinding and a mama who didn't love him, Rodgers turned that afternoon to a remake of "Home Call," an effusive paean to domesticity as close and overstuffed as a 1930's front parlor. As a shift from "Blue Yodel No. 10," it was not exactly going from the sublime to the ridiculous; "Home Call" does have a certain musty charm about it, and there's no denying that the song, in its inception, at least, carried special meaning for Rodgers as an expression of his feelings for Carrie and especially for Anita. By this time, however, the song had scarcely more relation to his life than did any other situation he sang about; the decision to re-record it was clearly dictated as much by dissatisfaction with the technical quality of the original and the lack of other usable material as by any sentimental motives. The least that can be said of the remake is that, without the musical saw and other cumbersome accompaniment, it is superior to the first recording three years earlier. Jimmie performs with strength and clarity; it is anyone's guess whether he felt a flicker of irony as he sang, "We're as happy as happy can be, in the evening just Carrie, Anita, and me."[36]

His plans for a partnership with Kell now discarded, Jimmie went to work immediately to align himself with some other touring tent company for the coming season. By mid-March he'd announced his intention of joining the J. Doug Morgan Show, scheduled to open in Jacksonville, Texas, around the end of the month.[37]

Morgan, like his fellow showman and good friend Skeeter Kell, was a Midwesterner who'd found a home in Texas. Like Kell also, he was an astute rep manager who'd enjoyed great success throughout the Twenties and now found himself hard pressed to keep his operation afloat. There the resemblances ended. Kell was tall and gangling, a rumpled, raw-boned character who clowned off stage as well as on; Morgan could hardly have presented a more sedate and distinguished mien had his middle name been Pierpont. Portly and greying at the temples, always immaculately dressed, he might have passed for a small-town banker. Beneath that conservative appearance, however, was a flamboyant showman. The J. Doug Morgan Show in the Big Circus Tent—to give it the full billing he insisted on—was one of the most colorful in the country.[38]

Originally from Iowa, Morgan had started as a prop boy with the old Howard-DeVoss Company before the turn of the century, and later he toured with various canvas attractions before organizing his own rep show after World War I. An actor by inclination, he preferred drama over vaudeville and insisted to the bitter end that "the play's the thing." At the same time, he was more flexible and progressive than most tent managers and had realized early that the standard old rep format would have to be modified and embellished if it were to compete with movies and radio. "I have always been on the lookout for new ideas," he said in 1929, recalling how in the early Twenties he'd saved an otherwise losing season by booking a group of musicians from a circus that had closed.[39] That alone was a radical departure for a rep show in those days, but the fact that the musicians were black only compounded the protests from Morgan's white actors, who resented the professional encroachment and feared even more the consequences of touring Texas in a racially mixed company. However, Morgan's adroit handling of the situation and the band's immediate success as a "draw" quickly established them as permanent fixtures. From that time on, the show regularly carried presentation acts, vaudeville specialties, and "added attractions."

By the late 1920's Morgan was mounting as many as four units, often equipping one or two with a full carnival section including rides, midway, and minstrel show. His rep units, painted in "the famous Morgan red," became familiar attractions along an established route from Texas to Iowa, playing such standbys as "The Whole Town's Talking," "Why Girls Walk Home," "Ten Nights in a Bar Room," and

"Uncle Tom's Cabin." The basic character of the show was still that of rep theater, but Morgan played heavily on the ornate mystique of the circus big top to publicize it, outfitting the show with gaudy pennants, balloons, barkers, and a huge calliope to "play 'em into the tent." When showtime came, the normally somber and dignified Morgan underwent a metamorphosis, striding down the center aisle with a ringmaster's whistle to announce each act, bellowing out a welcome to the crowd in a voice which, according to one fellow showman, "you could hear into the next county."[40]

In the summer of 1930 Morgan had suffered the same fate that befell Swain's Hollywood Follies and most other shows on the road. Renewed emphasis on variety acts and extravagant ballyhoo did little to offset the effects of the Depression; within a year Morgan was down to one unit, fending off competitors for his old territory and trying desperately to put together a show that would click. "I believe if a manager had some special feature he would do business," he told *Billboard*—but, failing to find one, he had closed the 1931 season early and had gone off to Hollywood to relax and make plans for next year. "Believe me, the same old show will not attract the public any more," he said, and it was clear from this and similar statements throughout the winter that the idea had become almost an obsession.[41] By February the show began to take shape, and Morgan announced an early opening for what he hoped would be his longest season ever. "High-class talent will be featured," he said, "and real plays will be used this season, instead of the Toby, slap-stick kind that failed to please the customers last year."[42] But all the brave talk about "new ideas and new equipment" was singularly lacking in detail, and it soon became obvious that Morgan had not really found a combination that pleased him. The highly touted "minstrel first part and high class colored band and orchestra," for example, consisted of the same group he had carried several seasons earlier—profitable enough back then, but certainly nothing novel. The announcement several weeks later that Jimmie Rodgers would open with the show on March 30 was a more encouraging sign.[43]

As it turned out, bad weather delayed the opening several weeks, and when the show was finally ready, America's Blue Yodeler shared headline billing with someone known as "Miss Helene, Mentalist."[44] If Jimmie Rodgers saw in that any evidence that he was slipping, there was no indication of it; nor did he take the show's delayed opening as an omen of things to come. After all, things were tough all over. Vernon Dalhart had not made a record for Victor in more than two years—his career there was virtually over—and, out in Chicago, Gene Austin was singing without pay on local daytime radio in a last-ditch attempt to revive his fading popularity. The man who'd made dozens of national hits and set everyone humming "My Blue Heaven" barely five years earlier was dismissed in the trade press as "just another tenor."[45]

The Morgan show opened in Jacksonville, site of its winter quarters, during the second week in April. Business was dutifully reported as "very encouraging," and the troupe set out to play Morgan's established East Texas territory, including such towns as Longview, Kilgore, Tyler, Carthage, and Lufkin.[46]

Jimmie traveled in his big blue Cadillac, accompanied only by his driver, Cliff Bass, whom he'd come to rely on for a variety of services. In addition to driving and keeping Jimmie's cars in prime condition, on the road Bass took care of travel arrangements, kept account of Jimmie's expenses, bought his whiskey and medicine, saw that he was stocked with his favorite Picayune cigarettes, and served as bodyguard, valet, male nurse, and general factotum. By this time Jimmie was avoiding hotels because of his illness, preferring instead to stay at tourist camps where he and Bass could prepare their own meals and he could come and go without attracting a crowd. Morgan arranged a special tent, with screens and roll-up walls for ventilation, to serve as a dressing room and a place where Rodgers could rest. As usual, the tent became a center of social activity between shows. During the day Jimmie could be found in front of it, in a chair tipped back against an end pole, joking and carrying on with members of the company, townspeople, and almost anyone who wandered by.

In late April he left the show briefly to meet Peer in Dallas and renew his contract with Victor, a ritual that had been taking place each spring since 1928. As Jimmie told it, under the terms of the new contract he was to be paid $25,000 for twelve monthly releases (twenty-four sides) during the coming year—the implication being that the money was merely a cash advance, in addition to which he would also receive royalties. Again he had inflated the sums involved, but the actual terms were undoubtedly substantial, given current conditions in the recording business. Peer said later that by the time of his last session Rodgers was being paid an advance of $250 per side; even that was a figure which few other solo artists could match in those days. For his entire orchestra of twelve musicians, Guy Lombardo was reportedly receiving only $350 a side.[47]

Having agreed with Peer on tentative plans for another recording session in the summer, Jimmie rejoined Morgan. As in the past, he felt obliged to explain why a star of his stature would travel with a tent show. "It's something different," he told an interviewer in Lufkin, but he went on to admit that "my health is bad." Touring with a show like Morgan's "gives me a chance to be in the open, keeps me away from crowded theatres and strenuous performances throughout the day. I only have to go on stage once a day now. When you play with the 'Big Boys' you have to make about four or five appearances each day, and it goes pretty hard for a fellow in bad health."[48] Even performing only once a day, Jimmie was exhausted after every show and had to rest for an hour or so in his tent before he could even remove his makeup.

A young reporter, Carl Biggers, came out to interview him, but made several return trips before he found Jimmie in condition to talk. Then the interview took place in the blue Cadillac, as Cliff Bass drove them around town. "Jimmie was very nervous and wanted to be on the move," Biggers recalled later. "I would like to think that I was wrong, but I got the impression that he was either drinking or taking dope. I know he was on medication. I remember seeing a number of medicine containers around his quarters." The tragic state of his health was clear enough, but Biggers sensed a further twist to Rodgers's bitter plight—the financial urgency of the situation that no amount of brave talk about $25,000-a-year contracts and elaborate tours abroad could cover up. "I got the impression that he was needing money," said Biggers. "That he was broke."[49]

It soon became obvious that Morgan had not been able to mount a production of the quality he'd boasted, and by this time Jimmie was in no shape to carry the show alone. Beset by his ever-worsening health and distracted by a dozen other things, he performed erratically, shortening his appearances and often failing to go on at all. In Lufkin he'd opened strong, and even Biggers was impressed that a man so ill could perform as he did. "I was amazed with the ease he performed on the first night," Biggers said. "He would sing and with no visible effort go right into his specialty, the yodel."[50] But later several performances had to be cut short, and by the end of the week he was barely able to perform.

Attendance hovered at the break-even point as the show struggled on through the Big Thicket country of East Texas. Finally, in mid-May, Morgan decided to jump the show north to Iowa in hopes of finding better pickings in his old territory.[51] He encouraged Rodgers to stay with the tour, but the singer shook his head. It was too far from his familiar stamping ground, and he'd never felt at ease "up Nawth," even in the summertime. He was tired of the tour anyway, and he had other things on his mind. One was Stella's lawsuit, which was scheduled for a final court hearing in Oklahoma City in early June. He and Morgan parted amiably, agreeing that they might try another tour together later if conditions improved.

On June 9, the U.S. District Court reached its verdict in the matter of Stella Harkins and Kathryn Rodgers, a Minor, vs. Jimmie Rodgers. Both parties had waived a jury trial, and Judge Edgar Vaught set to work examining the extensive evidence before him, including stacks of depositions taken from character witnesses, physicians, and various other people who claimed to have knowledge of the circumstances surrounding the birth of Kathryn Rodgers.

One of the more curious aspects of the proceeding was that while both parties had raised serious questions concerning the time of the child's birth, neither side introduced any substantial proof or attempted to establish a specific date that might have bearing on the time of conception, a crucial issue in Rodgers's defense. The questioning of the doctor who delivered the baby was typical. Rodgers's chief counsel, his brother-in-law, Nate Williamson, extracted the rather vague statement that "to my recollection, the year was 1917"—thus strengthening the defense's claim that the child was conceived prior to the marriage in May of that year.[52] Rather than pursuing the matter to establish a more specific date, Williamson took up another line of questioning and let the subject drop. Stella's witnesses, assuming the stand to support her contention that the birthdate was in February, 1918, offered equally vague and inconclusive information.

In his decree Judge Vaught ruled simply on the condition of the marriage itself. That, he found, was clearly legal. Consequently, the child had been born in "legal wedlock" and was thus declared the legitimate daughter of the defendant. Rodgers was ordered to pay $50 a month as child support until Kathryn reached the age of eighteen, a sum amounting to $2,650.[53] Although a substantial burden to one in Jimmie's precarious condition, it was still far less than the $15,000 originally filed for; in addition, the court denied outright Stella's claim for reimbursement for her past services in caring for the child. Later there would be rumors of a huge trust fund set up by Jimmie for both of his daughters, but as far as Kathryn was concerned there is no tangible evidence that she received anything more than the stipulated $50 a month until Rodgers's death the following May. Although his will made no provision for her, it seems reasonable to assume that Carrie made a nominal settlement of some sort, to avoid further and more drastic claims against the estate. In any event, Kathryn's marriage and subsequent death in 1938 rendered the matter closed.[54]

Just how all this may have affected Jimmie Rodgers is another matter for conjecture. The situation is clouded by a mass of contradictions and enigmas: why he first acknowledged the child and then contested the suit; the extent to which Carrie and her brother, Nate Williamson, influenced his actions; why Stella insisted that "he asked me to sue him," when the evidence points to a bitter and prolonged contest; why his first wife felt compelled to take such action in the first place, in view of Jimmie's notorious generosity with everyone—and especially, one would assume, with the child he'd so openly welcomed as his own and on whom he'd lavished gifts and attention at their first meeting.

Perhaps Jimmie's strongest reaction to the court's decision was simply a feeling of great relief that the whole affair was over. There can be little doubt that he had been pulled in many directions, torn not only between his two "families" but harried as well at trying to marshal what little physical strength he had left in order to maintain some sort of professional life in the midst of it all.

NOTES

1. *Billboard,* June 27, 1931, p. 22.
2. Interview, Mar. 12, 1975, Huntsville.
3. *Billboard,* Sept. 5, 1931, p. 35.
4. *Ibid.,* Nov. 21, 1931, p. 22.
5. *MHJR,* p. 242.
6. *San Antonio Express,* Nov. 5, 1931, p. 13.
7. *MHJR,* p. 228.
8. Interview, May 21, 1976, Kerrville.
9. Confidential source.

10. See D. Russell Connor and Warren Hicks, *BG on the Record* (New Rochelle, N.Y.: Arlington House, 1969), p. 89.

11. *Billboard*, June 12, 1926, p. 30; Dec. 22, 1928, p. 30; June 27, 1931, p. 22; July 4, 1931, p. 21.

12. *Ibid.*, Dec. 12, 1931, p. 22, and Jan. 9, 1932, p. 24.

13. See *Houston Post-Dispatch*, Dec. 24, 1931, p. 14.

14. *Billboard*, Jan. 9, 1932, p. 24.

15. *Ibid.*

16. *Ibid.*, Jan. 23, 1932, p. 22.

17. *Ibid.*, Jan. 16, 1932, p. 24.

18. *Ibid.*, Feb. 6, 1932, p. 22.

19. Mrs. Rodgers, however, visited the company on Feb. 20 (*Billboard*, Feb. 27, 1932, p. 22), suggesting that Jimmie may still have had some connection with the show. In any event, her presence is further evidence that the parting between Rodgers and Kell was neither abrupt nor acrimonious.

20. *Billboard*, Mar. 12, 1932, p. 22.

21. Jimmie Rodgers to Raymond Hall, Jan. 22, 1932; copy in my files.

22. See *San Antonio Light* radio listings for Jan. 19, 1932, *et seq.* Prior to the beginning of Rodgers's program, the KMAC log carried only generic headings: "variety program," "popular tunes," "dance music," etc. For a time the only other artist to have his own show was Louis Armstrong (on records, of course). By March, KMAC was featuring, in addition to Rodgers, recorded programs of Wayne King, Ethel Waters, Nick Lucas, the Happy Chappies, Bert Lown, Eddie Dunstadter, and a "classical hour."

23. For representative listings and news stories, see *Tulsa World*, May 19, 1929, sec. 4, p. 15; *Memphis Commercial Appeal*, Nov. 18, 1928, sec. IV, pp. 6, 8; *Atlanta Constitution*, Nov. 13, 1928, p. 10; *Ft. Worth Record-Telegram*, June 3, 1929, p. 9; *Dallas Morning News*, June 9, 1929, p. 7, and June 10, 1929, p. 5; *Houston Post-Dispatch*, June 25, 1929, p. 14, and June 27, 1929, p. 9; and *Birmingham Post*, July 20, 1929, pp. 3, 12.

24. Bob Coltman, "Across the Chasm: How the Depression Changed Country Music," *Old Time Music*, no. 23 (Winter, 1976/77), 6.

25. Randle, "History of Radio Broadcasting," p. 463.

26. Coltman, "Across the Chasm," pp. 11–12.

27. Gelatt, *Fabulous Phonograph*, p. 255. See also Oliver Read and Walter L. Welch, *From Tin Foil to Stereo* (Indianapolis: Howard W. Sams, 1959), p. 291.

28. See *Billboard*, Oct. 3, 1931, p. 20.

29. A few companies, notably Columbia and Decca, would continue to make commercial recordings in the field as late as the 1940's.

30. In singling out Brown and Wills, I do not mean to diminish the other, less well known members of the original Light Crust (a.k.a. "Fort Worth") Doughboys, Durwood Brown and "Sleepy" Johnson, both of whom had long and influential careers in Western swing.

31. Mrs. Bill Boyd to NP, Apr. 6 and 28, 1976. Boyd's reason for remaining silent about his work with Rodgers was related to me by Jim Evans, who discussed it with Boyd some years ago.

32. Burkes to NP, Jan. 23, 1977. Victor's logs show only one date for "My Time Ain't Long," but (as other evidence indicates) the company's files are not always authoritative.

33. "Ninety-nine Year Blues," words and music by Jimmie Rodgers and Raymond Hall. © 1932 by Peer International Corporation. Copyright renewed. Used by permission.

34. "Down the Old Road to Home," words and music by Jimmie Rodgers and Carey D. Harvey. © 1934 by Peer International Corporation. Copyright renewed. Used by permission.

35. "Blue Yodel No. 10," words and music by Jimmie Rodgers. © 1932 by Peer International Corporation. Copyright renewed. Used by permission.

36. "Home Call," words and music by Jimmie Rodgers and Elsie McWilliams. © 1932 by Peer International Corporation. Copyright renewed. Used by permission.

37. *Billboard*, Mar. 26, 1932, p. 42.

38. See Neil Schaffner, with Vance Johnson, *The Fabulous Toby and Me* (Englewood Cliffs, N.J.: Prentice-Hall, 1968), pp. 129–30.

39. *Billboard*, Mar. 23, 1929, p. 65. See also Dec. 12, 1925, pp. 18, 134; Dec. 20, 1919, p. 45; Feb. 3, 1923, p. 28; Apr. 30, 1927, p. 30; Dec. 22, 1928, p. 30; June 28, 1930, p. 45.

40. Schaffner, *Fabulous Toby and Me*, p. 130.

41. See *Billboard*, Sept. 12, 1931, p. 20; Nov. 7, 1931, p. 22; Jan. 23, 1932, p. 22.

42. *Ibid.*, Feb. 13, 1932, p. 22.

43. *Ibid.*, Mar. 26, 1932, p. 42.

44. *Ibid.*, Apr. 23, 1932, p. 24.

45. *Ibid.*, July 23, 1932, p. 17. For a favorable review of Austin's earlier, short-lived efforts on another Chicago station, see *Variety*, May 3, 1932, p. 50.

46. *Billboard*, Apr. 23, 1932, p. 24.

47. *Variety*, June 31, 1932, p. 61.

48. *Lufkin* (Tex.) *Daily News*, May 3, 1932, p. 6.

49. Carl Biggers to NP, Jan. 29, 1978.

50. *Ibid.*

51. *Billboard*, Aug. 6, 1932, p. 22.

52. Interrogatories and answers of J. D. Weeks, M.D., *Stella Harkins and Kathryn Rodgers* v. *Jimmie Rodgers*, Law 4502 (1932).

53. Journal entry of judgment, *Harkins and Rodgers* v. *Rodgers*.

54. Rodgers's will, dated May 11, 1931, stipulated a trust fund of $3,000 for Anita, "for her schooling and education," to be administered by her mother. There is no mention of Kathryn. See *Will Book of Lauderdale County, Mississippi*, 6:464; also filed in *Probate Dockets, Bexar County, Texas*, Estate No. 21329, June 28, 1933. Rodgers's daughter by Stella Kelly died Oct. 15, 1938, in what officials termed an "accidental suicide." Following a spat with her husband, she apparently drank disinfectant in an attempt to frighten him, but unintentionally swallowed a fatal dose. See the *Shawnee* (Okla.) *Morning News*, Oct. 16, 1938, p. 1.

17 *July–September, 1932*

"I Heard the Gang Singing 'Bury Me on the Lone Prairie' "

The shabby experience of J. Doug Morgan's Show in the Big Circus Tent had signaled only another downward step in the slow, descending spiral. Early in Rodgers's career Peer had told him that the average life of a recording artist was only three years, a prophecy that held true for hundreds of other phonograph stars who'd risen to popularity in the flush Twenties and soon vanished with the onslaught of the Depression. In many parts of the country customers still gathered at music stores to greet the monthly Jimmie Rodgers release; but the crowds were much smaller now, and there were other signs that the bloom on the Rodgers rose had begun to wilt. By 1932 the once novel and distinctive aura of America's Blue Yodeler was only a comfortable, familiar reminder of better days, and the wave of attention that had greeted him a few years earlier settled into a quiet deference as the nation went about the more pressing business of trying to stay alive. Yodelers were a dime a dozen now, and although some years would pass before the Gene Autrys and Ernest Tubbs would find a true national audience, the net effect of so many imitators was to dilute the already diminished market for Rodger's records. At the same time, his illness limited his exposure and diffused his impact upon the public.

With Stella's lawsuit finally settled, Jimmie went to Meridian, supposedly to rest for a month or so. But within days he was up again and roaming the country, traveling to see old friends, booking spur-of-the-moment performances in small-town theaters and high school auditoriums, accompanied by Cliff Bass and one old crony or another. Conferring with Peer by phone, he began to plan his summer recording session, which by now had become something of an annual event—one big push in the studio during which he could stockpile a year's supply of releases in a single concentrated period. The February sessions in Dallas had produced only eight sides, and again Victor was down to only a few titles from which to select his monthly releases. Yet Jimmie detected a certain coolness when the conversation turned to the subject of where they would record. A few years earlier Peer would have been on his way to Atlanta or New Orleans or Dallas, but now there was little interest in the bother and expense of a field session, even to record America's Blue Yodeler.

It mattered little to Jimmie: if Victor wouldn't come to him, he'd go to Victor. He was always on the road anyway, and a trip back east to Camden would be a pleasant diversion. He hadn't been there since 1929, and there were old acquaintances to renew and numerous other attractions. As an added inducement, Peer mentioned that he was again thinking of a foreign tour, to England maybe, after the recordings were made; there was also the possibility of a radio show that would originate from New York on one of the major networks. For this they would need additional talent, and Peer suggested that Jimmie line up two or three musicians to accompany him. The whole plan was characteristically vague, but Jimmie's old optimism bubbled again. He assured Peer that he was feeling better than ever and would have everything worked out when he reached Camden.

While playing scattered local dates in the South, Rodgers had learned that his old friend Clayton McMichen had left Tennessee and was working at WHK in Cleveland. From Gadsden, Alabama, he wired Mac:

> 1932 JUL 21 3:20 AM
> GC 14 10NM GADSDEN, ALA
>
> CLAYTON MCMICHEN VIOLIN PLAYER
> CARE RADIO STA WHK CLEVELAND
>
> CAN YOU WORK WITH ME ADVISE CARE MORRIS HOTEL=
>
> JIMMIE RODGERS[1]

McMichen called him almost immediately and indicated a willingness to listen to any proposition. He had only recently split with Gid Tanner and the Skillet Lickers and was fronting the first of several groups he would call the Georgia Wildcats—comprised at the time of himself and guitar players Johnny Barfield, Pat Berryman, and Hoyt "Slim" Bryant. Things had not been going well for them in northern Ohio, and they were about to move on when Rodgers's wire arrived. McMichen tried to persuade him to take the entire band, but since Jimmie would be paying the musicians out of his own pocket, he insisted that he wanted only McMichen. Mac countered with a plea that Rodgers at least hire Bryant, a fellow Georgian whom McMichen especially liked, but Jimmie agreed only to think about it. He'd already lined up a five-string banjo player named Oddie McWinders, an old vaudeville hand who'd had some previous recording experience; with McMichen's fiddle and his own guitar, Jimmie felt he would have a suitable trio, one that would meet Peer's requirements and still keep his own expenses to a minimum.

A few days later he wrote to McMichen, confirming the travel arrangements and recording dates. Scrambling for material as always, he encouraged Mac to bring anything he'd written. "Mr Peer says he wonts me to do at least 10 numbers so if you have any thing of your own be sure to bring it along because Im pretty sure I can get several of your Songs Recorded." Regarding Bryant, he would say only that he'd do what he could to persuade Peer to use him, but could not guarantee it. "But I will pay his expenses if he cares to come along with you and take chances on working. I mean eating and sleeping expenses as long as he is with us."[2]

As arranged, McMichen and Bryant met Jimmie in Washington, at the home of Carrie's sister and brother-in-law, Annie and Alex Nelson. Leaving Anita with the Nelsons, Jimmie and Carrie and the two musicians were chauffeured to Camden by Cliff Bass, with a stopover in Baltimore to visit Jimmie's legendary uncle, Rawl Bozeman. McWinders joined the group in Camden, and they set to work rehearsing.

The initial session, a day-long affair in Studio 2 at the Old Trinity Church, turned out to be little more than a trial run for the musicians and their material. Peer had come down from New York with some new material from Tin Pan Alley that he wanted Jimmie to try, and he had also rounded up a couple of extra musicians—a steel guitarist named Dave Kanui, and George Howell, who played string bass. Slim

Bryant was quickly incorporated into the group, on the basis of both his ability and Peer's desire to back Rodgers with as much accompaniment as possible. Unfortunately, the musicians were mismatched and ill at ease, having never worked together before. McWinders, in particular, had problems; although an adept and versatile musician, he was rather slow in picking up new material and, according to Bryant, "had to take everything home and memorize it."[3] Later there were also rumors of friction between McMichen and the black bass player, Howell.

To compound their difficulties, Victor's engineers were testing new equipment and experimenting with various recording techniques. A year earlier, as part of the Depression retrenchment, chief engineer Raymond Sooy had ordered that only one wax master of each matrix number be processed.[4] However, because the wax of a desired take sometimes became defective before it could be made into metal, Sooy's staff had undertaken to develop means of recording simultaneously on two or more machines to provide spare waxes of each take; it was hoped that this process would reduce the need for retakes of an otherwise acceptable performance that was spoiled by flaws in the wax itself. But the machines and techniques for achieving this had to be tested and perfected under a variety of conditions, and, if one judges from what ensued on the day when Rodgers and his scratch band began, the men in the control booth were more concerned with the performance of their cutting lathes and dubbing circuits than with the aesthetic quality of what was taking place before the microphone. Further complications outside the studio resulted from the growing tensions between Peer and Oberstein, who by this time was "overseeing" sessions produced by Peer.

The musicians worked from mid-morning until past the dinner hour to record only one title, a slick Tin Pan Alley item called "In the Hills of Tennessee." Yet of the five takes—three of which were made simultaneously on two machines—none was considered satisfactory, and the number was shelved. Peer's ideas for "doing something different" clearly weren't working. Sensing also that the musicians might get along better without the two outsiders he'd brought in, he dismissed Kanui and Howell. Rodgers and the others turned back to their own material in preparation for the next session.

They were in the studio again early the following day, and by noon things were beginning to click. Even with frequent breaks to allow

Jimmie to rest, by the time they finished at 6:30 that evening they'd
gotten down four sides—"Mother, the Queen of My Heart" "Prohibition Has Done Me Wrong," "Rock All Our Babies to Sleep," and
"Whippin' That Old T.B." While none of these is really of the first
rank, all are musically interesting; quite apart from Peer's efforts to do
something "different," they contribute still another dimension to the
Rodgers idiom—a sound that is distinctively modern and ahead of its
time. The result largely of Bryant's advanced guitar work and the
bright, upbeat fashion in which Rodgers delivers several of the songs,
it is a sound that prefigures much of what was to happen to country
music in the Thirties. Yet in another important sense, it looks
backward, too. Nowhere is this happy tension more evident than in
McMichen's fiddle, grounded in oldtime grandeur, simplicity, and
ease, yet temperamentally attuned to contemporary swing licks and
itching all the while to break loose. One senses that, on these sides
with Rodgers, McMichen's talents were never really allowed to reach
their potential.

As the only song commercially recorded by Rodgers but never
released, "Prohibition Has Done Me Wrong" later became the source
of endless conjecture. The faintly shady nature of its title, coupled with
the subsequent loss of the master, has led to speculation about the
presumed offensiveness of the lyrics and rumors of high-placed
skullduggery in suppressing it. The fact is that the song, a second-rate
reworking of McMichen's earlier, unissued "Prohibition Blues"
(Columbia master 150319) with cursory emendations by Rodgers, simply isn't particularly good—no worse than others Jimmie recorded, but
burdened by limp, awkward lines and rather simple-minded preach-
ments about the hypocrisy of the Eighteenth Amendment. In view of
Rodgers's increasing dependence on pain-killing drugs—it was during
these sessions, as McMichen related later, that he administered
morphine shots to Jimmie—Peer perhaps felt a little uneasy with the
song's declaration that if people don't get whiskey "they'll take to
dope, cocaine, and morphine,"[5] but it is doubtful that he would have
withheld the song solely on these grounds. Some commentators have
also pointed out that Prohibition was on the verge of repeal by the time
the song would have been ready for release, thus diffusing its
topicality. There had, in fact, been a spate of such songs on the market
for several years, notably "Goodbye, Mr. Dry, You're All Wet," a
1931 hit. It is even more likely that, from its very inception, the master

was judged inferior on the basis of material, performance, and recording quality. Peer may also have decided that it was simply too close to McMichen's original to allow a new copyright in Rodgers's name. In any event, the master sat on a shelf in Victor's vaults, gathering dust; it was eventually destroyed in a rather routine house-cleaning in 1944, when metal was at a premium.[6] While the loss may be mourned, it is doubtful that "Prohibition Has Done Me Wrong" would add much to our appreciation of Jimmie Rodgers or the other musicians involved.

"Rock All Our Babies to Sleep," recorded the same day, has little to recommend it save what we hear of McMichen, Bryant, and McWinders. The song would eventually pass into both folk and recording tradition, but whether from Rodgers's performance or Riley Puckett's 1924 version (Columbia 107-D, supposedly the first hillbilly record to employ the yodel) is difficult to determine. Similarly, "Whippin' That Old T.B." owes most of its merit to McMichen's fiddle, and to whatever consolation it may have given Rodgers's audiences, especially the fellow "lungers" among them. The lyrics of "Whippin' That Old T.B." suffer in comparison with its prototype, for where "T.B. Blues" had confronted its subject honestly and imaginatively, the sequel seems little more than commercialized bravado, wholly admirable for what it attempts, but woefully misnamed and doomed in its determination to impose platitudinous good cheer on what was in fact a hopeless situation. At this stage Jimmie's manful assertion that "happiness and sunshine" have "done me all the good"[7] must have had a hollow ring, even to him. Fortunately, the song ultimately rises above its twisted banalities, and the net effect is to affirm Rodgers's true stance, a far more incisive perception of the everyday reality with which he lived: don't worry that you're going to die, because you surely will; take what ease you can, and don't feel sorry for yourself.

The day's session had begun with "Mother, the Queen of My Heart." Despite its syrupy sentimentality, or perhaps because of it, the song was destined to be one of Rodgers's most popular numbers and one that has been covered by numerous artists over the years. Aside from the cloying if rather clever situation—a gambler who reforms when his dead mother's face appears on a poker card—the song shows the touch of a professional in its tight construction and narrative development. It was Slim Bryant's composition, of course, and

Jimmie was quick to recognize the young guitar player's talents as a songwriter. "Let's give ol' Slim a break and put his name first on the record as composer," he told Peer, in a characteristic gesture. Bryant, like many others, was impressed by Jimmie's generosity and humility, remarking later that "he was a very congenial fellow and not the least uppity for being a great star."[8]

After a long weekend to rest up, Jimmie returned to record "Hard Time Blues" with Bryant, followed by a number that Rodgers had entitled "I'm Always There on Time," accompanied by Oddie McWinders. Both were tentatively designated Blue Yodels, but, as finally released by Oberstein, "Hard Time Blues" was given the more accurate (and, in those Depression days, more commercially appealing) title of "No Hard Times," while "I'm Always There on Time" became "Long Tall Mama Blues." The talents of Bryant and McWinders fairly sparkle on their respective sides, with the result that these are two of the best numbers to come from the Camden sessions. Bryant's licks on "No Hard Times" are especially fine, highlighted in the clean, progressive break between the second and third verses—a sound like nothing that had been heard before on a Jimmie Rodgers record, and a bright augury of things to come in country music.

That afternoon McMichen rejoined the group for "Peach Picking Time Down in Georgia," one of Mac's own tunes that has since become another Rodgers standard. Lyrically the song is no great shakes, but the band recorded it with an appropriate lilt, wafted along by McMichen's firm and resonant fiddle. Paired with "Prairie Lullaby," it had the distinction of being the last record to be issued while Rodgers was still alive.

The band sounded even better on "Gambling Bar Room Blues," recorded the following day. But the material was also better—far superior to either of Rodgers's previous gambler songs, "Those Gambler's Blues" and "Gambling Polka Dot Blues." Supplied by Shelly Lee Alley, "Gambling Bar Room Blues" also had its roots in "St. James Infirmary" and a dozen other traditional variants in black folk music; however, Rodgers assimilated it into his own idiom and experience, the rowdy netherworld of the down and out, of trainmen's dives and gin mills where "flatfooted cops" are sometimes the best customers. He knew the scene well, and rendered it with the appropriately mournful note, a wailing minor key and the falsetto chant in place of his usual jaunty yodel.

As so often happened in his sessions, the repertoire meandered from one extreme to another. From the sublimities of "Gambling Bar Room Blues" the group moved on to close out their work in Camden with "I've Only Loved Three Women," a pathetic old ballad that was already filtering into tradition when Carey D. Harvey ("Down the Old Road to Home") came up with a version for Jimmie. Peer was already unhappy with both the quality and quantity of what they'd recorded, and, according to Slim Bryant, the musicians weren't particularly pleased, either.[9] "I've Only Loved Three Women" surely did not improve matters.

Peer hoped to stockpile at least a dozen sides, but his reserved block of studio time had expired, along with the material at hand. Only ten masters were "in the can," and he knew that several of those would probably never be released. Realizing also the serious state of Rodgers's health, Peer was more concerned than ever about building up a backlog against the uncertain future. A source close to the situation said, "Don't quote me, but I think Peer knew Jimmie wasn't going to last much longer, and they wanted to get all the recordings they could."[10] At any rate, Peer began to arrange for another session in New York, knowing that Jimmie was going there to discuss various business matters and perhaps attempt a brief vacation before returning to Texas. McMichen and the other musicians were told to come along. A session was scheduled for August 29, almost two weeks away, to give Rodgers a chance to rest and organize additional material.

When the time came, however, he produced only two numbers— "Miss the Mississippi and You" and "Sweet Mama, Hurry Home," both put together from bits and pieces he'd been carrying around in his briefcase. "Miss the Mississippi and You" originated with Bill Halley, who'd written "Roll Along, Kentucky Moon." "Sweet Mama" came from Jimmie's San Antonio buddy Jack Neville, co-author of "Jimmie the Kid" and "What's It?" In addition to these, Peer scheduled a remake of "In the Hills of Tennessee." Despite the trouble they'd had with it in Camden, he was determined to have the song properly recorded in order to earn the mechanical royalties, for he'd already published the sheet music and assured the composers, Sam Lewis and Ira Schuster, that it would appear on record. Still, that left them with only three songs for the session.

While Rodgers and the musicians were in Peer's New York office discussing the situation, a young songwriter who called himself

George Brown came along, hawking his wares. Peer hurriedly scanned a batch of manuscripts that Brown handed him, picking out a number called "Prairie Lullaby." Jimmie went to work with the composer to learn it on the spot. When they'd finished, Brown pulled out more songs and tried to get Peer to listen to them, but he was waved away. "Why didn't you listen to his songs?" the musicians asked when he'd gone. "We could use plenty more." "I'm not that hard up," Peer replied. "There's a million song hacks in New York, and if I listened to one, I'd have 'em all pounding on my door."[11]

But "George Brown" had gotten his foot in the door. As a result of his initial success with "Prairie Lullaby" and other rural- and Western-oriented songs, he reverted to his real name—which, by interesting chance, formed a spoonerism of "hillbilly," although the fellow himself was Boston bred and educated at the New England Conservatory of Music. As Billy Hill, his true cognomen, he became rich and famous as the composer of such popular hits as "The Last Roundup," "Wagon Wheels," "Empty Saddles," "Have You Ever Been Lonely?," "The Glory of Love," "In the Chapel in the Moonlight," and dozens more.[12] Ersatz Western as "Prairie Lullaby" may have been, Jimmie Rodgers's recording of it helped popularize a musical genre that was to flourish as staple fare in cowboy films and on records for decades to come.

Just as "Prairie Lullaby" is often slighted for its supposed commercialism, "In the Hills of Tennessee" has been dismissed as the work of "mediocre Tin Pan Alley writers." In fact, composer Sam Lewis had to his credit such hits as "Five Foot Two, Eyes of Blue," "Rock-a-Bye Your Baby with a Dixie Melody," "How Ya Gonna Keep 'Em Down on the Farm," "Dinah," "I'm Sitting on Top of the World," "My Mammy," and a host of others. Admittedly, "Hills of Tennessee" was something of a hurried effort with a minor collaborator, and in recording it, Peer's old yen for diversity led him to back Rodgers with one more hastily assembled "uptown ork." That accompanied performance resulted in another misuse of a self-contained talent whose best work was done solo. Still, with all its handicaps, "In the Hills of Tennessee" survives as an altogether pleasant piece of work, perhaps because the anonymous musicians sent over by the union on the spur of the moment were much better than some of the ones Jimmie had been stuck with. Their performance was, to say the least, professional, faithful to the song's substance and the era's ambience.

The nominal leader was the piano player, who set the tempo for the group, and Peer wisely chose Slim Bryant to work behind Jimmie, to guide him along and protect against the timing errors that so often plagued his efforts to record with accompaniment. Thus Bryant, who'd originally joined Rodgers purely on speculation, became the only one of those who had backed him in Camden to be retained for the New York session. "Jimmie was a little hard to accompany," Bryant said later, modestly understating his own function. "Timing was something he cared little about. He would stick in an extra bar here and there, and you had to watch his every movement to be with him." Predicting just what Rodgers would do, and when, was no easy matter, but in only a short while Bryant had gotten so good at it that he was allowed to work with the union musicians on the basis that, as Peer told them, "he's Jimmie's regular guitar player."[13]

If nothing else, the four sides produced by their joint efforts demonstrate Rodgers's versatility as an entertainer. In Louisville the previous summer he'd hoked it up with the Carter Family, doing the sort of downhome grits-and-gravy routine that would enshrine him as the father of it all in the Country Music Hall of Fame; in New York a year later, without really altering his essential stance, he was as slick and easy as any of the new radio crooners. In fact, Peer had been trying to promote a network radio show for Jimmie, and it may well have been with an audition in mind that he arranged for the "uptown ork." In any event, the distinctive flavor of the performances—polished, upbeat, "modern" in every sense save Jimmie's characteristic yodel— suggests the trend his career might have taken had his health ever permitted him to become a national star. Regardless of the criticisms of redneck purists on one side and academic critics on the other, the recordings which resulted from that brief afternoon session in New York are of substantial merit. All except "Sweet Mama, Hurry Home" sold well at first, and (ironically) this song now seems to be the most enduring, cropping up every now and then. It has been performed on albums such as Leon Redbone's *On the Track* (Warner BS 2888), and a 1975 movie, *Rafferty and the Gold Dust Twins*, featured Jimmie's original recording.

In the two-week interval between the Camden and New York sessions, McMichen, Bryant, and McWinders picked up free-lance work in New York. In addition to playing several vaudeville dates in the city, they managed to contact Bob Miller, prolific composer-arranger ("Twenty-one Years" and hundreds of other hits) and sometime recording director for Columbia. Through Miller they were signed to record some twenty sides for Crown, one of the many independent cut-rate labels then struggling for existence. But the highly touted radio program failed to materialize—Bryant said he never knew anything about it—and Jimmie's ambitious plans to take the group to London for a lengthy personal appearance tour were finally set aside. (Peer had him examined by New York specialists and was told that the singer's ravaged lungs were in no shape to withstand the damp English climate.) Back in Camden, Rodgers had spent most of the time between sessions in bed, though it was during this period that he told McMichen, "I'm not going to lay in one of these hospital rooms and count the fly specks on the wall. I want to die with my shoes on."[14] But however much he might ignore the seriousness of his condition and persist in making fanciful plans, the musicians at last realized that they had little or no future with Rodgers and began to drift away. Oddie McWinders disappeared, so far as is known, into the mists of history; McMichen and Bryant went to Louisville, where Mac reorganized the Georgia Wildcats and got them on the staff of WHAS. Some months later, back in San Antonio, Jimmie Rodgers arose early one winter morning, unable to sleep, and tuned in the distant station. Moved at hearing his old friends again, he wrote Slim Bryant a card: "Sure did make me feel good to hear you. Wasent very clear but I heard the gang singing 'Bury Me on the Lone Prairie.' My kindest Regards to you all. Yo' friend, Jimmie Rodgers."[15]

By late 1932, the institution once known as the Victor Talking Machine Company was no longer the darling of the home entertainment business. As part of a national conglomerate, its status now was more nearly that of a chimney-corner stepchild. If RCA was the wicked stepmother in this corporate version of the Cinderella tale, her namesake, radio, had somehow perversely become the belle of the ball. The phonograph had grown passé, along with buggy whips and high-button shoes. Record sales were practically at a standstill, although hillbilly discs continued to withstand the Depression better than some others: "'Billy Tunes Still Bullish," reported *Variety* in undisguised amazement, noting in particular that Sears, Roebuck's "hick disc" market had tripled since 1930.[16] Mail-order sales would play a major role in sustaining Rodgers's reputation after his death, when Montgomery Ward reissued virtually 90 percent of his recorded repertoire on its own label and sold the recordings in substantial quantities for years. But the initial, faddish rage for new talent from the mountains and hinterlands had passed its apogee. Victor no longer placed a premium on blues singers, balladeers, and string bands—and as their value diminished, so did the demand for the special services of Ralph Peer.

This turn of events was of relatively little consequence to Peer. Although he had profited considerably from his involvement in blues and hillbilly music, he'd never really been satisfied with a business that threw him into the company of house painters, hobos, mountain illiterates, jug blowers, and sickly brakemen. He could take pleasure in the financial rewards of hillbilly music and try to bask in his role as its discoverer, but he never quite came to terms with the fact that his fortune and his place in cultural history rested on the likes of Jimmie Rodgers and the Carter Family. They made money, but they never really gave him the respectability which he coveted.

While Peer was running Victor's field operations involving hillbillies and blacks, he was also angling on his own for the popular market and doing all he could to establish himself as a prestigious music publisher. Rodgers and the Carters were a means of paying the bills while Peer built what he hoped would one day be a substantial general catalog and searched desperately for the one glorious pop hit that would propel him into the ranks dominated by Shapiro-Bernstein, Irving Berlin, DeSylva, Brown and Henderson, Mills Music, M. Witmark, and others. This long-range goal had motivated him, back in 1928, to hand over control of Southern Music to RCA, with the understanding that Victor's A&R department would funnel its pop material into Southern's catalog, whose profits and copyrights Peer continued to share. To his great disappointment, however, the agreement was never really honored; the company's session directors in New York continued to ignore him, and it was largely by chance that he got his few popular tunes—notably Hoagy Carmichael's "Lazy Bones" and several Don Redman numbers, including "Cherry," which McKinney's Cotton Pickers had made into a hit. By 1931 Oberstein was steadily encroaching on Peer's hillbilly and race business, meddling in the selection of material to be recorded, overriding plans for field trips, promoting new artists of his own, and eventually, according to Peer, resorting to various shady tactics to discredit his colleague entirely and force him out. This included spreading the word that he was padding his expense accounts and otherwise cheating the company, Peer later charged.

Apparently few Victor executives believed Oberstein, but the situation caused serious internal problems, eventually reaching the attention of RCA's grand mogul, David Sarnoff. Matters came to a head in September, 1932; anti-trust investigators in the Department of Justice were taking a hard look at the burgeoning growth of certain entertainment conglomerates, and Sarnoff was only too aware that RCA's expansion into records and talking pictures, through the acquisition of Victor and R-K-O, had placed the corporation in jeopardy of violating anti-monoply statutes. "Mr. Sarnoff woke up to the fact that, for example, Southern Music owned copyrights and license agreements," said Peer, "while on the other hand, R-K-O, which he had purchased in the meantime, were buying the synchronizing rights from publishers. In other words, he was on both sides of the fence, and he had heard of the Justice Department in Washington, and was just a little afraid that he shouldn't be on both sides of the fence at the same time. A very astute man, this fella."

Sarnoff's simple and ingenious solution settled both the anti-trust problem and the Peer-Oberstein wrangle in one stroke: he ordered the sale of Southern Music, and saw that it was offered immediately to Ralph Peer. This fit precisely into Peer's plans; furthermore, because he could make a show of doing RCA a favor by taking its unwanted subsidiary and stepping away from the conflict with Oberstein, he got the company for substantially what he'd sold it for in 1928, adjusted downward into Depression dollars ("book value" was Peer's term). Over and above this windfall, Peer received the full value of all copyrights acquired by Southern in the intervening four years. "I've always been sort of thankful to Oberstein," Peer said later. "He really didn't get much out of the deal, because I had all these people [Rodgers, the Carters et al.] signed to me in my original arrangements with Victor, so it all sort of kicked back on him. In fact, I think Victor cancelled one of my notes which I was paying to the company, just because of what Oberstein had done."

As his statement suggests, Peer's connection with Victor did not end when he resumed sole ownership of Southern Music. Working through and around Oberstein, he continued to arrange sessions, select material, and oversee promotion for a number of the artists he'd originally signed—a loose arrangement which actually lasted almost until his death. But the immediate consequence of Sarnoff's shrewd maneuver was to redirect Peer's energies and attention to the music publishing business and away from the day-to-day careers of the people, such as Jimmie Rodgers, whom he'd guided to stardom. Some, like the Carter Family, might have cause for complaint; as Peer himself admitted, "They went off on their own when I didn't do anything for them." But in the case of the Blue Yodeler, it was of little consequence. Everyone knew he was dying.

NOTES

1. In Clayton McMichen's scrapbook, Country Music Foundation, Nashville.

2. Jimmie Rodgers to McMichen, July 27, 1932, in McMichen's scrapbook. See also Shelton and Goldblatt, *Country Music Story,* p. 65.

3. Hoyt "Slim" Bryant to NP, Feb. 28, 1977.

4. See Rust, *Victor Master Book, Vol. 2 (1925–36),* p. 416.

5. "Prohibition Has Done Me Wrong," words and music by Jimmie Rodgers and Clayton McMichen.

6. Brad McCuen's worksheets for *My Time Ain't Long* (RCA LPM 2865), Feb. 11, 1964; McCuen to NP, Mar. 12, 1976.

7. "Whippin' That Old T.B.," words and music by Jimmie Rodgers. © 1933 by Peer International Corporation. Copyright renewed. Used by permission.

8. Hoyt "Slim" Bryant to NP, Feb. 28, 1977.

9. *Ibid.*

10. Confidential source. Also Nat Vincent, interview by Johnny Bond, Aug. 20, 1975, La Crescenta, Calif. (copy in my files); Bond to NP, Oct. 3, 1976. See also Bond, *Recordings of Jimmie Rodgers,* p. 53.

11. Hoyt "Slim" Bryant to NP, Feb. 28 and Mar. 10, 1977.

12. For an account of Billy Hill's career, see *Billboard,* June 10, 1950, p. 41; also Lee Hill Taylor to NP, Jan. 17, 1978.

13. Hoyt "Slim" Bryant to NP, Feb 28, 1977.

14. Clayton McMichen, interview by Bob Shelton, Mar., 1964, Louisville; transcript in the files of the John Edwards Memorial Foundation, UCLA. Also quoted in Shelton and Goldblatt, *Country Music Story,* p. 60.

15. Jimmie Rodgers to Hoyt "Slim" Bryant, Jan. 15, 1933. See *Pittsburgh Press Roto,* Jan. 30, 1977, p. 5.

16. *Variety,* Nov. 8 and 29, 1932, both p. 53; see also *Billboard,* Oct. 3, 1931, p. 20.

18 *Autumn, 1932–May, 1933*

Yodeling My Way Back Home

Unlike Gene Austin, Vernon Dalhart, and dozens of lesser contemporaries, Jimmie Rodgers would not live long enough to outlast
his popularity. Perhaps he was fortunate in this respect. Only one in
thousands—the rare Bing Crosby or Clark Gable or Groucho Marx—is
granted a long and successful life at the top in show business, with
none of the changing fortunes, dips into obscurity, and lamentable
comeback attempts that afflicted the careers of even such stellar lights
as Al Jolson and Judy Garland. The professional lives of country artists
are notoriously enduring, yet it is possible to envision Jimmie Rodgers
as a has-been, fading away from the scene by the late Thirties, little
known to new generations of audiences, perhaps surfacing again
briefly in the wave of nostalgia that gave Austin a very minor second
fling, or being rediscovered along with other oldtimers in the "folk"
craze of the Fifties. At the time of his death, Rodgers's style was still
being copied widely, and his records continued to sell as well as any
others. But, from the standpoint of his immediate professional life, it
now seems clear that by mid-1932, the Blue Yodeler's career had
peaked and begun to dip. Any star attraction can expect a certain
leveling-off of popularity once his initial novelty has worn away, but
in Rodgers's case worsening health had to be a major factor in his
decline. If general business conditions contributed to the situation, he
had certainly fared better than most during the Depression. The
obvious speculations are hard to resist: What if Jimmie had been
healthy? What if there had been no Depression? Perhaps he would
have flourished into old age, securely notched in the public

consciousness somewhere between Bing Crosby and Roy Acuff. But ultimately such predictions are pointless. Whatever the social, economic, or personal reasons, in the late summer of 1932 Jimmie Rodgers was beginning his longest period of inactivity since Bristol, and at the time of his death the following May, the few scattered obituaries mentioned nothing of his career after 1931. The most prominent account pointedly referred to "the height of his career a few years ago."[1]

The strain of the Camden–New York sessions had been excessive; back in Texas to rest and gather his strength once more, Rodgers found recovery slow in coming. Gone were the old jauntiness, the spring in his step, and the yodeling chuckles that once punctuated his conversation. As usual, Jimmie tried his best to keep up a cheery front, but Carrie was struck by how grave and solemn he'd become. "He'd be bedfast for weeks," she wrote of this period. "Then he'd be up. More trouping. Another recording."[2]

Telling the story the way she wanted it to happen, she also added, "And as soon as I could, I'd join him, on such rare occasions as I hadn't accompanied him all the way." This was not her only lapse from reality; there were, in fact, no more recording sessions until the final one, in May of the following year, and precious little touring. But by mid-October, after spending most of the autumn in bed, Jimmie convinced himself that he was feeling well enough to resume occasional live broadcasts over KMAC in San Antonio. What appeared to be renewed energy was probably only the high nervous tension characteristic of tuberculosis in its terminal stages, but Jimmie was on his feet again and that was what mattered most. Carrie viewed it all with a certain equanimity. After nearly a decade of worrying over his health and dreading the worst, she had almost begun to believe that he would, after all, beat the odds. They traveled to Meridian that fall for her parents' golden wedding anniversary, and as usual the old hometown was a tonic for Jimmie's jangled nerves and depression. Revived once more, he returned to San Antonio with still another scheme for booking a vaudeville tour, an old dream that had been shoring him up for several years now.

But if his dream had not faded, vaudeville surely had. By this time even the venerable Palace in New York, a grand bastion of variety theater, had thrown in the towel and gone over to the movies. Out in the hinterlands, the once-flourishing "wheels" of R-K-O, Loew's,

Publix, and even lowly Gus Sun, the scourge of the West, had all but ground to a halt. The scattered dates that Jimmie Rodgers was able to book across the Lone Star State that bleak winter of 1932-33 were nominally "independent vaudeville"—a trade paper euphemism for any nickelodeon or neighborhood house whose manager could be persuaded to book a live act between movies. When Rodgers played Dallas's Joy Theater in January, for example, it was "vaudeville" by only the severest stretch of imagination and vocabulary. The Joy was a ten-and-fifteen-cent burlesque house on Elm Street, at the fringe of the city's notorious "Deep Elem" district of seedy hotels, pawnshops, brothels, and second-hand stores—a long way from the Earle in Washington, or even Loew's State on Canal in New Orleans. But if Jimmie Rodgers felt he had come down in the world, he showed no sign. Instead, he proudly boasted of big business at the box office, and told *Billboard* that entertainers "at liberty" could find plenty of work if they'd get out of New York and look for it.[3]

In East Texas, Jimmie ran across his old friend J. Doug Morgan, who suggested that they team up and try a tour of small towns in the area. Normally Morgan's show would have been off the road and in winter quarters, but business had grown so bad in recent years that he was willing to risk adverse weather and other hazards in search of any income, however meager. He and Jimmie decided that two-night stands might flush out enough business to make a tour worth their while, and, despite frequent rains and chilly temperatures, receipts for the first several weeks were promising.

But Jimmie had ignored the elements and jeopardized his health once too often. While they were playing Lufkin during the second week of February, he collapsed and was rushed to Methodist Hospital in Houston.[4] Fearing the development of pneumonia and further complications, the attending physician placed him in an oxygen tent, ordered round-the-clock nursing care, and refused to allow visitors. Jimmie, chafing over the restraints and longing for a friendly face, got in touch with Mrs. Cora Bedell, a nurse at a small private hospital in Carthage, Texas, where he'd been treated on several earlier occasions when playing that area. Mrs. Bedell, a gregarious, matronly blond whom Jimmie affectionately called "Ole Pleasin'," agreed to come to Houston and replace the special-duty nurse supplied by the hospital. "She was a real professional," said Ray Hall, who met Mrs. Bedell later when she visited him at Huntsville. "She had a lot of experience caring for show business people, especially those with T.B., and she said she only catered to professional people. Jimmie was a real trouper in her eyes. They were quite a pair."[5]

Mrs. Bedell soon had her hands full. The minute he could breathe freely long enough to issue his own orders, Jimmie had insisted that the oxygen tent be taken away, and he quickly found all sorts of ways to defy the no-visitors rule. Soon the floor was alive with old railroad buddies, show business friends, and random will-wishers. He even found a way to smuggle in his Boston bulldog, Mickey, who was adopted as a mascot by the nurses and staff despite the havoc he created. Jimmie himself received much the same treatment, and he reciprocated by playing and singing for the other patients and their visitors whenever he had enough strength.

Billy Burkes went up to see him and found Jimmie in a philosophical mood. "I don't give a damn how much money you got in your pocket," he told Burkes. "If you only got a dollar, and you want a steak, and that steak costs a dollar—buy it."[6] It was an attitude that had changed little from the days when he was an impecunious railroader, spending, loaning, or giving away his weekly paycheck and trusting that luck would see him through. But of course this was more than merely an economic opinion, it was also Jimmie Rodgers's credo: enjoy life while you can, and let the devil take the hindmost.

In March a new President took office, telling the nation that all it had to fear was fear itself. Franklin D. Roosevelt had been elected on his promise of "a new deal for the American people," and after more than three years of deadening Depression, the American people responded with fresh hope and energy. Perhaps this new national spirit affected Jimmie Rodgers, too; it may have somehow restored his faith and given him the will to leave his sickbed one last time and return to the work he had not finished. But even when he'd managed to convince the doctor to release him from the hospital, Jimmie had concerns other than national politics and long-range recovery programs. Time was running out. For him there was no long-range anything, as he knew all too well.

Despite the freewheeling advice he'd given Billy Burkes, by this time Rodgers was worried about the drain on his finances. Money did not mean much to him personally—it never had, really—but now he was increasingly anxious about those he would leave behind, especially twelve-year-old Anita. Said a close family friend, "I think that little girl and his bulldog were the only ones he really loved."[7] Kathryn, his daughter by Stella, was also on his mind; but he had never really known her, and he was confident that she'd be in good hands with her mother, for Stella was a survivor if there ever was one. Carrie, too, would manage; the duplex in San Antonio was paid for, and she could depend on her family for help if it was needed. But he wanted more for Anita, some assurance that she would never suffer the uncertainties of his own childhood, that she would grow up with at least the genteel advantages he'd been able to provide up to that time.

It disturbed him also that life at home had become increasingly hectic and disordered, first by his professional life and now by his worsening health and frequent hospitalizations. Jimmie and Carrie had already felt it best to send Anita off to her grandparents in Meridian to finish the school year, and concern for his daughter's welfare was added to Jimmie's worries over money problems. Just meeting their living costs was an increasing burden; in the long period of inactivity since the previous summer his royalties had hardly been sufficient to pay current household bills, and now medical expenses and other debts were piling up. Mrs. Bedell's services alone cost him fifteen dollars a day plus her expenses, a substantial sum at that time. Assets from his plush years were rapidly being drained away, and there was, of course, no question of life insurance. By the time he'd been able to afford any, no company would issue a policy.

At about this time Jimmie heard from his old friend Billy Terrell, who was in Paducah, Kentucky, gamely trying to make a go of his old rep show route through the Mississippi Valley.[8] Terrell's last three seasons had resulted in heavy losses, and the accumulated debts and continuing poor business were threatening him with bankruptcy. Despite the advanced state of his illness and his own financial worries, Jimmie wired Terrell immediately: "Am coming on fast as this Cadillac can make it. Put in every chair available. Charge 75¢ on front seats, 50¢ reserve, 50¢ concert. Wire when open." Not without misgivings, Terrell followed instructions and on opening night received what he called "the big thrill of my life" when the boss canvasman reported, long before showtime, that the tent was full and "they are lining up and down the sidewalks." Said Terrell later, "Yes, Jimmie sang and pulled me out of a bad place."

Rodgers paid a high price for such selflessness; the medium of exchange was not merely money, but also irreparable damage to his

"America's Blue Yodeler"

JIMMIE RODGERS

EXCLUSIVE VICTOR RECORDING STAR

ENROUTE:

"BLUE YODEL"

SOMTHING ABOUT YOU MAMA THAT SHO GIVES ME THE BLUES.

IT AINT YOUR DROP STITCH STOCKINGS AINT YOUR BLUE BUCKEL SHOES.
HEY HEY HEY
YODEL

YOU KNOW SWEET MAMA IM BOUND TO LOVE YOU SOME. TRUTH HONEY

CAUSE I DONE MORE FOR YOU THAN ANY BODY EVER DONE.
YODEL

GOT ME A PRETTY MAMA GOT ME A BULL DOG TOO.

MY PRETTY MAMA DONT LOVE ME BUT MY BULL DOG DO. SHO HAVE
YODEL

THERES BEEN A GROUND HOG ROOTIN ROUND MY YARD AT NIGHT. HEY HEY

AND FROM THE WAY MY MAMA BEEN TREATING ME HE MUST BE ROOTIN ALR'
LAWD HONEY HE DOS BE ROOTIN ALRIGHT

I AINT NO SHEEK MAN DONT TRY TO VAMP NO GIRL.

ITS MY REGULAR GRINDING GETS ME BY IN THIS WORLD.
YODEL

Recorded in Dallas 2/6/32
accomp Self.

Rodgers's lyric sheet to "Blue Yodel No. 10," recorded simply as another Blue Yodel and later assigned a number in the sequence at the time of release. Discographical notes at the bottom are in Rodgers's hand.

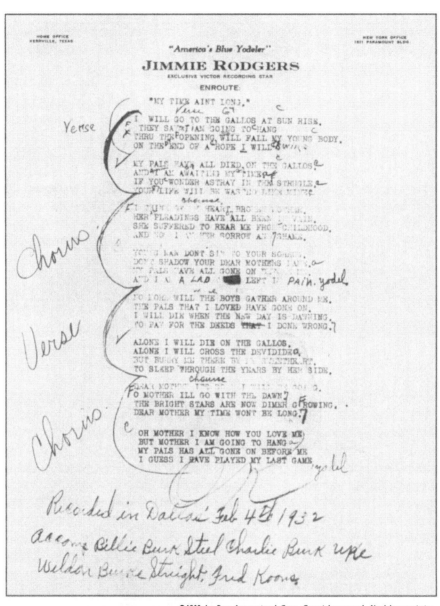

Graphic example of Rodgers's revisions is this lyric sheet for "My Time Ain't Long," showing chord changes, performance notes, and discographical information in Rodgers's hand.

JIMMIE RODGERS

NATIONALLY KNOWN

VICTOR RECORDING AND RADIO ARTIST

WASHINGTON, D. C.

YODELING MY WAY BACK HOME.

(1)

I've Been Away Just A Year, To-day,
But soon I Will Cease To Roam:
And I'm Traveling Along-Doing No Harm,
Yodeling My Way Back Home:

(2)

The Birds Are Singing Up In The Trees,
Their Songs Are For Me Alone;
Listen To Me-I'm Homesick You See,
I'm Yodeling My Way Back Home:

(3)

Folk's That I Love Will All Be There,
Under That Bright Southern Moon;
Soon I'll Be Back-In My Ole Mammy's Shack,
Yodeling For Her This Old Tune:

I've Traveled HERE AND IVE TRAVELED THERE,
Searching For Bluebirds In Vain:
I'm Weary To-Day-So That's Why I Say,
I'm Yodeling Home Again:

Ready 2

Recorded in N.Y. 5/18/33 J.R. Guitar.

Rodgers made these notations on the lyric sheet of "Yodeling My Way Back Home" and sang from this page in the studio scarcely a week before his death. The letterhead is from the Washington, D.C., period five years earlier, indicating that the song had its origins as early as mid-1927. The notation "Ready 2" is unexplained. Possibly the number is merely a check mark, indicating that the song had been satisfactorily rehearsed and approved for recording.

From Blue Yodeler's Paradise, the Rodgers family moved to this comfortable bungalow in the San Antonio suburb of Alamo Heights.

Gaunt and somber, Rodgers posed with Billy Terrell for what is possibly the last photograph taken of America's Blue Yodeler.

Mr. Mickey, Jimmie's favorite bulldog, poses with the master in another of his many cars.

frail and pain-wracked body. Home again in Texas, he went reluctantly to bed, fretting over accumulating debts and his growing inability to reduce them. Before, the chance of some sort of personal appearance had always been in the offing when money ran low, but now all that was simply out of the question. Jimmie no longer tried to appear for even the KMAC broadcasts, which once again had reverted to airing his records.

The Victor contract was about all he had left, and it would be up for renewal in May. There had also been feelers from the American Record Corporation, a cheap-label conglomerate which had taken over Brunswick in 1931 and would eventually absorb Columbia and its subsidiary, Okeh. From his sickbed Rodgers called Peer to discuss the situation and to make preliminary arrangements for the annual recording session, usually planned for midsummer. Without revealing his real concerns to Peer, Jimmie urged him to schedule a session no later than May, under the terms of the current contract, which guaranteed Jimmie an advance payment of $250 for each side recorded. As far as Rodgers was concerned, that was money in the bank. Considering the way business was going, the next contract— whether with Victor or someone else—might not be so liberal. Once he'd recorded a dozen or so sides for Victor and gotten his cash advance, he could decide what future course to take.

Peer later implied that, at the time, Victor had at least a year's supply of Rodgers masters still in its vaults, and therefore was in no particular hurry to record any more. As of April, 1933, there were in fact fourteen unissued sides on the shelf—but twelve had already been passed over for release and, with one or two exceptions, were clearly inferior. (Victor would not hesitate to put them on the market later, though, when all sides from the last session had been issued.) Peer did acknowledge, however, that he'd been receptive to a new session that spring since "there were one or two masters to be remade because of technical defects."[9] As it turned out, none was redone. As far as Jimmie was concerned, the real inducement for holding an early session was the $250 advance. "What he wanted to do was come up to New York and record about ten selections and get $2,500," said Peer. "I couldn't see any objection to it."

That remark, made years later, suggests that Peer was less than enthusiastic about the session but agreed to it largely to accommodate Jimmie. He would also emphasize that Rodgers had assured him he was in good shape for the trip. There is little doubt that, over the phone, Jimmie had painted a less than realistic picture of his condition; but Peer's supposedly casual approach to the session and his repeated insistence that "I didn't realize he was so terribly ill" both run counter to prevailing rumors, some substantiated by close associates of both Peer and Rodgers, to the effect that efforts were being made as far back as the 1932 Camden–New York sessions to stockpile as much Rodgers material as possible before Jimmie died. That both Peer and Victor were grooming various would-be successors (notably Dwight Butcher) is a matter of record. What Peer really *didn't* know, of course, was that Rodgers was sick enough to die almost in the midst of a session. No one—except perhaps Jimmie himself—could know that.

The recording session was scheduled for mid-May, and Rodgers began to make arrangements to sail from Galveston to New York by ocean steamer. The trip was to be a special treat for Mrs. Bedell, who'd agreed to accompany him. In the meantime there had been a windfall of sorts: on March 18, in the wake of Roosevelt's bank holiday and renewed confidence in the national economy, Blue Yodeler's Paradise was finally sold, after almost two years on the market. The buyer, a prominent Kerrville businessman, paid $9,100 for the house, less than half its original cost. Of course these were Depression dollars, with considerable more buying power than those of 1929. Rodgers realized only $3,900 from the sale; the rest was indebted to Ralph Peer in the form of a mortgage, payments on which were assumed by the new owner. Jimmie's share, however, was enough to meet current expenses and bankroll the New York trip. The excess, together with the advances he received for his last session, constituted the bulk of his estate when he died.[10]

The relationship between Jimmie and Carrie at this crucial juncture is largely a matter of speculation. To explain why she did not accompany him to New York, when death was so clearly imminent, Carrie later wrote[11] that she was caring for her older brother, Covert Williamson, who had come to Texas seeking treatment for what she implied was tuberculosis. (It was actually cancer of the throat, from which he died two years later.[12]) Another, more important reason, she said, was "frankly a question of expenses"—they simply couldn't afford her fare and other travel costs. In light of the recent sale of the house, this seems a bit strained, although it is true that ready cash had long been a problem. A persistent, although unverifiable, story among members of the Rodgers family was that she and Jimmie had in fact separated some time earlier; Jimmie reportedly wrote to his brother Talmage from New York, telling Tal that he intended to return to Meridian when the recording session was finished and live whatever was left of his life there, "away from that woman."[13] It seems plausible to assume a complex combination of these circumstances, and to conclude that, while they were no longer really close, Jimmie himself found agreeable reasons to travel without his wife during these last few months, not merely because of any mutual animosity, but also to spare her, if he could, that last grim scene which he knew was imminent.

Jimmie and Mrs. Bedell left Galveston aboard the S. S. *Mohawk* during the second week of May and arrived in New York on May 14. When Rodgers showed up at the offices of Southern Music the next day, Peer was shaken by his haggard appearance and the obviously advanced state of his illness. Accompanying him back to the Hotel Taft (formerly the Manger, Jimmie's customary stopping place), Peer saw to it that the singer went to bed to rest for a day or two before they started recording. He assigned one of his office employees, a young Mexican boy named Castro, as a sort of "go-fer" to help Mrs. Bedell look after Rodgers—"if he needed more whiskey or whatnot," as Peer put it.

Throughout his performing career, beginning with E. T. Cozzens and J. R. Ninde back in February, 1928, one of the continuing paradoxes involved Peer's repeated efforts to record Rodgers with "variegated" accompaniments, despite the fact that it had been Jimmie's singular, highly individual style which first attracted Peer, as well as the record-buying public. Except for a few happy accidents when Jimmie and one or another scratch band somehow picked up on each other—the Louis Armstrong date immediately comes to mind, along with the sides recorded in Atlanta in October, 1928—the Blue Yodeler's strongest, most memorable performances had been solo. Yet for every session after the first two, some motley lot of musicians was assembled to accompany him (although Jimmie invariably found ways to include his own solo cuts along the way). Rodgers had sanguinely accepted it all, sometimes even rounding up the musicians himself, at Peer's behest and in the interest of selling records. But he was never completely at ease with a back-up group; at best it was a discomfort, at worst a severe strain. Moreover, it cost money. Now, with everyone's finances badly stretched, that consideration probably weighed most

heavily in Peer and Rodgers's ironically fortuitous decision to dispense
with accompaniment for the current sessions. On that final, weary day
they would have to call in some help; but how very poignant and fitting
that Jimmie Rodgers should make his last records as he had his first
and exit as he'd begun, alone before the microphone, just "me and my
old guitar."

Whatever the circumstances that determined he should go it alone,
Jimmie's solo performances are the singular strength and special
distinction of these last sessions, which began on Wednesday, May 17,
in Victor's studios at 153 East 24th Street. All the old flair was there,
the heady energy, the familiar yodel, the bright, solid guitar work with
its incessant little noodles, eccentric chords, and unorthodox runs:
listen to "Barefoot Blues" (released as "Blue Yodel No. 12") or the
driving introduction to "Cow Hand's Last Ride." Even such kitsch as
"Dreaming with Tears in My Eyes" and "I'm Free from the Chain
Gang Now" is redeemed by the unique fusion of instrument and voice
that was Rodgers's particular genius.

In two days of long, strenuous labor in the studio, he recorded six
numbers, topped off by the tragically ironic "Yodeling My Way Back
Home" and "Women Make a Fool out of Me," fated to be retitled by
Oberstein and released as "Jimmie Rodgers' Last Blue Yodel." Those
six were half of the sides he'd planned to make, and while a casual
listener might be unable to distinguish the quality of his voice from that
on his earliest discs, the strain was beginning to tell. On a couple of
takes he'd barely been able to disguise the rasp, turning it to advantage
on one raw, bluesy line ("she's never coming home")[14] of "Barefoot
Blues" and altering the yodel more and more to hold the range. The
miracle was that Rodgers was able to perform at all; his lungs were
literally in shreds and racked with pain beyond all relief, the rest of his
body sedated almost into a stupor in a desperate gamble to stay alive
until his work was done. At the end of the second day, during which he
tried to recuperate by alternating in the studio with Bert Lown's
Orchestra, Jimmie was so weak he had to be carried to a cab.

Somehow both Peer and Oberstein found themselves busy with
other matters at this rather crucial time. Perhaps they both merely
experienced the instinctive human desire to shun the presence of death;
but, for whatever reasons, supervision of the sessions had been given
over to Fred Maisch, a Victor underling.[15] More than a little disturbed
by Rodgers's condition, Maisch got in touch with Bob Gilmore, Peer's

assistant, and explained the situation, urging that further sessions be postponed. When Gilmore phoned Rodgers at his hotel, however, Jimmie assured him that he'd be fine after a day's rest and asked that the Saturday session be held as planned. Gilmore acquiesced and Jimmie, true to his word, managed to show up in the afternoon to record "The Yodeling Ranger" and "Old Pal of My Heart," even though he was so weak that he had to be given an easy chair and propped up with pillows before the microphone. When the session ended, Gilmore vetoed the idea of continuing on Monday and insisted that Jimmie take a few days off before they tried to resume.

Restless and impatient despite his illness, Jimmie agreed only reluctantly. Gilmore suggested that he leave town for a day or two, and Rodgers decided that a short trip into New England might do him good. There he could also do some additional work on the material he and Peer had lined up to finish the twelve sides they'd agreed on.

The bulk of this material had come from other songwriters, for by now Jimmie's own resources, always meager and spotty, were truly depleted. He had no energy for the task anyway. Because of the music business's time-honored practice of the cut-in, Rodgers received composer credit, in whole or in part, for ten of the twelve numbers recorded during the last session; but in fact he was only minimally involved in composing even the three songs for which he received sole credit. Although Jack Neville's name appeared on "Mississippi Delta Blues," it was scratched from the lyric sheets of "Barefoot Blues"; similarly, someone named Arza Hitt was largely responsible for "Cow Hand's Last Ride" but received credit only on the original-issue labels. "Dreaming with Tears in My Eyes" originated with Waldo O'Neal, and Ray Hall had written "The Yodeling Ranger" back in 1931 on the occasion of Jimmie's honorary induction into the Texas Rangers. Hall and others contributed verses to the Blue Yodel (thirteenth and last in the series) which Jimmie knew as "Women Make a Fool out of Me." Elsie McWilliams undoubtedly had a hand in "Yodeling My Way Back Home," for Rodgers had been working on it since his Washington days, when extra verses began to evolve out of "Brakeman's Blues" (originally subtitled "Yodeling the Blues Away"). "Old Pal of My Heart," a successful imitation of "My Old Pal," came from John B. Mason, another amateur source like O'Neal, Hitt, Hall, and Walter Ryan, who helped compose "Somewhere Down below the Dixon Line."

The non-professionals who wrote for Jimmie generally served him better than Peer's Tin Pan Alley hacks, old steady tigers like Lou Herscher, a Philadelphia tunesmith who was responsible, along with Peer's song plugger, Saul Klein, for "I'm Free from the Chain Gang Now" and "Years Ago."[16] Herscher was also called in to doctor "Old Love Letters" by Dwight Butcher, the young Tennessean who was being touted by Peer and Victor as Rodgers's possible successor.

After a few days on Cape Cod, Jimmie returned to New York and called Peer's office to schedule the final four sides. However, Peer was in Camden, where (among other matters) he was negotiating a new contract for Rodgers. Bob Gilmore made the arrangements in Peer's stead, scheduling studio time for the afternoon of Wednesday, May 24. He also suggested that they hire a musician or two to accompany Jimmie and spare him as much exertion as possible. Two old hands, John Cali and Tony Colicchio, were summoned. Both had "jobbed around" in recording studios for years; between them they had recorded with literally hundreds of artists, good, bad, and indifferent, ranging from Ben Selvin's Novelty Orchestra and Bailey's Lucky Seven to Bix Beiderbecke, Red Nichols, and the Dorsey brothers. Cali had even worked with Vernon Dalhart in his heyday.

Cali and Colicchio met with Jimmie in a rehearsal hall that morning to go over the material. A cot was set up there, so that Rodgers could rest from time to time, but as usual he was impatient with any special attention. When it came time to record, he insisted on standing before the mike as if everything were normal.

One of the more appealing legends surrounding this session, a story blandly perpetuated by Dwight Butcher, has it that "Old Love Letters" was the last song Jimmie Rodgers recorded. To be sure, it is the best of the love ballads that he did, a rich and elegant melody hauntingly accented by Cali's steel guitar. Jimmie's heartfelt rendition is touched with just enough strain and barely concealed physical anguish to make it an appropriate *memento mori* for those who seek some morbid, dramatic significance in a dying man's last words. Much as we might like to believe that he made his professional exit on that note, however, the master numbers indicate that "Old Love Letters" was not the last but the first of four sides to be recorded that day.

The song which followed, "Mississippi Delta Blues," might have been an even more fitting finale, combining as it does so many elements intrinsic to the phenomenon that was Jimmie Rodgers—slick stage-work rooted in an earthy reality, sentimentality that is nevertheless an expression of genuine emotion, the bluesy sadness that grows lighthearted in its rendering. By whatever measure, "Mississippi Delta Blues" ranks with the best of Rodgers's work, and there is an even greater (if perhaps melodramatic) reason for wishing it were his final effort: on the lyric sheet he has written, "hold till last." But again, the master numbers must be heeded. "Last" meant merely "later on, near the end." The order in which he approached his material in the studio never mattered much to Jimmie, passing as he did from the best to the worst and back again. It would be reaching too far to suppose that now, only because he knew the end was near, he would deliberately concern himself with what number would be "last," any more than he would be responsible, as some wanted to believe, for such a clearly morbid and theatrical title as "Jimmie Rodgers' Last Blue Yodel." For all the heightened aura that occasion may now have, there was precious little self-conscious drama in those final, desperate hours at the microphone—he was far too sick and benumbed for that. To attempt to find some deliberate pattern or intent in the order in which the last songs were recorded is to forget that the gentle but disputatious art of discography was yet to flower. As far as those in the recording business were concerned, all that mattered was what issued from the stamping machines. Interest in sequence of recording, take numbers, variants, and even the identities of the accompanying musicians was inconsequential, if not completely nil.

As the day wore on, Jimmie began to tire. After three straight hours in the studio that afternoon, he was forced to rest on the cot that had been set up in the rehearsal hall. When he felt strong enough to continue, Cali and Colicchio joined him for "Somewhere Down below the Dixon Line," a pleasant but tragically prophetic tune in which Jimmie bids goodbye to the icy Northland and anticipates the journey back to his beloved South, "where warm, warm breezes blow."[17] At 4:45 they'd done the customary two takes to everyone's satisfaction, and the musicians were dismissed. Jimmie rested a few minutes on his cot again, and then came back to the studio alone to do one more side, a rather feeble and synthetic convict ditty by Herscher and Klein. "Years Ago" did not provide an especially distinguished end to the Blue Yodeler's recording career, but, appropriately enough, he did it alone, just as he'd begun, and when it was over, he was still on his feet and able to walk to the waiting cab.

That night Rodgers slept fitfully, but he awoke the next morning in good spirits. With the recording session completed, he planned to stay on in New York a few days to rest up and treat himself to whatever fun he could manage. That included at least one more trip to Coney Island; still a boy at heart, he loved the carnival atmosphere and preferred an afternoon there over anything else the city had to offer. After that there was some shopping to be done, for gifts for Anita and other family members; then he and Mrs. Bedell would take the train down to Washington, stopping over for a day or so with the Nelsons before going on to Meridian. In fact, Alex Nelson had come up to New York earlier in the week to drive them down, but the schedule had gotten mixed up as a result of the delays caused by Jimmie's illness, and Nelson's brother, who'd accompanied him on the trip, was anxious to get back to Washington. Jimmie assured them that he'd rather travel by train anyway, but he persuaded Nelson and his brother to stay one more day and go with him to Coney Island.

Accompanied by Mrs. Bedell and chauffeured by Peer's man Castro in a rented car, they drove out through Brooklyn. (The vaunted Dodgers were in Cincinnati that afternoon, losing 4-1 and dropping into seventh place in the National League.) Most of the day was spent on the beach. Lunch was hot dogs and newly legalized 3.2 beer, after which Jimmie dozed in the fine spring sun. Showers forecast for the afternoon did not materialize, and on the way back Jimmie was feeling so good that he stopped the car several blocks from the hotel and got out for a walk, accompanied by Alex Nelson. After only a short distance he suddenly sagged and had to be helped over to a fire hydrant, where he sat for several minutes until his vision cleared and he could breathe easily. "Let me take a blow," he told Nelson, wheezing for air.

Back at the hotel he went to bed immediately, but there was nothing out of the ordinary about that. Alex Nelson left to return to Washington, sure that he'd see Jimmie there in a few days. Castro, who'd left the desk clerk a number where he could be reached, also went home for the night, after giving Jimmie an alcohol rubdown to ease his now constant fever.

On her way back from a late dinner alone in the dining room, Mrs. Bedell stopped outside Jimmie's room and heard him coughing. The unusually severe spasm lasted half an hour or more, and before it was over he'd begun to hemorrhage. Mrs. Bedell was not particularly alarmed, however, for that had happened many times before; when the bleeding appeared to stop after a time, she thought no more about it. Then, just before midnight, the deep, spasmodic coughing began again, and this time the hemorrhaging came in bright, violent surges. The house physician could not be located immediately; Castro was called but arrived too late to do anything but stand by and watch. Mercifully, the inevitable end came soon, in the early hours of Friday morning. Slipping into a coma, Rodgers simply drowned in his own blood.

The final trip south to his homeland was made aboard one of the mighty trains Jimmie Rodgers loved so well. A special baggage car was added to the Southern's Washington–New Orleans run, and the casket, covered in lilies, rode on a raised platform in the center. Many of the train's crew were old friends and acquaintances; Engineer Homer Jenkins had known Jimmie and Carrie since their courting days and would serve as pallbearer at the funeral, along with J. M. Martin and R. J. Strobel, whose names had appeared on the callboard with Jimmie's in his only movie.

Hundreds gathered around Meridian's Union Station in the darkening summer night to meet the train and pay their respects, many of them weeping openly. From far away they heard the low, funereal moan of the engine's whistle, the sound that had been so much a part of Jimmie Rodgers's life and music. He'd had a special love for the train whistle, so special that he'd learned to imitate it on his records. Now it sounded a fitting requiem, building to a long, high wail as the train rumbled slowly into the station and rolled to a halt. When at last Homer Jenkins stepped from the cab into the throng that crowded near, he carried in his hand the framed portrait that Jimmie had autographed for him, a picture of the Singing Brakeman in his railroad garb, giving the jaunty "thumbs up" signal. A universal sign of good fortune and a job well done, the gesture is used by brakies to tell the engineer to start the train and "go ahead, everything's okay." As Homer Jenkins watched the pearl-grey coffin carried from the baggage car, he was reminded of still another meaning. In its older, original use, the railroader's "thumbs up" signified simply, My work's all done.

Jimmie Rodgers had not quite literally died alone, but it was very much the same thing. To his family and friends, his death had been imminent for years, yet all of them were far away when the time came.

Ralph Peer, the man who through chance and acuity had made Rodgers's career possible, was in Camden, attending to business. Reached by phone, he is said to have told Castro to keep the news of Jimmie's death quiet until he could conclude the new contract with Victor, calling for increased royalties on reissues and containing a clause prohibiting the company from disposing of any Rodgers masters.[18]

As for the public, they might mourn the Blue Yodeler briefly when word of his passing finally went out across the land, but other, more momentous events filled the news those days. In the East, where he'd died, business and politics dominated the headlines. Almost daily the new President announced major steps to revive the economy; that week he'd moved to repeal the gold standard, and stock prices shot up to their highest level in more than two years. Wall Street and the *New York Times* followed closely the Senate's investigation of J. P. Morgan & Co. for alleged shenanigans in international financing, while Americans of more modest means—those in breadlines, for example—may have taken wry interest in the news that Mahatma Gandhi was ending another lengthy fast in protest against British policies in India. The Japanese were settling down in Manchuria and threatening to take over Ch'eng-te as well. Closer home, 1,200 American clergymen signed a protest against something called "Hitlerism" in Germany. In Manhattan, Duke Ellington's Cotton Club Review of 1933 moved from Harlem and into the big time at the Capitol Theater; out in Chicago the World's Fair opened. Little wonder that, in the city where he died, news of the passing of Jimmie Rodgers, "a singer of 'hillbilly' songs," was relegated to a few lines of type in the back pages of the *Times* and the *Herald-Tribune*.[19] All his life Jimmie Rodgers had fretted over bill-printers and reporters who misspelled his name; in its two-paragraph obituary on page 13, the *Times* committed the error twice, and referred to him as "a radio singer." That description was a sign of the times. Nobody listened to phonograph records anymore, and a "radio singer" who never starred on New York's WEAF or any of the networks could hardly expect serious attention from some bored copyeditor on the *Times* obit desk.

In lesser metropolises like Memphis and Dallas the reaction was much the same. There, instead of government and high finance, the standard front-page fare had always been sex and violence—rapes, kidnappings, lynchings, plane crashes, and the more sordid divorce cases. Now Roosevelt's farm bill and the establishment of a government agency to insure bank deposits were capturing headlines, leaving little space to mark the demise of a frail, tubercular ex-brakeman-turned-singer. Even in San Antonio, in the area where he'd lived for most of his professional life, the story ran "inside," on page 2. It was a long and sympathetic account, however, plaintively noting that "at the height of his fame a few years ago, [he] was one of the foremost entertainers in the United States."[20] Hours after his death on May 26, KMAC broadcast its regular program of "Jimmie Rodgers Records" as usual, but by the following week the line in the log for that time slot had been reset to read simply "Records."

The trade papers gave his passing scant attention. In *Billboard*, where his name had appeared so often over the years, there was only a brief, impersonal notice in "The Final Curtain," the paper's alphabetized list of show business obits. *Variety*, which had practically ignored him in his heyday, was actually more generous, but both items were obviously culled from the metropolitan papers.[21]

Only in Meridian and Kerrville did Rodgers make the front page—and in towns their size, of course, almost everything made the front page. All day Monday, May 29, his body lay in state in the Scottish Rite Cathedral while lines of mourners filed through. At four o'clock that afternoon, accompanied by an escort from the Hamasa Temple Shrine, Scottish Rite Masons, and Knights of Pythias Lodge, he was moved to the Central Methodist Church for funeral services and then taken to nearby Oak Grove Cemetery in quiet little Bonita, to be buried beside his baby daughter, June, on a gentle knoll looking across the pine-shaded hills.[22]

Out in Wewoka, Oklahoma, Stella Kelly learned of his death only that evening. In her small house on Seminole Avenue she sat through the night, playing his records over and over. "It was not at all like me to do something like that," she said. "But I was awfully upset. It seemed like he was there in the room."

NOTES

1. *San Antonio Light*, May 26, 1933, p. 2A.
2. *MHJR*, p. 281.
3. *Billboard*, Jan. 28, 1933, p. 20.
4. *Ibid.*, Feb. 4, 18, and 25, 1933, all p. 20.
5. Interview, Mar. 12, 1975, Texas State Penitentiary, Huntsville; Hall to NP, Apr. 29, 1975; also Bennie Hess, interview, June 3, 1976, Nashville.

6. Billy Burkes, interview by Jim Griffith, Mar. 11, 1976.

7. Confidential source.

8. *America's Blue Yodeler*, 2:2 (Spring, 1954), 3. Although this is the accepted chronology, Terrell only implies that the incident occurred at this time. His account does not agree with other events of that period. It is my strong belief that it took place the previous spring or fall, but an extensive search of newspapers and other documents in Paducah has failed to produce any record of Terrell's or Rodgers's appearance there in either 1932 or 1933. Lacking tangible evidence to the contrary, I have followed the standard sequence.

9. *Meridian Star*, May 26, 1953, p. 24.

10. For details of the sale of Blue Yodeler's Paradise, see *Deed Records of Kerr County, Texas*, 55:378. See also *Billboard*, Apr. 8, 1933. When Rodgers's will was probated in June, 1933, his estate was valued at approximately $4,000. This consisted mainly of postal savings deposits of $1,500 and cash in a lock box at the Gunter Hotel, San Antonio. The family residence was valued at $2,500, and he also owned two lots in Meridian valued at $2,000, but these were encumbered by a deed of trust for $2,500. Not considered, of course, was the estate's most valuable asset: Rodgers's copyrights and royalty contracts, which Peer later said (in the Borgeson interviews) "will turn in two or three thousand dollars a year, no matter what happens"—almost indefinitely, it seems. The probate documents further reveal the range and extent of Rodgers's generosity with friends and relatives. Owed to the estate were some thirteen personal notes, ranging from a few dollars to Paul English's $1,200, and totaling almost $2,000. According to the probate officer, "The above notes were given Deceased by theatrical people, with the exception of one or two loans. These people are hard to locate and the value of the notes to the estate are nominal" (*Will Book of Lauderdale County, Mississippi*, 6:471).

11. *MHJR*, p. 252.

12. Elsie McWilliams, interview, Jan. 7, 1975, Meridian.

13. Confidential sources.

14. "Blue Yodel No. 12," words and music by Jimmie Rodgers. © 1933 by Peer International Corporation. Copyright renewed. Used by permission.

15. See liner notes to *When Evening Shadows Fall* (RCA LSP 4073e).

16. Klein had co-authored "Make My Cot Where the Cot-Cot-Cotton Grows," one of the more popular of dozens of "stutter" songs that flourished in the Twenties (*Billboard*, Oct. 22, 1927, p. 23). Herscher, who'd been around for years, was best known for "Dream Daddy" (1923), touted as "Radio's First Popular Song Hit." For a profile, see *Billboard*, Feb. 25, 1928, p. 20; also Oct. 29, 1927, p. 24.

17. "Somewhere Down below the Dixon Line," words and music by Jimmie Rodgers and Walter Ryan. © 1934 by Peer International Corporation. Copyright renewed. Used by permission.

18. Nat Vincent, interview by Johnny Bond, Aug. 20, 1975, La Crescenta, Calif.; Bond to NP, Oct. 3, 1976.

19. *New York Times*, May 27, 1933, p. 13; *New York Herald-Tribune*, May 27, 1933, p. 15.

20. *San Antonio Light*, May 26, 1933, p. 2A.

21. See *Billboard*, June 3, 1933, p. 52; *Variety*, May 30, 1933, p. 62.

22. *Kerrville Mountain Sun*, June 1, 1933, p. 1; *Meridian Star*, May 26, 1933, p. 1; May 28, 1933, p. 3; May 29, 1933, p. 1.

19

Endings, and Beginnings

I gleaned the barebones facts of Jimmie Rodgers's life from census reports and deed records and obligatory interviews with the few people still living who knew him. I read Confederate Army rolls in the National Archives to find his grandfathers, and I sat at the big round kitchen table in the home of Mr. and Mrs. M. G. Harvey in Meridian, sipping good strong Southern coffee while Mr. Harvey told me about old days on the railroads—he retired off the "Queen" after thirty years—and Mrs. Harvey showed me the courting letters of Rodgers's mother and father and told me stories about her Cousin Jimmie, stories she heard from the aunt who raised them both, twenty years apart. I prowled the woods around Pine Springs, Mississippi, and found Jimmie's mother's grave in a tiny, neglected cemetery, and in the early summer heat I followed a rutted dirt road up a wooded lane to an old-fashioned country house, cool and open and immaculate beneath a grove of cottonwoods, where Mrs. Pearl Bozeman Harris, another cousin, hushed the yard dogs and took me into her parlor and cautioned me lovingly against cigarettes and hard drink and told me, full of laughter, how little Jimmie had taken to smoking and wearing his shirttail out, and had stolen a bale of cotton from his uncle when "he still wasn't more'n a tad, not biggern a minute." I scanned old print in fragile bindings in the cluttered backshops of newspapers, and squinted at microfilm in dozens of hushed libraries. I flew to both coasts, drove six thousand miles tracing Rodgers's itineraries through the South and Southwest, hung out in Nashville, talked to broken-down musicians, lit-up ladies, and sweet old folks aged fourteen to eighty-one. I read and pondered, and listened to all of Rodgers's records time and again, records that I have been hearing since I was ten and already knew every word and note and inflection of. I gave up trying to explain the object of my quest to foreigners, Yankees, youthful aesthetes, and folklorists; but before that I had some pleasant surprises, like the twenty-three-year-old socialite from Ohio who, quicker than I could reluctantly launch into my father-of-country-music routine, yodeled up the original "T.B. Blues" in its entirety. I filled desk drawers, file cabinets, manila envelopes, and index folders with clever, incisive notes gleaned from the whole of Western knowledge, scribbled down in brilliant sentences on desk pads, bar napkins, check stubs, Kleenex boxes, any loose and pocketable writing surface, even note cards occasionally, sat up long, empty nights trying to figure them out, tuck them in somewhere, nurtured and preserved, shuffling them over and over like so many tattered, misshapen Tarot cards. They are still around somewhere, unused and useless, in the bottom of a closet or wedged behind the file cabinet. I endured the good-natured gibes of friends and colleagues, and a music professor who inquired, with treacherous warmth, how I intended to write about a hillbilly singer "*qua* musician." To which I replied, limply seeking a soft answer that would turn away wrath, "Oh, I don't think anyone ever accused Jimmie Rodgers of being a musician," and then hated myself for days.

Put down like this, it all begins to sound a bit unhealthy, tinged with the faint whiff of fanaticism. True, I had my private stake in it, my own sweet demons and fevers, my own harbored love; but it was curiosity as much as obsession that kept me going, a simple wish to clear the muddle of myth and rumor, the pleasures of research, pure pedantry, and worst of all just the old Puritan ethic. It went on over a period of years, hit and miss, and in between I took out the garbage and went to see Willie Nelson and watched the paint peel off the back fence. Surely all but the most crazed and voracious biographers sometimes grow tired of their subjects, and there were days when I felt engorged, like a fat-livered goose, and was grateful for diversion.

But mostly I suffered it gladly, sometimes ecstatically, because I knew that out of all the musty records and hours of interviews and crazy, endless note-scribbling I would finally be able to distill some pithy, trenchant conclusion and at last explain, if only to myself, the grand phenomenon that was Jimmie Rodgers.

I was wrong, of course. When it was time for an end, I was still writing beginnings.

The thirty-five years, eight months, and eighteen days of Jimmie Rodgers's life covered a period of vast social and cultural change—greater, perhaps, than in any other such era in our history. In the entertainment world, his life spanned the rise of the phonograph, the flowering of motion pictures and radio, the decline and fall of live entertainment in the United States. More than any other entertainer, Rodgers was actively involved in all of it from the grass-roots level to the big time, and for a while it seemed that he was destined to be the first truly national superstar. Fate, in the form of a deadly disease and the Great Depression, was against him, but he faced that doom with gallant spirit and moving grace. There is as much inspiration in the way he lived and died as in the enduring music he created.

Once Rodgers was dead, it was only natural that his presence in the national consciousness should begin to wane. A plethora of "tribute" songs helped keep his name alive for a time, at least among the faithful, and Victor continued its Rodgers releases throughout 1933, sometimes rushing out two in one month. Then, after December, they stopped, and no records were released in all of 1934. The following year, however, Carrie Rodgers wrote and privately published her romanticized but endearing "biography," *My Husband, Jimmie Rodgers*, and with record sales reviving in the general economic upswing, his previously unreleased material began to appear again, at the urging of Peer-Southern. Two new records were issued in 1935, one in 1936, three in 1937. The last appeared in May, 1938, on the fifth anniversary of his death. As late as 1936, the Victor catalog still carried twenty-two Rodgers titles in their original pairings, and many others were being reissued on the Bluebird and Montgomery Ward labels throughout the late Thirties. By 1941 Jimmie's listing in Victor's catalog had shrunk to one record (unaccountably, it was "Blue Yodel No. 6"/"Yodeling Cowboy"), and soon even that was deleted. The coming of the war sent some enterprising executive into the archives for a reissue of "The Soldier's Sweetheart" paired with "The Sailor's Plea," and for several years that poor moldy fig bore alone the burden of sustaining whatever image of the Blue Yodeler that remained among a new generation to whom his former glory was only a dim memory. A decade and more after his death, it seemed that the story of Jimmie Rodgers was a quietly closing chapter in the history of popular entertainment. Not even Valentino's rabid fans and swooning soulmates had remained faithful that long.

But the story was only beginning. No one who had been touched by his spell ever forgot, and out among the hard core, time's passing only burnished and deepened the enthrallment. In the late Forties and early Fifties, Victor reissued some of his 78's in three-record sets for what they considered a rather limited market. With little promotion, the albums sold steadily if unspectacularly. Then in 1956, again nudged by Peer, the company cautiously put together a long-playing album of what they considered the best sides, gingerly releasing it as a one-shot deal. A year later sales were still climbing, and a second LP went into the works. By 1960 sales had surpassed 60,000 copies and were still building. That prompted still a third album. By this time Rodgers's stature as a pioneer in the field was clearly reestablished, and his induction into the newly formed Country Music Hall of Fame—the first performer to be so honored—was occasion for another album of reissues. By August, 1962, *Country Music Hall of Fame* (RCA LPM-2531) was in second place on the C&W charts, and *Jimmie the Kid* (RCA LPM-2213), issued the previous year, was still moving along in fourth position, in a league with Ray Charles, Jim Reeves, Marty Robbins, George Jones, and Hank Williams. Such popularity was nothing short of phenomenal for an oldtimer in competition with the new world of Nashville. Each year from 1960 to 1964 saw the release of a new Jimmie Rodgers album, until RCA had at last mined everything from the lode—and then, in accord with the usual grubby practice, the company began to reissue the reissues, in ever-changing formats and combinations.[1]

During this time published commentary on the Blue Yodeler remained largely in the hands of liner-note hacks and idolatrous but uninformed fans mostly concerned with promoting Rodgers's candidacy for sainthood and proving that he was better/richer/more famous than Elvis Presley/the Beatles/Bing Crosby or some other supposed paragon. Until recently, serious scholars and cultural historians largely ignored him or, on those rare occasions when they deigned to take notice, managed to slight him in petty ways. In *The Country Blues*, a pioneering and otherwise eloquent study, Samuel Charters identified him only as "Jimmy Rogers, a railroad brakeman living in Nashville" who recorded "dozens of blues that he'd heard in the mountains."[2] (In the sole other reference to Rodgers, Charters confused him with the black guitarist of the same name.) Ironically, one effect of Jimmie's growing popularity in the Sixties and Seventies has been to produce a sort of weary blacklash amid the cliques of oldtime music enthusiasts, who tend to recognize and dismiss him in the same fell swoop.[3] Much of this, one detects, is because he had the effrontery to sing the blues—which, as everyone knows, is not white man's music.

A serious attempt to deal realistically and forthrightly with Rodgers appeared in Goldblatt and Shelton's *Country Music Story*. In *Country Music, U.S.A.: A Fifty-Year History*, now considered a standard reference, Bill Malone correctly assessed Rodgers's impact on the entertainment world, asserting that "one would be hard pressed to find a performer in the whole field of 'pop' music—whether it be Al Jolson, Bing Crosby, or Frank Sinatra—who has exerted a more profound and recognizable influence on later generations of entertainers."[4] Hank Snow and Ernest Tubb put it in specific terms: "He made it possible for cowboy or country singers to get employment on radio stations. He was responsible for the sale of more guitars than any other man. He made the value of country songs and records into a commercial product that since then has been recognized as an important part of the music industry. He made it possible for hillbilly entertainers to play theatres and first rate entertainment places."[5]

The basis for his popularity was simply Rodgers's broad appeal to so many diverse audiences, and no one has written of this more perceptively or eloquently than his wife:

> Family groups delighted in his sentimental ballads. The poverty-stricken, gripped by sickness and troubles almost more than they could endure, knew that here was a fellow who understood; who had "been there." Far, lonely cabins on western plains, on the high ranges, in distant forests; isolated dwellers in such places knew that this boy knew them too. Railroad men and their families thrilled to his songs of the silver rails. Army men—hard-boiled, grim-faced he-men—scoff and wisecrack though they might . . . sailors and their sweethearts . . . even the "rowdies" in poolrooms and barrooms—yes, he knew them, too.
>
> He talked the language of them all. Sweethearts—mothers—fathers—hobos—husbands and wives—even cops! For each some gift of cheer, of sympathy, of broad or tender humor. Jimmie Rodgers reached them every one with his sobbing, lonesome yodels; held them with his whimsy, his deliberate audacity.[6]

But these were audiences of his own time and place. What of his continued popularity today, in a vastly altered world? What of the English and Australian fan clubs, the deluxe boxed LPs in Japan, the stack of Rodgers 78's in an Eskimo hut in Point Barrow, the Kipsigis' fertility dance? What of me, and my lifelong, bumbling, inexplicable love for Jimmie Rodgers and his music?

The source was intrinsic to the man himself. It defies scholarly imperatives, categories, musicology, social science, footnotes, carefully hewn lists of origins, analogs, and influences. Jimmie Rodgers transcended past and future referents, crossed immense cultural barriers, touched the lives of millions who shared with him nothing more than their basic humanity.

Given the nature of the arts and "culture" in this country, it may have been easier to reach the Kipsigis than some people closer to home. No one suffered the stratification more than Ralph Peer, and if he never quite prevailed against it, it is to his credit that he developed larger sympathies and a truer vision. I have touched on the biases, unwitting and otherwise, of music professors and the scholarly establishment at large. Henry Pleasants's experience, recounted in *The Great American Popular Singers*, is a telling one, all the more poignant because Pleasants writes about Rodgers with unabashed affection and understanding, and with more intelligence than anyone I have read. A professional musician trained at Philadelphia's Curtis Institute, an expert on opera who describes himself as "classically educated and European-oriented," Pleasants confesses his early contempt for country music ("and I probably called it 'hillbilly'") as being "beyond the pale"; he then relates how a chance encounter with a Jimmie Rodgers album changed all that. "I took it home," he writes, "put it on the turntable and—as one says nowadays—flipped! . . . Here was a white country boy singing a classical twelve-bar blues. But where a black bluesman would have been interposing a blues riff on the guitar between verses, Jimmie Rodgers was yodeling! And how he yodeled! I had heard plenty of yodeling during tours of duty with the Army and the Foreign Service in Switzerland, Bavaria and Austria, but never anything quite like this. It was sweeter than any yodeling I had ever heard, more melodious, wider in range—a true falsetto extending upward to the E flat above high C—more accurate in pitch, more imaginative in its figuration, and somehow compellingly and uniquely plaintive."

"Wistful," he decides, is a better word than "plaintive": "I am reminded of how many other great singers have expressed that same sense of loneliness and vulnerability: Judy Garland, Billie Holiday, Edith Piaf, Frank Sinatra, Hank Williams." Noting the limitations of Rodgers's voice, Pleasants makes the simple, obvious point: "Well, great voices do not great singers make. Great singers are made by what musically creative men and women do with the voices God gave them."[7]

Hundreds of stories attest to what Jimmie Rodgers did with his voice, but the one that is most vivid to me is the short, simple one that Dick Furman in Kerrville told me about his father's death. Not long ago, more than forty years after he'd rambled the Texas Hill Country with Jimmie Rodgers, fishing and hoorawing and sipping drugstore bourbon, John Furman lay dying, alert but speechless, immobile, all but his right hand paralyzed from a massive stroke. By a system of squeezes with the one good hand, he made it known that he wanted to hear music from the phonograph. Said Dick Furman, "Of course I knew that meant Jimmie's records. I asked him, and he said yes. While the record played, he closed his eyes and died, squeezing my hand in time to the music."

NOTES

1. Had there ever been any long-range plan or commitment to the project, the corpus of Rodgers's work might have been shaped into an imposing and valuable uniform set—as with the fine Japanese Victor issue of 1973 (RCA [Japan] RA 5459-66). Instead, RCA depended on each album to prove its marketability before going ahead with the next one.

2. See Charters, *Country Blues*, pp. 153–54, 169.

3. Typical is this line from a review of one of the later reissues: "The repercussions of [Rodgers's] versatility were to resound through country music history and influence its development—for the worse, some would say, but that's no reason for not knowing just what it was that Jimmie Rodgers had" (*Old Time Music*, no. 4 [Spring, 1972], 23).

4. Malone, *Country Music, U.S.A.*, pp. 91–92.

5. *Billboard*, May 16, 1953, p. 20.

6. *MHJR*, pp. 175–76.

7. Henry Pleasants, *The Great American Popular Singers* (New York: Simon and Schuster, 1974), pp. 115–17.

Sources and Acknowledgments

This book was first envisioned more than twenty-five years ago, in the impassioned but woefully inadequate mind of a Texas farm boy. At that time, only a generation after Rodgers's death, the memories of those who had known him were still fresh, and I surely would have found the research path less cluttered with legends, detours, and dead ends. Several of the principals—notably Carrie Rodgers and Ralph Peer—were still alive; dozens of others might have been traced and found, to reveal valuable insights now forever lost.

In other ways, however, it was perhaps fortunate that I then lacked the resources to undertake such a task. In those days—and for some years to come—a book about "America's Blue Yodeler" would have had no home except in a bottom drawer of the author's desk, among his other stillborns and orphans. No one took "hillbilly music" seriously in academic and publishing circles; even among its natural audiences and loyal fans it was generally considered subcultural, irrelevant, and not very respectable. I remember how, as college freshmen, we labored arduously to understand the daily lives of the ancient Greeks and Romans. The subject absorbed me, but I was tied to my own age, too. When I ventured a modest essay on the world I inhabited, the paper came back from the professor marked "trivial" and "mere local color." (It was, I clearly recall, an awkward boy-and-his-horse saga, innocently swiped from Montana Slim's recording of "The Fate of the Strawberry Roan" and relocated on the windy West Texas plains of the Fifties, a time and place I loved and hated with equal ferocity.)

Quarrels between the Ancients and the Moderns are long standing. For at least two centuries, from the time when intellectual elitists in the Age of Reason began to make artificial distinctions between "high" and "low" culture, students (and some professors) have struggled with notions of what is and what isn't pedantically respectable. Complaints about this curious disjunction are nothing new, but only in relatively recent times has anyone done much about it. I confess to lingering confusions about the study of so-called popular culture. In many ways it is a great shaggy dog, friendly and warm and a joy to the heart—but after all, which end *is* which, and is it really housebroken? I am as uneasy as anyone with deep analyses of mother pillows, filling-station architecture, bottle caps, and yes, even country music. (Too often the problem is that the analyses aren't "deep" at all, but only declarations of the obvious in high-jargon nostalgia, the academic mother tongue.) But like Borges's wonderful, demented Pierre Menard, I believe that every man should be capable of all ideas, and I know the efficacy of a good Nashville heart song. In a time that is, admittedly, overly taken with fad and trivia, we also may be learning again how to study our lives and understand the spiritual and intellectual values of the commonplace events and experiences that are ignominiously labeled "pop culture"—the sight and feel of our time through the shared awareness of its music, its films, its language, its fashions, its fevers and fears and tremblings. To those who have shown the way in recent years, this book is deeply indebted.

Changes in the general atmosphere began to take place in the 1960's, with the growth of American studies and popular culture programs at schools across the country. Concurrently, for students of commercial music and recordings, two important centers were being established: the John Edwards Memorial Foundation at UCLA, and the Country Music Foundation's Library and Media Center in Nashville. My work owes a great deal to both institutions; some acquaintance with their unique holdings and their knowledgeable staffs seems mandatory for anyone studying or writing about country music.

A signal event was the publication in 1965 of a whole issue of the *Journal of American Folklore* (78, July-September) devoted entirely to studies of hillbilly music by leading scholars. Unabashedly proclaiming itself the "Hillbilly Issue," this collection has become a cornerstone for much subsequent research. The following year saw publication of the first, and in several respects the best, of the pictorial histories: Burt

Goldblatt and Robert Shelton's *Country Music Story* (Indianapolis: Bobbs-Merrill, 1966). Although occasionally marred by errors (several of which I contributed), it remains a lucid, interesting, and comprehensive survey of the subject.

During this time there appeared a work that has now become the standard reference. Bill Malone's *Country Music, U.S.A.* (Austin: University of Texas Press, 1968) is at once an engrossing narrative and a model of scholarship. I am grateful for the opportunity to acknowledge not only the influence of his book, but also Professor Malone's valuable advice and other direct contributions to my own work.

Archie Green has been a guide and an inspiration to many. In the early Sixties, I happened upon an article of his about the Carter Family (*Southern Folklore Quarterly,* 25 [December, 1961]) and got my first hint that it was okay to appreciate the lilting, lovely music that had been filtering into my half-conscious head since I was a child, when I played around my grandfather's chair as he sat late into the night, tuning his old Philco Cathedral radio to the Carter Family's broadcasts over the Mexican border stations. No one I'd known had ever talked seriously about such music—where it came from or who performed it, or why—and nothing about it appeared in the books and magazines that came my way. "Hillbilly" was beneath the contempt of everyone around me, although it was virtually all they listened to. Now here was a professor from a famous university, writing about that music with loving care and telling me more than I'd ever hoped to know. Some years later I was fortunate enough to meet the author, and his immediate enthusiasm for a book about Jimmie Rodgers convinced me to undertake the project in earnest. Professor Green remains a good friend and a constant source of help and encouragement.

In the past decade publishers have brought out serious biographies and discographies of entertainers and musicians once dismissed as "popular" or "hillbilly": Louis Armstrong (*Louis;* Boston: Little, Brown, 1971); Benny Goodman (*BG on Record;* New Rochelle, N.Y.: Arlington House, 1969); Bix Beiderbecke (*Bix: Man and Legend;* New Rochelle, N.Y.: Arlington House, 1973); Tex Ritter (*The Tex Ritter Story;* New York: Chappell, 1976). References to some of these will be found in my notes; I am spiritually indebted to them all. In this respect I wish to acknowledge the particular impact of Charles

Townsend's *San Antonio Rose: The Life and Music of Bob Wills* (Urbana: University of Illinois Press, 1976). Truly a trailblazer, this book will become a major source for generations of future scholars. I am further indebted to Professor Townsend for direct contributions to my work; among other assistance, he put me in touch with his sister, Dorothy Long, who shared her childhood memories of Jimmie Rodgers in the family home.

Although generally shunned by music histories and broad cultural studies, Rodgers has been the subject of considerable scribbling, if one cares to dig up the fan magazines, obscure foreign journals, and pop encyclopedias in which it usually appears. However, very little has been written about him that is both reliable and of much consequence. Exceptions include the Rodgers chapters in Malone and Goldblatt-Shelton, John Greenway's pioneering article, "Jimmie Rodgers—A Folksong Catalyst" (*Journal of American Folklore,* 70 [July-September, 1957]), and Bob Sanders, "America's First Big Time Country Singer," *Auburn Circle* (Winter, 1974), a somewhat arch yet lively analysis, obscure but available in the files of the JEMF. No one interested in Rodgers can overlook Mike Paris and Chris Comber, *Jimmie the Kid* (London: Eddison Press, 1977), the first book-length study, with many rare pictures and a substantial discography.

My account of Rodgers's life and work has been produced mainly from primary sources—letters, public documents, and newspaper accounts, augmented wherever possible by interviews with those who knew him or were otherwise immediately involved in his career. I have also attempted to explore in some depth, through general sources, the cultural and historical currents of his era. In this respect the files of *Billboard* and, to a lesser extent, those of *Variety* have been invaluable. While many interviews were both obligatory and enlightening, I found them generally less satisfactory and reliable than local newspaper files and other written records; too much time has passed, and too many other life stories are in search of a biographer.

A few informants asked to remain anonymous, but most sources, primary and secondary, are fully identified in notes at the end of each chapter. For this reason I have chosen not to burden the book with a formal bibliography, which in most instances would only repeat information from the notes. Except in the few cases where indicated, I conducted the interviews, and tapes of all interviews are in my possession. My files also contain many photocopies of the letters, pictures, documents, and newspaper stories cited, together with my own extensive correspondence, field notes, and other materials relating to this book. At the earliest opportunity, I hope to place my entire archive in a public depository—presumably the Country Music Foundation library or that of the John Edwards Memorial Foundation. In the meantime, my files are available to any serious scholar or student. I welcome corrections and additions.

Despite the encouragement of Archie Green and others, a clear plan or commitment to this book had not really crystalized when I happened to pass through San Antonio in early 1973 and, almost on impulse, called Rodgers's daughter, Anita Rodgers Court. She graciously agreed to meet me, and in the course of several hours' conversation she left me with valuable insights and sources of information that no one else could have provided. Tapes of our interview and her subsequent communications were added to the material I had been collecting at random while involved with other projects. Coincidentally, at about that time I heard from Mike Paris and Chris Comber in England; the two were then in the final stages of their important study, *Jimmie the Kid,* and were just completing an article drawn from it for Bill C. Malone and Judith McCulloh's *Stars of Country Music: Uncle Dave Macon to Johnny Rodriguez* (Urbana: University of Illinois Press, 1975; paperback ed., New York: Avon, 1976). The resulting exchange of information, at times voluminous, not only served as a sounding board but also became for me a valuable incentive and source of encouragement. Mike Paris shared further insights with me following the completion of their book.

Perhaps the single most important event of my early research was the discovery of Jimmie Rodgers's boyhood correspondence with his Aunt Dora Bozeman, some two dozen letters and other items in the possession of Mrs. M. G. Harvey of Meridian, Tom Bozeman's daughter and Rodgers's cousin. I had believed that the details of Jimmie's formative years were lost forever; but, in addition to personal accounts of his whereabouts in Rodgers's own voice and handwriting, the letters provided many leads to other documents and interviews that would otherwise have been overlooked. For access to the correspondence and for other important information, I am especially grateful to Mr. and Mrs. Harvey. A few of these early letters have been placed on display in the Jimmie Rodgers museum at Meridian; photocopies of all of them, my taped interviews with the Harveys, and related field notes are in my possession.

Another gracious lady, Mrs. Pearl Bozeman Harris of Pine Springs, shared memories of her cousin Jimmie's boyhood and helped me sort out and identify the many Bozemans in his life. Tapes of our interviews (May 22, 1975, and May 29, 1976) and her correspondence are also in my files.

The staff of the Meridian Public Library provided valuable assistance in researching Rodgers's early years and the history of Meridian. I am particularly indebted to Randl W. Ockey, assistant director, and to Mrs. Mary Smith, who guided me to special sources in the library's Mississippi Collection, where, among other items, I found a rare copy of the Reverend Joseph Bozeman's genealogy of Rodgers's maternal ancestors (*Sketches of the Bozeman Family;* Meridian: Mercury Publishing Co., 1885). Information concerning Aaron Rodgers's family was obtained from the National Archives in Washington and from the Alabama Department of Archives and History in Montgomery; the contributions of Milo B. Howard, Jr., director, are gratefully acknowledged.

Any study of Rodgers's early years requires some knowledge of railroading and show business in the South during that era. Few subjects have been as eagerly and thoroughly studied as American railroads; thousands of pages document the roles of major lines in the romantic days of westward expansion, and coffee tables overflow with glossy nostalgia bemoaning the loss of Pullman luxury along the Eastern Seaboard. But one looks in vain for a reliable survey of local railroading in the South after the turn of the century, when Jimmie Rodgers was a novice on the high iron. One source, valuable as background but of limited use to me because of its chronological scope, is John F. Stover, *The Railroads of the South, 1865-1900* (Chapel Hill: University of North Carolina Press, 1955). Also helpful was H. Stafford Bryant, Jr., *The Georgian Locomotive* (New York: Weathervane Books, 1952). But knowledge of routes and division points, train make-up, line mergers, wages, and schedules—a sense of the railroader's daily life on the NO&NE, the Mobile Road, or even the mighty Southern in Rodgers's time—can be had only in bits and pieces, from occasional articles and obscure, specialized studies—or, in rare instances, from knowledgeable and sympathetic sources on the railroads themselves. In this respect I was fortunate to discover two executives whose interests in railroading extend beyond matters of everyday commerce. Clearly taken with his topic, Robert W. O'Brien of Illinois Central–Gulf supplied valuable information about the Illinois Central and the Gulf, Mobile & Ohio (successors to the M&O); William F. Geeslin of the Southern Railway performed a similar service in generously answering my questions about the Southern, the NO&NE, and the VS&P, as well as providing excerpts from railway operating rules and other useful details. A special note of gratitude is due Mrs. May Alexander of the Florida East Coast Railroad, who, at some expense of time and trouble, diligently traced Rodgers's employment records there.

Once the Hollywood picture books are removed, show business is subject to a similar void. The nineteenth century is amply recorded, but, like so many other aspects of our recent history, accounts of grass-roots entertainment are largely in the hands of worshipful amateurs and diarists of the my-forty-years-in-the-sideshow school. A rough beginning, at least for tent repertoire, has been made with William L. Slout's *Theatre in a Tent* (Bowling Green, Ohio: Popular Press, 1972) and Jere C. Mickel, *Footlights on the Prairie* (St. Cloud, Minn.: North Star Press, 1974), but the subject deserves more thorough treatment. Robert C. Toll's timely and well-written *On with the Show* (New York: Oxford University Press, 1976) offers a broad overview of the national scene. For my purposes I have relied largely on local newspapers and the trade journals of the day, especially *Billboard*. Newspaper accounts of Rodgers's appearances in Oklahoma were traced for me by Mrs. Mary Moran of the Oklahoma Historical Society, and by Elwyn Isaacs of the Will Rogers Memorial Commission. In Texas I owe similar debts to the public libraries in San Antonio and Kerrville, and to Mickey Pearce, who helped me locate details of Rodgers's appearance in O'Donnell.

For other vital information concerning the Terrell and Swain shows in the heyday of tent rep, I am indebted to Al Lindberg of Temple City, California. Lindberg, an alumnus of Chase-Lister, Justus-Romain, and other prominent rep companies in the Twenties and Thirties, also worked in radio and recording; his wide-ranging interests in show business and the world at large have opened many avenues for me in the almost thirty years of our friendship. Long ago Al quietly endured a country boy's naive boast that "Jimmie Rodgers is the best guitar player there ever was." For many such acts of love and generosity, he shares the dedication of this book.

Notes from my interview with Stella Kelly, June 6, 1975, are in my files, together with letters and other papers pertinent to her role in Rodgers's life. Notable among these are the briefs and court depositions relating to the case of *Stella Harkins and Kathryn Rodgers* v. *Jimmie Rodgers,* No. 4502 Law, documents which are also on file at the Federal Record Center, Fort Worth, Texas, under Record Number 106247.

Although unreliable in many respects, Carrie Rodgers's *My Husband Jimmie Rodgers* (San Antonio: Southern Literary Institute, 1935) places the early years of their marriage in close perspective and provides personal details not found elsewhere. Long out of print, this volume is now available from the Country Music Foundation, Nashville. Mrs. Rodgers's sister, Gladys Hunt of Meridian, shed further light on this period, as did her brother, Nate Williamson.

Despite serious illness, Waldo O'Neal answered my inquiries in detail and sent me letters and other materials relating to his association with Rodgers.

Raymond Hall, who died in Memphis in 1982, was a ready and valuable informant. Dr. Don Kirkpatrick of the Texas Department of Corrections made possible my initial interview with Hall prior to the latter's release from Huntsville; I am also indebted to Dr. Ronald J. Waldron and Lonnie Laqua of the T.D.C., who helped me review Hall's records there and provided useful background material.

Although Rodgers's name appeared only infrequently in local newspapers while he was in Asheville, the back files of the *Asheville Citizen* and *Asheville Times* are a rich source for any researcher seeking to reconstruct his activities there just prior to the first Bristol recording session. The *Citizen-Times* librarian, Mrs. Lucille D. Hearn, gave me gracious assistance, as did the staff of Pack Memorial Library on my many visits to the fourth floor of that wonderful old building.

My account of the Tenneva Ramblers, a.k.a. the Jimmie Rodgers Entertainers, would have been woefully incomplete without the help of Glenn Sellers. At the time a graduate student at East Tennessee State University, Sellers generously shared tapes of his interviews with Claude Grant, answered my many additional questions, and enabled me to correspond briefly with Grant before the latter's death in late 1975. Sellers's video interviews with Grant, in the Southern Appalachian Video Ethnography Series (Broadside Video), are in the Archives of Appalachia, ETSU, Johnson City, Tennessee. Charles Wolfe put me on the trail of James "Mac" Sievers, who shared his memories of Rodgers at Johnson City just prior to Bristol; those interested in this event will want to consult Sievers's earlier interview with Professor Wolfe, in the latter's possession.

The standard histories of the phonograph, indispensable to any student of the subject, are Roland Gelatt, *The Fabulous Phonograph* (Philadelphia: J. B. Lippincott, 1955), and Oliver Read and Walter L. Welch, *From Tin Foil to Stereo* (Indianapolis: Bobbs-Merrill, 1959), now back in print. Both, however, have limitations. Gelatt, concentrating on "the more ambitious and durable musical repertoire . . . entrusted to the phonograph," confesses to a bias against popular music and even jazz; for him the hillbilly recording industry, with all its innovations and contributions to native culture, never existed. The Read and Welch book is a veritable encyclopedia of technical information and morning-glory horns, but, in their relentless zeal to defend Edison and the acoustical era, the authors skip only lightly across corporate machinations and cultural developments during the late Twenties and early Thirties. Apparently finding the enclosed horn a bore, they almost totally ignore the interesting models and cabinets of that period, while illustrating dozens of turn-of-the-century machines.

In many ways, Brian Rust's *American Record Label Book* (New Rochelle, N.Y.: Arlington House, 1978) excels either of the above in detailing the histories of the various recording companies, their studio operations, their artists and catalogs, and their methods of conducting business. (However, one must watch for occasional errors—Rust is not above referring to the Carter Family as "a team of two girls and their father.") Like his major discographies (*Jazz Records, 1897–1942; The American Dance Band Discography, 1917–1942*), Rust's *Victor Master Book, Vol. 2* (Hatch End, Middlesex: By the author, 1969) has been a great asset to the present work; my account of the Victor Talking Machine Company could not have been constructed without it. On the same subject, E. R. Fenimore Johnson's curious little biography of his father, *His Master's Voice Was Eldridge R. Johnson* (Milford, Del.: Privately printed, 1974), is eccentric but whimsically rewarding, mostly concerned with family history and the elder Johnson's troubled efforts to cope with his millions, but valuable for its discussion of Johnson's patents and his early days in the phonograph business. I have also relied on Victor catalogs and brochures from 1912 to 1948, in my possession, augmented by frequent dips into Roger Kinkle's *Complete Encyclopedia of Popular*

Music and Jazz, 1900–1950 (New Rochelle, N.Y.: Arlington House, 1974), which I recommend as a browser's delight to anyone interested in Tin Pan Alley and its impact on our culture.

Of paramount value to my work was the discovery, through Archie Green, of what I have labeled simply the Peer-Borgeson interviews. These constitute more than fourteen hours of taped conversations between Ralph Peer and Lillian Borgeson, recorded at Peer's home in Hollywood between January and May, 1959. Little is known of this project's origin, but it was apparently undertaken with the idea of producing a series of magazine articles or a biography of Peer. The original tapes, partially transcribed, are at the JEMF; my files contain complete copies and a full transcript.

On the first of my many trips to Meridian, I was graciously received by Elsie McWilliams, a warm and delightful lady who contributed materially to my research in its early stages. Other members of her family in Meridian also gave generously of their time and knowledge. In Fort Worth I interviewed Annie Williamson Nelson and Mildred Williamson Pollard, eldest and youngest of Carrie Rodgers's sisters; Mrs. Nelson helped me reconstruct Jimmie's early days in Washington, and I am especially grateful to George and Mildred Pollard for their help and hospitality.

In my behalf, Armand Beard interviewed Julian R. Ninde, Sr., just prior to Mr. Ninde's death in December, 1975. Beard also shared his considerable discographical knowledge of Rodgers and other artists, assistance that I acknowledge with pleasure.

My debts to Bill Bruner and Bennie Hess (and, I hope, my affection as well) are obvious. Bruner's son and daughter-in-law, Jim and Faye Bruner, generously allowed me access to Bruner's rare original recordings. Almost everyone I met in Meridian was equally courteous and helpful; I especially want to thank W. R. Swain of the All-Star Record Shop, James Skelton, and the officers of the Jimmie Rodgers Memorial Festival.

Among her many other contributions, Judith McCulloh put me in touch with Billy Burkes. For that rare bit of good fortune I am also indebted to Jim Griffith, who first found Burkes, interviewed him, and made his tapes and notes available to me. Later Mr. Burkes bore my intrusions with good cheer, patiently answered my many questions, and contributed in the process a veritable archive of Rodgers-related material, as cited in the notes to Chapter 11.

My query to Will Rogers, Jr., was answered immediately with

interest and enthusiasm, and in my behalf Mr. Rogers generously enlisted the aid of Dr. Reba Collins, curator of the Will Rogers Memorial. I am grateful for the opportunity to thank them both.

Rodgers's lyric sheets are in the possession of Jim Evans, to whom all fans of the Blue Yodeler are indebted. Jim has done perhaps more than any other individual to keep the Rodgers story alive; for allowing me to make copies of the lyric sheets and for many years of friendship and encouragement, I owe him more than I can acknowledge here.

The late Johnny Bond helped me gain access to sources and materials I would otherwise have missed. He was a fine, rare man who loved his profession and understood its historical consequences; I cherish his friendship and all that I learned from him.

Bob Pinson probably has more country music discography in his head than most of us have on paper. A patient and indefatigable well of information, Bob also read portions of the manuscript and gave sage counsel. I hope someday to find another lode of rare records with which to reward him. Bill Ivey at the Country Music Foundation was also a source of support and encouragement, along with Doug Green, Danny Hatcher, and Kyle Young. Others in Nashville to whom I am indebted include Ernest Tubb, Chet Atkins, and especially Brad McCuen, one of the best people in the industry. Brad invariably fit me into his busy schedule, and he contributed materially to the discography by supplying files for the Rodgers reissues which he produced.

The ubiquitous Charles Wolfe was always available to share his store of knowledge and to lend support; I treasure our many communications and the memory of my visits to Murfreesboro.

Norm Cohen published an early section of this work in the *JEMF Quarterly*. Other members of the JEMF staff were also helpful during my trips there, especially Patty Hall, now at the American Association for State and Local History.

Permission to quote from the songs of Jimmie Rodgers was generously extended by Peer International Corporation. I also wish to thank ATV Music Corporation for permission to quote from Roger Bowling's "I'd Like to Sleep 'til I Get Over You," and Bennie Hess for permission to quote from "Tennessee Mama Blues."

An earnest note of thanks to my old friend Don Cotten and to others who bore my whimsies, covered my trail, and offered aid and comfort along the way: John Bierk, Henry Sessoms, Fred Goodwin, Roy Dawson, Peter Hilty, Charles Hearn, Bob Hamblin, Kay McBride, Herb Scott, and especially Larry Grisvard, friend and colleague, who "tramped the dusty Alabama roads," and H. O. Grauel, who helped me locate the details of Rodgers's Masonic affiliations. A substantial portion of my work was made possible by grants from the Research Funding Committee and the College of Humanities of Southeast Missouri State University, which also provided other support. The staff of Kent Library, especially Alan Nourie and Linda Duckworth, were always helpful in locating materials from near and far; Dr. Jack Thompson of the University Computer Center devised ingenious ways of keeping up with the mass of discographical information and enabled me to present it in its final form. At crucial moments, Bob Cox and Betty Black copied photos and processed graphics.

Although I must state it more briefly, my gratitude to the following people is no less heartfelt. Thanks go also to Mrs. Paul H. Albright, Carl Biggers, Mr. and Mrs. Bill Boyd, Jim Boyd, Fred Cox, Cap Duncan, Jack Dunigan, Carl Echols, Jr., David Freeman, Dick Furman, Ed Goodman, Jim Hadfield, Ken Harrison, Dr. Bob Healy, Harvey Hecht, Fred Hoeptner, Ellen Fraser Kiker, Leo Leriche, Spence Lyon, R. F. "Peg" Meyer, Julian R. Ninde, Jr., John L. Pestell, William Randle, Tony Russell, Brian Rust, Clenton Sanders, Boyd Senter, Pauline Slover, Mr. and Mrs. J. Roy Slover, Lee Hill Taylor, Carrel T. "Tony" Thomas, Dirk P. Vogel, T. C. Walker, Marybeth White, and Henry Young.

Valuable research assistance came from Cynthia Anne Boren, whose interest in the project and contributions to it were above and beyond the call of duty. My thanks also to Cindy Blest, Debbie Burris, and Diane Morgan, who at various times helped with the manuscript.

I began with a glance at the state and progress of the art. One of the more recent and vital developments in that art is the Music in American Life series of the University of Illinois Press, a source of knowledge and inspiration to all who are involved with this aspect of our cultural roots. I count it an honor to be included in the series, and am prouder still for the opportunity to know and work with Richard L. Wentworth and his fine staff. Judith McCulloh gave support and encouragement to the project almost from its inception, long before she had any reason to believe in it; when it was done, Ann Lowry Weir worked her considerable magic as an editor and saw to it that my manuscript eventually said what I meant to say. No book was ever in better hands.

In the time since the original edition of this book was published in 1979, I have heard from readers—all avid Jimmie Rodgers fans—in forty-six states and a number of countries abroad. Only recently, in Liverpool, England, I met W. Ralph "Hank" Walters, considered by many to be "the father of British country music," and a loyal disciple of Rodgers, whom he credits with being his major influence. He told me a wonderful story, which I think expresses the force of Jimmie Rodgers's continuing appeal, across time and national boundaries.

It seems that while on tour Hank and a couple of other musicians were passing the time in a small pub in a remote part of northern Wales. The conversation turned to Rodgers, for whom all of them expressed great admiration. But as sometimes happens in barroom discussions, reaction began to set in, and after a few more pints, someone allowed that while Rodgers was great, maybe he wasn't all *that* great. The others chimed in: "Oh, 'e was smashin' and all that, but 'e really wasn't so much," one would say, and the rest would nod sagely. " 'E was OK, but 'e didn't last, did 'e then?" another would say.

An old Welshman sat close by, puffing his pipe and taking it all in, and finally he could keep still no longer. "Oh, bloody good," he said, his voice heavy with sarcasm. "Ah don't know how far 'tis from here to that place Jimmie Rodgers was born, and 'e's been dead for over fifty bloody years, but here we are sitting all this way, up in the hills of Wales, and we're talking about him. Who'll be talking about *you* in fifty bloody years?"

Finally, then, my gratitude to all those, here and abroad, who are still talking about Jimmie Rodgers.

The Recordings of Jimmie Rodgers

Collected Works

The Rodgers recorded canon, as first released domestically between 1927 and 1938, consists of 110 separate and distinct songs originally identified with Rodgers, plus the remastered "Rodgers' Puzzle Record" (a total of 111 sides). Of these, 108 were paired together in their initial release, 98 titles (49 records) on the Victor "scroll" label and 10 titles (5 records) on Bluebird. The remaining 3 sides appeared initially on separate Bluebird issues, paired with titles by Mrs. Rodgers, Jesse Rodgers, and the Monroe Brothers. Thus 57 single-issue 78 rpm records comprise "the complete work." All except the Puzzle Record have been reissued at least once on EP or LP recordings, and all remained in RCA's catalog into the 1980's.[1] The definitive reissue, now in progress and scheduled for Spring, 1992, is from Bear Family Records (Germany). It contains everything except the Puzzle Record,[2] plus the soundtrack of "The Singing Brakeman" and many outtakes.

To these may be added "Prohibition Has Done Me Wrong," unissued and now presumed lost; "The Pullman Porters," currently circulated among collectors on tape and an unauthorized LP; and as many as 17 titles of questionable origin, thought to have been recorded privately or as an experiment in the studio (see below).

Recording Sessions

On 17 occasions, for periods ranging from a day to several weeks, Rodgers traveled to a specific location primarily for the purpose of recording. These sessions[3] took place in 9 cities across the country, including Bristol, Tennessee; Camden, New Jersey (on four occasions); Atlanta (twice); New York (three times); Dallas (three times); Hollywood; San Antonio; Louisville; and possibly New Orleans. The following chronology may be helpful in charting the course of Rodgers's recording career:

Year	Session	Date	Place	Number of known masters recorded	Resulting number of sides issued	
1927	1	Aug. 4	Bristol, Tenn.	2	2	
	2	Nov. 30	Camden, N.J.	4	4	
						6
1928	3	Feb. 14-15	Camden, N.J.	8	8	
	4	June 12	Camden, N.J.	9	7	
	5	Oct. 20-22	Atlanta, Ga.	4	4	
						19
1929	6	Feb. 21-23	New York, N.Y.	5	5	
	7	Aug. 8-12	Dallas, Tex.	7	5	
	8	Oct. 22	Dallas, Tex.	6	6	
	9	Nov. 13	New Orleans, La.[4]	1	1	
	10	Nov. 25-28	Atlanta, Ga.	8	8	
						25
1930	11	June 30–July 17	Hollywood, Calif.	15	14	
						14
1931	12	Jan. 31	San Antonio, Tex.	3	3	
	13	June 10-17	Louisville, Ky.	11	11	
						14
1932	14	Feb. 2-6	Dallas, Tex.	8	8	
	15	Aug. 10-16	Camden, N.J.	10	8	
	16	Aug. 29	New York, N.Y.	4	4	
						20
1933	17	May 17-24	New York, N.Y.	13	12	
						12
			Totals	118	110	

(plus Puzzle Record)

Sales Figures

How many copies of Rodgers's records were sold? Perhaps no aspect of his career has been the subject of more controversy, exaggeration, and guesswork. Published speculation ranges from "more than five million records" to a high of 20,000,000.[5] The actual figure was somewhere comfortably in the middle of these extremes, probably in the area of 12,000,000 records sold in the United States during Rodgers's lifetime and the ensuing 15 years or so.

As with other matters, much of the confusion originated with Rodgers himself. In early 1929 he asserted that "Sleep, Baby, Sleep" had sold 2,000,000 copies within a year of its release, and by December of that year he was claiming total sales of 12,000,000, on the basis of some 14 records then in the stores.[6] Several of these had just been released and thus could not have contributed much to the total; hence the first dozen or so would have to have sold more than 1,000,000 each by that time in order to reach the figure claimed. Most informed observers agree that such sales would have been quite unlikely, in spite of Peer's casual assertion that "for at least three or four years, any Jimmie Rodgers record would be expected to sell a million eventually." Just how long "eventually" might be was not explained, and this points to a central issue in any discussion of record sales: while many fans and commentators have been anxious to offer some impressive total as testament to Rodgers's popularity, few have been willing to consider such difficult factors as selling duration or catalog life (i.e., the period of time each record was available for sale), the degree to which Victor's budget labels may have affected sales—and Rodgers's royalties—in competition with its premium line, and the widespread economic fluctuations across the entire phonograph industry during the time Rodgers was active.

It was long understood that all of Victor's files pertaining to Rodgers's sales figures were lost in a warehouse fire, but later Brad McCuen told me he'd invented the story out of embarrassment when he discovered that most of the information had simply been thrown away. More recently, however, some rudimentary data have come to light, largely through the diligent efforts of David Freeman.[7] Unfortunately, the basic problems remain. Not only do Freeman's figures cover fewer than half of Rodgers's original releases, but his sources apparently carry no clear indication of the period they cover;

nor is there certain evidence that the figures for any given release actually represent the final compilation for that issue. Pressing orders, if available, might produce a better understanding of Rodgers's popularity and his position in the industry. As a starting point, however, Freeman's data at least provide a concrete basis for calculations, in an area too often at the mercy of random speculation and emotional guesswork.

Freeman was able to compile approximate sales figures for 25 of Rodgers's 49 original Victor releases—figures which reflect a steady, sometimes precipitous decline in sales of those records issued between 1929 and 1933. The first record for which a figure is available is Vi V-40014, "Waiting for a Train"/"Blue Yodel No. 4" (released 2/8/29). While its exact selling life is not known, the record had disappeared from the catalog by 1936; yet it sold at least 365,000 copies. The last release shown by Freeman, Vi 23840, "Old Love Letters"/"Somewhere below the Dixon Line" (released 10/20/33), appeared only in the 1934 and 1935 catalogs and apparently sold a mere 1,200. Total sales for the 25 Victors shown by Freeman were 1,146,000, an average of about 46,000 per release. Applied to all 57 original Victor and Bluebird releases, this average would produce a total of only 2,622,000; but in light of the important omissions from the list and the extremely variable economic conditions during those years, that is obviously not a very reliable method of estimating the combined total. Missing from Freeman's compilations are Rodgers's first 9 records (including the original "Blue Yodel") and most of the releases for 1929 and 1930, all presumed to be substantial sellers. Also missing are all releases for the second half of 1932 and everything released after October, 1933, including all sides originally released on Bluebird.

Rodgers's releases up to about 1930 are thought to have averaged at least 350,000 each. It is generally agreed that "Blue Yodel" alone "eventually" sold at least 1,000,000 copies, and a couple of other early issues probably came close.[8] Hence the first 9 issues, including "Blue Yodel" (all missing from Freeman's figures), would easily account for sales of over 4,000,000. Applying the average derived from Freeman's incomplete figures—roughly 50,000 per issue—to the remaining 48 initial releases would increase the figure to about 6,500,000. It should be stressed that this is strictly a bottom line, conservatively calculated from actual figures. Allowing for the record companies' standard practice of deflating sales figures in their ledgers (to minimize royalty payments) and for other variables in reporting and accounting, it seems entirely reasonable to estimate that sales for the original Victor and Bluebird releases "eventually" reached at least 7,000,000.

Freeman's figures for 44 of the 61 Montgomery Ward reissues show a total of 313,000, an average of 7,120. But again, many of Rodgers's biggest hits are missing from the list, and the period covered by the data is not known. A figure of 1,000,000 would seem to be a conservative estimate for all Montgomery Ward releases, considering their relative popularity and long catalog life. (As late as 1938, Ward's catalog still carried 82 Rodgers titles). The 54 reissues on Electradisk, Sunrise, and Bluebird (especially popular in the late Thirties and early Forties), together with the RCA Victor 78 rpm albums in the early Fifties, may easily account for another 3–4,000,000.

Clearly, the above figures are only informed guesses, but they represent an effort to determine Rodgers's sales on some logical basis from the best evidence available, however thin and inadequate. These calculations are liberal in some respects, conservative in others, but they generally support the figure of 10–12,000,000 for all of Rodgers's 78 rpm records, originals and reissues, released in the United States and on sale variously between 1927 and the early 1950's. Foreign sales, impossible to calculate, might well equal or exceed that amount. Domestic EP, LP, and tape reissues are in the range of 1,000,000. Each of the seven "primary" LPM (U.S.) album reissues has sold between 50,000 and 100,000 copies, for a collective total in excess of 500,000. An eighth album, DPL 2-0075, offered exclusively by mail, accounted for sales of another 100,000 copies within months of its release in 1974, and four other "re-reissue" albums on sale since have done proportionately well. Although the first of the 7 primary LPMs appeared over 20 years ago, all of them remain in RCA's catalog, selling at a steady rate. Together with the 5 "re-reissues" they constitute, according to an RCA executive, "one of the largest intact bodies of non-classical releases from that period by an RCA artist."[9]

Finally, one must note the futility of trying to compare Rodgers's sales with those of other artists—and, even more problematic, the insignificance of numbers as a measure of an artist's audience, influence, or intrinsic merit. Norm Cohen has commented on the illusionary magic of the Gold Record: in the popular mind, "a hit record means a million seller; less than a million, conversely, means a flop. This is not a very useful pair of definitions."[10] Today, "hitting gold" (and even platinum) is so commonplace as to have become a bore. In Rodgers's time the concept scarcely existed, and in an era when sales of even 50,000 were exceedingly rare, the 1,000,000 mark had real meaning. Applying it now to compare prewar and postwar recording artists is about as useful as counting buggy whips versus radiator caps.

The social and cultural factors which set Rodgers apart from a modern-day phenomenon such as Elvis Presley—the artist with whom Rodgers loyalists most often try to rank him—are too complex and numerous to deal with adequately here. But no learned analysis is necessary to understand that Presley's career drew its initial momentum from a youth cult which simply did not exist in Rodgers's day; the growth of his popularity was assisted by advanced promotional techniques, television exposure, and a general resurgence of the music and phonograph industries, all in a time of expanding population and greater disposable income. Presley's premature death may also obscure the fact that his career actually spanned more than twenty years, in contrast to Rodgers's brief five and a half.

Entertainers such as Frank Sinatra and Bing Crosby clearly enjoyed a more broadly based popularity than did Rodgers, but again, their careers both lasted much longer. Crosby enjoyed over half a century at the top, and while all the Old Groaner's records sold well, a few phenomenal hits on the order of "White Christmas" account for the astronomical dimensions of his lifetime record sales. (Indeed, no one has yet suggested that the records Crosby made during Rodgers's lifetime outsold the Blue Yodeler's, even though Crosby began recording a year earlier. Crosby's first million-seller, "Sweet Leilani," did not appear until 1937, and his second—of all things, "San Antonio Rose"—came out in 1941.)

Similar perspectives are necessary even when Rodgers is seen exclusively within the context of his own time. If he had only one million-seller in that era, no more could be said for such luminaries as Al Jolson and Gene Austin. Jolson, despite his popularity on stage and screen, was never a consistent success on records until the Forties, when the entertainment world was expanding radically and his career had taken a brief reprise. Although he began recording in 1911 and made dozens of sides throughout the Twenties and Thirties, "Sonny

Boy" (1928) was his only million-seller in that era. Austin hit gold only with "My Blue Heaven" in 1927 ("Ramona," the following year, may have come close). Not to be outdone by anyone, Austin later, in the 1950's, claimed lifetime sales of over 90,000,000—at a time when even Crosby's known total was less than half that amount. The actual number was probably about 10,000,000, roughly the same as for Rodgers. The fact is that until about 1930, all of them put together had been outsold by Vernon Dalhart ("the John Denver of old-time music," says Bill Ivey of the Country Music Foundation), whose lifetime sales are conservatively estimated at 75,000,000. Today, the average Dalhart 78 rpm record, in mint condition, will fetch perhaps 50¢ at a yard sale, and he survives in reissue only on a very few obscure LPs put together by small specialty labels. So much for million-sellers.

If one insists on ranking Rodgers according to sales figures, perhaps there's some comfort in Peer's observation that when the Blue Yodeler sold 1,000,000 records in the early days of his career, it was easily the equivalent of 5,000,000 or more today—but even that equation should be handled with care, considering the infinite variables that stand between his day and ours. Similarly, Rodgers's supposed decline must also be seen in relative terms. According to Freeman's figures, by mid-1932 sales had dropped below 10,000 per release, and the last 4 items he cites sold less than 2,000. This has led some observers to question the data, or to shake their heads mournfully over the tragic fall of the once-great Blue Yodeler. They forget, however, that by 1931, scarcely 10,000,000 records were sold by the *entire recording industry*. (In any given year in the Twenties, the figure had been well over 100,000,000.) During the Depression, any record that sold 5,000 copies was a smash hit—and there were precious few of those. When Rodgers sold 1,200, he was still on top; most artists were lucky if their records sold half that amount. In any event, as Cohen has pointed out, Rodgers's sales figures—even if the exact totals were known—would ultimately have little bearing upon his stature or his reputation. Perhaps a better index would be the number of times his records were listened to and passed from hand to hand, household to household, generation to generation. Today one rarely finds a Rodgers original that is not worn grey, scratched and battered, patched and proudly cherished. Those records were *played*.

Discography

As with so many other matters pertaining to Jimmie Rodgers, research into the history of his recordings originated with Jim Evans, who in the late 1940's began to supply members of the Jimmie Rodgers Society with a printed compilation of all the Blue Yodeler's original recordings. Strictly speaking, this was not a discography—the art scarcely existed in country music in those days—but simply a list of the songs as they were paired for issue, arranged in order of release, with dates of recordings. While this tabulation contained no information concerning master and take numbers, places of recording, or accompaniments, it provided a valuable overview of Rodgers's recording history, at a time when any published information was rare and only a few of his records were available to a new generation of enthusiasts. I can recall poring over the list avidly, relishing the titles of songs I'd never heard.

The appearance of John Edwards's detailed Rodgers discography in the Fall, 1955, issue of *International Discophiles* not only constituted a landmark in Rodgers scholarship but also became an inspiration and a model for country music discography in general. While the Edwards work contained occasional errors, omissions, and faulty speculation (notably with regard to session personnel), it was the first full listing of germane information, including all foreign and domestic release numbers up to that time. For more than a decade it remained the definitive Rodgers discography and is still useful as a guide to the pattern of reissues abroad.

In the mid-1960's, in connection with research at RCA for his dissertation on radio broadcasting, William Randle compiled a Rodgers discography directly from company files, with valuable annotations concerning session times, copyrights, and relevant information surrounding the recording and release of various takes. Working independently from the same sources, Rodney McElrea assembled a similar but less comprehensive discography which appeared in the April, 1966, issue of *Country News and Views*. Randle's work has not been published, but a copy is on file at the John Edwards Memorial Foundation, UCLA.

Paris and Comber's *Jimmie the Kid* (1977) took matters a step further by showing detailed take information and by adding new data in several areas. On occasion, however, their discography is curiously at variance with the narrative of the book, and certain inaccuracies remain.

All of the above served as source material for the late Johnny Bond's *Recordings of Jimmie Rodgers: An Annotated Discography,* published by the JEMF in 1978. Largely a synthesis of recording data previously available, this work is most valuable for Bond's personal insights, set down in hodgepodge but engaging fashion, and for Norm Cohen's lucid and incisive introduction.

The following discography of Rodgers's recordings attempts to expand, correct, and bring up to date all previous such compilations, acknowledging an indebtedness to each of them. It generally conforms to standard discographical format, incorporating one or two minor alterations suggested by the special nature of Rodgers's recording history. (An effort has been made, for example, to emphasize the places and dates of recording for easy reference, and the relatively small number of masters makes possible the inclusion of such additional information as original release dates and pairings.) Entries begin with the master number, suffixed by the total number of takes. Beneath each title, in parentheses, is the name of the composer or composers, followed by that of the original copyright holder. These are determined from all available information: generally composers' names are those shown on the original records, but not always in the same order; copyright data are based on Victor's files and thus do not always agree with other published sources, such as Peer's 1967 Memorial Folios. Spelling and punctuation have been regularized throughout.

In the column following the title-composer-copyright entry, catalog numbers are shown for each released take, employing standard label abbreviations (see key below). Numbers in the first block are domestic 78 rpm releases; indented immediately beneath them are foreign 78s. Next below are domestic LP and EP issues, beginning with the album title of the initial ("primary") U.S. 12-inch LP reissue. Foreign LPs and EPs, as with foreign 78s, are again indented beneath. The order in which catalog numbers are listed remains constant throughout; they are arranged alphabetically according to the abbreviations in the key except for the initial entry in the following categories: U.S. 78s begin with the original release; U.S. LP and EP reissues begin with the primary album, by title; and foreign LP and EP reissues begin with the Japanese "complete works" set. The final column at the right shows the date and pairing of the original (Vi or Bb) release.

Key to Label Abbreviations

DOMESTIC:

ACL   Pickwick/Camden LP albums

ANL   RCA LP albums

ANS   RCA eight-track tapes

Bb   Bluebird 78 rpm singles

CAL   RCA Camden 12″ LP albums

CPL   RCA 12″ LP stereo-effect albums

DMM   RCA Special Products 12″ LP albums for Neiman-Marcus

DPL   RCA Special Products double-record 12″ LP album, sold by mail

El   Electradisk 78 rpm singles, from Vi and Bb masters for Woolworth
      chain (1932–33)

EP–   RCA 45 rpm albums

ES   Endangered Species 12″ unauthorized LP album

LPM   RCA 12″ "primary" LP albums:
      1232 *Never No Mo' Blues* (released August, 1956)
      1640 *Train Whistle Blues* (released December, 1958)
      2112 *My Rough and Rowdy Ways* (released April, 1960; now
            renumbered ANLI–1209e)
      2213 *Jimmie the Kid* (released May, 1961)
      2531 *Country Music Hall of Fame* (released July, 1962)
      2634 *The Short but Brilliant Life of Jimmie Rodgers* (released
            May, 1963; now renumbered AHMI-3094)
      2865 *My Time Ain't Long* (released July, 1964)
      [LPMs 2633 and 2564 contain Rodgers's selections overdubbed by
      the Rainbow Ranch Boys.]

LPT   RCA 10″ LP albums

LSP   RCA 12″ LP stereo-effect albums

MW   Montgomery Ward 78 rpm singles, budget line from Vi and Bb
      masters

NW   New World Records 12″ LP album

Sr   Sunrise 78 rpm singles, budget line from Vi and Bb masters for
      dime-store chains (1933–34)

TT   Timely Tunes 78 rpm singles, short-lived budget line from Vi and
      Bb masters (April–July, 1931)

Vi   Victor Talking Machine Company and (on labels after 1945) RCA
      Victor Records:
      20000, 21000, 22000,
        23000, 24000, and
          V-40000 series   Rodgers's original releases on 78
                                  rpm[11]

Vi   (*continued*)
          18–6000 (sole issue)   78 rpm "picture record"
          20–6000 series   RCA 78 rpm singles, with overdub-
                                   bing by the Rainbow Ranch Boys
          21–0000 series   in RCA 78 rpm albums P-244, P-282,
                                   P-318
          27–0000 series   in RCA 45 rpm albums WPT-21,
                                   WPT-22, WPT-23
          47–6000 series   in RCA 45 rpm album of titles over-
                                   dubbed by the Rainbow Ranch Boys
          420–0000 series   in RCA 78 rpm album PT-3035
          447–0000 series   RCA 45 rpm albums
          599–0000 series   in RCA 45 rpm album SPD-3
          947–0000 series   in RCA 45 rpm album EPBT 3073
VPS   RCA 12″ LP double-record stereo-effect albums

FOREIGN:

AP   RCA 12″ LPs, Japan
CMH   Country Music History 12″ LPs, West Germany
Col   Columbia 78 rpm singles:
               IFB   Ireland
               MZ   France
DPM   RCA 12″ LP double-record set (mono), England
DPS   RCA 12″ LP double-record set (stereo), England
EP   RCA 45 rpm album, Australia
HMV   His Master's Voice 78 rpm singles:
               EA   India
               HR   New Zealand
               MH   British Isles
               N   India
          His Master's Voice 45 rpm albums:
               7EG   England
HP   RCA 10″ LP albums, Japan
L   RCA 12″ LP albums, Australia
RA   RCA 12″ LP albums, Japan
RCX   RCA 45 rpm albums, England
RD   RCA 12″ LP albums, England
RZ   Regal Zonophone 78 rpm singles:
               G   Australia (ca. 1937)
               IZ   Ireland
               ME   England
               MR   England

RZ   (*continued*)
        MR 20000
            series   India
        T   England; Australia, if not previously released
                           there in Zo EE series (ca. 1928–34)
SRA   RCA 12″ LP albums, Japan
Tw   Twin 78 rpm singles, India (ca. 1928–37)
Vi A   RCA 78 rpm singles, Japan (ca. 1948–54)
Vi JA   RCA 78 rpm singles, Japan (ca. 1936–40)
Zo   Zonophone 78 rpm singles:
        4000, 5000,
            6000 series   England
        EE series   Australia

408-10 State Street
Bristol, Tennessee
August 4, 1927

Vocal with own guitar:

Take 4:

1. BVE 39767-4 **The Soldier's Sweetheart**   Vi 20864, Bb 33–0513, MW M–4452   Oct. 7, 1927,
                (Rodgers)   HMV EA1400, RZ G23197   with "Sleep,
                ©1927, R. S. Peer   *Country Music Hall of Fame*   Baby, Sleep"
                                                (LPM 2531), DMM 4–0343,
                                                DPL 2–0075
                                                    RA 5459, DPM 2047,
                                                    RD 7505

Vocal with own guitar:

Take 3:

2. BVE 39768-3 **Sleep, Baby, Sleep**   Vi 20864, Bb B–6225, MW M–4452,   Oct. 7, 1927,
                Public Domain[12]   Vi 21–0180 (in P–318)   with "The
                ©1953, Peer Intl. Corp.   HMV EA1400, RZ G23197,   Soldier's
                                                   RZ MR2795, Tw FT8585,   Sweetheart"
                                                   Vi A1466
                                                Jimmie the Kid (LPM 2213),
                                                CPL 1–2504(e), DMM 4–0406,
                                                EPAT 23, LPT 3038,
                                                Vi 27–0104 (in WPT–23)
                                                    RA 5459, DPS 2021, RA 5176,
                                                    RA 5510, RA 9037, RD 27241

Victor Studio 1
114 North Fifth Street[13]
Camden, New Jersey
November 30, 1927

Vocal with own guitar:

Take 2:

3. BVE 40751-2 **Ben Dewberry's Final Run**
(Andy Jenkins)
©1928, R. S. Peer

Vi 21245, Bb B-5482
  HMV EA1543, RZ G23117,
  RZ IZ495, RZ MR2241,
  Tw FT8185
Train Whistle Blues (LPM 1640),
ANL 1-1052, ANS 1-1052,
CPL 1-2504(e)
  RA 5459, DPS 2021, RD 27110

Apr. 6, 1928,
with "In the
Jailhouse
Now"

Vocal with own guitar:

Take 1:

4. BVE 40752-2 **Mother Was a Lady**[14]
(Edward B. Marks and
Joseph Stern)
[©1896, Edward B. Marks
Music Pub. Co.]

Vi 21433, Bb B-5482, MW M-4224
  HMV EA1382, RZ G23193,
  RZ IZ495, RZ MR2241,
  Tw FT1808
My Time Ain't Long (LPM 2865)
  RA 5459, RD 7644

Aug. 3, 1928,
with "Trea-
sures Untold"

Vocal with own guitar:

Take 2:

5. BVE 40753-2 **Blue Yodel**
(Rodgers)
©1928, R. S. Peer

Vi 21142, Bb B-5085, MW M-3272,
Sr S-3172, Vi 21-0042 (in P-244)
  RZ G22792, RZ IZ310,
  RZ IZ414, RZ MR1918,
  RZ T5158, Tw FT1980,
  Zo 5158[15]
My Rough and Rowdy Ways
(LPM 2112; ANLI-1209e), ACL 7029,
CPL 1-2504(e), DPL 2-0075,
EPA 5097, EPAT 21, LPT 3037,
LPT 6, LSP 3315(e), Vi 27-0017
(in WPT-6), Vi 27-0098 (in WPT-21),
Vi 599-9020 (in SPD-3), VPS 6091(e)
  RA 5459, DPM 2047, EP 20219,
  HMV 7EG 8163, L 10883,
  RA 5176, RA 5510, RA 9037,
  RCX 1058[16]

Feb. 3, 1928,
with "Away
Out on the
Mountain"

Vocal with own guitar:

Take 2:

6. BVE 40754-2 **Away Out on the Mountain**
(Kelly Harrell)
©1928, R. S. Peer

Vi 21142, Bb B-5085, MW M-3272,
Sr S-3172, Vi 21-0042 (in P-244)
  RZ G22792, RZ IZ310,
  RZ IZ414, RZ MR1918,
  RZ T5158, Tw FT1733,
  Tw FT1980, Zo 5158, Zo EE109

Feb. 3, 1928,
with "Blue
Yodel"

November 30, 1927 (continued)

My Rough and Rowdy Ways
(LPM 2112; ANLI-1209e), ACL 7029,
DPL 2-0075, EPA 5097, EPAT 21,
LPT 3037, LPT 6, LSP 3315(e),
Vi 27-0017 (in WPT-6), Vi 27-0098
(in WPT-21), Vi 599-9020 (in SPD-3),
VPS 6091(e)
  RA 5459, DPM 2047,
  EP 20219, HMV 7EG 8163,
  L 10883, RA 5501, RCX 1058

Victor Studio 1
114 North Fifth Street
Camden, New Jersey
February 14, 1928

Vocal and own ukulele, with Ellsworth T. Cozzens, steel guitar, mandolin;
Julian R. Ninde, guitar:[17]

Take 1:

7. BVE 41736-2 **Dear Old Sunny South**   Vi 21574, Bb B-6246, Vi 21-0182   Oct. 5, 1928,
                by the Sea   (in P-318)   with "My
                (J. Rodgers-E. T. Cozzens)   HMV EA1228, HMV N4336,   Little Old
                ©1928, R. S. Peer   RZ G22792, RZ G23188,   Home Down
                                             RZ IZ317, RZ IZ414,   in New
                                             RZ MR1918, RZ T5341,   Orleans"
                                             Tw FT1980, Vi A1454, Zo 5341
                                             Never No Mo' Blues (LPM 1232),
                                             DPL 2-0075, EPAT 410, LPT 3039,
                                             Vi 27-0106 (in WPT-23),
                                             VPS 6091(e)
                                               RA 5459, DPM 2047, RA 5176,
                                               RA 9037, RD 27138, RA 5510

Vocal, with Ellsworth T. Cozzens, steel guitar; Julian R. Ninde, guitar:

Take 2:

8. BVE 41737-2 **Treasures Untold**[18]   Vi 21433, Bb B-5838, MW M-4217   Aug. 3, 1928,
                (J. Rodgers-E. T. Cozzens)   HMV N4310, Tw FT9115,   with "Mother
                ©1928, R. S. Peer   Zo EE139   Was a Lady"
                                             Train Whistle Blues (LPM 1640),
                                             VPS 6091(e)
                                               RA 5459, DPS 2021, EP 20176,
                                               RA 5176, RA 5510, RD 27110

Vocal and own guitar, with Ellsworth T. Cozzens, ukulele:

Take 1:

9. BVE 41738-2 **The Brakeman's Blues**   Vi 21291, MW M-4214,   May 4, 1928,
                (Rodgers)   Vi 21-0044 (in P-244)   with "Blue
                ©1928, R. S. Peer   HMV EA1542, HMV N4364,   Yodel—
                                             RZ G23116   No. II"
                                             My Rough and Rowdy Ways

February 14, 1928 (continued)

(LPM 2112; ANLI-1209e),
ACL 7029, ANL 1-1052,
ANS 1-1052, EPA 5097, EPAT 21,
LPT 3037, Vi 27-0100 (in WPT-21),
VPS 6091(e)
    RA 5459, EP 20219,
    HMV 7EG 8163, L 10883,
    RCX 1058

Vocal and own guitar,[19] with Ellsworth T. Cozzens, steel guitar;
Julian R. Ninde, guitar:

Take 1:

10. BVE 41739-2 **The Sailor's Plea**   Vi V-40054, Bb B-6246,   Apr. 19, 1929,
    (Elsie McWilliams–   Bb 33-0513, MW M-5036   with "I'm
      Jimmie Rodgers)   HMV N4327, RZ IZ321,   Lonely and
    ©1928, R. S. Peer   RZ T5401, Zo 5401   Blue"
                            Country Music Hall of Fame
                            (LPM 2531)
                            RA 5459, RD 7505

Victor Studio 1
114 North Fifth Street
Camden, New Jersey
February 15, 1928

Vocal and own guitar, with Ellsworth T. Cozzens, banjo:

Take 1:

11. BVE 41740-2 **In the Jailhouse Now**   Vi 21245, Bb B-5223, El 2109,   Apr. 6, 1928,
    (Rodgers)   MW M-4721, Sr S-3306   with "Ben
    ©1928, R. S. Peer   HMV EA1406, HMV N4309,   Dewberry's
                      RZ G23202, Zo 4342   Final Run"
                      The Short but Brilliant Life of
                      Jimmie Rodgers (LPM 2634;
                      AHMI-3094), DPL 2-0075,
                      VPS 6091(e)
                      RA 5459, RD 7562

Vocal and own guitar, with Ellsworth T. Cozzens, steel guitar:

Take 2:

12. BVE 41741-2 **Blue Yodel—No. II**[20]   Vi 21291, MW M-4214,   May 4, 1928,
    (Rodgers)   MW M-8121, Vi 21-0181   with "The
    ©1928, R. S. Peer   (in P-318)   Brakeman's
                      HMV EA1542, HMV N4309,   Blues"
                      RZ G23116, RZ IZ1004,
                      RZ MR3122, Tw FT8775,
                      Vi A1454, Zo 4370
                      Jimmie the Kid (LPM 2213),
                      EPAT 23, LPT 3038, Vi 27-0105
                      (in WPT-23)
                      RA 5459, DPS 2021, RD 27241

February 15, 1928 (continued)

Vocal with own guitar:

	Take 2:	
13. BVE 41742-2 **Memphis Yodel**	Vi 21636, MW M-4450,	Nov. 2, 1928,
(Rodgers)	MW M-4725, Vi 21-0042	with "Lullaby
©1928, R. S. Peer	(in P-244)[21]	Yodel"
	HMV EA1540, HMV N4291,	
	RZ G23114, RZ IZ315,	
	RZ T5283, Zo 5283	
	Jimmie the Kid (LPM 2213)	
	RA 5459, DPS 2021, RD 27241	

Vocal with own guitar:

	Take 2:	
14. BVE 41743-2 **Blue Yodel No. 3**	Vi 21531, MW M-4213,	Sept. 7, 1928,
(Rodgers)	Vi 21-0177 (in P-282)	with "Never
©1928, R. S. Peer	RZ IZ314, RZ T5247, Zo 5247	No Mo' Blues"
	Jimmie the Kid (LPM 2213),	
	ACL 7029, EPAT 22, LPT 3037,	
	Vi 27-0103 (in WPT-22)	
	RA 5459, DPS 2021, RD 27241	

Victor Studio 1
114 North Fifth Street
Camden, New Jersey
June 12, 1928

Vocal with own guitar:

	Take 1:	
15. BVE 45090-2 **My Old Pal**	Vi 21757, Bb B-5609, Vi 21-0176	Dec. 2, 1928,
(McWilliams–Rodgers)	(in P-282)	with "Daddy
©1928, Southern Music	RZ G22792, RZ IZ318,	and Home"
Publishing Co., Inc.[22]	RZ IZ414, RZ MR1918,	
	RZ T5356, Tw FT1756,	
	Tw FT1980, Zo 5356, Zo EE150	
	Jimmie the Kid (LPM 2213),	
	ACL 7029, EPAT 22, LPT 3037,	
	Vi 27-0102 (in WPT-22),	
	VPS 6091(e)	
	RA 5460, DPS 2021, RD 27241	

Vocal with own guitar:

[83.] BVE 45901-2[23] **Mississippi Moon**	Unissued
	[Remade Feb. 4, 1932]

June 12, 1928 (continued)

Vocal with own guitar:

Take 1:

16. BVE 45093-2   **My Little Old Home**   Vi 21574, Bb B-5609, MW M-4218   Oct. 5, 1928,
               Down in New Orleans   HMV N4336, RZ IZ317,   with "Dear
               (Rodgers)[24]   RZ T5341, Zo 5341, Zo EE139   Old Sunny
               ©1928, SMP   *Train Whistle Blues* (LPM 1640),   South by
                                   DPL 2-0075   the Sea"
                                   RA 5460, DPS 2021, RD 27110

Vocal with own guitar:

Take 1:

17. BVE 45094-2   **You and My Old Guitar** Vi V-40072, Bb B-5083, El 2009,   June 7, 1929,
               (McWilliams-Rodgers)   MW M-4224, Sr S-3170,   with "My
               ©1928, SMP   Vi 420-0028 (in PT-3035)   Little Lady"
                                   RZ IZ323, RZ T5423,
                                   Tw FT1276, Zo 5423
                                   Never No Mo' Blues (LPM 1232),
                                   CPL 1-2504(e), EPAT 411,
                                   LPT 3039, Vi 447-0028
                                   RA 5460, DPM 2047,
                                   EP 21002, RD 27138

Vocal with own guitar:

Take 1:

18. BVE 45095-2   **Daddy and Home**   Vi 21757, Bb B-5991, MW M-8109, Dec. 2, 1928,
               (McWilliams-Rodgers)   Vi 20-6408, Vi 21-0043 (in P-244) with "My
               ©1928, SMP   RZ G22792, RZ IZ318,   Old Pal"
                                   RZ IZ414, RZ MR1918,
                                   RZ T5356, Tw FT1756,
                                   Tw FT1980, Zo 5356, Zo EE150
                                   Never No Mo' Blues (LPM 1232),
                                   EPAT 409, LPT 3038, LSP 3315(e)
                                   Vi 27-0099 (in WPT-21),
                                   Vi 47-6408, VPS 6091(e)
                                   RA 5460, EP 21002, RD 27138

Vocal with own guitar:

Take 1:

19. BVE 45096-2   **My Little Lady**   Vi V-40072, Bb B-5838,   June 7, 1929,
               (McWilliams-Rodgers)   MW M-4731, Vi 420-0029   with "You
               ©1928, SMP   (in PT-3035)   and My Old
                                   HMV N4371, RZ IZ323,   Guitar"
                                   RZ T5423, Zo 5423
                                   Never No Mo' Blues (LPM 1232),
                                   EPAT 411, LPT 3039, Vi 447-0029
                                   RA 5460, RA 5501, RD 27138[25]

June 12, 1928 (continued)
                    Vocal with own guitar:

[25.] BVE 45097-2 **I'm Lonely and Blue**   Unissued
                    (McWilliams–Rodgers)   [Remade Oct. 22, 1928]
                    ©1928, SMP

                    Vocal with own guitar:

                                                    Take 2:
20. BVE 45098-2 **Lullaby Yodel**   Vi 21636, Bb B-5337,   Nov. 2, 1928,
                    (McWilliams–Rodgers)   MW M-4218, Sr S-3418   with "Memphis
                    ©1928, SMP   HMV EA1540, HMV N4291,   Yodel"
                                                        RZ G23114, RZ IZ315,
                                                        RZ T5283, Zo 5283
                                                    Train Whistle Blues (LPM 1640)
                                                        RA 5460, DPS 2021, RA 5176,
                                                        RA 5510, RA 9037, RD 27110

                    Vocal with own guitar:

                                                    Take 1:
21. BVE 45099-3 **Never No Mo' Blues**   Vi 21531, Bb B-6225, Vi 20-6408,   Sept. 7, 1928,
                    (McWilliams–Rodgers)   Vi 21-0043 (in P-244)   with "Blue
                    ©1928, SMP   RZ IZ314, RZ T5247,   Yodel No. 3"
                                                        Tw FT1733, Zo 5247,
                                                        Zo EE109
                                                    Never No Mo' Blues (LPM 1232),
                                                    EPAT 409, LPT 3038, Vi 27-0099
                                                    (in WPT-21), Vi 47-6408,
                                                    Vi 599-9020 (in SPD-3),
                                                    VPS 6091(e)
                                                        RA 5460, EP 21002, RA 5176,
                                                        RA 5510, RD 27138

                    Peachtree Road
                    Atlanta, Georgia
                    October 20, 1928

                    Vocal, with Dean Bryan, guitar; C. L. Hutchison, cornet; John Westbrook,
                        steel guitar; James Rikard, clarinet; George MacMillan, string bass:
                                                    Take 3:
22. BVE 47215-3 **My Carolina Sunshine Girl** Vi V-40096, Bb B-5556,   Aug. 22, 1929,
                    (Rodgers)   MW M-4451, Vi 21-0180   with "Desert
                    ©1929, SMP   (in P-318)   Blues"
                                                        HMV N4351, RZ T5495,
                                                        Zo 5495
                                                    My Rough and Rowdy Ways
                                                    (LPM 2112; ANLI-1209e),
                                                    DPL 2-0075, EPA 5097, EPAT 23,
                                                    LPT 3038, Vi 27-0104 (in WPT-23),
                                                    VPS 6091(e)
                                                        RA 5460, DPM 2047,
                                                        EP 20219, L 10883,
                                                        RA 9037, RCX 1058

October 20, 1928 *(continued)*

Vocal, with Dean Bryan, guitar; C. L. Hutchison, cornet; John Westbrook, steel guitar; James Rikard, clarinet; George MacMillan, string bass:

Take 4:

23. BVE 47216–4 **Blue Yodel No. 4**
(Rodgers)
©1929, SMP
	Vi V–40014, MW M–4722,
	MW M–8124, Vi 21–0175
	(in P–282)
	    HMV MH192, RZ G22792,
	    RZ IZ320, RZ IZ414,
	    RZ MR1918, RZ T5380,
	    Tw FT1980, Zo 5380
	Never No Mo' Blues (LPM 1232),
	EPAT 409, LPT 3038, Vi 27–0101
	(in WPT–22), VPS 6091(e)
	    RA 5460, RA 9037, RD 27138
		Feb. 8, 1929,
		with "Waiting
		for a Train"

Peachtree Road
Atlanta, Georgia
October 22, 1928

Vocal, with Dean Bryan, guitar; C. L. Hutchison, cornet; John Westbrook, steel guitar; James Rikard, clarinet; George MacMillan, string bass:

Take 4:

24. BVE 47223–4 **Waiting for a Train**
(Rodgers)
©1929, SMP
	Vi V–40014, Bb B–5163, El 2060,
	MW M–8109, Sr S–3244,
	Vi 21–0175 (in P–282)
	    HMV MH192, RZ IZ320,
	    RZ T5380, Zo 5380
	Never No Mo' Blues (LPM 1232),
	ANL 1–1052, ANS 1–1052,
	DPL 2–0075, EPAT 409, LPT 3038,
	LSP 3315(e), Vi 27–0101
	(in WPT–22), VPS 6091(e)
	    RA 5460, AP 3004, HP 526,
	    RA 5501, RA 9037, RD 27138
		Feb. 8, 1929,
		with "Blue
		Yodel
		No. 4"

Vocal, with Dean Bryan, guitar; C. L. Hutchison, cornet; John Westbrook, steel guitar; George MacMillan, string bass:

Take 3:

25. BVE 47224–5[26] **I'm Lonely and Blue**
[Remake of (McWilliams–Rodgers)
BVE 45097 ©1928, United Music
—see session   Pub. Co.
of June 12,
1928]
	Vi V–40054
	Take 5:
	Vi V–40054, MW M–4047,
	MW M–4217
	    HMV N4327, RZ IZ321,
	    RZ T5401, Zo 5401
	The Short but Brilliant Life of
	Jimmie Rodgers (LPM 2634;
	AHMI–3094)
	    RA 5460, RD 7562
		Apr. 19, 1929,
		with "The
		Sailor's Plea"

Victor Studios
46th Street
New York, New York
February 21, 1929

Vocal, with house orchestra of unknown violin, cornet, clarinet, tuba,
    piano, trapman, conducted by Leonard Joy:[27]

		Take 3:	
26. BVE 48384-3	**Desert Blues**	Vi V–40096, MW M–4451,	Aug. 22, 1929,
	(Rodgers)	Vi 21–0176 (in P–282)	with "My
	©1929, SMP	HMV N4351, RZ T5495,	Carolina
		Zo 5495	Sunshine
		Jimmie the Kid (LPM 2213),	Girl"
		ACL 7029, EPAT 22, LPT 3037,	
		Vi 27–0102 (in WPT–22)	
		RA 5460, DPS 2021, RD 27241	

Vocal and own guitar, with house orchestra of unknown violin, cornet,
    clarinet, tuba, piano, trapman, conducted by Leonard Joy:

		Take 1:	
27. BVE 48385-2	**Any Old Time**	Vi 22488, Bb B–5664,	Sept. 5, 1930,
	(Rodgers)	MW M–4730	with "Blue
	©1929, SMP	HMV N4215, RZ T5780,	Yodel No. 7"
		Zo 5780, Zo EE221	
		Train Whistle Blues (LPM 1640),	
		DPL 2–0075, LSP 3315(e),	
		VPS 6091(e)	
		RA 5460, DPS 2021, RA 5176,	
		RA 5510, RA 9037, RD 27110	

Victor Studios
46th Street
New York, New York
February 23, 1929

Vocal with own guitar:

		Take 2:	
28. BVE 49990-2	**Blue Yodel No. 5**	Vi 22072, MW M–4212	Sept. 20, 1929,
	(Rodgers)	RZ IZ326, RZ T5548,	with "I'm
	©1929, SMP	Tw FT1824, Zo 5548	Sorry We Met"
		Zo EE185	
		Train Whistle Blues (LPM 1640)	
		RA 5460, DPS 2021,	
		RD 27110	

Vocal with own guitar:

		Take 2:	
29. BVE 49991-3	**High Powered Mama**	Vi 22523	Oct. 17, 1930,
	(Rodgers)	RZ IZ334, RZ T5808, Zo 5808	with "In the
	©1929, SMP	*Train Whistle Blues* (LPM 1640)	Jailhouse Now
		RA 5461, DPS 2021, RD 27110	No. 2"

February 23, 1929 (continued)

Vocal with own guitar:

Take 1:

30. BVE 49992-2 **I'm Sorry We Met**   Vi 22072, Vi 21-0177 (in P-282)   Sept. 20, 1929,
(Rodgers)   RZ IZ326, RZ T5548,   with "Blue
©1929, SMP   Tw FT1824, Vi A1466,   Yodel No. 5"
Zo 5548, Zo EE185
Jimmie the Kid (LPM 2213),
ACL 7029, EPAT 22, LPT 3037,
Vi 27-0103 (in WPT-22)
RA 5461, DPS 2021, RD 27241

Banquet Hall
Jefferson Hotel
Dallas, Texas
August 8, 1929

Vocal, with Billy Burkes, guitar; Joe Kaipo, steel guitar; Weldon Burkes,
ukulele:

Take 2:

31. BVE 55307-2 **Everybody Does It in**   Vi 22143   Nov. 22, 1929,
    Hawaii[28]   HMV N4364, RZ IZ327,   with "Frankie
(McWilliams-Rodgers)   RZ T5577, Zo 5577, Zo EE189   and Johnny"
©1929, SMP   *The Short but Brilliant Life of*
Jimmie Rodgers (LPM 2634;
AHMI-3094), DPL 2-0075
RA 5461, RD 7562

Vocal, with Billy Burkes, guitar; Joe Kaipo, steel guitar, Weldon Burkes,
ukulele; Bob MacGimsey, harmony whistling:

Take 1:

32. BVE 55308-3 **Tuck Away My Lonesome** Vi 22220, Bb B-5664, MW M-5036, Jan. 3, 1930,
    Blues   Vi 21-0181 (in P-318)   with "My
(Rodgers-Kaipo-McWilliams)   RZ T5983, Tw FT1356,   Rough and
©1929, SMP   Zo 5983, Zo EE269   Rowdy Ways"
Jimmie the Kid (LPM 2213),
EPAT 23, LPT 3038, Vi 27-0105
(in WPT-23)
RA 5461, DPS 2021, RD 27241

Vocal, with Billy Burkes, guitar; Joe Kaipo, steel guitar; Weldon Burkes,
ukulele:

Take 2:

33. BVE 55309-2 **Train Whistle Blues**   Vi 22379, MW M-4223   June 5, 1930,
(Rodgers)   HMV EA1539, HMV N4345,   with "Jimmie's
©1929, SMP   RZ G23113, RZ T5697,   Texas Blues"
Zo 5697
Train Whistle Blues (LPM 1640),
ANL 1-1052, ANS 1-1052
RA 5461, DPS 2021, EP 20176,
RA 9037, RD 27110

Banquet Hall
Jefferson Hotel
Dallas, Texas
August 10, 1929

Vocal, with Billy Burkes, guitar; Joe Kaipo, steel guitar:

Take 2:

| 34. BVE 55332-2 | **Jimmie's Texas Blues**
(Rodgers)
©1929, SMP | Vi 22379, MW M-4212
HMV EA1539, HMV N4355
RZ G23113, RZ T5697,
Zo 5697
Train Whistle Blues (LPM 1640)
RA 5461, DPS 2021, RA 9037,
RD 27110 | June 5, 1930,
with "Train
Whistle Blues" |

Vocal with own guitar:

Take 2:

| 35. BVE 55333-2 | **Frankie and Johnny**
(arr. Rodgers)[29]
©1929, SMP | Vi 22143, Bb B-5223, El 2109,
MW M-4309, MW M-4721,
Sr S-3306, Vi 21-0044 (in P-244)
HMV N4371, RZ IZ327,
RZ T5577, Zo 5577, Zo EE189
Jimmie the Kid (LPM 2213),
ACL 7029, DPL 2-0075, EPAT 21,
LPT 3037, Vi 27-0100
(in WPT-21), VPS 6091(e)
RA 5461, DPS 2021,
HMV 7EG 8163, RA 5501,
RA 9037 | Nov. 22, 1929,
with "Every-
body Does It
in Hawaii" |

Banquet Hall
Jefferson Hotel
Dallas, Texas
August 12, 1929

Vocal, with unknown cornet, piano, saxophone, banjo, string bass:

| [35.] BVE 55344-3
[Remake of
BVE 55333—
see session of
Aug. 10, 1929] | **Frankie and Johnny** | Unissued | |

Vocal and own guitar, with Joe Kaipo, steel guitar; L. D. Dyke, musical saw:[30]

| [86.] BVE 55345-3
[Takes 1-3—for
takes 4 and 5,
see session of
Feb. 6, 1932] | **Home Call**
(Rodgers-McWilliams)
©1929, SMP | [78 rpm issues from take 4]
Take 2:
Jimmie the Kid (LPM 2213),
CPL 1-2504(e), LPT 3073,
Vi 947-0225 (in EPBT 3073)
RA 5465, DPS 2021, RD 27241 | |

Banquet Hall
Jefferson Hotel
Dallas, Texas
October 22, 1929

Vocal, with Billy Burkes, guitar; Joe Kaipo, steel guitar; Weldon Burkes,
ukulele:

Take 3:

36. BVE 56449-4 **Whisper Your Mother's**
Name
(Rodgers)
©1929, SMP

Vi 22319, Bb B-5057, El 1983,
MW M-4207, Sr S-3142
HMV EA1382, HMV EA2242,
HMV N4310, RZ G23193,
RZ IZ496, RZ MR2242,
Tw FT9115
When the Evening Shadows Fall
(LSP 4073e)
RA 5461, DPM 2047

Apr. 4, 1930,
with "A
Drunkard's
Child"

Vocal with own guitar:

Take 1:

37. BVE 56450-4 **The Land of My Boyhood**
Dreams
(Rodgers)
©1929, SMP

Vi 23811, Bb B-5337, MW M-4450,
MW M-4728, Sr S-3418
HMV EA1303, HMV N4259,
RZ G23190
Take 4:
My Time Ain't Long (LPM 2865)
RA 5461, RD 7644

July 14, 1933
with
"Southern
Cannonball"

Vocal with own guitar:

Take 3:

38. BVE 56453-3 **Blue Yodel No. 6.**
(Rodgers)
©1929, SMP

Vi 22271, MW M-4211,
Vi 21-0182 (in P-318)
RZ IZ329, RZ T5623, Zo 5623
Never No Mo' Blues (LPM 1232),
EPAT 410, LPT 3039, Vi 27-0106
(in WPT-23)
RA 5461, DPM 2047, RD 27138

Feb. 21, 193(
with
"Yodeling
Cowboy"

Vocal with own guitar:

Take 3:

39. BVE 56454-3 **Yodeling Cowboy**
(Rodgers-McWilliams)
©1929, SMP

Vi 22271, Bb B-5991,
MW M-4058, MW M-4213
HMV N4381, RZ IZ329,
RZ T5623, Zo 5623
Country Music Hall of Fame
(LPM 2531), LSP 4073(e)
RA 5461, RD 7505

Feb. 21, 193(
with "Blue
Yodel No. 6"

October 22, 1929 (continued)

    Vocal and own guitar, with Joe Kaipo, steel guitar:

                     Take 1:

40. BVE 56455-3 **My Rough and Rowdy Ways**
(Rodgers-McWilliams)
©1929, SMP
	Vi 22220, MW M-4215
	   RZ T6022, Tw FT1808,
	   Zo 6022, Zo EE269
	My Rough and Rowdy Ways
	(LPM 2112; ANLI-1209e),
	DPL 2-0075, VPS 6091(e)
	   RA 5461, L 10883, RD 27203
		Jan. 3, 1930,
		with "Tuck
		Away My
		Lonesome
		Blues"

    Vocal with own guitar:

                     Take 3:

41. BVE 56456-3 **I've Ranged, I've Roamed, and I've Travelled**
(Rodgers-McWilliams)[31]
©1929, SMP
	Bb B-5892, MW M-5013
	   HMV EA1566, HMV N4377,
	   RZ G23205
	Take 1:[32]
	My Time Ain't Long (LPM 2865),
	DPL 2-0075
	   RA 5461, RD 7644
		Apr. 10, 1935,
		with "Why
		Did You
		Give Me
		Your Love?"

New Orleans, Louisiana
November 13, 1929[33]

    Vocal, with Billy Burkes, guitar:

                     Take 1:

42. BVE 56528-3 **Hobo Bill's Last Ride**
(Waldo O'Neal)
©1929, SMP
	Vi 22421, MW M-4210
	   RZ IZ333, RZ T5724,
	   Tw FT1784, Zo 5724,
	   Zo EE213
	Train Whistle Blues (LPM 1640),
	ANL 1-1052, ANS 1-1052
	   RA 5461, DPS 2021, EP 20176,
	   RA 5176, RA 5510, RA 9037,
	   RD 27110
		Aug. 1, 1930,
		with "That's
		Why I'm
		Blue"

Atlanta Women's Club
Atlanta, Georgia
November 25, 1929

    Vocal, with Billy Burkes, guitar:

                     Take 3:

43. BVE 56594-4 **Mississippi River Blues**
(Rodgers)[34]
©1929, SMP
	Vi 23535, Bb B-5393, MW M-4722
	   HMV EA1402, HMV N4207,
	   RZ G23199, RZ T5983,
	   Tw FT1356, Zo 5983
	Country Music Hall of Fame
	(LPM 2531)
	   RA 5462, DPM 2047,
	   RA 9038, RD 7505
		Apr. 24, 1931,
		with "T.B.
		Blues"

November 25, 1929 (continued)

Vocal, with Billy Burkes, guitar:

Take 4:

44. BVE 56595-4 **Nobody Knows but Me**   Vi 23518, MW M-4724   Mar. 13, 1931,
    (Rodgers-McWilliams)   HMV EA1401, HMV N4322,   with "The
    ©1929, SMP   RZ G23198, Tw FT9116   Mystery of
                                           The Short but Brilliant Life of Number Five"
                                           Jimmie Rodgers (LPM 2634;
                                           AHMI-3094)
                                               RA 5462, RD 7562

Atlanta Women's Club
Atlanta Georgia
November 26, 1929

Vocal and own guitar, with Billy Burkes, guitar:

Take 1:

45. BVE 56607-3 **Anniversary Blue Yodel**[35]   Vi 22488, MW M-4210   Sept. 5, 1930,
    (Rodgers-McWilliams)   HMV N4215, RZ T5780,   with "Any
    ©1929, SMP   Zo 5780, Zo EE221   Old Time"
                                           Jimmie the Kid
                                           (LPM 2213), LPT 3073,
                                           Vi 947-0226 (in EPBT 3073)
                                               RA 5462, DPS 2021, RD 27242

Vocal with own guitar:[36]

Take 1:

46. BVE 56608-3 **She Was Happy Till She**   Vi 23681, Bb B-5057, El 1983,   July 1, 1932,
                Met You   MW M-4207, MW M-4324,[37]   with "Home
    (Rodgers-McWilliams)   Sr S-3142   Call"
    ©1929, SMP   RZ IZ388, RZ MR1335,
                                                 Tw FT1723, Zo EE352
                                           Country Music Hall of Fame
                                           (LPM 2531)
                                               RA 5462, RD 7505

Atlanta Women's Club
Atlanta, Georgia
November 27, 1929

Vocal and own guitar, with Billy Burkes, guitar:

Take 1:

47. BVE 56617-4 **Blue Yodel Number**   Vi 23796, MW M-4726   June 30, 1933
                Eleven[38]   [No foreign 78s]   with "Sweet
    (Rodgers)   *The Short but Brilliant Life of* Mama Hurry
    ©1933, Peer Intl. Corp.   *Jimmie Rodgers* (LPM 2634;   Home"
                                           AHMI-3094), NW 287
                                               RA 5462, DPM 2047, RD 7562

Atlanta Women's Club
Atlanta, Georgia
November 28, 1929

Vocal, with Billy Burkes, guitar:

Take 1:

48. BVE 56618-3 **A Drunkard's Child**
(Andrew Jenkins-
Jimmie Rodgers)[39]
©1929, SMP

Vi 22319, MW M–4221
  HMV EA1385, RZ G23194,
  Zo 4343
*The Short but Brilliant Life of
Jimmie Rodgers* (LPM 2634;
AHMI-3094)
  RA 5462, DPM 2047, RD 7562

Apr. 4, 1930,
with
"Whisper
Your Mother's
Name"

Vocal, with Billy Burkes, guitar:

Take 1:

49. BVE 56619-3 **That's Why I'm Blue**
(Rodgers-McWilliams)
©1929, SMP

Vi 22421, Bb B–6198, Mw M–4222
  RZ IZ333, RZ IZ422,
  RZ MR2049, RZ T5724,
  Tw FT1784, Zo 5724,
  Zo EE213
My Time Ain't Long (LPM 2865)
  RA 5462, RD 7644

Aug. 1, 1930,
with "Hobo
Bill's Last
Ride"

Vocal, with Billy Burkes, guitar:

Take 3:[40]

50. BVE 56620-4 **Why Did You Give Me
Your Love?**
(Rodgers)
©1929, SMP

Bb B–5892, MW M–5013
  HMV EA1566, HMV N4377,
  RZ G23205
My Time Ain't Long (LPM 2865),
LSP 3315(e)
  RA 5462, DPM 2047, RD 7644

Apr. 10, 1935,
with "I've
Ranged,
I've Roamed,
and I've
Travelled"

Victor Hollywood Studios
7000 Santa Monica Boulevard
Hollywood, California
June 30, 1930

Vocal, with Bob Sawyer's Jazz Band: Bob Sawyer, piano; unknown cornet,
  clarinet,[41] banjo, tuba:

Take 2:

51. PBVE 54849-3 **My Blue-Eyed Jane**
(Jimmie Rodgers-
LuluBelle White)
©1930, SMP

Vi 23549, Bb B–5393, MW M–4222
  HMV EA1399, HMV N4302,
  RZ G23196, Tw FT9114
My Rough and Rowdy Ways
(LPM 2112; ANLI-1209e),
DPL 2-0075
  RA 5462, L 10883, RD 27203

June 5, 1931,
with "Jimmie
the Kid"

June 30, 1930 (continued)

Vocal, with Lani McIntire's Hawaiians:[42] Lani McIntire, guitar;
unknown steel guitar, ukulele, string bass:

Take 3:

52. PBVE 54850-3   **Why Should I Be**   Vi 23609, Bb B-5082, MW M-4204,   Dec. 4, 1931,
          Lonely   Sr S-3169   with "What's
          (Jimmie Rodgers–   HMV N4221, RZ IZ336,   It?"
            Estelle Lovell)   RZ T6102, Zo 6102, Zo EE305
          ©1930, SMP   *The Short but Brilliant Life of*
                                 Jimmie Rodgers (LPM 2634;
                                 AHMI-3094), LSP 3315(e)
                                 RA 5462, RA 9038, RD 7562

Vocal, with Lani McIntire's Hawaiians: Lani McIntire, guitar;
unknown steel guitar, ukulele, string bass:

Take 3:

53. PBVE 54851-3   **Moonlight and Skies**   Vi 23574, Bb B-5000,[44] El 1830,   Oct. 23, 1931.
          (Jimmie Rodgers–   El 1958, MW M-4216,   with "Jimmie
            Raymond E. Hall)[43]   MW M-4720, Sr S-3104   Rodgers Visits
          ©1930, SMP   Col IFB341, HMV MH187,   the Carter
                                   HMV N4322, RZ IZ469,   Family"
                                   RZ MR2200, Tw FT9116,
                                   Zo EE369
                                 The Short but Brilliant Life of
                                 Jimmie Rodgers (LPM 2634;
                                 AHMI-3094), DPL 2-0075,
                                 LSP 3315(e)
                                 RA 5462, RA 5510, RD 7562

Victor Hollywood Studios
7000 Santa Monica Boulevard
Hollywood, California
July 1, 1930

Vocal with own guitar:

Take 2:

54. PBVE 54852-2   **Pistol Packin' Papa**   Vi 22554, MW M-4316,   Dec. 5, 1930,
          (Rodgers–O'Neal)   MW M-4730, Vi 420-0027   with "Those
          ©1930, SMP   (in PT-3035)   Gambler's
                                   RZ T6011, Zo 4342, Zo 6011,   Blues"
                                   Zo EE232
                                 Never No Mo' Blues (LPM 1232),
                                 EPAT 410, LPT 3039, Vi 447-0027,
                                 VPS 6091(e)
                                 RA 5462, DPM 2047, RD 27138

Victor Hollywood Studios
7000 Santa Monica Boulevard
Hollywood, California
July 2, 1930

Vocal, with Lani McIntire's Hawaiians: Lani McIntire, guitar;
unknown steel guitar, ukulele, string bass:
Take 3:

55. PBVE 54854–3   **Take Me Back Again**   Bb B–7600   May 25, 1938,
(Rodgers–Hall)[45]   HMV N4422   with
©1930, SMP   *The Short but Brilliant Life of*   "Dreaming
Jimmie Rodgers (LPM 2634;   with Tears in
AHMI-3094)   My Eyes"[46]
RA 5462, RD 7562

Victor Hollywood Studios
7000 Santa Monica Boulevard
Hollywood, California
July 5, 1930

Vocal, with Lani McIntire, guitar:
Take 1:

56. PBVE 54855–3   **Those Gambler's Blues**   Vi 22554, MW M–4211   Dec. 5, 1930,
(arr. Rodgers)   RZ MR911, Zo 4344, Zo EE232   with "Pistol
©1930, SMP   *My Time Ain't Long* (LPM 2865)   Packin' Papa"
RA 5463, RD 7644

Victor Hollywood Studios
7000 Santa Monica Boulevard
Hollywood, California
July 7, 1930

Vocal, with Lani McIntire's Hawaiians: Lani McIntire, guitar;
unknown steel guitar, ukulele, string bass:
Take 2:

57. PBVE 54856–3[47]   **I'm Lonesome Too**   Vi 23564, Bb B–5739,   July 17, 1931,
(Rodgers)   MW M–4220   with
©1930, SMP   HMV EA1253, RZ G23189,   "Travelling
RZ IZ401, RZ MR1599,   Blues"
Tw FT1822
Country Music Hall of Fame
(LPM 2531)
RA 5463, RD 7505

Vocal, with Lani McIntire's Hawaiians: Lani McIntire, guitar:
unknown steel guitar, ukulele, string bass:
Take 1:

58. PBVE 54857–3   **The One Rose**   Bb B–7280   Dec. 1, 1937,
(Lani McIntire)   [No foreign 78s]   with "Yodeling
©1929, Charles P.   *My Rough and Rowdy Ways*   My Way Back
Loveland and   (LPM 2112; ANL 1-1209e)   Home"

July 7, 1930 (continued)

Del Lyon—	RA 5463, L 10883, RA 5176,
assigned to	RA 5510, RA 9038, RD 27203
SMP, 1938	

Victor Hollywood Studios
7000 Santa Monica Boulevard
Hollywood, California
July 8, 1930

Vocal, with Lani McIntire's Hawaiians: Lani McIntire, guitar;
    unknown steel guitar, ukulele, string bass:

[59.] PBVE 54860-2	**For the Sake of Days**	Unissued
[Takes 1 and 2]	**Gone By**	[Remade July 9, 1930]

Victor Hollywood Studios
7000 Santa Monica Boulevard
Hollywood, California
July 9, 1930

Vocal, with Lani McIntire's Hawaiians: Lani McIntire, guitar;
    unknown steel guitar, ukulele, string bass:

		Take 3:	
59. PBVE 54860-2	**For the Sake of Days**	Vi 23651, Bb B-5784, MW M-4221	Apr. 8, 1932,
[Takes 3 and 4-	**Gone By**	HMV N4281, Vi A1430,	with "Roll
for takes 1 and	(Jimmie Rodgers-	Zo EE363	Along,
2, see session of	Jack White)	*Country Music Hall of Fame*	Kentucky
July 8, 1930]	©1930, SMP	(LPM 2531)	Moon"
		RA 5463, DPM 2047, RD 7505	

Victor Hollywood Studios
7000 Santa Monica Boulevard
Hollywood, California
July 10, 1930

Vocal and own guitar, with Bob Sawyer's Jazz Band: Bob Sawyer,
    piano; unknown banjo, clarinet, cornet, tuba:

		Take 3:	
60. PBVE 54861-3	**Jimmie's Mean Mama**	Vi 23503, MW M-4723,	cà. Feb. 6, 193
	Blues	Vi 420-0027 (in PT-3035)	with "Blue
	(Waldo O'Neal-	HMV EA1541, RZ G23115,	Yodel No. 8"
	Bob Sawyer)	RZ T5859, Zo 5859	
	©1930, SMP	*Never No Mo' Blues* (LPM 1232),	
		EPAT 410, LPT 3039, Vi 447-0027	
		RA 5463, RD 27138	

Victor Hollywood Studios
7000 Santa Monica Boulevard
Hollywood, California
July 11, 1930

Vocal with own guitar:

Take 3:

51. PBVE 54862-3 **The Mystery of**   Vi 23518, Bb B-5739, MW M-4223   Mar. 13, 1931,
                 Number Five   HMV EA1401, RZ G23198,   with "Nobody
                 (Rodgers)   RZ IZ401, RZ MR1599,   Knows but
                 ©1930, SMP   Tw FT1822, Zo 4343   Me"
                                     My Time Ain't Long (LPM 2865),
                                     LSP 3315(e)
                                     RA 5463, DPM 2047, RD 7644

Vocal with own guitar:

Take 1:

62. PBVE 54863-3 **Blue Yodel No. 8**   Vi 23503, Bb B-6275,   ca. Feb. 6, 1931,
                 (Rodgers)   MW M-4723, MW M-8235,   with "Jimmie's
                 ©1930, SMP   Vi 20-6205   Mean Mama
                                     HMV EA1541, RZ G23115,   Blues"
                                     RZ T5859, Zo 5859
                                     My Rough and Rowdy Ways
                                     (LPM 2112; ANLI-1209e),
                                     CPL 1-2504(e), LPM 2633,
                                     LPT 3073, LSP 3315(e)
                                     Vi 47-6205, Vi 947-0226
                                     (in EPBT 3073), VPS 6091(e)
                                       RA 5463, L 10883, RA 5176,
                                       RA 5510, RA 9038, RD 27203

Victor Hollywood Studios
7000 Santa Monica Boulevard
Hollywood, California
July 12, 1930

Vocal with own guitar:

Take 1:

63. PBVE 54864-3 **In the Jailhouse Now—**   Vi 22523, MW M-4315, Vi 20-6092   Oct. 17, 1930,
                 No. 2   HMV MH193, RZ IZ334,   with "High
                 (Rodgers)   RZ T5808, Zo 5808   Powered
                 ©1930, SMP   *My Rough and Rowdy Ways*   Mama"
                                     (LPM 2112; ANLI-1209e),
                                     CPL 1-2504(e), LPM 2564,
                                     LPT 3073, Vi 47-6092,
                                     Vi 947-0226 (in EPBT 3073),
                                     VPS 6091(e)
                                       RA 5463, L 10883, RA 5501,
                                       RD 27203

Victor Hollywood Studios
7000 Santa Monica Boulevard
Hollywood, California
July 16, 1930

Vocal, with Louis Armstrong, trumpet; Lillian Hardin Armstrong,
    piano:

Take 2:

64. PBVE 54867-3   **Blue Yodel No. 9**   Vi 23580, MW M-4209,   Sept. 11, 1931
                   (Rodgers)   MW M-4724   with "Looking
                   ©1930, SMP   Col MZ315,[48] HMV MH194,   for a New
                                              RZ MR3208, Tw FT8832,   Mama"
                                              Zo EE300
                                          My Rough and Rowdy Ways
                                          (LPM 2112; ANLI-1209e)
                                              RA 5463, L 10883, RA 5176,
                                              RA 5510, RD 27203

Victor Hollywood Studios
7000 Santa Monica Boulevard
Hollywood, California
July 17, 1930

Dialog with I. N. Bronsen:

Take 1:

−PBVE 1302-1   **The Pullman Porters**   ES-13

Texas Hotel
San Antonio, Texas
January 31, 1931

Vocal and own guitar, with Charles Kama, steel guitar:

Take 3:

65. BVE 67133-3   **T.B. Blues**   Vi 23535, Bb B-6275, MW M-4067,   Apr. 24, 1931
                  (Rodgers-Hall)[49]   MW M-4729[50]   with
                  ©1931, SMP   HMV EA1402, RZ G23199,   "Mississippi
                                              RZ IZ616, RZ MR911,   River Blues"
                                              RZ MR2374, Zo 4344
                                          Country Music Hall of Fame
                                          (LPM 2531)[51]
                                              RA 5463, RD 7505

Vocal, with Charles Kama, steel guitar: M. T. Salazar, guitar; Shelly
    Lee Alley and Alvin Alley, violins; Mike Cordova, string bass:

Take 2:

66. BVE 67134-3   **Travellin' Blues**   Vi 23564, MW M-4729,   July 17, 1931
                  (Jimmie Rodgers-   HMV EA1514, HMV N4367,   with "I'm
                    Shelly Lee Alley)   RZ G23112   Lonesome
                  ©1931, SMP   *My Rough and Rowdy Ways*   Too"

January 31, 1931 (continued)

> (LPM 2112; ANLI-1209e),
> LPT 3073, Vi 947-0225
> (in EPBT 3073)
>   RA 5463, DPM 2047,
>   L 10883, RD 27203

Vocal, with Charles Kama, steel guitar; M. T. Salazar, guitar;
Mike Cordova, string bass:

		Take 1:	
67. BVE 67135-3	**Jimmie the Kid**	Vi 23549, MW M-4731,	June 5, 1931,
	(Jimmie Rodgers-	HMV EA1399, HMV MH194,	with "My
	Jack Neville)	HMV N4302, RZ G23196,	Blue-Eyed
	©1931, SMP	RZ MR3208, RZ T6022,	Jane"
		Tw FT8832, Tw FT9114,	
		Zo 6022	
		Jimmie the Kid (LPM 2213),	
		DPL 2-0075	
		RA 5463, DPS 2021,	
		RA 5501, RD 27241	

500-block Main Street
Louisville, Kentucky
June 10, 1931

Vocal duet with Sara Carter; Maybelle Carter, guitar:[52]

		Take 1:	
68. BVE 69412-3	**Why There's a Tear**	Bb B-6698, MW M-7138	Nov. 23, 1936,
	in My Eye	RZ IZ616, RZ IZ649,	with "We
	(A. P. Carter)[53]	RZ ME33, RZ MR2374,	Miss Him
	©1937, Peer Intl. Corp.	RZ MR2429, Tw FT8313	When the
		Take 3:[54]	Evening
		My Time Ain't Long (LPM 2865)	Shadows
		RA 5463, DPM 2047, RA 5501,	Fall"
		RA 5645, RD 7644	[Mrs. Rodgers]

Vocal duet with Sara Carter; Maybelle Carter, guitar:

		Take 2:	
69. BVE 69413-3	**The Wonderful City**[55]	Bb B-6810, MW M-7137	Feb. 17, 1937,
	(Rodgers-McWilliams)	RZ G23184, RZ IZ662,	with "I've
	©1950, Peer Intl. Corp.	RZ MR2455, Tw FT8313	Only Loved
		My Time Ain't Long (LPM 2865)	Three Women"
		RA 5464, DPM 2047, RA 5501,	
		RA 5645, RD 7644	

500-block Main Street
Louisville, Kentucky
June 11, 1931

Vocal with own guitar:[56]

Take 3:

70. BVE 69424-4   **Let Me Be Your**   Vi 23621, Bb B-5084,   Dec. 31, 1931
                       Side Track   MW M-4209, Sr S-3171   with "Rodgers
                   (Rodgers)   HMV N4209, RZ T6056,   Puzzle
                   ©1931, SMP   Zo 6056, Zo EE363   Record"
                                                Train Whistle Blues (LPM 1640)
                                                RA 5464, DPS 2021, RD 27110

Vocal and dialog, with A. P. Carter, dialog; Sara Carter, vocal,
   dialog, and guitar; Maybelle Carter, vocal, dialog, and mandolin:

[71.] BVE 69427-3   **Jimmie Rodgers Visits**   Unissued
   [Takes 1-3]   **the Carter Family**   [Remade June 12, 1931]

Vocal, dialog, and own guitar, with A. P. Carter, dialog;
   Sara Carter, vocal and dialog; Maybelle Carter, dialog:

[72.] BVE 69428-3   **The Carter Family and**   Unissued[57]
   [Takes 1-3]   **Jimmie Rodgers in**   [Remade June 12, 1931]
                        Texas

500-block Main Street
Louisville, Kentucky
June 12, 1931

Vocal and dialog, with A. P. Carter, dialog; Sara Carter, vocal,
   dialog, and guitar; Maybelle Carter, vocal, dialog, and mandolin:

Take 4:

71. BVE 69427-1   **Jimmie Rodgers Visits**   Vi 23574, MW M-4720   Oct. 23, 1931
   [Take 4—for   **the Carter Family**   HMV MH188, RZ ME34,   with
   takes 1-3,   (Rodgers)[58]   RZ MR3164, Tw FT8806,   "Moonlight
   see session of   ©1931, SMP   Zo EE369   and Skies"
   June 11, 1931]   *My Time Ain't Long* (LPM 2865),
                                                   DMM 4-0406
                                                   RA 5464, RA 5501,
                                                   RA 5645, RD 7644[59]

Vocal, dialog, and own guitar, with A. P. Carter, dialog;
   Sara Carter, vocal and dialog; Maybelle Carter, dialog:

Take 4:

72. BVE 69428-1   **The Carter Family and** Bb B-6762, MW M-7137   Jan. 20, 1937
   [Take 4— for   **Jimmie Rodgers in**   HMV MH188, RZ ME34,   with "Where
   takes 1-3,   **Texas**   RZ MR3164, Tw FT8806   Is My Sailor
   see session of   (Rodgers)   *My Time Ain't Long* (LPM 2865),   Boy"
   June 11, 1931]   ©1931, SMP   DMM 4-0406, DPL 2-0075   [Monroe
                                                   RA 5464, RA 5501, RA 5645, Brothers]
                                                   RD 7644

500–block Main Street
Louisville, Kentucky
June 13, 1931

Vocal, with Cliff Carlisle, steel guitar; Wilber Ball, guitar:
Take 2:

73. BVE 69432-3 | **When the Cactus Is in Bloom** (Rodgers)[60] ©1931, SMP | Vi 23636, Bb B-5163, El 2060, MW M-4216, Sr S-3244 RZ MR2795, Tw FT8585,[61] Zo EE345 *Country Music Hall of Fame* (LPM 2531) RA 5464, DPM 2047, RA 9038, RD 7505 | Feb. 26, 1932, with "Gambling Polka Dot Blues"

500–block Main Street
Louisville, Kentucky
June 15, 1931

Vocal, with Ruth Ann Moore, piano:
Take 2:

74. BVE 69439-3 | **Gambling Polka Dot Blues** (Rodgers-Hall)[62] ©1931, SMP | Vi 23636 Zo 4365, Zo EE345 *My Time Ain't Long* (LPM 2865) RA 5464, RD 7644 | Feb. 26, 1932, with "When the Cactus Is in Bloom"

Vocal and own ukulele, with Cliff Carlisle, steel guitar; Wilber Ball, guitar:
Take 3:

75. BVE 69443-3 | **Looking for a New Mama** (Rodgers) ©1931, SMP | Vi 23580, Bb B-5037; El 1966, MW M-4203, Sr S-3131 RZ ME15, RZ MR3002, RZ MR20215, Tw FT8694, Zo EE300 *Jimmie the Kid* (LPM 2213) RA 5464, DPS 2021, RD 27241 | Sept. 11, 1931, with "Blue Yodel No. 9"

500–block Main Street
Louisville, Kentucky
June 16, 1931

Vocal, with Ruth Ann Moore, piano:
Take 1:

76. BVE 69448-4 | **What's It?** (Rodgers-Neville) ©1931, SMP | Vi 23609, Bb B-5084, MW M-4208, Sr S-3171 Zo EE305 *My Time Ain't Long* (LPM 2865) RA 5464, RD 7644 | Dec. 4, 1931, with "Why Should I Be Lonely"

June 16, 1931 (continued)

Vocal, with the Louisville Jug Band: Clifford Hayes, violin; Cal Smith and Fred Smith, guitars; Earl McDonald, jug; George Allen, clarinet:

Take 3:

77. BVE 69449-3   **My Good Gal's Gone Blues**   Bb B-5942, MW M-5014   May 22, 193
(Rodgers)   Tw FT1925   with "Leave
©1931, SMP   *Train Whistle Blues* (LPM 1640)   Me Alone
RA 5464, DPS 2021,   Sweet Mama
RD 27110   [Jesse
Rodgers]

500-block Main Street
Louisville, Kentucky
June 17, 1931

Vocal with own guitar:

Take 1:

78. BVE 69458-4   **Southern Cannon-Ball**   Vi 23811, MW M-4728   July 14, 193
(Rodgers-Hall)   HMV EA1503, HMV N4259,   with "Land
©1931, SMP   RZ G23111   My Boyhood
My Rough and Rowdy Ways   Dreams"
(LPM 2112; ANLI-1209e)
RA 5464, DPM 2047, L 10883,
RA 5501, RD 27203

Victor Studios
Camden, New Jersey
October 27, 1931 (Takes 1 and 2)
November 11, 1931 (Takes 3 and 4)

Remastering session:

Take 3:

– BVE 69032-4   **Rodgers' Puzzle Record**[63]   Vi 23621   Dec. 31, 19:
HMV EA1489, HMV N4209,   with "Let M
RZ G23204, RZ T6056,   Be Your
Zo 4365, Zo 6056   Side Track"
[No LP reissues]

Junior Ballroom
Jefferson Hotel
Dallas, Texas
February 2, 1932

Vocal, with Dick Bunyard, steel guitar; Red Young, mandolin; Bill Boyd, guitar; Fred Koone, string bass:

Take 2:

79. BVE 70645-2   **Roll Along, Kentucky Moon**   Vi 23651, Bb B-5082,   Apr. 8, 193:
MW M-4219, Sr S-3169   with "For tl
(Bill Halley)   HMV EA1228, HMV N4281,   Sake of Day
©1932, SMP   RZ G23188, RZ IZ1004,   Gone By"

February 2, 1932 (continued)

> RZ MR3122, Tw FT8775,
> Vi A1430, Zo 4370
> *Country Music Hall of Fame*
> (LPM 2531), DPL 2-0075,
> LSP 3315(e)
> RA 5464, DPM 2047,
> RA 5501, RA 9038, RD 7505

Junior Ballroom
Jefferson Hotel
Dallas, Texas
February 3, 1932

Vocal, with Dick Bunyard, steel guitar; Red Young, mandolin;
    Bill Boyd, guitar; Fred Koone, string bass:
                    Take 1:

80. BVE 70646-2	**Hobo's Meditation**	Vi 23711, MW M-4205	Sept. 23, 1932,
	(Rodgers)[64]	HMV EA1374, HMV N4233,	with "Down
	©1932, SMP	RZ G23192, RZ IZ1065,	the Old Road
		RZ MR3313, RZ MR20064,	to Home"
		Tw FT8902, Zo 4374	
		The Short but Brilliant Life of	
		Jimmie Rodgers (LPM 2634;	
		AHMI-3094)	
		RA 5464, RA 9038, RD 7562	

Junior Ballroom
Jefferson Hotel
Dallas, Texas
February 4, 1932

Vocal, with Billy Burkes, steel guitar; Weldon Burkes, guitar;
    Charlie Burkes, ukulele; Fred Koone, string bass:
                    Take 3:

81. BVE 70647-3	**My Time Ain't Long**	Vi 23669, Bb B-5083,	May 20, 1932,
	(Rodgers–O'Neal)	El 2009, Sr S-3170	with
	©1932, SMP	HMV N4210, RZ T6159,	"Ninety-nine
		Zo 6159	Year Blues"
		Take 1:	
		My Time Ain't Long (LPM 2865)	
		RA 5464, DPM 2047, RD 7644	

Vocal and own guitar, with Billy Burkes and Weldon Burkes,
    guitars; Fred Koone, string bass:
                    Take 2:

82. BVE 70648-2	**Ninety-nine Year**	Vi 23669, MW M-4215	May 20, 1932,
	Blues	HMV N4210, RZ T6159,	with "My
	(Rodgers-Hall)	Zo 6159	Time Ain't
	©1932, SMP	*The Short but Brilliant Life of*	Long"

February 4, 1932 (continued)

Jimmie Rodgers (LPM 2634;
AHMI-3094)
RA 5464, RD 7562

Vocal, with Billy Burkes, steel guitar; Weldon Burkes, guitar;
Fred Koone, string bass:
Take 5:[65]

83. BVE 45091-2 [Takes 3 and 4—for takes 1 and 2, see session of June 12, 1928]	**Mississippi Moon** (Rodgers–McWilliams) ©1928 United Music Pub. Co.	Vi 23696, Bb B-5136, El 2042, MW M-4220, Sr S-3217 HMV EA1253, HMV N4252, HMV N4292, RZ G23189, RZ IZ410, RZ MR1853, Vi A1401, Vi JA708 *My Rough and Rowdy Ways* (LPM 2112; ANLI-1209e) RA 5465, DPM 2047, L 10883, RA 5176, RA 5510, RD 27203	Aug. 12, 1932, with "Blue Yodel No. 10"

Junior Ballroom
Jefferson Hotel
Dallas, Texas
February 5, 1932

Vocal and own guitar, with Fred Koone, guitar:
Take 1:

84. BVE 70649-2	**Down the Old Road to Home** (Jimmie Rodgers– Carey D. Harvey) ©1932, SMP	Vi 23711, Bb B-5081, MW M-4202, Sr S-3168 HMV EA1374, RZ G23192, RZ IZ404, RZ MR1725 *Train Whistle Blues* (LPM 1640) RA 5465, DPS 2021, RA 9038, RD 27110	Sept. 23, 1932 with "Hobo's Meditation"

Junior Ballroom
Jefferson Hotel
Dallas, Texas
February 6, 1932

Vocal with own guitar:
Take 1:

85. BVE 70650-2	**Blue Yodel No. 10** (Rodgers) ©1932, SMP	Vi 23696, MW M-4208, MW M-4725 Col MZ315, HMV N4292, RZ MR3257, RZ MR20010, Tw FT8858, Vi A1401, Vi JA708 *The Short but Brilliant Life of Jimmie Rodgers* (LPM 2634; AHMI-3094) RA 5465, RD 7562	Aug. 12, 1932 with "Mississippi Moon"

February 6, 1932 (continued)

Vocal with own guitar:

Take 4:

86. BVE 55345-2   **Home Call**   Vi 23681, MW M-4219   July 1, 1932,
    [Takes 4 and   (Rodgers-McWilliams)   HMV N4367, Zo EE352   with "She Was
    5—for takes   ©1929, SMP   [LP reissues from take 2]   Happy Till She
    1-3, see session   Met You"
    of Aug. 12, 1929]

Victor Studio 2
114 North Fifth Street
Camden, New Jersey
August 10, 1932

Vocal, with Hoyt "Slim" Bryant, guitar; Clayton McMichen, fiddle;
Oddie McWinders,[66] banjo; Dave Kanui, steel guitar; George
Howell, string bass:

[95.] BS[67] 58960-5   **In the Hills of**   Unissued
                       Tennessee   [Remade Aug. 29, 1932]

Victor Studio 2
114 North Fifth Street
Camden, New Jersey
August 11, 1932

Vocal, with Hoyt "Slim" Bryant, guitar; Clayton McMichen, fiddle;
Oddie McWinders, banjo:

Take 2A:[68]

87. BS 58961-2   **Mother, the Queen**   Vi 23721, Bb B-5080, El 2008,   Oct. 21, 1932,
                  of My Heart   MW M-4206, Sr S-3167,   with "Rock All
                  (Hoyt Bryant-   Vi 20-6205   Our Babies to
                  Jimmie Rodgers)   HMV EA1390, HMV N4239,   Sleep"
                  ©1932, SMP   RZ G23195, RZ MR1310
                                            Jimmie the Kid (LPM 2213),
                                            CAL 737, DPL 2-0075, LPT 3073,
                                            LSP 3315(e), Vi 47-6205,
                                            Vi 947-0225 (in EPBT 3073)
                                               RA 5465, DPS 2021, RA 5176,
                                               RA 5510, RA 9038, RD 27241

Vocal, with Hoyt "Slim" Bryant, guitar; Clayton McMichen, fiddle;
Oddie McWinders, banjo:

— BS 58962-2   **Prohibition Has Done**   Unissued
                Me Wrong
                (Jimmie Rodgers-
                Clayton McMichen)

August 11, 1932 (continued)

Vocal, with Hoyt "Slim" Bryant, guitar; Clayton McMichen, fiddle;
Oddie McWinders, banjo:

Take 1A:

88. BS 58963-2   **Rock All Our Babies**   Vi 23721, Bb B-5000, El 1830,   Oct. 21, 1932,
       to Sleep   El 1958, MW M-4201, Sr S-3104   with "Mother,
       (arr. Rodgers)[69]   Col IFB341, HMV EA1403,   the Queen of
       ©1932, SMP   HMV MH187, HMV N4239,   My Heart"
       RZ G23200, RZ IZ469,
       RZ MR2200, Zo 4378
       The Short but Brilliant Life of
       Jimmie Rodgers (LPM 2634;
       AHMI-3094)
       RA 5465, DPM 2047, RD 7562

Vocal, with Hoyt "Slim" Bryant, guitar, Clayton McMichen, fiddle;
Oddie McWinders, banjo:

Take 2:

89. BS 58964-2   **Whippin' That Old T.B.**   Vi 23751, Bb B-5076, El 1999,   Jan. 13, 1933
       (Rodgers)   MW M-4204, Sr S-3157   with "No
       ©1932, SMP   HMV EA1390, RZ G23195,   Hard Times"
       RZ MR1310
       The Short but Brilliant Life of
       Jimmie Rodgers (LPM 2634;
       AHMI-3094), CPL 1-2504(e)
       RA 5465, RD 7562

Victor Studio 2
114 North Fifth Street
Camden, New Jersey
August 15, 1932

Vocal and own guitar, with Hoyt "Slim" Bryant, guitar:

Take 2A:

90. BS 58968-3   **No Hard Times**   Vi 23751, MW M-4205   Jan. 13, 1933
       (Rodgers)   HMV EA1534, HMV N4251,   with "Whippir
       ©1932, SMP   RZ G23117   That Old T.B.
       Train Whistle Blues (LPM 1640)
       RA 5465, DPS 2021, RD 27110

Vocal and own guitar, with Oddie McWinders, banjo:

Take 1A:

91. BS 58969-1   **Long Tall Mama Blues**   Vi 23766, MW M-4202   Feb. 24, 193?
       (Rodgers)   HMV N4245   with
       ©1932, SMP   *My Rough and Rowdy Ways*   "Gambling
       (LPM 2112; ANLI-1209e)   Bar Room
       RA 5465, L 10883, RD 27203   Blues"

August 15, 1932 (continued)

Vocal, with Hoyt "Slim" Bryant, guitar; Clayton McMichen, fiddle;
Oddie McWinders, banjo:

Take 2A:

92. BS 58970-2	**Peach Pickin' Time**	Vi 23781, Bb B-5080, El 2008,	Apr. 7, 1933,
	Down in Georgia	MW M-4200, Sr S-3167,	with
	(Rodgers–McMichen)	Vi 20-6092	"Prairie
	©1932, SMP	HMV EA1403, HMV MH193,	Lullaby".[70]

    HMV N4242, RZ G23200,
    RZ IZ388, RZ MR1335,
    Tw FT1723
My Rough and Rowdy Ways
(LPM 2112; ANLI-1209e),
ACL 7054, CAL 737, DPL 2-0075,
LPT 3073, Vi 47-6092,
Vi 947-0226 (in EPBT 3073),
VPS 6091(e)
    RA 5465, L 10883, RA 5501,
    RA 5524, RA 9038,
    RD 27203, SRA 5040

Victor Studio 2
114 North Fifth Street
Camden, New Jersey
August 16, 1932

Vocal, with Hoyt "Slim" Bryant, guitar; Clayton McMichen, fiddle;
Oddie McWinders, banjo:

Take 3:

93. BS 58971-3	**Gambling Bar Room**	Vi 23766, Bb B-5037, El 1966,	Feb. 24, 1933,
	Blues	MW M-4203, Sr S-3131	with "Long
	(Rodgers–Alley)	HMV EA1514, HMV N4245,	Tall Mama
	©1932, SMP	RZ G23112, RZ ME15,	Blues"

    RZ MR3002, RZ MR20215,
    Tw FT8694
Country Music Hall of Fame
(LPM 2531)
    RA 5465, DPM 2047, RD 7505

Vocal, with Hoyt "Slim" Bryant, guitar; Clayton McMichen, fiddle;
Oddie McWinders, banjo:

Take 1A:

94. BS 58972-1	**I've Only Loved**	Bb B-6810, MW M-7138	Feb. 17, 1937,
	Three Women	RZ G23184, RZ IZ662,	with "The
	(Rodgers–Harvey)	RZ MR2455, Tw FT8334	Wonderful
	©1932, SMP	*My Time Ain't Long* (LPM 2865)	City"

    RA 5465, RD 7644

Victor Studio 1
153 East 24th Street
New York, New York
August 29, 1932

Vocal, with Hoyt "Slim" Bryant, guitar, unknown clarinet, two
  violins, piano:

Take 1:

95. BS 73324-2   **In the Hills of**   Vi 23736, Bb B-5784, MW M-4200   Dec. 2, 1932,
[Remake of   **Tennessee**   HMV EA1404, HMV N4234,   with "Miss
BS 58960–   (Sam M. Lewis-   RZ G23201, RZ MR2700,   the Mississippi
see session of   Ira Schuster)   Tw FT8538, Zo 4376   and You"
Aug. 10, 1932]   ©1932, SMP   *My Time Ain't Long* (LPM 2865)
       RA 5465, RD 7644

Vocal, with Hoyt "Slim" Bryant, guitar; unknown clarinet, two
  violins, piano:

Take 1:

96. BS 73325-2   **Prairie Lullaby**   Vi 23781, Bb B-5076, El 1999,   Apr. 7, 1933,
(Jimmie Rodgers-   MW M-4201, Sr S-3157,   with "Peach
George Brown   Vi 420-0028 (in PT-3035)   Pickin' Time
[Billy Hill])   HMV EA1405, HMV N4242,   Down in
©1932, SMP   RZ G23203, RZ 1Z404,   Georgia"
       RZ MR1725
       Never No Mo' Blues (LPM 1232),
       EPAT 411, LPT 3039, Vi 447-0028
       RA 5465, EP 21002, RD 27138

Vocal, with Hoyt "Slim" Bryant, guitar; unknown clarinet, two
  violins, piano:

Take 1:

97. BS 73326-2   **Miss the Mississippi**   Vi 23736, Bb B-5081,   Dec. 2, 1932,
and You   MW M-4206, Sr S-3168   with "In the
(Billy Halley)   HMV EA1404, HMV N4234,   Hills of
©1932, SMP   RZ G23201, RZ MR3257,   Tennessee"
       RZ MR20010, Tw FT8858,
       Zo 4376
       Jimmie the Kid (LPM 2213),
       LPT 3073, Vi 947-0225
       (in EPBT 3073)
       RA 5466, DPS 2021,
       RA 9038, RD 27241

Vocal, with Hoyt "Slim" Bryant, guitar; unknown clarinet, two
  violins, piano:

Take 1:

98. BS 73327-2   **Sweet Mama**   Vi 23796, MW M-4726   June 30, 193?
Hurry Home   HMV EA1406, RZ G23202   with "Blue
(Jack Neville)   *Country Music Hall of Fame*   Yodel Numbe
©1932, SMP   (LPM 2531)   Eleven"
       RA 5466, RD 7505

Victor Studio 1
153 East 24th Street
New York, New York
May 17, 1933

Vocal with own guitar:

Take 1/5R:[71]

99. BS 76138-1 **Blue Yodel No. 12**   Vi 24456, MW M-4727,   June 27, 1933,
                (Rodgers)   Vi 18-6000   with "The
                ©1933, SMP   [No foreign 78s]   Cowhand's
                                           Jimmie the Kid (LPM 2213) Last Ride"
                                             RA 5466, DPS 2021, RD 27241

Vocal with own guitar:

Take 1:

100. BS 76139-1 **Dreaming with Tears in** Bb B-7600, MW M-7139   May 25, 1938,
     [Take 1–for   **My Eyes**   HMV N4422   with "Take Me
     take 2, see (O'Neal–Rodgers)   [LP reissues from take 2] Back Again"
     session of   ©1933, SMP
     May 18, 1933]

Vocal with own guitar:

Take 1:

101. BS 76140-1 **The Cowhand's Last**   Vi 24456, MW M-4727,   June 27, 1933,
                Ride[72]   Vi 18-6000   with "Blue
                (Jimmie Rodgers–Arza Hitt)[73] HMV EA1362, RZ G23191 Yodel No. 12"
                ©1933, SMP   *Country Music Hall of Fame*
                                           (LPM 2531)
                                             RA 5466, RD 7505

Vocal with own guitar:

Take 1:

102. BS 76141-1 **I'm Free (from the Chain** Vi 23830, MW M-4453   Sept. 8, 1933,
                Gang Now)   HMV EA1489, HMV N4263,   with "The
                (Lou Herscher–Saul Klein)   RZ G23204, Tw FT9112   Yodeling
                ©1933, SMP   *Country Music Hall of Fame* Ranger"
                                           (LPM 2531)
                                             RA 5466, RD 7505

Victor Studio 1
153 East 24th Street
New York, New York
May 18, 1933

Vocal with own guitar:

[100.] BS 76139-1 **Dreaming with Tears in** [78 rpm issues from take 1]
       [Take 2–for **My Eyes**   *Take 2:*[74]
       take 1, see (O'Neal–Rodgers)   *Country Music Hall of Fame*
       session of   ©1933, SMP   (LPM 2531), NW 287
       May 17,   RA 5466, RD 7505
       1933]

May 18, 1933 *(continued)*

Vocal with own guitar:

Take 1:

103. BS 76151-2 **Yodeling My Way Back Home** (Rodgers) ©1933, SMP

Bb B-7280, MW M-7139 RZ MR2700, Tw FT8538 *The Short but Brilliant Life of Jimmie Rodgers* (LPM 2634; AHMI-3094) RA 5466, RD 7562

Dec. 1, 1937, with "The One Rose"

Vocal with own guitar:

Take 1:

104. BS 76160-1 **Jimmie Rodgers' Last Blue Yodel** (Rodgers) ©1933, SMP

Bb B-5281, El 2155, MW M-4415, Sr S-3362 HMV EA1567, RZ G23206, RZ MR1702, Tw FT1874 *My Rough and Rowdy Ways* (LPM 2112; ANLI-1209e), DPL 2-0075 RA 5466, DPM 2047, L 10883, RA 9038, RD 27203

Dec. 20, 1933 with "Years Ago"

Victor Studio 1
153 East 24th Street
New York, New York
May 20, 1933

Vocal with own guitar:

Take 1:

105. BS 76191-2 **The Yodeling Ranger** (Rodgers–Hall) ©1933, SMP

Vi 23830, Bb B-5556, MW M-4453 HMV EA1405, HMV N4263, RZ G23203, RZ IZ410, RZ MR1853, Tw FT9112 [No domestic LP reissues] RA 5466, CMH 106, DPM 2047

Sept. 8, 1933 with "I'm Free (from the Chain Gang Now)"

Vocal with own guitar:

Take 1:

106. BS 76192-2 **Old Pal of My Heart** (Jimmie Rodgers– John B. Mason) ©1933, SMP

Vi 23816, Bb B-5136, El 2042, Sr S-3217, Vi 420-0029 (in PT 3035) HMV EA1362, RZ G23191, RZ IZ496, RZ MR2242, Tw FT8185, Zo 4378 *Never No Mo' Blues* (LPM 1232), EPAT 411, LPT 3039, Vi 447-0029 RA 5466, DPM 2047, RD 27138

July 28, 193? with "Mississippi Delta Blues"

Victor Studio 1
153 East 24th Street
New York, New York
May 24, 1933

Vocal, with John Cali, steel guitar; Tony Colicchio, guitar:[75]

Take 1:

107. BS 76327-1 **Old Love Letters**   Vi 23840, Bb B-6198, MW M-4454   Oct. 20, 1933,
                 (Jimmie Rodgers–   HMV EA1303, HMV N4297,   with
                    Lou Herscher–   RZ G23190, RZ IZ422,   "Somewhere
                    Dwight Butcher)   RZ MR2049, Tw FT9113   Down below
                 ©1933, SMP   *Country Music Hall of Fame*   the Dixon
                                           (LPM 2531), CPL 1-2504(e)   Line"
                                           RA 5466, RD7505

Vocal, with John Cali, banjo; Tony Colicchio, guitar:

Take 1:

108. BS 76328-2 **Mississippi Delta Blues** Vi 23816   July 28, 1933,
                 (Rodgers–Neville)   HMV EA1385, RZ G23194   with "Old Pal
                 ©1933, SMP   *Train Whistle Blues* (LPM 1640) of My Heart"
                                            RA 5466, DPS 2021, RD 27110

Vocal, with John Cali and Tony Colicchio, guitars:

Take 1:

109. BS 76331-2 **Somewhere Down**   Vi 23840, MW M-4454   Oct. 20, 1933,
                 below the Dixon   HMV EA1503, HMV N4297,   with "Old
                 Line   RZ G23111, Tw FT9113   Love Letters"
                 (Jimmie Rodgers–   *Train Whistle Blues* (LPM 1640)
                    Walter Ryan)   RA 5466, DPS 2021, EP 20176,
                 ©1933, SMP   RA 5176, RA 5510, RD 27110

Vocal with own guitar:

Take 1:

110. BS 76332-2 **Years Ago**   Bb B-5281, El 2155, MW M-4415,   Dec. 20, 1933,
                 (Jimmie Rodgers–   Sr S-3362   with "Jimmie
                    Lou Herscher–   HMV EA1567, RZ G23206,   Rodgers' Last
                    Barry Richards)[76]   RZ IZ1065, RZ MR1702,   Blue Yodel"
                 ©1933, SMP   RZ MR3313, RZ MR20064,
                                            Tw FT1874, Tw FT8902
                                          The Short but Brilliant Life of
                                          Jimmie Rodgers (LPM 2634;
                                            AHM1-3094), DMM 4-0406
                                            RA 5466, RD 7562

Questionable Attributions:

Over the years, there have been repeated stories of unlogged recording
sessions and unissued masters of songs other than those Rodgers is known to

"Rodgers' Puzzle Record" contained dubbings of three previously recorded songs, remastered in parallel grooves. The supposed "puzzle" was that the listener did not know which of the three would play when the soundbox (tone arm) was set down on the record.

Rodgers's popularity abroad resulted in issues on many foreign labels, such as this Australian Regal Zonophone (*left*). "Jimmie Rodgers Medley," remastered from previous recordings, was issued only in England, Australia, Ireland, and India.

Cover of a rare Rodgers songbook from 1934, indicating that "Home on the Range" and "Man on the Flying Trapeze" were among the songs "written and sung on Victor records by Jimmie Rodgers." These numbers have not been found in Victor's files.

have recorded. In at least a dozen instances, such stories have been traced until they evaporated or otherwise failed to produce reliable evidence. The following, however, bear reporting:

[Date and place unknown]

[Origin unknown]	**The Man on the Flying Trapeze** **Hot Time in the Old Town Tonight**	Hoover Brilliant Special 38217 (Co 38827) ["Special Record for Radio Stations"]	[Date of issue unknown]

This is an item reported by a West Coast collector, who attempted to buy the record. The reluctant owner, rather than part with it, deliberately broke the disc, claiming that it was bootlegged and would cause legal problems if discovered in his possession. I have seen very hazy photographs of the record, establishing the information given above, but have only the word of the collector, who heard it played, that the performer was indeed Rodgers. Attempts to trace the Hoover label have been unsuccessful.

The possibility, however, that Rodgers did at least record "The Man on the Flying Trapeze" is supported by a 1934 Southern Music song folio, *Jimmie Rodgers Deluxe Album of Songs,* in which that song appears, according to the cover, "as written and sung on Victor records by Jimmie Rodgers." But while record release numbers are given for other songs in the album, the number for "The Man on the Flying Trapeze" is omitted. The sheet music page shows only "Arr. by Jimmie Rodgers." It is precisely the sort of old vaudeville chestnut he is known to have favored, as with "Hot Time in the Old Town," which he performed with Sara Carter on Victor master BVE 69427.

Interestingly, the same Rodgers song folio also contains "Home on the Range," words and music attributed to Mr. and Mrs. W. M. Goodwin, copyrighted by Southern Music, and recorded on Victor V-40186. That recording, however, was actually by a group called the Rodeo Trio, recorded July 15, 1929, in El Paso. How the song came to be included in a Rodgers folio is anyone's guess, but it is further evidence for speculation that Rodgers recorded songs other than those shown in the Victor logs.

Erroneously Attributed:

In early 1978 an issue of *Film Collector's World* carried an advertisement offering for sale a supposed Vitaphone soundtrack transcription entitled "The Pullman Porters," carrying the date 10-26-29 and attributed to Rodgers. The coincidence of the title and the proximity of the date to the filming of "The Singing Brakeman" suggested a possible variant and further light on the dialog skit recorded with I. N. Bronsen in Hollywood in 1930. However, a tape copy supplied by the owners proved that this "Pullman Porters" was recorded not by anyone even resembling Rodgers, but by an anonymous gospel/minstrel group.

NOTES

1. With the issuance of the seven primary LPs, RCA assumed that it had made all of Rodgers's titles available. It was then discovered that two titles—"Whisper Your Mother's Name" and "The Yodeling Ranger"—had been omitted from the reissues, and plans were made to include these on an eighth album, LSP 4073(e), otherwise comprised of tribute songs and covers by other artists. Unfortunately, "Yodeling Cowboy" was confused with "The Yodeling Ranger" and *re*-reissued in its place. Finally, in 1972, "The Yodeling Ranger" was reissued abroad by Country Music History (CMH 106) and later included in the complete set produced in Japan.

2. The Puzzle Record was, of course, largely a gimmick for manually operated 78 rpm phonographs. Moreover, the original record was itself a "reissue," comprised of Rodgers songs already released.

3. The term "session" is subject to varied application. In compiling his discography from Victor's files, Randle arbitrarily determined a session to be "a normal period of time (3 hours)." He numbered each accordingly, intending to divide those which exceeded that limit so long as they occurred on the same day. In most instances he followed this plan, but failed to do so for the Oct. 22, 1929, session in Dallas, which apparently began at 12:30 p.m. and ended at 10:00 p.m. Bond (*Recordings of Jimmie Rodgers*, p. 15), noting the discrepancy, attempted to correct it, so their session numbers do not coincide. (Randle shows a total of 62; Bond, 63.) In the narrative of the present work, the term "session" has been employed as determined by the context, so that in some instances it distinguishes the studio activity on a particular date (Randle's "normal period of time"), but more often it is used generically in reference to all sessions during those periods, sometimes spanning several weeks, when Rodgers was in a given city for the specific purpose of recording. In the interests of simplicity and convenience, and because of the discrepancies between Randle and Bond, the numbering system above follows this latter interpretation. In any event, Rodgers's sessions, whether singular or collective, are not numbered in Victor's files, and any such designation remains arbitrary.

4. Disputed; see pp. 216–18.

5. See, for instance, Shelton and Goldblatt, *Country Music Story*, p. 69. Some estimates run as high as 75,000,000.

6. Kerrville *Mountain Sun*, Apr. 25, 1929, p. 1; *Asheville Times* and *Asheville Citizen*, stories and ads throughout the week of Dec. 2, 1929.

7. See Bond, *Recordings of Jimmie Rodgers*, p. vi.

8. These figures are a consensus derived from discussions with Bob Pinson, Brad McCuen, Charles Wolfe, David Freeman, and others. In *78 RPM Records & Prices* (Des Moines: Wallace-Homestead, 1977), Peter Soderbergh lists "Blue Yodel" and, curiously, "The Brakeman's Blues" in his chapter entitled "They Sold a Million: 1919–1946." Other contenders are "Sleep, Baby, Sleep," "Daddy and Home," "In the Jailhouse Now," "Hobo Bill's Last Ride," and "Frankie and Johnny."

9. Confidential source, to NP, Nov. 22, 1978.

10. Introduction to Bond, *Recordings of Jimmie Rodgers*, p. v.

11. Most, if not all, of Rodgers's original Victors and Bluebirds were released

simultaneously in Canada. Canadian Victors carry the same release numbers as their U.S. counterparts but retain the so-called pre-scroll (or "batwing") label. All of Rodgers's U.S. Victor releases were, of course, on the famous "scroll" label. Canadian Bluebird labels are essentially identical to U.S. ones, but may be distinguished by Canadian patent numbers and the legend "Montreal, Canada" in small print in the rim of the label.

12. The record carries no composer credit. *Memorial Folio II* (1967) shows "Words and Music by Jimmie Rodgers" and the 1953 copyright date.

13. This, of course, was the site of the famous Trinity Baptist Church, taken over by Victor for recording purposes because of its exceptional acoustics.

14. Originally released as "If Brother Jack Were Here," with composer credit to Rodgers. Following notice from Marks that he held the copyright, the issue was withdrawn on Oct. 18, 1928; for that reason copies are considered rare and are now avidly sought by Rodgers collectors. After Oct. 29, 1928, Victor began a new issue labeled simply "Mother Was a Lady," but when that apparently caused confusion among dealers, a third and final label was printed, indicating "Mother Was a Lady" with the subtitle "If Brother Jack Were Here" in parentheses. Most copies seen today carry that combined designation.

15. Foreign 78s: four issues—RZ MR1918, RZ G22792, RZ IZ414, and Tw FT1980—contain segments of six songs dubbed from previously mastered recordings and issued only abroad, as "Jimmie Rodgers Medley, Parts 1 and 2." The songs are "My Old Pal," "Dear Old Sunny South," and "Blue Yodel No. 1" on side 1; "Daddy and Home," "Away Out on the Mountain," and "Blue Yodel No. 4" on side 2. Remastering was done in the studios of Columbia Graphophone Co. (E.M.I), London, on Oct. 28, 1935.

16. Some EP and LP issues contain an edited version of "Blue Yodel" in which the guitar solo after the fourth verse has been abbreviated. These issues include the following: domestic—LPM 2112 (ANLI-1209e), LSP 3315(e), EPA 5097, DPL 2-0075; foreign—all except HMV 7EG 8163.

17. Some labels show "Jimmie Rodgers, accompanied by the Three Southerners," which has led to much confusion and speculation. "The Three Southerners" were simply Rodgers, Cozzens, and Ninde. Rodgers on ukulele, speculated by Jim Evans and by Paris and Comber, among others, was confirmed by Armand Beard, who interviewed Julian Ninde shortly before Mr. Ninde's death. (Beard to NP, Oct. 6, 1975.)

18. Listed in Victor files only as "Treasure Untold," although all labels show "Treasures Untold." An unrecorded third verse appeared in *Cowboy Songs*, no. 18 (Sept., 1953), 7.

19. Paris and Comber omit Rodgers's guitar; aural evidence is inconclusive.

20. As shown on original labels. All subsequent Blue Yodels are designated in Arabic numerals.

21. Only by error, in some early issues, and labeled "Away Out on the Mountain." Corrected in later issues.

22. Hereafter shown as SMP.

23. Much speculation has surrounded the next master number—BVE 45092—in the sequence. However, information supplied to John Edwards by Brad McCuen suggests that the wax was used as a test by the engineer during a break in the session and indicates that the actual number was assigned to a German recording made on June 5, 1928. (McCuen to Edwards, undated, in JEMF files.)

24. One of several songs to which Elsie McWilliams contributed substantially but

for which she did not receive label credit. The title frequently appears in error (as on LPM 1640) as "My Little Home *Town* in New Orleans."

25. Opening notes of initial guitar run are unaccountably edited out on LPM 1232 and all foreign reissues.

26. When possible, it was standard practice at Victor to assign the same master number to retakes, but this is clearly an exception, perhaps because the original master number was not available to Peer in Atlanta. Similar instances are BS 58960 and BS 73324 (both "In the Hills of Tennessee") and BVE 55333 and BVE 55344 (both "Frankie and Johnny"). Compare BVE 45091 ("Mississippi Moon") and BVE 55345 ("Home Call"), in which the same master number was assigned to takes made several years apart.

27. Joy was a longtime staff director and arranger for Victor. Company files show "sax" rather than clarinet for this session, but it is generally agreed that none is heard and that instead the reed man plays clarinet on both "Desert Blues" and "Any Old Time."

28. One of the more curious but interesting covers of "Everybody Does It in Hawaii" was by King Oliver (Vi V-38109), recorded the following month.

29. As shown in Victor files. Vi 22143 gives no composer or arranger credit. Southern Music's *Jimmie Rodgers Deluxe Album of Songs* (1934) shows only "As Sung by Jimmie Rodgers." *Memorial Folio I* (1967) shows "Words and Music by Jimmie Rodgers."

30. Dyke on takes 1 and 2 only.

31. Generally attributed to Goebel Reeves, "The Texas Drifter." See Fred Hoeptner, "Goebel Reeves, The Texas Drifter," *Old Time Music*, no. 18 (Autumn, 1975), 13; Hoeptner to NP, Apr. 25, 1977, and Dec. 15, 1978. Rodgers's song seems to be essentially the same as the first side of a two-part recording which Reeves called "The Drifter" and recorded on several occasions (he is not known to have recorded a number entitled "I've Ranged, I've Roamed, and I've Travelled"). Yet in liner notes to CMH 101, Chris Comber describes "The Drifter" as "a protracted version of the Jimmie Rodgers song 'I've [R]anged, I've [R]oamed, and I've [T]ravelled,'" and asserts that "this is NOT, as is so often pointed out, the song written by Reeves and copied by Rodgers. It appears the other way around. . . ." The statement is at best ambiguous, allowing for, among other things, the possibility that Reeves may have written some other song called "I've Ranged, I've Roamed, and I've Travelled." In any event, Reeves first recorded "The Drifter" for Okeh (45365) in San Antonio on June 25, 1929, four months before Rodgers's recording. The version Comber refers to was recorded (for Melotone, Aurora, and other labels) in New York on Oct. 15, 1930, still four and a half years before Rodgers's recording was released. In view of the fact that it was not Rodgers's style to take material without at least giving label credit, all this points to the possibility that he had casually learned the song from Reeves when they were touring together in the early 1920's, or that their paths crossed again in Texas after Rodgers went there in 1929. In either case, this line of speculation suggests that by the time Rodgers used the song at the above session, he had again lost track of Reeves (who was even more peripatetic than the Blue Yodeler), and hence it was simply credited to the Rodgers-McWilliams "factory." Still another possibility is that it was basically Rodgers's composition from the beginning, one he had shared with Reeves in the early days, but there is no evidence for this view.

32. Take details not verified.

33. Date and place are in question, but are listed here as in Victor's files. It seems likely that "Hobo Bill's Last Ride" was recorded in Atlanta, but the gap in master numbers cannot be accounted for.

34. Another instance where Elsie McWilliams was clearly involved but did not

receive credit.

35. This, as the subtitle indicated, was No. 7 in the Blue Yodel series. The main title was apparently chosen to commemorate the second anniversary of the recording of the original Blue Yodel in Nov., 1927 (see Paris and Comber, *Jimmie the Kid*, p. 87).

36. Takes 2 and 3, unissued, were vocal by Rodgers, with Billy Burkes, guitar.

37. Title for Montgomery Ward issue: "She's More to Be Pitied Than Censored."

38. As shown in Victor files, the only Blue Yodel to be so spelled out. It was, of course, originally planned to be No. 8 in the sequence, which accounts for its listing under that designation in Brian Rust's *Victor Master Book*, p. 320. See also Bond, *Recordings of Jimmie Rodgers*, p. 19.

39. Details of the composition of this song are in Dorothy Horstman's *Sing Your Heart Out, Country Boy* (New York: E. P. Dutton, 1975), p. 75.

40. Take details not verified; also given as take 4. Brad McCuen's worksheets for the reissue indicate that only takes 1 and 3 were processed, and that take 3 was superior.

41. Definitely not Boyd Senter. (Senter to NP, Apr. 7, 1975.) Bond (*Recordings of Jimmie Rodgers*, p. 28) has established also that the cornet player was not Mickey Bloom, as originally shown by John Edwards and Brian Rust. Rust now agrees (Rust to NP, Dec. 8, 1975.)

42. Rodgers's lyric sheets show "Lani McIntire's Harmony Hawaiians," although the name was later shortened by Oberstein and appears simply as "Lani McIntire's Hawaiians" in Victor files and on labels. Although most of the group except for McIntire remain unknown, the steel guitarist may have been Sam Koki.

43. Hall's name is shown on record labels as "Hill," apparently on wired instructions from Rodgers (see Bond, *Recordings of Jimmie Rodgers*, p. 22). Why this occurred remains a mystery. In *Memorial Folio I*, Hall's name is deleted, with both words and music credited to Rodgers.

44. Bluebird issue: Although some special-market records in the Bluebird series were later given lower numbers, this was the record which inaugurated the Bluebird label. The popularity of "Moonlight and Skies" in the original issue is indicated by its release on all Victor subsidiary labels (in some instances twice) and the broad range of foreign 78 rpm releases, including a rare instance of Rodgers's appearance on Columbia (Ireland). This, of course, was not the Columbia organization familiar to American audiences, but an adjunct of British Gramophone (E.M.I.), with contractual connections to Victor.

45. Hall's name again changed to "Hill" on labels, although it is given correctly in *Memorial Folio I*.

46. The final issue of Rodgers's originals on 78 rpm.

47. Remastered in 1937 as BS 017103. The three original masters were destroyed during World War II. (Brad McCuen to John Edwards, Oct. 12, 1959.)

48. Rodgers's only French release, obviously prompted by the jazz accompaniment.

49. Hall's name is deleted from *Memorial Folio I*, which shows only "Words and Music by Jimmie Rodgers."

50. Some discographies show Timely Tunes reissues of "T. B. Blues," "Travellin' Blues," and "Jimmie the Kid," but those were actually by Gene Autry.

51. The cut of "T.B. Blues" on CPL 1–12504(e) is actually by Gene Autry, presumably an error in re-mastering.

52. Although Rodgers's lyric sheet shows "2 Guitars," Sara Carter reported that only Maybelle played on this session. (Interview by Henry Young, May 29, 1971.) Aural evidence supports her statement; if a second guitar was used, it is indistinct.

53. The song was written and copyrighted in 1928 by Carson Robison, under the

title "An Old Man's Story." See brochure accompanying JEMF LP 101, *The Carter Family on Border Radio*, p. 26.

54. Takes 1 and 3 are essentially the same except that take 1 is slightly faster. Brad McCuen's worksheets for the reissue indicate that take 3 is "best performance" and that metal parts for take 1 were marred by "ticks" and a tracking flaw at the end.

55. In *Memorial Folio II*, the title is given as *"That* Wonderful City." Although Elsie McWilliams is not credited in Victor files or in the song folios, her name appears on the original 78 rpm record labels. Rodgers's lyric sheet clearly indicates that the song is "by Elsie McWilliams."

56. Takes 1 and 2, unissued, were vocal and own guitar with Clifford Gibson, guitar.

57. Paris and Comber indicate (*Jimmie the Kid*, p. 186) that one of the two cuts of "The Carter Family and Jimmie Rodgers in Texas" on RA 5645 is presumed to be take 3, although it is identical to the issued take 4.

58. No composer credit is given on record labels. Victor files credit A. P. Carter, although copies of the working scripts among Rodgers's lyric sheets bear no evidence that Carter was involved. A further twist appears in *Memorial Folio I*, where, under the title "Jimmie Rodgers Visits the Carter Family," what is essentially twelve bars of "My Clinch Mountain Home" is credited "Words and Music by Jimmie Rodgers."

59. LPs: As Brad McCuen's worksheets indicate, reissues of "Jimmie Rodgers Visits the Carter Family" have been edited to remove Rodgers's repetition of the words "town tonight" near the end, and the spoken coda from take 3 has been dubbed in.

60. According to Wilber Ball, he and Cliff Carlisle supplied music to Rodgers's lyrics of "When the Cactus Is in Bloom." (Ball to NP, May 15, 1978.)

61. Title for Twin issue: "Round-Up Time in the West."

62. As with "T.B. Blues," Hall's name is deleted from "Gambling Polka Dot Blues" in *Memorial Folio I*.

63. Triple-track novelty recording made by dubbing segments of three previously recorded masters: "Train Whistle Blues," "Blue Yodel [No. 1]," and "Everybody Does It in Hawaii." Rodgers, of course, was not present.

64. Rodgers's lyric sheet shows "by Floyd D. Henderson."

65. As shown on records. It actually appears to have been the third take, but was erroneously numbered in Victor's files. A supposed take 3, unissued, was recorded the following day (Feb. 5) with Rodgers accompanied only by his own guitar and Fred Koone, guitar.

66. Spelled variously "McWindows" and "McWinters." Rodgers's lyric sheets show "McWinders"; presumably he was the same McWinders who had recorded for Victor in Memphis in Sept., 1929 (see Rust, *Victor Master Book*, p. 302). Earlier he had worked with Fiddlin' Sid Harkreader; see *Fiddlin' Sid's Memoirs: The Autobiography of Sidney J. Harkreader*, JEMF Special Series, 1976, p. 21.

67. The "S" (sometimes "SHQ") designated Victor's home studios, replacing the earlier "VE" ("Victor Electric"). The B-prefix was assigned to 10-inch issues.

68. The A-suffix, as shown on Vi 23721, indicates that the record was actually pressed from a master recorded simultaneously on a second machine during the second take. Some discographies show four takes ("1, 1A, 2, 2A") for "Mother, the Queen of My Heart," but of course the song was performed only twice in the studio. All songs during these sessions in Camden were recorded in the same manner; thus for each take number shown there exists (or existed) a duplicate master.

69. Probably written by George Vaughn. *Memorial Folio I* credits "Words and Music by Jimmie Rodgers."

70. The last pairing to be issued in Rodgers's lifetime.

71. The fifth dubbing from take 1. Information in Victor files concerning take numbers for this final series of sessions is often ambiguous, involving dubbings and takes recorded concurrently with take 1. Although it appears that in several instances two separate, distinct takes were made, the protection copy was often merely take 1A, recorded simultaneously on a separate machine but indicated in the files as "two takes." Thus the take details shown above for these sessions are not verified, but are based on a careful analysis of the information available.

72. This title is the subject of many variant spellings and arrangements on labels and in Victor's files. It is given here in what is presumed to be the final form.

73. Although Hitt's name appears on record labels, it was deleted from Victor files and from *Memorial Folio I*.

74. Take 1 differs substantially from take 2, notably in the inclusion of an extended guitar break (which Rodgers flubs) following the first verse. Why it was chosen for the original release is unknown. Some discographies reverse the order of takes, showing take 2 as the 78 rpm release and take 1 as the reissue, but Victor's files and Brad McCuen's worksheets clearly indicate the sequence shown above.

75. As shown in Rodgers's handwriting on his lyric sheet. It is interesting that, at this very late stage, he was still meticulously recording the names of his accompanists.

76. As the lyric sheets show, "Barry Richards" was actually Saul Klein.

Appendix I

The Blue Yodels of Jimmie Rodgers

RELEASED TITLE (AND SUBTITLE)	RECORDED
"Blue Yodel"	Nov. 30, 1927
"Blue Yodel—No. II" ("My Lovin' Gal, Lucille")	Feb. 15, 1928
"Blue Yodel No. 3"	Feb. 15, 1928
"Blue Yodel No. 4" ("California Blues")	Oct. 20, 1928
"Blue Yodel No. 5"	Feb. 23, 1929
"Blue Yodel No. 6"	Oct. 22, 1929
"Anniversary Blue Yodel" ("Blue Yodel No. 7")	Nov. 26, 1929
"Blue Yodel No. 8" ("Mule Skinner Blues")	July 11, 1930
"Blue Yodel No. 9" ("Standin' on the Corner")	July 16, 1930
"Blue Yodel No. 10" ("Ground Hog Rootin' in My Backyard")[1]	Feb. 6, 1932
"Blue Yodel Number Eleven"	Nov. 27, 1929
"Blue Yodel No. 12" ("Barefoot Blues")	May 17, 1933
"Jimmie Rodgers' Last Blue Yodel"	May 18, 1933

1. Subtitle scratched from the original label in Victor's files.
2. According to Victor's files, "Blue Yodel No. 12" was actually released 3 days *before* "Blue Yodel No. 11"! "Long Tall Mama Blues" (recorded Aug. 15, 1932) was originally titled (on Rodgers's lyric sheet) simply "Blue Yodel #—," suggesting that it was a candidate for "Blue Yodel No. 11 (or 12)." That notation provides further evidence that Peer (and Oberstein) kept

RELEASED	ORDER OF RECORDING	ORDER OF RELEASE	TITLE VARIANTS
Feb. 3, 1928	1	1	Later subtitle: "T for Texas"
Apr. 6, 1928			
May 4, 1928	2	2	
Sept. 7, 1928	3	3	Later subtitle: "Evening Sun Yodel"
Feb. 8, 1929	4	4	
Sept. 20, 1929	5	5	Original title: "Ain't No Blackheaded Woman Can Make a Fool out of Me"
Feb. 21, 1930	6	6	(in Victor files)
Sept. 5, 1930	7	7	
ca. Feb. 6, 1931	9	8	Original title: "Blue Yodel No. 9" (in Victor files and on lyric sheet)
Sept. 11, 1931	10	9	
Aug. 12, 1932	11	10	Original title: "Blue Yodel #—"
June 30, 1933	8	12	Original title: "Blue Yodel No. 8"
June 27, 1933	12	11[2]	Original title: "The Barefoot Blues"
Dec. 20, 1933	13	13	Other titles: "Women Make a Fool out of Me," "Why Don't the Women Let Me Be"[3]

the series going by stockpiling possible songs and just assigning the next number in the sequence when it came time to release a Blue Yodel.

3. Lyrics to this title, on the back of the lyric sheet for "Roll Along, Kentucky Moon" (recorded Feb. 2, 1932), suggest that "Why Don't the Women Let Me Be" was the original title.

Appendix II

Jimmie Rodgers's Personal Appearances

Jimmie Rodgers loved audiences, large or small. Throughout his career he always seized the slightest opportunity to "barnstorm a few dates," as he put it, hitting the road on a moment's notice, touring incessantly. Because many of his appearances were in small towns and rural areas, hastily booked at random, they have gone largely unrecorded. But he also played major cities in the East, South, and Southwest, headlining big-time vaudeville bills in first-class theaters. On still other occasions he was booked into the scheduled tours of leading tent repertoire companies, and, while his appearances were often interrupted by illness and other difficulties, these tour routes and schedules can be traced with some certainty. Perhaps someday access to Rodgers's press books (now in the hands of his daughter) will show the full extent of his travels; the following chart is an outline of what is now known of his personal appearances.

STANLEY-CRANDALL-KEITH CIRCUIT
Summer, 1928

> Earle Theater, Washington, D.C., Aug. 4-10

In his first appearance on a big-time circuit, Rodgers headlined the show. Others on the bill were Charlie Althoff, popular oldtime musician and rube comic known as "The Yankee Fiddler"; the Lovey Girls, a teenage sister act; dancer Frank Seifert; and the Kardo Brothers, "The Boys of 1,000 Songs." Joe Bonbrest performed as master of ceremonies.

   Rodgers also played suburban theaters of the Stanley-Crandall chain, but these dates have not been identified.

LOEW'S "SOUTHERN TIME" CIRCUIT
Autumn, 1928

> Loew's State Theater, Norfolk, Va., Nov. 5–11
> Loew's Capitol Theater, Atlanta, Ga., Nov. 12–18
> Loew's State Theater, Memphis, Tenn., Nov. 19–25
> Loew's State Theater, New Orleans, La., Dec. 3–9
> The Loew Theater, Houston, Tex., Dec. 10–16

For Loew's, Rodgers toured with what was known as an "intact unit," essentially a road show comprised of four or five acts which remained together throughout the tour and appeared in conjunction with a feature-length film. A modification of traditional vaudeville, this combination was known as "film presentation" or "vaudefilm." Rodgers's unit included Al Gordon's Dogs, the Three Ryans ("Frolics of the North and South"), comedians Faber and McIntyre, and Frank and Milt Britton's Brown Derby Orchestra. Jimmie headlined, appearing in the favored "next-to-close" spot.

The show went on to Evansville, Canton, Cleveland, Toronto, Montreal, and Boston, but after Houston, Rodgers's name disappeared from the route list in *Billboard,* and he shortly joined the Paul English Players in Mobile. A trade report noted "much turmoil in Loew booking offices" and indicated that the organization's road shows were about to be dropped or curtailed (*Billboard,* Nov. 24 and Dec. 8, 1928).

PAUL ENGLISH PLAYERS
Dec., 1928–Feb., 1929

> Mobile, Ala., week of Dec. 20
> Gulfport, Miss., week of Jan. 7
> Jackson, Miss., week of Jan. 14
> Vicksburg, Miss., week of Jan. 21
> Meridian, Miss., week of Feb. 4
> Hattiesburg, Miss., week of Feb. 11

Except for Meridian, dates are approximate. Plays were the mainstay of this organization, a tent repertoire company, but Rodgers was given extravagant billing as an "Extra Added Attraction." Other non-dramatic entertainers appearing on the bill were Eva Thomas, a blues singer; Happy Gowland, comedian; Buddy Baker, vocalist; and Happy Cook's Kentucky Buddies, a novelty band. The tour went on to Biloxi, Laurel, and other Gulf cities after Rodgers left to record in New York.

INDEPENDENT BOOKINGS
Spring, 1929

> Big Spring, Tex., week of Mar. 25
> Lynn Theater, O'Donnell, Tex., Apr. 6
> Palace Theater, Lubbock, Tex., Apr. 11 and 12
> Arcadia Theater, Kerrville, Tex., May 5

Rodgers appeared solo, in conjunction with various movie bills. It is highly probable that he played other dates in the region during this time, but the above are the only appearances for which evidence is available. Big Spring date not confirmed.

RADIO-KEITH-ORPHEUM "INTERSTATE" CIRCUIT
Summer, 1929

> Coleman Theater, Miami, Okla., May 16 and 17
> Orpheum Theater, Tulsa, Okla., May 18–24
> Orpheum Theater, Oklahoma City, Okla., May 25–31
> Majestic Theater, Fort Worth, Tex., June 1–7
> Majestic Theater, Dallas, Tex., June 8–13
> Majestic Theater, San Antonio, Tex., June 14–21
> Majestic Theater, Houston, Tex., June 22–28
> Orpheum Theater, New Orleans, La., June 29–July 5
> Majestic Theater, Little Rock, Ark., July 6–12
> Ritz Theater, Birmingham, Ala., July 13–19
> Georgia Theater, Atlanta, Ga., July 20–26

Another "intact unit," appearing with feature film bills. Rodgers again
headlined, supported by the Seven Nelsons, an acrobatic team; comedians
Morton and Stout; and the Shaw-Carroll Dance Revue. For the grand opening
of the new Majestic Theater in San Antonio, they were joined by Don Galvin,
"The Banjo Boy"; the Harrington Sisters, "Rays of Sunshine"; Vernon Geyer,
organist; and Eddie Sauer and the Syncopaters.

INDEPENDENT BOOKINGS
Autumn, 1929

> Municipal Auditorium, San Angelo, Tex., Oct. 3 and 4
> Beaumont and Port Arthur, Tex., week of Oct. 14

Accompanied by Billy Burkes, Weldon Burkes, and Joe Kaipo, known briefly
and informally as "Jimmie Rodgers's Guitar Hounds" (apparently they were
never billed in that fashion). Beaumont and Port Arthur dates not confirmed.

INDEPENDENT BOOKINGS
Winter, 1929

> City Auditorium, Asheville, N.C., Dec. 5 and 6
> Rex Theater, Spartanburg, S.C., Dec. 7
> Memorial Auditorium, Chattanooga, Tenn., Dec. 13 and 14
> Tupelo and Pontotoc, Miss., week of Dec. 16

Appearing with Rodgers in Asheville: Billy Burkes, Clayton McMichen,
Otis Elder, and Lee "Texas Tom" Holden; in Spartanburg: Burkes and
McMichen; in Chattanooga: Burkes, McMichen, Holden, Earl Van Arsdale,
William Krug, Hugh Cross, and Howard Campbell; in Tupelo and Pontotoc:
Burkes, McMichen, and Holden. Tupelo and Pontotoc dates not confirmed.

Just prior to this tour, a story in the *Kerrville Times* (Nov. 28, 1929) reported that Rodgers and his friend Jerry Gerard had returned "from a seven-week vaudeville tour in the larger cities of Texas, New Orleans, La., New York City, Washington, D.C., and other places on the Eastern Coast." During that period he had been touring West Texas and had recorded in Dallas and Atlanta. No evidence of appearances in the other cities named in the story has been uncovered.

INDEPENDENT BOOKINGS
Spring, 1930

Carthage Theater, Carthage, Miss., Mar. 13 and 14

Accompanied by the Freeny-Cannon Trio: Leslie Freeny, Hendrix Freeny, and A. F. "Fonzo" Cannon. A third show, scheduled for Mar. 15, was cancelled because of Rodgers's illness. Other dates were probably played in the area prior to this event.

SWAIN'S HOLLYWOOD FOLLIES
Summer, 1930

Independence, La., Mar. 29
Ruston, La., Apr. 2
El Dorado, Ark., Apr. 3
Smackover, Ark., Apr. 4
Camden, Ark., Apr. 5
Jefferson, Tex., Apr. 9
Marshall, Tex., Apr. 10
Mineola, Tex., Apr. 11
Terrell, Tex., Apr. 12
Athens, Tex., Apr. 14
Tyler, Tex., Apr. 15
Corsicana, Tex., Apr. 16
Ennis, Tex., Apr. 17
Greenville, Tex., Apr. 18
McKinney, Tex., Apr. 19
Bonham, Tex., Apr. 21
Clarkesville, Tex., Apr. 22
Paris, Tex., Apr. 23
Whitesboro, Tex., Apr. 24
Gainesville, Tex., Apr. 25
Nocona, Tex., Apr. 26
Henrietta, Tex., Apr. 28

Electra, Tex., Apr. 29
Vernon, Tex., Apr. 30
Quanah, Tex., May 1
Childress, Tex., May 2
Clarendon, Tex., May 3
Borger, Tex., May 4
Panhandle, Tex., May 5
Canadian, Tex., May 7
Woodward, Okla., May 8
Alva, Okla., May 9
Anthony, Kans., May 10
Kingman, Kans., May 12
Stafford, Kans., May 13
Peabody, Kans., May 14
Dwight, Kans., May 15
Herington, Kans., May 16
Caldwell, Kans., May 17
Ada, Okla., May 28
Wetumka, Okla., May 29
Henryetta, Okla., May 30
Holdenville, Okla., May 31

A grueling tour of forty-three one-night stands. After Rodgers left at Holdenville, the show played (or attempted to play) some two dozen additional dates down the Oklahoma-Arkansas border to Louisiana, limping into New Orleans in late June. The itinerary above was compiled from *Billboard* listings, Swain's own route cards, Rodgers's letters, and other documentary evidence; although it may vary occasionally from actual dates and places, most entries have been verified by local newspaper ads and publicity. One source of confusion is the Borger, Tex., May 4 date. It is not given in any *Billboard* list or shown on Swain's route card, yet a published photograph shows Rodgers standing in front of a six-sheet clearly advertising the appearance. The case is further complicated by Waldo O'Neal's report that he traveled to nearby Panhandle, Tex., that day and located the Swain show there, as advertised, but was told that Rodgers had gone to Borger "on business." A possible explanation is that Swain mounted two units whenever possible, working, as it were, both sides of the street. Bill Bruner is known to have stood in for Rodgers on this tour; perhaps on occasion they appeared simultaneously in two cities, both billed as Jimmie Rodgers. Performances may also have been given on dates missing from the above list, particularly between May 18 and 27, for which no route has been discovered. Evidence indicates, however, that during that period the company was engaged in reorganizing and "making the jump" from Kansas into southeastern Oklahoma.

Rodgers, of course, was the star attraction of Swain's Hollywood Follies until he was replaced by Ben Turpin in early June. Other acts included blues singer Eva Thomas (formerly with Paul English), comedian Jimmy Vann, and Frieta's Hawaiian Revue, also billed as the Waikiki Hawaiians.

INDEPENDENT BOOKINGS
Autumn, 1930

> Lufkin, Tex., Oct. 24

In Houston the following day, Rodgers notified *Billboard*, "I am booking a few barnstorm dates before Christmas." These were presumably solo appearances throughout East Texas, where, he reported, "business conditions seem to be better."

WILL ROGERS RED CROSS BENEFIT TOUR
Winter, 1931

> Austin, Tex., Jan. 26
> Memorial Auditorium, San Antonio, Tex., Jan. 26
> Municipal Auditorium, San Angelo, Tex., Jan. 27
> Abilene, Tex., Jan. 28

Breckenridge, Tex., Jan. 28
Municipal Auditorium, Dallas, Tex., Jan. 28
Oklahoma City, Okla., Feb. 2
University of Oklahoma Field House, Norman, Okla., Feb. 3
College Auditorium, Chickasha, Okla., Feb. 3
Convention Hall, Ardmore, Okla., Feb. 3

This list was compiled with the assistance of Will Rogers, Jr., and Elwyn Isaacs of the Will Rogers Memorial Commission, whose valuable help is gratefully acknowledged. Rodgers probably remained with the tour for several more days as it moved through northeast Oklahoma and into Arkansas, but his presence cannot be definitely established past Feb. 3. Also traveling with Will Rogers were his son, Will, Jr., world champion roper Chester Byers, and aviator Frank Hawkes. Various local acts appeared with the show in each city, and on at least one occasion—in Dallas—they were joined by the famous Revelers quartet, stars of network radio and recordings.

W. I. SWAIN SHOW COMPANY
Autumn, 1931

Central and South Texas, Sept.?

Exact dates and places unknown. Sole evidence is a brief notice in *Billboard* for Sept. 5, indicating that "Rodgers is the special feature of the show." The association is presumed to have been a brief one; within two weeks Rodgers was back in Kerrville, resting and attending to his new business enterprise —an Orange Julius franchise!

SKEETER KELL AND HIS GANG
Dec., 1931–Mar., 1932

Houston, Tex., Dec. 21–Jan. 23
Luling, Tex., Jan. 25–30
San Antonio, Tex., Feb. 1–Mar. 5

Rodgers's presence for the San Antonio stand has not been confirmed. During this period he traveled to Dallas for a week-long series of recording sessions and was also involved with his new radio program on KMAC in San Antonio. He may have appeared sporadically with the Kell show until it folded in early March. Various performers headlined the show in the course of its three-city run; in addition to Rodgers, they included fan dancer Holly Desmond, Texas Ann and her Wild West company, and John Mansell's Hollywood Revue.

J. DOUG MORGAN SHOW
Spring, 1932

>   Jacksonville, Tex., Apr. 4–9
>   Longview, Tex., Apr. 11–16
>   Lufkin, Tex., May 2–7

These are the only known appearances, but other towns in the area were undoubtedly included in the tour. Exactly when Rodgers left the show is not known.

INDEPENDENT BOOKINGS
Winter, 1933

>   Joy Theater, Dallas, Tex., Jan. 21

According to *Billboard,* Rodgers was "currently playing independent vaudeville in the Texas country." Although there were probably other dates, this is the only one thus far identified. Exact date not confirmed.

J. DOUG MORGAN SHOW
Spring, 1933

>   East Texas, Feb. 1–15

Itinerary is unknown, and dates approximate. In mid-February, Rodgers entered Methodist Hospital in Houston with severe pneumonia.

BILLY TERRELL'S COMEDIANS
Spring, 1933

>   Paducah, Ky., late March

Unconfirmed. Some evidence suggests that this appearance took place either the previous spring or fall.

OTHER PLACES where Rodgers is known or believed to have appeared (dates unknown): Annapolis, Md.; Greenville, S.C.; Olympia Theater, Miami, Fla.; Temple, Tex.; Victoria, Tex.; El Campo, Tex.; Beeville, Tex.; Ponca City, Okla.; Monroe, La.

Index

Items in the discography are indicated by a *d* following the page number and preceding the discographical sequence number; "406*d58*," for example, refers to entry 58 ("The One Rose") on page 406. Relationships of members of the Rodgers family to Jimmie Rodgers are shown in parentheses after their names.

Abilene, Kans., 242
Abilene, Tex., 276, 277, 437
Ackerman, Miss., 34
Actors' Equity, 231–32
Acuff, Roy, 4, 191, 343
Ada, Okla., 244
Adams, Jack, 158
Admission prices, 175–76, 225, 244, 346
Aeolian Vocalion Co., 89
"After the Ball," 122
"Ain't No Blackheaded Woman Can Make a Fool of Me." *See* "Blue Yodel No. 5"
Alabama, 10
"Alabama Moon," 146, 318
Alabama & Vicksburg Railroad, 121
Alamo Heights, Tex., 306
Albee, Edward F., 189
Alderman, Tony, 95
Al G. Fields Minstrels, 17
Al Gordon's Comedy Canines, 166, 433
Al Hopkins' Original Hill Billies, 90
Allen, George, 299
Allesandri, Arturo, 88
Alley, Alvin, 278
Alley, Shelly Lee, 278, 280, 334
Althoff, Charlie, 153, 432
Altus, Okla., 88
Amarillo, Tex., 88
American Record Corp., 347
American Red Cross, 273, 275, 276, 281, 436–37

Amos 'n Andy, 88, 260
Anglin, Margaret, 17
"Anniversary Blue Yodel." *See* "Blue Yodel No. 7"
"Any Old Place I Can Hang My Hat Is Home Sweet Home to Me," 55
"Any Old Time," 72, 187, 398*d27*
Apeda Studio (New York), 157
Appomattox, Va., 10
Ardmore, Okla., 281, 437
Ardmore (Okla.) *Ardmoreite*, 281
Arizona, 52, 60, 201
Arkansas, 249
Arkansas Shorty, 88
"Arkansaw Traveler," 88
Armstrong, Lillian Hardin, 260
Armstrong, Louis, 255, 258–60, 349
Arnold, Eddy, 126
"Around the Water Tank." *See* "Waiting for a Train"
Artesia, Miss., 15, 25
Asheville, N.C., 62, 65–82 *passim*, 105, 107, 114, 116, 140, 165, 201, 222, 227, 273; Chamber of Commerce, 67
Asheville (N.C.) *Citizen*, 69, 226
Asheville (N.C.) *Times*, 68, 70, 76
Ashley, Clarence, 66
Ask-Me Dodge, 57
Associated Glee Clubs of America, 88
Atlanta, Ga., 56, 92, 101, 159, 164, 167, 206, 217, 219, 349, 380, 434
Atlanta Constitution, 204

Atlanta Women's Club, 219
Atwood, John, 34
Austin, Gene, 88, 140, 150, 162, 170, 178, 194, 202, 210, 234, 236, 288, 318, 342; and Rodgers, 151–53, 159; early life, 151–52; in decline, 372; sales compared with Rodgers, 384
Austin, Tex., 274, 286–87, 436
Australia, 306, 364
"Away Out on the Mountain," 119-23 *passim*, 132, 139, 156, 162, 170, 201, 226, 244, 391*d6*
Aztec Theater (San Antonio, Tex.), 208

Bailey, Jesse James, 82*n2*
Bailey's Lucky Seven, 352
Baker, Buddy, 182, 433
Baker Hotel (Dallas, Tex.), 218
Baker-Lockwood Tent Co., 48
Ball, Wilber, 295–96
Baltimore, Md., 81, 330
Balzac, Honoré de, 266
Banjo, 31, 37, 44, 52, 54, 76
Barco, Steve, 170
"Barefoot Blues." *See* "Blue Yodel No. 12"
Barfield, Johnny, 330
Barker Hotel (Hollywood), 251
Barnum & Bailey Circus, 230
Barnum, P. T., 230
Bass, Clifford, 287, 322, 323, 329, 330
Battery Park Hotel (Asheville, N.C.), 226
Beatles, 362
Beaumont, Tex., 214, 434
Bedell, Cora, 344–49 *passim*, 354–55
Beethoven Maennerchor, 276
Beiderbecke, Bix, 352
"Ben Dewberry's Final Run," 119, 120, 153, 391*d3*
Benedict, Okla., 246
Benevolent and Protective Order of Elks, 268, 282*n4*, 287
Ben Selvin's Novelty Orchestra, 352
Berlin, Irving, 73
Berliner, Emile, 84, 87
Bernard, Al, 211
Bernie, Ben, 297
Berryman, Pat, 330
Bert Lown's Orchestra, 350
Biggers, Carl, 323

"Big Rock Candy Mountain[s]," 123
Big Spring, Tex., 199, 433
Bilbo, Theodore, 31, 231
"Bill Bailey, Won't You Please Come Home," 49. *See also* "I Wonder Why Bill Bailey Don't Come Home"
Billboard, 56, 57, 63*n8*, 72, 177, 180–81, 188, 213, 233, 235, 236, 242, 249, 252, 253, 273, 287, 288, 302, 307, 308–9, 344, 357, 433, 436, 437, 438
Billroy's Comedians, 47
Billy Terrell's Comedians, 48–52, 438. *See also* Terrell, Billy
Biltmore, N.C., 74
"A Bird in a Gilded Cage," 122
Birmingham, Ala., 22, 203, 204, 311, 434
Birmingham (Ala.) *Post*, 204
Blackface, 71, 124, 226, 231, 260, 261. *See also* Show business
Blevins, Sunny, 270
Blondin Shows, 42
Bloom, Mickey, 260
Blue and Gray Troubadours, 135, 139
Bluebird records, 361, 379, 383
Blue Heaven (yacht), 152, 202
Blues, 22, 138, 161–62, 206, 291, 317, 339; Rodgers quoted on, 26, 124, 294; popularity of, 42, 72; in Rodgers's early career, 49, 55, 112; first recordings of, 92; attitudes toward white singers of, 123–24, 299, 363; ironic voice in, 130*n39;* Rodgers's use of traditional lines from, 187–88, 211, 257, 280, 290, 316, 319; in country music, 312
Blue Yodeler's Paradise, 12, 202, 212, 269–70, 272, 276, 303, 304, 306, 348. *See also* Kerrville
"Blue Yodel [No. 1]," 75, 111–12, 117, 119, 120, 123, 124, 132, 139, 156, 162, 168, 170, 226, 227, 228, 262, 276, 294, 305, 382, 391*d5*
"Blue Yodel—No. II," 138, 149, 393*d12*
"Blue Yodel No. 3," 124, 138, 161, 394*d14*
"Blue Yodel No. 4," 160, 161–62, 205, 382, 397*d23*
"Blue Yodel No. 5," 187–88, 398*d28*
"Blue Yodel No. 6," 215, 361, 401*d38*

"Blue Yodel No. 7" ["Anniversary Blue Yodel"], 220, 403*d45*

"Blue Yodel No. 8," 221, 258, 408*d62*

"Blue Yodel No. 9," 72, 255, 258–60, 280, 292, 305, 409*d64*

"Blue Yodel No. 10," 315, 318–19, 415*d85*

"Blue Yodel Number Eleven," 221, 403*d47*

"Blue Yodel No. 12," 350, 351, 420*d99* *See also* "Jimmie Rodgers' Last Blue Yodel"

Blue Yodels, 49, 50, 70, 111–12, 117, 135, 175, 210, 292, 318, 334; named by Peer, 124–25, 131*n41*; Elsie McWilliams as co–composer of, 148; numbered by Peer, 161; sequence of recording and release, 172*n4*, 221, 430–31 (chart)

Bogalusa, La., 288

Bonbrest, Joe, 153, 432

Bond, Johnny, 387

Bonita, Miss., 52, 357

Bonner, Capt. M. J., 100

Borger, Tex., 235, 240, 436

Bostonians Light Opera Co., 72

Boswell Sisters, 88

Box office receipts, 22, 236, 277, 309

Boyd, Bill, 316

"A Boy's Best Friend Is His Mother," 151

Bozeman, Dora Virginia (aunt), 14–26 *passim*, 32, 36, 40, 115–16, 128, 140, 165, 244

Bozeman, Eliza. *See* Rodgers, Eliza Bozeman

Bozeman, Joe (cousin), 36

Bozeman, Joseph W. (great-uncle), 9–10

Bozeman, Lucy Carroll (great-grand-mother), 10

Bozeman, Meady (great-grandfather), 10

Bozeman, Meady (great-great-grand-father), 10

Bozeman, Samuel (grandfather), 10–14 *passim*

Bozeman, Samuel (uncle), 21

Bozeman, Tom (uncle), 20–22

Bozeman, Virginia Shine (grandmother), 11–14

Bozeman, Walter Raleigh "Rawl" (un-cle), 81, 183, 330

Bozeman family, 9–10, 12, 14, 18

Bracey, Ishman, 159

"The Brakeman's Blues," 137, 149, 153, 201, 351, 392*d9*

Breckenridge, Tex., 268, 277, 437

Bridgers, J. D., 66

Bristol, Va.-Tenn., 6, 71, 73, 74, 81, 87, 104, 105–14 *passim*, 156, 159, 180, 187, 301, 343, 380

Bristol (Va.-Tenn.) *Herald Courier*, 105

Bristol (Va.-Tenn.) *News-Bulletin*, 106

British Columbia, 309

Britton's Brown Derby Orchestra, 166, 433

Brockman, Polk, 92–98 *passim*

Bronsen, I. N., 260–61, 423

Brontë sisters, 266

Brooklyn, N.Y., 354

Brown, George. *See* Hill, William J. "Billy"

Brown, Milton, 314

Browning, Elizabeth Barrett, 266

Bruner, Bill, 174–79, 183, 202, 244, 248, 436

Brunk's Comedians, 207

Brunswick-Balke-Collender Co., 80, 87, 89, 104, 347. *See also* American Record Corp.

Bryan, Dean, 160

Bryant, Hoyt "Slim," 79, 330–35, 337–38

Buffalo Bill's Wild West Show, 244

Bunyard, Dick, 316

Burkes, Charlie, 317

Burkes, Weldon, 206, 207, 209, 212, 214, 218, 316, 317, 318, 434

Burkes, William T. "Billy," 79, 206–9 *passim*, 211, 212, 217–22 *passim*, 222*n15*, 226, 271, 316–18, 345, 434–35

Burr, Henry, 88

"Bury Me on the Lone Prairie," 338

Butcher, Dwight, 348, 352

"Buttons and Bows," 178

Byers, Chester, 275, 437

"The Cacklin' Hen," 227

Cagney, James, 262

Cahn, Sammy, 239

Cairo, Ill., 8

Cali, John, 352, 353

California, 39, 201, 249, 251, 261, 273
"California Blues." *See* "Blue Yodel No. 4"
Callahan brothers, 66
Camden, N.J., 78, 84, 85, 87, 95, 100, 101, 114, 118, 135, 141, 147, 185, 188, 216, 221, 329, 330, 334–38 *passim*, 343, 352, 356, 380
Campbell, Howard, 227, 435
Canada, 309
Canadian Kid, 57
Cannon's Jug Stompers, 159
Cape Cod, 352
Capt. Rives's Supporting Force, C.S.A., 7
Carlisle, Cliff, 295–96
Carmichael, Hoagland Howard "Hoagy," 149, 339
Carnivals. *See* Show business
"Carolina Moon," 318
Carolina Tar Heels, 101, 159
Carroll, Lucy. *See* Bozeman, Lucy Carroll
"Carry Me Back to Old Virginny," 88
Carson, Fiddlin' John, 55, 56, 88–101 *passim*, 227
Carter, Alvin Pleasant Delaney "A.P.," 16, 291, 292, 294
Carter, Jimmy, 3
Carter, Maybelle Addington, 291, 292, 294
Carter, Sara Dougherty, 291–94 *passim*
Carter Family, 16, 66, 90, 99, 104, 128*nl*, 219, 290–94, 337, 339, 340, 341
"The Carter Family and Jimmie Rodgers in Texas," 294–95, 411*d72*
Carthage, Miss., 234, 435
Carthage, Tex., 322, 344
Caruso, Enrico, 85, 101, 104, 150
"Casey Jones," 35, 120
Cash, Wilbur J., 5, 7
Castle, Irene, 86
Castle, Vernon, 86
Castro (Peer employee), 349, 354–56
C. A. Wortham Carnival, 207
Chalupka, Suzanne, 78
Chambers, C. M., 274
Charles, Ray, 362
"Charleston," 55, 71, 72, 75, 78, 228
"Charlestonette," 72

Charlotte, N.C., 104, 111, 291
Charters, Samuel, 92, 362
Chase-Lister Show Co., 47
Chattanooga, Tenn., 221, 226–27
Chattanooga Times, 226
Chekhov, Anton, 184
"Chemirocha," 200. *See also* Kipsigis
"Cherry," 339
Chicago, Ill., 91, 93, 100, 229, 322
Chilton, John, 258, 260
Choctaw County, Ala., 8
Choctaw County, Okla., 34
Chopin, Frederic, 266
Chriesman, Tex., 195
Christie Brothers Circus, 201
Churchill Downs (Louisville, Ky.), 297
Circuses. *See* Show business
City Auditorium (Asheville, N.C.), 225, 434
Civil War, 7, 8, 10
Clarendon, Tex., 238, 239
Clarion records, 306
Clarksville, Tex., 238
Classical music, 21, 37, 85, 313. *See also* Caruso, Enrico; Victor Talking Machine Co., Red Seal records
Clifford Hayes's Dixieland Jug Blowers, 297–99. *See also* Earl McDonald's Original Louisville Jug Band
Clinton, Larry, 256
Clinton, Tenn., 78
Cohen, Norm, 162, 383, 387
Coker, Elmer, 245
Cole, Nat King, 266
Coleman Theater (Miami, Okla.), 203, 434
Colicchio, Tony, 352, 353
Collins, Dorothy, 190
Colonial Beach, Va., 134
Colorado, 52
Colorado & Southern Railroad, 238
Coltman, Robert, 75, 94, 125, 312
Columbia Phonograph Co., 87, 89, 91, 92, 221, 338, 347. *See also* American Record Corp.
Columbia Pictures Corp., 188, 214, 261
Comber, Chris, 7, 386
"Companionate Marriage" (playbill), 176, 182
Company B, 14th Alabama Infantry, C.S.A., 10

Coney Island, 145, 165, 354
Conn, May, 30–31, 32
Conn, Tom, 30–31, 32
"The Conundrum (What Will I Play Next?)," 305
Cooksey, Robert, 100
Coolidge, Calvin, 88
"Coon song" tradition, 86
Cooper, Dr. Inman W., 179–80, 183–84, 273
Copyright, 90, 96–100 *passim*, 110, 111, 119, 186, 196, 211, 239, 253, 254, 289, 292, 307, 313, 314–15, 333, 339
Cordova, Mike, 278
Correll and Gosden. *See* Amos 'n Andy
Cottondale, Ala., 23
The Country Blues, 362
Country music, 2–5 *passim*, 21, 26, 55, 73, 80, 94, 95, 99, 124, 146, 148, 250, 257, 258, 279, 280, 312, 334, 364. *See also* Folk music; Hillbilly music; Radio; Western music
Country Music (magazine), 190
Country Music Foundation, 385
Country Music Hall of Fame, 337, 362
The Country Music Story, 363
Country Music, U.S.A., 363
Country News and Views, 386
Court, Anita Rodgers (daughter), 43, 52, 59, 62, 66, 107, 113–17 *passim*, 158, 270, 308, 319, 330, 345–46
Cover records: by Rodgers, 116, 257; of Rodgers's recordings, 138, 156, 172*n1*, 178, 333
Cowboy Ramblers, 317
Cowboy songs. *See* Western music
"Cow Hand's Last Ride," 350, 351, 420*d101*
Cox, Fred, 297, 298
Cox Hat Co. (Bristol, Tenn.), 105
Cozzens, Ellsworth T., 122, 134–39, 349
Crane, Stephen, 266
Crawford, Jesse, 88
Crockett, Davey, 122
Crosby, Bing, 200, 256, 262, 342, 343, 362, 363, 384, 385
Cross, Hugh, 227, 435
Crowley's Comedians, 42
Crown records, 338
Crumit, Frank, 88, 152, 211
Culver City, Calif., 251

"Cut-in," 239, 241*n23*, 351
"The Cyclone of Rye Cove," 219

"Daddy and Home," 145, 149, 164, 205, 262, 395*d18*
"Daddy's Little Girl," 55
Daleville, Miss., 14
Dalhart, Vernon (Marion Try Slaughter), 55, 86, 89, 101, 126, 150, 236, 253, 279, 288, 322, 342, 352, 385
Dallas, Tex., 203, 206, 214–18, 277, 278, 295, 310, 314–16, 322, 329, 344, 356, 380, 434, 437
Dallas County, Ala., 10
Dallas News, 204, 277
Dance music, 55, 75, 80, 108
"Danville Girl." *See* "Waiting for a Train"
"The Daring Young Man on the Flying Trapeze," 49, 140, 423
Davis, Jimmie, 314
Davis, Smokey, 71, 78
"Dear Old Sunny South by the Sea," 137, 139, 392*d7*
Decca records, 191
Decker, Peter, 93
"Deep Elem" (Dallas), 344
DeLeath, Vaughn, 88
Dell, Paperman, 57
Del Rio, Dolores, 169
Delta Point, La., 40
Dempsey, Paul, 157
Depression, 179, 189, 228, 240*n7*, 249, 261, 272, 273, 288, 290, 304–6 *passim*, 314, 321, 334, 338–48 *passim*, 361. *See also* Economy, national
"Desert Blues," 187, 398*d26*
Desmond, Holly, 308, 437
Desmond's New York Roof Garden Revue, 309
DeSylva, Brown, and Henderson Music Publishing Co., 339
Devers, Dorothy, 139
Dickey, James, 5
Didion, Joan, 279
"Dinah," 336
Disaster songs, 126
Discography, 260, 297, 353, 386–422
"A Distant Land to Roam," 219
Dixie Credit Co., 20
Dixieland jazz. *See* Jazz

"Dixie Moon," 318
Dixon brothers, 66
Doc El Vino, 57
Dok Eisenburg and His Sinfonians, 88
"Don't Fence Me In," 149
"Don't It Make My Brown Eyes Blue," 2
"Doo Wacka Doo," 55
Dorsey, Jimmy, 138, 352
Dorsey, Tommy, 138, 306, 352
Dostoevsky, Feodor, 266
"Do What You Did Last Night," 209
"Down the Old Road to Home," 315, 318, 335, 415*d84*
"Down the River of Golden Dreams," 80
"Dreaming with Tears in My Eyes," 350, 351, 420*d100*
"A Drunkard's Child," 220, 404*d48*
Duncan, Tommy, 296
Durant, Miss., 30, 32, 33
Dwight, Kans., 231, 232, 233, 249

Earle Theater (Washington, D.C.), 152–57 *passim*, 344, 432
Earl McDonald's Original Louisville Jug Band, 297, 298. *See also* Clifford Hayes's Dixieland Jug Blowers
East (U.S.), 329, 356, 432
Economy, national, 39, 167, 181, 214, 215, 218, 228–29, 242, 310, 348, 356. *See also* Depression
Edison, Thomas Alva, 90, 93
Edison records, 86, 89, 92
Edwards, John, 260, 386
"The 18th Amendment" (playbill), 308
Elder, Otis, 226
"The Elder Brother" (playbill), 182
Electradisk records, 383
Eliot, T. S., 5
Elite Theater (Meridian, Miss.), 17, 22
Elizabethton, Tenn., 73
Elks. *See* Benevolent and Protective Order of Elks
Ellington, Edward Kennedy "Duke," 356
El Paso, Tex., 26, 268
El Tivoli Club (Dallas, Tex.), 206, 208, 212, 213, 218
Emerson, Ralph Waldo, 266
"Empty Saddles," 336
England, 306, 329, 364
English, Paul, 42, 48, 172, 175, 176, 180–83, 201, 234, 236, 288, 306, 311, 433

Enterprise, Miss., 12
Ernest Phipps and His Holiness Quartet, 106
Evans, David, 162
Evans, Jim, 386
Evansville, Ind., 172, 433
"Evenin' Sun Yodel." *See* "Blue Yodel No. 3"
"Everybody Does It in Hawaii," 209–10, 293, 305, 399*d31*

Faber and McIntyre (comedy act), 166, 433
Falsetto. *See* Yodel
Fatty Martin's Orchestra, 88
Faulkner, William, 31–32, 45*n2*
Fawcett, W. A., 212
Fellowship Forum, 140
Ferguson, Ben, 299
Ferguson, James E. "Pa," 268–69
Ferguson, Miriam "Ma," 268–69
Field hollers, 125
Field recording, 93, 94, 96, 100, 104, 158, 159, 185, 313, 314, 315, 329. *See also* Peer, Ralph S.; *and various cities*
First Methodist-Protestant Church (Meridian, Miss.), 36
"Five Foot Two, Eyes of Blue," 336
Flat Iron Building (Asheville, N.C.), 68
Fleming, Mad Cody, 57
Flora DeVoss Shows, 47
Florida East Coast Railroad, 59
Folk music, 69, 72, 75, 77, 90, 112, 124, 125, 133, 161, 170, 187, 280, 312, 334, 342. *See also* Country music; Hillbilly music; Oldtime music
"Following the Cow Trail," 90
Ford, Burt, 199
"Forgotten," 72
Fort Pierce, Fla., 59
Fort Sam Houston (San Antonio, Tex.), 274
"For the Sake of Days Gone By," 252, 257, 407*d59*
Fort Towson, Okla., 245
Fort Worth, Tex., 206, 207, 208, 218, 434
Fort Worth Doughboys, 314
Foster, Gwen, 101. *See also* Carolina Tar Heels
Foster, Stephen C., 86

Fox, William, 205
"Frankie and Johnny," 51, 153, 159, 168, 177, 211, 223n23, 259, 400d35
Fraternal orders: Rodgers in, 268, 282n4, 287
Fred Waring and His Pennsylvanians, 120. *See also* Waring, Fred
Freeman, Charles J., 190
Freeman, David, 381, 385
Freemasonry, 268, 282n4, 287
Freeny-Cannon Trio, 235, 435
Fries, Va., 92
Frieta, Alfred, 236
Frieta, Lucille, 236
Frieta's Hawaiians. *See* Waikiki Hawaiians
Frizzell, William Orville "Lefty," 3, 280
Fuhri, W. S., 91
Fullam, Albert, 58–59, 63n9, 65, 66
Fullam, Jack, 66
Fullam, John, 65, 66
Fuller's Jazz Band, 86
Furman, Dick, 270–71, 305, 365
Furman, John, 270–71, 305, 365

Gable, Clark, 342
Gadsden, Ala., 329
Gainesville, Tex., 236
Galax, Va., 86, 95
"Galilee," 276
"A Gal like You," 179
Galveston, Tex., 62, 268, 348, 349
"Gambling Bar Room Blues," 334–35, 418d93
"Gambling Polka Dot Blues," 290, 296, 297, 334, 412d74
Garland, Judy, 342, 365
Gass, Theodore John Henry, 267
Gauguin, Paul, 266
Geiger, Ala., 12, 53, 60, 117, 164
Gelatt, Roland, 85, 87
Gem Theater (Meridian, Miss.), 17
General Phonograph Corp. *See* Okeh records
George Vanderbilt Hotel (Asheville, N.C.), 68
Georgia, 8, 10
Georgia Yellow Hammers, 101, 159, 219
Georgia Wildcats, 330, 338
Gerard, R. T. "Jerry," 213, 219, 435
Gettysburg, battle of, 10
Gibson, Clifford, 293

Gibson, Hoot, 216
Gilbert and Sullivan, 230
Gilliland, Henry, 88
Gilmore, Bob, 272, 350–52
Glander, Anita. *See* Peer, Anita Glander
Glenn, Wilfred, 275. *See also* Revelers
"The Glory of Love," 336
Gluck, Alma, 88, 96
Goldblatt, Burt, 363
Gold records, 383
"Goodbye, Dixie, Goodbye," 80
"Goodbye, Mr. Dry, You're All Wet," 332
Goodman, Benny, 306
GOSH. *See* Shepherd, G. O.
Gospel music, 21, 101, 292
Gowland, Happy, 175, 176, 182, 433
Graham, Charles, 220
Graham's Switch, Miss., 12
Gramophone (Berliner), 84
Grand Ole Opry, 2, 4, 159
Grant, Claude, 67, 71, 74, 77–82 *passim*, 107, 109, 114, 159. *See also* Jimmie Rodgers Entertainers; Tenneva Ramblers
Grant, Jack, 71, 81, 107, 129n9. *See also* Jimmie Rodgers Entertainers; Tenneva Ramblers
Grappelly, Stephane, 299
Grayson, George Banman, 56
The Great American Popular Singers, 364
Great Cosmopolitan Shows, 48
Green, Archie, 138
Green, Clarence, 66
Griffin, Lena (aunt), 11
"Ground Hog Rootin' in My Backyard." *See* "Blue Yodel No. 10"
Guitar, 43, 44, 52, 54, 58, 177; Martin, 76, 112, 157, 183, 192, 197n3, 218; Weymann, 153, 169, 217, 287, 299n7; Gibson, 174, 178, 208; Hawaiian (steel), 206
Gulfport, Miss., 182, 433
Gunter Hotel (San Antonio, Tex.), 271, 274, 278, 303
Gus Sun Vaudeville Circuit, 344

Hagar, Fred, 92
Haggard, Merle, 160, 220, 280
Hall, Raymond E., 56, 59, 239, 252–53, 269, 280, 289, 291, 296, 300n10, 302,

Hall, Raymond E. *(continued)*
310, 317, 344, 351
Hall, Wendell, 89
Halley, Bill, 335
Handy, William Christopher, 91, 124, 257
Hanks, Joe "Fine Arts," 57, 213
Happiness Boys, 88
Happy Cook's Kentucky Buddies, 182, 433
"Hard Time Blues." *See* "No Hard Times"
Hare, Ernest. *See* Happiness Boys
Harkins, Richard, 245
Harkins, Stella. *See* Kelly, Stella
Harlan, Byron, 86
Harley Sadler's Own Show. *See* Sadler, Harley
Harmony records, 306
Harmony whistling, 210
Harrell, Kelly, 66, 100, 119, 123, 130*n38*
Harris, Pearl Bozeman (cousin), 18, 359
Hart, William S., 216
Harvey, Carey D., 335
Harvey, Hortense "Virginia Shine," 359
Harvey, M. G., 359
Hattiesburg, Miss., 19, 35, 49–51 *passim*, 185, 433
"Have You Ever Been Lonely?," 336
Hawaiian music, 209, 312
"Hawaiian Whoopee" (musical show), 233, 236
Hawkes, Frank, 277, 437
Hayes, Clifford, 297–99
Hearst, William Randolph, 230
Heflin Hotel (Ackerman, Miss.), 34
Heineman, Otto, 95
Helton, Al, 67
Helton, Ernest, 67, 78–79
Helton, Harry, 67
Helton, Osey, 67
Helton's Old Time String Band, 69–70, 72, 77
Hemphill, Tex., 306
Hendersonville, N.C., 77
Henry F. Seal Agency, 157
Henry Grady Hotel (Atlanta, Ga.), 219
Herscher, Lou, 352, 353
Hersholt, Jean, 169
"He's in the Jailhouse Now," 178

Hess, Bennie, 190–96 *passim*
Hess, Festo "Cap," 194
Hess, Troy, 190
Hibbard, Charles, 93
Hibbler, Doc Zip, 57
High Island, Tex., 249
"High Powered Mama," 188, 398*d29*
Hill, Murray, 88
Hill, William J. "Billy," 336
Hill Billies. *See* Al Hopkins' Original Hill Billies
Hillbilly music, 3, 56, 69, 72, 75, 91–97 *passim*, 105, 110, 111, 118, 124, 136, 151, 161, 186, 258, 279, 291, 339, 356; characterized, 3; as pejorative term, 4, 226, 250, 274, 364; Hank Williams quoted on, 26; industry reaction against term, 73; term originated by Peer, 86; first recordings of, 88–90; developed at Victor by Peer, 98–101; early commercial appeal of, 133; modernized by Rodgers, 312–13; popularity in Depression, 313, 338; first yodel on recording of, 333. *See also* Country music; Folk music; Oldtime music; Western music
Hines, Earl, 260
Hiram and Hezekiah. *See* "The Pullman Porters"
"His Master's Voice," 85. *See also* Victor Talking Machine Co.
Hitchcock, Raymond, 88
Hitt, Arza, 351
"Hobo Bill's Last Ride," 216–18, 219, 238, 239, 255, 402*d42*
"Hobo's Meditation," 315, 317, 414*d80*
Hogan, Roy, 244
Holden, Lee "Texas Tom," 226, 227, 434–35
Holdenville, Okla., 245, 246–47
Holland, 10
Holiday, Billie, 365
Hollywood, Calif., 228, 229, 251, 253, 260, 261, 268, 321, 380
"Home Call," 211, 315, 318, 319; LP issues, 400*d86*; 78 rpm issues, 416*d86*
"Home on the Range," 423
"Home Sweet Home," 96
"Honey in de Comb," 276
Hooey, Herbert, 157
Hoover, Herbert Clark, 88, 167

Hopi Indian Chanters, 88
Hopkins, Al, 95
Hopkins, Joe, 95
Horwitz, Will, 270, 282*n8*
Hot Springs, Ark., 281
"A Hot Time in the Old Town Tonight,"
49, 75, 140, 294, 423
Houston, Tex., 100, 171, 172, 196, 204,
303, 307–12 *passim*, 316, 434, 437
Howard-DeVoss Show Co., 320
"How Come You Do Me Like You Do,"
55, 151, 162, 209
Howell, George, 330–31
"How Ya Gonna Keep 'em Down on the
Farm," 336
Hudson, Arthur Palmer, 163
Hughes County, Okla., 246
Hughes County (Okla.) *Tribune*, 245
Hugo, Okla., 34, 245, 249
Hunt, Gladys, 41, 52, 54
Hunt, Mose, 41, 52
Hunt, Prince Albert, 162, 163
Huntsville, Tex., 344
Hurt, Mississippi John, 162
Hutchison, C. L., 160

"I'd Like to Sleep 'til I Get Over You,"
2–3
"If Brother Jack Were Here." *See*
"Mother Was a Lady"
Illinois Central Railroad, 30
"I'll See You in My Dreams," 55
"I Love You Yet," 194, 196
"I'm Always There on Time." *See* "Long
Tall Mama Blues"
"I'm a One Man's Woman Now," 238,
240
"I'm Free (from the Chain Gang Now),"
350, 352, 420*d102*
"I'm Lonely and Blue," 146, 148, 149,
163, 397*d25*
"I'm Lonesome Too," 196, 252, 256,
406*d57*
"I'm Sitting on Top of the World," 336
"I'm Sorry We Met," 188, 399*d30*
"I'm Waiting for You, Liza Jane," 86
Independence, La., 236
Independence, Mo., 90
India, 306
Indiana, 58
International Discophiles, 386

Interstate Time. *See* Radio-Keith-
Orpheum
"In the Baggage Car Ahead," 122
"In the Chapel in the Moonlight," 336
"In the Hills of Tennessee," 331, 335,
336, 419*d95*
"In the Jailhouse Now," 137, 142*n4*,
152, 159, 168, 201, 205, 226, 228,
276, 311–12, 393*d11*
"In the Jailhouse Now—No. 2," 258,
408*d63*
Iowa, 320
Irving Berlin Music Co., 339
"I Scream, You Scream, We All Scream
for Ice Cream," 120
"It Ain't Gonna Rain No Mo'," 89
"I've Only Loved Three Women," 335,
418*d94*
"I've Ranged, I've Roamed, and I've
Travelled," 215, 220, 295, 402*d41*,
426*n31*
Ivey, William, 385
"I Wonder Who's Kissing Her Now,"
178
"I Wonder Why Bill Bailey Don't Come
Home," 22
Jackson, Jim (trainman), 40
Jackson, Jim (bluesman), 159
Jackson, Willie, 280
Jackson, Miss., 30–31, 42, 182, 433
Jacksonville, Tex., 319, 322, 438
James, Lewis, 275. *See also* Revelers
James, Skip, 162
J. & W. Seligman & Co., 87
Janis, Elsie, 86
Japan, 364
Jazz, 55, 73, 75, 86, 87, 124, 138, 211,
232, 251; criticized by Rodgers, 71–
72; in recordings of Rodgers, 72, 160,
161, 211, 252, 257–59 *passim*, 280,
297, 312. *See also* Blues
The Jazz Singer, 116
J. Doug Morgan Show. *See* Morgan,
J. Doug
"Jealous," 55
"Jeanie," 140
"Jeanine," 148
Jefferson, Blind Lemon, 123
Jefferson, Tex., 236
Jefferson Hotel (Dallas, Tex.), 206, 209
Jenkins, Andrew, 95, 120, 121, 221, 239

Jenkins, Homer, 355
Jenkins Family, 95
"Jimmie Brown the Newsboy," 219
Jimmie Rodgers and the Grant Brothers. *See* Jimmie Rodgers Entertainers; Tenneva Ramblers
Jimmie Rodgers Entertainers, 6, 75–82 *passim*, 107, 109. *See also* Grant, Claude; Tenneva Ramblers
"Jimmie Rodgers' Last Blue Yodel," 196, 350, 351, 353, 421*d104*
Jimmie Rodgers Memorial (Meridian, Miss.), 2, 4, 5, 178, 191
Jimmie Rodgers Society, 386
"Jimmie Rodgers Visits the Carter Family," 290, 294, 305, 411*d71*
"Jimmie's Mean Mama Blues," 72, 238, 257, 407*d60*
"Jimmie's Texas Blues," 124, 211, 400*d34*
"Jimmie the Kid," 238, 280–81, 335, 410*d67*
John Edwards Memorial Foundation, 386
John Mansell's Hollywood Revue, 309, 437
Johnson, Charles, 78, 80, 106
Johnson, Eldridge R., 84–87 *passim*, 101*n4*
Johnson, Paul, 78, 80, 106
Johnson, Robert, 123
Johnson City, Tenn., 70, 73, 78, 80
Jolson, Al, 86, 342, 363, 384
Jones, Ada, 86
Jones, Billy. *See* Happiness Boys
Jones, Fred, 66
Jones, George, 262
Jones, Max, 258–60 *passim*
Jones, Spike, 166
Joseph C. Smith's Orchestra, 86
Joy Theater (Dallas, Tex.), 344, 438
Jug bands, 159, 290, 291, 292, 297–99. *See also* Hayes, Clifford; McDonald, Earl
Jung Hotel (New Orleans, La.), 169, 170
"Just a Little Dream," 179
Justus-Romain Show Co., 47

Kaipo, Joe, 206, 208–15 *passim*, 218, 434
Kama, Charles, 278, 281
Kansas, 242, 248

Kansas City, Mo., 48, 90, 91
Kanui, Dave, 330, 331
Kardo brothers, 153, 432
Karnes, Alfred G., 106, 159
Keats, John, 266
"Keep to the Right" (playbill), 182
Keith, Benjamin Franklin, 189
Keith, Ward, 295
Keith-Albee-Orpheum (K-A-O) vaudeville circuit, 153, 189
Kell, Amber Wymore, 307
Kell, Leslie "Skeeter," 48, 303–10 *passim*, 316, 319, 320, 437
Kell, Leslie, Jr., 307
Kelly, George, 30, 33–34
Kelly, Hugh, 245
Kelly, Millie Catherine, 30
Kelly, Stella (first wife), 29–34, 38, 245, 282, 284–86, 303, 324, 325, 328, 346, 357
Kelly Field (San Antonio, Tex.), 274
Kemper County, Miss., 10
Kenton, Stan, 3
Kentucky, 58
Kerrville, Tex., 201–3 *passim*, 212–14 *passim*, 240, 268, 269, 270, 276–77, 302, 305, 357, 365, 433
Kerrville (Tex.) *Mountain Sun*, 202, 212, 272, 277, 287
Kiker, Ellen Fraser, 246
Kilgore, Tex., 322
King's Daughters Hospital (Meridian, Miss.), 54
Kipsigis (Africa), 200, 364
Klein, Saul, 352, 353
KLRA (Little Rock, Ark.), 311
KMAC (San Antonio, Tex.), 310, 312, 343, 347, 357, 437
KOMA (Oklahoma City, Okla.), 311
Koone, Fred, 316–18
KPRC (Houston, Tex.), 311–12
Krug, William, 227, 435
Kuykendall, Otis, 67–71 *passim*, 78
KVOO (Tulsa, Okla.), 205, 311

Lake Providence, La., 210
Lamar Hotel (Meridian, Miss.), 179
"Land of My Boyhood Dreams," 215, 295, 401*d37*
Lani McIntire's Harmony Hawaiians. *See* McIntire, Lani

La Plante, Laura, 153
"The Lass Mohee," 253. *See also* "Little Mo-Hee"
"The Last Roundup," 336
Lauder, Harry, 86, 120
Lauderdale County, Miss., 11
Lauderdale Springs, Miss., 55, 56, 75
Laurel, Miss., 34, 433
"Lazy Bones," 339
Lee, Robert E., 10
Leecan, Bobby, 100
The Legendary Jimmie Rodgers' 110 Collections, 379
"Legion" (Veterans Hospital), 201
Lehleitner, G. H., 170
"Let Me Be Your Side Track," 292–93, 305, 411*d70*
Lewis, Sam, 335, 336
Lewis, Walter "Furry," 123, 159
Lexington, Miss., 32
Lilac Time, 148
Lillie, Gordon W. "Pawnee Bill," 244, 302
Lindbergh, Charles A., 71
"Little Darling Pal of Mine," 294
"The Little Lost Child," 122
"Little Mo-Hee," 253
"The Little Old Log Cabin in the Lane," 92, 96
Little Rock, Ark., 203, 434
Loew's Capitol Theater (Atlanta, Ga.), 167, 433
Loew's Houston Theater (Houston, Tex.), 171, 433
Loew's "Southern Time" Circuit, 158, 165–71 *passim,* 203, 311, 343, 432–33
Loew's State Theater (Memphis, Tenn.), 168, 433
Loew's State Theater (New Orleans, La.), 169, 344, 433
Loew's State Theater (Norfolk, Va.), 165, 166, 433
Lombardo, Guy, 323
London, England, 338
London, Ontario, Canada, 68
Long, Dorothy, 237–38
"Long Tall Mama Blues," 334, 417*d91*
Longview, Tex., 322, 438
"Looking for a New Mama," 290, 296, 305, 412*d75*

Lost Gap, Miss., 12, 15
Louisiana, 249
Louisville, Ky., 289–98 *passim,* 301, 305, 315, 337, 338, 380
Louisville, Miss., 30–34 *passim*
Louisville Jug Band. *See* Earl McDonald's Original Louisville Jug Band
Love songs, 164, 221, 252
Lovey Girls, 153, 432
Lowndes County, Ala., 10
Lowndes County, Miss., 13, 15
Lubbock, Tex., 199, 200–201, 433
Lucas, Nick, 208, 220
Lufkin, Tex., 273, 322, 323, 344, 436, 438
Luling, Tex., 309, 437
Lullaby Larkers, 295. *See also* Ball, Wilber; Carlisle, Cliff
"Lullaby Yodel," 26, 146, 147, 149, 279, 396*d20*
Lunsford, Bascom Lamar, 66, 69, 77
Luther, Frank, 150

McClintock, Harry, 123
McCormack, John, 120
McCoy, Charlie, 159
McCreath, Ray, 141, 144, 152, 157–59 *passim*
McCuen, Brad, 381
McCurtain County, Okla., 245
McDonald, Earl, 297–98
McElrea, Rodney, 386
Maces Springs, Va., 104
MacGimsey, Bob, 152, 210
McIntire, Lani, 251, 254, 256, 263*n22*
McKinney's Cotton Pickers, 339
McMichen, Clayton, 221–22, 226, 329–38 *passim,* 434–35
MacMillan, George, 160
Macon, David Harrison "Uncle Dave," 89, 90
Macon, Miss., 23
McTell, Blind Willie, 159, 219
McWilliams, Edwin Richard, 143
McWilliams, Elsie, 54–56, 118, 135, 141–49 *passim,* 163, 206, 209–11, 217–18, 220, 221, 252, 292, 296, 297, 318, 351
McWinders, Oddie, 330–38 *passim*
Madisonville, Tex., 201
Mainer's Mountaineers, 66

Maisch, Fred, 350
Majestic Theater (San Antonio, Tex.), 205, 208, 434
"Make My Cot Where the Cot-Cot-Cotton Grows," 55
"Makin' Whoopee," 209
Malone, Bill, 125, 363
Mandola, 207
Mandolin, 168, 169
Manger Hotel (New York), 117, 145, 349
"The Man on the Flying Trapeze," 423
Marable, Fate, 211
Marion, N. C., 79
Marks, Edward B., 119, 122, 162
Marriages: Rodgers marries Stella Kelly, 32; divorces Stella, 38; marries Carrie Williamson, 40
Martin, C. F., I, 192
Martin, C. F., III, 262, 265*n44*
Martin, J. M., 355
Martinez, Eduardo, 275
Marvin, Johnny, 88, 150, 152
Marx, Groucho, 342
Maryland, 10
Masons. *See* Freemasonry
Mason, Walter B., 351
Mayfield, Alice, 276
Mayfield, Professor, 57
"Mechanicals." *See* Royalties
Medina Lake, Tex., 270
Melba, Nellie, 101*n4*, 104
Melton, James, 275. *See also* Revelers
Memorial Auditorium (Chattanooga, Tenn.), 221–22, 226, 434
Memphis, Tenn., 30, 31, 101, 159, 167, 249, 356
"Memphis Day," 168
Memphis (Tenn.) *Press–Scimitar,* 168
"Memphis Yodel," 138, 394*d13*
Meridian, Miss., 4, 8–11, 13, 15–22 *passim,* 34–44 *passim,* 48, 52, 55, 58–62 *passim,* 77, 115, 127, 140, 143, 145, 164, 168, 174, 175, 183, 201, 206, 288, 302, 303, 328, 343, 346, 349, 355, 357, 359, 433
Meridian Board of Trade, 16
Meridian Female College, 16
Meridian Male College, 16
Meridian Opera House, 16
Meridian (Miss.) *Star,* 1, 164, 165, 175

Methodist Hospital (Houston, Tex.), 344, 438
Miami, Fla., 59, 159
Miami, Okla., 203
Midwest, 230, 250
Miller, Bob, 337–38
Miller, Townsend, 236–37
Mills Music Co., 254, 339
Minstrel Club of Asbury Park Kiwanis Club, 88
"Miss Helene, Mentalist," 321
Mississippi, 50, 55, 141, 167, 246, 286
"Mississippi Delta Blues," 351, 352–53, 422*d108*
Mississippi Medical College (Meridian, Miss.), 16
"Mississippi Moon," 146, 148, 315, 317, 318, 415*d83*
"Mississippi River Blues," 217, 220, 255, 402*d43*
Mississippi State University, 30
"Miss the Mississippi and You," 335, 419*d97*
Missouri, Kansas & Texas Railroad, 238
Mr. Mickey (bulldog), 345
Mixon, Lottie Mae Rodgers (half-sister), 13, 14, 25, 113
Mobile, Ala., 172, 180, 433
Mobile & Ohio Railroad, 8, 9, 23, 25, 34, 194
Moffit–McLaurin Institute for Girls (Meridian, Miss.), 16
Monroe brothers, 379
Montgomery Ward, 216
Montgomery Ward records, 339, 361, 383
Moody, Dan, 205
"Moonlight and Roses" (revue), 153
"Moonlight and Skies," 251, 252–53, 279, 289, 305, 405*d53*
Moore, Earl, 270, 276
Moore, Ruth Ann, 297
Morgan, J. Doug, 48, 319–24, 328, 344, 438
Morgan, John Pierpont, 356
Mormon Tabernacle Choir, 88
Morphine, 180, 304, 332
Morton and Stout (comedy act), 203, 434
"Mother, the Queen of My Heart," 332, 333–34, 416*d87*
"Mother Was a Lady," 119, 120, 121–

"Mother Was a Lady" *(continued)* 22, 162, 391*d4*

Mountain music. *See* Hillbilly music

Movies. *See* Silent films; Talking pictures

"Movie presentations." *See* Vaudeville

Movietone Follies, 205

Muehlebach Hotel (Kansas City, Mo.), 232

Muldaur, Maria, 187

Muldon, Miss., 25

"Muleskinner Blues." *See* "Blue Yodel No. 8"

Municipal Auditorium (San Angelo, Tex.), 213, 277, 436

Murray, Billy, 86

Musical saw, 212

Musicology, 136, 147

M. Witmark Co., 339

"My Blue-Eyed Jane," 251–52, 404*d51*

"My Blue Heaven," 140, 151, 322, 385

"My Carolina Sunshine Girl," 72, 160, 226, 227, 396*d22*

"My Clinch Mountain Home," 294

"My Dog Faced Gal." *See* "What's It?"

"My Gal Sal," 122

"My Good Gal's Gone Blues," 72, 290, 297, 298–99, 317, 413*d77*

My Husband, Jimmie Rodgers, 361

"My Little Lady," 146, 149, 395*d19*

"My Little Old Home Down in New Orleans," 145, 149, 169, 395*d16*

"My Lovin' Gal Lucille." *See* "Blue Yodel—No. II"

"My Mammy," 55, 336

"My Old Home Town Girl," 179

"My Old Pal," 26, 146, 148, 149, 351, 394*d15*

"My Pal of Yesterday," 178

"My Rough and Rowdy Ways," 215, 402*d40*

"The Mystery of Number Five," 257–58, 408*d61*

"My Time Ain't Long," 315, 316, 414*d81*

Nashville, Tenn., 3, 5, 72, 159, 160, 190, 313, 359, 362

Nathan, Jukes & Calvin Circus, 230

Nelson, Alex, 147, 156, 330, 354

Nelson, Annie, 81, 114–15, 127, 147,

Nelson, Annie *(continued)* 156, 330

Nelson, Willie, 130*n39*, 360

"Never No Mo' Blues," 147, 148, 149, 217, 396*d21*

Neville, Jack, 281, 297, 335, 351

New Mexico, 52

New Orleans, La., 26, 30, 34–40 *passim*, 43, 48, 51, 56, 59, 100, 101, 168, 174, 195, 205, 216, 231, 233, 236, 249, 380, 434

New Orleans & Northeastern Railroad, 13, 19, 34, 35, 39, 40, 49–56 *passim*, 60, 121, 171

New Orleans (La.) *States*, 169, 170–71, 206

New Orleans (La.) *Times–Picayune*, 169, 206

New York, N.Y., 6, 42, 81, 85, 91–101 *passim*, 112, 116, 117, 141, 145, 151, 174, 179, 183, 185, 228, 229, 273, 309, 320, 329, 330, 335–43 *passim*, 348, 349, 352, 354, 380

New York Herald–Tribune, 356

New York Times, 356

Nichols, Bob. *See* McMichen, Clayton

Nichols, Ernest Loring "Red," 352

Niles, Edward Abbe, 124

Ninde, Julian R., Sr., 134–39, 349

"Ninety–nine Year Blues," 315, 317, 414*d82*

Nipper the Terrier, 85

Nixon, Richard, 4

"Nobody Knows but Me," 220, 403*d44*

Nocona, Tex., 237

"No Hard Times," 334, 417*d90*

Norfolk, Va., 158, 165, 170

North, Ted, 48

North (U.S.), 132, 171, 302, 353

North Fork (N.C.) Mountain Resort, 79, 80, 81, 107, 108

Northwest (U.S.), 309

"No Telephone in Heaven," 219

Novelty Grahams (carnival act), 17

Noxpater, Miss., 30

Oberstein, Eli, 299, 314–15, 331, 334, 339–40, 350

Odeon records, 306

O'Donnell, Tex., 198–200, 433

O'Donnell (Tex.) *Index*, 199

Ohio, 58
Okeh records, 56, 67, 89–101 *passim*, 104, 119, 174, 178–79, 258, 306, 314, 347. *See also* Columbia Phonograph Corp.
Oklahoma, 190, 201, 242–48 *passim*, 252, 302
Oklahoma City, Okla., 56, 252, 281, 324, 434, 437
Oklahoma State Penitentiary, 245
Oklona, Miss., 25
"The Old Hen Cackled and the Rooster's Going to Crow," 92, 96, 227
"Old Love Letters," 352, 382, 422*d107*
"An Old Man's Story." *See* "Why There's a Tear in My Eye"
"Old Pal of My Heart," 351, 421*d106*
Oldtime music, 55, 93, 107, 108, 186, 292, 312, 332; prejudices against, 69, 111; appeal of, 73, 99, 122; in Victor catalog, 86; Peer recognizes commercial value of, 94; Rodgers's attitudes toward, 107, 111. *See also* Country music; Hillbilly music
Old Trail Drivers Association, 274
Olympia Theater (Miami, Fla.), 159
O'Neal, Waldo, 216, 238–39, 240, 248, 257, 316, 351, 436
"The One Rose," 255–56, 406*d58*
Orange Julius, 272, 437
Original Dixieland Jazz Band, 86
Orpheum Theater (Tulsa, Okla.), 204, 434
Owens, Buck, 130*n39*, 190
Oxford, Miss., 32
Ozona, Tex., 213

Paducah, Ky., 346, 438
Paganini, Niccolo, 266
Palace Theater (Lubbock, Tex.), 200
Palace Theater (New York), 93, 113, 189, 343
Pampell, J. L., 212
Panhandle, Tex., 239–40, 436
"Panther of the Sea" (playbill), 50
Paramount Pictures, 204
Paris, Mike, 7, 386
Paris, Tex., 236
Parker, Chubby, 69
Parks, Lucien, 43
Parks Boarding House (Louisville, Miss.), 33

Parton, Dolly, 190
Patterson, Pens, 57
Paul English Players. *See* English, Paul
Pawnee, Okla., 244
"Pawnee Bill." *See* Lillie, Gordon W.
Peabody Hotel (Memphis, Tenn.), 249
"Peach Pickin' Time Down in Georgia," 334, 418*d92*
Peer, Abram, 90
Peer, Anita Glander, 105, 136, 137
Peer, Ralph Sylvester, 56, 72, 81–82, 84, 117, 128*n6*, 145, 153, 170, 171, 183, 209, 210, 240, 249, 250, 254, 261, 268, 290, 295, 299, 322, 328–31 *passim*, 336, 356, 361–62
—and hillbilly music: responsible for term, 86, 95; attitudes toward, 90, 94, 162, 186, 197*n14*, 339; first records of, 92–93
—attitude toward own success: 90
—early life and career: 90–92, 95
—achievements of: 90, 94, 96, 99, 132–34
—as businessman: 90, 92, 94, 98–100, 348
—and race music: 91, 92, 94, 159
—as "folksong collector": 92, 133, 187
—and field recording: for Okeh, 92–94; for Victor, 101, 104–13 *passim*, 136, 159, 206, 214, 219, 273, 278, 291, 314; financial arrangements, 104–5; decline of, 314, 339
—and Rodgers: "discovery" of, 107, 108–13 *passim*, 128*n6*; attitudes toward, 112, 118, 163, 185, 186–87, 200, 271–72, 313; as A&R man for, 118, 132–36, 162, 185, 186, 239, 291, 293, 331, 332, 335, 347–52 *passim*; names Blue Yodels, 124, 131*n41*; personal management of, 153, 157, 189–90, 329, 337, 338, 340–41
—and Southern Music: 150, 197*n15*, 314–15, 339–41
—and popular music: 186, 339
—and Louis Armstrong: 258–59
Pelgery, Brown, 78
Personal appearances, 432–38; with Terrell, 50–51, 346, 438; in Washington, D.C., 115, 140–141, 153–54, 432; on independent tours, 158–59, 183, 203, 212–14 *passim*, 225, 227, 234, 287–88, 328–29, 344, 433–36 *passim*, 438;

Personal appearances *(continued)*
on Loew circuit, 165–72 *passim*, 432–33; with English, 182–85 *passim*, 433; on R–K–O circuit, 201–6 *passim*, 434; with Swain, 236–48 *passim*, 302, 435–36; with Rogers, 273–82 *passim*, 436–37; with Kell, 308–10, 437; with Morgan, 322–24, 344, 438

Philadelphia, 85, 118

Philadelphia Rapid Transit Band, 88

Phipps, Ernest, 159

Phonograph, 42, 84–85, 229, 312, 313, 338, 361. *See also various record companies*

Piaf, Edith, 365

Piedras Negras, Mexico, 271

Pierce, Jack, 71, 74, 76, 77, 81, 114, 159. *See also* Tenneva Ramblers

Pine Springs, Miss., 9–20 *passim*, 194, 359

Pirated recordings, 195

"Pistol Packin' Papa," 238, 254, 405*d54*

Pleasants, Henry, 364–65

"Please Don't Holler, Mama," 299

Pogie O'Brien Circus, 230

Point Barrow, Alaska, 364

Police Gazette, 21

Polish National Orchestra, 88

"Polly of the Circus," 17

Pontotoc, Miss., 227, 434–35

Pope, Pearl. *See* Rodgers, Pearl

Poplar Bluff, Mo., 231

Popular music, 37, 42, 85–86, 96, 97, 99, 122, 124, 125, 168, 207, 209, 221, 280, 312, 313; in Rodgers's repertoire, 70, 75, 80; sought by Peer, 186, 339; Rodgers's influence on, 363. *See also* Jazz

Population Charlie, 57

Port Arthur, Tex., 214, 218, 434

Porter, Cole, 149

Porter, William Sidney (O. Henry), 65

Poulos, Sergeant, 57

"Prairie Lullaby," 334, 336, 419*d96*

Prescott, E. A., 212

Presidential election (1928), 167

Presley, Elvis, 237, 362, 384

Press notices, 70, 76, 123, 140, 154, 166, 167, 168–69, 201–6 *passim*, 278

Princeton, W.Va, 106

Princeton Seminary Male Chorus, 88

"The Prisoner's Song," 55, 89

Prohibition, 275–76, 308, 332

"Prohibition Blues," 332

"Prohibition Has Done Me Wrong," 193, 255, 332–33, 379, 416

Promotional techniques, 165–66

Publix theaters, 158–59, 208, 344

Puckett, Riley, 89, 111, 227, 333

"The Pullman Porters," 70, 194, 260–61, 379, 409, 423

Purvis, Miss., 19

Puzzle records, 305–6

Race music, 90, 91, 92, 99, 101, 133, 186, 291, 312, 339. *See also* Blues; Jazz

Radio, 51, 67, 174, 229, 307, 337, 338, 356, 361; country music programming on, 2, 3, 312; Rodgers on, 70–71, 140, 182, 203, 270, 310–13, 343

Radio Corporation of America, 87, 106, 151, 189, 315, 338, 339, 340, 362, 379, 386. *See also* Victor Talking Machine Co.

Radio–Keith–Orpheum (R–K–O) vaudeville and pictures, 189–90, 201, 202, 214, 251, 253, 302, 311, 340, 343, 434

Rafferty and the Gold Dust Twins, 337

Ragan Twins, 57

"Rag Opry," 243

Railroading, 4–12 *passim*, 24, 39, 44, 171. *See also various lines*

Railroad regulations, 16, 35, 168, 171

"Ramona," 152, 385

Randle, Bill, 312, 386

Randolph, Vance, 211

RCA Victor. *See* Radio Corporation of America; Victor Talking Machine Co.

"The Reckless Hobo." *See* "Waiting for a Train"

Record industry, 86, 90–96 *passim*, 99, 133; Rodgers writes to, 80. *See also various companies*

Recording sessions: in Bristol, 109–13, 128*n6;* in Camden, 119–24, 136–38, 147–49, 330–35; in Atlanta, 159–64 *passim*, 219–21; in New York, 186–88, 335–37, 349–53; in Dallas, 209–12, 214–15, 314–19; in Hollywood, 251–61 *passim;* in San Antonio, 278–81; in Louisville, 291–99 *passim;* difficulties in studio during, 112–13,

Recording sessions *(continued)*
130*n18*, 137, 223*n29*, 293–94, 316–
17, 331; statistics on, 250, 380 (chart);
characterized, 289–90
Recording techniques, 109–10, 142*n2*,
137, 305, 331
*Recordings of Jimmie Rodgers: An Anno-
tated Discography,* 387
Records: Rodgers learns from, 36, 42;
release of, 116, 132, 139, 156, 188,
250, 295, 305, 334, 347, 361–62;
sales of, 128, 139, 154*n10*, 162, 170,
202, 225, 249–50, 253–54, 303, 313,
328, 338, 361, 381–85; reissues, 362,
379; collected works, 379; questionable attributions, 422–24
Rector, John, 95
Redbone, Leon, 337
Red Cross. *See* American Red Cross
Redman, Don, 339
Reed, Blind Alfred, 106
Reeves, Goebel, 43, 426*n31*
Reeves, Jim, 362
Reinhardt, Django, 299

Reneau, Blind George, 56, 89, 151
Repertoire, 70, 71, 75, 80, 140; eclectic,
55, 56, 73, 76; limited, 95, 110, 118,
119, 136, 141, 188, 278, 289, 315,
330, 351; risqué, 209–10, 254, 292–93
Revelers, 88, 275, 437
Rhodes, Cecil, 184
"Right on Down through Birmingham,"
79
Rikard, James, 160
Ringling Brothers Circus, 17
Rio Rita (stage show), 182
Ritchie, A. B. "Samson," 78, 79
R–K–O. *See* Radio–Keith–Orpheum
Robbins, Marty, 362
Robert Fulton Hotel (Atlanta, Ga.), 159
Robertson, A. C. "Eck," 88
Robinson, Edward G., 262
Robinson, Virginia Shine. *See* Bozeman,
Virginia Shine
Robison, Carson, 279, 292
"Rock-a-Bye Your Baby with a Dixie
Melody," 55, 336
"Rock All Our Babies to Sleep," 332,
333, 417*d88*
Rock music, 72

Rodgers, Aaron Woodberry (father), 8–
13 *passim,* 15, 17, 19–26 *passim,* 62,
164, 165, 194
Rodgers, Carrie Cecil (second wife), 36,
40, 43, 53–66 *passim,* 74, 107, 145,
152, 158, 201, 206, 258, 271–72, 285,
308, 319, 325, 330, 346, 348, 355,
361, 379
—character of: 37–38
—quoted: 44, 52, 62, 75, 115, 118, 146,
244–45, 270, 274, 276, 303, 343; on
Tenneva Ramblers, 77; on oldtime
music, 111–12; on Rodgers's first
recording session, 113; on Rodgers's
appeal, 363
—works to support family: 54, 56, 115,
127
Rodgers, Eliza Bozeman (mother), 9–12,
41
Rodgers, Ida Smith (stepmother), 13, 15,
17, 20, 23
Rodgers, James Charles "Jimmie":
—attitudes of: toward misspelled name,
2, 356; toward blues, 26; toward
money, 33, 38, 40, 44, 107, 114–16,
117, 165, 213, 225, 272, 345; toward
marriages, 35, 44, 62–63; as professional, 42, 146, 183, 184, 317; toward
children, 44, 271, 346; toward oldtime
music, 56, 70, 71, 72, 75, 111, 117;
toward jazz, 71–72; toward own
music, 75–76; toward audiences, 78,
432; toward politics and society, 167,
268–69, 273–75 *passim,* 345; toward
old friends, 164, 167–69, 171, 213–
14, 226, 237; toward death, 184, 333
—myths about: 5, 6, 18, 23–24, 28*n19*,
45*n17*, 58, 170, 171, 192, 198, 199–
200, 202, 225, 240*n3*, 265*n44*, 281,
288, 352
—character and personality: 5, 7, 21, 33,
79, 112; habitual rambler, 7, 12–13,
39–40, 41, 52–53; high spirited, 16–
19; sociable, 23, 66; serious, 25–27;
optimistic, 26, 35–36, 39, 44, 62, 77,
82, 111, 132, 141, 184; happy-go-
lucky, 30, 33, 38–39, 63, 164, 345;
generous, 33, 165, 218–19, 226, 247,
272, 288, 289, 310, 325, 334, 346;
self–assured, 117; sentimental, 164;
sensitive, 310

—as musician: 5, 42–43, 121, 137, 220, 221, 259, 317, 318, 337, 365; with guitar, 21, 35, 49, 51, 52, 55, 75, 112, 121, 123, 163, 169, 186–87, 215, 257, 258, 262, 265*n45*, 318, 350; with banjo, 31, 37, 49, 52, 54, 55, 167, 169; with mandolin, 54, 55, 168, 169; with ukulele, 296

—influence of: as artist, 5, 279, 310; on folk tradition, 99, 125, 170; on popular music, 99, 127, 363; on country music, 118, 125, 254, 257, 279, 332, 334, 363; on other performers, 126, 313; on Western swing, 280; on singing–cowboy films, 295, 336; on rural radio programming, 312–13

—influences on music of: 14–15, 17, 21–22, 24, 37, 125, 170

—schooling: 15, 19, 23

—drinking: 16, 33, 35, 127, 238, 270–71, 305

—as performer: aspirations of, 17, 21–22, 24, 57, 58, 61; at dances, 55, 67, 80, 83*n31;* blackface, 57, 58, 261; style of, 75, 76, 79, 108–9, 146, 163, 261, 293, 337; solo, 258, 318, 336, 349

—health: 23–24, 40, 53, 59, 61, 80, 112, 115, 127, 171, 176, 182, 244–58 *passim,* 269, 286, 290–96 *passim,* 301–4 *passim,* 335–38 *passim,* 343, 348, 350–55 *passim;* in childhood, 15, 19, 25; attitudes toward, 53, 54, 184, 278–79, 323, 338; improves temporarily, 152, 251, 268, 272–73, 343; collapses, 179–80, 183, 344; given a year to live, 273; and decline of popularity, 328, 343; death, 355

—employment: as railroader, 23, 24–26, 35, 39–41 *passim,* 44, 52, 53, 56, 58, 60–61, 170–71; in other jobs, 24, 31, 41, 44, 45*n17,* 66

—personal problems: in career, 24, 26, 44, 62–63, 66–67, 77, 115, 128; in marriage, 35, 271, 302, 319, 346, 348–49; death of daughter, 77; with Tenneva Ramblers, 107–9

—image: 35, 165–66, 168–69, 209, 290; as Father of Country Music, 5, 21, 42, 137, 262, 337; as America's Blue Yodeler, 5, 118, 124–25, 126, 141, 142*n10,* 145, 158, 165, 168, 171, 180, 203, 216, 234, 238, 253, 321, 328, 329; as Singing Brakeman, 5, 139, 140, 153–54, 165–66, 168, 169, 171, 203, 216, 234, 355; as folk hero, 5, 238, 288; as Yodeling Brakeman, 166, 203; as Westerner, 291, 294; following death, 361–62; biased, 364

—physical description: 39, 237, 262, 304

—as yodeler: 43, 109, 111, 121, 125–26, 131*n44,* 163, 170, 220, 246, 257, 293, 317, 318, 337, 350, 364

—sources of appeal: artistic sensibility, 43, 136, 279, 310, 318–19, 350, 352–53, 361, 365; sincerity, 146; versatility, 337, 363–64

—popularity: 51, 76, 79, 80, 123, 149, 154, 156, 164–72 *passim,* 175, 182, 205, 220, 225–27, 234, 236–38, 250, 287–88, 289, 308, 312, 333, 344, 346, 362–65; abroad, 170; in decline, 328, 342

—finances: 66, 74, 77, 79, 275, 286, 348; salary as railroader, 36; problems with, 41, 61, 127, 272, 303–4, 323–25, 345–46; as businessman, 58, 60, 62, 107, 272; salaries as entertainer, 80, 158, 169, 172, 180–81, 190, 201; record royalties, 127–28, 132, 149, 156, 202, 272, 322, 347; salaries to musicians, 139, 212, 218, 223*n38,* 330; buys songs, 239; estate, 325, 327*n54,* 348, 358*n10*

—as "popular" entertainer: 73, 110, 112, 138, 256, 291, 312, 337

—as booking promoter: 77–80 *passim,* 157, 171, 172, 190, 212; prefers local tours, 78, 157, 308; plans foreign tours, 309, 329, 338

—as composer: 111, 118–19, 123, 146–48 *passim,* 215–16, 256, 291, 298, 315, 351; lyric sheets, 255, 257, 298, 316, 353

—as singer: blues, 123, 211, 257, 299; "hillbilly," 136, 275

—promotional techniques: 157, 165–66, 195, 203, 243, 287–88

—death: obituaries, 343, 356–57; public reaction, 355–57

—published commentary on: 362–65

See also Fraternal orders; Marriages; Personal appearances; Press notices; Radio; Recording sessions; Records; Repertoire; Royalties; Texas Rangers
Rodgers, Jesse (cousin), 316, 379
Rodgers, June Rebecca (daughter), 44, 51
Rodgers, Kathryn (daughter), 34, 247, 253, 284–86 *passim,* 324–25, 327*n54,* 346
Rodgers, Lottie Mae. *See* Mixon, Lottie Mae
Rodgers, Pearl (sister-in-law), 19, 20, 22, 34
Rodgers, Talmage "Tal" (brother), 12–21 *passim,* 27*n18,* 34, 165, 168, 217, 349
Rodgers, Walter (brother), 12, 13, 165, 203
"Rodgers' Puzzle Record," 305–6, 379, 413
Rogers, Charles "Buddy," 169
Rogers, Martha Woodberry (grandmother), 8
Rogers, Will, 67, 88, 273–78 *passim,* 281, 287, 303, 436–37
Rogers, Will, Jr., 274, 276, 281, 437
Rogers, Zachary (grandfather), 7, 8, 21
"Roll Along, Kentucky Moon," 315, 316, 318, 335, 413*d79*
Rollins, Widow, 57
Roosevelt, Franklin Delano, 345, 348, 356, 357
Roosevelt Hotel (New York), 183
Rose, Fred, 72
Rosenfeld, Monroe, 220
Rosenfield, John, 204
Rotary Clubs, 70, 287, 310
Royalties: record, 97–98, 100, 104, 106, 127–28, 131*n46,* 132, 139, 149–56 *passim;* composer, 97–98, 110, 123, 131*n46,* 139, 211, 220, 239, 289; "mechanicals," 97–98, 189, 313, 335
Rozell, Walter "Slim," 50, 54–56 *passim*
Rubiola, Joseph, 275
"Rule G." *See* Railroad regulations
Rust, Brian, 72, 260
Ryan, Walter, 351

Sachs, Bill, 233
Sadler, Harley, 47, 48, 207, 310
"The Sailor's Plea," 137, 141, 144, 361, 393*d10*

"St. James Infirmary," 254, 255, 334
St. Louis, Mo., 8, 100
"St. Louis Blues," 80, 227
Salazar, M. T., 278
"Sally Gooden," 88
Salt Lake City, Utah, 100
San Angelo, Tex., 213–14, 276, 277, 434
San Antonio, Tex., 61, 196, 213, 273, 274–76, 278, 303, 305, 306, 309, 314, 338, 357, 380, 434, 436, 437
San Antonio (Tex.) *Express,* 303
San Antonio (Tex.) *Light,* 205
"San Antonio Rose," 384
Sandburg, Carl, 211
"San Fernando Valley," 178
San Francisco Symphony Orchestra, 101
Santa Fe Railroad, 195
Saphia–Bosch, Mrs., 275
Sarnoff, David, 340
Savannah, Ga., 104
Sawyer, Bob, 251, 257, 260, 263*n22*
Schaeffer, Albert, 276
Schaffner, Neil, 48
"School Day Dreams," 179
Schreiner, L. A., 202
Schuster, Ira, 355
Scooba, Miss., 12, 164
Scruggs, Earl, 66
Sears, Roebuck, 4, 174, 313, 338
Seifert, Frank, 153, 432
Seminole County, Okla., 246
Senter, Boyd, 138, 260
Sentimentality in music, 35, 55, 110–11, 122, 146, 148, 151, 215, 220, 252, 292, 312, 318, 333, 353
Seven Nelsons, 203, 434
Seven Tennessee Ramblers, 78
Shapiro–Bernstein Music Co., 339
Shaw, Elliott, 275. *See also* Revelers
Shaw–Carroll Dance Revue, 203, 434
Shelley, Percy Bysshe, 266
Shelton, B. F., 106
Shelton, Robert, 363
Shepard, Burt, 88
Shepherd, G. O., 68–70, 76
Sherman, William Tecumseh, 8
"She Was Happy Till She Met You," 220, 403*d46*
Shilkret, Nathaniel, 100, 104, 117, 123
"Shoeboot's Serenade," 257
Short subjects. *See* Talking pictures

Showay Productions, 190
Show business, 17, 24, 47–48, 57, 116, 158, 189, 204, 228–29, 232–33, 361; minstrelsy, 21, 47, 86, 96, 119, 125, 163, 294, 320, 321; medicine show, 22, 47, 57, 58, 261; circus, 42, 47, 96, 228, 320, 321; carnival, 42, 47, 207, 228, 229, 320. *See also* Radio; Talking pictures; Tent theater; Vaudeville
Shreveport, La., 40
Side Liner Club (Tulane University), 169
Sievers, Fiddlin' Bill, 78
Sievers, James M. "Mac," 78–79
Sievers, Willie, 78
Silent films, 17
"The Silver Masked Tenor." *See* White, Joseph
"Silver Threads among the Gold," 96, 207
Sinatra, Frank, 200, 237, 363, 365, 384
"Singing the Blues with My Old Guitar," 178
The Singing Brakeman, 216, 261–62, 355, 423
"Sixteen Sections" (Bozeman home), 11, 14, 18
Skeeter Kell's Comedians. *See* Kell, Leslie
Skeeter Kell and His Gang. *See* Kell, Leslie
Skillet Lickers, 221, 330. *See also* Tanner, Gid
"Sleep, Baby, Sleep," 75, 76, 86, 111–12, 116, 126, 127, 129*n14*, 146, 202, 390*d2*
"Smiles," 178
Smith, Al, 167
Smith, Cal, 299
Smith, Ida Love. *See* Rodgers, Ida Smith
Smith, Jake (stepbrother), 13–17 *passim*
Smith, Mamie, 92
Smyth County Ramblers, 159
Snow, Hank, 178, 252, 363
Snow, Jimmie Rodgers, 178
Snyder, Leroy J., II, 88
"The Soldier's Sweetheart," 75, 110, 112, 116, 126, 127, 170, 361, 390*d1*
"Some Baby" (playbill), 182
"Somewhere Down below the Dixon Line," 351, 353, 382, 422*d109*
Songcopaters, 88
"Sonny Boy," 384–85

Sonora, Tex., 213
Sooy, Raymond, 331
Sound-on-film synchronization, 228–29, 251, 340. *See also* Talking pictures
Sousa, John Philip, 85, 86
South (U.S.), 1, 8, 10, 29, 33, 40, 48–56 *passim*, 101, 104, 167, 220, 228, 230, 231, 250, 306, 329, 353, 359, 432
"Southern Cannonball," 296, 413*d78*
Southern Music Publishing Co., 150, 155*n13*, 186, 197*n15*, 254, 314–15, 340, 349
Southern Pacific Railroad, 60–61, 121
Southern Railway, 34, 58, 65, 66, 171, 203, 355
Southern (Railway) *News Bulletin*, 171
"Southern Time." *See* Lowe's "Southern Time" Circuit
Southwest (U.S.), 174, 207, 228, 230, 242, 250, 273, 281, 306, 359, 432
Spaeth, Sigmund, 122
Spartanburg, S.C., 226, 434
Speyer & Co., 87
Sporting Life, 21
Sprague, Carl T., 89
Springfield, Mo., 306
S. S. *Mohawk*, 349
Stamps Quartet, 159, 219
"Standin' on the Corner." *See* "Blue Yodel No. 9"
Stanley-Crandall-Keith theaters, 153, 156, 432
Starkville, Miss., 23, 30
"Steamboat Bill," 22
Stentz, J. Dale, 68, 69, 76
Sterling, Ross, 269, 275, 310
Sterling, William W., 286, 287, 310
Stern, Joseph, 119
Stewart, Anita, 43
Stewart, Cal "Uncle Josh," 86, 88
Stokowski, Leopold, 120
Stoneman, Ernest V. "Pop," 95, 100, 106
Stoneman Family, 66, 100, 159
Streptomycin, 268
Strobel, R. J., 355
Stuart, Uncle Am, 89, 151
S:n Brothers Shows, 17
Sunrise records, 383
Suqualena, Miss., 11
Swain, W. I., 17, 42, 47, 48, 181, 182, 243, 248–49, 268; Dramatic Show,

Swain, W. 1. *(continued)*
42, 47, 231; Comic Opera Co., 230;
early life and career, 230–32; Hollywood Follies, 233–49 *passim,* 321,
435–36; Original Show Co., 302, 437
"Sweet Leilani," 384
"Sweet Mama, Hurry Home," 335, 337,
419*d98*

Taft Hotel. *See* Manger Hotel
Taggart, Charles Ross, 88
"Take Back Your Gold," 122
"Take Me Back Again," 56, 252, 406*d55*
Talking pictures, 51, 152, 188, 204, 214,
228–29, 251, 261, 307, 340, 343, 361
Tanner, Gid, 89, 221, 330
"T.B. Blues," 26, 260, 266–67, 278–80,
289, 317, 333, 360, 409*d65*
Ted North Players, 47
Teeter, H. B., 27*n1*
Temple, Tex., 195
Tennessee, 58
"Tennessee Mama Blues," 194, 196
Tenneva Ramblers, 71, 73–74, 104, 107,
109, 134, 136, 159
"Ten Nights in a Bar Room" (playbill),
182, 308, 320. *See also* "The 18th
Amendment"
"Ten Thousand Miles from Home." *See*
"Waiting for a Train"
"Tent rep." *See* Tent theater
Tent theater, 42, 47–48, 172, 174, 182,
207, 228–30, 233, 243, 306–7, 320–
21, 323. *See also* Show business; *and
various companies*
Terrell, Billy, 48–51, 54, 55, 124, 172,
346, 358*n8*, 438
Terrell, Bonnie, 48
Terrell, Brooks, 48, 50
Test recordings, 217
T. E. Swann Music Co., 199
Texas, 27, 39, 52, 190, 201, 202, 227,
238, 294, 295, 302, 309, 320, 335,
343, 347; West, 1, 198, 213; East,
198, 273, 322, 324, 344, 436, 438;
North, 218
Texas & Pacific Railroad, 238
Texas Ann's Wild West Show, 309, 437
"The Texas Drifter." *See* Reeves, Goebel
Texas Hill Country. *See* Kerrville
Texas Rangers, 289; Rodgers honored

Texas Rangers *(continued)*
as, 286, 289, 309, 351
Texas State Penitentiary, 253, 280, 291
"T for Texas." *See* "Blue Yodel No. 1"
"That's Why I'm All Alone," 179
"That's Why I'm Blue," 220, 255,
404*d49*
Thomas, Eva, 182, 236, 433, 436
Thomas, Tony, 249
Thoreau, Henry David, 266
"Those Gambler's Blues," 254–56, 334,
406*d56*
Three Ryans, 166, 433
Three Southerners, 136
Tilden, Bill, 69
Timely Tunes records, 383
Tin Pan Alley, 6, 55, 72, 97, 119, 148,
161, 290, 330, 331, 336, 352
Tipton, A. M., 35, 56
Toby comedian (stage character), 306,
307, 321
Topeka, Kans., 242
Toscanini, Arturo, 120
Townsend, Claude, 237
Townsend, Dorothy. *See* Long, Dorothy
Trade Exposition and Tri-State Fair
(Johnson City, Tenn.), 78
"Train Whistle Blues," 195, 211, 305,
399*d33*
"Travellin' Blues," 280, 409*d66*
"Treasures Untold," 122, 137, 139, 205,
392*d8*
Trinity Baptist Church (Camden, N.J.),
120, 330
Tubb, Ernest, 191, 194, 363
Tuberculosis, 12, 53–54, 59, 63*n5*, 115,
184, 201, 266–68, 273, 279, 282*n3*,
343, 348
"Tuck Away My Lonesome Blues," 210,
399*d32*
Tucson, Ariz., 60–61
Tuggle Brothers, 23
Tulsa, Okla., 204
Tulsa (Okla.) *World,* 205
Tupelo, Miss., 227, 434–35
Turpin, Ben, 248–49, 436
Tuscaloosa, Ala., 2, 3
"Twenty-one Years," 338
Two Black Crows, 260
Tyer, W. C., 60
Tyler, Tex., 322
Tyler Hotel (Louisville, Ky.), 293

Ukulele, 137, 207, 209
"Uncle Josh." *See* Stewart, Cal
"Uncle Tom's Cabin" (playbill), 321
Union City, Tenn., 48
Union Station (Meridian, Miss.), 56, 355
U.S. Copyright Office, 253
U.S. Department of Commerce, 68
U.S. Department of Justice, 340
U.S. Railway Administration, 39
Updike, John, 149
Utah, 52

Valentino, Rudolph, 362
Vallee, Rudy, 178
Van and Schenck, 86
Van Arsdale, Earl, 227, 435
Vann, Jimmie, 236, 436
Variety, 138, 154, 171, 209, 215, 338, 357
"Vaudefilm." *See* Vaudeville
Vaudeville, 17, 47, 57, 180, 188–90, 208, 212, 229, 231, 297, 302, 312, 337; "movie presentations," 152; "vaudefilm," 152; in decline, 152, 158, 204, 214, 343–44; efforts to revive, 153, 189; Loew circuit, 165–71 *passim;* R-K-O circuit, 189–90, 203–6; in tent rep shows, 233, 308, 320
Vaught, Edgar, 324
Velvet Tone records, 306
Vessey, Bernard, 88
Vicksburg, Miss., 182, 433
Vicksburg & Montgomery Railroad, 8
Vicksburg, Shreveport & Pacific Railroad, 40
Victor Talking Machine Co., 6, 72, 78–82 *passim*, 92, 114, 116, 117, 120, 127, 140, 141, 149, 170, 183, 188, 202, 216, 221, 250, 256, 273, 278, 290, 291, 305, 313–14, 322, 329, 331, 333, 338–41, 347, 350, 356, 361, 362; history of, 84–90; Red Seal records, 85, 87, 88, 150, 155n14; scroll label, 85, 379; catalog, 86, 88, 361; sold to New York bankers, 87; and hillbilly music, 89, 90, 100–101, 108; and Peer, 95, 99–101, 150, 186, 314, 339–41; and field recording, 100, 101, 104–5, 314; merged with RCA, 106, 151; West Coast operations, 251
Victrola, 87, 274, 289

Villa (Cuidad) Acuna, Mexico, 271
Virginia, 10
Vitaphone, 188
Vocalion records. *See* Aeolian Vocalion records; Brunswick-Balke-Collender records

Waco, Tex., 68
"Wagon Wheels," 336
Waikiki Hawaiians, 236, 436
"Waiting for the Robert E. Lee," 55
"Waiting for a Train," 57, 72, 160, 162–63, 201, 216, 226, 382, 397d24
Walcott, F. S., 183
Walcott, W. S., 42
Wallcott's Original Rabbit Foot Minstrels, 42, 183
Wallace, George, 4
Waller, Thomas "Fats," 149
Walsh, Dock, 66, 101. *See also* Carolina Tar Heels
Walt Whitman Hotel (Camden, N.J.), 118, 135
"Waltz of the Roses," 162
Wamboldt, Wickes, 76, 77
Waring, Fred, 88, 150, 152
Warley, Malcolm, 159
Warner Brothers, 188
Washington, D.C., 81, 114, 134, 139, 140–41, 144–45, 152, 156, 158, 201, 228, 330, 351, 354
Washington Post, 154
WBAP (Fort Worth, Tex.), 311
WBRC (Birmingham, Ala.), 311
WCOC (Meridian, Miss.), 288
WEAF (New York, N.Y.), 356
"Weary River," 227
Weeks, J. D., 34
West (U.S.), 344
West Blocton, Ala., 23
Westbrook, John, 160, 163
West Coast, 100
Western Electric, 109
Western Hotel (Asheville, N.C.), 74
Western music, 90, 125, 215, 295, 336. *See also* Country music; Western swing
Western swing, 280, 314, 332
West Point, Miss., 13
Wewoka, Okla., 245–48 *passim*, 357
WFAA (Dallas, Tex.), 278, 311, 316
WGCM (Gulfport, Miss.), 182

WHAS (Louisville, Ky.), 295, 298, 338
"What-cha Call-em Blues," 72
"What's It?," 293, 297, 305, 335, 412*d76*
"When My Sugar Walks Down the Street," 151
"When the Cactus Is in Bloom," 295, 412*d73*
"When the Work's All Done This Fall," 90
"Where the River Shannon Flows," 75, 110
"Whippin' That Old T.B.," 332, 333, 417*d89*
"Whisper Your Mother's Name," 214, 401*d36*
White, Joseph, 88
White, Lasses, 273
"White Christmas," 384
Whiteman, Paul, 88, 89, 150, 152, 170, 246
Whitman, Walt, 5
Whitter, Henry, 55, 56, 66, 89–99 *passim*, 102*n20*, 106, 159
WHK (Cleveland, Ohio), 329
"The Whole Town's Talking" (playbill), 320
"Who's Sorry Now?," 55, 80
"Who's Your Little Who-zis?," 297
"Why Did You Give Me Your Love?," 220, 221, 404*d50*
"Why Girls Walk Home" (playbill), 320
"Why Should I Be Lonely?," 251, 252, 405*d52*
"Why There's a Tear in My Eye," 292, 410*d68*
"Why Wives Worry" (playbill), 182
Wichita, Kans., 207
Wichita Falls, Tex., 252, 253
Wickersham report, 275
"Wild and Reckless Hobo." *See* "Waiting for a Train"
Wilgus, D. K., 162
Williams, Hank, 3, 26, 161, 362, 365
Williams, Sam, 26, 32, 45*n10*, 110
Williamson, Annie. *See* Nelson, Annie
Williamson, Carrie. *See* Rodgers, Carrie
Williamson, Covert, 348
Williamson family, 40–41, 62
Williamson, Jesse Thomas, 37
Williamson, Kizzie Ann, 37

Williamson, Nate, 40, 141, 285, 324, 325
Wills, Bob, 280, 296, 314
Wills, Nat, 88
Will Shade's Memphis Jug Band, 142*n2*, 159
Wilson, Woodrow, 31–32
Wintz, George B., 182
Wiseman, Skyland Scotty, 66
WLAP (Louisville, Ky.), 295, 297
WLS (Chicago, Ill.), 69
WMC (Memphis, Tenn.), 168, 311
Wolfe, Thomas, 65
"The Women Make a Fool out of Me." *See* "Jimie Rodgers' Last Blue Yodel"
"The Wonderful City," 221, 292, 410*d69*
Woodberry, Martha. *See* Rogers, Martha Woodberry
World's Fair (1933), 356
World War I, 30, 31–32
Wortham, Charles A., 48, 207
"Wreck of the Old 97," 55, 89, 120
"The Wreck of the Virginian," 106
WRR (Dallas, Tex.), 316
WSB (Atlanta, Ga.), 93, 311, 312
WTFF (Washington, D.C.), 140, 141, 145, 311
WWNC (Asheville, N.C), 68–71, 75–80 *passim*, 111, 170, 202, 225, 311
Wymore, Amber. *See* Kell, Amber Wymore

XED (Reynosa, Mexico), 270

"Yearning," 72, 140, 151
"Years Ago," 6, 352, 353, 422*dl10*
Yodel, 50, 86, 125–26, 328, 333, 334
"Yodeling the Blues Away." *See* "The Brakeman's Blues"
"Yodeling Cowboy," 215, 294, 295, 361, 401*d39*
Yodeling Messenger Boy. *See* Bruner, Bill
"Yodeling My Way Back Home," 350, 351, 421*dl03*
"The Yodeling Ranger," 351, 379, 421*dl07*
"You and My Old Guitar," 147, 148, 395*dl7*
Young, Red, 316

CPSIA information can be obtained at www.ICGtesting.com
Printed in the USA
LVOW131329241012

304262LV00001B/31/P